John Colet

John B. Gleason

University of California Press
Berkeley / Los Angeles / London

University of California Press
Berkeley and Los Angeles, California

University of California Press, Ltd.
London, England

Copyright © 1989 by
The Regents of the University of California

Library of Congress Cataloging-in-Publication Data

Gleason, John B.
  John Colet / John B. Gleason.
    p.   cm.
  Bibliography: p.
  Includes index.
  ISBN 0-520-06510-7 (alk. paper)
  1. Colet, John, 1467?–1519. I. Title.
BR754.C6G57 1989
230′.2′0924—dc19   88-32907
                                                   CIP

Printed in the United States of America

1 2 3 4 5 6 7 8 9

For My Wife

*uerum animo satis haec vestigia parua sagaci
sunt, per quae possis cognoscere cetera tute.*

—*Lucretius i.402*

Contents

Acknowledgments

It is a pleasure to acknowledge the help and encouragement received while this book was in preparation. The librarians of the University of San Francisco Library, with their enlightened acquisitions policy and their endlessly resourceful, learned, and sympathetic help at all stages and on all kinds of inquiries, have been my indispensable co-adjutors. Friends and colleagues have done their part, as only friends and colleagues can, to bring the book along. I am especially indebted for encouragement to my department chairman Hugh Dawson, and for practical help and encouragement in the past to my then dean Edmond Smyth. J. B. Trapp, hospitable and helpful during my visits to London, also read an earlier version of the whole book, catching several errors and adding his meed of encouragement.

For prepublication access to recent papers I am indebted to James D. Tracy and, again, J. B. Trapp; for consultation on several vexed points of Colet's Latinity, to James Hooker, the late Louis Mackay, and Giacinto Matteucig; for free access to the St. Paul's School manuscript of Colet's writings, to Patrick Hutton; for permission to use an argument from his unpublished Cambridge dissertation, to Michael J. Kelly; for help on the nature of Colet's final illness, to Ilza Veith; for calling several recent papers to my attention, to Guy Lytle; for information on Colet's vocabulary, to R. E. Latham; and, for procuring photostats from Continental libraries, to, again, Hugh Dawson.

The Librarians of the Guildhall Library and Lambeth Palace Library have provided valuable responses to my inquiries, as has the Archivist of the Mercers' Company, London. I am grateful for permission to study the Colet manuscripts in Cambridge, at the University Library, Corpus Christi College, Emmanuel College, and Trinity College; at all of these libraries I have enjoyed a courteous and helpful reception. The Editors of the Augustinus-Lexikon, Stuttgart, kindly authorized a computer search of the database for their edition of St. Augustine's works in the Corpus Christianorum series. The University of San Francisco subsidized transcription of the first draft of this book into computer-readable form for further revision. The staff of the University of California Press, especially Shirley Warren, have proved unflappable where occasional problems arose and consistently helpful in more normal times.

What I cannot even begin to say adequately is at least hinted at on the dedication page.

Abbreviations

Colet's Writings

The titles corresponding to the abbreviations listed below are in many cases mine; likewise, the titles of Colet's works in the published editions listed below are often editorial. In all these editions except those of EK, OCC, and P, Colet's Latin texts are accompanied by English translations. Unless otherwise indicated, citations using the abbreviations refer to the Latin text in these published editions; citations of the translations or other editorial material are distinguished by the use of "p." or "pp."

C On First Corinthians.
An Exposition of St. Paul's First Epistle to the Corinthians. Edited by J. H. Lupton. London, 1874. Also *John Colet's Commentary on First Corinthians.* Edited by Bernard O'Kelly and Catherine A. L. Jarrott. Binghamton, N.Y.: Medieval and Renaissance Texts and Studies, 1985. Page citations of the text of C are to both the Lupton and (in square brackets) the O'Kelly and Jarrott editions.

CM On the Mystical Body.
"De compositione sancti corporis Christi mystici, quae est ecclesia." In *Joannis Coleti opuscula quaedam theologica*: *Letters to Radulphus on the Mosaic Account of the Creation, together with Other Treatises*, edited by J. H. Lupton, 185–195. London, 1876.

DCH On Dionysius's Celestial Hierarchy.
"De caelesti hierarchia." In *Two Treatises on the Hierarchies of Dionysius*, edited by J. H. Lupton. London, 1869.

DEH	On Dionysius's Ecclesiastical Hierarchy.
	"De ecclesiastica hierarchia." In *Two Treatises. See* DCH (above).
EK	Letter to Richard Kidderminster.
	In Knight, 265–268. *See* Knight (below).
FEM	Marginalia in Colet's copy of Marsilio Ficino, *Epistolae*, Venice, 1495.
	In Sears Jayne, *John Colet and Marsilio Ficino*. Oxford: Oxford University Press, 1963.
G	On Genesis.
	"In principium Genesios." In *Opuscula*, 165–188. *See* CM (above).
OCC	Sermon to the Clergy in Convocation.
	"Oratio ad clerum in Convocatione." In Knight, 238–250. *See* Knight (below).
P	On the First Epistle of Peter.
	"Epistola Sancti Petri Apostoli." In *Opuscula*, 285–303. *See* CM (above).
R	On Romans, sixteen-chapter version.
	An Exposition of St. Paul's Epistle to the Romans. Edited by J. H. Lupton. London, 1873.
RO	On Romans, unfinished five-chapter version.
	"In Epistolam divi Pauli ad Romanos." In *Opuscula*, 199–281. *See* CM (above).
S	On the Sacraments.
	De sacramentis. Cited by page number of the Latin text in appendix 1 below, which is based on British Library Loan Manuscript 55/2 (Duke of Leeds).

Other Abbreviations

A	Letter from Erasmus to Joducus Jonas, 13 June 1521.
	In Allen, 4:507–527, Ep. 1211. *See* Allen (below). Cited by line numbers.
Acts of Court	*Acts of Court of the Mercers' Company, 1453–1527*. Edited by Letitia Lyell and Frank D. Watney. Cambridge: Privately printed, 1936.

Allen

Opus epistolarum Des. Erasmi Roterodami. edited by P. S. Allen, H. M. Allen, and H. W. Garrod. 12 vols. Oxford: Clarendon, 1906–1958. Cited by volume, page, and letter number.

ASD

Opera omnia Desiderii Erasmi Roterodami. 19 vols. to date. Amsterdam: North-Holland, 1969–. Cited by *Ordo* number, volume, and page.

CC, Ser. Lat.

Corpus Christianorum, Series Latina. 91 vols. to date. Turnholt and Paris: Brepols, 1953–.

CSEL

Corpus scriptorum ecclesiasticorum latinorum. 83 vols. Vienna, 1866–1971.

Knight

Samuel Knight. *The Life of Dr. John Colet, Dean of St. Paul's.* New ed. Oxford, 1823.

LB

Desiderii Erasmi Roterodami opera omnia. Edited by Jean Le Clerc. 10 vols. Leiden, 1703–1706.

Lupton, *Life*

Joseph H. Lupton. *A Life of John Colet, D.D.* London, 1887.

More, *C*

The Correspondence of Sir Thomas More. Edited by Elizabeth F. Rogers. Princeton: Princeton University Press, 1947.

More, *CW*

The Yale Edition of the Complete Works of St. Thomas More. 14 vols. to date. New Haven: Yale University Press, 1963–.

PG

Patrologiae cursus completus, Series Graeca. Edited by J. P. Migne. 165 vols. Paris, 1857–1866.

PL

Patrologiae cursus completus, Series Latina. Edited by J. P. Migne. 221 vols. Paris, 1844–1855.

STC^2

A Short-Title Catalogue of Books Printed in England, Scotland, & Ireland. Compiled by A. W. Pollard and G. R. Redgrave. 2d ed. Edited by W. A. Jackson, F. S. Ferguson, and Katharine F. Pantzer. 2 vols. London: The Bibliographical Society, 1976–1986.

VCH

The Victoria History of the Counties of England. London, 1900–.

Vies

Erasme, Vies de Jean Vitrier et de John Colet. Translated and edited by André Godin. Angers: Ed. Moreana, 1982.

Part I

Beginnings

1

A Case of Mistaken Identity

A generation after John Colet's death in 1519, he appeared to have lost the heavily handicapped contest with oblivion. His deanery of St. Paul's Cathedral had already known several later occupants; the part of his great fortune which was not earmarked for the endowment of his school had been dispersed; and his services to the Church and the Crown had long since been absorbed into the institutional fabric, leaving little distinctive impression behind. Where he was remembered at all it was as the founder of St. Paul's School in London. Hence when a controversialist tried to invoke his authority for a moment in 1566, his opponent retorted, "As for John Colet, he hath neuer a worde to shew, for he left no workes."[1]

About all this there is nothing unusual. What is unusual, however, is that three centuries later Colet's fame suddenly gained a new lease on life, which this time proved enduring. In 1867 the first of what were to be five volumes of Colet's supposedly nonexistent works was published, edited by the surmaster of the school that Colet had founded, the Reverend Joseph H. Lupton. By itself, this publication might have attracted little attention, for it was simply a slender volume containing a treatise on the sacraments, its crabbed Latin text unaccompanied by a translation. What excited broad interest was the appearance in the same year of a widely publicized book in which the hitherto obscure John Colet emerged as the captain of an intellectual venture in which he was joined by the illustrious figures of Erasmus and Thomas More. This book was *The Oxford Reformers*, by Frederic Seebohm. As Seebohm told the tale, Colet and his famous lieutenants had sought to lay the groundwork for a fruitful reformation of the church in England, a revolution that would have been nonviolent and nondoctrinaire. Seebohm called the three men the Oxford Reformers, a title that has stuck.

Until the appearance of Seebohm's book, Colet, besides having been recognized as the founder of a school, had been lumped among the distant harbingers of the Reformation. But Seebohm thought he saw in Colet a man who had tried to bring about a quite different type of reformation from the one which actually occurred. Seebohm found the raw materials for his interpretation in the pages of Erasmus; but the framework into which he incorporated them he supplied for himself. It happened that for special reasons, which I will examine shortly, Erasmus had deliberately emphasized the reformist element in Colet—a fact that helped make his portrait of Colet appear to be just what Seebohm was looking for. In order to understand how Seebohm's Colet came to be, we must therefore first turn back to the circumstances under which Erasmus wrote his biographical account. Having done that, we can return to the pressures that molded Seebohm's work.

Erasmus, aware that Colet had published only a single sermon, a very short devotional work, and some contributions to schoolbooks, was concerned that he would soon "drop from the sight of posterity."[2] After Colet's death he started canvassing mutual acquaintances for biographical materials, for he himself had not met Colet till both were in their thirties, and most of Erasmus's life had been spent far from Colet and England. Unfortunately Erasmus's correspondents were not helpful and the project languished. When it was revived two years later, in 1521, the times had changed and Erasmus had something more in mind than a graceful literary memorial.

During those two years the Reformation had made rapid headway on the Continent. Erasmus was increasingly distressed at the defection of promising young scholars to Luther's side, and he resolved to do what he could to stop it. He now enlarged his project of writing a memorial of Colet to include also a memorial of Jean Vitrier, a Franciscan who had died a few years before Colet[3] and who had once been important in Erasmus's life. The account he gave of these two men, which ran to some six thousand words, was addressed as a letter to Jodocus Jonas, a highly promising young theologian who, rumor had it, was on the point of going over to Luther. The letter, dated 13 June 1521 and published later that summer, was a last-ditch (and unsuccessful) attempt to keep Jonas within the old Church.[4] Looked at in the light of these circumstances, the letter is clearly intended to demonstrate in the persons of Vitrier and Colet how far a man could go in honest criticism and active sympathy with reform, while still remaining loyal to Rome. With this object Erasmus dwelt on Colet's hostility to abuses and his sensitivity to the need to purify the Church. Erasmus hoped this double portrait would induce Jonas to work for reform, as Vitrier and Colet had done, from within the Church: reform, he implied, had no necessary connection with Luther. Colet was asserted by Erasmus to have been accused of heresy by his bishop, an undocumented assertion to which we will return. And, not content with having defied his ecclesiastical lords, Erasmus's Colet preached a pacifist sermon to the assembled court at the very moment when the king was preparing for war against France. Again, the implication is clear. Colet, in defiance of all terrestrial authority, ecclesiastical or royal, dared to preach the undiluted Christian message—all this from within the Roman communion.

The touches that were intended to catch Jonas's imagination are exactly those that caught the Protestant Victorian imagination and led to Colet's rediscovery—if not his invention.[5]

By 1529 William Tyndale, seizing—and improving—on a story of Erasmus's about Colet, was declaring that Colet's little translation of the Lord's Prayer had got him into serious trouble with prelates afraid to let the people read the Gospel in a language they understood.[6] The story grew in the telling, and a sermon delivered by Hugh Latimer in 1552 had Colet in imminent danger of being burned at the stake as a heretic.[7] Colet actually died in his bed, but another ardent Protestant controversialist reported (1548) that unnamed prelates wanted Colet's body taken from its coffin and burned, a desecration he said was prevented only by the intervention of the king.[8] Meanwhile, at the beginnings of the English Reformation, a dialogue in which Erasmus described Colet's aversion to the commercialization of shrines and images was translated into English for propaganda purposes.[9] This accumulating picture of Colet as proto-Protestant naturally passed into John Foxe's vast *Book of Martyrs* (English version, 1563), where Colet has six pages.[10]

With these credentials he won a secure if minor niche in the pantheon of Reformers even though he was supposed to have "left no workes." Colet is one of several dozen figures associated with Reform in Henry Holland's *Herωologia* (1620). He has six pages in Donald Lupton's *The History of the Moderne Protestant Divines* (1637), an adaptation for English readers of Jakob Verheiden's *Praestantium aliquot theologorum, qui Rom. Antichristum praecipue oppugnarunt, effigies* (1602); the Continental original, however, does not mention Colet. He was noticed by English antiquarian writers; he has his four pages in Henry Wharton's history of the London bishops and deans down to the Reformation (1695);[11] and his single surviving sermon appeared in a collection of out-of-the-way documents in 1708.[12]

In a scholarly age that loved religious polemics it was only a matter of time until Colet found a biographer on the Low Church side. The learned antiquarian bishop White Kennett set himself to write "the Life of our great forerunner of the Reformation Mr. Dean Colet"[13] in the early 1720s. He collected materials for the biography, but it was not a high priority with him and he dropped the project when he became embroiled in other literary controversies.[14] He passed his materials on to Dr. Samuel Knight, another Old Pauline and a man whose father, like Kennett's and for that matter Colet's, was a wealthy London Mercer. Knight, a comfortably-off clergyman "at the Protestant end of the Anglican spectrum,"[15] thus became Colet's first full-length biographer with the *Life of Dr. John Colet* (1724). A highly patriotic partisan of the Reformation, Knight emphasized everything English while playing down Continental connections as likely to be "nauseous" to English readers.[16] His book, if rather "invertebrate,"[17] is a useful collection of documents enlivened by much anti-Roman commentary; but it is to be used, as the phrase goes, with caution. More than once a quotation from Erasmus is silently expanded, still within quotation marks, by an extensive passage from the pen of the biographer.[18] At the leisurely interval of ninety-nine years the Clarendon Press brought out in 1823 a reprint of Knight, described as a "New Edition" but with no mention of an editor; it seems to owe its existence to the Mercers.[19]

As late as 1823, then, Colet was still seen principally as a herald of the Protestant Reformation. As yet we hear nothing of the exegete whose Oxford lectures transformed biblical scholarship—a Colet quite unknown to his contemporaries, whose discovery was reserved to the year 1867.[20] Instead, in Knight and the writers before him whose mentions of Colet we have surveyed, there is no question that it is his connection with the Reformation that lent him distinction.[21] This is precisely why Colet had remained a minor figure. As the antiquarian writers saw things, Colet had shown where his sympathies lay, but his early death in 1519 deprived him of the chance to take part in the Reformation proper; his connection with it as a forerunner, while creditable to him personally, had done little for the cause. The glory of the English Reformation was naturally reserved for those who made it a reality.

However, the established consensus about the English Reformation began rapidly to disintegrate beginning in the 1820s. The churchmen and statesmen and sovereigns who had wrought the Reformation, their goals and their methods, were subject to increasingly critical scrutiny. Even earlier, within the Anglican communion, High Churchmen and Low Churchmen—the latter being the enthusiasts for Colet—had differed sharply about the character of the English Reformation. Now, in addition, Methodists and Roman Catholics, rationalists and Tractarians, were all having their noisy say on a question that Peel's proposed Catholic Emancipation had made acute. What was the nature of the Church of England, and what was its relation to the state?

Questions that remain purely theological can be agitated indefinitely, but the origins of the church and its relation to the state had in the end to be tackled as a legal and historical issue. The church now had to submit to the same scholarly scrutiny of its origins as was routinely brought to bear on other institutions. At once the figure of Henry VIII, with his sexual politics and his Reformation Parliament, began to assume an awkward prominence.

While he occupied the throne Henry was the unabashed *fons et origo* of the Reformation. Speaking in the Parliament of 1536 Sir Richard Rich (whose suborned testimony had sent More to the block in the preceding year) felt no hesitation in extolling Henry as "worthily and rightly to be compared to Solomon on account of his justice and wisdom, to Samson on account of his strength and courage, to Absalom on account of his form and beauty."[22] Three hundred years later, however, this ecstatic note could hardly be sustained. To present Henry as Christian hero in a land of sharply divergent religious persuasions and a free press was to ask for trouble; but the church's defenders could not disavow him either. And so long as Henry with his three children and their parliaments held center stage it was impossible to evade the sarcasm that "within a single generation, the relation Christ's flesh and blood bore to the bread and wine was changed five times by royal proclamation or act of Parliament."[23] It was already foreseeable that a standard study of the Reformation by a Regius Professor of Modern History at Oxford could begin with the sentence "The one definite thing that can be said about the Reformation in England is that it created a State-Church."[24] To forestall such a verdict a new framework had to be developed for understanding the church's origins.

The Oxford Movement attacked the problem through a reinterpretation of the church's history which edged the figure of Henry to one side. Instead of tracing the national church back to the Henrician revolution, the Oxford intellectuals argued that the independence of national churches had characterized Christianity from the earliest times. One effect of this approach was to "de-Protestantise the Church of England,"[25] an approach the more plausible because the English church was alone in breaking with Rome without embracing Reformed theology.[26] As its inner logic unfolded, however, the Oxford Movement threatened to lead to near-coalescence with Rome, and when its leader J. H. Newman actually went over to Rome in 1845 the movement rapidly lost credibility and influence.

The problem it had set itself to solve nevertheless remained. Attention now centered once again on the earlier sixteenth century, but with a difference. Instead of concentrating on the traditional central figures, King Henry and Pope Clement VII, Wolsey and Campeggio and Cromwell, it seemed more important to trace the reform to a genuinely religious impulse originating in sources that had been neglected by earlier historians.

Were there not men of a reformist tendency, without the fame of a Fisher or a More but equally influential in their own time, who before the Reformation led holy lives, denounced abuses, and even suffered for their unseasonable idealism? In the work of such men would be found the true spiritual origins of the Reform and the ultimate answer to the jeers of the church's enemies who persisted in deriving the Reform from Henry and his problems.

It was in this anxious polemical atmosphere that the hitherto little-known figure of John Colet was brought to the notice of the general public in Frederic Seebohm's *The Oxford Reformers John Colet, Erasmus, and Thomas More: Being a History of Their Fellow-Work.*[27] Seebohm's Colet was a fascinating discovery. Like other "neglected" figures then and now, he proved to exemplify the values of the age that rediscovered him. He was said to have inaugurated a new type of critical exegesis at Oxford by interpreting the Bible in historical perspective. He gave primacy to its literal meaning and brushed aside the fantastic allegorizing of medieval writers. It was self-evident that, as an interpreter of the text of the New Testament, he had a sound knowledge of Greek. He saw the need for a school that would combine with traditional piety a thorough grounding in the classics. He scorned superstition and left no money to finance prayers for his soul, thereby placing in doubt his belief in the Roman Catholic doctrine of purgatory. He defied convention by preaching reform to the unheeding prelates of his day, and in consequence of his plain speaking he was accused of heresy.

Nor was this all. Besides these remarkable personal achievements, Colet turned out to be (thanks in large part to a mistake of Seebohm's about year dates) the decisive influence on the intellectual and religious life of Erasmus. The public now learned that Colet had detached Erasmus from his absorption in belles lettres, impressed on the talented but flighty foreigner much of his own deep seriousness about theology, and given him priceless direction in developing this new-found interest. Indirectly, then, Colet's influence was immense: he was the teacher behind the most influential scholar of the age.

As we shall see, substantially all these assertions by the Victorian writer are mistaken. But if his revolutionary Colet bore little resemblance to the John Colet whom sixteenth-century contemporaries knew and who is the subject of this book, the rediscovered Colet answered exactly to the needs of 1867.

The great appeal of Seebohm's Colet is to be sought, I think, in two directions. Defenders of the church from within its communion welcomed the hitherto unknown spiritual and intellectual ancestor of the Reformation. And outside the institutional church, a diverse group of nondoctrinaire Christians also found in Seebohm's Colet inspiration for their effort to work out what they thought of as a rational Christianity. Though for some people these appeals overlapped, it will be convenient to consider them separately.

We have already seen the difficult position of the church's defenders, who sought to find the origins of the national church not in the actions of Henry VIII but in the witness of religious idealists among his subjects. The somber and bloated monarch of Holbein's unsparing late portrait made a devastating contrast with the few who dared resist him and went to their deaths—the Carthusians, Bishop John Fisher, Sir Thomas More. Moreover, the king's supporters whom history knew did not cut much of a figure morally. There must have been others who were more convincing religiously, but it was hard to know who they were. The Lollard movement of the early fifteenth century had been effectively stamped out among intellectuals and survived in Henry's age only among the masses, with no recognized leader.[28] Moreover, the sorry state of the pre-Reformation church guaranteed that there would be few candidates for the retrospective mantle of moral leadership which Victorian apologists were eager to bestow.

In view of these circumstances it is easy to understand the enthusiasm with which a reviewer in a journal having Anglican affiliations greeted the appearance of Seebohm's Colet: "We need nothing more to prove against Romish sneers, the necessity of a reformation, than the words of divines [like Colet] who lived and died in the communion of national churches which were themselves still in communion with the Roman See."[29] Seebohm's study of the Oxford Reformers working under the inspiration of Colet thus offered a welcome retort to "Romish sneers" at the church's historical origins and set the portrait of Colet in a frame that was to become classical.

Almost at once Seebohm's newly discovered Colet also took a pivotal place in the *Short History of the English People* (1874), by John Richard Green, the nineteenth century's most widely read English historian after Macaulay. Green was strongly influenced by Seebohm. He even wrote that "the awakening of a rational Christianity, whether in England, or in the Teutonic world at large, begins with the Florentine studies of John Colet."[30] It is true that scholars like the Tudor specialist J. S. Brewer promptly criticized Green as anachronistic in reading contemporary concerns and points of view back into the past,[31] but this was precisely what made Green's history important for nonspecialist readers. In attributing to Colet the development of a "rational Christianity" Green points to the significance of Seebohm's Colet for many thoughtful contemporaries who felt unable to accept all the freight that the historical Church of England carried but remained attached to what they conceived to be the essence of Christianity.

What this essence was, was a question of deep concern to Seebohm, a Quaker by upbringing. He opposed what, in a book dating to the period of *The Oxford Reformers*,[32] he called "sacerdotal and Augustinian theories of Christian dogma."[33] Instead he proposed to do what he thought Colet had done: go back to the scriptural texts themselves, especially the Pauline texts, which he considered Augustine to have distorted. He found that "in St. Paul's own Epistles, with one or two slight exceptions, miracles and the abnormal mental phenomena deemed miraculous are ignored or mentioned only to be emphatically subordinated to the moral objects of Christianity."[34] Seebohm was apparently not deterred by the fact that one of the "slight exceptions" was the Resurrection, concerning which Paul said, "If Christ did not rise [from the dead], then our preaching is useless and your believing it is useless" (1 Cor. 15:14). Seebohm tended to use Paul in the same way he used Colet, in support of a preconceived thesis. His key assumption is eventually expressed in terms that show exactly why he gave Colet's neglected Oxford lectures unprecedented prominence. Colet, he thought, was asking the same question of Paul's Epistles which he himself was asking:

> Half theology to this day rests upon the supposed infallible authority of texts from his epistles. But what was his attitude to his *own* theology? *He did not regard it in all its details as an essential part of Christianity.* . . . It was the moral sense itself and not its mental environments which was the essential and eternal thing.[35]

Thus the aid and comfort that Seebohm's discovery of Colet gave the apologists of the Church of England was real and important. Nevertheless Seebohm's personal objective was not to defend the historical church but to work back to what men like himself and Green regarded as the essential spirit of Christianity. As Seebohm's son reports:

> He was influenced by the belief that a better understanding of the past would shed light on the problems of the present and of the future. . . . In the endeavours that underlay the fellow-work of Colet, Erasmus, and More, described in [*The Oxford Reformers*] he found much that corresponded with the desires and difficulties of our own day. Added to this, his study of their thoughts and actions gave him a real admiration for all their independence, and love of their characters; his vivid historical insight made him feel they had been almost his companions and friends.[36]

In this large spirit men like Seebohm and Green worked for a Christianity that would be true to the spirit of Jesus but would recognize that he and the sacred writers were unavoidably entangled in an outlook and in customs that were now irrelevant, if not positively obstructive, to the "moral sense" of Christianity, which was "the essential and eternal thing." As the Anglican apologists did, but from a different angle, men of Seebohm's outlook wondered whether there had not been some far-sighted men in the days before the Reformation who likewise had seen the need to study the Scriptures from a historical point of view in order to prune away what no longer had meaning in changed historical circumstances. They looked for a man of upright life who had been indignant at the centuries-long accretion of abuses and formalism, a man who would vigorously winnow the Christian wheat from the medieval chaff and thereby discover a doctrine more worthy of the nineteenth century.

The movement in which men like Seebohm and Green enlisted Colet sought to stake out a ground between, on the one hand, the deistic and rationalist tendencies that regarded Christianity simply as a religion of enlightenment and good conduct and, on the other hand, the existing Church of England, burdened by traditions and doctrines that were seen as obscuring the message of Jesus. The movement that Seebohm and Green typify has been traced back to about 1850, when the reaction against the revolutionary forces briefly unleashed in 1848 threatened the recently emerged liberal element in the churches and forced it into becoming a loyal opposition.[37] In England the term "Broad Church" goes back at least to 1853,[38] and the party it designates goes back further still, to the time of Coleridge. Its outlook, both the positive and the negative sides, is summarized by the historian and Bampton Lecturer Hastings Rashdall:

> I think we might say that we adhere to the three great essentials of the Christian religion—belief in a personal God, in a personal immortality, and (while not limiting the idea of revelation to the Old and New Testaments) in a unique and paramount revelation of God in the historic Christ. But we recognise that to this one foundation there has, in the course of ages, been added much building-upon. Of the vast superstructure of doctrinal and ritual and ethical tradition which has been built upon and around the essential Christianity which we find in the moral and religious consciousness of Jesus the Son of God, not all is of equal value. There is a great deal of hay and stubble that has simply got to be cleared away.[39]

Workers in this tradition, who began to call themselves Modernists near the end of the century, were taught by Seebohm that Colet had brought to bear the same critical spirit on the reading of the Scriptures and had also distanced himself from the many features of the church of his day which he found incompatible with what Rashdall called the "great essentials of the Christian religion." Readers of the Modernists' organ, *The Modern Churchman*, were assured by one contributor that "whatever hope there is for true progress today is to be found in the existence of men of the type of Colet" as delineated by Seebohm,[40] while another contributor claimed that the Modernists were the "successors" of Seebohm's trio—Colet, Erasmus, and More.[41] Roman Catholic Modernists too were attracted by Seebohm's Colet. The first volume of what the Abbé Auguste Humbert intended as a multivolume work on *Les origines de la théologie moderne* included a section on Colet, though the author confessed he relied on the Seebohm tradition because he was unable to find copies of Colet's actual writings.[42] In the very year of publication, however, this book was denounced and placed on the *Index librorum prohibitorum*;[43] the author promptly submitted[44] and was heard from no more.

Seebohm's interpretation of Colet had deep personal meaning for him, and he rode his thesis hard. Misgivings on the part of specialists were drowned out by the acclaim of the wide educated public. He himself had a conspicuous tendency, while justifiably emphasizing his new insights, to ignore inconvenient evidence. His most important scholarly work deals not with the so-called Oxford Reformers but with medieval English communities and agricultural practices. Even here, however, where his reputation was more solid, he tended to downplay or ignore evidence that told against his interpretations. So much so, that the leading authority on Seebohm's subject expressed himself after Seebohm's death in what for an obituary notice are unusually candid terms:

> His method of collecting evidence was not entirely free from objections. He looked keenly for the facts suited to his arguments, and often succeeded in presenting disregarded points in an entirely new and striking light. . . . But he was sometimes colour-blind in regard to the sides of the subject which did not fit his theories.[45]

Seebohm's thesis supplied the ideological framework of what became the standard biography, *A Life of John Colet, D.D.* (1887), by the Reverend Joseph H. Lupton, surmaster, or second master, in the school that Colet founded. Lupton not only adds significantly to the factual record given in Knight's biography but offers a much less tendentious picture of Colet as reformer than his predecessor had done. His mild and kindly account naturally stresses Colet's educational work, though his ventures into the history of education were, as we shall see in chapter 9, poorly received by contemporary scholars. The greatest weakness of the biography, however, lies in its almost complete divorce of Colet's life from his writings. Instead of rethinking for himself the significance of the works he had edited, Lupton took on faith the conceptual framework that Seebohm had put forward twenty years earlier and confined his labors largely to the biographical record. Lupton and Seebohm refer to each other as friends in their prefaces, and Lupton in his more temperate way appears to have shared at least some of the Broad Church interests. In 1887 he gave a set of (unpublished) Hulsean Lectures,[46] lectures which were delivered almost exclusively by speakers of a pronounced liberal stamp.[47]

Lupton's attractive and well-written biography was reissued posthumously in a virtually unchanged "New Edition" in 1909, in connection with what was then thought to be the school's quatercentenary. The biography has always been readily available. Seebohm's study, after achieving four editions between 1867 and 1896, became a sort of minor classic by being included in 1914 in the series Everyman's Library, which contained what its editor regarded as the thousand best books in the world. *The Oxford Reformers* is no longer part of that series, but for a time it nestled into the history section alongside Gibbon and Thucydides, and it sold well.

The now century-old picture of Colet given by Lupton and Seebohm has proved surprisingly durable. The clamor of religious polemics in which it first appeared has long since died down. Scholarship has modified or obliterated many features on which the old interpretation was founded. New facts have gradually accumulated, and old errors have been corrected.[48] Nevertheless, in many quarters much the same things are said about Colet today as were said about him a hundred years ago, and Colet studies until the last few decades remained essentially where Seebohm and Lupton left them.

Part of the reason for this scholarly neglect is the simple fact that Colet's works were published in such small editions that they were already all out of print by 1887[49] and soon became very scarce even in England. Elsewhere they were not to be had at all during the period when confessional Reformation studies flourished, before the current ecumenical interests became dominant. Foreign scholars, though free of the pressures that had helped mold the Seebohm-Lupton account, had no way of correcting it or even of knowing that it needed correction. In 1929, for example, a German scholar expressly apologized for his second-hand account of Colet by explaining that he could not find his writings in the libraries or on the antiquarian book market;[50] and even as late as 1948 another German scholar repeated the complaint.[51] The printed catalogue of the Bibliothèque Nationale in Paris lists none of Colet's writings, and the Library of Congress did not number Lupton's editions of Colet among its millions of volumes until the situation was remedied by a 1966 reprint.

A further reason for the slow movement in Colet studies is that his place seemed to be so securely settled that there was little more to do. Erasmus's memoir of Colet, already mentioned, was long taken at face value with little if any allowance for its evident reformist bias. The hint already given by Erasmus's editor P. S. Allen in 1922 that the portrait of Colet may have had a "special purpose"[52] was not followed up. Now, however, the situation has begun to change. From the late 1960s on, Continental scholars have repeatedly pointed out that the letter on Colet needs to be read in the light of Erasmus's intent,[53] and the way is open for a reinterpretation, not merely of what Erasmus said about Colet but—much more important—of Colet's own works.

It is a curious fact that both Seebohm and Lupton paid very little attention to what Colet actually wrote, even to the point of passing over in silence—not to say suppressing—some of the most revealing evidence. A curious fact admittedly, but not inexplicable. A close look at what Colet wrote will give us quite a different picture of what he was like and what he was doing from the picture his Victorian admirers offered. As we will see in the pages that follow, Colet was definitely an early Tudor intellectual, not a Victorian one. It is not surprising that his aims and methods diverged sharply from theirs, so much so that at times later writers preferred to avert their eyes from what there was to see.

The present study offers a fresh look at Colet's achievement. It aims to take him on his own terms, unfamiliar and sometimes even uncongenial as they are, as far as the evidence permits. We will see him in the familiar role of preacher, but we will see him also in less familiar roles—active in putting down heresy and judging heretics, highly political, and, like most successful people, markedly deferential to those above him in church and state. I will consider Colet as founder of a school often supposed to be advanced and humanistic in orientation but, as planned by Colet, actually quite conservative. Even in the most familiar of all his roles, that of the interpreter of Scripture, we will see that he was working on altogether different lines from those he is usually supposed to have been following. We may well find that the sixteenth-century John Colet is, as compared with his Victorian namesake, the more interesting man. He is certainly the more real.

2

"As the Tree Is Planted . . ."

"As the tree is planted, so it grows" ("Qualis plantacio, talis est arbor"; DEH, 272). Colet was speaking here of the deep influence guardians could have on their wards; but this judgment clearly applies even more closely to the influence that he knew a child's heredity, home life, and schooling have on his later development. This and the following chapter are focused on Colet's family background and his growth to young manhood.

The obvious point of departure for Colet's early life is Erasmus's sympathetic and well-informed biographical letter to Jodocus Jonas. Erasmus met Colet on his first visit to England in 1499, when both men were in their early thirties. On his later visits, their friendship ripened gradually, and they maintained a high regard for each other though exchange of letters was only intermittent. When Erasmus learned of Colet's death he wrote to an English friend that "there is no man in the last thirty years whose death has so afflicted me."[1] It is probably a mistake to take this statement as literally as most scholars have done, for on such occasions Erasmus was not given to understatement.[2] It is nevertheless thanks to Erasmus's wish to commemorate Colet that we know details about Colet's early life such as survive for very few persons born in the fifteenth century.[3]

John Colet, Erasmus tells us, was the oldest of twenty-two children, eleven girls and eleven boys, born to Henry and Christian Colet (A, ll. 256–258). One piece of sixteenth-century evidence would make the children twenty in all,[4] but Erasmus repeated his figure more than a decade later,[5] and other friends of Colet give the same number,[6] so that twenty-two is probably right. Even more striking than the size of the family was its mortality. As Erasmus remembered it, John was the only surviving child when he met him in 1499, all his sisters and brothers having died in infancy or youth. Erasmus's imagination, however, was so struck by the mortality among Colet's siblings that he forgot a fact of the first importance to the Colet family: one of John's brothers, Richard, did survive to reach manhood.

Richard Colet, a dozen years younger than John, entered Lincoln's Inn in 1493,[7] a year before Thomas More entered New Inn. More was about sixteen at that point, after two years spent at Oxford. If Richard, not having gone to Oxford, entered Lincoln's Inn at the then perfectly normal age of fourteen he would have been twenty-one in 1500. This chronology squares well with two dates known from other sources.

First, on 1 May 1500 Richard made his first known appearance with his father as party to a real estate transaction;[8] by that date, then, he was of age. Second, documentary evidence places John Colet's birth in early January of 1467.[9] Markedly religious from an early age, John nevertheless waited till the unusually late age of thirty-one before taking his vows as priest on 25 March 1498, after receiving the diaconate on the preceding December 17.[10] It looks as if the family insisted that he wait to take irrevocable vows until Richard, who was being groomed to succeed his father in managing the family's business interests, had safely reached manhood. In placing their hopes on Richard, however, the family was to be disappointed. Richard continues to appear in business documents until 1503,[11] but then no more. His name does not appear in his father's will of 27 September 1505.[12]

Thus two—not, as Erasmus said, only one—of the Colet sons lived to attain their majority. But this does little to attenuate the terrible fact that John, as the oldest, lived out his entire boyhood and adolescence amid a continuing "procession of cradles and coffins."[13] The age was of course inured to infant mortality, to the point that in some families children remained unnamed until the passage of several years gave some likelihood to their survival.[14] In a single family the same given name might be reused again and again as one bearer of it after another died. In the family tree of Colet's own cousin William we find among the names of his children the drily touching record:

Willyam,
Willyam,
Willyam,
all dead.[15]

Statistical realities notwithstanding, it is painful to imagine the atmosphere of such a household, quickened to near-panic from time to time as yet another child fell ill.

Psychohistorical speculation is notoriously risky, but in the face of such a childhood it seems unavoidable. What we will see of Colet's early years will seem at times to invite Freudian commentary, yet the Freudian model has taken hard knocks in recent years,[16] and in fact we have no satisfactory model of childhood against which to interpret Colet's. Though John and Richard grew up in the same household with the same parents, their early experience seems to have affected them very differently. Richard studied the law and was no doubt expected to marry in due course and have a family. John studied theology, and his attitude toward marriage and sex, and in general to this world, was, to put it mildly, different.

He never tired of insisting that marriage, which he curtly defined as "sleeping with one woman" (C, 189 [128]), had no positive value at all but was at best only a "concession" to those unable to lead the heroic life of celibacy. According to this contemptuous definition, while marriage is better than promiscuity, that is all that can be said for it. He recoils from "the pollution of intercourse," which "stains" the wife and leaves the husband's body "dirty" (P, 294). Nor is it marriage only against which he inveighs. Repeatedly he cites 1 John 5:19 as proof that this "whole world lies in the power of the Devil" (C, 208 [162]; R, 180, 200); his insistence on this text gives as good a clue as we have to his character. In all his writings he has not a single favorable word to say of the world here below. In contrast to the other clergy of his station, who regularly wore purple, Colet always wore black. Erasmus was sufficiently struck by this habit to mention it (A, ll. 333–334), and it was so much a part of Colet's image that he was depicted wearing black in the colored effigy on his tomb.[17] Yet this vehement rejection of the world and its ways came from a very rich man who enjoyed his comforts and showed considerable fondness for money. The scornful dismissal of marriage came from a man whose parents clearly did not share his outlook on it. We know that as a grown man Colet was fond of his mother and spent lengthy periods with her in the country. We do not know what he thought of his father.[18]

Clearly something here requires explanation, but that of itself does not mean that adequate materials for an explanation are forthcoming. In this chapter I wish to set forth such facts as we have about Colet's parents and home, the practices of child rearing in their social class, and the like. Tentative patterns will emerge, but I trust they will emerge from the relatively numerous facts, which will serve as a continual check on speculation. Moreover, anyone who has grown up among siblings knows that environment explains only so much. Even if we knew how John Colet spent every day of his childhood we might still find it hard to explain why he turned out so different from Richard. It may be after all, as has been argued recently,[19] that the biology of brain development is as decisive a determinant of a child's moral and emotional life as anything that happens in his early environment. What is said of Colet's parents in this chapter, there-fore, is not intended to oversolve the problem. The growth of a youngster remains mysterious.

Fortunately for John, his mother, Christian, was a quite remarkable woman, vigorous, abundantly healthy, resilient, and (I would guess) happy. She came from an old and eminent Buckinghamshire family, the Knyvets, or Knevets.[20] In 1340, under Edward III, Sir John Knyvet was lord chancellor of England, the only professional lawyer to hold that office before Colet's friend Sir Thomas More assumed it in 1529, under Henry VIII.[21] Christian Knyvet was the daughter of Sir John Knyvet and Alice (née Lynn); Elizabeth Clifton, who Lupton thought was Christian's mother, actually belongs one generation earlier.[22]

Christian had only one sibling, a brother who shared her good genes and died in 1516 at the then-patriarchal age of seventy-six. Thus he was born about 1440 and his sister, who was six years younger, about 1446.[23] Since her first son was born in January 1467, her marriage to Henry Colet may be put around 1466, when she was nineteen or twenty, the typical age of marriage for women in early modern England,[24] while her hus-band, as we shall see, was about thirty-five.

Christian Knyvet was a very good catch. Her father already enjoyed a large patrimony and his only son, William, Christian's brother, married a nobleman's daughter—also an heiress, of course. Upon her death he was in a position to aspire to the daughter of the first duke of Buckingham.[25] With this marriage the Knyvets, and ultimately therefore the Colets, acquired a connection with the royal family itself: Bucking-ham's third son, Henry, married the widowed Lady Margaret, Countess of Richmond and Derby and mother of the future King Henry VII. Thus Christian Knyvet brought her husband not only a suitable dowry but an impressive network of connections.

In the hard-bitten world of fifteenth-century England such a bride had to be earned. Colet's Victorian biographer comments demurely that the marriage "must have been a most advantageous one for young [Henry] Colet,"[26] but of course the lady's family were as well aware of this fact as he was. They would be careful to see that the advantages were not all on one side, so that by the time he was realistically able to claim such a bride "young Colet" was not so very young.

Henry Colet was the third (or fifth)[27] son of Robert Colet of Wendover, Bucks.[28] The family was a good one and had a coat of arms from an early date.[29] Nevertheless, ambitious Colets had been making their way to Lon-don, and specifically to the Mercers' Company, for quite some years be-fore the youthful Henry set out for the capital. Already in 1442 a John Colet was admitted to the freedom of the company (after some ten years' apprenticeship), and Henry's older brother John, who died in 1461, was admitted to the freedom in 1450.[30] Clearly there was ample precedent on the Colet side for the name that Henry gave his oldest son, besides the fact that the oldest son in each generation of Christian Knyvet's family was regularly named John.[31]

The mercery was an attractive trade and, as with all such guilds, entrance was restricted. Applicants would have to prove they could read and write, for the internal organization of the great livery companies was very similar,[32] and in 1469 we find the Goldsmiths restating and stiffening an existing requirement to that effect.[33] Applicants had not only to be sixteen but to look it. Documentary evidences of birthdate were still uncommon, and "dayly" the Company was besieged by lads who claimed they had attained the minimum age but looked to skeptical eyes "verrey litill in growing and stature."[34] We may fairly suppose, then, that Henry Colet was and looked sixteen when he was admitted as an apprentice to the Mercers' Company in 1446–1447.[35] His birth must therefore be put in 1430, ten or fifteen years earlier than Lupton assumed.[36] In theory and usually in practice apprenticeship lasted ten years; Henry Colet followed this pattern, for we find him "issuing," on completion of his apprenticeship, in 1456–1457.

The core of the Mercers' trade lay in finished cloth and especially luxury apparel, but with time it had branched out into a great many related, and even unrelated, areas.[37] It is probably not too much to say that whenever a remunerative cargo could be had, or disposed of, the more prominent mercers would be interested. Earlier scholars tended to idealize the brotherhood of the guild merchants and suppose there was virtually no price cutting and no attempt to expand one's own business at the direct expense of anyone else in the fellowship,[38] but the records of the companies tell a more realistic story. Despite all the ecclesiastical prohibitions of usury, lending money at interest was not unknown.[39] Attempts to lure away the customers of one's brothers in the guild were also common enough.[40] Moreover, despite agreed-upon prices, deliberate underselling was rife.[41] Widespread too was poaching on trade that in principle belonged to another company. For the Mercers the Goldsmiths were an inviting target. The core of their trade was making straightforward gold plate, while the Mercers dealt in gold objects of ostentation,[42] but the dividing line was a wavering one. Already in 1372 the Goldsmiths were having so much trouble from the poaching by other companies that they were granted the right to search the premises of presumed offenders.[43] This was more easily said than done, of course; Mercers and even Haberdashers continued to encroach on the exasperated Goldsmiths. On another front the Mercers were busy defending their own territory against similar encroachments by the Goldsmiths and, especially, the Grocers. These characteristic examples suggest that the original concentration of the guild companies on specific crafts had seriously eroded.

Corresponding to the changing positions of the companies relative to one another were important internal changes. The collegial atmosphere of trust was increasingly subject to challenge. In principle the freemen of the Mercers, like the freemen of other companies, were equal, but in practice a two-tier system had evolved. Those who had a large business had become a sort of company within the company, a distinction signalized by their wearing of the company's livery. As befitted the Mercers' trade the livery was handsome; it was also expensive and was moreover changed every few years to different colors. A not-unintended effect was the exclusion of the lesser men from those who were "in the livery." In Henry Colet's own time the lines between mercers and mercers continued to be drawn ever more rigidly. By 1478 a man who wanted to have his own shop not only had to pay a substantial 40s. fine, or fee, to the company but had to prove that he had £100 in capital and how he had come by it.[44] Even the greatest mercers still retained a presence on the retail side of the trade, but there was a widening gulf between the "mercantile" and the "handicraft" members of the company.[45] The latter, basically shopkeepers and artisans, were crowded out of its more important affairs. The governing body, the master with his Court of Assistants, was open only to those who were in the livery. Those not in the livery could attend the quarterly general meetings and the feasts but could not be members of the crucial committees that ran the company's affairs.

These two phenomena—increasing differentiation between the important and the minor members of a given company, and blurring of the lines defining the scope of the great companies vis-à-vis one another—were reflected in the rise of a sort of supercompany that occupied much of Henry Colet's thoughts, though it is not mentioned by Lupton at all, namely, the Company of Merchant Adventurers. Its members were drawn from the upper echelons of the more important companies, with the Mercers predominating. So close were the ties of the Mercers' Company with the Merchant Adventurers that the minutes of the meetings of both companies were entered in the same book. Indeed for reasons of convenience the headquarters of the Merchant Adventurers was on the ground floor of Mercers' Hall, then as now in Ironmonger Lane. The clerk of the Merchant Adventurers, from 1487 to at least 1497, was another John Colet.[46] Wealthy Grocers and Mercers and Fishmongers and Goldsmiths had more in common with one another than they did with the little people in their own trades; they were the ones who specialized in international and wholesale trade, where the big profits were to be made.

It was soon clear to young Henry Colet that his future lay with this far-ranging side of the trade. Apprentices were not permitted to trade on their own account,[47] but of course some demonstrably did so anyway.[48] Henry had relations in the company and was probably apprenticed to one of them, so that collusion would be easy and undetectable. There is no direct evidence that Henry Colet got a flying start in business before he had acquired his formal credentials, but it is hard to imagine him dutifully hanging back while fellow apprentices were already making their first deals.

Once Henry Colet emerged from the obscurity of apprenticeship in 1456–1457, it was not long before he began to appear in the records of the company. Within five years he was already in the livery, at about the age of thirty-one.[49] He emerges from these early mentions as a hardworking, loyal, popular member of the fellowship. Especially at the beginning of his career we see him performing, and no doubt performing well, duties that others avoided. On great ceremonial occasions, such as the entrance of the monarch into London or his return to the capital after a victory, the city companies were expected to ride out to greet him. This duty was unpopular with the merchants: it was expensive, since they had to be dressed and mounted with appropriate elegance, and the leisurely pace of such ceremonial actions cut heavily into the working day. So unpopular was this duty that on one major occasion, out of twenty-four Mercers assigned to ride out to meet the king no fewer than eight simply did not appear, to the embarrassment of the company, which levied heavy fines on the truants.[50] On 5 June 1461 Henry Colet was one of the twenty-four "goodely horsemen" who represented the company in the coronation procession of Edward IV and were expected to reflect credit on the city and the company ("likly for the worsship of the Citie & of the same felyshipp").[51] He was assigned to a similar delegation two years later, and needless to say he was there.[52] He clearly intended to show himself a conspicuously faithful member of the company, willing to begin his climb up the ladder by doing things others would rather not do. At this stage, though he was in his earlier thirties, marriage and his very large family were all still ahead of him.

The contemporaneous Wars of the Roses leave little trace in the records of the company. As we have seen, the company welcomed Edward IV on his coronation. In the course of time they welcomed Edward V, his youthful heir who was to lose his life in the Tower under mysterious circumstances;[53] after Edward they greeted his uncle, now King Richard III. And after Bosworth they rode out once again, this time to greet Henry VII. They discussed the obvious political problem and coolly decided to play no favorites but to follow, in greeting Henry, "the president [i.e., precedent] in receyvyng yn of Kyng Richard the iijth."[54] Henry Colet was no longer deputed to these ceremonies; he had not only got older but had greatly raised his position in the company during the twenty-four tumultuous years between the coronation procession of Edward IV and the crowning of Henry VII.

A series of levies, mainly for compulsory loans to the Crown, permits us to measure the rapid increase of Henry Colet's wealth. On the first such occasion on which he is mentioned he is assessed only 10s, while at least a few were assessed as much as £4.6s.8d.; around the same time his share of another assessment was 5s. while some others were paying as much as 40s.[55] Within the same week as the latter loan the Mercers were suddenly required to contribute to yet another loan, "a preste of D marc graunted to the Kyng . . . for the spede of therle of Warwik." The Mercers contributed their share, grudgingly.[56] This time the maximum assessment was £13.6s.8d., the minimum 3s.4d., and the median 20s. Colet subscribed 33s.4d., well above the median, when he had had the freedom for only five years.[57] By 1477, sixteen years later, in an assessment for the Mercers' contribution toward rebuilding the city walls, Colet and three others paid 10s.; only two men were assessed more, while all the others paid less, those in the livery being generally assessed 5s. each and those out of the livery 1s.8d. None of those assessed 10s. or more held office in the company at the time; the assessments were based not on "room," or office, but on wealth.[58]

Henry Colet's increasing wealth, and no doubt his personal popularity also, put him in the company's inner circle. By 1476 he was one of the wardens,[59] and in 1480 he was elected to the first of what were to be five terms as master of the company.[60] The company at whose head he now stood was preeminent among the city companies, as shown by the ever-reliable index of assessments for compulsory loans to the Crown. Of the eighty-two companies assessed for this purpose on 19 January 1489, the Mercers had to pay £740, followed at a great distance by the Grocers (£455), the Drapers (£420), the Fishmongers and the Goldsmiths (£280 each), and so on down to the lowest six of the eighty-two companies, which were assessed "nichill."[61]

The notoriousness of the company's wealth had occasional drawbacks. The Mercers had become accustomed to giving splendid suppers at the installation of new wardens, suppers to which influential guests from outside the company were also invited. Somehow these shrewd merchants failed to foresee that the luxurious scale of their feasts would be bound to cause their share of general imposts and loans to rise. When in the summer of 1491 they came to realize this fact, they decided not to hold the supper at all but to limit themselves instead to an "honest, convenyent drinking," accompanied only by venison, sturgeon, strawberries and wafers, ale, and "Wyne red & claret"[62]—the clerk being apparently an ale drinker.

The Mercers' wealth was, most of the time, prudently understated. Like the members of the financial community today they were notable for understatedly luxurious clothes and conservative hair styles. When an occasional maverick appeared in their midst, like Robert Carswell, he soon felt the company's displeasure. Robert was refused his request to be sworn a shopholder until he promised to "sadly dispose hym [i.e., behave himself gravely] and manerly both in his arreye & also in Cuttynge of his here and not to go lyke a gallaunt or a man of Courte."[63] The same dislike of the profligates at court seeps into the clerk's account of William Pickering's presentation of his case before a panel of the company. William, it seems, was not so easily daunted as Robert had been. William, "alle hawty and Roiall, full of pride disdeyned to stond bare hed but boldly did his cappe on his hed and so tolde his tale."[64] On most days the honest clerk was no wizard with words, but here in his indignation he gives us a zestful foretaste of Elizabethan English.

As we have seen, the company over which Henry Colet had come to preside was highly conscious of the image it presented to the outside world. Its inner workings, however, while generally grave and prudent, sometimes reflect deep tensions. Committees appointed to assess fellow members for a loan to the king could be expressly instructed not to let themselves be swayed by "hatred, malis or evyll"—a sign that the caution was needed.[65] The levels to which hostility could rise within the company are illustrated by an incident in which two members of the fellowship, at odds after a judgment had gone against one of them, went after each other "not oonly with wordes but also in dedes . . . to geder fraying with edge toles."[66] This dangerous brawl was no doubt fully discussed by the combatants' fellows, but another far more lurid and sinister case throws it into the shade, a case that involved illicit sex and conspiracy to commit a murder within the company.

One mercer, Thomas Wyndout, bribed another mercer to marry the wife of yet a third, Thomas Shelley. From the facts scattered throughout the unusually long account of this scandal we can make out that Wyndout, himself a married man, and Shelley's wife were in love. The go-between whom Wyndout bribed was not married and thus could marry Mistress Shelley—once she became a widow. He would then presumably have been the complacent husband when Wyndout paid his visits. However, this scenario presupposed the murder of Shelley. When the conspiracy was accidentally discovered, the intended victim, at first sight surprisingly, petitioned the king to allow the company to determine the matter intramurally. The records do not say so, but Shelley must have been under pressure not to force mercers to wash their dirty linen in public. Henry Colet, a member of virtually every important committee within the company, was also on the tribunal that handled this case. Its judgment was anything but ferocious. Wyndout escaped with a very heavy fine and had to ask pardon of Shelley (and his wife) on his knees; he also had to free Shelley from a burdensome debt. But that was all. The Shelleys resumed their previous domestic relations, whatever they had been; Wyndout, far from being expelled from the fellowship, remained in the livery[67] and two decades later was an alderman.[68] If one wonders what a member of the fellowship would have had to do to be expelled, the only such action the existing records contemplate is for a member to have been detected, repeatedly, in presenting a falsified bill of lading to customs officials.[69] The Shelley-Wyndout matter, by contrast, was glossed over to the apparent satisfaction of all, including the king, who had in effect retained jurisdiction to ensure that justice was done.

A curious sidelight on the affair, not mentioned in the company's records, is that Wyndout had entered the company as the apprentice of Henry Colet.[70] Hence Colet's presence on the tribunal that was judging him seems at least anomalous. In any case, as apprentices lived with their masters, the lusty apprentice and John Colet, still a boy, would have known each other, though we do not know how sober John looked on the roustabout Thomas.

Henry Colet's rapid rise to distinction in the Mercers' Company is paralleled by his rise to prominence in the city. By 1476 he was highly enough thought of to be nominated alderman, his name being proposed by the incumbent sheriff and an ex-sheriff. As he had done within the company, Henry Colet was willing to take his seat in the Court of Aldermen as the representative of the ward generally thought of as least prestigious, Farringdon Ward Without,[71] on 15 November 1476;[72] in the following year we find him a sheriff.[73] By 7 March 1487, a decade later, he had worked his way up to be the alderman of the most desirable ward, Cornhill. In the course of his ascent he was translated (that is, nominated to and elected by a ward to which he was willing to move) from Farringdon Without to Bassishaw Ward. Bassishaw was a Mercers' stronghold, so that his election there is further testimony to his strong position within the company. When it was time to move on again he accepted discharge from his duties at Bassishaw on 15 February 1482 but made a very handsome parting gesture, a gift of 200 marks toward the repair of the Cheap Cross.[74] His new seat, from 1 February 1483, was as alderman for Castle Baynard, from which in 1487 he made his final move to Cornhill.

Shortly before this point, on 13 October 1486, his career in the city reached a climax with his installation as lord mayor.[75] He was knighted on the following 13 January, which must have been very close to his son

John's twentieth birthday.[76] During his tenure of the office he had the additional satisfaction that he ranked, for purposes of precedence, as an earl.[77]

As if his cup were not already running over, he was elected to Parliament, representing London, on 9 October 1487.[78] At the close of this first term he was reelected, on 2 December 1488, for the 1489 term.[79] Still in the future lay the unusual honor of a second term as lord mayor; this time the office was pressed upon him, and he may have accepted reluctantly.[80]

Certainly he ran some danger of being overcommitted. The company's records show him fully involved in its affairs, and his wealth continued to grow. His term as lord mayor was over and above all this and was followed by two terms, perhaps less onerous, in Parliament. To get all this done well, in addition to the demands of his home life, he must have budgeted his time efficiently. Like his wife, he clearly enjoyed excellent health; even in the last summer of his life, in his mid-seventies, he was serving yet again as master of the company and was active in its affairs. His career was vastly successful, and more than any other London merchant of his time his success was built on money he himself made rather than on inheritance or a rich marriage.[81] But the earlier stages of his career had for that very reason taken time. When he had reached the point where an heiress's father and brother would take him seriously as a suitor he was already thirty-five.

For a man who was to father twenty-two children after marrying in midlife this long preparation for an advantageous marriage must have caused some strain. It is true that in his day no fewer than eighteen brothels were lined up across the river in Bankside.[82] It is also true that prostitution, though immoral, was accepted as a practical necessity by churchmen; at this period the Bankside brothels were licensed by the government. Even homosexual activity and masturbation, though severely reprehended by theologians, were dealt with surprisingly lightly in manuals for confessors, who had to deal with the world as it was.[83] No matter how philopolyprogenitive he proved in marriage, the heavy demands on his time and his continued excellent health suggest that as a single man he relied mainly on his fundamental decency, plenty of hard work and long hours, and a steady self-discipline. It is more than likely that as a father he expected the same self-restraint from his son John, who, as Erasmus tells us (A, ll. 391–392, 396–398), found his own sexual drives very troublesome in adolescence and later.

When Henry Colet did marry and brought his bride to his house in Budge Street, the house of a well-off merchant was very different from what it would be even a century later. The age of privacy had not yet arrived, and the house had none of the multiple room divisions a wealthy family would later take for granted. The house of a successful merchant at that period would have a hall and a large bedroom for the whole family. In the bedroom the master and mistress would share a curtained and canopied four-poster, while everyone else would settle down somewhere else in the room. A kitchen, pantry, and buttery (sometimes separate, often not), with perhaps a countinghouse or a storeroom, would complete the inventory of the rooms, even when the family were numerous and the number of servants correspondingly large.[84]

Given the physical closeness, where everyone's doings were subject to everyone else's inspection and comment, youngsters would learn the facts of life early and for the most part take them for granted. One remembers the good-natured bawdy of Mercutio or Juliet's Nurse, but it is worth remembering also that the Nurse's sallies on the score of impending marriage brought no blush to the cheeks of her thirteen-year-old charge. Youngsters would likewise soon know that at every pregnancy a woman ran a real risk of death. John Colet, his mother pregnant again and again though her children seemed fated to die, would soon know, to cite the nurse again, that "women grow by men." The intelligent and observant boy would think his thoughts.

As we have already noticed, Colet seems to have been fond of his mother in his adult years, and through Erasmus we catch a glimpse of her as she looked in old age. Naturally Erasmus was struck by the fortitude with which she endured the tragic mortality of her children. Somehow she remained cheerful and kind, and even as an elderly lady her skin was smooth and unwrinkled.[85] Her son spent time with her in her house in Stepney, then in the countryside though near London; there she was occasionally Erasmus's hostess on his visits to England in 1504–1505 and again in 1511-1512. Erasmus seems to have been fond of her and she of him. She asks after him, Colet tells his friend,[86] and Erasmus returned the interest. They managed to circumvent the linguistic barrier—of course her language was English, and Erasmus's knowledge of that language, to judge by his published comments on it, must have been exceedingly shaky.[87] One imagines that at her table Erasmus ate better, and had his cup filled more frequently, than when dining with her son at the deanery. In the abstemious dean's presence they may even have exchanged a few confidences, or perhaps a conspiratorial wink, about their shared preference for beef over crackers and for wine over water—the sort of comradeship that translates with a minimum of words.

Besides having this glimpse of Dame Christian in serene old age we are fortunate in knowing at least something of the circumstances under which she grew up. She was raised in her family's house in Allwelthorp, Buckinghamshire; however, it seems likely that she spent her later girlhood in the Benedictine priory at nearby Carrow, for she learned to read and write. It is true that a document she signed on 19 November 1519 bears only her two initials, and these rather scrawled,[88] but a lady in her seventies might well have a touch of arthritis. The fact that she was appointed co-executrix successively in the wills of her son Robert,[89] her husband,[90] and finally her remaining son, John,[91] strongly suggests that she had practical literacy as well as business sense. The latter two estates were exceedingly large and complex, and family members must have thought she discharged her responsibilities creditably.

Responsibility must have been thrust on her from an early age, since her brother, the only other child in the family, was often away.[92] The sturdy independence of the women in the family was epitomized in an event that doubtless became a favorite part of the family lore. One day when Christian's father was away in London a royal commission appeared before the castle demanding its surrender to the king. Her mother rejected the demand as unjust, as in the sequel it proved to be. But with nothing to rely on at that moment but her own fighting instinct, she and her people pulled up the drawbridge, and she appeared on the parapets alongside her retainers, all of them armed with missiles and clearly meaning business. Confronted with this militant demonstration from the castle's lady, the commissioners, all of them men of course, slunk off ignominiously.[93]

Her mother's plucky stand set an example of activity, self-confidence, and loyalty to her husband's interests that was not lost on the daughter. When Christian married a not-so-young and already successful merchant she threw herself into her new duties with characteristic energy. We have already seen that she ran a large household and bore a large number of children. For all their fifteen years' difference in age she became a wife whom Sir Henry could talk to about his affairs and whose comments he probably came to respect. As already mentioned she showed aptitude for business, and like her husband she identified with the company first and last. Indeed our final glimpse of her is near the close of her life, having survived her husband and all of her children, as she presents to the Mercers two valuable cups.[94]

The emotional temperature of the Colet family in John's early years is hard to gauge, and of course the mellow serenity of a time when the son is a middle-aged man and his mother is on in years does not necessarily tell us much of what it felt like to grow up in the house in Budge Street forty years earlier. Some scholars find in the late middle ages an increased affection for children, at least among the rich.[95] Two Italian travelers in the 1490s, however, were struck by how little affection parents in England seemed to show their children.[96] It is tempting to write off the latter observation as an instance of cross-cultural incomprehension. After all, one of the same travelers, attending a banquet for the installation of a London sheriff, thought the affair was almost preternaturally quiet, while the Londoners must have thought they were having a good time.[97] Moreover, English parents and children would have their own cultural expectations, whatever the livelier customs in vogue in Italy. Before concluding that visitors from the South were simply mistaken, however, it may be well to consider the child-rearing practices current among the upper middle class. These are surprisingly well documented from the later fifteenth century on. With the increasing prominence of the bourgeoisie, books on raising children multiplied and were eagerly consulted.[98]

For what it is worth, Colet's mother probably did not nurse him or his siblings but put them out to a wet nurse. The mere fact of her twenty-two pregnancies would suggest this, since breast feeding has a contraceptive effect and weaning often extended over two or three years. In addition, the books on child rearing uniformly discountenance a mother's feeding her child herself. (Conservatives, though, held out for the old practice because a baby was supposed to drink in the qualities of its nurse. A woman who put her children out to nurse was not a mother but a "cruel stepmother" according to one critic who, however, had to add in the next breath that "manye mothers are there at this present" who put their children out to nurse anyway.)[99] Toilet training was started early with harsh suppositories. Another odd sidelight on child rearing may be implied by Colet's referring with approval to an etymology that derived the word *mentula*, "penis," from *mens* (stem *ment-*), "mind" (RO, 224; bowdlerized in Lupton's translation). He took this, along with several other etymologies, from the humanist Latin dictionary *Cornucopiae*, by Niccolò Perotti,[100] who explained the etymology as follows: "Mothers or nurses of infants, caressing [*blandiendo tangentes*] their male member, have the habit of calling it *paruam mentem* [little mind], in much the same way that they kiss the child and call it *animulam*, that is, 'little soul,' or *corculum*, that is 'little heart.' "[101] As Colet read this passage in Perotti, did it sound familiar?

The authors of the volumes on child rearing (all of them men) regularly advocated the withdrawal of affection as an effective means of getting a child to obey. The results of this method, in extreme form, can be seen from the account of his own childhood by the early Spanish humanist Juan Luis Vives, who was one generation younger than Colet. Vives's mother rejected his instinctive childish appeals for love unless he was "good." Under these conditions, even when the mother does show affection and the child feels approved he knows that the approval is only conditional, so that it brings no real security. Vives's own reaction to this upbringing was a textbook case. By psycho-logic he became convinced as a child that his mother was very good and withheld love from him only because he was unworthy. He became fixated at this level of fundamental insecurity, always trying to propitiate the just but offended parent and find acceptance. Because what was really sought was the security of love, the effort was foredoomed to fail. When Vives offered his own contribution to the literature of child rearing, *Institution of a Christian Woman* (1536), he ironically proved he was his mother's son. Despite the suffering his mother's methods had caused him, he recommends the same methods to other mothers.

Certainly nothing so drastic occurred in Colet's life. His mother was kindly and loving, and one tantalizing passage suggests that in later years he recalled from time to time scenes of play from his childhood. The recollection, if such it was, was triggered by a mention in Dionysius the pseudo-Areopagite of "many-colored horses" and "warriors carrying lances."[102] Colet pauses for a moment to evoke the image of "girls playing with dolls" and "boys astride toy rocking horses"; though he immediately gives the image a theological turn, it remains as a solitary possible hint of childhood pleasures in his own boyhood. But in the Colets' social class the prevailing wisdom on child rearing did not encourage doting, and fifteenth-century English had no term corresponding to "the kids."

For whatever reasons, John Colet's outlook in later life was notably somber. He remained celibate, he ate and drank little, and he looked with disfavor on lavish hospitality. As he ate his scanty meals an attendant read biblical passages aloud, preferably from St. Paul.[103] Guests were offered chiefly intellectual and spiritual nourishment — to the distress of Erasmus, who was no enemy of a good meal and enjoyed his burgundy. Colet led a vigorous, useful, and interesting life as an adult, but it seems that the emotional start he got in life made his achievement more difficult and left marks of strain.

The scenes of death which shadowed his most formative years would almost of themselves lead a boy of his stamp to some rejection of the world — a rejection that was to be a very prominent element in Colet's thought. A thoughtful child would soon conclude, even before he read Paul, that "here is no continuing city." He would discipline himself to renounce the joys he might so easily not live to experience, and happiness under these circumstances would be almost surreptitious.

Colet was healthy, handsome, and in many obvious ways fortunate, and some irrepressible untheoretical voice did occasionally break through, for Erasmus testifies to odd bursts of hilarity and horseplay (A, l. 392) which — rarely — diversified the dean's grave demeanor. For that unreflecting but unintegrated vitality he was as deeply indebted to his hearty parents as for anything they consciously tried to teach him during the years in the family home in Budge Street.

Certainly the center around which the family revolved was Colet's overpoweringly successful father. As we have seen, Henry Colet was exceedingly busy, and his comings and goings at home were attended with a respectful bustle that would leave his son rather on the emotional side-lines. If his father spoke, silence would fall, not only from respect but because he had tales to tell of the glamorous world of high finance and sometimes the court.

The Mercers, as we have seen, deprecated aping the ways of the court, but they often found it necessary to know their way around there. When the company was confronted in 1480 with Edward IV's demand for the enormous sum of £2000, they turned in the emergency to Henry Colet. Colet decided the best approach would be through the queen. As the records of the company's governing body tell the story, "Maister Colet of his grete Curtesie, gretely by his meanes laboured the quenes grace to be oure speciall good & gracious lady, though whos labour the Kyng released and pardoned v^c marcs." But the company seems to have expected that he would get more than this one-sixth of the total demand remitted, and their disappointment showed. Decidedly piqued, Colet offered to step aside in favor of someone else, whereupon "the hole felyship besought him" to continue as their ambassador to the court. Colet at the same time was making secret appeals to other influential court figures, to the point that the lord chamberlain had to caution the Mercers not to overdo it: "to be more secrete of theyre frendes and that non avaunt be made who that is frendly and laboureth for vs Except the quenes good grace oonly."[104] The further abatement of 500 marks that resulted from these approaches encouraged the Company to make an offer much below the remaining 2,000 marks, "trustyng to haue satisfied the Kynges good grace with the Summe of a Ml marcs, or ellese with a Ml li." Well aware that their proposed highest offer of £1,000 was still only two-thirds of the king's final figure, the Mercers anxiously discussed "what maner & fourme it may be best borne for to be presented,"[105] but they soon found that the king had made his final concession, and they paid the full 2,000 marks with the best grace they could muster.

The reference to Henry Colet's "grete Curtesie" is not in the usual bald style of the records, and reads like an insertion intended to mollify him after he in effect demanded a vote of confidence. It suggests the able strategist, who made sure that in the difficult negotiations ahead he would have the company behind him. In part his annoyance—verging on petulance—may have been genuine. He thought his labyrinthine efforts at court were not appreciated back in Mercers' Hall, and the record suggests that by being straightforward about his emotions he could turn them to his advantage—one of his secrets of success.

The hint of petulance in the preceding scene is again struck in another scene, this time one internal to the company. A prominent mercer, Hugh Clopton, had been fined for an infraction, and Henry Colet was urging that he be forced to pay. The others, however, hung back, and their reason is interesting. "But for asmuche as grete gruge betwene Master Colet and Maister Clopton hath ben & yitt is for the mater of John Hart, the Chaumberlayns Clerke, for the whiche a dowte is and also lyklyhode that Maister Clopton shulde deme the observyng of the said sentence nowe to be of Malise than otherwise," a committee was formed—not including Colet—to forge a compromise with Clopton. The company obviously felt that enough was enough and recorded the hope "by grace of god . . . to have them bothe the soner in good accorde, unytie & Rest."[106] But the unity and rest were not forthcoming. Two months later Colet prodded the company into taking official notice that Clopton had not yet fulfilled his part of the compromise agreement, but its court avoided siding with Colet and limited itself to sending the recalcitrant merchant a tactful reminder.[107]

Christian Colet, at home where there was no need for the head of the house to keep his feelings muffled, probably knew these moods better than the mercers did. The children, too, would know when their father was not having a good day.

If Henry Colet had foibles, it is nevertheless clear that his fellows admired both him and Hugh Clopton and simply wished they would compose their difference about John Hart, of which unfortunately no trace remains in the records. Henry Colet was a Mercer through and through and identified thoroughly with the company, right or wrong. When the company suffered an affront, as it did several times in 1477 from the Grocers, we may be sure Colet's whole household knew of the master's indignation and his subsequent triumph at the Grocers' humiliation. According to the Mercers' one-sided account the Grocers had forced their way into the place traditionally reserved for the Mercers on ceremonial occasions, "which hath caused rancure & grete Malice, specially by mean of uncurteyse langage on theire partie." Uncourteous words soon led to blows, and push came literally to shove. Henry Colet was a member of the indignant delegation that sought redress from the lord mayor. It may have helped that the lord mayor that year was a Mercer, for the fracas was settled to the company's satisfaction.[108] Such battles centering on a company's prestige were common enough—the Goldsmiths staged a notable brawl with the Butchers at much the same time—but they could lead to bloodshed and even death, a reminder of the intertwining of ceremony and violence in late medieval times. Roughness and majesty and petulance could flicker disconcertingly in the daily life of a great London merchant.

We are fortunate in being able to reconstruct, mainly from the company's records, the concerns that were typical of Henry Colet's life. Many of them are not earthshaking in themselves, but cumulatively they suggest the background against which Henry's eldest son grew up. Perhaps there is no other London family of the time for which we can reconstruct even some of the dinnertable conversations.

One of Sir Henry's greatest moments came in the spring of 1496, when he had also the satisfaction that his oldest son, recently returned from Italy, was there to see it. The king's policy, eminently acceptable to the business community, was to promote trade and peace. In the earlier months of 1496 he negotiated the great treaty known as the Magnus Intercursus, between England and the Low Countries. The leading trading cities of both parties were expected to affix their seals to the treaty as a guarantee that they would abide by its provisions, but for complex reasons the Corporation of London refused to do so. Though they placed the king in the embarrassing position of seeming unable to guarantee adherence to the treaty in his own kingdom, the corporation continued to temporize. The king stepped up the pressure by sending a delegation to the city consisting of the lord treasurer, the lord chief justice, and the master of the rolls; but they returned from Guildhall empty-handed. In anger and perplexity the king turned to Henry Colet. At this juncture Colet took a momentous and perhaps unprecedented step. "At the requeste and commaundment of my said sovereigne lorde," he gave on 1 May 1496, under his seal, the pledge of his entire fortune, present and to come, for the faithful observance of the treaty.[109] What this magnificent gesture cost the prudent merchant in well-dissimulated anxieties we cannot know. But its effect was dramatic and a welcome relief to the king. Colet's single bond was accepted as sufficient, and the treaty was ratified. The king did not forget.

Sir Henry himself may have profited mainly, as Knight suggested, by being freed from the exactions of Sir Richard Empson and Edmond Dudley, the king's hated financial agents who plagued and even endangered many another mayor and sheriff. But certainly an indirect beneficiary of Sir Henry's splendid gesture was his eldest son, who was destined for the church. When the deanery of St. Paul's in London fell vacant Colet had been only six years a priest and was still in his thirties. The grateful king nevertheless signified to the cathedral chapter his pleasure that they elect to this eminently desirable position young Dr. Colet. He became a member of the chapter by being collated to the prebend of Mora on 5 May 1505,[110] and on 2 June 1505 the chapter obediently elected him its dean.[111] Later in the same year Dr. Colet inherited from his father one of the great London fortunes and had no need, and as a native Londoner probably no desire, to make his way up the episcopal ladder by being translated all over the kingdom. It could not have escaped his notice that the bishop of London was thirty years older than he.

Thanks to his father, Dr. John Colet was very rich and also enjoyed the elegant austerity of the deanery of St. Paul's, set in its own spacious

grounds though in the heart of the capital. While a person similarly situated today might feel it necessary to emerge from his father's shadow
by some striking personal achievement, in Tudor times such signal good
fortune called for gratitude rather than guilt. Colet was fully aware that
he owed the distinction he now enjoyed—if for the moment we leave aside
the much-discussed Oxford lectures—to his father.

In less obvious ways, though, the oldest son was also the product of
influences outside the home. The mere fact that he began to study Latin
already made him part of a world unknown to his father, who had only
an elementary schooling in English and had worked for his living from
the time he was sixteen. It is noteworthy that the only committees in the
Mercers' Company in which Henry Colet does *not* figure are those concerned with legal and financial intricacies.[112] Thus without either father's
or son's being conscious of the fact, every time John left home in the morning for the grammar school—the grammar being Latin—he was moving
toward a position of his own in which he would enjoy a standing denied
to his father. We may now therefore turn to the educational structures
within which John Colet slowly developed his own potentialities.

3

"... So It Grows"

Colet's home was exceptional in important ways, and we are fortunate to have vital facts and even revealing anecdotes concerning both his parents. We shall have to suppose, however, from a complete absence of details about his schooldays, that his early education was typical.

This is probably a safe assumption. Almost all the schoolwork was memory work and much the same things had to be memorized whatever school the child attended. The teachers' emphases and penchants no doubt differed somewhat, and upwardly mobile parents complained at times that texts or teaching methods differed from one school to another; nevertheless, from the standpoint of the present day the impression is one of uniformity, not to say monotony.

Schools were still few when Colet was a boy.[1] Two or three generations earlier they had scarcely existed at all, except for schools, like the long-established cathedral school of St. Paul's in London, where choirboys learned what they needed to know in order to take their part in divine services.[2] The London mercantile class, with newly heightened ambitions for their sons, started petitioning for schools early in the fifteenth century. They understood that access to literacy, and especially to Latin, was essential as preparation for administrative positions. Young people studied Latin then for much the same reason they now study computer science — to prepare themselves to play a role in a rapidly changing society. The Wars of the Roses during John Colet's youth had significantly undermined the influence of the old aristocrats who despised learning and contemptuously left administration to churchmen. In John Skelton's rough-and-ready but contemporary verse:

> Noblemen born
> to learn have scorn
> but hunt and blow a horn,
> leap over lakes and dikes,
> set nothing by politics.[3]

At about the same time a Spanish scholar voiced in tidier language a similar complaint about "noblemen born":

> No ponen sus hijos doctrina aprender
> y han en las letras muy gran negligencia.[4]

But as society moved toward greater centralization there was increasing need for legists and administrators—from justices of the peace all the way to the Court of King's Bench and the Royal Council itself. The confident middle class was poised to make deep inroads into the Church's traditional monopoly of cultural institutions, but to do so it had to have access to formal education.[5]

What the pupils' parents mostly wanted, in the candid words of a mid–fifteenth-century German schoolmaster, was "[s]ola utilia et necessaria."[6] These are the terms in which evening business schools advertise their curricula today, and the resemblance is not accidental. Humanistic elements had yet to be infused into the school; for the present it was concerned "only" with what it saw as "useful and necessary." This meant, basically, grammar—Latin grammar—and religion. The teaching of grammar did not aspire to classical niceties, the idea being simply to understand Latin and be understood. The grammatical examples did double duty by serving also as maxims of worldly prudence. The distichs ascribed to Publilius Syrus—two-line metrical precepts of conduct—had been popular since the late Roman Empire and were among the first books to be printed, the classic in this pedagogical genre being the *Disticha Catonis*. Notwithstanding the title, it is not the work of the much earlier Cato Uticensis but a collection from the third or early fourth century which distilled the principles of practical ethics into some 130 hexameter verses.

The collection reveals "how the silent majority thought they ought to behave,"[7] or, more accurately for our purposes, how their teachers and parents wanted them to behave. There was a ready market for this standardized wisdom, especially when it was clothed with the prestige of Latin. It amounted to a sort of Stoic philosophy adapted to the needs of the unspeculative middle-class reader who wanted authoritative guidance. The teachers advertised and the boys got "Only What Is Useful and Necessary." To get the flavor of this pedagogic routine one student of fifteenth-century schools suggests we would have to "imagine English taught in schools to-day entirely as a vehicle for self-expression [a prophetic note not intended in 1940], with no writers studied except for Paley's *Evidences of Christianity*, a book of parsing, and some selections from Pope."[8] If we imagine such a regimen in Latin we can form an idea of the curriculum of the grammar school John Colet attended. This no-

nonsense approach left his Latin with a rugged made-in-England quality that it never lost; indeed Erasmus says Colet's consciousness that his own Latin style was poor was the reason he did not publish (A, ll. 524–525).

We do not know what the future founder of a school thought of his curriculum and teachers, or what the teachers thought of him. He was probably sent to either the school of St. Antholin's (or Anthony's) Hospital in Threadneedle Street, or the Hospital School of St. Thomas of Acon.[9] His father's house was in St. Antholin's parish and the school was considered a good one; but as the school was a feeder school for Eton and Colet's name is not among the matriculants there it is more likely that John attended the school of St. Thomas of Acon. The school was already closely associated with the Mercers, and after the Reformation it became the Mercers' School, so that St. Thomas of Acon seems a natural choice for the family to make.

When Colet founded his own school he specified that before a child was admitted he must demonstrate that he "canne [i.e., knows] the catechyzon, and also that he can rede and wryte competently, elles let him not be admittid in no wyse."[10] In Colet's own school days, however, the tendency to require this elementary preparation before entering grammar school had barely begun. When he entered school, the first order of business was probably to learn to read and write English well enough to study the catechism and the other basic religious formularies, before he went on to the Latin grammar that gave the schools their name and distinctive function. He would have entered at the age of six or seven and remained there for eight years.[11]

When Colet entered school printed texts still lay in the future; the master dictated, in both senses of the word, while the boys copied and memorized. Motivation may have come from a desire to please the teacher, but if that failed the ever-present birch rod was a reliable substitute. Tudor pictures of schoolmasters regularly show them with the birch;[12] at Oxford too, the grimly candid insignia of the grammar masters was not a book but the birch and ferule.[13]

Indeed, while such amenities as the blackboard were more than a century in the future, instruments of punishment enjoyed a precocious development. Besides the birch, some schools had developed a ferule with a circular end suited to slamming down into the culprit's outstretched palm; a further refinement was to pierce the circular end with a hole so as to raise blisters. At Eton the accoutrements of punishment included a special block at which unruly boys were "swished," or flogged.[14]

These fifteenth-century schools may have induced little nostalgia in their graduates, but they managed to do the jobs assigned them. They taught an unabashedly utilitarian Latin that nevertheless equipped the pupil for later work in administration or the learned professions. Latin was also the language of diplomacy and early forms of the grand tour; even texts in practical arts like navigation or agriculture were often in Latin. Since the late eighteenth century the scope of "the classics" has shrunk to an almost purely belletristic content, but in Colet's day Latin was the medium through which almost all learning worth having was transmitted.

The one respect in which English approached Latin in importance was in the schools' other main task, that of instilling in the pupils a knowledge of their religion. There was only one church, of course, so the pupils did not have to trouble themselves with looking into its claims to adherence, and still less with the arguable claims of religion in general. The church was taken perfectly for granted, a structure parallel to the state with its own codes, offices, courts, official publications, and hierarchical power structure. Under these circumstances the boys' religious studies would concentrate more on objective forms than on piety, though there was no necessary sense of tension between the two.

Reading began with the catechism and familiar prayers. A contemporary summary of what the master was supposed to drill into his charges leaves no doubt about where the emphasis lay:

> In the first place he would teach the boys the alphabet, the Lord's Prayer, the Salutation of the Angel [i.e., the prayer beginning "Hail Mary"], and the Apostles' Creed, and all other things necessary for serving the priest at mass, together with the psalm *De Profundis* and the collects, in addition to the customary prayers for the dead. Also he would teach them to say grace as well at dinner as at supper. Then he should teach the boys in English the fourteen articles of faith, the ten commandments of God, the seven mortal sins, the seven sacraments of the church, the seven gifts of the Holy Spirit, the seven works of mercy, corporal and spiritual, the five bodily senses, and the manner of confession.[15]

Childhood was not explicitly recognized as a distinct period of life with its own characteristics, and child psychology as a theoretical consideration did not exist. A boy dressed in scaled-down versions of a grown man's clothes. He was thought of as a junior version of a man, and his duties were as unmistakably clear as his father's.[16] The school reflected the hierarchical value system that obtained beyond its walls. The master was almost literally enthroned on a raised dais; the boys' inferiority was signalized by their sitting at his feet. The system relied heavily on memory work to inculcate established values and severely punished lapses of attention. The master's natural sympathy with his charges may have mitigated the rigors of the scheme, but in principle the schoolroom was a model in little of the great world outside, in which duty and punishment were objective categories acknowledged even when they were evaded.

More cheerful or more careless boys probably shrugged off the dark side of the system. But for those made in a different mold this would not be easy. John was a serious child and turned out to be a very serious man indeed. As a youngster he was no rebel, and, though he probably did not internalize every last detail of the elaborate patterns he had to commit to memory—he was too intelligent for that—he certainly absorbed the fateful assumption that the universe was thoroughly patterned and that someone had the key to it. The future founder of a school was at the moment still a powerless pupil; the hierarchical severities entailed in schoolmastering of the sort he knew became a conspicuous feature of his own value system. The manuscripts he left behind reveal his preoccupation with hierarchy not only in their text but in the diagrams, tables of correspondences, and bracketed pairs and triplets in which they abound—schemes that make disorderly reality look a great deal neater. The published editions include some of these as samples, but diagrams and tables are considerably more prominent a feature of Colet's writing, and also his thinking, than the reader of the printed page only might suppose.[17]

In this kind of school, religion and bourgeois values went comfortably hand in glove. The desired outcome was useful participation in an ordered state, and because the industrious schoolboys of middle-class London wanted in the end what their parents and teachers wanted, the system worked. There was little friction between the success and profit envisioned by their parents and the virtues encouraged on the religious side. The church remained officially committed to unworldliness, but for practical purposes it had long since made a separate peace on that front. Evangelical poverty had been condemned as heresy by Pope John XXII as early as 1317, and the reckless virtues of the saints, while they enjoyed official admiration, were quietly supplemented by virtues more to the taste of the middle class.

Teachers found themselves commending many of the same virtues in schoolwork that the boys' fathers practiced in business. Among these quite unmedieval virtues were thrift and sobriety, prudence (hardly distinguishable now from caution), budgeting one's time, and especially saving money.[18] These new virtues were held up for imitation at home and at school, though they were laughed to scorn by the traditionally-minded aristocracy. Rich families like the Colets did not parade their wealth as their unthrifty betters tended to do. Lavish "housekeeping," or hospitality, was downplayed, and the bibulous four-hour dinners in vogue among the English who could afford them[19] did not fit the routine of the busy merchant. In later years John Colet showed in many ways that he had assimilated the careful, rational outlook he learned as a boy. But he was to find it hard to transplant this outlook from its native soil in the business world to the less congenial climate of the church.

As John's school days drew to a close a decision had to be made about his future course. Regarding his own wishes at just this time we are fortunate in having the testimony of Polydore Vergil, a contemporary of Colet's (born about 1470) who came to England from Italy in 1502 as a deputy papal collector, an office that brought him often to London. There he was, with Colet, More, and other learned and influential men, a member of Doctors' Commons, or more formally the Doctors of the Arches, a society whose members were concerned in one way or another with the work of the ecclesiastical courts.[20] What Polydore Vergil knew of Colet's bent during his later school days he obviously heard from Colet himself:

> By nature holy and religious, as soon as he passed from boyhood and finished the studies by which boys are made civilized young people, he set himself to the study of divine letters. For his preceptor he chose Paul, and both at Oxford and Cambridge, and then later in Italy, became deeply versed in him.[21]

Seebohm's tag "the Oxford Reformers," though there have always been scholars who rightly objected to it,[22] has nevertheless stuck, and with it the association of Colet with Oxford. Anthony à Wood's biographical dictionary, *Athenae Oxonienses* (London, 1691–1692), says Colet attended Magdalen College, but the college registers for the period in question were already lost in Wood's time, and he cites no authority. The contemporary evidence points instead to Colet's having studied up to the M.A. level at Cambridge. As we have just seen, a friend of Colet's says he studied at both universities. More recently attention has been drawn to the fact that John Colet appears in two published grace books of Cambridge University (a "grace" being the official action taken on a student's petition, often for a waiver). In *Grace Book A* John Colet appears twice, in the academic year 1484–1485 as a "questionista," meaning that he was on the point of taking his baccalaureate after what was normally a four-year course;[23] and again in 1486–1487 as working toward an M.A. In *Grace Book B* he is already, under date 1488, an "inceptor," or master of arts.[24]

The chronology fits the other known facts. Having been born in early January 1467 and presumably having entered school around the age of six, in 1473, Colet would have finished eight forms by 1481. By the Michaelmas term at Cambridge he would have been a few months short of fifteen, a normal age for going up.[25] The grace books show him as bachelor in 1485 and master of arts in 1488. At Cambridge, then, rather than Oxford, Colet apparently got his earlier university education. This may be the reason that Sir Henry Colet was later placed on a very short list of notable people, including the king, to whom officials of Cambridge

University appealed for funds to build the church of Great St. Mary's.[26] His son the dean's connection with the university might be thought to warrant the appeal.

On reflection the family's decision that Colet should attend Cambridge looks logical enough. Cambridge was at this time very much on the upswing, a serious rival to the larger University of Oxford. Ever since Oxford's infiltration by Wyclifite sympathizers early in the century, Cambridge had enjoyed increased royal favor;[27] this fact alone would weigh heavily with a family that consistently made the right moves.

The Cambridge of Colet's day does not seem especially exciting, especially since university students were on the average three years younger than today's undergraduates and correspondingly less demanding. Erasmus, writing in 1516 after having taught at Cambridge for several years himself, told a friendly English correspondent: "At Cambridge, about thirty years ago [the period of Colet's student days] nothing was taught but Alexander and the so-called 'Small Logicals' [*Parva Logicalia*] and those ancient Aristotelian rules, with the *Questions* derived from Duns Scotus."[28] In other words, both the Latin and the philosophy taught at Cambridge in the 1480s were barbarous. The Alexander in question is Alexander de Villa Dei, or Villedieu, the early thirteenth-century writer of a grammar in verse. Alexander was a favorite target of northern humanists;[29] his Latin was so poor that Erasmus claimed it was "half Latin and half French."[30] Erasmus was an excellent judge of Latin, but on the *Parva logicalia* he was by no means an expert. It was, like Alexander's grammar in verse, another thirteenth-century textbook that had worn well, being a section of the *Summulae logicales* of Peter of Spain (Petrus Hispanus), later Pope John XXI. The portion of the larger work called *Parva logicalia* was intended by Peter to introduce teenage students to notions contained in the logical works of Aristotle, after which the author added a section that summarized advances in medieval logic. For the latter purpose Peter and other writers on logic coined new technical terms to correspond to the new concepts. Humanists who cared little about post-Aristotelian logic were repelled by the patently unclassical new terms, and Peter of Spain himself became, as a recent historian of logic has put it, "the humanists' bogie," who "defines negatively the aims of Renaissance humanism. When the humanists, particularly those of northern Europe, descend to particulars in their recriminations against scholastics, there is no name they cite with such regularity and cold fury as that of Peter of Spain."[31] Even less acceptable than the book's Latinity was its program, which Peter announced in his provocative opening sentence: "Dialectic is the art of arts and the science of sciences, possessing the way to the principles of all disciplines [*methodorum*]."[32] *Grammatica*, for Peter, was merely a handmaid to dialectic, while poetry and rhetoric were relegated to a still lower level.

To the teenage John Colet, though, Peter of Spain and even Alexander de Villa Dei may have seemed quite an improvement over the texts he had been used to in the grammar school. Since both authors had lasted for more than two centuries their texts must have proved teachable, and it by no means followed that because Erasmus expressed contempt for them when he was fifty, Colet as a youngster would have felt the same way. He was never so keen on the arts of language as Erasmus was, and he was never strongly drawn to literature. If Colet was hesitant about poetry, he was still more distrustful about rhetoric. He felt it wrong to argue on both sides, or all sides, of important questions, their truth-value being to him all-important. If Colet objected to Peter of Spain the reason would have been that such subtleties led away from Christ, not that they led away from poetry and rhetoric. Indeed it is likely that Colet neither rejected nor accepted the texts at the time, but simply sighed and studied. It is possible to take too seriously the atmosphere in which the *Parva logicalia* was taught by newly minted M.A.'s eighteen or twenty years old to boys just a few years younger.[33]

All was not quite so dark in those distant days "thirty years ago" as Erasmus had been told it was. For example, Richard Brinkley, who arrived in Cambridge just a year before Colet, owned a Greek New Testament and seems to have studied the Psalter in Hebrew as well as in the Septuagint translation.[34] Alongside the rigid arts curriculum were growing up informally and tentatively literary studies that were distinctively modern. The situation of the English universities in the late fifteenth century has been aptly compared to their situation in the late nineteenth century. In the latter period the natural sciences and economics were being taught long before they became part of the official degree programs.[35] Thus, to take an example from among Colet's friends, William Grocyn, newly returned from Florence, was lecturing on Greek at Oxford from 1491 to at least 1493, though the lectures had nothing to do with the official curriculum.[36] Testifying to the new extracurricular interests here and there are the Greek and Hebrew grammars and dictionaries that began to turn up from 1450 on among the books of members of the universities.[37] Naturally the revival of learning that flourished in Italy was echoed only timidly, but what response there was was genuine.

There is no telling how interested Colet was in this new wave, or ripple. Most of those just referred to were mature men, while he was still quite young and had to spend most of his time on the prescribed studies that led to a degree. We do have, however, a single word in his own handwriting that points to a negative verdict on his Cambridge years. Not long after he was graduated he encountered in his reading the unusual word *philopompi*. From the context the word means sciolists (by contrast with *philosophi*, true lovers of wisdom). In the margin of his book the recent graduate glossed *philopompi* with the significant word "Cantabrigienses" ("Cambridge men"; FEM, 98; cf. 9).

Impatience comes naturally to able students, however, and one need not take this expression of scorn too seriously. The curriculum that he had now completed was certainly hoary, but it had given him academic competence, and perhaps even the stimulus to do more besides. His decision to follow up his M.A. with a couple of years of study in Italy suggests that friends and masters at Cambridge at least helped to turn his mind in that direction. Colet's Cambridge, if not exciting, was not quite a desert.

After he earned his master's, there still remained the obligation to lecture in the university for two years, called the necessary regency. This institution has to be understood against the background of a very different university structure from today's:

> Nowadays in all universities (including Oxford and Cambridge) there is a very clear distinction between those who teach and those who are taught, between professors and students; and it goes without saying that every university has to supply a permanent body of salaried professors and other teachers. At medieval universities like Oxford and Cambridge . . . there was not at first such a clear distinction. There was on the contrary an ingenious—and economical—system by which the very process of performing the exercises necessary for a degree automatically supplied the necessary teaching for the rest of the students; it was rather like the "pupil-teacher" system [in American universities, "teaching assistants"]. At the beginning of his career the pupil played of course a purely passive part, attending lectures; but soon he had to take part in disputations (a very important means of instruction); when he became bachelor of a faculty, the student had himself to give lectures; and finally when he graduated master of arts or doctor of theology, etc. ("inception"), every candidate had to give lectures during the two following years—this was called "necessary regency" (*regentia necessaria*).[38]

As we have seen, Colet was "inceptor" in 1488, so that the two subsequent years would be those of his necessary regency, in which as "regent" he would "rule" his school starting at the great age of twenty-one. He would have had little choice about what he was to teach. The system was designed to provide lectures over the whole ground covered by the curriculum, and the books they were to teach were simply assigned to the new M.A.'s.

Concerning Colet's activities after completing his necessary regency in 1490 we have no evidence. Some regents remained to lecture voluntarily, but if Colet did so his lectures would have had to be within the arts curriculum because he had as yet no theological qualification. Nor is illness to be excluded for a conscientious student who had been working hard in the damp climate of the fenlands. Health was a precarious possession even for the young, and recovery from a serious illness could drag on for months. Certainly his parents, with the experiences they had had with their other children, would insist that if their son was ill he should rest until he was thoroughly well. And it is true that we next catch sight of Colet in the warm climate of Rome.

Nevertheless, amid the uncertainties the simplest conjecture is that he moved to Oxford and began working on his doctorate in theology. This pattern—earlier work at Cambridge followed by doctoral study in theology at Oxford—was common enough at the time.[39] The doctorate in theology was a very long course of study, extending nine or ten years beyond the M.A.[40] If his health posed no problems, Colet may have made a start on his doctoral studies during the two years beginning with the Michaelmas term of 1490. If on his return from Italy he resumed his studies in the autumn of 1496 and pursued them without further intermission for eight years more, he would have received his doctorate in 1504, the year before he become dean of St. Paul's. The exact date of his inception remains uncertain, but we have seen that when elected dean on 2 June 1505 he was referred to as "professor of sacred theology," the title given at Oxford to doctors of divinity.

Long before this point, however, and before he was even a priest, he had begun—thanks to his Knyvet relations and his father—to accumulate desirable benefices. While Colet was still in his late teens a cousin on his mother's side presented him with the lucrative living of Dennington, situated midway between Cambridge and Oxford. This living he held for the rest of his life. A few years later Sir Henry acquired a substantial country property and gave the living attached to it to his son, still not ordained as a priest or even deacon, and later gave him yet another living. With time Colet became a notable pluralist, even though unlike many other pluralists he could not plead financial need[41] for assuming livings involving the cure of souls. One other such pluralist deplored wittily that in the four bishoprics he had successively held—two of which he had never seen—he was spiritually responsible for "innumerable sawles whereof I neuer see the bodyes."[42] One feels that he was partly consoled for the sad fact by the satisfying turn he had given to its expression.

By the time Colet set out for Italy the souls for which he was spiritually responsible, if not "innumerable," were many. His travels were amply funded, quite apart from whatever his father gave him, by revenues from the livings of Dennington and Thurning, as well as prebends in York, Salisbury, and St. Martin's le Grand, along with the free chapel of Hilberworth in Norfolk and of course the valuable living attached to his father's country home in Stepney.[43]

At first sight it seems a little puzzling to find Colet vigorously denouncing pluralism (OCC, 241–242). Nor was he the only upright ecclesiastic to express such paradoxical sentiments. In the next generation Reginald Pole compiled an even more spectacular record. As cousin of the king, he was already a dean at eighteen and enjoyed rich and numerous benefices and prebends; yet he was not ordained deacon until he received the cardinal's hat and did not become a priest until he was made archbishop of Canterbury. Nevertheless he too condemned nonresident pastors, who as he complained "gather the wool diligently without regard of the profit of their sheep."[44] Pluralism was a means of compensating favored persons without having to take the money from one's own pocket, and as such it was understandably popular. It was so much a fact of life that when we find the institution condemned by notorious beneficiaries of it we must consider the condemnation as, so to speak, structural—condemnation of the system itself rather than of those who happened to benefit by it. So it was, doubtless, with Pole, and also with Colet, who was now able to set out for Italy in considerable style.

Several older friends had recently returned from extended study in Italy. Thomas Linacre, some ten years his senior, had studied at Padua from 1487 to 1492 and is regularly mentioned as a possible influence on Colet's decision to travel to Italy. Linacre too was supported by the income from benefices, though his interests were in medicine rather than sacred studies. In later years Colet commissioned him to draw up a Latin grammar for the school he was founding, but his interests seem to have been decidedly more secular than Colet's, and some early stories told of him suggest a degree of religious indifference that would not have amused Colet.[45]

More likely as an influence on the sober-minded Colet was William Grocyn, an accomplished scholar though he did not publish. He was some twenty years older than Colet, having already held a lectureship in divinity at Magdalen which he resigned to go to Italy. He remained in Italy three years and returned to Oxford to lecture on Greek there, as we have seen. We know the two men were close in later years. When Colet was dean he invited Grocyn to lecture at St. Paul's, and when he founded his school it was Grocyn's godson, William Lily, whom Colet chose for the unusually well paid post of headmaster there. (Lily too, it appears, returned from Italy in 1492.)[46] Thus it is likely that Grocyn was a major influence on Colet's Italian plans.[47]

Concerning what Colet did with his three years in Italy—or, in regard to Greek, what he did not do—Erasmus is not very helpful. In keeping with the reformist thrust of the whole biography he reports simply that Colet studied the Fathers of the Church in preparing himself to preach the Word when he returned to England. For the same reason, Erasmus continues, Colet also studied the English writers who, he assures his readers, correspond "to Dante and Petrarch among the Italians"—a way of referring to Hoccleve and Lydgate which if it is not deliberately comic must have been a pure shot in the dark. Apart from these preparations Erasmus vouchsafes nothing of consequence from Colet's Italian *Wanderjahre*. Erasmus was not interested in playing the annalist. He was writing a sharply focused portrait for Jodocus Jonas, at a critical moment in Jonas's life, and he left the background of Colet's Italian stay mostly a blur.

We are thus reduced to the guidance of stray and meager facts, fleshed out with surmise. By September 1492 at the latest Colet was in Rome.[48] The upright young Englishman could hardly have arrived at a darker moment, for in August Alexander VI had been installed in the Vatican. Despite the depravity of the Holy City, Colet remained there a year at least, residing in the English Hospice, where Linacre had served as warden in the previous year.[49] The permanent members of the hospice were organized under a modified Augustinian rule; they worked in hospitals, cared for foundlings, and assisted indigent English pilgrims.[50] The visitors tended to be well-situated men who looked forward to significant careers in the Church. In 1490 alone the hospice admitted, among others, Thomas Linacre; William Warham, the future archbishop of Canterbury and lord chancellor; and Grocyn's godson William Lily; and in 1493 it welcomed Christopher Bainbridge, the future archbishop of York.[51] Colet formally became a member, or *confrater*, at the annual reception of new members on 3 May 1493.[52] On 13 March of the same year he enrolled not only himself but his parents and his brother Richard in the Fraternitas S. Spiritus et S. Mariae de Urbe.[53] Not that they were present, but their names on the fraternity's books—accompanied by a payment—would ensure their participation in the spiritual benefits accruing from the fraternity's good works. It is worth noting that enrolling absent family members to benefit from an organization's prayers and good works was a late-medieval innovation that Colet accepted unhesitatingly.[54]

Though Colet spent the year 1492–1493 in the hospice it was not at that period a happy place. The troubles were personal and centered around Dr. Hugh Spaldyng, who had been popular enough to be elected chamberlain in 1474 and had been *custos*, or warden, since 1477 but now was the rallying point for bitter infighting; in the end it took an appeal to the king himself to have Spaldyng removed, and by that time, in 1496, the treasury had been emptied and the institution was unable to carry on its basic mission to those in need.[55]

The records of the English Hospice show that men who stayed more than one year were reentered annually on the rolls, but Colet's name appears only once. Until the surrounding marshes were drained in this century the summer was malaria season in Rome, so Colet, distressed perhaps by the strife-ridden atmosphere at the hospice, probably left soon after his official installation as *confrater* in May 1493. No further documentary evidence for his stay in Italy has been found,[56] but until recently scholars had always taken it for granted that Colet made a long stay, in fact probably made his headquarters, in Florence. Savonarola is invariably listed as one of the attractions of Florence for a man of Colet's stamp, and the supposition may be justified. One wonders, however, whether Colet's Italian was up to Savonarola's sermons. A definite attraction of Florence, similar to that of the English Hospice in Rome, where he had stayed the previous year, would be that his friends who had studied in Florence would have given him letters of introduction, as well as practical advice about lodgings and the like. Nor should we forget the prosy fact that Florence, besides sheltering writers and artists, was a capital of the textile industry. The Mercers worked closely with the Medici agents in the Low Countries,[57] and Colet's father, who also had direct connections with Genoese merchants,[58] could procure letters that would be helpful in Florence.

In Florence too, or rather at his handsome villa just three miles outside the city, resided the hero of Colet's intellectual life at that stage, Marsilio Ficino. For decades Ficino had presided over the Platonic Academy that had been established under Cosimo de' Medici and fostered under successive Medici rulers, most memorably under Lorenzo the Magnificent; though for Colet, Ficino would have been primarily the gifted translator who had put both Plato and Plotinus into Latin. Erasmus was not particularly interested in neoplatonic philosophy, and he does not bring out how intensely Colet admired Ficino at this time. Along with Erasmus himself and Pico della Mirandola, Ficino is the only contemporary whom Colet quotes in his writings.[59] Even if the neighborhood of Florence offered nothing else to the traveler, Colet would have wanted to go there to see Ficino.

Even the facts of geography made Florence an all-but-unavoidable destination. All the land routes from England to Italy ran near or passed through the city.[60] In particular the "Dutch" (i.e., German) Road, widely used by English travelers in the fifteenth century, passed directly through Florence.[61] Moreover, no matter by which route Colet came to Rome, he knew that once he was there, Florence would be only five or six days' ride distant[62]—even freight took only eleven days.[63]

Under these circumstances, for Colet not to visit Florence during three years in Italy would amount to a boycott for which there is no imaginable reason. All this would be too obvious to mention were it not that a notation has come to light which has made some scholars think that, inexplicably, Colet waited till he was back in England to write to Ficino. On this assumption a chronology of Colet's entire literary production has been drawn up which has led to serious misunderstandings of Colet's writings and career. The notation therefore requires detailed analysis; carefully read, it throws much light on Colet's aims during the *Wanderjahre* that are our present subject. This analysis now follows.

The Dating of Colet's Correspondence with Ficino

The notation referred to is in Colet's copy—now in the Library of All Souls College, Oxford—of Marsilio Ficino's *Epistolae* (Venice, 1495). Colet obviously studied the volume carefully. His annotations in the margins run to some five thousand words, plus underlinings and other indications of interest. Moreover, on the flyleaves Colet has copied out the body of two previously unknown letters that he received from Ficino. The volume also contains two very rough drafts of Colet's reply, in which he declares in the strongest terms how keenly he desires to see Ficino—to see him, not merely to read him. Neither the letters nor the drafts are dated, and the order in which they are written is not certain. Sears Jayne, who published the annotations and letters, along with translations and commentary, proposed to date the letters between 1496 (the date of Colet's return to England) and 1499 (the date of Ficino's death), for reasons that are discussed below. I put the correspondence in 1495, while Colet was still in Italy, and my reasons likewise follow. I will try to show that the new evidence bearing on the dating is readily reconciled with the commonsense assumption that Colet did not incomprehensibly wait until he was back in England to write to Ficino but wrote when he was half an hour's ride from the master's villa.

To appraise the evidence we must see it within the framework of the exchange of letters. Obviously it was Colet who began the correspondence, in a letter that does not survive. Apparently he took the occasion of the publication of Ficino's *Epistolae*, which appeared in Venice on 11 March 1495[64] and would be known in Ficino's Florence very soon afterward. Encouraged by seeing from this book that Ficino wrote letters even to strangers who sought his opinion on specific points, Colet took his courage in his hands and wrote to the great scholar as many another obscure student had done. He asked, to judge by Ficino's response, about the relation between intellect and will—a question that genuinely interested him, as we shall see, but also afforded a suitable pretext to bring himself to Ficino's notice. Ficino's reply—but minus salutation, formal closing, and date—Colet proudly copied onto the front flyleaf of his copy of the *Epistolae*. He himself was now one of Ficino's correspondents.[65]

Ficino's response called for a fervid thank-you letter, and the two drafts preserved in the *Epistolae* volume are drafts of such a letter. The first is a false start only two lines long; the second tries again, taking up the same idea in much the same words, but though it runs a little longer it also soon crashes. The style is singularly tormented, so that it will be convenient to print the Latin, in Jayne's transcription, followed by my translation, which differs from Jayne's in a number of points. (The words in italics were canceled by Colet.)

Tuos libros legens, ut videor *viso* vivo, ~~quanto~~ quanto magis te videns viverem vidende et colende Marsile. Tua *epla* epistola non solum vivo, ut videor, sed bene vivo. Te ipsum si iam videre et cernere potero, beatus erro [i.e., ero]. Spe vivo videndi tui et spem [*sic*] morior, expectans (ut videor) ~~nimium~~ nimium contemplationem tui. At interea *interea* ~~me~~ *me* sustine in ea ~~vita~~ vita tui partiali. Hunc annum tua epistola me temuisti [i.e., tenuisti] in vita. Ei alteram adde et alter~~um~~ ann~~um~~ am vivam. Tu *si ab hinc tertium vixeris* Tu si deinde tertio vixerero vixero anno

At which point he gave up.
This draft may be tentatively rendered:

As while I am reading your books I seem to live, how much more would I live if I were to see you, Marsilio, whom I long to see and pay homage to. Through your letter I seem not only to live but to live well. If now I shall be able to see you and get to know you I shall be happy. I live in the hope of seeing you and am dying of expectation, having waited too long, as it seems, to bask in the sight of you. But meanwhile sustain me in this life bereft of you.[66] This year by your letter you have kept me alive. Add another to it and I shall live for another year. Then [*canceled:* if you live till the year after that] if I live till the year after that, you

A man who had gone all through the M.A. curriculum must have been able to turn out a passable Latin letter; Colet's problems arose from a bad case of literary stage fright and also from trying to ring all the changes he could on the *v*'s in *vivo* and *video*, with "ut videor" brought in three times for good measure. What he finally sent, if in the least deserving of Ficino's polite epithet "felicitous" ("eligans"),[67] must have been a fresh start. By the ostentatious alliteration on *vivo*, "I live" and *video*, "I see," Colet was trying hard to suggest that only if he could "see" Ficino could he "live"—reading him, however salutary, was not enough. Moreover the draft contains no fewer than three words for seeing: "*videre*," "*cernere*," "*contemplationem*." It looks very much as if Colet was angling for an invitation to the great man's villa at Careggi.

From the use of the singular noun "letter" ("epistola") it is clear that Colet had not yet received the second of Ficino's letters. When it came it did not contain the hoped-for invitation and merely deprecated politely the unknown graduate student's desperate admiration. Nevertheless it too was inscribed in the volume, on the rear flyleaf since the front flyleaf was already filled with the first letter. Ficino's second letter did not leave much opening for a reply and the exchange of letters lapsed. If Colet was in the neighborhood of Florence at the time, the whole little exchange could have been completed in a week or less. Ficino's letters—he was an inveterate correspondent—went by express messenger,[68] and Colet's would be carried by his servant.

In the foregoing account I have assumed, contrary to Jayne's view, that Ficino's more substantive letter, that on the relation between intellect and will, came first, and the letter that merely deprecates the young man's enthusiasm came second. Ficino's *Epistolae* are in actuality less letters than brief essays on philosophical topics; Colet, lacking a pretext to bring himself to the famous scholar's notice, would want to have something definite to say or at least to ask, and the simplest approach would be to imitate previous unknown correspondents by asking the master's views on a specific problem. When he received Ficino's response Colet had no way of knowing he would ever receive another letter from Ficino and would, I think, naturally give it the place of honor in the front of his copy. Jayne's proposed order of the letters requires us to suppose that Colet put what was at that point his one and only letter from Ficino in the back of the volume. He does not argue for his assumption or appear to recognize its improbability. The whole question would be hopelessly minor if it were not that Jayne has used his assumption about the order of Ficino's letters as the cornerstone of a highly improbable chronology of Colet's writings.

Jayne mentions two considerations that he sees as pointing to a time for the little exchange of letters when Colet was already back in England. The first of these is a note on the recto of the rear flyleaf: "Divi Pauli epistola quae est prima ad Corinthios Jo. Colet die lune proxime sequente quam melius poterit deo aspirante conabitur expl[ic]are, loco et hora solita" ("With God's help John Colet will endeavor on Monday next to explicate as well as he can St. Paul's First Epistle to the Corinthians, at the usual place and hour").[69]

Without discussion, Jayne assumes that this jotting is an "announcement" of Colet's Oxford lectures; as these were given in 1496–1499 according to Erasmus, it would follow that the notation was written in England. This much being in his view certain, Jayne constructs a scenario according to which the notation just quoted would have been written after Colet received the first letter from Ficino and before he received the second. Having assumed that the notation refers to Oxford lectures, Jayne further assumes, because the ink and handwriting look the same, that Colet wrote the notation "immediately after" he copied the Ficino letter that is above it on the same page. Still a further assumption is that "after scribbling the note, Colet seems then to have turned the page and written [his draft letter]."[70]

This suggested sequence of events is open to serious objections. First, the notation is probably though not necessarily later than the Ficino letter above it, but by how much it is impossible to say: to assert that it was written "immediately after" the letter was copied is quite arbitrary. Second, the notation about a lecture on First Corinthians, on a back page of one of the writer's own books, is not an "announcement"; it is more in the nature of a doodle, since no one but Colet could see it. Young people often imagine themselves at some desired point in their future and write as if it had come already, and this may be what the young graduate student is doing here. Third, the notation, whatever its character, makes no mention of Oxford or indeed of England. If we see Colet's European *Wanderjahre* in a European context we must recall that in Italy and generally on the Continent a Pauline revival was in progress.[71] Indeed one qualified scholar has declared, in words obviously applicable also to 1495, "One can safely say that during the first thirty years of the sixteenth century there is not an author more widely read and more popular, more often cited in season and out of season, even in the conversation of laymen, than St. Paul."[72] If Colet's notation does refer to a definite occasion (though there is something oddly indefinite about "the usual place and hour"), it could at least as well refer to a lecture he was getting up for his fellows in another religious sodality such as the one he had stayed in in Rome. The notation could refer merely to the place and hour usual for the lecture series in which he was to take his turn—perhaps a sort of fifteenth-century Italian Monday Club whose members presented papers for discussion. In the absence of any reference to Oxford (or even England), it is natural enough to refer the doodle to the circumstances of his life in Italy, where he bought and read the book in 1495.

Cumulatively the three points so far raised show, at the least, that nothing in our evidence requires the supposition that Colet wrote the notation under discussion after his return to England. We may now turn to the reasons supporting the natural assumption that he wrote to Ficino while he was still in Italy.

I have given reasons for thinking that Ficino's substantive letter was the first and the letter that was merely a polite response was the second and last. Now, if this order is right, then the scenario proposed by Jayne is not merely improbable but impossible. For if, as my reading of the evidence has it, the letter that Colet copied at some point on the rear flyleaf, whose bottom portion contains the notation under discussion, is the second that Colet had from Ficino, Colet could not have "then . . . turned the page and written [his draft letter]," for that letter expressly says that at the time of writing Colet had received one letter only, referred to in the singular. Thus, if the sequence of Ficino's letters is what I conceive it to be, the order of events is simply this: (1) Colet receives and transcribes on the front flyleaf Ficino's first (substantive) letter; (2) Colet receives and transcribes on the rear flyleaf Ficino's second (merely polite) letter; (3) Colet makes a notation about a lecture or talk he will give next Monday on First Corinthians. The date of (3) has nothing to do with the date of (2) or (1). (1) and (2) could perfectly well have happened in Italy even on the assumption—which is far from certain—that (3) happened in England.

Still to be discussed, however, is the other consideration that has led Jayne and other scholars to doubt that Colet took up residence in Florence, however strong the antecedent likelihood of his having done so, and to put him already back in England by the time of the Ficino correspondence. Colet's draft letter shows that he longed to "see" Ficino, but that as of March 1495 or a little later he still had not met him and thought that perhaps a year, perhaps two or three years, might have to pass before his desire could be fulfilled. Jayne, followed by other writers, assumes that what kept Colet from seeing Ficino was distance, which would have been decisive only if he were back in England. On this theory the reason Colet might not have been able to see Ficino for a year or two, or even three, would be that his studies would have kept him in England for the foreseeable future.

In fact, Ficino's inaccessibility is readily explained by a glance at the tumultuous political history of Florence. Ficino's entire career had been bound up with the patronage of the Medici. Cosimo had discovered the promising lad at a time when Marsilio was destined by his physician-father for medicine and persuaded old Diotifece to let his son pursue instead the literary and philosophical career that ultimately led to the translations of Plato and Plotinus which enraptured Colet. Also under Cosimo arose the grand project of a revived Platonic Academy, to be presided over by Ficino. The seat of the Accademia Platonica was the handsome villa of Careggi, in the hills just three miles to the north of Florence, where Ficino also lived. The academy was generously fostered by successive Medici rulers of Florence and especially by Lorenzo the Magnificent. With the death of Lorenzo in 1492, however, Ficino's position abruptly changed. For forty years his work had prospered under the patronage of the Medici; now, with the advent to power of Lorenzo's unworthy son Piero, Ficino soon became involved in the intense hatred the Florentines felt for their new master. Ficino withdrew to a voluntary exile in his villa at Careggi, and for practical purposes the Accademia Platonica ceased to exist in 1492.[73] Florence's political situation deteriorated rapidly. Early in 1494 Piero was driven from the city. Meanwhile Charles VIII of France stood poised to invade Italy. On 17 November 1494, coincidentally the day of Pico della Mirandola's death, Charles entered Florence unopposed. Ficino remained immured in his villa at Careggi during his final years, for during his lifetime the Medici did not return.

This, then, is the state of affairs to which Colet alluded in 1495. We know that he spent his first Italian year in Rome, and afterward he may have visited Padua, the "graduate school"[74] where some of his friends had studied and where he would find at the university a large English "nation." Given his enthusiasm for neoplatonic philosophy[75] Florence had probably been all along his final goal, but by the time he was settled there, Ficino was off to a self-imposed exile of indeterminate duration. Colet wrote ruefully to say that he had indeed "waited too long, as it seems, to bask in the sight of you." He is still hopeful, however, as is shown by his use of the simple future ("potero") rather than a contrary-to-fact subjunctive. The political situation had changed rapidly once and might change rapidly again. "Meanwhile" he expresses his hope for another letter, if not the invitation he clearly desired. In any case, Colet continues, perhaps next year, or the year after that, Ficino would again be visible. If, that is, he survived that long. The thought, which Colet lined out immediately after writing it, was nevertheless a natural one concerning a man in his sixties. Even the bust of Ficino still mounted on the wall of the Duomo of Florence, though posthumous and probably somewhat idealized, shows him with deeply furrowed brow and sagging skin; in the living man the marks of age were probably still more evident. Ficino's already advanced age is yet another obvious reason why Colet would not unaccountably wait until his return to England to write to the scholar whom he burned to see in Italy.

Thus there is no need to doubt that Colet passed in Florence at least a good part of the two years or more after he is last heard of in Rome. The studies that he emphasized during his whole Italian stay—the Fathers of the Church, along with neoplatonic philosophy and apparently some readings in English to fit him for preaching—did not lend themselves to formal study in European universities, and so his journeys left little trace. His name is not among those matriculated in the Studio, or university, in Florence;[76] and if Colet had specialized knowledge of canon law, as Erasmus intimates (A, ll. 275–276), he apparently did not acquire it in Padua.[77]

Colet and the Hussite heresy

We learn from Erasmus (A, ll. 276–277) that Colet made it a point to read whatever histories he came across. Of these histories we can name with certainty only one, but it is an unusually interesting work. In the late summer or early fall of 1492 Christopher Urswick, about to leave Rome for England, asked Colet to look in Rome for the *Historia Bohemica* of Aeneas Silvius Piccolomini, which gives a sympathetic account of the Hussites.[78] That John Hus was a heretic did not trouble Colet: he liked to say that he often profited from reading heretical works more than he did from conventional orthodox ones.[79] In due course he wrote to Urswick to say that he had found the printed book and was sending it on.[80]

At first sight it seems odd that a busy churchman and diplomatist like Urswick, a man very much part of the establishment, would be interested in Hus and the wars in which his followers became engaged. In fact, however, the conservative Urswick was simply expressing an interest in Hus that was widely shared far beyond the heretic's native Bohemia.[81] An articulate and self-confident scholar, Hus proclaimed the "dominion of grace," that works performed by those in a state of sin were inherently dead and that divine grace could be transmitted only through truly spiritual men. This side of his doctrine at once entangled him in a controversy that lay near the heart of the ecclesiastical system. In real life priests were often in both points the opposite of those in Utopia, whom Thomas More described as exceedingly holy and therefore exceedingly few; actual priests' moral shortcomings were often so obvious as to call into question whether the sacramental actions they performed could be efficacious. The institutional church had to assert that the sacramental grace depended not at all on the moral character of the minister but simply on the proper performance of the sacramental action in keeping with the church's intention. As the technical language had it, the efficacy of the sacrament depended *ex opere operato*, on the correct performance of the sacramental action itself, and not *ex opere operantis*, on any personal contribution by the person who performed it. To declare otherwise would have been to declare worthless many sacramental actions of many priests. Nor had the faithful, convinced that their salvation depended in great part on the sacraments, any way of telling whether a given priest was in a state of grace or in a state of perhaps secret sin. The nature of the ecclesiastical system, which divided priests from laymen by an absolute distinction conferred at ordination, would have been fatally undermined by any distinction between good priests, whose sacramental actions were valid, and wicked priests, whose sacramental actions were invalid. The church was thus forever in the unhappy position of having to guarantee the validity of sacraments conferred by all priests, whether of good or evil life, though this broke the ideal existential link between a person's life and his work, gave ammunition to scoffers, and puzzled men of good will.

For all the dangerous implications of Hus's teachings, their intended thrust was positive. He envisioned a Christian community in which the priest's good life, spent in the imitation of Christ, would be the foundation for the good worked by Christ through him. His doctrine was irrefragably scriptural but manifestly impossible to translate into reality in the existing church. Hus was condemned at the Council of Constance, but many would—and did—agree at least privately with Erasmus's judgement: "Hus may have been burned, he was not refuted" ("Hus . . . cum . . . exustus fuerit, non revictus").[82] This comment is from 1518—two or three years later Erasmus could not have written it for publication—and it caught the eye of readers in Bohemia and the German-speaking countries.[83] A delegation of Hussites besieged Erasmus, giving him a printed summary of their principles published under the suggestive title *Apologia sacre scripture* [Defense of Sacred Scripture] (1511), which they begged him to endorse. Erasmus evaded their entreaties, but he also evaded the demands of the orthodox that he come out publicly against Hus.[84]

The shortcomings of the clergy and the *ex opere operato* doctrine that protected all priests' status had also been strongly criticized in England in the first decades of the fifteenth century. Vigorous suppression by royal and ecclesiastical authority had largely eradicated these Lollard doctrines from the universities, but they survived among the common people. Documentary evidence shows that after becoming a preacher, the goal toward which he had trained in his Italian years, Colet seemed to the Lollards of his time a sympathetic voice—so much so that one suspected Lollard declared on examination that he had been sent up to London to hear Dr. Colet preach.[85]

Not only did Colet look up the *Historia Bohemica* for Urswick; his specific comments on its subject and style imply that he read it himself, as do his quotations on the value of history; moreover he knew that Urswick was especially interested in this particular book. It could well have been Colet's first exposure to a sympathetic picture of Hussite, and thus to some extent also Lollard, doctrines. We shall see below that a number of doctrines of John Hus were akin to Colet's opinions—although, as we shall also see, Colet, unlike Hus, did not broadcast his more controversial opinions (a fact attested by Erasmus but regularly neglected by nineteenth- and twentieth-century writers on Colet). Naturally there can be no suggestion of a direct cause-and-effect relation between reading about Hus's views and professing some partially similar views later in life.

Nevertheless the *Historia Bohemica*, by the future Pope Pius II, caught Colet's attention. It cast the condemned heretic John Hus and his fellow-sufferer Jerome of Prague in a surprisingly sympathetic light. Aeneas Silvius dutifully vituperates the heresies that Hus "vomited forth," but Hus's strongly antipapal views are treated with remarkable objectivity, even admiration. He acknowledges that Hus was "known for the purity of his life,"[86] as was his associate and follower Jacobellus Misnensis, whom also he describes as "remarkable for his scholarship and the excellence of his character."[87] At the Council of Basel, which was to decide the fate of Hus and Jerome of Prague, the two men, he reports, claimed that *they* were the Church; the Church, they held, consisted exclusively of the righteous, past, present, and to come. As for the institutional church, it had "moved far from the teachings handed down by the Apostles; instead it sought after wealth and pleasure, lordship over the people, and the first place at feasts, while prelates raised horses and dogs and consumed in lust and luxury the property of the church, which belonged to Christ's poor."

Both Hus and Jerome of Prague were condemned to be burned, lest such doctrines infect the rest of the church. The future pope then reports:

> Both endured with constancy the death to which they were sentenced, and hastened to the flames like guests invited to a banquet, uttering no word that would indicate they were downcast. When they began to burn, they sang a hymn to which even the flames and the roar of the fire could scarcely put an end. None of the philosophers is reported to have encountered death so stoutheartedly as they did the flames.[88]

Objective about Hus's and Jerome's heresies and warm in his praise of their personal nobility, he concludes his account of their death by recommending further reading: "Poggio [Bracciolini] of Florence wrote to his fellow citizen Niccolò Niccoli an elegant letter on the death of Jerome [of Prague]."[89] If any doubt could remain about how Aeneas Silvius regarded Hus and Jerome, it would be resolved by his admiring reference to Poggio's description of how Jerome met his death, a description so impressive that it produced a forged companion piece regarding the death of Hus himself which was long regarded as genuine.[90]

Poggio pays his devoirs to the officially established fact that Jerome was a heretic, but he does so minimally:

> It is sad that such a noble and excellent mind was turned to those heretical studies, if such they are [*si tamen vera sunt*]: as for the charges brought against him, it is not for me to judge in so grave a case. I acquiesce in the opinions of those reputed wiser [*qui sapientiores habentur*].

Having thus protected himself while leaving his true opinion easily guessed, Poggio goes on to express repeatedly his admiration for Jerome's learning and acuity, and the weight of patristic evidence he had adduced in his own defense. This was the more remarkable because Jerome had been kept for 350 days in a filthy, stinking dungeon and deprived of his books. At the Council of Basel his accusers had no time limit in their attacks upon him, while Jerome was not granted a single hour to make his defense systematically. Instead he was put on the defensive by having to reply impromptu, one by one, to a dossier of charges drawn up against him. Poggio's reaction was unambiguous:

> It is incredible with what warmth he replied, and the arguments by which he defended himself. Never did he express anything that would be unworthy of a good man—to the point indeed that if he genuinely believed what he said he believed [si id in fide sentiebat quod in verbis profitebatur] there could be found no reason for the slightest punishment, not to speak of the death penalty.

Scorning an offer of forgiveness on condition that he confess his errors and submit, Jerome broke out instead into a eulogy of John Hus, "calling him a saintly man who had not deserved to die, and saying that he himself was prepared to endure any torment with a firm and steadfast spirit." Hus's only crime, Jerome continued, had been to cry out "against the abuses of clerics, and the pride and luxury and pomp of prelates." With this Jerome's fate was sealed. Poggio's account of his noble death ends as follows:

> When the executioner wanted to light the fire behind his back so that he would not see it, he cried, "Come here, and light the fire in my sight. If I were afraid I would never have come here when I could have fled instead." So this man, remarkable for his faith [propter fidem egregium], was burned to death.[91]

Poggio's letter to Niccoli circulated widely, as Aeneas Silvius's reference to it several decades later testifies. The readers who preserved it and copied it were personally sympathetic, but they found its candor impolitic. Leonardo Bruni, the future chancellor of the Florentine Republic, wrote on 1 April 1417 to warn his colleague the author to be careful:

> You appear to attribute to [Jerome] more than I should wish, and though you frequently qualify your regard for him [judicium tuum saepe purgas], yet you do show for him a special esteem [nescio quid majoris affectionis prae te fers]. I believe it would be better to write more cautiously on subjects like this.[92]

For intellectuals like Urswick and Colet, men committed to the existing order of things but committed also to the prospect of the Church's renewal, the career of John Hus and Jerome of Prague was uncomfortably suggestive. They knew, as Erasmus said later, that Hus could not be refuted from the Scriptures, but they also knew that his and Jerome's views were irreconcilable with the Church not only in its existing form but in any then imaginable future form. No one can say now whether Aeneas Silvius's account of Hus made an impact on Colet in 1492, but Hus's views coincide in part with views that, as we will see in chapter 10, Colet came to hold. At the very least Aeneas Silvius's account of John Hus, supplemented perhaps by Poggio's account of the noble death of Jerome of Prague, which he also recommended, would make heady reading for the young Englishman.

The account of Hus and Jerome of Prague may even have stirred some latent dispositions that the serious-minded student brought with him from his London home. Certainly nothing suggests that his parents were not completely orthodox in their religion; nevertheless there are tantalizing suggestions here and there that the Mercers' Company, or at least some of its members, were in two minds about the institutional church. As early as 1496 we find that "certain English merchants" not otherwise identified offered the very large sum of two hundred gold ducats to have translated from Italian into Latin Savonarola's series of forty-eight sermons on the Book of Amos, which were published shortly afterward in Florence, on 8 February 1497.[93] Prosperous merchants in England would not flaunt any anticlerical feelings they may have harbored, of course. Their practical interests were so intertwined with those of the monasteries that as a practical matter they had to get along with the monks.[94] Nevertheless we find Mercers a little later importing Luther's books into England, first legally and then, after Luther's books were burned in May 1521, illegally.[95] All this has made a church historian suggest that "a study of early Protestantism in the Mercers' Company would prove rewarding."[96] Clearly any influence from home which Colet brought with him to Italy would be now indemonstrable, but quite independently of the wisps of fact gathered here it has been thought "just possible" that a Savonarola manuscript written by Colet's regular scribe may have been commissioned by him.[97]

In later years, when the beleaguered Lollards thought that for once they heard a sympathetic voice among the higher clergy, they may have imagined Colet felt more sympathy for some of their positions than he did. Nevertheless we shall see that the Lollards did hear what they thought they heard—not often and certainly not maintained formally, but as a strong undercurrent on the many occasions when the dean denounced the vices of his time. Long before he was dean, while still in his twenties, Colet was already giving criticism a hearing.

Colet's Lack of Interest in Learning Greek

Though he could give a hearing to reformist sentiment, Colet apparently saw no connection between it and the study of the Greek New Testament, for while he was in Italy he showed no interest at all in studying Greek. The widespread notion that Colet stressed the need for interpreting Scripture on the literal level has led many writers to assume that he knew Greek.[98] As we have noticed, a sprinkling of men during Colet's undergraduate days were already interested in the Greek New Testament. Also, at least a few bishops could read their New Testament in Greek already in the 1480s.[99] But not until the appearance in 1516 of Erasmus's edition of the Greek New Testament with a new Latin translation did Colet understand that Greek was essential for the serious study of Scripture. In that year he wrote to Erasmus, "Now I regret that I did not learn Greek, without a mastery of which we are nothing."[100] He promptly set himself to learn the language, as Thomas More reported to Erasmus;[101] but Erasmus, though sympathetic, seems to have found the attempt to learn Greek at Colet's time of life a little pathetic. He wrote to Johannes Reuchlin, "Colet is working hard at Greek, though now an old man [*senex*—he was forty-nine]."[102] In fact it was too late. In 1517 Colet was still ignorant of Greek,[103] and in 1519, the year of his death, a list of seven important Englishmen who supported Reuchlin ends with the notation "Omnes sciunt Graece excepto Coleto" ("They all know Greek except for Colet").[104] But though Colet came to regret bitterly that he had not learned Greek while he was young, a glance at the circumstances of that earlier time makes his failure to tackle Greek understandable.

A few men were indeed learning Greek, but only a few. Mainstream scholars of Colet's generation regarded the Latin translation of the Bible as perfectly adequate. If ever a text met the famous standard that Vincent of Lérins developed in the fifth century to distinguish canonical from noncanonical books of the Bible— "*quod ubique, quod semper, quod ab omnibus*" (a canonical book is one that has been accepted as the Word of God "everywhere, always, by all")[105]—it was St. Jerome's Latin translation of the Old and New Testaments. When Erasmus asked an opponent rhetorically where the authority of the Vulgate came from, he drew an angry reply that nevertheless makes a telling point:

> You ask which council approved the Vulgate version . . . I did not say, Erasmus, that it was expressly approved by any one council, but that a great many councils, whenever a knotty question arose concerning the faith, turned to this one version. You know this is so if you ever looked at the Decretals.[106]

Scholars knew perfectly well that they were using a translation. They were also aware that in the course of copying and recopying variations inevitably arose among texts. When errors were striking, *correctoria* were circulated to eliminate them,[107] but since there was no received text, even the best scholars could judge among variant readings only by good sense, or what they considered such.[108] For all the inescapable textual differences, scholars believed that the version of the sacred texts in general use was guaranteed in its essentials; God would not fail to protect the Church from error. Erasmus's question finally received its answer at the Council of Trent, which, despite a minority attempt to head off this determination, affirmed the existing consensus that the Vulgate version was "authentic" and replaced the original in every respect.[109] If this could happen in the mid–sixteenth century, when there was a much higher level of sophistication in Greek studies, it is small wonder that a well-informed mainstream scholar like Colet assumed, more than half a century earlier, that he could rely entirely on the Vulgate and need not undertake the labor of learning Greek.

Learning Greek, not easy even now, was then a formidable task, with competent teachers hard to come by and texts very scarce in the West. The Greek text that interested Colet most was already available in a translation by a saint and Doctor of the Church. Moreover, even someone who had made a good start on the language would find that there was almost nothing for him to read outside the Scriptures; hardly a dozen Greek texts were available before Aldus set up business in 1494,[110] and few of these were suited to Colet's interests. If Colet remained ignorant of Greek under these circumstances, he was typical of his generation.

Homeward Bound

On his homeward journey overland Colet paused for a time in the university cities of Orléans and Paris. When Archbishop Parker stated in his *Antiquitates* (London, 1572–1574) that "Colet studied for a long time in universities overseas [*in transmarinis Academiis*],"[111] he must have meant that in the cities he visited he followed such courses of lectures as seemed of interest, not that he was formally matriculated. From a chance reference in the correspondence of Erasmus we learn that Colet followed lectures in canon law for a time at Orléans. The university there was already distinguished and was to number among its graduates in the next generation such figures of the Reformation as Johannes Reuchlin, Melchior Wolmar, Etienne Dolet, Beza, and Calvin himself.[112] As to literature, however, Erasmus said that at Orléans "the Muses meet with a pitifully

cool reception [*misere frigent*]";[113] but here, as on the Cambridge undergraduate curriculum, Colet's opinions probably did not coincide with Erasmus's. Colet was not one of the Muses' devotees in any case, and he
was at Orléans for a different reason. François Deloynes, a distinguished
legist whose career in the law was to take him to the Parlement of Paris,
told Erasmus that he and Colet "studied together at Orléans,"[114] without
specifying the date or the subject studied. Erasmus says that Colet went
to France before going to Italy (A, ll. 268–270), and it is possible that
it was on the outward journey, rather than on his way home, that Colet
studied alongside Deloynes. In any case Deloynes's whole career was in
the law,[115] which means that Colet's "studying together" with him refers
to legal study.

Not detained by Orléans's reputation as a major center also for the
study of Greek,[116] Colet moved onward to the University of Paris. If he
found the university as a whole severely scholastic for his tastes,[117] he
found other circles that were deeply congenial. From 1494 the city had
an active circle of devotees of Ficino,[118] and we may be sure that the
prized letter from Ficino to Colet on the relation between intellect and
will did not go undiscussed in their meetings. Another of Ficino's correspondents, Robert Gaguin, was the center of a prestigious group of rather
conservative humanists whom Colet also knew.[119] (The membership of
the several groups often overlapped.)

Gaguin was the general of the Mathurin (Trinitarian) Order, which had
hundreds of houses throughout Europe, among them forty-three in
England.[120] Much favored by Louis XII, Gaguin had had an illustrious
career. Though his doctorate was in canon law he occupied the chair of
rhetoric in the University of Paris until he became general of his order
in 1474. Like many of his opposite numbers among the English prelates
he was frequently sent on diplomatic missions, two of which, in 1489 and
1491, had brought him to London. His *Gesta Francorum* (1495) is remembered mainly because it contains the first published work of Erasmus, a
eulogy of Gaguin's history. Gaguin found in Erasmus, over thirty years
younger than himself, an enthusiastic supporter of the idea that ecclesiastical subjects should and could be treated in elegant language.[121] Erasmus and Gaguin wrote off the Latin of the preceding two hundred fifty
years as barbarous and went back to the twelfth-century Bernard of
Chartres for stylistic models. From the time of Augustine down to Bernard of Chartres a fit balance had obtained between style and content;
then the victory of the scholastic method in theology had introduced a
new barbarism into ecclesiastical language which placed it at an infinite
remove from that of theologians who were also *grammatici*. Colet shared
the enthusiasm for Ficino's neoplatonic theology which he found in the

circle around Gaguin and elsewhere in Paris. With their stylistic preoccu-
pations as such he would be less concerned, but he shared their desire
for a biblical theology such as the older writers exemplified.

On another subject much discussed in Gaguin's circle it would be most
interesting to know what line Colet took. The question of the Immaculate
Conception of the mother of Jesus was much discussed during the fifteenth century. All agreed that she was sanctified in the womb, but one
school argued that this took place only when the soul was infused into
the embryo, while others contended that she was free of sin from the moment of conception. Because the greatest of the Dominican doctors had
taken the former position the controversy had become at one level, like
so many other controversies, a contest between the Franciscans, who took
the latter position, and the loyal *confratres* of St. Thomas. On another
level, the low esteem in which the theologians held the sexual act, even
in marriage, served also to darken counsel. Gaguin's contributions to the
controversy were characteristically twofold. On the plane of piety he
wrote an ardent yet elegant poem in elegiacs celebrating the Immaculate
Conception of Mary. On the scholarly plane he wrote a treatise in refu-
tation of the attack on the doctrine in 1481 by Vincenzo Bandello, the
general of the Dominicans. Bandello cited no fewer than 216 arguments
of Fathers, Doctors of the Church, and other theologians against the doctrine. For good measure he added refutations of thirty-five arguments advanced by the doctrine's defenders.[122] At least one of Gaguin's counterarguments had a certain ingenuity that would appeal to Colet. To break
the connection between Mary's conception and sex, Gaguin argued that
when her future parents learned from the angel what Mary's destiny was
to be they retired to their chamber so filled with devout thoughts that
when the seed was emitted it was "like perspiration,"[123] bringing no particular sensation of pleasure.

Colet must have preached on Mary at appropriate times in the liturgical
year and on her many feasts, and also in the series of sermons that he devoted to a running commentary on the Gospel of Matthew which Erasmus
mentions. Mary is nevertheless almost entirely absent from his surviving
writings, where the few references to her are brief and incidental (RO,
205; S, 302 [referred to, though not by name]). The most substantial piece
is a prayer to Mary written in English in the margin of Colet's copy of
Ficino's *Epistolae* (FEM, 103). The absence of Mary is probably attrib-
utable to Colet's preoccupation with Paul and Dionysius, contexts in
which there was no occasion for speaking of her. It is impossible to decide
what position Colet took on the question of the Immaculate Conception,
but while he was in Paris he must have had heard a great deal about the
controversy. Perhaps his thoughts were already turning to his now-

imminent return home and he was not deeply involved in the question; or, with his fondness for absolute positions, he may have accepted Gaguin's poetic argument:

> Congruit hoc Gnato penitus lucescere Matrem;
> Si decuit, voluit; si voluit, quid obest?

(It was fitting that her Son should in this way make his Mother wholly radiant; if it was fitting he willed it; and what hindrance could there be to his will?)

Gaguin instinctively gives his graceful verses the structure of an enthymeme. In this northern world, where religious feeling was central and Italian preoccupation with style only peripheral,[124] Colet would feel at home.

Did Colet return to England, perhaps in time for his twenty-ninth birthday in January 1496, an appreciably different man from the twenty-five-year-old whom we found in Rome in September of 1492? My answer would be a qualified no.

It is true that he developed. With three years at his disposal and a well-filled purse he traveled where he wished and read widely and deeply. He laid the strong foundations for the *doctrina* that contemporaries admired in him. He came to know the Church Fathers well—though not so well as Erasmus did, as their famous controversy about Christ's passion was to show before the decade was out. It goes without saying that he studied and restudied the Scriptures. Among secular writers he was strongly drawn to the lofty visions of Plato and Plotinus, who indeed for him were hardly secular writers at all; he read them, of course, in the Latin translations of Ficino. He read whatever histories he came across and one supposes that he learned of the astonishing geographical discoveries that were being made by his contemporaries; but if so they left no mark on his writings. These, as we shall see, are pointed resolutely heavenward, with not even a side glance for the achievements of the age he was living in.

Though Erasmus's biographical letter belongs to 1521, twenty-five years after the point we have now reached, the character traits that can be gleaned from it were at least beginning to be prominent back in 1496. The highly intelligent oldest son of very rich parents apparently saw no reason for much humility. Now and then he had disconcerting bursts of what sounds like horseplay (A, 1. 392), but he was entirely without a sense of humor and took himself very seriously. For him there was no virtue in detachment. Instead of humor he came to prefer searing sarcasm, and with time even this mocking vein shaded into the more congenial mode of straightforward denunciation, as his writings show at every turn. And his undoubted holiness could sometimes be more inspiring at a distance. At large gatherings he made it a point to speak Latin in order to avoid frivolity, and also to avoid women (A, ll. 402–412). He felt, especially no doubt in later years, that "all eyes were trained upon him" (A, l. 412), a conviction that suggests a lively sense of his own importance. He had also, one may suspect, a lively sense of his own holiness, dramatized in mature years by the customary suits of solemn black which he wore when other clergymen of his station wore purple (A, ll. 333–334). Erasmus reports that Colet was "by nature singularly haughty and utterly unwilling to accept any affronts" (A, ll. 390–391)—another trait that more recent writers do not linger on. Even his friends agreed that he would reject good advice, knowing that it was good, simply because it came from someone else.[125] Naturally he struggled against his pride (A, ll. 398–400), but with indifferent success. In the singularly low esteem that we shall see he had for the human race, he may sometimes have made an unconscious exception for himself. He could proclaim the Pauline doctrine that "the desire for wealth is the root of all evils" (OCC, 242) without even suspecting what the nudges and glances among his listeners might mean; and he could denounce men who chased after benefices secure in the knowledge that he did not chase after them—they came to him. Erasmus's final appraisal of his friend's character is balanced and equitable: "It was a fine thing for Colet, with his ample fortune, to follow unwaveringly the call of Christ rather than the call of nature. . . . But Colet did have certain qualities that reminded one that he was, after all, a human being" (A, ll. 622–627).

The erudition that Colet brought back from Italy, which he built on in later years, was an old-fashioned, solid erudition. It was founded on the Bible and the Christian classics, including among them the Greek Fathers, especially St. John Chrysostom and later Origen, in translation. It was also entirely a Latin erudition, except for the writers he read in his native language. In any language he much preferred religious to secular writers and was not a man to sprinkle his writings—all religious—with elegant tags from the Augustan poets, even the chaste ones. Though he spent years in Italy he seems not to have cared for the Italian people,[126] and he shows no interest in their literature—unless we include two appearances of the word "vestibulum" that just might imply he had looked into the first few cantos of the *Inferno* (C, 198 [142]; DEH, 251).

For a student still in his twenties his selectivity is a little dismaying. He knew from the start what he wanted to study, and he studied it. He makes no mention of architecture, and his only reference to painting is the exception that proves the rule: a painting of Christ and the seraphim (DEH, 230). The Roman poetry that enthralled other young men makes no appearance in his writings. Even Vergil appears only twice, and then at his most allegorizable.[127] Colet screened out not only what was un-Christian, such as some of Ovid, most of Catullus, and practically all of the satirists and Lucretius, but also what he simply saw no particular reason to be interested in—among many other things Italian literature and Greek literature. He also remained uninterested in developing a good Latin style.

Within the limits he set himself Colet made excellent use of his opportunities abroad, but the limits remain narrow. It seems that even before he set out for the Continent at the age of twenty-five he had a fixed agenda—to preach Christ. He had settled also on how to reach that goal and was little affected by experiences that to another young man who had the chance to travel in Italy would have been deeply exciting. The reasons for his inflexible otherworldliness must go back in good part to his boyhood and adolescence. It is hard to decide just how deep this otherworldliness went. Most of the time, as later chapters will show, he had nothing good whatever to say about the world in which he was living very comfortably. But once, just once, he let slip a comment—typically, in the form of a prayer—that makes one wonder a little. In concluding his "Statutes" of St. Paul's School he adjured the Mercers' Company to take seriously its responsibility for the school, and in gratitude he prays that its members will enjoy the very best things he can ask for them from God. The reader who knows his Colet might expect that he is going to ask for the usual transcendental religious rewards. And they are indeed mentioned, but in strange company: "And finally praying the great Lorde of mercy . . . now and all way to sende vnto theme in this worlde muych welth and prosperite and after this lyff muych Joy and glorie."[128] Surely there is something not quite integrated here, testimony to a this-worldly side of his own character that Colet nowhere else acknowledged but that continued to give him trouble. The tension within him told, and his character structure began to lose flexibility rather early in life. By the time he left home it was firmly fixed and would not alter much. He was a good and upright man, learned and serious, but already in his twenties he was settled in his views and something of a puritan.

PART II

A World of Thought

4

The Colet Manuscripts: Dating and Chronology

Upon his return to England, Colet returned to his graduate studies. At the same time, he embarked on the lectures on St. Paul's Epistles which were to become, thanks to Seebohm, the most famous episode in his life. Erasmus, however, who actually attended some of the lectures, gave them in the biography only eight lines out of 357, and we shall see that Colet would have been astonished to read about these early lectures in *The Oxford Reformers*. Seebohm, followed unquestioningly by Lupton, assumed without evidence that the surviving manuscripts give us the texts of the lectures as Colet delivered them at Oxford between 1496 and 1499, the year in which Erasmus heard him. After publishing his first edition, however, Seebohm came upon evidence that at least one of the Colet manuscripts was in fact very late, three years or less from the end of Colet's life. This unwelcome discovery unavoidably raised the possibility that the other manuscripts, on which Seebohm had been relying for the Pauline lectures, might also be late. His radical solution was to try to discredit the evidence and thereby preserve his gratuitous assumption that the surviving texts of the Pauline lectures go back to the late 1490s.

Lupton was unconvinced, and as we shall see he said so at the time. Nevertheless, when he published his biography of Colet fourteen years later he for some reason ignored his own elaborate rebuttal of Seebohm and silently accepted the latter's dating. During the century since Lupton wrote, this dating of the manuscripts has remained the conventional wisdom. The evidence set forth below will show, however, that the conventional wisdom is badly in need of reexamination. If we are to determine what Colet said and when, we will have to consider the evidence afresh, independently of Seebohm's and Lupton's assumptions.

The body of this chapter is necessarily concerned a good deal with detail. The chapter shows that the Colet manuscripts are datable to late in his life, and that in most cases they are private rather than public in character. These conclusions are fundamental to our turning away from the Victorian Colet to the real Colet of the early sixteenth century, for it is essential to know what kind of evidence we are dealing with as we seek to determine how he thought. The reader needs to be aware of the conclusions reached here, but if he prefers not to delve into the evidence that underlies them he will find these conclusions stated briefly at the end of this chapter, under the heading "Tentative Chronology of Colet's Writings."

It will be convenient to begin with the manuscript that Seebohm tried to discredit in order to determine for ourselves its documentary value. Next we will examine the external evidence for the dating of the other manuscripts and their relative chronology. Finally we will examine the texts themselves for further evidence bearing on their dating.

Colet's Authorship of Trinity College, Cambridge, Manuscript o.4.44

Between his first edition (1867) and his second edition (1869) Seebohm became aware that Trinity College, Cambridge, Manuscript o.4.44, attributed to Colet by a seventeenth-century scholar's note written at the head of the manuscript itself, contains quotations from the "Annotationes" appended to Erasmus's *Novum Instrumentum* published in March 1516.[1] The quotations came from three different Epistles of Paul and amounted to a very strong argument for a date not earlier than 1516 for the manuscript. Lupton supported this conclusion by drawing up a list of close parallels of thought or language between Colet's other writings and Manuscript o.4.44. Faced with this evidence for a late date Seebohm could come up with only one counterargument. He noted that Erasmus's 1516 edition reads at one point "hymbribus," whereas the manuscript attributed to Colet uses the more common spelling "imbribus," a spelling that was not used by Erasmus in this passage until his 1522 edition, after Colet's death; from this frail argument Seebohm concluded that the author of the manuscript could not be Colet. Lupton, aware that spelling was not an exact science in the sixteenth century, and that in any case the manuscript's borrowing from Erasmus merely moved from an uncommon spelling to the usual one, found this counterevidence "so extremely slight, as not to admit of any conclusion being based upon it."[2]

The verdict Lupton pronounced on Seebohm's effort to get rid of inconvenient evidence can only be confirmed if we turn now to the credentials of the scholar whose note ascribes the manuscript to Colet.

The author of the note is Dr. Thomas Gale, high master of St. Paul's School during the quarter-century 1672–1697.[3] Before this appointment he had been a fellow and tutor of Trinity, where the manuscript still remains, and then Regius Professor of Greek at Cambridge. Like many other scholars of his day he was a passionate antiquarian and edited among other works *Historiae Britannicae scriptores*. Manuscript o.4.44, whose date proved so critical to Seebohm, was of no special consequence to Gale. When he encountered it he simply furnished the manuscript with the following factual note on the flyleaf: "This appears to be the work of John Colet, Dean of St. Paul's in London: much that is in it is clearly identical with what Colet wrote in his own hand in the volume preserved in the Chapter house of St. Paul's church: and accordingly this work is as it were a revised version." As further indication of Colet's authorship Gale adds, "The text contains many errors, a characteristic problem of Colet's."[4] Though an earlier version that Gale knew is lost, the testimony of a good scholar who had access to the library of the chapter house of St. Paul's for twenty-five years is quite sufficient of itself to guarantee that the manuscript is Colet's—all the more so as Gale had no imaginable reason not to tell the truth.

If the flat statement of a disinterested scholar who had at his disposal evidence now lost were not enough, the manuscript's contents would confirm the ascription. It may therefore be worth adding to Lupton's already impressive list of similarities between Manuscript o.4.44 and Colet's other writings certain further coincidences. Just as Colet's chapter 7 in C is much the longest in that work, the "Abbreviation" of First Corinthians, chapter 7, is much the longest of all the Pauline chapters in Manuscript o.4.44 (40^{r-v}). Again, in S Colet finds at least six times that certain apparently differing terms used by Paul are in reality "the same" ("idem"),[5] and in Manuscript o.4.44 we read similarly that the three different terms "templum," "sacerdotium," and "oblacio" in reality are "idem" (P, 290). A final addition to Lupton's list seems to me very nearly conclusive. Colet uses no fewer than seven times the unusual term "vicissitudinarius" in the sense, defined by the context, of "reciprocal" (R, 185; DCH, 175; DEH, 199, 238, 249; S, 000, 000). Not a classical word, Colet's adjective is cited by DuCange from feudal documents of the thirteenth century. In England *vicissitudinarius* seems to have been used mainly if not only in the sense of "recurring"; it is used in that sense in citations dated circa 1170 and circa 1293.[6] The word appears also in a nonclassical dictionary of 1500, but unfortunately the definition ("prebens vicem") is too general to be helpful here.[7] As a theological term, employed by Colet to describe the relations between God and man, the word seems to be virtually unknown: it is absent from the two standard dictionaries of Latin religious writers of the middle ages,[8] and it never appears, for example, in the works of

Colet's favorite Latin Father, St. Augustine.[9] The word is therefore decidedly unusual in a theological context. We do find "vicissitudinarius," nevertheless, not only in Colet's acknowledged writings but also on folio 40[r] of Manuscript o.4.44.

Once Colet's authorship of Manuscript o.4.44 is vindicated, several important consequences follow. We learn that Colet was still working on St. Paul in the last few years of his life. This fact in turn demonstrates that we should be very chary of the assumption, silently made by Seebohm and Lupton and by later writers, that the Pauline writings of Colet give us the text of work he was doing at Oxford as much as twenty years before 1516. It would be only natural to assume that a scholar who is continuously interested in his subject will continue to work on it as his knowledge increases and his perspectives widen. Thus it is hardly surprising that Colet, closely identified in his contemporaries' mind with Paul,[10] continued to work on his favorite author after he left the university. All of which makes it seem likely that the manuscripts that we possess give us not the lectures of a graduate student but the matured thinking of a riper scholar.

Dating and Chronology of the Colet Manuscripts

The surviving manuscripts that are fundamental to the text of Colet's surviving works are five. We have already discussed Trinity College, Cambridge, Manuscript o.4.44, a handsome paper manuscript professionally written and decorated. Another paper manuscript, this one mainly if not entirely in Colet's own hand,[11] consists partly of fair copies and partly of drafts of the following works: R, EK, CM, C, and DCH. Preserved as Cambridge University Library Manuscript Gg.iv.26, this manuscript is naturally of the highest interest and will be considered below in detail. Finally, we possess a group of three professionally executed manuscripts on vellum, also to be considered below in detail. One — Emmanuel College, Cambridge, Library Manuscript 3.3.12 — contains a fair copy of C; the others contain works for which, with one exception, Colet's original drafts have not survived. British Library Loan Manuscript 55/2 (Duke of Leeds) contains the fair copy of the draft of DCH already mentioned, along with DEH and S. The third vellum manuscript — Corpus Christi College, Cambridge, Parker Manuscript CCCLV — contains RO and G. These three vellum ("parchement") manuscripts are, or are among, those referred to in Colet's testament as "oder books of myne own making in parchement, as Coments on Paulis Episteles and Abbreviacions with many other such."[12] They appear to have been intended by Colet to constitute a "collected edition"[13] of those of his writings by which he set most store.

In seeking to date these five Colet manuscripts as closely as possible it will be convenient to list first the considerations bearing on the *terminus post quem*.

(1) Some of the arguments to be brought forward are necessarily rather technical, but we may begin with an argument from ordinary experience. The very fact that an author has collected his most important writings and has had them recorded on vellum suggests that he feels his writing days are largely behind him.

(2) The copyist of the three vellum manuscripts was Peter Meghen, a scribe from Brabant whose presence in England is not attested until February 1503, when however he was working for Christopher Urswick, not yet for Colet.[14] Meghen's earliest datable work for Colet was a copy of the Vulgate translation of all the Epistles executed in 1509.[15] At unspecified times Meghen worked for Colet copying manuscripts that belonged to the Chapter library of St. Paul's;[16] this copying is hardly to be dated before Colet came to London to assume his duties as dean in mid-1505 and could equally well belong to any period thereafter during which Meghen was in England. When Meghen was assaulted and robbed in 1516 it seemed natural to Erasmus to ask Colet to help Meghen out even though the crime occurred while Meghen was in the Low Countries;[17] at this time, therefore, Erasmus knew that Colet and Meghen were reasonably close. Similarly, in March 1518 Erasmus expected that when Meghen returned to the Low Countries he would bring with him a letter from Colet.[18] In short, the known relations between Meghen and Colet can hardly be dated earlier than mid-1505, and the first definite date that connects the two men is 1509; the evidence for a rather close connection between them is from 1516.

(3) The texts offered by our manuscripts contain, notoriously, a number of blasts at the higher clergy. During the period of the Oxford lectures to which Erasmus attests, 1496–1499, Colet was an unknown M.A. without even a bachelor's degree in divinity. During most of that period he was not even a priest, having been ordained only in March 1498. It would be a venturesome M.A. indeed who would publicly denounce "the disease of avarice and the lust for money" that was spreading throughout the whole church and especially "its leading members" (R, 218), some of whom were sitting in his audience (A, ll. 286–288). The lecturer demands that bishops serve God "instead of the kings and earthly princes to whom they prostrate themselves like vile serfs" because "they would rather look up to the king in his court than to God in his churches" (RO, 206–207). Nor is this all. In the same treatise Colet, still supposedly a graduate student lecturing in public, calls the clergy "bloodsuckers" interested only in the "golden blood" of the laity; when they have drunk their fill they leave their lay victims "empty of pocket whilst they them-

selves are swollen with their thefts and robberies." They are "torturers and tormentors of men," yet "because of the position they falsely hold in the church it is not safe for anyone to criticize [*despicere*] them openly"; instead everyone must submit to their "fines and extortions" (RO, 280). These expressions alone show that anyone venting such criticisms would have to have a well-protected place in the church from which to do so. Had such things really been said publicly in 1496–1499 by a graduate student we should hardly expect Erasmus to report, as he does, that the lectures were well received by such dignitaries as "all" the abbots of Oxford.

In real life a young man who still has his career to make in the church does not deliver himself of such sentiments in public. Besides being imprudent, such behavior on Colet's part would have been out of character. It is too often forgotten that the same letter that mentions the lectures tells us (A, ll. 512–515) that Colet made it a point to be circumspect in public. When he disagreed profoundly with current practices he would discuss his true views in a circle of friends; but "when other people were present he dissimulated his true opinions, so as not to make matters worse and lose his reputation into the bargain." Colet's reluctance to antagonize publicly men of whom he privately disapproved is illustrated in his well-known Convocation Sermon. By the time he delivered this sermon he was an established figure in his forties, a doctor of divinity, dean of St. Paul's, and one of the richest men in London. Yet he deemed it prudent to begin by declaring his sense of the unseemliness that he should presume to address his "fathers" and "masters" though he was only their "son" and "servant." Indeed, he continued, it would seem in him "almost arrogant" to address "men so great" were it not that the command to preach had been laid upon him by the archbishop himself (OCC, 239). The prudent caution that Colet actually exercised in 1510 offers a suggestive contrast to the intemperate and insulting terms he supposedly used in public as a virtual nobody in the 1490s. In this contrast we find further reason to wonder about the date of the Pauline commentaries preserved in our manuscripts and what stages of his thinking they really represent.

(4) Colet's holograph manuscript (Cambridge University Library MS. Gg.iv.26) is earlier in date than at least two of the three vellum manuscripts, for they contain fair copies from it. Yet in that manuscript the author writes himself "Sacrae Theologiae Professor" (DCH, 165), the title given at Oxford to doctors of divinity, a degree that we have seen he could have received no earlier than the last months of 1504.

(5) At the beginning of one of the vellum manuscripts (Corpus Christi College, Cambridge, Parker MS. CCCLV), the author is styled Dean of St. Paul's, which he became only upon his election on 2 June 1505.

(6) In the five manuscripts under discussion Colet cites or refers to at least six different passages in Origen's works. It is now fairly well estab-

lished, however, that Origen did not begin to be quoted in England before 1503 at earliest;[19] the evidence for France and for Venice points similarly to 1503–1506 as the period during which Origen came to be quoted at all markedly,[20] though an occasional Greek scholar like Ficino knew him earlier.[21] Even so well-read a scholar in patristic literature as the following chapter will show Erasmus to have been did not know Origen's writings until 1501; in that year an acquaintance with Origen was so unusual that it remains uncertain how Jean Vitrier himself, who introduced Erasmus to Origen,[22] came to possess the latter's writings.[23] Colet's relatively free use of Origen suggests for his manuscripts a period when citation of Origen was already well accepted.[24]

Taken together these six considerations put the *terminus post quem* of the five substantive manuscripts no earlier than 1505–1506. The three vellum manuscripts of the collected edition, executed by Peter Meghen, may well belong to a period much later still. Indeed I shall argue below, on the basis of their contents and compositional genetics, that these three manuscripts probably belong to roughly the period between 1516 and 1518. First, however, we may turn to the considerations that help determine a *terminus ante quem* for the three vellum manuscripts as such. I have noticed only two, but they are interesting.

(1) We have already seen that Trinity College, Cambridge, Manuscript o.4.44 contains a number of passages based on the "Annotationes" to Erasmus's *Novum instrumentum* of 1516. The other side of the same coin is that Colet's other Pauline writings do *not* contain any material from this work. The edition so impressed Colet that he even made a belated though unsuccessful effort to learn Greek. Thus, while we see from the Trinity manuscript that Colet was still working on Paul in 1516, we learn from the other Pauline manuscripts that he did not incorporate any of Erasmus's fresh material into the latter.

These facts raise the interesting possibility that it may be precisely the appearance of the *Novum instrumentum* that put an end to Colet's work on the Pauline commentaries. In that case the publication of Erasmus's Greek New Testament would be the occasion for Colet's decision to give to the work he had already done a permanent form on vellum. Colet now realized that he would have to learn Greek if he was to pursue the study of Paul on the linguistic level that was state-of-the-art. By 1517, as we have seen, he appears to have given up the attempt. He was now also suffering recurrent bouts of the dreaded sweating sickness, which left those who survived it seriously weakened—another reason, along with advancing age, for thinking of giving final form to the work he had done. Without Greek he could not develop it further, and even with Greek he would know his works would require a thorough reconsideration. All these circumstances may have conspired to make Colet give his works permanent form while there was still time, aware as he now was that his exegesis could not be pushed much further without Greek. In the nature of things the effect of Erasmus's Greek Testament on Colet's decision to give his work permanent form can be only a suggestion, but it is a suggestion consistent with the rest of our evidence concerning the dating of the manuscripts.[25]

(2) A very curious fact is that all three vellum manuscripts of the "collected edition" require further attention from the scribe that they never received. The evidence is of four kinds: the presence or absence of decorative initial capitals; the extent of authorial correction; the extent to which the scribe did or did not erase properly the guidelines he had drawn to keep his lines of writing straight; and gaps, due to erasure of an error or inability to read the copytext, which were never filled in.

Of the three vellum manuscripts the one most nearly provided with the finishing touches is the Emmanuel manuscript containing C. Here in all the indented blocks of space left for ornamental initial capitals the initials have been supplied. Colet made one substantive change in the text, replacing "velis" ("you should wish to") by "debes" ("you must"; k5^v); and he added a few indications of chapter breaks in the margins (k4^r, m4^r). The penciled guide lines that extended out irregularly beyond the margins are erased, though not so carefully as they might have been. The only sign that the manuscript remains unfinished is that twenty-five gaps remain where Meghen could not make out the original. One would have expected that Meghen would contact Colet to find what the readings should be, but that was never done.

The second vellum manuscript, the property of the Duke of Leeds and now on loan to the British Library, contains DCH, DEH, and S; it is much less finished in appearance. The large spaces left for decorative initials remain empty. While a certain amount of authorial revision is evident in the first two-thirds of the manuscript—Colet filled a blank that Meghen had left and corrected a verb form (both on h5^r), and in one place where his text had read simply "humana natura" he could not resist adding "stulta" ("stupid")—Colet's corrections give out entirely after i4^r, though dozens of blanks remain in the rest of the manuscript. Moreover even in the earlier portion authorial correction was desultory, with corrections bunched in a few places and many blanks remaining unfilled even before i4^r. The scribe's guidelines are left unerased and make an ungainly appearance as they project randomly into the margins. After only a few perfunctory corrections here and there Colet never returned to this manuscript.

The third and last vellum manuscript, the Corpus Christi College manuscript, which contains RO and G, also lacks the finishing touches that the other two lack. What gives it a special additional interest is that it appears to contain a clue to its date which bears likewise on the date of the other two vellum manuscripts.

The Corpus manuscript, unlike the other two, is heterogeneous in origin. The longer work with which it begins, RO, is in the hand that Peter Meghen used for the other vellum manuscripts we have discussed. Then follows in a quite different hand the short treatise G. Except for a decorative initial at the beginning of RO which is notably small for the space reserved for it, the large spaces left for initial capitals throughout RO were never filled. It shows very little authorial correction; a few dropped words are supplied by Colet on leaves a1 and a2, but thereafter the only corrections are Meghen's, which are fairly thorough. The number of blanks due to the illegibility of the copytext is here smaller, some six or seven. But what makes the manuscript of RO unique is that the copyist has stretched it out to make it fill the pages that separate it from the beginning of G, which follows it.

Until signature d Meghen had proceeded in the same manner as with the other two vellum manuscripts. But at that point he became aware that the remainder of the text he was copying was not long enough to occupy the space left for it unless he took special measures. From there on he made the paragraphs markedly shorter, and left wider spaces between them. Moreover he now began to create large patterns of white space on each page. The stretching is done artistically, sometimes with flowing yin-yang effects of script against empty space, and sometimes with varied geometrical patterns of, in effect, black against white. The copyist's stretching of his text would be unaccountable except on the supposition that G, the text that follows RO, was already written in the volume when Meghen began copying RO into it.

Because G, though it is a work by Colet, is executed in a writing style different from that of its neighboring RO, it has been assumed that the scribe of G was not Meghen. Unlike the other vellum manuscripts it is written twenty lines to the page, as against their twenty-two; nor does it present the markedly unfinished character that they present. It sets off scriptural quotations from the surrounding text in a gothic hand and by means of indentation. The interesting point about these differences is that while they separate G from the other vellum manuscripts, they bring it into suggestive conjunction with the Trinity manuscript, datable to 1516 at earliest. The latter manuscript also runs twenty lines to the page. It also treats scriptural quotations in similar gothic style. Both the Trinity manuscript and G are by the same author, Colet, so that the scribe of these two similar manuscripts is likely to have been the same man, and—still more important—the manuscripts are therefore likely to be close to each other in date. The Trinity manuscript is in or shortly after 1516, so that

G also will belong to about the same date. Then, since RO was written after G, RO too is datable to 1516 at earliest. And, more generally, the collected edition, of which RO forms part, will likewise belong to much the same period. This conclusion regarding the dating of the collected edition is consistent with the results of the independent lines of evidence already discussed.

A possible further confirmation of this result is suggested by inquiry into the identity of the scribe who wrote both the Trinity manuscript and G for Colet. As has already been mentioned, the differences of style between these two works on the one hand and the works that belong unmistakably to the collected edition on the other have been assumed to exclude the otherwise natural assumption that Colet would use Meghen, his regular scribe for years, to write also the Trinity manuscript and G. In fact I think it possible that he did use him. It is worth noting that the latter manuscripts exhibit strong stylistic affinities with a non-Colet manuscript that is known to have been written by Meghen. This manuscript is Bodleian Manuscript Rawl. A.431 (not dated).[26] If specialists in palaeography were to endorse this suggestion, then it would be safe to say that all the writings that Colet had professionally written would be from the hand of his well-tried Peter Meghen.

Whatever the merits of this suggestion, the important fact remains that the professionally written Colet manuscripts, whether by one scribe or two, have as their likely *terminus post quem* the year of publication of Erasmus's Greek New Testament.

As to the lower limit for the dating of the Meghen manuscripts other than the Trinity manuscript and G, recent evidence would put it in late 1517 or 1518. Andrew Brown has shown that over time Meghen altered certain features of the angular humanistic hand in which most of the Colet manuscripts were written. The most unmistakable of the changes is Meghen's substitution of one form of the letter *h* for another during the year 1517;[27] the later form of the letter is not found in the Colet manuscripts. While this fact unfortunately does not give us an absolutely firm date — Brown observes that for a time after Meghen altered the form of any given character he tended to go back and forth between the old form and the new[28] — it is likely that the transition would be complete by 1518.

Now that we have considered the evidence that bears on the dating of the Colet manuscripts, we may turn next to the different but related question of the dates of the works these manuscripts contain. Absolute dates will not be easy to come by, but I think we may hope to fix with tolerable precision the chronology of the Colet writings with respect to one another. For this purpose we shall have to examine closely the texts of the works themselves. We shall seek to decide how much revision the texts underwent before they were given their final form in the manuscripts we have already studied. Finally, we shall look at certain passages whose content seems to refer to a datable series of public events.

Evidence for Revision, Especially in the Writings on Romans and First Corinthians

The obvious starting point for our inquiry is the Cambridge University Library manuscript, which is mainly, if not entirely, in Colet's handwriting.[29] The first of the five works it contains[30] is R, one of Colet's two surviving works on Romans. Lupton's edition of R declares on the title page that the work was "delivered as lectures in the University of Oxford about the year 1497," but it is evident that the text that Lupton prints dates from a later period.

First and most important, Colet himself says so. At the end of chapter 11 of R he explains that he had originally concluded his interpretation at that point. However, "certain friends" who had been "faithful listeners when I was interpreting Paul" (where or when is not said) "begged me long and hard" to continue the treatment of the Epistle to the end. "Finally I was induced to promise that in the near future [*modo*][31] I would continue with what I had begun" (R, 175). By this account the elapsed time between the original set of lectures that ended with chapter 11 and its later continuation was considerable, a matter of something between several months and several years. First Colet delivered the lectures, then he communicated them in written form to certain enthusiastic hearers. The friends, impressed anew, had to work on him for a "long" period before prevailing on him to undertake a sequel. Even then, the sequel belonged, as I read the passage, to the "near future." His reluctance to continue the work may have been due to his gradually realizing that the work would take longer than he had anticipated. At the end of the original eleven chapters, in a paragraph that amounts to a preface to chapters 12–16, Colet states that the work had turned out to be "much longer than I envisioned when I began" (R, 174), and when he did embark on a continuation the chapters he added were on a still more substantial scale (fifty-two pages for the last five chapters, as against thirty-seven for the first eleven). We do not know how fast a worker he was; but if the first part of the work took him longer than he had expected, the second must have taken him longer still.

Furthermore, internal evidence confirms that the text as we have it is a copy of an earlier manuscript—a fact that Lupton's edition obscures. Lupton (R, 174-175), after closing the original eleven chapters with "FINIS" written on a separate line, inserts a new paragraph: "There follows the rest of the *enarratio*," etc. Only after a further space below this heading of his own devising does he begin the text of Colet's continuation. The manuscript tells a different story. The text of the original part concludes, as it happens, near the beginning of a line. The copyist, Colet himself, simply writes as the next word "finis" and fills the rest of the line, in the same unhurried hand, with the first words of the second part of the work. It is evident that he was simply transcribing an already existing text. If confirmation were needed that our manuscript is a copy of a version that arose earlier, it would be found in the fact that at one point (R, 170) Colet absentmindedly copied a passage from the following page, which must therefore already have existed. In much the same way, a crossed-out word in the manuscript (fol. 12^r)—"aut ~~illiciti~~ a corporis illecebris alliciti"—shows that Colet glanced ahead in his existing copytext and promptly made a Freudian slip, automatically associating "allured by the enticements of the body" with what is "illicit."

Other evidence shows that either the text we have has become detached from any original oral context or else it simply originated outside an oral context. Even before the break following chapter 11 Colet refers to his audience as "readers" (R, 168, 174); in fact he soon leaves the idea of any audience behind and professes that he is writing "not so much for others as for myself" (174). If he was ever thinking in terms of a lecture audience he is thinking now in other terms. He considers himself embarked on a more exploratory enterprise, writing, as he was to put it nicely in a later work, "rather in a freely inquiring than in a doctrinaire spirit" (S, 284). The same assumption that what he was writing was meant to be read rather than heard appears in the text of the added five chapters also (R, 182).

The look of the text in the Cambridge holograph suggests that Colet felt that his text, prepared for readers, was now pretty much in its final form. In writing it out he even left blocks of space to indicate where ornamental initials would go. Second thoughts about the content are confined to a few comments marked for insertion near the end. For example, at some time after copying his earlier statement, based on St. John Chrysostom and [pseudo-]Ivo of Chartres, that St. Paul had journeyed as far as Spain, Colet wrote in the margin alongside the passage, "but how far he actually got I cannot say on any weighty authority" (R, 224, but not identified by Lupton as an insert). Apart from this the writing runs smoothly and evenly from beginning to end of the transcription. The word "Oxonie," written at the end in the same hand, would seem to refer to the writing just completed. The easiest assumption is thus that the text of R was completed by mid-1505, when Colet moved from Oxford to London.

After R our next concern among the Pauline writings is with C. It is not possible to determine just how much time intervened between the completion of the transcript of R and the beginning of work on C, but it is likely to be considerable. Between these works in the manuscript are two shorter pieces that differ markedly in writing style from either what precedes them or what follows. The first of these pieces, EK, is a letter in a small, fine, spikily upright hand that might be Meghen's, in which case we should have to recall that there is no evidence definitely connecting Colet with Meghen before 1509. EK was followed by three leaves that have been removed—perhaps another letter. This gap in turn is followed by the quite short treatise CM, written in a different hand from that of EK, a hand that is possibly but not certainly Colet's. After CM is another gap, this time consisting of one missing leaf. Only then do we reach the text of C.

The first six chapters of C are written in a hand with such marked affinities to that in which R is written as to make it very probably Colet's. It differs from the hand of R, however, in that abbreviations, as for example "qq" for *quanquam*, regularly lack the tilde that equally regularly is used for them in R. Another feature that would imply an appreciable lapse of time between R and the first six chapters of C is the noticeably more pronounced rightward slant of the latter, along with the absence of secretary features in the text proper (interlineations, by contrast, are in a normal secretary hand).

After the first six chapters, neat and uniform in writing style, the remainder of C dissolves into a remarkable variety of handwriting styles. They are generally as different from one another as are the contents they record—a degree of difference which, as we shall see, is great indeed. At this point we are prompted to look back with greater curiosity at the title of the treatise—or, more precisely, the title that is set at the head of the first six chapters. Though the editors of the treatise have shown no curiosity about it, the title surely invites comment: "Hic latius tractantur ea que in prima parte continentur prime epistole ad Corinthios" ("Here is treated at length what is contained in the first part of the first letter to the Corinthians"). We have read Colet's own testimony that in treating Romans he initially intended to treat only a part of the work, not the whole. Something very similar seems to be true of his work on First Corinthians. The evidence of the manuscript points to his original intention's having been to treat the first five chapters; only later, and at intervals, did he add chapters to correspond to the remaining eleven chapters in Paul. Moreover, Colet's treatment of First Corinthians becomes fuller as he goes along (the first five chapters run to twenty-three printed pages in Lupton's edition, the last eleven to eighty-four)—another feature reminiscent of his work on Romans.

Before we turn to evidence for revision based on individual chapters, it may be well to record a few chance details from C which imply that at least part of the treatise as we have it was not intended for a university audience, or indeed for hearers at all. In chapter 13 (only) we find several instances of *tu* rather than the *vos* to be expected in a lecture. When we recall that a number of Colet's writings are expressly addressed to individuals (G, EK, RO, dedicatory letter to DCH), we may begin to suspect that here too we have material originally addressed to a specific person which has been preserved in the framework of a commentary on First Corinthians. Another pointer to material that originated elsewhere is a passage from chapter 10 which would have drawn an unintended laugh from a university audience: "Nolite fieri vos philosophorum lectores, socii demoniorum" ("Do not you become readers of the philosophers, companions of demons"; C, 239 [219]). Again, in commenting on 1 Corinthians 3:15, Colet expressed his puzzlement because the text he was using seemed to make no sense (C 180 [106]). The trouble was that it erroneously had *si* for *sic*. There is no critical tradition for *si* here; it is simply a copyist's error,[32] and had Colet expressed his perplexity in public a member of the audience with a better text would have been able to come to his aid.[33]

Like R, then, C has long since slipped any moorings it may have had in the lecture format. Close scrutiny shows that C as we have it was a long time in the making. First and most obvious, though hitherto ignored, is the shift from a declared intention to treat only "the first part" of the Epistle, to a treatment of the whole. Even between the writing of almost-adjacent chapters, like 6 and 8, a considerable time must have elapsed. The lesson that chapter 8 draws (230–231 [200, 202]) from Paul's remarks about eating food previously offered to pagan idols is quite different from the lesson that the discussion of the same topic had yielded two chapters earlier (190–191 [130, 132]). In chapter 8 Colet makes no mention of his own earlier discussion of the problem, and—oddly enough for someone who is supposed to have taken a historical approach to Scripture—he never mentions the long passage in Acts 15 where the Council of Jerusalem officially settled the question. It is hard to resist the conclusion that these differing discussions were taken out of their original differing contexts, in lecture or sermon or letter, and placed in the framework of First Corinthians as a handy place to preserve them.

Coming between Colet's differing treatments of an identical problem in chapters 6 and 8 is his enormous chapter 7. This chapter runs to a good third of the whole treatise, out of all proportion to the corresponding chapter in Paul. What gives Colet's chapter its great length is a long digression, amounting to an essay in itself, which examines the difference between commandments and counsels. Moreover this digression, acknowledged as such by Colet, contains a lengthy sub-digression on yet another topic. That the digression and the sub-digression originated as separate essays appears from the fact that both repeat the same reference to Luke 11:28, followed in each case by the same observation that true kinship is not in family but in Christ (C, 210, 221 [156, 164]).

Another instance of revision is chapter 14, or rather the chapters 14, for there are two. In the manuscript, though not in Lupton,[34] they are readily distinguished. The first is written in a loose, flowing script with wide intervals between the letters and wide spaces between the lines. On a separate line below the section so written we read, "finis xiiij" (Cambridge MS, Gg.iv.26, fol. 149^v). There follows immediately, but in a tighter script and with different ink and pen, the heading, on a line by itself, "In capud xiiij prime epistole ad Corinthios" (fol. 150^r). After this section, at the bottom of the same page and again on a separate line, is written, once more, "finis xiij capitis," to which another j has been added to make "xiijj." Faced with all this, the tactful Peter Meghen simply suppressed the extra headings and conclusion; but he showed his awareness that the two parts of the resulting single chapter are unrelated by leaving a wide space between them.

Nor is chapter 14 the only chapter present in two versions. Paul's chapter 6 is short. Its theme is simple: that ideally Christians should not dispute among themselves about worldly matters, but if they must do so the issue is to be adjudged within the Christian community; in no case are Christians to hale fellow-Christians before the secular courts. This chapter of Paul, which is less than a page in an average Bible, has grown manifold in Colet (C, 185–193, [120–134, where pages of Latin text and English translation alternate]). The most obvious join is at page 190 [128], where a centered subheading reads, "Omnia mihi licent sed non omnia expediunt. — Pri. ad Corin. 6." On this Lupton notes the obvious fact that the heading quotes verse 12, but he shows no curiosity about why what looks like a chapter heading should abruptly appear in the middle of the chapter. The portion of "Chapter 6" before the subheading deals with an entirely different subject from that of the portion following it. The former is an unmeasured denunciation of the clergy, specifically "including those considered highest [*primarii*] in the church," for their folly in defending the church's property rights to the exclusion of every other consideration. This is the tone of a well-situated cleric addressing others of like status (cf. "we," "ours," 187 [124]) and of course implies a date when the writer is safely installed in St. Paul's. The subheading within chapter 6 means that Colet is in effect starting over. This time his theme seems at first to have more relevance to Paul's topic, for he begins with the conventional declaration that Christians should constitute a single community steadily imitating Christ. But this soon turns into a tirade on the more familiar reverse situation in which the Christian clings to his own pleasures. The fervor with which Colet denounces gluttony actually causes him to misread his author.[35] From gluttony Colet passes to the lure of sex, which he is never tired of denouncing. For him the sense of touch is "the vilest and least spiritual—the sense that is, so to speak, most physical" ("vilissimus et crassissimus et, uti dicam, maxime corporalis"). Touch, he continues, is "the source of venereal filth": it causes "lust and filthy titillation" (C, 192 [132])—a passage that Lupton (p. 48) understandably but silently bowdlerized in translation. Thus the latter portion of "Chapter 6," though it begins with a bow to Paul's actual text, is in effect a denunciation of the objects of the physical senses. The two sections of this "Chapter 6" have little to do with each other, and little to do with Paul. They evidently originated in different contexts and have been arbitrarily joined together for the author's convenience.

Colet's chapter 12 is different in method from any other chapter on First Corinthians. It alone is preceded by its own heading: "Capud duodecimum." It follows the movement of Paul's thought much more closely and systematically than does any other chapter, and is an interesting piece of work, which will repay examination in chapter 7 (below). For the present it is enough to note that Colet claims with an evident sense of triumph that by the end of the chapter he has "rewoven" Paul's text so as to bring out its hitherto hidden meaning. Nevertheless he does not employ the "reweaving" approach anywhere else in his treatise—another indication that the chapter originated elsewhere.

Finally we may notice that the last two chapters, 15 and 16, differ greatly from each other in handwriting. The latter is very loose and open, with only seventeen lines to the page, whereas the tight, neat hand of chapter 15 gets twenty-nine lines onto the same size page. It is evident that these chapters were entered at different periods.

From this survey of the manuscript of C it appears, first, that the opening five chapters do not exhibit the evidence for revision which is so prominent in the remainder of the treatise. It is likely that together they constitute the originally intended commentary on the "first part" of the Epistle. By the time he returned to the manuscript his intentions had changed. While in the first five chapters he had stayed fairly close to ideas arising directly out of Paul's text, those that followed were conceived of along different lines. Colet apparently decided to use the commentary on First Corinthians as a framework within which to anthologize passages from his own writings—sermons, letters, notes on reading—which he thought worth preserving.

In a sense this project amounted to a retrospective appraisal of his life's work. It is not surprising that it took time, and that intervals, even long intervals, intervened between most of the chapters that he added on this new plan. His countrymen spoke of him as "another Paul,"[36] and it was by his work on Paul that he wished to be remembered. The work that he finally produced used the order of Paul's chapters as its external framework, but from chapter 6 on the contents could be better described as "Collected Essays on First Corinthians."

As the work progressed, especially toward the end of it, Colet must have become uneasily and increasingly aware that the current in Pauline studies was setting strongly toward work based on the Greek original. The work of Jacques Lefèvre d'Etaples on the Epistles of Paul, bearing the date 15 December 1512, could have come to Colet by early 1513. The same work was reprinted, apparently without the author's permission but because there was a market for it, in 1515. Also in 1515, Lefèvre himself published a revised version.[37] And less than a year later, in March 1516, came Erasmus's Greek New Testament. At first, as the Trinity manuscript shows, Colet hoped to be able simply to incorporate some of Erasmus's results into his own pattern of thought. Then, as he came to understand that he would have to begin anew on a solid textual foundation, Colet made a belated effort to learn Greek himself; but this proved unsuccessful. He was too good a scholar not to see that a new philological approach to Pauline scholarship was beginning to be established, but he was too human not to wish his own work preserved too. Hence, one supposes, the project of the collected edition.

Before we are in a position to pull together the results of our inquiry thus far, we must turn our attention to another treatise on Romans, RO, which as we have seen forms the first half of the vellum Corpus manuscript which also contains G. Both Lupton in 1876 and Sears Jayne in 1963, for different reasons, assumed that RO is an earlier draft while R preserves for us Colet's final views on Romans. We must now look at those reasons. Both writers seem to have been impressed by the fact that although R covers all sixteen chapters of Paul, RO includes only the first five; but as an argument for priority this fact could cut either way. Moreover, Lupton's position when he came to edit RO, as part of his final volume of Colet's writings, was distinctly awkward. He had to admit in print that when he had edited R three years earlier he had not even bothered to read RO. He had merely noted that it began with a summary of Romans, which he appropriated for R without noticing that it was actually the summary of a different work.[38] It is easy to understand that he passed over this admission hastily and simply assumed that the work he had not troubled to read was less important than the one he had already published.

Jayne's reason for thinking RO earlier is that its "exegetical method is the old method of quotation and explication, and it shows little if any interest in Platonism."[39] The reader who cares to read in RO after the first few pages—after Colet has hit his stride—will be able to decide for himself about the accuracy of this characterization of Colet's method. The assertion about platonism is question-begging in any case, but it loses all its force as a criterion for priority when one asks what "old" method means in this context. On Jayne's own showing there would be no time for Colet to have an old method that would distinguish RO from R. He puts both works in the same year—1498, January and October respectively. And this is simply part of a chronological scheme that squeezes all Colet's writings into twenty-three hyperactive months between January 1498 and November 1499.[40] During these months this chronology has him continuing his studies as a full-time graduate student, writing five or six hundred pages of Latin (essentially all the surviving works), lecturing, studying such extracurricular works—not light reading—as Pico's *Heptaplus* and Ficino's *Theologia Platonica*, carrying on a written disputation with Erasmus concerning Christ's Agony in the Garden, and preparing by prayer for his ordination to the priesthood. Fortunately we need not think of Colet as condemned to such a schedule.[41] A reviewer of Jayne's work promptly reported that at one point (DEH, 178–179) Colet unmistakably quotes in abridged form a passage from the edition of Dionysius which Lefèvre d'Etaples published in Paris on 6 February 1499.[42] Thus the date proposed for DEH in this rushed chronology is impossible. Moreover, the premise for the whole chronology is that Colet read Ficino's *Epistolae* and wrote to its author not when he was within three miles of the author's house but only after he completed the forty days' return journey to England. As we saw in the previous chapter this assumption will not bear scrutiny. For both reasons the proposed chronology must be abandoned, and we are happily not under the necessity of finding time within it for Colet also to write his numerous lost works.[43]

Though RO gets down only to chapter 5 of Romans, its treatment is on a much fuller scale than the corresponding chapters of R: the five chapters of RO fill seventy-seven pages, while all sixteen chapters of R together run to only ninety-one pages. If anything, this fact argues for a later date for RO—as Colet himself mentions elsewhere (R, 174), he found as he warmed to his work that he had more and more to say. The likelihood that it is RO, not R, that gives us Colet's matured views on Romans is all but proved by the fact that it is RO which Colet elected to have transcribed onto vellum. All writers on the subject agree that RO and R are entirely distinct works, neither showing the influence of the other. Hence to continue to suppose that RO was a trial run for R would force one to assume this decidedly awkward sequence: Colet worked out RO on a relatively very full scale; he then abandoned it and wrote the briefer R instead, consigning RO, of which he made no use, to the wastebasket—after which he paid no further attention to R and instead retrieved RO from the wastebasket in order to have it inscribed onto vellum.

The Hunne Affair and
the Dating of Colet's Manuscripts

Two decades ago H. C. Porter noted in his reading of Colet a perplexing problem that made him think back to Sherlock Holmes:

> *Watson:* "Is there any point to which you would wish to draw my attention?
> *Holmes:* "To the curious incident of the dog in the night time."
> *Watson:* "The dog did nothing in the night time."
> *Holmes:* "That was the curious incident."[44]

The curious incident of which Porter was thinking was the striking perti-
nence of passages in RO and DEH, supposedly written in 1498 and 1499,
to a pair of interrelated crises that were convulsing the London ecclesiastical world from 1512 to at last 1515.[45] Relying perforce on the chronology that we have now found to be untenable, Porter was obliged to leave
the anomaly unexplained. His discovery of the parallelism between the
two Colet writings and the contemporary crises deserves a second look,
however, in view of our findings that the manuscripts are relatively late
and certainly not from the 1490s.

In 1512 Parliament withdrew the immunities from prosecution in the
civil courts which clergy in minor orders enjoyed. This development,
though it did not directly affect those in major orders—subdeacon, deacon, priest—was understandably viewed as ominous by the higher clergy.
Its anticlerical implications were soon intensified by a case in the ecclesiastical courts that began as a routine matter but grew to unprecedented
dimensions.[46]

In March 1511 Richard Hunne's baby son, Stephen, died at the age
of five weeks. The priest who buried him, Thomas Dryffeld, made a routine claim for the child's burial cloth as a mortuary. In theory a mortuary
was a solicitous effort on the part of the church to ensure that the departed
soul not be punished in the afterlife for having unintentionally failed to
pay financial obligations to the church during life. To compensate for such
a possible oversight it became the custom to offer something of value on
behalf of the deceased at burial—hence the term "mortuary." What began as a voluntary offering soon came to be regarded by the officiating
priest as a customary right.[47] Little Stephen's father, as a prominent member of the Merchant Taylors' Company, was well able to pay, but he refused Dryffeld the burial cloth. Hunne was known to be anticlerical, and
Dryffeld, probably correctly, saw in his refusal a challenge. He sued
Hunne in the court of the archbishop's chancellor and was granted judgment in May 1512. Nothing daunted, Hunne countered by charging Dryffeld with having brought him into a "foreign" court and thus with being
guilty of *praemunire*.[48] Such a countercharge was not without precedent

in such cases, and the common-law judges eventually ruled against Hunne, apparently late in 1514; but his making this serious charge raised the stakes in the controversy greatly.

It is not certain whether Hunne was under suspicion of heresy independently of the mortuary matter,[49] or whether instead, as contemporary opinion almost unanimously held, the charge of heresy was in retaliation for the charge of *praemunire*. In any case Hunne, though not the most prudent of men, saw that he had got into more serious difficulties than he had reckoned on. The charge of heresy resulted in imprisonment in a tower of St. Paul's for several months, after which Hunne seemed willing to admit his fault and ask pardon of the bishop. But it would appear that he refused to withdraw the charges of *praemunire* and that negotiations for a mutually acceptable solution broke down. What is certain is that soon afterward Hunne was discovered hanged in his cell.

The coroner impaneled a jury who were "ryght honest men" according to even the pro-clerical Thomas More but "perjured caitiffs" according to Richard Fitzjames, bishop of London; the jury speedily brought in a true bill indicting the bishop's chancellor, Dr. Horsey, on a charge of murder, along with two of Horsey's servants. Whether it was suicide or murder is still argued. But Hunne's fellow Londoners were sure it was murder, and this popular conviction is attested by Fitzjames himself. Fitzjames felt sure that if Horsey were tried in the secular courts he would be lost, yet because the chancellor was only in minor orders the recent act of Parliament had stripped him of clerical immunity and the privilege of pleading instead in the ecclesiastical courts. Fitzjames wrote an urgent secret appeal to the lord chancellor which casts a remarkable light on his cure of London souls: "If my Chancellor be tryed by any XII men in London, they be so maliciously set *in favorem heretice pravitatis*, that they will cast and condempne my[50] clerk, though he were as innocent as Abell." The letter was "leaked" to the City Corporation, whose members were outraged to read that because they were indignant at what looked to them like murder and were in favor of bringing people charged with murder before the same courts that had jurisdiction over themselves, they were promoting heresy.

Far from apologizing, Fitzjames dug in more deeply. He published the charges of heresy against the dead Merchant Taylor at Paul's Cross on the next Sunday, December 10. On the Saturday after that he presided over a court of bishops which tried the charges of heresy and found Hunne guilty. The trial could not have taken long, for there was time the same afternoon to pronounce a formal sentence of heresy over the corpse in the Lady Chapel of St. Paul's Cathedral (was the dean present? or conspicuously absent?). If this was not revenge it certainly looked like it.

At this point the specifics of the Hunne case intermesh with the wider question that then worried the ecclesiastical authorities intensely, that of clerical immunities, which, as already mentioned, Parliament had stripped from those in minor orders. Parliament's act of 1512 had only a temporary force, it being left to the next parliament to decide whether the clerical immunities should be removed permanently; and that crucial parliament was summoned for February 1515, two months after Hunne's posthumous condemnation and before Horsey's trial. On the day before the parliament was to convene, Bishop Fitzjames arranged for a public defense of the unpopular immunities by the abbot of Winchcombe, Richard Kidderminster. "The most distinguished English monk of the Tudor period"[51] and one of the four English representatives at the Fifth Lateran Council, Kidderminster was a respected churchman whom Fitzjames could rely on to defend the Church's legal position.

The role of Kidderminster as champion of the Church's stand illustrates the dilemma in which Colet found himself. The two men were friends. It was to Kidderminster, only some five years older than he, that Colet had written a letter containing an exegesis of Romans 1 by which he wished to be remembered, the only one of his letters which we know he wanted saved; this is the letter (EK) entered between R and C in the Cambridge University Library holograph. The letter is not dated, but its inclusion at this point in the manuscript shows that the two men, now both important churchmen, were on excellent terms in middle life. Both of them regarded ecclesiastical law as resting on divine authority and beyond the reach of Parliament; indeed Colet repeatedly declared ecclesiastical law superior to any secular authority whatever (RO, 262, 263, 266; DEH, 197). He would have had less than no sympathy with the position of an anticlerical like Hunne; however, he saw more clearly than most that the claimed divine origin of ecclesiastical law cut both ways. If its authority was binding because it derived from Christ, equally binding was Christ's mandate of charity and brotherly love. His dilemma was that, on the one hand, he could not waive any of the church's claims to authority over its members, because the authority was of divine origin, while on the other hand, he was aghast at the abuse of the Church's authority in open contempt of the mandate of charity.

The issues that troubled Colet had little to do with possible carnal failings of the clergy or even with routine anticlericalism. Instead they lay deep in the structure of ecclesiastical society. As formulated by H. C. Porter, they included "the liberty of the church; the obligations of the temporalty to the spiritualty; the reformation of the church, 'never more needed'; the defects of ecclesiastical justice, springing from covetousness."[52] These issues, which emerge from the Convocation Sermon probably datable to 1510, are not yet discussed there in the language of crisis which we first meet in DEH and especially RO, works we have found reason to think late. In the last-named works, with a passion rare even in so passionate a man, Colet denounces the "princes of iniquity," "the Devil's servants," who "sell" bishoprics to unspiritual and unworthy men. Though he knew that "God will one day repay them according to their works" (DEH, 247), he also knew that no lesser agency could be expected to root out this structural evil. Hence the despair with which he says that if Christ himself does not come to the rescue of the Church it is in danger of perishing altogether (DEH, 255, 265). The bitter fruit of the Church's worldliness was the crisis he saw besetting it at that moment. "Pseudo-Christians," who were worse than pagans, condemned themselves by the words of the Gospels in which they pretended to believe. What Paul said in Romans 2 could be applied "verbatim" to the present simply by exchanging one set of names for another:

> Virtually the same kind of strife that once existed between Jews and Gentiles is now ubiquitous in the Christian Church itself, between priests and laymen, between the so-called spiritual part of the church and the laity. Each accuses the other; they battle in the most deplorable way. Both sides are proud, vain, boastful. (RO, 227, 228)

By a terrible paradox, he continues, "because of priests the name of God is blasphemed by laymen" (RO, 228). Colet begs the priests, for their part, to endure even undeserved criticisms, returning blessings for hatred: "Priests, particularly . . . by returning to their ancient virtue, will recall laymen to their ancient obedience." On this follows a plea to laymen to

> have compassion on the lost and profligate priest; and mourn as you behold the light extinguished by which you were supposed to see, the example you were to follow gone, the salt with its savor lost. You will weep to see, once the captains in the war are slain, how Christians succumb to the Devil, who carries them off again into slavery; while, with the helmsman lost, the bark of the Church wallows amidst the billows of this world. (RO, 228–229)

Later in the same treatise Colet makes his indictment specific by denouncing merciless legalistic administration of canon law that makes a travesty of Christian compassion (266). In a similar vein he closes the treatise with a passage that, coming as it does in the work on Romans which he wanted copied onto vellum, may be the last surviving words he wrote under the inspiration of his beloved St. Paul.

The beginning of this passage (RO, 280) has already been quoted;[53] in it Colet asserts that the high position that evil men hold in the church makes it "not safe for anyone to criticize them openly." In this perhaps final effort, in a work addressed only to a single person, Colet next protests the perversion of church law by "petty-minded legists, experts in the law, who continually encourage lawsuits, spouting formulas, insisting on technicalities, weaving nets to trap the unlearned, and then extorting money from them in order to get rich." Such men would do far better

to set aside their professional cunning and insatiable avarice and concentrate instead on Christ and his Church, . . . to observe the law themselves before they punish others who transgress it, to bring men to know the law instead of punishing them when they offend unwittingly, . . . so that when they do impose punishment it is clear that they do so not because the accused was simply imprudent but because he was deliberately wicked, . . . and obvious also that they grieve that there should be occasion for punishment, which they impose only as a last resort. (RO, 280–281)

The gravamen of this passage is unmistakable. It is directed against those who exercise ecclesiastical authority in one capacity or another. Colet is outraged by the bishops and other prelates who ignore the souls committed to their charge and truckle instead to the court (RO, 206–207). This is, I think, the only passage in the works published by Lupton in which bishops are singled out for attack; and we have seen reason to think that this second of Colet's commentaries on Romans is a late work. But in the "Abbreviations," which remain in manuscript and date from 1516 or later, it is as if Colet had developed a conditioned reflex to the word "bishop." Within the space of nine leaves of this work, which isolates key ideas from the Epistles, we find the heading "Episcopus" three times and "Episcopatus" once. The bishop is to exercise his ministry "temperately" ("sobrie"; Trinity MS. o.4.44, fol. 9^v). Editorializing on a passage in Second Timothy in a direction that Paul did not take, Colet chooses to paraphrase Paul thus: the bishop is "not to go to law or to engage in battles of words" ("non litiget nec pugnet verbis"; fol. 9^r)—exactly the opposite of Bishop Fitzjames's behavior during the Hunne crisis. A few pages further on, Colet enlarges on this already clear mandate. The bishop is to be "not litigious, averse to strife and dispute, not greedy or avaricious and without concern for wealth or base lucre" ("non litigiosum, alienum a pugna absque iurgio, non cupidum, non avarum sed alienum ab argenti cupiditate, non turpilucrum"; fol. 11^r). And under the heading "On Bishops and Priests Who Exercise Authority" ("De episcopis et sacerdotibus qui presunt") he comes very close to drawing a distinction, which he also draws in another late work,[54] between bishops and priests whom the faithful are bound to "honor" and those who though they have the title of bishops are in fact simply "tyrants." Having spoken of the honor rightly due to bishops who fulfill their office creditably, he remarks, "Here note carefully which bishops and priests we are bound to hold in honor—not those, assuredly, who preside in pomp by virtue of their empty titles, and act like tyrants rather than bishops" ("Hic nota diligenter quos episcopos et sacerdotes debemus habere in honore, non eos quidem qui habent inanos titulos, qui fastu presunt, qui magis tyrannidem quam episcopum agunt"; fol. 18ᵛ). A further reason for Colet's intense criticism of unworthy bishops is his bitter conflict with his own bishop, Richard Fitzjames, which as we shall see (chapter 10) also came to a head in 1515.

Colet's datable and very pointed statements about what a bishop must be and not be are parallel in spirit to the comments that Porter twenty years ago noticed as curiously pertinent to the Hunne case, comments bunched in writings that our survey of the manuscripts puts late in Colet's career. Certainly the parallels of thought do not amount in themselves to proof of the manuscripts' dates, but I agree with Porter that they are suggestive. If they are taken to reflect Colet's horrified reaction to the scandals of the Hunne case, they will be consonant with the evidence for the dating of the manuscripts and their contents which we have surveyed in this chapter.

Tentative Chronology of Colet's Writings

In a duly tentative spirit we may now draw together the implications of our analysis of the manuscripts for the chronology of Colet's writings.

The three manuscripts written on vellum—the Emmanuel, the Duke of Leeds, and the Corpus—which we have been calling the collected edition cannot be earlier than 1505 or 1506. They were written by a scribe whom we cannot definitely connect with Colet until 1509. They exhibit no influence from the annotations to Erasmus's Greek New Testament of 1516, and they do not exhibit the changes in Peter Meghen's scribal style which are datable to late 1517–early 1518. Thus, the texts—in the form in which we have them—all fall between 1505–1506 and 1516–1518.

To determine their place within these limits we may next recall the strong stylistic similarity between G in the Corpus manuscript and the Trinity manuscript containing principally the "Abbreviations" of Paul's Epistles. The latter is definitely datable to 1516 or later; but RO (also in the Corpus manuscript), which belongs stylistically to the collected edition, was written into the manuscript after G. Both treatises were composed by Colet, and they were probably transcribed at no great distance in time. So, if G too is to be dated around 1516 and RO was written later than G, then the likely dates for RO are approximately 1516–1517.

To determine the approximate date of DEH we may best begin by considering that of C. The Cambridge University Library manuscript containing the latter demonstrates that C underwent a painful and long period of gestation. On the assumption that the vellum manuscripts of the collected edition all belong to much the same period, we can attribute the Emmanuel College manuscript, which contains the transcript of C, to 1515–1517. This transcript shows no textual variations from the draft of C in the Cambridge University Library manuscript. But Colet, like most people who work continuously on their subject, was a rewriter. Hence the absence of variation between holograph and vellum copy means that no long time elapsed between them, and therefore that the finishing touches were put on C in the holograph not long before it joined its companions in the vellum edition of 1515–1517. Now, DCH follows C in the holograph, and Colet tells us he composed it in a few days; thus DCH too belongs to the same period. DEH regularly follows DCH, both in the Duke of Leeds manuscript of Colet's treatises on Dionysius and in the copy of it in the Library of St. Paul's School, London. It is an easy inference that, since the last pages of the holograph remain blank, DEH had not yet been written at the time DCH was completed but that it followed its companion piece not long after.

The date for S is indicated by the fact that it follows both DCH and DEH in the vellum manuscript (and in the St. Paul's School manuscript copied from it). Moreover, these are the three among Colet's works which are saturated with Dionysian influence—another indication that they belong together.

Regarding RO we have already observed that it represents a completely fresh attack on Romans, with no noticeable similarities to R. That RO is later than R is shown by the fact that Colet chose it and not the entirely different treatment of Romans in R for preservation on vellum. If RO's seeming responses to the Hunne case and related crises, noted by Porter over twenty years ago, really are what they seem, they will tend to confirm the late dating.

For C in its final form, the safest anchor for dating is the Emmanuel College vellum transcription, which we have dated to about 1516. It is, however, not easy to say when the "first part," corresponding perhaps to the smoothly transcribed first five chapters of the holograph, was written. The short works that separate C from the preceding R in the holograph are in different hands from each other and from C. But this is not of much help since solid evidence for the dating of the intervening treatises is wanting, while the date of R too is somewhat indeterminate. Perhaps the most we can do in dating the earlier part of C is to say that it is likely to be at least a couple of years after R, because of the different styles of writing of the intervening pieces, but also at least a couple of years before the second "part" of C itself, that part which we have described as essentially "Collected Essays on First Corinthians."

All we can safely say of R is that—in the form in which we have it—it does not report the text of lectures. It is specifically addressed to "readers"—moreover, readers who had to plead with the author for "a long time" before he consented to continue the work, and who had then to wait again until the continuation was actually written. We have noticed that the state of the text in the holograph suggests that at the time of writing Colet thought it was ready for professional transcription, since he left spaces for decorated initials. But beyond that there can be, I think, only speculation. A reasonable guess, but still only a guess, is that R in its present form dates to the point in late 1504 or early 1505 when Colet was wrapping up his work in Oxford and preparing for his definitive removal to London.

In sum, the textual and bibliographical evidence in the foregoing discussion offers the scaffolding for a general chronology of Colet's writings in the form in which we have them. The chronology, which includes for convenience a few works discussed more fully later, will look something like this:

Middle to Later Oxford Period *(1499–1505)*	"Disputatiuncula" with Erasmus concerning Christ's Agony in the Garden (see chap. 5 below) On Romans, sixteen-chapter version (R) Letter to Richard Kidderminster (EK) (see chap. 7 below)
Earlier London Period *(1505–1511)*	On the Mystical Body (CM) On First Corinthians (C), chapters 1–5 Convocation Sermon (OCC) (see chapter 7 below)
Middle London Period *(1512–1516)*	On First Corinthians, chapters 6–16 On the first four chapters of Genesis (G) On Romans, unfinished five-chapter version (RO) On Dionysius's Celestial Hierarchy (DCH) On Dionysius's Ecclesiastical Hierarchy (DEH) On the Sacraments (S)
Final Period (1516–1519)	On the First Epistle of Peter (P) "Abbreviations" of Paul's Epistles in Trinity College, Cambridge, Manuscript o.4.44

5

Erasmus and Colet: First Encounters

Having brought Colet back from Italy to England, we could have wished to turn to the lectures he delivered after his return, the lectures that are so often said to mark an epoch in biblical exegesis in England. We have seen, however, that the Pauline commentaries that survive date from later years. Thus, if we possessed nothing besides the five volumes of writings which Lupton edited it would not be possible to recapture the Colet whom Erasmus knew and heard in late 1499.

In fact, however, though Lupton decided not to print it, we possess a work by Erasmus entitled "Disputatiuncula," which preserves a fully developed example of Colet's exegetical work dating from 1499. For reasons that will soon become clear, Seebohm and Lupton averted their eyes from this work, yet it deserves the closest scrutiny. It offers an unimpeachable example of Colet's intellectual style at the time of the much-discussed Oxford lectures, along with revealing glimpses of his personality which are available nowhere else. As Lupton acknowledged, the "Disputatiuncula" is in substance Colet's: it is Colet who propounds the theory under discussion, while Erasmus largely confines himself to responding, developing his own views only to the extent necessary to refute Colet's.[1] Nevertheless, as Erasmus was keeping the minutes of the controversy its style is incomparably better than anything from Colet's pen.

The controversy centered on the causes of the sadness and dread that Christ felt at his impending Passion, a classical problem among theologians.[2] Already the Fathers of the Church had been struck by the seeming paradox that while many a Christian martyr had gone cheerfully to a terrible death, Christ himself was in an agony of apprehension at the torments that awaited him. Colet on a later occasion (RO, 230) saw the courage of the martyrs as a sign of their unshaken faith; how then could it be that Jesus had apparently not attained such a degree of resolution himself? The question troubled Colet enough to make him attempt an answer, and he took the occasion of a dinner party in Oxford to present his theory. Present, among others, were Richard Charnock, prior of the Augustinian College of St. Mary the Virgin, the residence of Augustinians studying at the university; the newly arrived Augustinian canon Erasmus of Rotterdam; and Colet himself. Of the discussion that began that day we possess several records.

Erasmus sent Colet a letter, dated on the day following the discussion itself, summarizing their opposed positions; of this communication, however, only his covering letter survives (Allen, 1:249–250, Ep. 109, ll. 1–36).[3] Colet made a reply, still extant (1:253–254, Ep. 110), that provoked a lengthy rejoinder from Erasmus, also extant (1:254–260, Ep. 111). From this last-mentioned 1499 letter Erasmus worked up the version that he published as the "Disputatiuncula," in a volume of shorter works, *Lucubratiunculae*, dated February 1503. In its new form Erasmus's record of the controversy with Colet is expanded to the equivalent of about fifty pages of average size.

Very fortunately Erasmus decided to reproduce not only the intellectual framework of the controversy but also its atmosphere. He cast it in dialogue form, with each man expressing himself in his characteristic way. Thus at a number of points we have a unique chance to see Colet in action, and to glimpse his reactions especially when the argument was going against him. It is noteworthy that this invaluable document has been given exceedingly short shrift by the dean's biographers,[4] who have almost nothing to say about the way the argument develops and even less about the insights into Colet's personality. It is clear that they found in this strictly contemporary document no support for their thesis that Colet reformed scriptural exegesis at Oxford. It shows the Oxford lecturer coming off second-best in a controversy about Scripture at the very moment when he is supposed to have been teaching Erasmus how to interpret Scripture. It also gives glimpses of his manner which, while not necessarily discreditable, are not the stuff of hagiography either.

The "Disputatiuncula" gives us what the extant Colet manuscripts do not, namely, an extended specimen of Colet's exegesis in 1499; for Erasmus's Epistle 111, datable to October of that year, serves as a check on the substantial accuracy of the fuller version dated February 1503. It is true that when Erasmus eventually sent Colet a copy of the latter he said it was "so altered that you would scarcely recognize it."[5] By this he meant, however, as the context shows, only that the controversy was now set forth much more fully than was possible in a letter. On the occasion of their original exchange Colet acknowledged that Erasmus had given a "faithful account" of his position (1:254, Ep. 110, October 1499), and Colet must have accepted also the accuracy of the presentation of his views in the "Disputatiuncula," for though Erasmus often revised his works he continued to reprint the "Disputatiuncula" without change.[6]

By the diminutive suffix[7] in the title of the piece and in the description of it as a "conflictatiuncula" in the first paragraph, Erasmus downplays any suggestion of hostility; but both opponents took their positions seriously. I propose to call the work, a little periphrastically, "A Dispute between Friends."

As there is, so far as I know, no translation into any modern language, I offer in the pages that follow a close and full summary that follows the whole course of the discussion, but focuses especially on Colet's contributions and quotes the passages where Erasmus describes his opponent's manner as the dispute continues. The summary follows the give-and-take of discussion. Direct quotations are indicated as such, and editorial interpolations are in square brackets. References are to column numbers in LB, volume 5.

Disputatiuncula de taedio, pavore, tristitia Jesu, instante supplicio crucis: Deque verbis, quibus visus est mortem deprecari, Pater, si fieri potest, transeat a me calix iste (A Dispute between Friends Concerning the Weariness, Dread, and Sadness Felt by Jesus at His Impending Passion)

Prefacing his account of the previous day's discussion, Erasmus recalls that it had grown "quite heated" (1265). As Erasmus was leaving, Colet's parting remark was that he felt sure that Erasmus, when he reconsidered, would find Colet right. Erasmus now reports that he did reconsider, looking also at the pertinent books that were available, but found nothing material to change in his own position. He now proposes to present his own response more methodically than was possible without advance notice.

He begins by summarizing Colet's position, in fact "as you yourself will admit" (1266) putting it more forcefully than Colet himself had done [even though Colet had had the advantage of preparing his presentation].

Colet rejected the traditional interpretation of Jesus' words "Father, if it is possible, let this cup pass from me," in which, though Jesus immediately added, "Yet not my will but yours be done," theologians saw a human horror at his imminent death. Colet argued that Christ's love of man was so great and his charity so perfect that he would not shrink from

death. Otherwise, he said, one would be in the absurd position of con-
tending that Christ's own charity was less than that of many of his martyrs,
who met their deaths joyfully. Christ was love, and he had become man
solely to free other men from the bonds of death by his own guiltless
death. It was in the nature of such love, Colet continued, to exclude all
terror. Furthermore, Colet denied the commonly held notion that there
are degrees in love and that it is natural to give oneself the preference
over one's neighbor. This, he said, would be to take away the very essence
of love, which is to care for others rather than for oneself, as witness
Christ, Moses, and Paul (1266). Therefore Christ's undoubted symptoms
of dread (his sweating blood and the words he addressed to his Father)
must have another explanation. Colet opted to follow Jerome in saying
that Christ's sufferings were due to his knowledge that his death, which
he wished to be universally salvific, would instead prove fatal to the Jews,
who were responsible for it.

Erasmus replies that he can accept the opinion of Jerome on which Colet relies as one possible meaning in the scriptural passage, because "I
know the manna did not taste the same to everyone" (1267); but not if
Colet so interprets Jerome's view as to exclude every other significance
in the passage. It was the virtually unanimous opinion of the other Fathers
that in his human nature Christ did indeed experience the fear of death.
Erasmus now informs Colet that besides the opinion Colet had cited, Jerome also expressed the consensus view, indeed oftener than he did the
view that had impressed Colet. The reason, Erasmus explained, is that
Jerome and Ambrose generally follow the example of Origen in offering
differing explanations in cases where opinions differ. If Colet rereads the
passage in question he will see that Jerome accepts also the interpretation
that Colet rejects.

In the absence of a suitable theological library Erasmus proposes that
they look at the problem simply in the light of reason. If Christ always
knew the effect of his death on the Jews why should he choose precisely
this moment to lament it? And why in such unclear terms, by comparison
for example with his tears before Jerusalem? Moreover Christ says, "Let
the cup pass from *me*"—he is not speaking here especially of the Jews.
Erasmus urges Colet to put aside his preconceptions and interpret the passage in its immediate context. He draws Colet's attention to the force of
the pronoun in the phrase "calix iste" ("that cup of yours"), which must
refer to the Father whom he is addressing and who has prepared the cup
for him, not to the Jews (1267–1268). In short, a close textual analysis
of the passage makes Colet's interpretation untenable.

From a textual analysis Erasmus now turns to theological considerations. It is surprising to him that theologians, such as "your" Jerome,
Augustine, and Hilary, though they acknowledge in Christ both a divine
will and a human will, hesitate to recognize that these wills may run

counter to each other, as in this case.[8] The terms of Christ's prayer have to be referred to his human will, for his divine nature foreknew that the cup would not pass from him. Similarly, it is only from the human viewpoint that Christ could say "if possible" to God (1268). As Ambrose says, Christ took on not only the appearance but the reality of human nature; hence it is fitting that he felt grief, to overcome it rather than exclude it.

"I know you are usually willing enough to part company with the latter-day theologians, but let us try what Plato recommends in the *Parmenides* [136 A–B] and see whether any absurd consequences follow from my interpretation. If not, why look for forced explanations, abandoning what is simple, pertinent and obvious in favor of something that is nowhere to be found in the literal meaning [quod nusquam est in litteris]?" (1269). [In view of the primacy of the literal meaning that Victorian scholars read back into Colet, Erasmus's first-hand reaction is instructive. It helps explain also why these scholars averted their eyes from the "Disputatiuncula."]

Erasmus anticipates that in responding to the challenge of the principle from the *Parmenides*, Colet will reply that Erasmus's interpretation detracts from Christ's perfect love for mankind and his perfect obedience. Erasmus counters by saying that this rock, on which Colet, like Jerome, is so afraid of foundering that he takes a very circuitous way around it, may after all prove to be merely a cloud. But for the present Erasmus will not attack Colet's view but simply state his own (1269).

[Erasmus then appears to suggest a stubbornness and closed-mindedness on Colet's part:] "But you, meanwhile, must take a little more objective view of that position to which you are so strongly attached and to which you are striving to bring me around, not so much by arguments as by appeals, at least long enough to give a hearing to such arguments as I bring forward." ("At tu interim, ab ista tua sententia, quam nimis impense deamas, et in quam ut discedem pedibus, non tam argumentis quam precibus obtinere niteris, tantisper abducas animum, dum quae a me ducuntur, cuiusmodi sint, consideres"; 1270.)

He asks Colet to concede that Christ assumed not only human nature as it was before the Fall but also the disabilities ("mala") that, though not sinful in themselves, are associated with sin as a consequence of the Fall—such disabilities as infancy, hunger, fatigue, grief, or sleepiness. Erasmus contends that the fear of death belongs in this class. Death is so utterly opposed to life that the fear of it is a fundamental quality in man. Even the Stoics, with their high opinion of man, allowed in him a dread of death, to the point of reckoning that dread among the basic elements of his nature. Hence it is natural that the fear of death should be in Christ the man as well. In him, in fact, three factors made it more intense than in other men: the value of the goodness that was injured, the extent of the injury, and Christ's own awareness of both these factors. We ordinary men, Erasmus continues, are greatly distressed at anything that threatens us with death, yet we are infinitely less in value and nature than Christ. Also, because we, unlike him, do not know for certain that we are about to die, we always contrive to hope, thus lessening our agony.

Erasmus writes that he knows what objections Colet will raise as he reads Erasmus's argument. While admitting that there were reasons to dread death, Colet would insist that Christ's perfect love and obedience lead us to anticipate that he would show readiness and even alacrity in his solicitude for others rather than for himself. Erasmus answers that he will defer for the moment the question of love and obedience and ask instead what Colet means by bravery. Would he deny that a man is brave if he is disheartened at imminent suffering? According to Socrates, fortitude involves knowing which things are to be endured and which are unendurable. In order not to feel natural dread a person would have to be a block rather than a man; one is all the braver for conquering natural dread. Also it belongs to a brave man to take a realistic view of what he is up against. Erasmus presses hard with many examples of heroes in Homer and Vergil and historical figures of Roman antiquity (1271–1273). He asks Colet, If you saw a soldier in the front line grow pale, while his hair stood on end and he groaned, would you taunt him with cowardice? No, a coward would be the man who ran from the battle. Would you deny that a man was brave if just before battle was joined he lost control over his face and voice, "or even could not manage to contain—what it would not be polite to mention?" (1273). Such emotional symptoms are neither virtues nor vices; they belong to the order of nature and necessity. "A soldier is twice brave who, for the love of his fellow citizens, conquers not only the danger but his own emotions, and, what is finer still, conquers himself before he seeks to conquer the enemy" (1273).

But, Erasmus continues, you will probably cite various impassive gladiators and warriors mentioned in Roman writers, or even convicted warlocks who joke with the spectators on the way to execution and greet their death with scorn, like drunkards. This is not bravery but simply absence of feeling. Following Scotus, Erasmus distinguishes between primarily physical pain ("dolor") and the sadness ("tristitia") that is primarily interior even though it may be expressed in the face (1274). He reminds Colet that it is a heresy to say that Christ was incapable of suffering. It is natural to avoid suffering: according to Aristotle even sponges, somehow aware that they are about to be culled, contract so as to protect themselves if possible. Would you "deny to a man what nature has implanted even in sponges?" (1274). [This caustic comparison is not the language of a disciple.]

Erasmus denies that Phocion's and Socrates' imperturbability in the face of death is a proof of virtue: it is simply the way they were made, some people being less susceptible to imagination and less warm-blooded than others. "If nature has made me more phlegmatic does that make me braver?" (1274). In fact Quintilian thinks it is nothing against an orator if he shows some nervousness when he begins a speech, for both Demosthenes and Cicero did (1275).

"Colet, I can see that you've been shaking your head for some time now and are still not satisfied. Hold on a bit; I won't rest till I have rebutted all your arguments. You say, 'What do I care about the Stoics? I'm talking about Christ!' In fact, though, since we are speaking of Christ, who is truth, if the Stoics offer an argument that is not at variance with the truth there is no reason not to make use of it. 'How truly they may have spoken has nothing to do with my point,' you say. But it is not irrelevant to cite the Stoics when we are speaking of Christ if what they said has truth in it" (1275).

Colet now rises to the challenge and seeks to turn Erasmus's own argument from the Stoics against him. Even if the Stoics grant that a wise man may be frightened at the sudden appearance of a seeming evil, they expect him to recover in short order. And in any case they would not grant that a wise man should fear death, which is as much a part of the natural order as birth is and is in fact the source of all our good. Erasmus is in effect putting Christ below the Stoics and moreover representing him as afraid of the very death that was of all works the most pleasing to God and the most meritorious (1275–1276).

"You overwhelm me, Colet, with a shower of missiles. But I can repel all of them at once by saying that while Christ had the same emotions as we do, he did not have them in the same manner or to the same effect [*sed non eodem modo, eoque non idem efficere*]." As Scripture teaches [Wisd. 1:13], "God did not fashion death, nor does he delight that living things cease to be." As God is the source of all things good, but not of death, death is evil. Hence Christ shrinks from death for the same reason the Stoic shrinks from wrongdoing, because it is evil. "Like a true human being Christ shrank from death, as from something evil in itself and evil in its origin," for it is through the malice of the Devil that death entered the world. [Erasmus then draws a distinction appropriate to the scholastic method in which both he and Colet had been trained:] Jesus "did not recoil from his death in respect of its being a fruitful work pleasing to God, but in respect of its being death" (1276). Thus he felt the conflicting emotions appropriate to his "complete human nature—fear, grief, hope, joy, desire, wrath, hatred, and whatever other emotions can subsist without sin" (1276).

If Colet charges him with attributing to Christ emotions that incline a person to evil, Erasmus replies that while such emotions might have this effect upon us, in our fallen state, they did not so affect Christ because he was free of the consequences of original sin. This, he explains, is what he meant in saying that while Christ had the emotions we have he did not have them in the same manner or to the same effect. It does not derogate from Christ's dignity to say, for example, that he felt hatred, for in him hatred was nothing but a rejection of evil (1276–1277).

[Having analyzed the sense in which Jesus felt human emotions, Erasmus now returns to Colet's contention that Erasmus's appeal to the Stoics would backfire.] Colet asserts that the Stoics admit the possibility of fright in a good man only for a short period, after which reason would reassert its dominion. This may be true, Erasmus replies, if by fright is meant something akin to panic, but he himself is far from attributing any such feeling to Christ. However, he says, if by fright is meant "a troubled and tormented dread of an imminent evil which arouses intense apprehension though without causing the mind to lose control," fright in this sense does not always arise from actually seeing terrifying things; in fact it originates in the mind and manifests itself only secondarily in the body. Fright does not exclude reason, being actually the consequence of a person's reflecting on a formidable and imminent evil. Erasmus sees no reason why fright so defined should not be long lasting. Even the kind of fright which he does not attribute to Christ, the fright akin to panic, causes some people to lose their mental faculties permanently. The kind of fright he is discussing is bound to last as long as the impending evil looms (1277). Because of original sin man must struggle almost continuously in the moral realm. Both "head and members" experience this sense of struggle, each in a different manner (1277–1278). [Later (1280) Erasmus expressly refers to Christ as head and the martyrs as members.]

"This would be more than enough, Colet, if you were not so attached to that theory of yours. But even now you keep shaking your head [the second reference to this mannerism] and claim you are not satisfied." Erasmus represents Colet as saying, "You are playing the rhetorician, and defending a bad cause with a good deal of skill" (1278). Despite Erasmus's counterarguments Colet continues to insist that it is of the nature of perfect love to overcome every difficulty with joyful eagerness; hence Christ must have done so.

Erasmus's reply is bold: "What ordinary human love effects in us, what greater eagerness their admittedly divine but still finite love effects in the martyrs, this I deny was effected by Christ's divine and infinite love. I deny it however not absolutely but insofar as it would preclude a sense of dread" (1279). The reason is that in us our several faculties and emotions conflict, and only one of them can predominate. But in Christ, who had the perfection of human nature, perfect love did not preclude intense dread. Erasmus then retorts Colet's objection upon him by observing that the fact of Christ's dread is itself enough to prove that Colet must be wrong

about the nature of perfect love, for Christ's perfect love was not inconsistent with his thinking of himself as well as others. Moreover he adds
that if Colet's stipulation regarding the nature of perfect love were admitted, then even some barbarians and slaves, of whom he gives examples,
would have loved more truly than Christ (1279). Actually Christ suffered
more than the most timorous men do: they may break out in a sweat, but
he sweated blood, which ran down onto the ground in drops. In short,
the logical consequence of Colet's position is that "a silly adolescent loves
his girl-friend more than Christ loves his bride [the Church]" (1280). [It
is hard not to think that Erasmus is carried away here by rhetorical over-
kill, unless this comparison is a sign of his impatience with Colet's stubbornness.]

Erasmus anticipates that Colet will reply that the intensity of Christ's
sufferings was due to concern not for himself but for others. This Erasmus
concedes but finds irrelevant: the point is that Christ did experience grief
and anguish, for whatever reason. Colet, Erasmus declares, is reduced
to saying that Christ's love was strong enough to make him suffer death
for our sake but not strong enough to make him do it cheerfully. On this
showing Christ endured his sufferings patiently, but he did not welcome
them wholeheartedly (1280).

"You answer" that the martyrs were sustained by a power not their
own, while Christ was destitute of his divinity. "Now," Erasmus declares,
"you have hit it" (1281). But before I explain my meaning, he continues,
I will turn against you the weapon that you were confident would vanquish
me all by itself. Christ certainly loved more ardently than the martyrs,
though many of them bore their sufferings more gladly. And even if Christ
put aside his divinity he still felt perfect love. So if you insist that the mark
of love is to put concern for others over concern for oneself, you would
have to say that other men's love was greater. Also, by the way, Jesus'
love, like the martyrs', came from God (Christ). Jesus differed from us
only in that while both we and he receive all good things from God, we
men also receive concomitant evils (1281). Unbounded love does not necessarily make sufferings lighter; nor does the absence of sufferings necessarily betoken unbounded love. A blush, for example, is only a sign of
shame, not a cause; so pallor of fear, cheerfulness of joy, and the like;
in any case these indices are not invariably associated with the corresponding emotion. The real proof of Christ's love is that he freely took
upon himself to die for us, though he owed his death neither to nature
nor to sin. It is for me, Erasmus concludes, a particular proof of his love
that he met his death in grief, likening himself to the weaker members
of his Church rather than the stronger (1282).

But you still insist that dread of death is a proof that a man is anxious
for himself. In fact, it argues Christ's perfection: he submitted to his

death, dreadful because undeserved, for our sake. Although he became thirsty no one thinks less of him for that sign of self-awareness; instead we are impressed that he endured the thirst for us. The greater the sufferings one attributes to him, the more glorious one shows his love. "Which of us is diminishing his love—you, who deny that he accepted an evil more grievous almost than death itself, or I, who maintain that for love of us he accepted even death?" But you will reply that while it would be more appropriate to his love to rejoice at his own death, he nevertheless grieved because certain men by putting him to death were bringing damnation on themselves. I grant you that these thoughts were a terrible part of his sufferings; indeed far from arguing against that idea I enlarge upon it (1282). Erasmus now explains that Christ's love is all the more apparent from his having been willing to take on the full implications of the human condition, with all its weaknesses; and he cites patristic passages in support of his contention (1283).

He then declares that Christ both did and did not fear. He suffered the emotions we suffer, in consequence of having taken on our nature; his sufferings were real but voluntary, while our sufferings and our fear of death belong to the order of necessity. "He feared not his evil death but ours, not for his own sake but for ours" (1283). [This is the true answer to Colet's contention that Christ suffered because of the Jews' anticipated punishment: he suffered not for them only but for all men, by taking on the nature of man and all that goes with it (except evil), including the dread of death.] Erasmus now sees Colet protesting that he is "propounding a Platonic riddle" in this distinction between fearing and not fearing. Erasmus explains: "The feeling of dread was ours, yet it was his. Ours because he took on our human nature, for our sake; his because he suffered truly in his own body and spirit, not in ours" (1283). The thread to follow in extricating yourself from this labyrinth of paradoxes is that he did not fear of necessity, as we do, but voluntarily.

[In elaboration of this key concept he explains further:] Christ feared death because [as demonstrated earlier] it is an evil in itself and not because it was inimical specifically to the human nature that he now shared. Moreover, as his faculties of body and spirit were immeasurably finer than ours, he felt every torment incomparably more acutely. He disdained the shifts by which we distract ourselves from our troubles and concentrate instead on a reward to come, means that even pagan sages used. In addition, he felt each of a thousand torments in its full horror, whereas with us at least the greater pain overwhelms the lesser. And in his great love he would not abate one jot of the terrible sufferings to which the perfection of his nature laid him open (1284–1285).

But as we continued our dispute you kept asking in exasperation, "What is the point of dwelling on the atrocities that Christ endured? It was primarily his love that made his death meritorious, and I prefer to dwell on that, not on the brutal horrors [*carnificinam*]"—indeed that was the very word you used. In fact, your argument decreases the love Christ showed while mine increases it, the very opposite of what you assumed at the outset. "Virtue is the greater as it is expressed in more difficult circumstances [*crescit virtus, crescente materia*]," and his death was to supply the treasury of merits for all mankind, furnishing moreover an example that would warm even the lazy and indifferent to devotion. "His was the most terrible grief that ever was or could be endured," and this is why theologians emphasize the bitterness of his sufferings.[9] Hence Erasmus cannot accept Jerome's explanation of Jesus' sufferings as a "propassion,"[10] a suffering in anticipation of what was to happen later (1285). Erasmus also interprets the phrase starting "He began" in the Gospel account as referring not to a transitory condition but to one that lasted as long as he lived (1286).

I think I have said more than enough to satisfy you, Erasmus continues, but since you insist so strongly on Christ's love I will add that I believe none of the martyrs ever met his death so cheerfully as Jesus did. At the very moment of his most intense suffering, while he was sweating blood, he felt a deep interior joy that the hour ordained by his Father for the reconciliation of the human race with himself had at last come. "No one was ever so desirous of life, no one so much wanted to live, as Christ wanted to die" (1286).

In explanation of this paradox Erasmus states that he follows certain theologians in distinguishing three wills—divine, rational, and carnal—all of which could be said to be one insofar as they refer to the same object, as people who are in agreement are said to be "of one mind." Moreover it is a common experience to be pulled simultaneously in opposite directions, truly desiring both to do something and not to do it (1286); even Paul speaks of the "law of his members" without our being justified in thinking that his recognition of this "law" involved him in sinful acquiescence in its behests, any more than it did Jesus. Erasmus sees the divine will in man as inclining him to things invisible and good, while the carnal will inclines him toward base things as such. The rational will is not of its nature inclined to either good or base things, but inclines man to natural goods that procure his safety or simply his peace of mind. While a good person could not be drawn to evil as such, "he could shrink from something neutral in itself, or even something good [*pium*] under the circumstances but repugnant to the natural feelings" (1287). Examples include dying for the sake of Christ, or the hunger due to fasting, or labor enjoined by brotherly love. "There is nothing to prevent a purely natural repugnance from existing in the most perfect man, even in Christ himself" (1287). Addressing himself directly to Colet, Erasmus adds, "I should not mind your despising these concepts as simply my fancies [*somnia*] if it were not that I have St. Augustine on my side." According to Augustine,

"Peter approached his suffering unwillingly but conquered it willingly, the unwillingness to die being a natural emotion that even age could not take from him." Erasmus concludes that Christ's human dread was of the same kind he foresaw in Peter, a purely natural one (1287–1288).

"So that you won't protest that dividing man into three parts, spirit, flesh, and reason, is merely something that came into my head [*meum commentum*], I will mention that the author I am following is Jerome. Jerome followed Origen, and Origen Paul, while Paul must have followed the Holy Spirit" (1288). [Erasmus is obviously pleased with himself as he administers this crushing blow to Colet's reliance on Jerome.] Of course Erasmus attributes to Christ only the two higher wills, and suggests moreover that of these he inherited the second from his mother (1288).

Erasmus does not regard this line of argument as entailing a distinction between what God wills and what Christ wills. Christ submits entirely to his Father's will. Further, even his recoiling from death is perfectly in keeping with his Father's will, since death is the penalty of sin and associated with the author of sin, the Devil. Remember, Erasmus tells Colet, that it was God who said, "I will not the death of the sinner"—still less the death of the just man. Yet Christ endured his death because it belonged to the human condition that he had assumed (1288).

Yet you insist ("efflagitas"), Erasmus continues, that I explain how Christ could be simultaneously eager to die and in dread of death. In fact it seems to me that I have already done so. Erasmus takes this opportunity for a peroration that leads to a final explanation of why, if Christ rejoiced inwardly, he manifested only his dread. The reason must be that he wished to give an example of patience, gentleness, and obedience rather than one of high-spirited courage ("animositatis")—an example for men to love and imitate. This kind of love was after all the theme of his last discourse with his disciples and of his whole Passion (1289). Moreover this tone comported better with the oracles of the prophets, who presented him under the aspect of the lamb led to slaughter (1290).

Erasmus concludes by saying that he has not tried to work up his case with all possible completeness, since he felt he was writing to a friend. He does not know whether he has convinced Colet, but he believes he has shown that his view, which is also that of contemporary theologians, is consonant with the Fathers, Scripture, and reason, and also more in keeping with our experience of human nature. This view of Christ's sufferings, far from detracting from the Redeemer's merits, adds to them.

"But how rash I am, a mere beginner, to venture to engage with a commander on so delicate a theological question, especially since I am, as you put it, merely a rhetorician and out of my field! But I thought there was nothing I would not risk in your presence, . . . who have brought forth from Italy such treasures in both the languages that for that reason alone Colet could hardly receive high enough tribute from the theologians."

Therefore, Erasmus continues, I have decided to cast our discussion in "the free-flowing fashion used of old," "rather than the pedantic superstitious style now in vogue which you so much dislike." And perhaps, Colet, you are right. "Nevertheless, in accordance with the saying Μῆδε Ἡρακλῆς πρὸς δύο [Not even Hercules should take on two opponents], be careful lest you find yourself unable to hold your ground against so many thousands. Farewell."

Underlying the specific point at issue was ultimately a clash of christologies.[11] The Council of Chalcedon (in 451) had anathematized those who, in order to preserve Christ's dignity, denied that he was really a man and asserted instead that while the Jesus of the Gospels seemed to have a man's body he was in reality spirit only—whence the designation of their heresy as Docetist, from the Greek word for "seems." Chalcedon affirmed in the one person of Jesus Christ two natures, divine and human, both of which he possessed in their fullness. Obedient to this definition and the consent of the Fathers, Erasmus took the classical position that Christ's agonies of apprehension were the expression of his human nature's recoiling from the ordeal that lay ahead.[12] Erasmus found it no derogation from the divine dignity that Christ shared with his fellow men the disabilities that are inseparable from human nature, such as infancy, fatigue, or hunger. In Christ's sharing with his fellow men also the horror that almost all of them would have felt at having to endure his torments and degradation, Erasmus saw a further proof of his loving solidarity with the poor imperfect human race.

Colet's Christ, by contrast, had to rise triumphantly over all the disabilities that were the concomitants of his human nature. He never thought of himself; he thought only and always of others. So marked is Colet's refusal to believe that Christ could behave like other men that recently a theologian has described his position as having "docetist tendencies."[13] Something in Colet made it unthinkable for him that Christ should have chosen to participate fully in that human nature that he himself always regarded with some measure of horror. Not that he never enjoyed himself, of course; still less that he was indifferent to money or comforts and position. But he never saw these good things as having any common ground with the world that matters, the world beyond the grave. This antihumanistic denial of value to human realities has been well called his "annihilation of the natural."[14] It is prominent in the "Disputatiuncula" and seems to be the underlying reason for the singular position that he took in his controversy with Erasmus about the Passion, and also for his tenacity in maintaining his view no matter what an opponent could say.

Colet's conviction, as it was not founded on reason, proved impervious to reason. It was not that Jerome's argument convinced him; it was that his own prior conviction made him cling to the authority of Jerome. Erasmus must have assumed that with the basis of Colet's appeal to Jerome undermined and no other patristic support available for his theory, he would have to abandon it. The root of Colet's position was not, however, logical but lay in his revulsion from a Christ submitted to the human condition. Erasmus may have demonstrated that Colet's theory was gratuitous. He may have pointed out that it also contradicted the literal meaning of the prayer that the cup might "pass from *me*."[15] But neither these arguments nor the theological reflection that Christ died for all men alike, all of humanity being his true concern, could budge Colet. Erasmus felt he had done enough and concluded, as we have seen, with a proverbial caution against taking on antagonists that even a Hercules, as he said ironically, could not handle.

Erasmus applied this proverb to his overambitious antagonist on another occasion in 1499, as we shall see, and he used it to end his fuller 1503 version of their dispute on the Passion in 1499. Exactly what Erasmus meant by the proverb we know from his own explanation of the saying, published in June 1500. It means, Erasmus explains, that "no one man is so surpassingly strong as to be able to stand alone against a number of others; nor need even the bravest man be ashamed to retire in the face of a multitude of opponents."[16] Whether Colet had proved himself the Hercules of theologians, Erasmus politely leaves an open question. But even if he was, or thought he was, it would be sensible for him to retire from a battle that he could not win.

Colet did not take the broad hint, and in the course of a single month Erasmus again had occasion to apply the same proverb to him. Again Prior Charnock was present, along with others unnamed. The conversation this time turned on why God accepted Abel's sacrifice but not Cain's. Colet was presiding at the table, and it was probably he who steered the conversation toward the subject, for he had been mulling over the passage in Genesis 4 and had ready a novel solution of the problem. Cain, the agriculturalist, lacked confidence that God would give him all he needed and turned to farming to provide for himself by his own industry, while his brother was satisfied to be a shepherd and trust to the sufficiency of whatever God gave. Both Erasmus and another divine attacked Colet's theory, "he with his syllogisms and I with my rhetorical analysis."

Erasmus soon saw that their host was getting angry. Seebohm takes at face value Erasmus's description of Colet at this juncture, but the passage deserves a second look. "He was single-handedly conquering us all," Erasmus reports. "He seemed to be raging with some sort of divine madness, giving the impression of something loftier and more august than mere man. His voice seemed different; his eyes had a different look; his face and expression were different; he seemed larger than life, inspired by a divinity." Predictably this fit of inspiration threw a pall over the previously lively gathering. Like a good guest Erasmus came to the rescue with an improvised "fable" about Cain[17] that diverted the company and gave Colet, who was after all the host, time to shake off his divine madness, or simply to recover his temper. Cheerfulness was restored and Erasmus obviously felt he had done a good day's work.

Erasmus's account of the occasion is given in a letter to a Frisian acquaintance at Oxford who had also been invited but luckily for us could not come.[18] Erasmus's high-spirited letter was written to give John Sixtin an idea of what he had missed. With a fellow countryman Erasmus could be more candid than he cared to be when writing to the English. His account of the scene maliciously echoes a passage from the *Aeneid*, lines 42–51 of Book VI. At this point Aeneas is about to venture into the underworld to seek the shade of his father and asks guidance of the Sibyl, the priestess of Apollo. From her lofty shrine, perforated with a hundred openings, the Sibyl makes a dramatic entrance:

> Here, as the men approached the entrance way,
> The Sibyl cried out:
>   "Now is the time to ask
> Your destinies!"
>   And then:
>   "The god! Look there!
> The god!"
>   And as she spoke neither her face
> Nor hue went untransformed, nor did her hair
> Stay neatly bound: her breast heaved, her wild heart
> Grew large with passion. Taller to their eyes
> And sounding now no longer like a mortal
> Since she had felt the god's power breathing near,
> She cried:
>   "Slow, are you, in your vows and prayers?
> Trojan Aeneas, are you slow? Be quick,
> The great mouths of the god's house, thunderstruck,
> Will never open till you pray."
>   Her lips
> Closed tight on this. A cold chill ran through the bones
> Of the tough Teucrians.

Had Sixtin any doubt as to the purport of the comparison of Colet's behavior with the Sibyl's, he need only have recalled the passage thirty lines further on, in which her behavior is described with imagery drawn from taming a wild horse:[19]

> But the prophetess
> Whom the bestriding god had not yet broken

Stormed about the cavern, trying to shake
His influence from her breast, while all the more
He tired her mad jaws, quelled her savage heart.[20]

Erasmus's description of the scene at the dinner party signaled the allusion to the *Aeneid*, if that were necessary, by the position of the conjunction *quando* at the end of a clause, a position possible only in a verse
quotation. Very little research would have shown that the allusion was
to Vergil, but Lupton chose not to notice the allusion or its implication.
For all Lupton's services to the subject of his biography, one must add
that he repeatedly looks away from documents that show another Colet
than the hero of *The Oxford Reformers*. In this chapter we have seen that
he passed over the argument of the "Disputatiuncula" in silence though
it is critical to the theory that Colet taught Erasmus how to interpret Scripture. He also chose not to understand Erasmus's parody of Colet's behavior when he met opposition to his theories. In chapter 7 we will meet another embarrassed aposiopesis of a similar kind; there too the document
that Lupton refuses to look at concerns Colet's method of interpreting
Scripture.

Regarding the occasion when Colet's behavior made Erasmus com-
pare him slyly with the Sibyl in Vergil, Seebohm, like Lupton, ignores
the allusion to Vergil and reports to his readers that Erasmus found Colet
"like one inspired. In his voice, his eye, his whole countenance and mien,
he seemed raised, as it were, out of himself."[21] As we have now seen,
this version of Erasmus's reaction contains a good deal less than half the
truth. In reality the observant visitor had already noticed Colet's predilection for novel theological theories that did not so much refute as ignore
the consensus of established scholars, coupled with an unwillingness to
budge from his position or to tolerate disagreement. "Let us reason together" was not one of Colet's favorite scriptural quotations.

When Erasmus finished his initial letter (Ep. 109) in October 1499 he
must have felt he had disposed of Colet's contention about the nature of
perfect charity so thoroughly that his opponent would have to admit defeat. But he soon found he was mistaken. The next mail (so to speak)
brought an astonishing response.

Erasmus had concluded his letter by inviting Colet to refute him and
show where he was wrong; Colet, aware that he had to say something but
unable to confess himself worsted, seized in this quandary on a conciliatory throwaway comment Erasmus had made in passing. Alluding to the
accepted doctrine that the divine origin of the Scriptures made them
"fruitful" of meanings, Erasmus had said simply that Colet's point might
have some truth in it too—though not if taken to preclude every other
interpretation of Christ's agony. Colet now claimed that the "fruit-

fulness" of Scripture, by which it could give birth to more meanings than one, was Erasmus's main point, the "front line" of his "battle array." Moreover, after seeking to replace the real issue with a side issue, Colet did not even attempt to address himself to the latter. He simply announced, "I cannot agree," his only counterargument being that such low creatures as ants and flies were also fruitful. With no attention at all to Erasmus's critique of the actual issue as formulated by himself, Colet then hastily sought to close the correspondence by pleading the pressure of other engagements. His entire letter (Allen, 1:253–254, Ep. 110) runs only to twenty-nine lines.

The irrelevance of Colet's attempt at a reply disconcerted even Lupton. In his mild and careful way he remarks of Colet, "In calling [the fruitfulness of Scripture] the front line of the defence, he appears to exaggerate the importance attached to it by Erasmus. For it is only allowed by him, in passing, as a theory under cover of which he might accept Colet's interpretation as one possible one."[22] Erasmus's own response was blunter. He ignored Colet's intimation that the topic might now be considered closed. Instead he replied in a long letter of some two thousand words (1:254–260, Ep. 111), written in a decidedly sharp tone, as his editor observes.[23] Erasmus's tough response to Colet's attempt to escape was not discovered and published until 1906; had it been known earlier its tone as well as its content might have given pause to even the most dedicated partisans of the notion that Colet taught Erasmus how to interpret Scripture.

The air of good humor and even subdued amusement in the "Disputatiuncula"—Lupton too noticed its tone of "raillery"[24]—abruptly disappears. In the fulsome if also subironic close of the "Disputatiuncula" Erasmus had affected to regard Colet as a great general and himself as the merest novice, "a rhetorician out of my own field." But when Erasmus found that Colet was trying to change the whole point at issue and ignore his searching critique of Colet's own original contention, he was no longer amused and laid aside his modest professions. The military metaphor reappears in this reply, but much transformed. Erasmus now has his own army and thus has promoted himself to general. The opposing general, Colet, is informed flatly that in supposing he had breached what he called the front line of Erasmus's position he was mistaken:

> You have not taken by storm the front line of my army but have captured some unarmed soldier, or rather sutler who chanced to stray too far from the rest of the army. What you do with him is not my affair but yours. When I mentioned in passing and at an appropriate point that esoteric writings [*arcanis litteris*] may yield various meanings, and that no meaning should be rejected provided it is supported by authority [*probabile*] and consistent with the respect we owe to the divine [*nec a pietate abhorreat*], I did not

make the assertion without supporting it by arguments, and these you do
not refute. Moreover I made the assertion not by way of affirmation but
as an accommodation; in the last analysis I said it not for my sake but for
yours. I wanted my campaign to cause as little bloodshed as possible and
to conduct it in such a way that neither Jerome nor anyone else should receive a wound. But you, I see, have preferred to run greater risks, with the
result that if you could prove Jerome's theory all the others would be wiped
out, while if I proved victorious then your Jerome would fall. (1:255, ll. 11–
25)

Erasmus's accommodativeness, by contrast, would not cause one of Jerome's opinions to cancel out another. It is Colet who is attacking Jerome's
authority, not Erasmus, for to Erasmus Jerome's various surmises are all
acceptable.

Erasmus sees no point in responding point by point to Colet's conten-
tions "since they have nothing to do with the subject under discussion"
("quoniam extra controversiam sunt"). You keep telling me, Erasmus
says to Colet, to look at what you say is as plain as day, but you can hardly
deny that there must be some obscurity in a passage about which so many
great men have been uncertain. "Why should you be surprised at my being in the dark when according to you Augustine, Ambrose, Leo, Gregory, and virtually everyone else have all without exception failed to see
the light?" (1:256, ll. 63–65).

Instead of insisting on one's own theory in a case in which no one opinion is clearly right, Erasmus advises Colet, it is best to give due weight
to all the surrounding circumstances and especially to those words of
Christ whose meaning is not disputed. If everything favors the interpretation almost universally held by the Fathers, while no circumstance tells
against it,

> why should we distort the words as referring to the Jews? . . . I don't know,
> Colet, whether I wrote this, but I certainly thought it—that in so clear a
> case with so many famous writers unanimous, one should not rashly side
> with Jerome against the settled and widely received interpretation unless
> one has not merely some arguments but arguments that are utterly convinc-
> ing. To proceed otherwise is daydreaming, not exegesis. [*Alioqui somniari
> est istud, non interpretari.*] (1:256–257, ll. 89–90, 94–98)

This devastating dismissal by Erasmus of Colet's effort deserves much
more attention than it gets.

At greater length than in the "Disputatiuncula" Erasmus demonstrates that the literal meaning of *calix* and *iste* cannot in context be what
Colet thinks. From a principle that is, as Erasmus significantly says,
"widely known and long established" among rhetoricians and logicians,

he goes on to disprove Colet's contention that Christ could not both will to die and recoil from death. This Erasmus mentions not because it is relevant to his own position but as an example that he hopes will set Colet thinking about the "numerous" ill-founded arguments he has introduced (1:259, ll. 211–212).

In concluding Erasmus reiterates, "So far you have not even touched the structure of my argument" (1:259, ll. 212–213). While he likes Colet's idea that from the clash of their opposing flints sparks may be struck that could provide illumination for them both, he is bound to state that this has not happened yet. As he coolly asserts in closing, "I don't believe you have yet touched my flint with yours. Do you think a truth hidden deep within its veins will flash out at a feeble first scratch? Even by vigorous and repeated contest it is hard to bring it out. Farewell, my dear Colet."

The "Disputatiuncula" and the letters we have just examined are the crucial texts for the intellectual relations between Erasmus and Colet in 1499. They do not speak the language of discipleship. Erasmus's letters of the period, intended for the eyes of English addressees, are naturally rich in the adulation expected from a clever indigent foreigner who was searching for a patron. When serious discussion arose on issues of substance, however, Erasmus's exchanges with Colet show basic disagreements between the intelligent, rich, and well-connected Englishman and the even more intelligent but poor and unknown visitor.

Familiarity with the texts of 1499 which we have been studying enables one to take with the necessary grain or two of salt the elegant flattery that Erasmus dispensed so freely during his short stay in England. He had no way of knowing in advance which new acquaintances might prove helpful and set himself to be highly agreeable to everyone. So when he first met Colet he was ecstatic, according to the letter he wrote to that very Colet. He would rather have even the silent approval of Colet alone, he claimed, than "a whole Roman Forum" filled with less judicious admirers. England, he continued, "abounds in men deeply versed in literature," but of them all Colet is "easily the first." Much of this extravagance was built into humanist Latin, of course, where elative forms came all too readily to the pen and "doctissimus" was almost the least one could say of a man. Nevertheless Colet's biographers rarely fail to quote from another of Erasmus's paeans of praise of Englishmen, written to an Englishman and likely to be passed around: "When I hear Colet it seems to me that I hear Plato"[25]—a Plato, he probably added privately, who does not know Greek, though unlike me he had ample opportunity to learn it. They have not noticed that comparison to Plato had become a humanistic commonplace, since Cicero called Plato the most eloquent of writers.[26] Biographers who have taken Erasmus's effusion literally have also not noticed that Erasmus found in England not only a Plato but a poet comparable to Homer or Vergil—none other than John Skelton. In Erasmus's recklessly encomiastic verses, just as Maeonia was famous as the birthplace of Homer and Mantua as the birthplace of Vergil, so England owed its renown to being the birthplace of Skelton.[27] These verses were written in the same month as the letter comparing Colet to Plato, and they were equally sincere. The author of "The Tunning of Elinor Rumming," a good scholar and a gifted drinker, was less literal-minded than Colet's Victorian biographers. When he heard of Erasmus's accolade he must have laughed good-humoredly and guessed that the verses had something to do with his being the tutor of Prince Henry.

The necessity of applying flattery with a trowel exacted a price from Erasmus. One scholar feels that his largely fruitless foray into England in quest of a patron and the poverty he endured in 1500 and 1501, which deepened his sense of protracted dependence, "left their mark on him. He now knows that to get what he wants he has to flatter adroitly. He has learned to distrust everyone and to put his interests above his feelings."[28] This judgment may be a little strong, but it reminds us not to build too confidently on the glowing account of England that Erasmus gave to Englishmen.

When once back across the Channel he spoke to intimates in a different vein. He scorned men who thought they could teach theology without knowing Greek, a notion he called "madness." He described contemptuously "some theologian" he had met who "spun out a long story [*fabulam*]" based on a misunderstanding of Psalm 50:4 (51:3) due to ignorance of Greek; warming to his work he went on to develop an imaginary and absurd misunderstanding of Psalm 91 (92):14 that he would not put past such one-language scholars. Though already at the Council of Vienne (in 1311) it had been declared that the universities should teach the three languages, Erasmus found that two centuries later "we are still perfectly satisfied with the rudiments of Latin" and rely "on Scotus alone as on a horn of plenty."[29] One of his *Adagia* published in the first collection of June 1500 speaks of those who, ignorant of the original languages, still presume to discourse on the mysteries of theology, as seeking to enter the temple with "unwashed feet."[30]

Erasmus thus saw clearly that for a person who wanted to do good work in theology, Scripture study in translation was a dead end. He and Colet may well have discussed the subject while Erasmus was still in Oxford, but if so he did not convince Colet. While Erasmus was waiting for a moment when it would be possible to leave England—he was detained by bad weather and by a temporary royal prohibition against leaving the country—he received a letter from Colet proposing that he remain at Oxford to teach poetry and rhetoric or, better yet, do for Moses and Isaiah what Colet was doing for Paul. Erasmus's reply was as blunt, for all its elegance of expression, as his disagreement with Colet had been in the "Disputatiuncula." Colet was quite wrong to reproach him, he replied, for he had never led Colet to suppose that he intended to devote himself to teaching literature or rhetoric. He had done such teaching while it was necessary, but happily that time was past (Erasmus had in his purse the twenty gold pieces that were to finance study in Paris, eighteen of which would be confiscated by a customs officer at Dover because it was forbidden to export specie from England—a calamitous reversal of his fortunes that still lay in the future). As for Colet's other proposal, that Erasmus should expound the Bible as he himself was doing, Erasmus replied that to expound the Bible was at present as much above his powers as the other proposal was beneath them. He could not teach what he had not yet learned, he told Colet. To do an adequate job of interpreting the sacred authors he would need to study them in their original language. Far from associating himself with Colet's kind of Scripture scholarship, Erasmus made it plain to his correspondent that he did not propose, as he expressed it a few months later, to approach the mysteries of theology "with unwashed feet."[31] His answer to Colet was a decisive No.[32]

Instead of following Colet's example Erasmus threw himself into the study of Greek immediately on his return to the Continent. If his English sojourn gave him a lasting stimulus it may well have been, as recent scholars have suggested, that he was exhilarated by the tone of lay society and scholarship into which he was thrown for the first time.[33] Also, the company and example of good Greek scholars like Grocyn and Linacre would stimulate him to acquire a solid knowledge of the language himself. Erasmus knew he cut an impressive figure with his Latin learning, but he assuredly felt a sense of inferiority alongside men who knew Greek well, an inferiority he determined to remove.[34]

It is Erasmus's immersion in Greek studies on his return to the Continent, not any awakening of religious interests,[35] that is the chief discernible result of his stay in England. The texts we have studied in this chapter demonstrate the breadth and seriousness of his religious interests before coming for the first time to England.[36] He had also been collecting proverbs for some time and published in Paris in June 1500 *Adagiorum collectanea*, containing 818 adages, some of them Greek. By the summer of the following year he was deep into an ambitious verse translation of two plays by Euripides; only the Italian humanist Francesco Filelfo had even attempted such a translation before Erasmus, who by 1501 felt he had overtaken him.[37]

There is no reason to suppose that Erasmus was already planning an edition of the Greek New Testament.[38] However, his sacred studies in the years immediately following the English visit were influenced by his ardent study of Greek. It is revealing that the Greek theological writer whom Erasmus discovered at this time and who remained a major influence throughout Erasmus's life was Origen—the last writer whom, on Seebohm's premises, Erasmus should have been studying.

The influence of Origen, greatest of the allegorical interpreters of Scripture, runs deep throughout the *Handbook of a Christian Knight* (*Enchiridion militis christiani*), dated 1503.[39] Its pervasiveness in the *Enchiridion* shows how far Erasmus was from having been converted by John Colet to a literal exegesis of Scripture several years before—if a reader of the "Disputatiuncula" needed to be shown. The influence of Origen is explicit and unignorable, so that even the resourceful Seebohm was left floundering. He admitted, though only in a footnote and in a question-begging form, "It is evident that Erasmus had not appreciated as fully as he did afterwards the *historical* method which Colet had applied to St. Paul's Epistles."[40] Seebohm is thus in an unacknowledged dilemma. If Erasmus did understand Colet's supposedly historical method of interpretation, how could he have forsaken it for Origen and allegory? And if, as Seebohm claims to think, Erasmus did not understand it, how could Colet's other hearers be expected to have understood it? Seebohm's problem disappears, however, when one sees on the one hand that there is no evidence that Colet exercised any special intellectual influence on Erasmus in 1499 and on the other hand that, as the following chapters will show, Colet's method of interpreting Scripture was altogether different from what Seebohm conceived it to be.

When Erasmus left England he did not suppose he would return any time soon, if at all;[41] moreover he was deeply embittered by the confiscation of almost all his money on his departure and the poverty into which this loss plunged him.[42] In late 1504, however, he thought he saw the prospect of a valuable benefice in England and prepared to return there after all. Though he had not kept in touch with Colet, he had recently been informed by English friends with whom he was still in regular correspondence that Colet, a newly minted doctor of divinity, had just added to his other advantages of wealth and station the nomination to the most desirable deanery in England. It was an opportune moment to reopen communication with the dean-designate of St. Paul's, whose ecclesiastical career was very much in the ascendant, but two difficulties stood in his way that might have given a less confident writer pause. Correspondence with Colet must have ceased at least three years earlier, for the letter Erasmus now set himself to write contains an account of his own activities for the past three years.[43] The fact that they had not been in touch for so long would take some graceful explaining. However, letters renewing acquaintances under similar circumstances, if awkward, are of the kind many people have to write now and then and would pose no difficulty to Erasmus's ready pen. The other problem he faced was potentially more difficult.

During the period when he did not expect to return to England and correspondence with Colet had ceased, Erasmus had published the "Disputatiuncula." The mere fact of publication shows that he considered he had carried off the honors of the disputation, as indeed he had; Colet came off looking not only weaker in argument and poorer in learning but without the skill and self-control of a seasoned disputant. If Colet did not happen on the book himself he certainly had his attention directed to it by common acquaintances, especially since the volume including the "Disputatiuncula" contained also the *Enchiridion*, which rapidly became one of Erasmus's best-known works. Erasmus's letter confirms that Colet did not write to him after the publication of the "Disputatiuncula"—a silence Erasmus could readily interpret. With his letter Erasmus now sent a copy of his *Lucubratiunculae*, a volume of miscellaneous writings containing the "Disputatiuncula" and the *Enchiridion*, as a "little gift," without alluding to the possibility that Colet was already familiar with it.

In the accompanying letter the future author of *De conscribendis epistolis* rises to the occasion. He begins in a sadly submissive tone, venturing to reproach the newly nominated dean because "for quite some years now [*compluribus iam annis*] I have had no letters from Colet."[44] He prefers to ascribe the fact to Colet's "being busy, or his uncertainty as to where to reach me, or for that matter any other reason than that he has forgotten his humble friend [*amiculi*]." As if to offset this rather obsequious beginning Erasmus now passes to a tone of unforced authority. Well aware that Colet was a student of St. Paul, Erasmus coolly remarks that he himself had begun to work up a commentary on Romans three years earlier but gave over the project because "at a number of points I felt the need of Greek." He continues, "Of this one thing I am now convinced, that literary studies are impossible without Greek. It is one thing to conjecture but another to decide, one thing to believe your own eyes and another to have to believe someone else's." The circumstances show that Erasmus had no wish to be rude. He simply takes for granted, interestingly enough, that the Greekless Colet's services to the Bible do not come under the heading of scholarly studies at all.

Erasmus then glides very rapidly over the "Disputatiuncula" itself, mentioning only that in preparing it for publication he had been unable to locate either Colet's reply to his own original formulation of the issue or his reply to Colet's reply (both of which did, however, turn up later). Instead of speaking of the "Disputatiuncula" itself he turns to the other works published in the same volume with it and another more recent publication also enclosed. He does not explain why he did not send a copy of the book on its first publication, though his usual habit was to make liberal use of presentation copies for literary-political purposes;[45] indeed he dedicated no fewer than forty works to English friends and patrons, present or prospective.[46]

The date of publication of the *Lucubratiunculae* is unfortunately not quite certain. Its publisher, Thierry Martens, gives February 1503, but Allen points out that in dating his volumes Martens sometimes reckoned the year from January 1 and sometimes from March 25 (the date of the conception of Jesus, nine months before Christmas).[47] Virtually all writers known to me take the date of the "Disputatiunculae" to mean February 1503, not 1504; but they do not discuss the question, and whether they are unaware of Allen's caution or have reasons for disregarding it, I do not know.[48] One of the two writers who give 1504 as the date bases his dating on a mistake;[49] hence February 1503 may be taken provisionally as the month when Erasmus's account of the disputation with Colet first appeared. The point is of some importance for the relation between the two men because of the long lapse of time—some twenty-two months if we follow the bibliographers' consensus—between the book's publication and Erasmus's writing to Colet about it. During this lengthy period Erasmus published a controversy that reflected credit on himself but left his erstwhile English acquaintance looking decidedly second-best. During the same period Erasmus's energies were bent on mastering Greek, a language in which Colet showed no interest. Moreover Erasmus's discovery of the Greek exegete Origen was due to the influence of another theologian, the Franciscan Jean Vitrier,[50] whose life Erasmus described to Jodocus Jonas in the same letter in which he described Colet's. When a return to England suddenly became imminent and Erasmus broke the years-long silence between himself and Colet he had moved into a realm of studies unknown to his correspondent and could report with conscious understatement that in concentrating on Greek he had "not wasted" his time.

Thenceforward the relations between the two men inevitably changed. On their first meeting Colet had been decidedly the more important of the two. The balance, however, soon began to shift. When they met again during Erasmus's visit of 1505–1506 Colet, as Erasmus knew, was already poised for a significant ecclesiastical career in England. But in the international world of scholarship Erasmus was no longer an unknown and had several published works to his credit, among which the *Adagia* in its first form and the *Enchiridion* had attracted considerable attention. During this second English sojourn it was to Thomas More that Erasmus gravitated when he could call his time his own. He and More enjoyed making translations from Lucian, which they then published jointly—a scholarly recreation from which the Greekless, humorless, and puritanical Colet was trebly excluded. Nor would Colet have been the perfect audience for Erasmus's *Praise of Folly* (*Moriae encomium*), written not long afterward and containing in its title a mild pun on the name of More. Erasmus doubtless paid his respects to Colet, but in his exultation at his new mastery of Greek he would tend to look elsewhere for full intellectual companionship.

It was, I think, mainly during Erasmus's third and last stay in England—a sojourn that lasted, with interruptions, from 1511–1516—that Colet and Erasmus laid a solid basis for their friendship. This was the period of what appears to have been a serious falling-out between Colet and the bishop of London, which is discussed in chapter 10 below. Regarding this affair Erasmus's biographical account of Colet and other evidence show that he sided warmly with Colet on issues that were important to both. Further, during Erasmus's third visit Colet was very busy with the planning stages and then the actual inauguration of his new school. In their different but equally intense concern with education[51] they seem to have come close to each other in this venture: each making a contribution the other could not have made, they met at last as equals.

From this period on, what evidence there is suggests that Colet occupied a special if rather narrow niche in Erasmus's life. It is true that once Erasmus returned to the Continent communications were only intermittent. Colet complained that Erasmus neglected him, and he could not disguise his chagrin about the way that the now-celebrated Erasmus, writing to Fisher, had asked his correspondent, in a kind of p.s., to say hello for him to Colet.[52] Nevertheless the long biographical letter, meditated though not written immediately after the news arrived of Colet's death, shows that Erasmus regarded himself as a faithful friend. In October 1519 he published no fewer than nine of his letters to Colet, along with one, dating back to 1499, from Colet to himself[53]—a publication planned before he learned that Colet had died in mid-September.

For all this show of interest during Colet's late years, the main literary connection between the two men continued to be the "Disputatiuncula"; and the twelve reprints of it during Erasmus's lifetime show that the estimate of Colet as exegete which he had formed in 1499 remained unchanged. The implication of this fact for the nature of Colet's exegesis has never, to my knowledge, been drawn; but it is worth pondering. It is, I think, that Colet accepted the image of himself which Erasmus had formed: he did not think of himself as engaged in biblical exegesis as it was practiced in professional circles.

We noticed above that when Erasmus saw fit to renew his acquaintance with Colet he mentioned that he had put aside his own work on the Epistle to the Romans because he felt he needed to know Greek if he was to do the work properly. In that letter he certainly had no wish to offend his correspondent; he assumed, and assumed that Colet assumed, that the sort of thing which Colet was doing fell outside the scope of exegesis altogether. Similarly, if Colet had taken serious offence at the "Disputatiuncula" Erasmus would probably have withdrawn it as a sacrifice to their renewed friendship. Naturally Colet could not have been pleased with the record of their controversy—he was not a good loser. But the point is that he had no reputation as an exegete at stake, even in his own mind. He was carrying on what both he and Erasmus thought of as the work of a "theologian." Erasmus always recognized that in one sense of the word "theologian," the theologian's job was to "move" his hearers. In that sense Colet was, for Erasmus, definitely a theologian, for in the *Paraclesis*, the treatise on preaching which Erasmus published near the close of his life in 1535, he declared that a "theologian" could do good work "even in English."[54] What Colet was trying to do, as we shall see in detail in chapters 6 and 7, was something altogether different from what scholarly exegetes were doing, and both he and Erasmus knew it.

The "Disputatiuncula," then, while it demonstrates Erasmus's unquestionable superiority as an interpreter of Scripture, did no fatal harm to Colet's sense of his own work, for he and Erasmus both understood that the two of them were working along different lines. In fact, the "Disputatiuncula," far from harming Colet's reputation, was to give it a dramatic turn that neither he nor Erasmus could have foreseen.

As already mentioned, Erasmus stated to Colet that in preparing the record of their disputation for publication in February 1503 (or possibly 1504) he had not been able to lay hands on Colet's reply to his long criticism of Colet's position. Much later the reply did turn up, however, and Erasmus appended it to the 1518 edition without comment, on the assumption that it spoke for itself; it was automatically reprinted in all later editions. This was the reply, written in 1499, in which Colet, without acknowledging the fact, tried to change his line of argument altogether, and claimed to think that the principal point at issue was Erasmus's remark that the literal text on Christ's Agony in the Garden might have more than one explanation. Colet denied this possibility, asserting that the fruitfulness of Scripture did not mean that a passage had more meanings than one, at least "in any one kind" ("uno in aliquo genere").

Lupton failed to refresh his memory about Seebohm's correct analysis of this expression and assumed that by denying a plurality of meanings "in any one kind" Colet was denying the familiar fourfold sense of Scripture, one literal and three allegorical. He went on to discuss this topic at considerable length, thus muddying the waters badly and throwing into obscurity Seebohm's accurate interpretation of what Colet meant. Seebohm saw that what Colet was denying was that "the words of the same passage might, in their *literal* sense, mean several different things, and be used as *texts* in support of statements not within the direct intention of their human writer," in short, "that the *literal sense was manifold.*"[55] To be sure, Seebohm thought such a notion was self-evidently preposterous, as his incredulous italics show, but he was right about the issue on which Erasmus and Colet differed.

The *duplex sensus litteralis* had in fact a long and respectable lineage and had been formulated in response to a genuine problem. It was necessary to explain how certain Old Testament texts that have a satisfactory literal meaning in their original context are given a quite different meaning by New Testament writers (e.g., Gen. 1:2; Gen. 47:31; Ps. 2:7; Isa. 53:5; Hab. 3:2). It appeared also that even a New Testament passage could have a twofold literal meaning; for example, in John 11:51 the prophecy of the high priest Caiphas that it was expedient that Jesus should "die for the nation" had one meaning for him, another in the context of Jesus' universally salvific mission.[56] Moreover, Jesus' citation of various Old Testament prophecies as referring to himself proved that these passages too had an additional sense, unknown to their original authors. The divine authorship of the Bible guaranteed that both literal meanings were true; the fertility of meanings, far from being regarded as an embarrassment, was considered to belong to the unique dignity of Scripture and was recognized by the Fourth Lateran Council.[57]

Passages where an additional literal meaning is in this sense actually guaranteed are few. But as words were merely signs of the realities that it was God's intention to convey, it remained possible that other passages, even many others, also carried latent additional literal meanings. Developing a doctrine that goes back to Augustine,[58] Aquinas, among others, proposed to distinguish basic meaning ("sensus principalis") from adapted meanings ("sensus per adaptionem"). The basic meaning known to God can be only one, but the linguistic integuments by which the idea is accommodated to a passage may be multiple. Such accommodated meanings, provided that they respect the text, are known to the Holy Spirit and therefore necessarily true.[59] This line of thought was well known to scholars of Colet's generation.

Nevertheless the recognition of the *duplex sensus litteralis*, though it seemed required by the unique nature of the Bible, entailed difficulties that brought many scholastic writers either almost to ignore it or to confine it within narrower limits than Aquinas and his followers did.[60] It was acknowledged that certain Old Testament injunctions could no longer be taken literally; moreover even certain New Testament injunctions, if taken literally, would contradict other commandments (e.g., Matt. 5:29, 19:12). Hence by the early fifteenth century a distinction was growing up between an apparent literal sense (*superficies*), or "mere grammatical sense," and the "true literal sense" concealed beneath it.[61] The strong nominalist influence in the universities at that period led to a systematic distrust of words as such; in such a climate it was necessary to distinguish Scripture in principle from other texts that offered a "mere grammatical sense" that could be deceptive; for Scripture the *duplex sensus litteralis* tended to be invoked when the "mere grammatical sense" had for one reason or another to be rejected.[62]

With his conciliatory suggestion that Colet's argument too might have some truth to it, Erasmus was thus simply referring to a widely accepted tradition of the *duplex sensus litteralis*, which increasingly found favor with ecclesiastical intellectuals of the fifteenth century. If one is to judge by the "mere grammatical sense" only, Colet's reply to Erasmus's challenge to show him wrong denies the same doctrine. It must be remembered, however, that at this point in the disputation Colet was in an unenviable position. His original contention had been shattered by Erasmus, and in this predicament he tried to avoid acknowledging defeat by raising another issue altogether. As on other occasions, he did not argue for his position but simply asserted it. A reader is left unsure whether his was a principled rejection of the familiar doctrine or simply a grasping at a side issue when he found himself faced with the need to answer the unanswerable.

What little evidence there is for the "true literal meaning" of Colet's riposte to Erasmus tends to favor the latter possibility. Colet's writings show that he himself admitted the *duplex sensus litteralis*—silently—on at least two occasions. Matthew 8:17 was recognized as a passage in which the twofold sense was required,[63] and we find that in P, in the late Trinity manuscript, Colet gives a meaning to Isaiah 53:5 which is quite different from the meaning it had been authoritatively given in Matthew 8:17 (P, 292) and thus acknowledges in this text at least two literal meanings. Again, setting himself to wrestle with the first three chapters of Genesis, Colet concedes, "All this is so obscure as to afford a basis for innumerable interpretations and expressions: and on it virtually anyone may say what he wishes, provided that what he says is internally consistent" (G, 167).[64] In these passages at least, Colet associates himself with the well-known tradition of multiple literal senses, though how deliberately it is not easy to say. In any case he employed, or came to employ, in practice, the theory he reproached Erasmus for holding.

As we have seen, Colet's attempt to escape from Erasmus's analysis of his position by raising the unrelated issue of the manifold literal sense promptly drew a long and severe reply. But Erasmus's letter did not see print until 1906, and thus Colet's attempted diversion stood uncontested in edition after edition of the "Disputatiuncula" from 1518 on. Thanks to this fact his letter had a circulation and readership incomparably greater than did anything else he ever wrote. Because of this letter his reputation took an unexpected turn, even a series of unexpected turns, without which his fame would probably have remained confined to the circle of antiquarians and Old Paulines.

In England there is no sign that contemporaries of Colet thought of him as excelling in biblical exegesis. The "Disputatiuncula" and its sequel in Colet's letter, followed in turn by Erasmus's reply, tell plainly enough why. Moreover, even apart from other considerations, Colet's lack of acquaintance with the original languages of the Scriptures would increasingly have operated to disqualify him from these studies. A valuable but neglected sign of contemporary opinion dates back to only fifteen years after Colet's death. From 1524 on, George Stafford, of Pembroke College, Cambridge, then a B.D., had lectured on books of the Bible. Stafford was well versed in the three languages, and his exegesis of Scripture based on the original texts not only proceeded without interference until his death from the plague in 1529 but attracted large audiences. When in 1534 the Cambridge University authorities determined to incorporate such exegetical lectures into the curriculum it was the model of Stafford that they expressly cited as having demonstrated the right way to proceed.[65] In the following year Stafford's method was endorsed by royal injunctions emanating from Cromwell.[66] It would seem that George Stafford was actually doing in pre-Reformation Cambridge what much later times supposed Colet was doing in Oxford, though unfortunately none of Stafford's writings are known to survive. The choice of Stafford rather than, say, Colet as an example of the right way to interpret scriptural texts, a choice made by experts in theology in 1534, deserves much more attention than it has received.

Erasmus's two references to Colet's lecturing at Oxford, if read without preconceptions, confirm that neither at the beginning of their acquaintance in 1499 nor in the posthumous tribute he paid Colet in 1521 did Erasmus represent Colet as having opened new paths to the exegesis of the Bible. Erasmus's 1499 letter to Colet, in whom he perhaps hoped to find a patron, was full of the praises that he scattered in all directions. But even there his verdict about Colet's lectures was significantly judicious. He himself had lectured on Scripture at some point before he left the Collège de Montaigu in the spring of 1496,[67] so that as he listened to Colet he would have made private comparisons; more important, he would certainly have caught any novelty in the lectures. Had they been anything like so significant as Seebohm wished to think, Erasmus could not have hesitated, as he does hesitate, about whether to attribute the good turnout to the lecturer's merits or the Oxford doctors' zeal for learning (A, ll. 288–290). It appears that John Fisher too heard some of Colet's lectures in the latter part of 1499, but on him also they apparently made no special impression.[68]

To Colet himself, of course, Erasmus sang a different song:

> There is not a doctor in this famous university who has not listened atten-
> tively to the lectures on the Pauline Epistles which you have been giving
> for three years now. In this connection it is hard to say which is more de-
> serving of praise, the lack of vanity that makes it possible for those who
> themselves teach all the rest to appear as pupils of a young man not fortified
> by the authority of the doctorate, or your own remarkable learning, elo-
> quence, and probity of character, which make them consider you worthy
> of this honor.[69]

The same alternative explanations are offered in the biographical tribute; like the early letter, with which it has in common an encomiastic tone, it does not go so far as to imply that the lectures were sufficient in them-selves to explain the good attendance. An eighteenth-century writer who expanded a little on the latter passage catches accurately Erasmus's bal-anced judgment:

> [B]ut whether this particular Encomium of [Colet] was in Reality owing to
> the Fame he had acquired, or to the Ingenuity of his Hearers, who, in more
> honorable Degrees and Years, were not ashamed to receive Instruction
> from one younger than themselves, and in other Respects their Inferior,
> I shall not take upon me to determine.[70]

It is evident from the words, "and in other Respects their Inferior" that in the writer's time, the mid–eighteenth century, there was no tradition that the lectures of Colet had offered anything really new. Just over a cen-tury later, however, Seebohm did for the first time make that assertion.

Seebohm was responding not to the English tradition regarding Colet but to the Colet who was much better known, at least as a name, on the Continent. In its own way Colet's reputation seems to have bifurcated much as Thomas More's did. Over against the More of the later years, author of vast antiheretical tracts written in English and known only in England, was the humanistic More of the *Utopia* and the other Latin writ-ings who was celebrated on the Continent.[71] In similar fashion, two dis-tinct Colets came to exist. On one hand in England itself Colet was known as dean of St. Paul's and as a preacher of great eloquence and purity of life; later generations of Englishmen remembered him as the founder of St. Paul's School. On the other hand the Continental Colet, unknown there in the capacities in which he was familiar to Londoners, owed his very existence to Erasmus. His substantial appearance in Erasmus's published correspondence would almost alone have guaranteed him a measure of fame in an age when scholars rated their importance by whether Erasmus found space for them in his published collections of letters.[72] Moreover the "Disputatiuncula," because it was regularly republished along with the widely read *Enchiridion*, ensured that Colet, even if on the losing side in the controversy, would remain associated in the mind of the scholarly public with the fame of the master. It will be remembered that from 1518 onward the record of the controversy was followed by a letter from Colet to Erasmus in which Colet rejected the widely acknowledged *duplex sensus litteralis*.

We are fortunate in possessing the reactions to Colet of two Continental readers who knew of him only through the connection with Erasmus. In a letter dated only "April" but probably from 1520, a canon of Mainz who was acquainted with Erasmus, Markwert von Hatstein, addressed an enthusiastic letter to Colet, of whose death some months earlier he was unaware.[73] He expresses his full sympathy with Colet's urgent call for peace, of which he had heard from Erasmus.[74] He also expresses admiration for Colet's determined stand against unspecified enemies, another episode of which he knew from Erasmus. He adds, significantly for our purposes, that while Erasmus no doubt gained from knowing Colet, Colet should be thankful to Erasmus "for making publicly known those virtues which before were unknown to us."

A further reference to Colet by an important Continental writer much influenced by Erasmus seems to have escaped the notice of writers on Colet. Even while still a Dominican the reformer Martin Bucer was an avid reader of Erasmus. He may have remembered Colet's name from texts that Erasmus wrote for St. Paul's School; from a saying of Colet's, "We are what our daily conversation is," quoted in the *Adagia*;[75] from the *Colloquia*;[76] from the dedication to Colet of Richard Pace's *De fructu qui ex doctrina percipitur* (1518), which was in Bucer's library;[77] or of course from the "Disputatiuncula." The latter work was, as mentioned, published with the *Enchiridion*, of which Bucer already possessed two copies as of 30 April 1518;[78] he must have acquired also one of the later editions in which Colet's letter appeared, for it is to this letter that Bucer refers specifically.

In the preface to his *Enarrationum in Evangelia Matthaei, Marci & Lucae, Libri Duo* (Strasbourg, 1527), Bucer takes occasion to decry the dangers and absurdities of uncontrolled allegorizing. In support of this view he adds, "On this subject the divine and learned Englishman John Colet, whom Erasmus of Rotterdam repeatedly and rightly praised, was quite correct, as his letter to Erasmus testifies."[79] The same tribute to Colet was repeated in the preface to the enlarged edition of 1530.[80] Because Colet's letter was not published until 1518 it was read almost from the beginning in a Reformation context; by 1527 Colet's assertion about the text he and Erasmus were discussing had taken on a significance appropriate to the changing direction of biblical studies. With the emphasis now increasingly on textual study and thus strongly against allegorizing, Colet's statement now meant to Bucer, as to Protestant writers generally, that, as a modern scholar paraphrases the idea, "the Scriptures admit of only one interpretation, the true interpretation, and any other method beyond that true interpretation misinterprets the singular and true sense of Scripture, and leads to abuses, as can be seen by the distorted allegoric 'fancies' of [Bucer's] time."[81]

Bucer must have cited Colet for the prestige the Englishman derived from association with Erasmus; there was of course nothing by Colet for him to read and thus no possibility of influence.[82] Had Colet published, Bucer might have seen in him something of a kindred spirit, for their views on education were broadly similar,[83] and Bucer too was interested in exegesis that was "theological and homiletical rather than grammatical" as the medieval doctors understood the latter term,[84] sharing with Colet a tendency to "de-historicise the Gospel" for homiletic ends.[85] Such broad similarities as may link the two men are overwhelmed, however, by the fundamental contrasts between Bucer's huge volumes and his solid Greek learning, and Colet's much briefer and less systematic writings, dependent entirely on the Vulgate and Latin learning. Already in the late 1520s, when Bucer published his vast commentaries on the Gospels, Colet's work belonged to a kind of scholarship no longer possible in advanced circles.

The scattered references to John Colet in Erasmus's works that caught the eye of Markwert von Hatstein and Martin Bucer also caught the eye of Frederic Seebohm. Seebohm was naturally alert to the presence of Englishmen in Erasmus's pages, not only the well-known figure of Thomas More but the less familiar figure of John Colet. Colet's letter appended to the "Disputatiuncula" obviously impressed Seebohm, and his fertile mind soon conceived the idea of a group of "Oxford Reformers of 1498" centered on the two Englishmen and Erasmus. As we noticed above, Seebohm himself was aware that the chronology on which his theory was built was shaky, though he mentioned the fact only in a footnote. He assumed that Erasmus and Colet were together in Oxford for more than a year, from 1498 till late in 1499, long enough for Colet to exercise gradually a fundamental influence on Erasmus and for the supposed band of reformers to develop. In fact Erasmus was there only a month, and even before the month was over he was ready to leave, his departure prevented only by bad weather and certain temporary restrictions on leaving the country. But by the time the true chronology was worked out at the end of the nineteenth century, Seebohm's account of the association of Erasmus with

Colet, according to which Erasmus was in important ways Colet's disciple, had assumed the status of fact.

Seebohm's portrait, written with charm and verve and quite free of disabling doubts, became a popular classic. The English Colet whom his early sixteenth-century contemporaries knew and respected, if for quite different reasons from Seebohm's, was meanwhile thrust into the shadows. His name was regularly and respectfully invoked, but his writings, confined to small editions and never reprinted, were known mostly at second hand; and it must be added that when those writings did not fit the picture of the Oxford Reformer which Seebohm had distilled from his reading of Erasmus, they were ignored. As the literary historian Sir Adolphus Ward observed already in 1916, Seebohm formed his conception of Colet "on the basis of the letters of . . . Erasmus."[86] The English Colet remained in the shadows; in his place the brightly lit and unambiguous figure created by Seebohm held the field. Through Seebohm, the Continental Colet was re-imported into England as an Oxford Reformer.

6

The Enterprise of Exegesis: Colet's Principles

To describe one of his own interpretations of Scripture, Colet used the term "enarrare" (R, 175), a term that Lupton seized on gratefully to describe Colet's biblical interpretations overall. In theory the term's meaning is clear: it is defined by Sixtus Senensis (1520–1569), as Lupton observes,[1] as "an exposition of divine Scripture delivered publicly to the people." According to Sixtus *enarratio* has two subdivisions, *homilia* (or *tractatus*), "which in a relatively familiar style leads hearers to understand the meaning of Scripture and act upon it," and *concio* (or *declamatio*), which pursues the same aim in a loftier style. *Concio* differs from *homilia* also in digressing more frequently from the course of the exposition to discuss moral and other questions, and in denouncing wrongdoing.[2] The beguiling neatness of these distinctions begins to blur, however, as soon as one turns to actual practice. When manuscripts of Augustine were copied, the term *enarratio* was often replaced by *expositio, sermo, tractatus, commentum*, and *explanatio*[3]—a record showing that *enarratio* covers a great deal of ground indeed. Over the centuries the term remained very flexible, and in Colet's day it was practically a synonym for *expositio, tractatus*, or *commentum*, among other terms.[4] In this chapter, therefore, instead of trying to go by the arbitrary label *enarratio*, it will prove more useful to investigate what Colet himself said an interpreter of Scripture should be and do.

Was Colet a Historically Minded Critic?

But before we can turn to the real Colet we must look at the evidence for the widespread notion that Colet interpreted Scripture, in particular

St. Paul's letters, in the light of their historical circumstances and with a special desire to establish their literal meaning. We have seen that this notion does not appear until Seebohm's *Oxford Reformers* of 1867. Why it did not appear in the preceding four hundred years will become clear if we now consider what I believe is a comprehensive list of the passages where Colet shows any interest at all in the historical circumstances under which the Epistles were written.

1. Colet remarks that "there was much difference of opinion on how to behave toward the pagans, in whose midst [the Christians] were and under whose rule they lived" (R, 135).

2. Near the beginning of his treatment of Romans 13 (R, 200–201) Colet gives a historical summary of Paul's career in fifteen lines. He suggests that fear of persecution made Paul deliberately say that Christians should submit to secular authorities, because he was afraid his letter might fall into pagan hands. In the same place Colet also conjectures the order in which four major Epistles were written.

3. In connection with Paul's apologizing to the Romans for writing to them before he even visited Rome, Colet says that according to Clement of Rome's "history" sent to James the Bishop of Jerusalem, the first of the apostles to come to Rome was Barnabas. Colet traces the line of teachers at Rome down to Peter, who he says lived there twenty-five years, and surmises that the Roman Christians were annoyed at the authoritative tone Paul took toward them when they already had Peter as their teacher (R, 223).

Most of the "history" here is false, taken by Colet from the document now known as the pseudo-Clementine *Recognitions* (I.7), then often attributed to Pope Clement I but later recognized as "the first genuine Christian novel."[5] In Colet's day opinions on the authorship of the work were divided, doubts having arisen already in the Latin west in the time of St. Jerome.[6] But it would appear from the context of a letter written in 1527 that Erasmus had at least not ruled out the possibility that the *Recognitions* were genuine.[7]

4. Colet identifies the Prisca of Romans 16:3 with the Priscilla of Acts 18:2 (R, 226).

5. On revision Colet corrects his earlier acceptance of St. John Chrysostom's statement that Paul fulfilled his wish to go to Spain and decides instead that the evidence is insufficient to settle the question (R, 224).[8]

6. Colet suggests that the residual loyalties of the Roman Jews made it impossible for Paul to express his true, low, opinion of the Law; otherwise they would have been alienated by his teaching (RO, 232).

The foregoing six passages constitute all the evidence for historical interest on Colet's part culled from two and a half volumes of Pauline commentary. To complete the record we may add all the evidence for historical interests of any kind from the two and a half volumes of his writings which deal with non-Pauline subjects.

1. Colet is struck by the differences between the form of baptism described by pseudo-Dionysius the Areopagite and the form current in his own time (DEH, 210–211). (He does not ask, however, when or why the form of baptism changed.)

2. At one point he appears to allude to the legalization of Christianity under Constantine (DEH, 212).[9]

3. He refers to the differences between the meanings attached by Dionysius to the terms *pontifex*, *sacerdos*, and *diaconus* and their current meanings (DEH, 241).

4. He also notices the fact that in the early church minor orders, those below subdeacon, were conferred by solemn consecration, whereas in subsequent times that practice lapsed (DEH, 254).

Against this meager compendium of Colet's historical interests we may usefully set a quite incomplete list of passages in which historical perspective seems needed but is not provided.

1. In treating Paul's discussion of whether Christians might eat meat that had been sacrificed to idols (e.g., C, 230–231 [204,206]), Colet appears to regard the question as open and makes no mention of the Council of Jerusalem in Acts 15, which settled it officially.

2. Taking for granted the historical primacy of Peter and Rome, he fails to observe that at the same Council of Jerusalem it was James, not Peter, who made the final decision about meats that had been sacrificed to idols; similarly he pays no attention to the fact that Paul rebuked Peter to his face in Galatians 2:11–21.

3. Colet takes the rivalry of Apollo and Paul out of its clear historical context in 1 Corinthians 3:5ff. and instead, in treating 1 Corinthians 13, speaks of them together as God's "instruments" and as coworkers in building up the church in Corinth (C, 259 [263]). He shows no interest in the agitated state of the church there, which so distressed Paul.

4. In discussing 1 Corinthians 16 (C, 268 [280]) Colet refers to a passage in Acts 11:28 mentioning a prophecy by Agabus but says nothing about the quite different prophecy attributed to Agabus in what appears to be the same context in Acts 21:10–11.

5. Colet says nothing, in discussing 1 Corinthians 16:2–4, of the political reason why Paul was anxious to collect money in Corinth to send to Jerusalem, even though it is evident from Galatians 2:1–10 that tensions in the Christian community at Jerusalem made Paul anxious to have Jerusalem ratify his mandate to preach to the Gentiles.

6. Colet asserts (RO, 243) that bishops have the right to alter decedents' wills; he ignores the fact that Galatians 3:15 says exactly the opposite.

7. Colet cites Colossians 1:15 as if its meaning were generally agreed on (S, 290, 298); but in fact, Eusebius of Caesaria's proposal to incorporate the phrase "the firstborn of all creation" from this verse into the creed of the all-important Council of Nicea in 325 was rejected because there was serious controversy about the passage's meaning.[10] Colet, by contrast, shared the indifference to the history of these patristic controversies which characterized the high and late medieval period.[11]

8. Romans 1:18–20 attributes a knowledge of God even to the wicked in a passage to which Colet repeatedly refers (RO, 203, 210, 213–214); but he pays no attention to Old and New Testament passages that seem to assert the opposite: Psalms 13 (Vulg.), 1 Corinthians 2, and especially Matthew 11:27.

9. Commenting on Paul's citation of the verse from Habakkuk 2:4 in the famous passage on justification by faith, Aquinas, for example, carefully notices that the translation from the Septuagint differs in important ways from the translation directly from the Hebrew ("Justus autem meus ex fide vivit" and "Justus ex fide sua vivit," respectively);[12] Colet, by contrast, seems unaware of or uninterested in the existence of an alternative reading (R, 137; RO, 208–209).

10. Colet asserts without qualification that Paul was unmarried (C, 223 [188]; S, 310, 312). He does not notice that 1 Corinthians 9:5, on which he relied, had been interpreted by such Fathers as Ignatius[13] and Clement of Alexandria[14] to mean that Paul was in fact married (Ignatius adds Peter too). The question was discussed by such contemporaries of Colet's as Erasmus and Lefèvre d'Etaples, not to mention the Sorbonne.[15]

11. In speaking of the levies on Christians in Paul's Rome (R, 198–199) Colet simply repeats Paul's two words "tributum" and "vectigal" (Rom. 13:7), adding nothing to them from other historical sources.

12. Colet repeatedly cites Romans 5:14 (S, 290; RO, 275), a passage famous because it explains the origin of sin in man. The major commentators in the Latin tradition, including Ambrosiaster, Hrabanus Maurus, Peter Lombard, and Thomas Aquinas among others, knew that many Greek manuscripts said that original sin came also "to those who had *not* sinned," even though their Latin manuscripts omitted "not."[16] Colet however takes no notice of the differing readings.

13. Similarly, Colet paraphrases Romans 1:4 (R, 136) using the Latin translation "*prae*destinatus," whereas already three centuries earlier Aquinas knew from Origen of the Greek manuscript tradition that would yield the translation "destinatus"[17]—another important textual difference in which Colet shows no interest.

14. In his compendium of Dionysius's *Celestial Hierarchy*, chapter 7, Colet simply omits a problem arising from the text of Isaiah 63 which Dionysius discusses and finds "surprising."[18]

15. Colet shows no interest in the argument of his friend William Grocyn, discussed below, that the works that go under the name of Dionysius the Areopagite were not written by him.

16. Colet tries (C, 267 [279]) to explain the text of 1 Corinthians 15:51 without paying any attention to the much-discussed fact that three different versions of the Latin translation were current.[19]

In short, Colet proves himself much less interested in interpreting Paul's text than, for example, the theologian Richard of St. Victor had been already back in the twelfth century, at the beginning of the Scholastic period. Richard's "Explanation of Some Difficult Passages in the Apostle [Paul]" comments on a text of Paul to which Colet gave prominence and which he took at face value, "All things are permitted to me" (1 Cor. 6:12); Richard's discussion was sensible and cautious, beginning "Some things, but not all . . ." Richard also tackles the difficult problem, ignored by Colet, of Paul's seeming self-contradiction in asserting in some places the sufficiency of faith alone and in other places the importance of works.[20] Had Seebohm or Lupton looked into such early scholastic writers as Richard and the other Victorines they might have changed radically their notion of what medieval theology was like; more important still, they would have been forced to ask in a more meaningful way what Colet was actually doing.

The three lists just given—the first two together constituting a list of passages where Colet shows some historical interests, and the third, being a partial list of passages where he fails to use existing knowledge or to take account of historical considerations—speak for themselves. It is well to add, however, that on closer look even the skimpy list of seemingly historically minded passages probably needs to be retrenched.

The two most interesting passages in this regard are R, 200–201, and RO, 232 (see items 2 and 6 in the first list). It seems not to have been observed that each of these concerns a scriptural text in which Paul is saying something unacceptable to Colet. The first text is at the beginning of chapter 13 of Romans, where Paul inculcates into the Christians of Rome the duty of obedience to pagan rulers and pagan law. To Colet it seemed obvious that Paul could not have meant seriously what he said, that he must have had something else in mind. Colet found it inconceivable that people who possessed Christian truth should actually be told to follow instead the orders of their pagan rulers in all matters not actually sinful. Now, Colet had marked antinomian leanings. In chapter 4 above we saw that 1 Corinthians 6:12 gets a heading to itself in the middle of the holograph manuscript's treatment of that chapter: "For me there are no forbidden things" ("Omnia mihi licent"). From this it followed, as he said elsewhere, that "the law is given only to the unjust and the sinful" (CM, 188). Further, his consternation at Paul's directing the Roman Christians to obey pagan rulers was deepened by his own conviction that ecclesiastical law was incomparably above any worldly law, even in a Christian state, not to speak of pagan Rome (RO, 263). In this case, then, where his own instinctive certainty conflicted with the apparent meaning of the text, he set himself, not to change his own views but to explain away Paul's text.

To extenuate a doctrine that commands Christians to subordinate their institutional forms to pagan edict, Colet looked for something in the circumstances in which Paul was writing that would explain why he spoke as he did. Since the Christians of Rome were unpopular and in danger of persecution Colet came up with the uncharacteristically devious theory that Paul may have had reason to suppose his Epistle would fall into pagan hands. He therefore slyly—still according to Colet—talked up for pagan consumption what good Roman citizens the Christians were. Anxious to undercut Paul's doctrine without expressly denying it, Colet seems unaware of the Pandora's box that such an interpretive principle would open up for scriptural exegesis.

In the passage at RO, 232, Colet follows the same approach. Again he was confronted by Paul's declaring for a point of view that he could not accept. In this case it was Paul's insistent reverence for the Old Law, an attitude that was anathema to Colet. Once again he sought to find in the surrounding circumstances a proof that Paul did not mean what he was saying. Here he decided that Paul did not dare express his true opinion of the Law to the Jews of Rome, for that opinion must have been very low (as Colet's was), and if Paul had been candid he would have risked alienating his hearers.

Naturally Colet never contradicted Paul—but he did ignore him. When Paul opined that "nature is the best teacher" Colet dutifully repeated the words without enthusiasm (C, 240 [222]) but paid no real attention to them. He took the same approach to Paul's interest in natural religion based on the conclusions reached by human reason. Obediently he repeated what Paul said on the subject (R, 137), but he dropped the idea immediately and later strongly controverted the possibility of knowing God by reason (RO, 258–259). Colet even brings himself to repeat that reason is the link between "the body" and "God" (R, 176)—he is under the necessity of explaining the famous phrase *obsequium rationabile*, "a rational service"—but it is not long before he abandons the doctrine, uncongenial to him, that human reason links man to God, assigning its role instead to "vital spirits" (R, 185–186). In his system, reason is regularly and harshly decried (R, 192; RO, 224–225). As a means to understanding, Colet declares that simple faith is far superior to reason (RO, 202). Colet's anti-intellectual bias put him in yet another quandary when he found Paul acknowledging, "I am indebted to Greeks and barbarians" (Rom. 1:14). Mainstream theologians of Colet's day imperturbably took the words in their literal sense and set about deciding the nature and extent of the indebtedness. To Colet, however, it was inconceivable that an Apostle in possession of Christian truth could acknowledge any "indebtedness" to non-Christians. He preferred to regard Paul as meaning that he had a duty to preach to them and convert them (R, 223; RO, 208)—which view turns the notion of indebtedness on its head. Aware perhaps that his interpretation was not cogent, he returned to the question by suggesting that Paul deliberately exaggerated the merits of the Gentiles as an implicit rebuke to the Jews (RO, 220)—another arbitrary and devious way out of a position unacceptable to him personally.

We see that Colet could bring considerable ingenuity to bear when he found the admired apostle apparently asserting the unthinkable. He seemed to know aprioristically the limits within which Paul was to be taken at face value. When Paul's more speculative mind ranged among ideas unacceptable to Colet, his interpreter was driven to use arguments from historical conditions and substitute for the literal meaning of Paul's text a hypothesis thought up by himself to explain unwelcome differences between Paul's thought and his own.

If, then, the most interesting passages in the short list of Colet's historical interpretations turn out on closer look to be cases of special pleading, what is left in the list is meager indeed. Whatever Colet was, he was not a historically minded critic plying his craft. In fact there was no reason why he should be a historically minded critic. He was quite unaware of what the nineteenth century would expect of him and was calmly pursuing his own interests in his own way. He belonged to his own time, like everyone else, and it is by the standards then current that his work must be approached. As historians of exegesis have reminded us:

> An exegesis does not come into being by an exegete's addressing himself without presuppositions to a text. The exegete stands in a definite tradition of exegesis whose character he accepts, against which he defines himself, but by which he is influenced. His exegesis thus becomes fully intelligible only when one is in a position to see it as part of an intellectual tradition.[21]

In this spirit we may now turn to the exegetical enterprise as Colet and many of his contemporaries saw it.

Implicit Premises
of Colet's Thought

The great fact from which all exegesis then took its starting point was that the Bible was the word of God, written by the Holy Spirit. The Bible's divine authorship guaranteed its truth; indeed the very greatness of its authority and truth carried certain corollaries important for an interpreter.

The Bible, given its authorship, had to be inexhaustibly meaningful. In the sweeping principle of St. Anselm, "What Scripture does not expressly deny, it may be said to assert."[22] Not, of course, always on the surface. In many places the surface or literal meaning was regarded less as a revelation in itself than as a veil drawn over the true, underlying meaning to protect it from the prying eyes of the profane. This conclusion followed by a kind of necessity from the principle that the Bible, though finite in its literal integument, was the self-revelation of the infinite God. As nothing could be lacking to God, so nothing could be lacking in his revelation, for what he revealed was himself. This is the reason, for example, that Colet declares that only "the spiritual man" can interpret "God," where the context shows that by "God" Colet means the Bible (C, 172 [88]). In the Bible are to be found, says St. Bonaventure, figures or signs of all things that are to come to pass, though usually in a form that permits their recognition only after the fact; their number is thus "in a sense definite." But in addition to the hidden signs of future realities are "virtually infinite" numbers of "seeds," in each one of which are "forests of forests." As plants produce ever more seeds, "so from the Scriptures arise new considerations [*theoriae*] and new meanings [*sensus*]." "When all the considerations have been drawn out [*eliciuntur*] it is as if one drop had been taken from the sea, by comparison with what remains to be drawn out."[23] To the challenge of Scripture's inexhaustible meaningfulness as set forth quite typically by Anselm and Bonaventure, Colet responded with enthusiasm.

A further consequence of the divine authorship of the Scriptures was that they could contain nothing trivial. If they seemed to do so this was a signal that the true meaning lay deeper. Colet often insisted that God's truths revealed through the Bible were not to be thrown like "pearls before swine." His opinion of the mass of men was in any case very low: they were "dregs" ("feces") (C, 175 [94]), and he agreed with Ficino's characterization of the populace as a beast with many legs but no head (FEM, 95). This conviction gave Colet yet another reason to assume readily that Scripture deliberately concealed its meaning from unworthy, which is to say unspiritual, eyes.

Thus Colet was by choice and temperament a homiletic rather than an academic exegete.[24] The latter tradition, which centered on the literal meaning, reigned unchallenged in the schools from the thirteenth century on. Homiletic exegesis, on the other hand, went back to the early centuries of the church and continued to nourish the monastic tradition, which sought to integrate scriptural study, prayer, and the growth of the spiritual life.[25] The academic and the homiletic traditions existed in different contexts and for different purposes, but they ran side by side and were not felt to be competing. No book in Colet's lifetime did more to set the literal exegesis of Scripture on a sound philological and historical basis than Erasmus's Greek New Testament of 1516. Yet Erasmus too continued to work in the parallel tradition of homiletic exegesis. For example, in 1525 we read in his interpretation of the Fourth Psalm that the "rind" of the literal meaning is "bitter" but that underneath it is the "sweet fruit" of the spiritual sense.[26] Well over half of the sermon is devoted to the "sensus moralis," applicable to his hearers' own quest for salvation. This particular sermon is by no means unique for Erasmus for the 1520s; nevertheless it has a particular claim on our notice because the Fourth Psalm was used as the foundation of Colet's only substantial work that is not a commentary, his *De sacramentis*. Colet's and Erasmus's treatments of the same psalm have nothing in common in the way they are worked out or even in the specific teachings they find in the psalm. This does not mean that either man was wrong or right, but it illustrates the assumption that both were developing a few among the infinite "seeds" that St. Bonaventure found in the Scriptures. Erasmus's treatment of the Fourth Psalm was dedicated to John Longland, bishop of Lincoln, whom Thomas More, a friend of both men, called "a second Colet."[27] Thus we learn that a work composed in an elaborately homiletic and allegorical spirit was also a work Erasmus expected would please "a second Colet."

The homiletic and academic traditions should not be opposed as black to white, after the fashion of many Victorian scholars. The exhausting hundred years' war of the nominalists and realists had left the better men of both persuasions eager to find common ground once more in the patristic period. This fact is borne out by study of late medieval academic libraries. As one historian of theology has remarked, "The basic sources for theological discussion, in addition to the Bible, were the works of the Fathers, and from the twelfth century onwards the catalogues of medieval libraries contain a high proportion of entries for such works"—a trend that gained momentum in the fifteenth century.[28] Indeed, as a distant relation of the dean has shown recently, a humanistic scholarship, "grounded in a study of Latin, Greek, and literature, and applied to a study of the Bible, St. Paul, and the Fathers, especially the Greeks," was already current in Italian Benedictine circles well before Colet even arrived in Italy.[29]

The bifurcation of exegetical methods that we have been considering is due essentially to the differing weights the two traditions placed on the literal and spiritual senses. The doctors of the schools, on one hand, for all their other differences, tended to agree in seeing the distinction between the letter and spirit as parallel to the Aristotelian distinction between body and soul. For them the letter did not conceal the meaning but expressed it,[30] and accordingly they showed less interest in the hidden significances with which in principle Scripture abounded. They were concerned to accommodate revelation to the body of ancient Greek philosophy, especially Aristotle's, both to obviate the danger that would be posed by two unreconciled bodies of truth that were both authoritative and to develop a system whereby Christian revelation could be applied to a mode of life increasingly urban and secular. The spiritual doctors, on the other hand, shared Colet's suspiciousness of pagan wisdom and turned from it in disdain. One of the greatest of them, Hugh of St. Victor, flatly stigmatizes "philosophi gentilium" as "reprobi," while the "philosophi Christianorum"—the seekers after wisdom within the Christian tradition—are the "electi."[31] Thus a homiletically oriented student of Scripture like Colet looked with a very different eye on the literal meaning of the sacred text than did the system-building doctors of the schools. Like building contractors, the latter saw in the great trees of the scriptural forest, deeply rooted in rich soil and offering ever-new prospects to the contemplative mind, simply so much potential first-quality lumber. Cut and stripped of their bark and branches, the divinely nourished truths of Scripture which delighted the spiritual writers were sized and dried by the scholastics to fit their needs. In the process they became also sapless—but they could carry weight.

Though four senses were commonly distinguished in Scripture texts, in essence these reduced to two—the literal and the allegorical. "Allegory" here carries its etymological sense, according to which the literal text "is speaking otherwise," saying something else besides its surface meaning. The three allegorical senses are basically classifications according to the fields to which the allegory applied: the tropological[32] sense concerned the truths of faith, the moral sense concerned right action, and the anagogical sense concerned divine realities. Once one delves beneath the literal sense, however, it is soon clear that this neat classification of meanings is a comforting illusion, for there is ample room for overlap among them. The essential distinction is whether one works on the literal level or moves into the realms of allegory. If one chooses to take the latter way it makes little difference how many senses there are in that vast region: "C'est le premier pas qui coûte."

As often happens with Colet, his expressed conformity with the prevailing outlook masks a distinctly personal idiom. Like everyone else, he accepted the general principle that "where there is a literal sense there is not always an allegorical sense, but on the other hand where there is an allegorical sense the literal sense always underlies it" (DEH, 235). Also like everyone else, Colet took for granted that "we have a fourfold method of expounding [exponendi] the Bible" (DEH, 238). (It may be worth adding that though Colet's manuscripts almost never use capital letters for emphasis, he gives each of the three allegorical senses a capital letter apparently in token of its prestige, while leaving "literalis" with only the small letter.) His other references to the four senses (G, 167, and especially DEH, 235) make it clear that he accepted them fully, a fact so evident as to make Lupton, in one of his very few disagreements with Seebohm, acknowledge candidly that Colet's views as set forth in DEH, 235, are in all essentials the same as St. Thomas Aquinas's (DEH, pp. 105–107).

The "Literal Meaning" of Scripture

That the literal meaning is primary in the sacred text is a formula that looks simpler than it is. Important qualifications are necessary if we are to take the formula in the sense it had for those who appealed to it. Though Seebohm did not realize the fact, the exegetes of the twelfth and thirteenth centuries were quite well aware that one had to begin by determining the intention of a sacred writer if one hoped to determine his meaning. The principle was given classic formulation by Nicholas of Lyra: "One must begin with the intention of the author, for on this depends the understanding of the book." To add to the complexity of the matter, one soon finds that for these exegetes the sacred writer's intention is not invariably expressed in the literal meaning of the text. We may take as an example their approach to Isaiah 37:29, which reads, "Because . . . your insolence has come to my ears, I will put my ring through your nostrils, my bit between your lips, to make you return by the road on which you came." Since the context shows that the prophet was thinking of Sennacherib, St. Albert the Great states flatly, "The literal meaning refers to Sennacherib, even though the image is that of a bull."[33] Serious theologians centuries before Colet were aware, in short, that "the literal sense of the Bible is itself an interpretation of the facts." The sacred writer operates "with specifically religious intentions, isolating from the crowd of events those which seem to him pregnant with religious significance."[34] Already one begins to see that the literal meaning as then understood was not so distant from the level that "speaks otherwise" as one might have thought.

A more fundamental difficulty in deciding what the literal meaning of a passage is lies in the nature of language itself. People use words in the sense in which other people use them, and medieval writers were aware that language is conventional, its literal meanings an invention by which speakers contrive to communicate and to achieve their purposes. Measured by this criterion language is a success. But God uses this merely instrumental system of communication to convey realities not part of man's world and not expressible in his language. From this insight into the inadequacy of human language to carry a weight of revelation it was never meant to bear, the notion of "literal meaning" becomes radically problematic; for human language can never answer to the full intention of the ultimate author of the Scriptures, the Holy Spirit. What the words "literally" mean is therefore simply what they mean to men and women, a meaning at an indeterminate remove from the intention of the divine author.[35] Colet seems to have had a sense of the incommunicability of the divine by means of words when he comments that God imparts himself to man "indirectly, by means of a host of images [*multiplici racione simulacrorum*]." The Old Testament is full of such images, and the New Testament too "is not lacking in such similitudes" (DEH, 202).

From the inherent disparity between necessarily conventional language and a revelation that is instinct with truth, it follows that the *true* literal meaning (often called also the historical meaning) is that which is intended to be designated by the words, not necessarily that which ordinarily the words do designate.

Thus Aquinas points out that the literal sense of the expression "God's arm" is not that God has an arm but that he has the operative power of an arm (in scholastic terminology, he has an arm "virtually").[36] From this elementary example it is an easy further step to conclude that the truth that the divine author intended to convey in other parts of the Bible must be arrived at by a similar interpretive operation. One knew already that God is pure spirit; hence reading that he has an arm one necessarily concluded that what the author meant to designate by the words he used was God's operative power. Analogously, one knew that the Messiah whom the Jews expected had already come; when one read the messianic prophecies in the Old Testament one therefore knew that by them their divine author intended to designate Christ. On this principle Christ is their literal rather than their allegorical meaning.[37] By a further extension of the same principle the Old Testament as a whole is the "literal" stage of which the New Testament is the symbolic realization. As one theologian puts it neatly, "If Scripture is a history in course of actualization, one must read it 'historically.' "[38]

This is exactly what Colet assumed. "Whatever Moses wrote," he declared, "pertains to Christ" (R, 171). Nor is this true of "Moses," meaning the Pentateuch, only. According to Colet, "The meaning of the Holy Scriptures is spiritual through and through, all of which Jesus made clear to his followers." From this he concludes, in a formula that certainly minimizes the official primacy of the literal meaning as conventionally understood, that "that spiritual meaning which requires the spirit of prophecy for it to be understood is the wisdom and foundation of the entire superstructure of our Christian church" ("sapiencia et racio est totius fabricatae ecclesiae nostrae Christianae"; DEH, 197).

Scriptural interpretation so understood becomes not the fruit of scholarly study in the ordinary sense but something in the nature of a revelation to the interpreter. Colet did not flinch from this implication: "To the first and best among men are granted more revealing insights, and into their minds comes a more direct enlightenment from God" ("Primis et summis hominibus apertiores sunt visiones ac in mentes eorum irradiatio simplicior deitatis"; DCH, 174).

If such is the path to the understanding of the Scriptures, even exegetes more sympathetic to the literal level than Colet was would have to conclude that study alone could avail little. Those who had no access to the true but unobvious meaning of the letter could devote endless study to the letter and yet have no glimmering of its all-important subtext, or rather supertext. For this reason, Colet's contemporary Lefèvre d'Etaples logically concluded that "God has smitten with blindness" all the rabbis, for despite all their devoted study of their Scripture they failed to discern its most fundamental meaning.[39] Confronted by the rabbis' incomprehensible failure to see the true meaning of the Bible, which he assumed was the prophecy of Christ's coming as redeemer, Colet similarly concluded that for all their knowledge of the surface meaning they did not possess the key that could come only from a revelation. They "did not understand the divine language," and that is why they did not see the truth it proclaimed (R, 139). If Moses did "foresee" the coming of Christ (R, 209), the fact presumably was a part of the revelation God gave him on Mount Sinai and thus becomes another confirmation of the necessity, for Colet, of a revelation if one is to read the Bible with understanding.

Colet's Attitude toward the Use of Secular Scholarship

Since scholarly study of the literal meaning—as the example of the blinded rabbis showed—gave no dependable access to the true literal meaning, the meaning intended by the Holy Spirit, it was an easy further step to renounce, and then to denounce, the aid of secular scholarship. The Holy Spirit was quite enough for Colet. A comparison with Lefèvre d'Etaples shows how far Colet pushed reliance on grace. Lefèvre uses almost the same words as Colet to express his reliance on the Spirit,[40] for the doctrine was in fact classical.[41] What makes the difference is that Lefèvre took it for granted that the exegete uses also all the philological and historical learning he can muster. Colet, however, repudiates the aid of secular learning in terms that are violent and suspicious even for a man as little given to understatement as he was. He rejects the "often expressed idea" ("quod dici solet") that "reading pagan books will help one understand the sacred writings" — a way of expressing himself that shows he knew his was a minority position among intellectuals. But to defer to such books was for him "sacrificing to demons, not to God." In pagan books "there is nothing that smacks of Christ, nothing that does not smack of the demon." Not content with this, Colet adds the gratuitous assertion "No one reads pagan books except out of distrust or scorn of the Scripture" (C, 238 [218]).

Aware that this tirade required comment, Lupton did what he could to extenuate it in a long, embarrassed note. He suggests that Colet's overreaction could be a reflex from the years he spent among the cultivated but licentious and irreligious Italians. But history has not been kind to this interpretation of the Italian renaissance, a caricature concerning which the less said the better. Lupton adds, as an alternative palliation of Colet's militancy toward secular scholarship, that such denunciation was not unknown even in ecclesiastical writers who had personally benefited from the learning they now decried. He had to add, however, that such denunciation was far more characteristic of the ignorant than of men in Colet's position. Lupton seems to have realized that his attempts in Colet's behalf were not very convincing, for he was candid enough to ask plaintively, after doing his best to make allowances for his subject, "Is nothing further to be looked for from the friend of Erasmus and More?" (C, p. xxxvi).

The friend of Erasmus and More may have had personal reasons too for rejecting philological scholarship. The passage of Colet that Lupton was trying to make acceptable comes from the later, heavily revised portion of C (chapter 10), which on other grounds we have concluded dates from about 1512 to 1516. Such a dating locates Colet's diatribe in a period when trends in scriptural interpretation were changing rapidly. Erasmus's epochal Greek New Testament was published in 1516. As already mentioned, Lefèvre d'Etaples, a good Greek scholar, used his philological and historical learning in a commentary on Paul's Epistles published in 1512. We cannot know whether Colet had yet seen either work when he wrote these harsh words, but he would at least have known that editions of Scripture were on the way that made the fullest possible use of secular learning — including, especially, Greek. His dismissal out of hand of what better scholars than he were doing sounds defensive.

At all events Colet set himself defiantly against what had become the accepted tradition of the Greek and the Latin churches regarding the role of secular scholarship in sacred studies. The cultivated Greek Fathers, educated in their own splendid literature and philosophy, could not be expected to renounce it without a pang. St. John Chrysostom, whom Colet cites expressly,[42] was remarkable for his cultivation of the Greek rhetorical tradition;[43] the epithet by which he was known, "the Golden-

Mouthed," testifies to his congregations' admiration of his eloquence. In principle, nevertheless, the defense of pagan studies was uphill work for the Greek Fathers. The gods of their fathers were now thought of as devils. The philosophers before Christ could not know his revelation in its fullness, even if many thought that Plato had learned his wisdom from Moses.[44] To meet these charges and turn their edge the Greek patristic writers developed subtle rationales, but very little of this literature was known in the West in Colet's time.[45]

In the West the best-known Greek document was the *Paraenesis*, or "piece of advice," in which St. Basil recommended to young men the study of the classic Greek writers. As a saint and a Doctor of the Church Basil's authority was great, and his "piece of advice" had the additional advantage of being short. It was not among the works of Basil selected for translation by Rufinus in the fifth century, but at last it was translated in 1400–1402 by no less a hand than that of the chancellor of the Florentine Republic, Leonardo Bruni.[46] Thenceforward its diffusion was rapid. The first dated copy of Bruni's translation is from 1403;[47] by 1450 Aeneas Silvius, the future Pope Pius II, whom we have already met as the author of the *Historia Bohemica*, was citing it in a letter to King Ladislas of Hungary on the education of children.[48] Starting with the first printed edition (Venice, 1470) the little work enjoyed in Italy alone at least twenty-eight editions by 1500, with another seven following during the next thirty years,[49] after which point the battle was effectively won.

In the West the prestige of St. Augustine himself was committed to the defense of pagan learning as a means of elucidating Scripture. The core of his *De doctrina christiana*[50] constitutes the classic defense for the Western church of the studies that Colet denounced; yet Augustine did not carry Colet with him on this vital question. Whatever may be thought of the reasons for Colet's resistance to the position represented by Augustine and Basil, there can be no doubt that the resistance was deep.

Colet acknowledged indeed that the philosophers of Greece and Rome had arrived at a natural knowledge of God from the creation all about them, but he turned this achievement into an indictment:[51]

> Starting with the senses, they arrived at understanding and at God, but they impiously failed to worship the God they had come to know: their wisdom made them actually irreligious to God and unjust to men. For they worshiped idols and lived wickedly. Bathed in light, they were cold;[52] filled with wisdom, they were utterly evil. Impressive in their words, in their actions they were plain fools [*in verbis gloriosi, in factis stultissimi*]. (RO, 203; cf. also 210)

Even in his last years he continued to warn, "Be careful lest some worthless self-proclaimed philosopher [*philosophator inanis*] should try to influence you with subtle snares [*occultis insidiis adortus*] and lead you out of the true path of faith into error and evil and slavery" (Trinity College, Cambridge, MS. o.4.44, fol. 21ʳ). Colet must have known from Clement of Alexandria, Eusebius, Tertullian, and other early writers[53] that Paul had quoted Menander (1 Cor. 15:33), who in turn was probably quoting Euripides,[54] and had thus introduced pagan literature into the pages of Scripture itself, even though he is silent about the fact. But we have seen that Colet could ignore passages in Paul that went against his personal convictions; moreover, his own deafness to the muses probably made them seem to him a lesser threat than the philosophers were.

Colet and Scholasticism

Colet relied on divine grace (cf. DCH, 175) to the brusque exclusion of the customary tools of scholarship (RO, 209, 267–268) and with disdain for insights won by the systematic use of reason. How extreme was his rejection of the academic approach to Scripture study we learn from Erasmus's account of discussions he and Colet had on this topic. Erasmus begins by emphasizing that it was "among his friends and the learned that [Colet] would very freely avow his opinion" (A, ll. 424–425). (It is worth emphasizing again Erasmus's emphasis on Colet's circumspection: far from declaiming his views to all and sundry, as Seebohm assumed, Colet actually expressed himself freely only "among his friends and the learned.")

> The Scotists, whom the ordinary run of men thought peculiarly subtle, he used to say were stupid and dull-witted, anything but clever; for going on and on [*argutari*] about other people's words and opinions, gnawing now at this and now at that, and taking everything apart in detail, he considered the sign of a poor and barren mind. (A, ll. 425–429)

"For some reason," Erasmus continues, "he was more prejudiced against Thomas than against Scotus." Erasmus was of the opposite opinion,[55] and in conversation with Colet he argued in favor of Thomas. Though Erasmus persisted, Colet said nothing, "maintaining a significant silence" ("*dissimulauit obticiscens*"). But not long afterward, when Erasmus praised Aquinas even more highly, Colet could no longer restrain himself:

> He looked closely at me, as if to determine whether I was speaking seriously or ironically. When he realized that I was speaking sincerely he exclaimed, as if filled with some spirit, "How can you praise such a man? If he were not decidedly arrogant he could not so rashly and haughtily have defined everything; if he hadn't had in him something of the spirit of this world he

could not have contaminated the teaching of Christ with his profane philosophy." (A, ll. 435–441)

As we saw in chapter 5 above, Erasmus had described such an outburst at the time he first met Colet, in 1499, when Colet flew into a "sacred rage" at opposition to his theory about the sacrifice of Cain, to the point that Erasmus had to save the social situation by diverting attention to a little "fable" of his own about Cain. There we saw that ironic amusement was signaled by the parody of a passage from the *Aeneid*. Here Erasmus is more concerned with the reaction of Justus Jonas, to whom his biographical letter is addressed; hence to describe his own reaction he takes refuge behind a Greek word that a reader can take in whatever sense he wishes: "I marveled at his transport" ("admiratus sum hominis ἐνθουσιασμοῦ").[56] No enthusiast himself, Erasmus was sufficiently impressed to reconsider the question, upon which he found his high esteem for Aquinas dropped "to some extent" for a while (A, ll. 442–444).[57] Colet's bursts of prophetic fervor, intemperate as they were, may have been a part of his charm for his greater but drier friend.[58]

After all this it might seem surprising to find Erasmus reporting in the same biographical letter that Colet "nevertheless did not fail to read Scotus and Thomas and others of that stripe when occasion required" (A, ll. 274–75). The paradox is, however, only superficial. Colet was by no means alone in his antipathy toward Aquinas and the scholastic doctors associated with him. Many objected to their pretentious determination to define everything, and also to their adulteration of Christ's teachings with Aristotelian philosophy— the specific points that angered Colet. Many objected also to the cold intellectuality of scholasticism and its lack of human qualities. And scholars more sensitive to such matters than Colet was felt revulsion at the scholastics' barbarous diction and bald syntax.[59] Finally, many rejected scholasticism because they did not find it made men better.[60]

Despite the weight of these charges scholasticism continued to hold sway in the universities during Colet's time and beyond. Colet and his contemporaries were in no danger of making the mistake that was often made later, that of equating scholasticism with doctrinal content. They were fully aware of the sharp differences of opinion among the multifarious philosophers who used the scholastic method. They could not have foreseen that pale avatar of their scholasticism, the neoscholasticism developed in the nineteenth century on the basis of Aquinas's doctrines alone and intended to provide a rational support for the teachings and practices of the Roman Catholic Church—a development that has helped give to scholasticism misleading connotations of medievalism and religion. For students in Colet's time, scholasticism was essentially a method.

Frustratingly enough, even scholasticism's critics, if they wanted to do professional philosophy at all, had to use the scholastic method. One stated a problem, then marshaled the evidence against the position he wished to defend. Next he set about systematically replying to each separate argument that could be advanced against his theory, one after the other. When all had been refuted he turned to the positive side and marshaled in similar fashion all the arguments that told in favor of his doctrine, concluding usually with a summary statement of his own opinion. The main repertories of arguments were the Bible—every single verse of which, because inspired, could be used as a proof text—the Fathers, the philosophers, philosophical axioms, in short whatever materials could pretend in some measure to authority; it was essentially these authorities that were pitted against one another. It is easy to see how such a method could lead to charges of contentiousness, vanity, quibbling, and intellectual pride; in fairness it should be added that the method also forced one to take account of all the available evidence and not simply the points favorable to one's own view. If we remember how Colet reacted when his favorite views were attacked, and recall the instances in which he simply ignored passages that told against his view, it is difficult to believe that scholastic disputation was an exercise in which he shone. His preferred forum was, literally and metaphorically, the pulpit.

But however uncongenial the scholastic method may have been to some, it survived for the good reason that "early humanism did not provide a substitute in the form of a real philosophy." Critics of scholasticism knew what was wrong with it, but they had no alternative at their disposal, no "philosophical concept, method or system, but only general tendencies and orientations. Whoever wanted to study philosophy was driven to return to the only philosophical system then existing, *i.e.*, scholasticism."[61] There was a real danger that hostility to scholasticism's many shortcomings could leave one without any way of contributing to reasoned philosophical discourse at all. Erasmus acknowledged that the scholastic method as applied to theology was often "frigid and strife-ridden," but he added realistically that "it has surely to be tolerated until some more suitable method is available."[62] Meanwhile he was unwilling to "condemn all the accepted studies of the schools": "Just as I do not think well of those who place no value at all on literary studies, I also disapprove of those who condemn out of hand the work of the latter-day theologians"[63]—critics like Colet. Colet's tirade against Aquinas may have prompted Erasmus to reconsider the matter, but he soon recovered all of his former esteem for Thomas. He continued to regard him as among the *recentiores* "incomparably the best, at least in my judgment,"[64] and to extoll him as "the most learned among the more recent theologians," a "most notable writer," "beatus," "sanctus."[65] He paid him moreover the practical compliment of citing him over forty times in the *Annotationes* to his New Testament.[66] Erasmus could give scholastic philosophers only limited and conditional approval, but he acknowledged that in the existing state of things the scholastic method was indispensable.

Colet, however, was not a man to live in halfway houses. The thoroughness with which he reprobated the most scholarly of the scholastics meant that he cut himself off from the patient, orderly study of the Scriptures' literal meaning by the only methods likely to produce generally acknowledged results. For him there was something impious in seeking to read the divine Word by the light of human reason. Instead he commends another way, the one that he himself doubtless took: "Truth . . . is understood by grace. Grace is granted when prayer is heard, and prayer is heard when it is whetted by devotion and strengthened by fasting" (C, 239 [219]). This fascinating passage establishes for Colet a nexus between asceticism and exegesis which, like his dismissal of the scholastic method, inclines him to be impatient of the "carnal and slavish letter" (Trinity College, Cambridge, Ms. o.4.44, fol. 31ʳ) and to seek elsewhere for the truth. We can be quite sure that when Colet was preparing to interpret a scriptural text he would feel that fasting prepared him to hear the communication of the Spirit that lay often beneath the surface. For the same reason he would be more likely on these occasions to spend hours on his knees in fervent prayer rather than hours ransacking the shelves of libraries.

Hermetic Interests

Scripture, obviously, was the great and, in a sense, the all-sufficient fount of truth. Nevertheless Colet, following Paul, accepted that God had revealed himself through other channels as well. Parallel to the written Word, God had granted the Church an unwritten deposit of tradition. And outside these two main channels of revelation, Colet thought he saw still other channels less authoritative and more diffuse, by which God communicated with men.

Already in his annotations of Ficino's *Epistolae* Colet showed interest in Ficino's statement that all the pagan lawgivers had ultimately received from God the laws they gave their respective peoples. The prophet Mohammed received his "laws" (presumably the Koran) from the archangel Gabriel. Even Greek and Roman legislators—Solon of Athens, Lycurgus of Sparta, Numa of Rome—drew their wisdom from the same divine source (FEM, 88). Colet may have been more interested than convinced—he later gave ecclesiastical law preeminence over any secular law whatever (RO, 262–263, DEH, 197)—but it is noteworthy that he was attracted to the idea of a multifarious revelation.

Given the nature of Colet's writings—his starting point was almost always the words of others—we can expect only scattered hints of what he thought concerning such revelation. What is important is that the hints are there and cumulatively testify to a range of hermetic interests that feed into his manner of regarding Scripture. Such hints fall into two broad classes, the manifestations of God in the nature of the universe, and the Law that he gave to the Chosen People.

First were testimonies pointing to the divine which were built into the constitution of nature itself. At least once and probably twice Colet makes unselfconscious use of alchemical language: unmistakably in "the flower of decoction" ("decoctionis flos"; C, 257 [258]) and less clearly but more interestingly in saying that adversity subjects our love to a trial by fire which proves it "golden" (R, 143). It was fundamental to alchemical theory that success depended on the practitioner's spiritual state. He was to approach his work free of sin and in a prayerful frame of mind; otherwise the transformation from base metal to gold would not occur. To an allegorizing age the spiritual significance of alchemy, whose techniques were, however, firmly rooted in the constitution of physical nature, was obvious.[67]

Colet's interest in alchemy recalls naturally a fact about which Colet's biographers have been singularly incurious, that he had as a houseguest in 1510 the famous alchemist and hermetic writer Henricus Cornelius Agrippa of Nettesheim. Though only twenty-four at the time, Agrippa (1486–1535) was already widely known through the circulation in manuscript of his *De occulta philosophia*, written when he was twenty-one though not printed until 1531.[68]

While staying with Colet, Agrippa wrote a tract defending himself against charges made by the Franciscan Jean Catilinet. Agrippa entitles his defense *Henrici Cornelii Agrippae Expostulatio super expositione sua in librum de verbo Mirifico cum Joanne Catilineti fratrum Franciscanorum per Burgundiam provinciali ministro, sacrae Theologiae doctoris*. According to Lupton, in this work "there is much to remind us of Colet's Lectures on St. Paul";[69] but if so I have failed to find it. What is, however, clear is that young Agrippa had been accused by Catilinet of "Judaizing." The charge was based on public lectures he had given at the University of Dôle before a large and distinguished audience. The lecturer discussed in detail the recent book *The Wonderworking Word* (*De verbo mirifico*), by Johannes Reuchlin—in whose work as we shall see shortly Colet was also keenly interested. Agrippa rounds on his accuser in no uncertain terms: "In your ignorance even of the very name of the cabbala and lack of knowledge of the Hebrew teachings you have called me heretic and Judaizer and on top of that consigned me to hellfire. But I rejoice that I endure these insults for the sake of our Lord Jesus Christ," whom on the same page Agrippa styles "ipse . . . pentagrammus Iesus Christus."[70] Agrippa's *Expostulatio* is dated "Ex Londino Angliae celebri emporio, Anno M.D.X."[71]

Biographers assume that Agrippa wrote his treatise while staying in Stepney with Colet's mother, but I see no reason why he should not have been staying in the deanery in London, from which city the *Expostulatio* is dated. It is unfortunate that Agrippa says little of his visit, but what he does say gives food for thought to those interested in Colet's intellectual sympathies. In the previous year Agrippa had given the public lectures on Reuchlin which drew Catilinet's attack. Then,

> crossing over to Britain, I worked hard on the epistles of St. Paul while staying with [*apud*] John Colet, a man deeply learned in Catholic doctrine and of blameless life, and under his tuition [*illo docente*] I learned much that I did not know, even though the business I had with the English was something completely different and highly confidential [*occultissimum* — obviously a favorite word with Agrippa].[72]

Who brought the young visitor to Colet's notice we do not know; but whoever it was, knowing Agrippa's *De occulta philosophia*, his involvement with the cabbala, and his interest in Reuchlin's *Wonderworking Word*, must have thought Agrippa was the kind of man that Colet would like to meet. The meeting was clearly a success on both sides. Agrippa, who under Colet's roof wrote of Christ as a "pentagram,"[73] shared his ideas and knowledge with his older host and in turn was excited by Colet's explorations of the subsurface meanings of Paul. Agrippa's statement that he "learned much that he did not know" from Colet's teaching is the clearest testimony we possess from any source that Colet's approach to Paul offered something new. This something new, however, was altogether different from what the Victorian scholars supposed who imagined that Colet was a pioneer of textual criticism in their sense of the term. In the following chapter I will investigate the methods that Colet worked out which yielded hidden results that were new to his youthful guest. It was the hermetic side of Colet's approach to Paul that interested him, an approach that brought to light deep-lying themes and significances in a sacred writer whom Agrippa would initially have thought he knew well.[74]

Agrippa returned to the Continent after completing his "highly confidential" business in England,[75] while Colet, eminently a Londoner, returned to his own duties, though refreshed and encouraged by the young savant's interest and admiration. Their conjuncture—the astrological term seems appropriate here—is not likely to have lasted long. Agrippa's hopes for patronage centered elsewhere; he had been in the train of the emperor Maximilian before coming to Dôle, the second university in Burgundy after Louvain, and he hoped to regain the patronage of Margaret of Austria, regent of the Netherlands, which he had lost after Catilinet's attack[76]—all considerations that forbade him to linger in London. Another indication that his visit to Colet was short is that while he was there he did not meet Erasmus, who was living at the time in England;[77] moreover Colet is not mentioned among the many friends whom Agrippa and Erasmus had in common.[78] But if theirs was a brief encounter, at its heart lay an interest that very few among Colet's contemporaries shared. With the exception of John Fisher (and perhaps Thomas More in virtue of his translating Gianfrancesco della Mirandola's life of Pico), Colet was the only man of that generation in England known to have had any interest in the cabbala.[79] To an unusual extent Colet was alert to mysterious meanings.

If, as Agrippa charged, Catilinet was "ignorant even of the very name of the cabbala," Colet was not. Agrippa was full of the controversy during the period when he was with Colet, and so from that date at latest Colet will have been aware of the cabbalist traditions. Because he did not know Hebrew, however, he always remained on the sidelines of cabbalist studies, impressed but unable to participate; when Colet write the word he uses what looks like an oral spelling: "quae scientia capule & receptionis dicebatur" (Corpus Christi College, Cambridge, Parker MS. CCCLV, fol. 1ᵛ; Lupton, RO, 232, partially normalizes the spelling). In writing to Erasmus on that subject in mid-1517 Colet seems hardly to have advanced from the level of understanding which he had at the time of Agrippa's visit. He tells Erasmus that he had "run through" ("percursus") Reuchlin's *De arte cabalistica*. "I admit my ignorance, and how blind I am in such recondite matters and the works of such a great man. Nevertheless as I was reading I sometimes felt that here were greater wonders of words than of realities." This passage is often quoted to imply that Colet the student of the literal meaning disdained such studies and saw through them; instead, however, he at once backs away from this criticism by confessing again that he does not know "what mysteries Hebrew words may contain in their characters and combinations."[80] Hebrew being the language God spoke with Adam, its every jot and tittle was significant.[81] Not knowing Hebrew at all, Colet could only marvel; but he would hardly wish to be ironic about God's language. In fact Colet remained interested in Reuchlin's work to the end, for in the last year of his life he is mentioned in a document as among Reuchlin's influential supporters in England.[82] Given Erasmus's relations with Reuchlin well before Agrippa's visit to Colet, it is tempting to surmise, though impossible to prove, that it was Reuchlin himself who advised his youthful supporter to look up Dean Colet.[83]

With his interest in Reuchlin, in Agrippa of Nettesheim, and at least to some extent in the cabbala, Colet went far beyond most of his contemporaries in the quest for mysterious meanings built by God into the realities of this world. More conventionally, he also shared the widespread conviction that "the heavens proclaim the wonderful works of God" (Ps. 18:2), often referred to as the "caeli enarrant" tradition.[84] Starting from Paul's assertion that the evidence for God's existence and power is everywhere, Colet speaks of the "two books of God": his works, through which the pagans knew him though they failed to follow through by worshipping him, and the "oracles" ("eloquia") to the Jews (RO, 201), which we will consider below.

Colet's own interest in the manner in which God had manifested himself to the pagans appears from his industrious annotations of one of the *Epistolae* of Ficino (FEM, 122–23, 143). Its title tries to guard against astrological determinism while still allowing for the possibility that God's will is revealed through the stars: "Divine law cannot be prescribed by the stars, but may perhaps be signified by them" ("Divina lex fieri a coelo non potest: sed forte significari"). Though divine law stands in no need of earthly aid, Ficino declares, the star that announced Christ's birth at Bethlehem (Colet underlined the account of the star) suggests that God himself may govern and guide the stars' motions. "Perhaps indeed this is what David meant in saying, 'The heavens proclaim the glory of God and the firmament announces the work of his hands.' "[85] And Colet finds that even the pharaoh and Nebuchadnezzar were granted true dreams brought by angels (DCH, 183–184)—a further proof that God makes himself known to all.[86]

For Colet, God had revealed himself both through the proclamation that the heavens made of his glory and in the pages of the Old Testament. The failure of men generally to understand the first of these revelations, and the Jews' incomprehension of the second taught a lesson essential for the exegete. The constitution of the universe pointed unmistakably to God, yet men did not understand, and even the rabbis who had been given the Old Testament were smitten with blindness and unable to read the "literal meaning" of their own Bible, which was its foretelling of Jesus the Messiah. Such failures could only be the effect of God's plan. God did not wish to communicate himself to those who were spiritually unprepared to receive him. Though the Jews had the Law, the mere possession of it had not made them worthy to comprehend it. In St. Paul's image (2 Cor. 3:12–18) God himself had placed a veil over the revelation he had granted which obscured its meaning from almost all Jews; Colet returned to this passage again and again because he saw in it proof that only Christians could read the Old Testament rightly (C, 247, 250 [236, 240]; DCH, 170, 171, 172). In so reading the passage Colet was not alone; it was widely regarded as a charter authorizing allegorical interpretation of the Old Testament.[87]

Going even further, Colet decided that it was intrinsically necessary that the sacred realities be concealed from the unworthy:

> By their own inner logic [*suo jure secreto*] things divine require to be concealed, for if they are vulgarized they lose their divinity. Indeed God does not wish to communicate himself to the many, for there are not many to whom he could communicate himself. Brightness, beauty, virtue, fragrance — all are lost if you reveal the secrets to ordinary men. (DEH, 228)

A later passage in the same work develops the theme: "Those sacred mysteries under the bark and rude surface of the words of the law, those secrets, that is, of the loftiest divinity . . . —to have laid them open to the ignorant mob [*stultae plebi*]" would be "to throw pearls before swine" (237). No wonder, then, he continues, that "it was the holy custom of all the wise saints, by means of enigmatic knots, to keep mystical doctrines inviolate from the profane multitude." In fact Plato too — profiting presumably from what he had learned from Moses — is careful to conceal his true meaning; the only persons who can interpret him are those who "bring their own light with them" (FEM, 93). The prophets, who according to Colet are rightly called "theologians" (DCH, 176), taught through symbols and analogies, for they "sought to instruct men while at the same time preserving the dignity of the divine mysteries."[88] This crucial conception is emphasized by its position: it is the concluding sentence of Colet's commentary on Dionysius's *Celestial Hierarchy* in its original form.

Closely related to the principle that divine realities are concealed from the profane is the likewise classical principle of accommodation. Again using "theologi" to mean sacred writers (cf. DCH, 172, 173), Colet states as a matter of principle that "Moses and the prophet-theologians [*prophetae illi theologici*] used allegory for all communication [*allegoria omnia significarunt*], commonly employing terms which were suitable by virtue of their likeness" to the realities to which they mysteriously point (C, 253 [250]). Theology as thus defined "takes full account of human weakness" (DCH, 169). Here too, as in so many other ways, Colet is simply working in a time-honored tradition of exegesis that is found already in the Fathers of the Church. Interpreters of scriptural books felt that they had to take into consideration the capacities of those to whom the writings had been addressed, especially in the case of Genesis.[89] Colet expressly recognized anthropomorphic language in the Bible: "God does not grow angry, but simple man [*homocolus*] speaks of God in human language . . . and ascribes man's emotions to God" (RO, 210) (though even the dean could occasionally forget himself, as he did when he wrote, "God was so delighted at Abraham's faith and hope that he promised him many great things" [RO, 265]).

Allowance had to made for people who, until Moses came to them, were absorbed in making bricks: "Moses wanted to lead them gradually to see their own nature and destiny [*ut . . . qui sint ad quidque nati doceat*], to bring them to a loftier life and the worship of God." To do this he had to "bear in mind the outlook of simple rustics"; hence in his account of the creation he "feigns successiveness," whereas in reality God the great "artificer" (a reminder of the *demiourgos* of the *Timaeus*) created the world in an instant (G, 170). After expatiating further on the concessions that Moses had to make to the capacities of the "stupid and dim-witted [*macra*] masses" (G, 172, 173), Colet explains that when Moses was writing about realities with which ordinary people were familiar he made it a point to write on their level, "in a popular, unspiritual style" ("populariter et crasso calamo"; G, 181). Moses even made use of something very like Plato's golden lie: "In making use of their conceptions he is trying by a perfectly honorable and pious fiction [*honestissimo et piissimo figmento*] to draw them on to the service of God" (G, 182). Even more strikingly, the ultimate author of this fiction is God, according to a long passage from Pico's famous *Oration on the Dignity of Man* transcribed by Colet without acknowledgment (DEH, 236) but noted by Lupton. Besides the written law in the Pentateuch God gave Moses also "the secret and true explanation and interpretation of the whole Law," commanding him on no account to reveal it to anyone but Joshua the son of Nun, who in turn "commanded the first priests to observe concerning it a holy, strict, and religious silence." As for the common people, God directed that the written law be made known to them "by means of a simple story" "in which now the power of God is shown, now his wrath toward the wicked, now his mercy toward the good, and everywhere his justice toward all."[90] The words are Pico's, but they had Colet's enthusiastic assent.

This passage from Pico has a further interest. It refers also in unmistakable terms to the doctrine that came to be known as the *disciplina arcani*.[91] In his wide reading in theological and historical writers Colet would often have noticed injunctions not to divulge the full meaning of Christian revelation, especially in fourth-century writers. He would find that even pagan religious teachings were made known in their fullness only to the initiate. All this was to be found in such accessible writers as Julius Firmicus Maternus, a convert to Christianity whose *De errore profanarum religionum* is full of information on pagan cults,[92] as well as in Apuleius and Plutarch. Josephus testified to the *disciplina arcani* among the Essenes, so that Colet found it practiced by Jews and Gentiles alike. Present-day scholars realize that initiates were seeking to protect their practices against profanation, not prohibiting communication of them to outsiders (who appear to have been uninterested in them anyway); but this last idea would hardly have occurred to Colet. He was impressed also by the importance of the formal catechumenate in the early Christian church, with its concealment of mysteries until the aspirant should have proved himself worthy. He likewise fully sympathized with the turn that Dionysius gave to the *disciplina arcani*—that the prohibition is directed not so much against the unbaptized as against those, initiates as well as catechumens, who still cling to earthly things. Both in his own commentary on First Corinthians (C, 182 [110]) and in the commentary he borrowed from Pico (DEH, 237), Colet strongly emphasized Paul's assertion (1 Cor. 2:6) that he "speaks wisdom" only to those who are "perfect." Such arcane wisdom, not the scholarship of "this world," was the real goal of Colet's interpretative quest.

7

"Living Wisdom": Colet's Exegesis in Practice

We have seen that Colet rejected secular scholarship and pagan philosophy in interpreting the Scriptures. He rejected at least as decisively the scholastic method in which he himself had been trained as it applied to theology, even though by so doing he cut himself off from the accepted methodologies of the schools. Disdaining such aid, he struck out largely on his own. He appears to have been quite aware of the difficulties that lay ahead for him. The modes of God's self-revelation that he like many others found imbedded in the very constitution of nature often required hermetic skills for their understanding. He had also to take account of the pervasive accommodation by means of which the Scripture spoke to simple people in their own pictorial terms, reserving for the expert the hidden underlying sense. He was aware too that the early church had practiced a *disciplina arcani* that further complicated the task of the interpreter of Scripture. An interpreter such as Colet wanted to be relied heavily on divine grace; he prayed for illumination, which was granted only to the "highest and best" and even to them only when their minds were "whetted with devotion and sharpened by fasting."

The Indispensability of "Spiritual" Interpretation

In view of all this it can be no surprise that for Colet the first and overridingly important qualification for an interpreter of Scripture—without which nothing else mattered—was that he be "a spiritual man." Only the spiritual man can interpret "God," by which interesting periphrasis the context shows that he refers to the Bible (C, 172 [89, 91] — a long and un-compromising passage). This is because "the meaning of the Holy Scriptures is spiritual through and through, all of which Jesus explained to his followers" (DEH, 197) in discussions to which we will turn shortly. Not that Colet necessarily denies all value to "grammatical" study (RO, 222), but the exegesis he aspires to has a different aim. He feels that like the preacher, the exegete "should not go into side issues [*non aliquo se conferat*] except for the purpose of 'imparting spiritual grace' [Rom. 1:11] by word or example, in order that from them may be born the fruits of righteousness"; there are to be no philological or historical excursuses that do not have a moral end in view (RO, 201). We have seen that the holograph manuscript of C contains two chapters 14, though the fact is not reflected in Lupton's text. The second of them emphasizes that the real purpose of interpreting Scripture is to get at the "spiritual meaning," without which the surface words remain "mere sound, airy breath, something without soul, without meaning, the words and spirit of man rather than of the divine spirit, which alone understands the words of prophecy" (C, 265 [275]).

According to Colet, Paul himself disdained the paraphernalia of scholarship and brought out instead the spiritual meaning that lay concealed in the Old Testament. Authority does not come from piling up quotations and citing authorities, he decided. Paul would say merely, "as Scripture says," with the unforced assurance of a man who knows (RO, 209, 267–268). Paul's exegetical principles could be inferred also from the practice of Dionysius. Colet believed that Dionysius was Paul's "pupil" (C, 171 [89]); hence Dionysius's exegetical techniques reflected those of Paul (DCH, 176). In a long chapter (13) of the *Celestial Hierarchy* which Colet did not comment on but certainly read, Dionysius declares, "Such were the teachings of my master, and I for my part am content to pass them on."[1] The unnamed master in question could actually have been Hierotheus, but Colet would think of Paul. Hence Colet decided that Dionysius's quest for hidden meanings and allegorical interpretations reflected the teachings of Paul and was the right way to proceed.

Thus Colet aligned himself firmly with what has been called the old hermeneutic, in which the exegete was simply unaware of the temporal, cultural, and stylistic distance between his text and himself. His method assumed that the sacred text and its reader were in "a single universe of discourse wherein no cultural distance could exist."[2] Such being the nature of the Scriptures and the relation of the exegete to them, it is not surprising that Colet regularly describes the exegetical enterprise by the terms "eruo" ("dig out" or "unearth"), "excudo" ("hammer out" or "forge"), "elicio" ("bring out by the application of skill"), "excutio" ("discover by scrutiny"), and "depromo" ("bring out") the first three of them exemplified in the single passage (C, 236–239 [214, 216, 218]) summarized in the following paragraph. He took for granted that no significant cultural barriers interposed themselves between the text and the reader who set himself in the proper way to "dig out" its meaning. He felt strongly, however, the difficulty of the great enterprise, indeed its impossibility if unaided by grace.

A typical example of this approach is C, 236 [214], where in the middle of chapter 10 he says, "Now let us see what remarkable principles and maxims can be dug out" ("quam insignia proloquia et sententiae erui possunt videamus"). Stimulated by Paul's saying in verse 6, in reference to the forty years the Jews spent in the desert under Moses' leadership, that "all these things are symbols for us," Colet finds, for example, that the manna and the water that gushed from the rock are "the flesh and blood of Christ." This meaning still lies fairly near the surface of Paul's text; digging deeper he finds that "Christ is the rock who steadfastly endures and, when struck on the cross, poured forth life-giving blood that satisfies thirst for all eternity"—a reference to the moment in which traditionally the church was founded, but such a reference as only a spiritual interpreter could have "dug out."

The Ambiguous Status
of the Old Testament

The Old Testament too could contain truths concerning Christ. Nevertheless, for a critic like Colet, sensitive to the part that accommodation played in the Old Testament and eager to hurry on to the fuller revelation of the New, one would expect that the former would hold relatively little interest; and such is the case. By far his favorite Old Testament book was the Psalms, which in common with his age he regarded as sung by David and as referring to Christ. He also tried his hand on the earlier chapters of Genesis. There he tackled an especially vexing problem, how it was that plants were created on the "third day" while the sun and other stars were created only on the "fourth." Colet laid down four conditions that any solution would have to satisfy: it must by worthy of God; it must take account of the fact that on matters lying within the apprehension of the common people Moses wished to meet them halfway ("vulgo satisfacere"); it must observe the logical order of events (the great difficulty in the present case); and, above all, it must be consistent with Moses' desire "to bring the people to true religion and the worship of the one God" (G, 177). Colet's requirements are derived aprioristically from the conception of God, not from the nature of the text. In any case, like many other writers, he soon found that it is one thing to set up conditions and another thing to meet them oneself; the actual solution he offered at some length (177–180) is pretty lame.

Besides the creation account and many references to the Psalms, Colet's references to the Old Testament are mostly explorations in allegory. We have already seen several allegorical references he "dug out" from the account of the years the chosen people spent in the desert under Moses. None of his surviving writings other than the four chapters on Genesis deal expressly with the Old Testament, where Christian interpreters traditionally found allegorical riches (though there is a lost work on Proverbs).[3] For this reason the following examples of incidental and unselfconscious allegorizing give us an idea of how hospitable Colet was to allegorizing even when his context did not encourage it. The samples that follow are simply mentioned in passing, and all of them come from the writings either on the New Testament or on Paul's "pupil" Dionysius. One can only surmise what riches might not have been "dug out" had Colet applied himself systematically, in any extant writing, to an Old Testament book.

The "triple cord" of Ecclesiastes 4:12 refers, according to Colet, to the three theological virtues of faith, hope, and charity (C, 206 [158]).[4] At the wedding feast of Cana the water of Moses was turned into the wine of Christ (C, 238 [216]).[5] Circumcision is "nothing else but" "cutting off all unbelief from the mind" so that it can appear "naked" (that is, not partly covered) and "complete" (R, 140). The prohibitions against eating unclean animals in Leviticus 11 "are only pointers and signs of what is meaningful for the soul, as Moses also clearly states when after the prohibitions he adds, Do not contaminate your souls [Lev. 11:43ff.]." By following these regulations the Jews would be made ready to follow the "teacher of truth" whose coming Moses "foresaw" and who would one day teach "true holiness of soul" (R, 208–209). When we read "He not only says, Lord, Lord, but adds a third Lord," the reference is to the three theological virtues (RO, 248). Isaac was the "type" ("figura") of Christ, who is "the spiritual Isaac" (R, 162, 163). Abraham saw "in his spirit" the typological significance of his sacrifice of Isaac; similarly Adam saw "in his spirit" that he would one day recover his felicity through Christ, while Adam's "clinging to his wife" (Gen. 2:24) refers to Christ's marrying the Church (RO, 248–249). Abel's offering of the first fruits of his flock to God signified "nothing other than" that Jesus would also be a shepherd of a flock, who would offer himself, the firstborn, to his Father. God therefore received Abel's offering favorably "because of what it signified" (RO, 249). When Enos, Adam's grandson, called on the name of the Lord, "what other name was he calling on than the name of Jesus?" (RO, 249). Noah's building an altar for sacrifice shows that he was "profoundly meditating" on the future sacrifice of Jesus and the martyrs, who were "burning" in love like a holocaust (RO, 250). The mention of Noah leads Colet to add that the ark is like the Church, because it contains both clean and unclean (RO, 250). God bade Abraham to look up toward the stars as an image of his vast posterity because he wished to show that Abraham's posterity would be heavenly, not earthly, men (RO, 253). The man in Isaiah 63 who "trod the winepress alone" and later came to be seen in terms of eucharistic imagery "is" Jesus (DCH, 179). As a final example we may take Colet's statement "Christ, being single, could not wear a coat having two parts [DEH, 213]." The rather terse expression of this idea ("Non patitur Christus simplex duplicem tunicam") misled Lupton, who thought it referred to the two cloaks that according to Matthew 10:10 and Mark 6:9 one is not to take along when fleeing the day of wrath. Actually it refers to the "seamless cloak" of Jesus, for which the soldiers cast lots. The mention of its seamlessness naturally attracted the interest of earlier exegetes. Many offered allegorical interpretations, but some of the early commentators asked good historical questions, such as, What did poor people actually wear at the time?[6] Not Colet, however. For him the meaning was clear: Jesus' cloak was seamless because his nature was—these are favorite words with him in De sacramentis— "undivided" and "single" ("individuus," "simplex").

The allegorizing we have surveyed is mainly of Old Testament passages. For students of Scripture in Colet's day the interest of the Old Testament depended largely on its foreshadowing the Christian dispensation. In its often colorful pages the devout imagination of the Fathers ranged freely in the search for types that foreshadowed what was to come, and it is evident that Colet sympathized with the quest. Indeed for him and the scholars of his time the question was not whether the Old Testament could be interpreted allegorically but rather what independent significance, if any, attached to the Old Testament now that what it prophesied darkly was fully revealed in the New.[7] The early church had still justified the Old Testament's survival because of its "prophecies," but even this argument left the great bulk of the Old Testament without any very obvious purpose under the New Law.

Of the Old Law Colet had a poor opinion. Throughout his one independent treatise of some length, De sacramentis, runs the leitmotiv that the Old Law is a mere "shadow" that is nothing alongside "the truth." Moreover the Old Testament failed in what was for the homiletic exegete the principal task of the Law: to make men better. Much struck by Paul's paradoxical remark that the Law had caused sin to abound (Rom. 7:7–14) Colet drew his own paradox, that the Law was a moral failure because it did not raise men to the moral level to which it nevertheless insisted they rise: "The Mosaic Law required [for its implementation] men who were righteous, without, however, making them such" (CM, 186). At best it was a basically "sound prescription" but addressed to people too "weak" to respond adequately (RO, 258). The contrasts he draws between the two Testaments demonstrate that the older has for him almost nothing that remains precious under the Christian dispensation. "The difference between the Old Testament and the New Testament is this, that the Old is incomplete and provisional, while the New is complete and eternal." Furthermore, "the Old was indulgent toward human emotions and permissive to a considerable degree, while the New virtually extinguishes [carnal] emotions and gives free, spontaneous enjoyment on a higher level," that of spirit (RO, 244). The exaltation of spirit over flesh is for Colet unfailing evidence of superiority.

Colet's answer to the question of what significance still attached to the Old Testament was characteristically decisive. The two Testaments were weighed in moral scales only, and by that standard the older was found sadly wanting. He paid it the incidental tribute of allegorizing it here and there, but he was clearly impatient to get on with the work of interpreting the Christian revelation. Though Moses was "God's scribe" (RO, 257) God had dictated clearer messages elsewhere—clearer, that is, to those who had eyes to see and ears to hear.

The Esoteric Strain in the Gospels

Reading the New Testament rightly was not a simple business. We have seen that the apparently simple notion of literal meaning conceals a series of subtle qualifications required by the fact that the author is God. Every time that Colet offered the mass he would read again Paul's words "O the depth of the riches of the wisdom and the knowledge of God! How incomprehensible are his judgments, and how unsearchable his ways!"— words that would give any exegete pause as he considered the apparently simple words of the text before him. The problems posed by Scripture's divine authorship were nevertheless widely recognized problems and Colet could draw on much earlier work for help.

Much in the New Testament, preeminently in the Epistles, seems to carry its full meaning in its literal sense. Even here, however, Colet had a strong personal sense of the final hiddenness of truth. He set himself to work out the methods we will consider below for discovering it in the Pauline texts. But the hiddenness of truth he found also in the very core of the New Testament, the account of Jesus' teachings given in the Gospels. His commentary on Matthew is, unhappily, lost; it would be of great interest to read what he made of the passage (Matt. 11:25) in which Christ says to his Father, "I thank you, Father, for hiding these things from the learned and the intelligent and revealing them to mere children," paralleled word for word in Luke 10:21. But from the writings that survive there can be no doubt that Colet was deeply impressed by the esoteric strain in the Gospels, which he saw reaching its height in the practice of Jesus himself.

Throughout the Gospels, but especially in Matthew, Jesus is represented as rereading texts of the Old Testament with a creative insight that brings out at last their full meaning. Through his exegesis of them it became clear that they had all the while been "speaking otherwise." Christ was God, so that the meanings he discerned in the Old Testament, though hidden, were indisputably there.

Even more remarkable texts that "spoke otherwise" were Jesus' own parables. Far from being the simple stories they might appear, they are riddling and paradoxical. It is often forgotten, but it was not forgotten by Colet, that when Jesus, gathered with his immediate followers around a campfire after a day of preaching, was asked why he taught in parables, his answer was straightforward and startling: So that "they" will not understand. The full passage runs:

> When he was alone, the Twelve, together with the others who formed his company, asked what the parables meant. He told them, "The secret of the Kingdom of God is given to you, but to those who are outside everything comes in parables, so that *they may see and see again, but not perceive; may hear and hear again, but not understand; otherwise they might be converted and be forgiven.*" (Mark 2:10–12)

This is not a beloved passage in a democratic age, but it is paralleled in both the other synoptic Gospels.[8] The italicized words in the quotation from Mark are a prophecy of Isaiah[9] which the evangelists all invoked, seemingly to explain the limited success of Jesus' preaching; outside the parable context it is applied to Jesus by John also.[10] Finally, Paul hurls the same prophecy after the departing Jews who had spent a whole day arguing with him about Jesus' message but remained unconvinced; he calls after them the words of their own prophet Isaiah and announces that he will address himself henceforward to the Gentiles instead of the Jews. On this dramatic note the Acts of the Apostles ends.[11]

Such passages concerning Jesus' manner of teaching made a strong impression on Colet. Allusions to eyes that do not see and ears that do not hear are very frequent in his writings. At bottom, Colet's sensitivity to this side of Jesus' teaching is the reason why Colet believes the interpreter of Scripture must above all other qualifications be a spiritual man. It is precisely the burden of the Gospels that the wise and cultured among those who listened to Jesus often remained unbelievers; hence the recourse to Isaiah's prophecy. After Paul's explanation of Christianity delivered on the Areopagus in the cultural capital of the Roman world, he found he had made exactly one convert, the famous Dionysius. Access to the inner meaning of the sacred texts, Colet concluded, must require something more than appeals to reason and the apparatus of scholarship. From this perspective his denunciation of secular scholarship and secular philosophy becomes not perhaps more attractive but more intelligible and even logical. And when Colet had hold of a congenial truth, or partial truth, he pressed it hard and took little notice of passages that told for another view; he retained the mental habits he had already demonstrated in the "Disputatiuncula."

Such an approach to the mysterious meanings of Scripture looks like a recipe for trouble in a dogmatic and heresy-minded age. For Colet, however, it was not; for he did not proclaim his discoveries from the rooftops. We learn of his ideas mainly from the essentially private medium of writings intended for "friends and the learned" and in the last analysis for himself, writings in which he expresses himself with considerable freedom. His range of speculation and quest for underlying significances was bounded, however, by another line of thought which he entertained with equal conviction.

The Extrabiblical Esoteric Tradition

Colet's overmastering desire was for revealed truth in all its fullness. The Church taught, and Colet eagerly assented, that parallel to the written revelation contained in Scripture was an unwritten revelation committed to the Church and transmitted orally from age to age. We have noticed that in commenting on Genesis Colet contrasted the "simple story" delivered in pictorial terms to the uninitiated common people with the true and deep interpretation given by God to Moses and transmitted by him to Joshua, with the prohibition against disseminating it or writing it down. The same was true of the New Testament:

> In addition to [the books of the New Testament] there was a certain secret system [*racio*] of wisdom not committed to writing by the Apostles but preserved with reverence and holiness in their minds and hearts. This these worthy men had learned from Christ Jesus, and thenceforward they transmitted it to none but the worthy, men like themselves, and commanded them not to reduce it to writing. (DEH, 203)

Typically, this description of the parallel revelation known as "tradition" is followed by yet another warning not to throw pearls before swine.

If alongside the New Testament there was, as Colet believed, a parallel revelation, likewise originating with Jesus Christ but fully known only to the Church, it followed that only the Church was in a position to judge authoritatively among rival interpretations of the written revelation, the New Testament. By drawing on tradition thus understood, the Church could and did condemn interpretations of Scripture found to be in error and confer on the correct interpretation an authority thenceforward unchallengeable.

His firm adherence to the dogma of tradition is part of the reason for Colet's notable lack of historical curiosity. We have seen him recording differences between the ancient and the contemporary forms of baptism, for example, but because the Church possessed authoritative unwritten traditions the changes must be right. Emphasizing the divine origins of the Church, Colet concludes:

> Hence we must believe that the sacrifices, rites and customs [in use] in the Church, and the Church itself have grown from the laws laid down by the Apostles. After his resurrection Jesus himself revealed what the Scriptures meant regarding the founding and establishing of the new Church in himself.

He then quotes (with a textual reference, contrary to his professed custom but in apparent tribute to the doctrine's importance) Pope St. Leo the Great: "Whatever has been devoutly received as custom by the Church comes down to us from the Apostles and the teaching of the Holy Spirit"; hence these laws and customs "are all obediently to be observed" (DEH, 197). As we have come by now to expect, this passage is followed a few lines later by a warning against casting pearls before swine.

The Church's Authority and the Limitations on "Spiritual" Interpretation

Colet's quotation from Pope St. Leo pointed, though unintentionally, to the ultimately problematical nature of the Church's position. Its essence required that it be the authority that guaranteed interpretations of Scripture, even though Scripture, being the self-revelation of the Infinite, was radically polysemous. This meant that the Church, which itself arose in consequence of the interpretation of certain symbolic meanings of scriptural texts, had at some stage to call a partial halt to the very process to which it owed its own origins. It could not allow the continued free operation of interpretation, with its unpredictable consequences. The Church sought to halt the process by converting symbolism, which does not have an agreed code, to allegory, which may or does. "But the problem remains: Quis custodiet custodes?"[12]

Colet may not have thought out the problem in these terms, but he accepted the position that the Church's final authority extended not only to the interpretation of biblical texts but to all formal changes introduced under its aegis. Colet knew that the powers contained in tradition had been exercised against positions he might be supposed to have sympathized with, but when the chips were down he sided with the authority of the Church. And we shall see in chapter 10 that Foxe the martyrologist was quite right in numbering Colet among the "persecutors" of heretics and Lupton quite wrong in pooh-poohing Foxe's assertion.

Among the most famous cases, close to Colet's time, in which the Church exercised its right to determine the meaning of Scripture was that of the Spiritual Franciscans. The Franciscans of the fourteenth and early fifteenth centuries were sure they could demonstrate from the text of Scripture that as a matter of historical fact Jesus and his Apostles did not hold property either individually or in common, nor did they enjoy the usufruct of property held on their behalf. The stakes were high in the controversy. If the Franciscans were right then they were almost the only religious still following Christ's teaching on property; their fidelity to Christ would be a standing reproach to the comfortable lifestyle of ecclesiastics on the higher levels. Pope Nicholas III indeed agreed with the Franciscans, but John XXII later reversed that determination and—citing the Church's authority to determine the meaning of the Scripture committed to its care—condemned the Franciscan view of evangelical poverty.

The case of John Hus, which interested Colet and his clerical circle,[13] provided another object lesson in interpreting Scripture correctly. Hus and his followers were convinced that the Bible spoke of a universal church composed solely of those predestined to be saved. For them the visible church, even to the extent that its members were predestined to be saved, was only a portion of that larger church made up of all the saved of all the ages, past and future. Only this church, they concluded, was the true church, which could read aright the revelation of God. Hus's array of passages from the Gospels and Epistles did not convince the Council of Constance, where the same passages were authoritatively interpreted otherwise. Refusing to accept the new official interpretation of the texts in question, Hus was burnt as a heretic.[14]

In both these cases interpretations of the scriptural texts which threatened the institutional structure of the Church were uncompromisingly condemned, no matter how plausible they might be in scholarly terms. These epochal cases from a few generations earlier must have pulled Colet in opposing directions. On the one hand, his ardent and absolutist temperament would respond to the idealism of the Spiritual Franciscans and of Hus. He was intensely alive to the mysterious dimensions of revelation. In himself he thought he discerned the workings of the Spirit which he believed essential to insightful biblical interpretation. On the other hand, as a working churchman Colet knew that structure and law are also indispensable if the Church is to carry on day by day with its teaching and ministry, and keep things going between the unscheduled visits of the Spirit. The wavering frontiers between Spirit and authority testified to the real claims of each position. The Spirit that bloweth where it listeth could certainly be inconvenient to administrators, and yet without it the Church would become desiccated and formalistic.

In the end, Colet regularly came down on the side of authority. Men in the mass, without authoritative guidance, were for him a kind of monster with many feet and no head (FEM, 88). Moreover his extravagant exaltation of ecclesiastical law above all other law probably had deeper roots than its rather sketchy official pedigree traced all the way back to Jesus. A personality like Colet's, with plenty of insurgent affect, would sympathize from experience with the need for structure and repression.

The Ultimately Practical Idealism of Colet's Exegesis

It is important to remember that Colet's own exegesis, to which we may now turn, is intended not for the man in the street but for intimates who, like himself, are "spiritual" men. Only under the guidance of the Holy Spirit, Colet was convinced, could one read the Scripture with understanding and profit. As Paul himself had said, the average Christian was still at the stage of imbibing "milk" like a baby, while "solid food" was reserved for the few.[15] Writing as he did for the latter audience, Colet expressed ideas or at least used formulations that if pressed could have led to charges of heresy against the enthusiastic exegete. But in public his expressions would have been tempered by the awareness that most professed Christians could not digest "solid food." Thus for all his hermetic interests Colet's fundamental concern remained practical. His ultimate aim had nothing to do with theorizing. It was identical with what he said Paul's aim was: to raise up progeny for the Church (C, 228 [196], 232 [204]).

Though often Colet enthusiastically searched out allegory, his notes on Dionysius's *Celestial Hierarchy* show how different his more practical Western temper was from that of Paul's Greek "pupil." In chapter 6 Dionysius worries at the question of exactly how each of the nine celestial hierarchies acquires the consecration to its appointed task, a question that Colet brushes aside impatiently with the comment, "Only God knows everything" (DCH, 176). Uninterested in Dionysius's speculations concerning the compatibility of free will in man with God's omnipotence, he simply decided the question was "too hard" (183). In chapter 12 Dionysius works out at length general principles that serve to explain how qualities that characterize higher essences in the hierarchy can be predicated of lower ones also, a problem that Colet ignores entirely. Another aspect of the same problem is discussed at length in chapter 13; Colet omits the entire chapter. In chapter 14 Dionysius speculates on the vast numbers mentioned in Daniel 7:10; Colet omits this chapter too. In the long chapter 15 Dionysius tries to penetrate to the invisible realities signified by a very long list of terms the Bible uses to designate or describe angels; Colet gives a perfunctory summary in one page of Dionysius's ten (187). Colet, the pragmatic idealist, seems always to be asking, "Yes, but what do we actually see when the veils of mystery are plucked aside?" He is interested in everything that could point to Christ, but in metaphysical speculation he shows no interest whatever.

The same practical indifference toward what to others were deep theological problems appears in his account of faith and its relation to works. He was certainly not indifferent to faith as such; it is simply that for him it did not present problems. He seems not to have thought of it as the shattering, revolutionary experience it had been for Paul. His neoplatonic bent made him see grace as working not violently but gradually and gently (C, 223 [188]), and his portrayal of its action in terms of neoplatonic rays (C, 199, 200 [146]) tells against any absolutist, either-or conception. He operates on the unargued assumption that the several terms by which faith is designated in the two Testaments are essentially equivalent (cf. R, 261), and for that matter he twice uses the definition of faith provided by Cicero (R, 230, 261)—a proof of how natural and instinctive he assumed faith to be. For him the biblical *locus classicus* on faith is "that definition of faith which the apostle Paul has in his letter to the Hebrews [11:1]," the splendid passage beginning in the Authorized Version, "Faith is . . . the evidence of things not seen."[16]

This definition does not confront the faith-works problem at all, and the evidence suggests that the problem held no interest for Colet. Quoting the key text Romans 1:17; he says of the last few words, "But what he means by adding 'to faith' [*in fidem*] I frankly confess I do not know" (RO, 209). Lupton points out rightly (RO, p. 62 n.1) that with very little trouble Colet could have found the reason in Clement of Alexandria or other early writers; he simply was not interested. It seems never to have occurred to him that faith alone could suffice for salvation, as Luther was to argue. He took for granted that Romans 1:17 must be perfectly compatible with the Church's carefully developed tradition according to which faith and works were essentially complementary. Sir Henry Colet's son and a born Londoner, John Colet had an instinctive regard for works. The importance of Romans 1:17 had been clear for centuries before

Luther; because it attributed man's salvation to faith it attracted a huge volume of commentary during the Middle Ages,[17] but for Colet the question that fascinated the academic exegetes scarcely existed. To him it was self-evident that "everyone is rewarded according to his works" (C, 170 [86]), and he quotes John and James at length to the effect that good works will necessarily follow if faith is genuine. How little he thought anything important was at stake in the matter of faith and works is shown by his making the perfectly casual statement "The just man lives by faith [the words of Rom. 1:17] and by the true worship of God" while on the same page adding, with no sense of contradicting Romans 1:17, that "man's business and merit reside entirely in doing" ("res et laus hominis tota est posita in actione"; R, 137). Neither justification nor faith is even mentioned in the two-page introduction he prefixed to his second work on Romans (RO, 199–200).

Theological subtleties were not a preoccupation of Colet's. He was deeply suspicious of speculative scholarship and regarded the scholastic method in theology as almost impious. "Knowledge puffeth up" was a Pauline insight that Colet thoroughly endorsed. He had a vision of the exegete's true work which looked in different directions altogether from most of the ecclesiastical activity he saw around him. At the close of his "Proemium" to Romans he lashes out yet again at "those secular would-be philosophers" ("illi philosophiculi mundi") and declares his sense of what learning and preaching should actually aim at. The phrase in which he distills this personal vision is "viva sapientia" ("living wisdom"; RO 203).

"Living wisdom"—the stress is on the first word—turns away from ostentation and pride and vain curiosity. "Living wisdom makes man worship God humbly, and live temperately, and lovingly serve his fellow man." In this fine description Colet at last succeeds in doing justice to himself. His positive aims are often in danger of being swamped by the negative tone, dismissive and hostile and often intemperate, in which so many of his pages are written. In the concept of "living wisdom," however, he turns to a positive goal, one that gives unity to his own work as both exegete and preacher. We shall have to consider the exegete and the preacher successively, but in principle their aims were intimately one: to reconcile man with God and thus with himself through the knowledge that would kindle love. The exegete proffered knowledge while the preacher kindled love; both were needed in principle, but Colet had no doubt that "ignorant love can do a thousand times more than a frigid wisdom" (DEH, 219).

If for convenience one speaks of the "method" of Colet's exegesis it is important to remember that he was convinced that the deeper meaning of the Scriptures was deliberately concealed from common eyes by its divine author. It followed that scholarship could play at best only a subordinate role, for the exegete's dependence is finally on the illumination he is granted. Of method in the sense of technique there can hardly be a question, so subordinate is every other factor to spiritual insight that comes from above if it comes at all.

The exegete who hopes for the good gift of spiritual insight knows that it comes, like "every good gift and every perfect gift," "from above" (R, 179). He can, however, do something for himself, by approaching his work in a prayerful frame of mind and by exciting devotion through fasting. Colet's ascetic mode of life must have been motivated at least in part by the desire to render himself a fitting vessel for the divine grace that he needed in order to read the Scripture with spiritual insight. His meals were few and meager, and while he ate he had a servant read aloud from some favorite author, usually Paul. The needs of the carnal man were barely met, in the evident hope that the insights of the spiritual man would be sharpened by self-abnegation. This connection between exegesis and asceticism, already noticed, is rarely stated, but one feels that it was a major element in Colet's mode of life.

The emphasis on asceticism shades into another pattern that we occasionally glimpse in Colet's work. The prayerful frame of mind just mentioned was part of a three-stage pattern in common use in the spiritual and monastic tradition to which Colet in basic ways belongs. In that tradition it assumed the form *lectio—meditatio—oratio*.[18] First the passage is read, slowly and repeatedly, to discern the literal shape and meaning of the pericope. This reading leads to a meditation that is in effect a spiritual or allegorical interpretation; this in turn culminates in a prayer refreshed by the insight the interpreter has gained through the process. In this manner, for example, Colet reads the passage in Genesis 22 describing the journey Abraham made as he took his son Isaac to the destined place of sacrifice. The literal meaning is acceptable and does not necessarily call for allegorical interpretation. Nevertheless Colet sees in the literal account a spiritual significance as well: the ram that Abraham sacrifices is the "old" man so often evoked in Paul; the thorns in which it is entangled are "the cares of this world," freed from which the ram becomes "a pleasing victim." This spiritual meditation leads to a prayer: "May every Christian, as a spiritual son of Abraham, imitate Abraham, and one day rest in felicity in Abraham's bosom" (RO, 225–226). Later in the same treatise one finds Colet employing a formal prayer of some length to close the significances that his meditation has found in the course of Romans 3—a prayer beginning, "O ineffable, admirable, and adorable Mediator Jesus," and concluding with "Amen" (245). One catches a glimpse of the pattern also in the conclusion to chapter 5 of the *Ecclesiastical Hierarchy*, with its prayer to "merciful Jesus" (DEH, 248). The later section on infant baptism[19] is similarly given by Colet a form, not in Dionysius, according to the three-stage process we have discussed. Only the *lectio* comes from Dionysius; the spiritual significance discovered by his *meditatio* is Colet's own, as is the concluding *oratio* (DEH, 272).

Not only did Colet train his own mind to make a flight heavenward when he read or heard a text of Scripture, but he taught his pupils the same approach. In the colloquy "Pia confabulatio" (1522), written shortly after Colet's death, Erasmus has a former pupil of Colet's describe a method he had learned from the dean:

> Suppose [during the Mass] the Epistle is read on "Purge out therefore the old leaven, that ye may be a new lump, as ye are unleavened." With respect to these words I speak inwardly to Christ in this manner: "May I be truly unleavened, pure of every leaven of sin. But thou, Lord Jesus, who alone art pure of all sin and without stain, grant that every day I may more and more purge out the old leaven." Again, if perchance the Gospel is read about the sower sowing his seed, I pray by myself thus: "Happy the man who deserves to be good ground: and I beg that he without whose blessing nothing at all is good may by his kindness make good ground of me, who am barren earth." These are examples . . .

When asked, "What Thales taught you this philosophy?" the speaker, called Gaspar in the colloquy, replies that as a boy he had been a member of the "household of the worthiest of men, John Colet." He adds moreover, again in the spirit of his mentor, "What I read in Sacred Scripture and the Apostles' Creed I believe with complete confidence, nor do I search further [*nec ultra scrutor*]."[20] It is likely that "Gaspar" stands for Thomas Lupset, who was for years a pupil in Colet's household.[21] The important point, in any case, is that it is not scholarly scrutinizing but prayer and implicit faith that Colet inculcated into the pupils who lived in his house, even lads of scholarly inclination like "Gaspar."

Colet brought the same meditative approach to the writings of the Dionysius whom he thought Paul's disciple. Lupton admitted, though belatedly, that what he had been calling "abstracts" of Dionysius were not really abstracts (DCH, p. xlv). Instead they are Colet's selective and strongly personal responses to his text. We have already noticed places where he paid little attention or none at all to chapters on subjects that interested Dionysius but not him, while elsewhere he dwells lovingly on topics not present in Dionysius. Always he reads his text with an eye to its usefulness in leading man to Christ.

The Distinction between "Interpreter of Scripture" and "Grammarian"

Colet further specifies the kind of exegesis he is working in by making an important distinction—a distinction that deserves far more attention than it has received. The context adds to the interest of the passage. In RO, Colet recounts for a friend the results of a study of Romans which he made for the benefit of a young man named Edmund; Colet was so pleased with the results that he recorded them for the friend and later had them inscribed permanently on vellum. The distinction he drew here was a distinction basic to his approach, yet Seebohm and Lupton chose not to notice what Colet was saying.

Coming upon a word unfamiliar to his pupil, "privaricator" in Colet's spelling, he explains its meaning to Edmund. He adds carefully, however, that in giving this explanation he is making an exception: "It is not the business of an interpreter of Scripture to do a commentator's job and scrutinize too minutely [individual] words" ("interpretis scripturarum non est grammatici officium agere, scrupulosiusque verba examinare"; RO, 222). The close scrutiny of his text is exactly what nineteenth-century scholars did expect of the "interpreter of Scripture," but Colet had in mind something quite different.

However surprising the idea that the *interpres scripturarum* need not concern himself with every detail of his text, Colet's distinction between the commentator, who of course must discuss every point in his text, and the "interpreter," who need not "scrutinize too minutely [individual] words," has precedent in a writer known to have influenced him deeply. Marsilio Ficino prefaces each dialogue of Plato by what Colet would call an "interpretation." A close parallel to Colet's thought is found in Ficino's preface to Plato's *Meno*. There Ficino tells the reader that his preface, or "Argumentum," passes over the geometric figures that are a notable feature of that dialogue. An "argumentum," he explains, "seeks to bring out the whole argument in general terms and to get at its essence" ("Argumentum autem summam rei caputque requirit"). To clarify this operative definition Ficino then draws the same distinction that Colet does: "Discussing details is the business not of a preface [*argumenti*] but of a commentary."[22] Ficino regarded the "preface" as giving the "interpreter" a good deal of freedom to point out to the reader the "essence" of the work he was treating. Ficino's translation of Plotinus likewise contains prefaces to orient the reader; in pursuing this aim Ficino does not hesitate, for example, to propose for *Ennead* I.iii a title giving a clearer idea of its actual contents than the traditional title does.[23]

On the "Track"
of Scripture's Meaning:
Colet as Hunter and Pastor

With Ficino's prestigious example as a clue, we may profitably turn now to a second main cluster of metaphors that Colet adopts to describe the work of the "interpreter of Scripture" as he understands that term. We have already seen that, profoundly convinced that the meaning of the sacred texts was concealed from common eyes, Colet uses a cluster of metaphors reflecting the activity of digging out, extracting, hammering out, and the like. He uses this group of metaphors in connection with the meaning of individual passages or shorter units of text. To bring out larger patterns, which Ficino thought the special province of the interpreter, Colet uses metaphors of the hunt. And since his ultimate interests were always homiletic, we shall see that he was always searching for ways to make the insights he hunted out spiritually fruitful for his audience.

An interesting example of the metaphor of the hunt comes at a critical point in R. His original intention, one will remember, was to conclude after the first eleven chapters of Romans. When he finally consented to continue to the end of the Epistle, he took the occasion to look back on what he had been doing in the first eleven chapters and to speak of what he intended to do in what would now follow. In so doing he sought also to justify what looked like a penchant for digression. He saw himself as prepared once again to "follow in Paul's footsteps, as I did earlier. And if at times I wander from the matter at hand, to the extent necessary for clearer explanation, I will nevertheless return to the path in such fashion that it will become clear that I never actually departed from the track of Paul" (R, 175). Sometimes Paul's "footsteps" lead through open country, and then the "path" ("via") is easy to follow. At other times it will disappear to the inexperienced eye, and it will look as if one's guide is simply wandering about none too sure himself of where the trail is. But in due time he will be vindicated by triumphantly recovering the "track" ("semita") of Paul and it will be clear that he knew what he was doing all along.

The conviction that Paul's argument is often latent and needs a spiritually keen eye to discern it came to Colet early. We find it expressed in the margins of the copy of Ficino's *Epistolae* that he annotated while a graduate student: "It is the sagacious man who selects and gets to know the byways, and finds what was hidden" (FEM, 99). Another passage in the Ficino volume expresses the same conviction in Ficino's own rapturous language—a passage that, significantly, comes from the one of Ficino's letters that Colet annotated more heavily than any other. In it we hear again of the sage, Colet's "sagax," and the hunt: "O hunter most sage, who in this deep forest that is the world tracks down the most completely hidden traces of God and brings them to light!"[24]

Having hunted out a scriptural passage's meaning, Colet then tried to pass on to the reader this understanding by orienting him to the main theme of what he was about to read. Colet does this so frequently—medieval exegetes had tried to do it too[25]—that a few specimens must suffice. He opens his work on First Corinthians by putting the reader in possession of what he sees as the leading ideas, adding that "if these things are known and attended to the Epistle once read will be more easily understood" (C, 159 [64]). Rather like the outline a lecturer might put on the blackboard, the summary Colet offers divides the Epistle into eight sections, each unified by a key idea. Where he differs from more conventional guides to the Epistle is in the themes he highlights, themes he feels sure were more important for Paul than they might seem. Chapters 9 through 11, for example, Colet sees as a unit, which he describes in the following terms:

> The Apostle says something about himself, asserting that he has the right to do many things that he does not do; he had the right to a living from preaching the Gospel, but while among the Corinthians he deliberately decided not to claim it, so that people would not think he was teaching in order to get food. Likewise in this part is that women should have their heads covered in church and men their heads uncovered. In this mention of a small matter deep mysteries are hidden. Likewise about the meeting of the Corinthians at the Lord's supper, and their communicating there, which Paul wishes done in a holy, sober, and loving manner. (C, 160 [66])

The reader who has these three chapters in mind and thinks he knows them, will be a little disconcerted. Gone are the well-known quotations, "Many indeed run the race but only one receives the crown," or "lest having preached to others I myself should become a castaway." Instead Colet takes up and recombines elements that he finds more important than the unaided reader might suppose. The followers of Moses in the desert, Paul says, "all ate the same spiritual food and drank the same spiritual drink" (Rom. 10:3), a passage followed almost immediately by the one that whetted Colet's interest: "[T]hese things all happened as symbols for us." Taking this as a hint that other things mentioned by Paul may be "symbols for us" too, he turns to the "small matter" that women, unlike men, are to cover their heads in church. Paul finds "deep mysteries" indeed in this prescription, but in his own commentary Colet finds a further deep mystery that Paul had not expressed, or at least not openly. "Paul seems, though he is talking of something else and uses roundabout language," to wish to inculcate another lesson without being ostentatious about it:

if women's hair is loose in church it will stimulate their vanity and also arouse sexual interest in young men, for "by women's hair as by bait young men are taken [*adolescentes capiuntur*]" (C, 240 [222])—a bit of unintended autobiography. In his handling of this three-chapter unit Colet is convinced that the Spirit has guided him in his hunt for Paul's "track" and helped him to read in the norms about head coverings a lesson that might otherwise have been missed.

Colet's pastoral concerns turned his discoveries of hidden truths into guidance for the serious Christian. An example of his ultimately homiletic interests is his treatment of chapter 2 in Romans, which also begins with a statement of the chapter's latent theme. Colet was very fond of ternaries, and sees Paul as proclaiming three aspects of the three persons of the triune God: his goodness, his prudence, and his justice (RO, 215). But the real goal, as usual, is not metaphysical but homiletic. By the end of the chapter (227) Colet is making Paul's doctrine yield moral fruit for contemporary Christians. He applies Paul's concern with the relations between Christians and pagans to those whom Colet regards as "pseudo-Christians." Quite naturally this application leads to the scandalous strife within the contemporary Christian community itself (RO, 227–229).

A further example of the overall pattern by which Colet announces at the outset the unit's leading themes and then draws them out in detail, with homiletic applications to the present day, is his treatment of 1 Corinthians 10. As in Romans 2, he states at the outset that 1 Corinthians 10, while seemingly concerned with the persistent problem of whether Christians could eat food sacrificed to idols, has as its real purpose to lead the Corinthians to "sincere . . . communion with Christ" (C, 235 [210]); and to do this Paul tries to persuade his hearers of three pertinent theological truths on which Colet descants at length. Colet pays no attention to the concrete historical situation to which Paul addressed himself. Instead, the three theological truths Colet sees as underlying the chapter's argument are then specifically applied to his own day. To this extent Colet's treatment of 1 Corinthians 10 is similar to that of Romans 2. In the chapter from Corinthians, however, Colet now adds a further method he found useful in his homiletic approach, the use of *sententiae*.

Colet's use of *sententiae*, or detached aphorisms, was at least in part a response to a problem that must have worried him a good deal. Even the person who prays is continually beset by the distractions of this world. He seems to have thought that by distilling the teachings of Paul into *sententiae* he could at least give the busy and distracted layman a truth in portable form which he could meditate on in a brief interval of leisure and keep ready as a principle of conduct. In this manner he could meet the needs of the well-disposed but harried Christian without compromising or diluting the message itself.

Though the use of *sententiae* seems to become more conspicuous in the later writings, it is evident as an intellectual habit already in the volume of Ficino's letters that Colet annotated while still in Italy. There he extracts three *sententiae* from a letter entitled "Amidst Evils the Only Refuge Is to the Highest Good," namely God (FEM, 119). Ficino himself liked *sententiae*, and Colet transcribed or paraphrased several in the margins (FEM, 99–100). Even from Dionysius's *Celestial Hierarchy* Colet, ever alert for moral applications of what he read, took five maxims that applied the implications of hierarchy to the individual's moral life (DCH, 174). He extracted *sententiae* not only from entire epistles but also from single chapters. The Trinity College, Cambridge, manuscript, datable as we have seen to mid-1516 at the earliest, is rich in groups of *sententiae*. It opens with a solid page and a half of miscellaneous aphorisms. The same manuscript also contains (49^v–50^r) a group of *sententiae* drawn from Romans 11, and concludes with three pages of carefully written propositions under the heading "Ex primo ca: ad Ro" (62^r–63^r). These overtly moralistic *sententiae* were not what the nineteenth century expected of an "Oxford Reformer." Lupton arbitrarily left the whole Trinity manuscript unpublished except for P. Its handsome form, however, shows that near the end of his life its author was of a different opinion from his Victorian admirers'.

Seebohm's Censorship of Colet's Triumph

Not only did Seebohm and Lupton ignore Colet's Trinity manuscript with its collections of *sententiae*. They censored a letter by Colet containing a further collection of *sententiae* even though Colet himself thought it was one of the best things he had ever done and wanted it to serve as a memorial to him when he was dead. The context is worth recalling.

One of the works in the Cambridge holograph is a letter from Colet to Richard Kidderminster, abbot of Winchcombe. The letter is long and circumstantial, recounting an incident that obviously pleased Colet greatly. A fellow priest had called on him the previous evening and brought along his own handwritten copy of St. Paul's Epistles. He told Colet how much the latter's lectures had helped increase his admiration of Paul and was soon begging him to bring out extempore some of the meanings that Colet told him were latent in almost every word of the apostle's writings, awaiting the reader who would "carefully consider" them. Up to this point both Seebohm and Lupton dwell enthusiastically on every detail of the scene, as an instance of the impact of the Oxford lectures. Seebohm gives this first part of the letter one and a half pages of combined quotation and close paraphrase, and Lupton translates every single word.

When it comes to what Colet actually found in Romans, however, both informants unexpectedly grow mute. Lupton cuts Colet off after seven lines: "After a long string of similar 'propositions,' Colet concludes"— and only then returns to word-for-word translation for the whole of the rest of the letter.[26] For Seebohm, even the seven lines that Lupton allows Colet's exegesis of Romans 1 is too much. Seebohm's book runs to 543 pages; to include the whole of the passage from Colet that he suppresses, from one of Colet's very few surviving letters, would have made it only one page longer.[27] But the reason for the complete suppression of the content of Colet's exegesis becomes clear as soon as one turns to what it says.

Colet reports both himself and his fellow priest as using the vocabulary of exegesis which we have seen to be characteristic of his extant writings: "eruere" ("dig out"), "depromere" ("draw forth"). His visitor hoped to learn from him some hints of "method" ("rationem") that he could apply when reading Paul on his own. Though the letter is not dated, it belongs at some point between the winter of 1498–1499 (they are sitting by a "winter fireside") and that of 1504–1505. The earlier limit is established by the fact that Colet, who was ordained on 25 March 1498, speaks of his visitor as a "fellow priest"; the latter, by a reference to his lectures on Paul "during the previous term," since he would no longer allude to the academic calendar after leaving Oxford to take up his duties as dean in London. A hint that the letter may belong to 1503 or later is Colet's saying to his correspondent near the end of the letter that he hopes this letter, which he wants returned to him, may after his own death "help preserve some memory of me." If it seems odd that a man in his mid-thirties would already have his mind fixed on his own death, I would suggest that Colet may have been writing in the wake of his brother Richard's death in the flower of young manhood in 1503 or 1504.

Everything we know about the letter signals its exceptional importance in Colet's own eyes. This is the only letter of his which has been preserved not by someone else or merely by chance but by his own positive act. He inserted it in the Cambridge holograph manuscript between his work on Romans (R) and that on First Corinthians. He says in the letter that though he usually does not keep copies of his own letters he wants this one back, to "help preserve some memory of me." Most important of all, the letter unquestionably dates from the period of his lectures at Oxford. Uniquely, it displays the features of his exegesis which inspired his caller to visit him in the first place and of which the lecturer himself was obviously proud.

Paradoxically, it is the letter's uniqueness as a record of the Oxford public lectures that ensured its suppression by Seebohm and Lupton. The reader who quickly refreshes his memory of Romans 1 will see there is plenty of work there for the historically minded critic. Instead, what Colet does, and what the visitor who had actually heard the Oxford lectures clearly expected him to do, is to "try to find how many and what kind of golden maxims [*aureae sententiae*] can be gathered [*colligi*] from only the first chapter of the Epistle to the Romans." Eager to make a record of the *sententiae* that Colet would "dig out" and "draw forth" from the text, the visitor proposed that he write down the *sententiae* as Colet dictated them. The part of the letter that comes next is the record of what Colet "dug up" from Romans 1. The key portion of this record—so important to Colet if so little to the taste of nineteenth-century writers on him—has never been printed in English. The only previous writer to quote the Latin original was Samuel Knight in his biography of 1724 (from the 1823 reprint of which I translate). Knight did not claim that Colet had launched an exegetical revolution; he merely tucked the letter into a long documentary appendix. For all its curious history this text is very instructive for anyone who wants to learn from Colet himself what his Oxford lectures were like. Lupton and Seebohm have translated the framing narrative; here is the centerpiece that Colet was so proud of and that his interpreters suppressed:

Faith in Christ comes from a calling by grace. Preaching Christ comes from being set apart. Paul was selected and sent by Christ. But all Christians are loved by God and holy. Grace and peace with God are what is most to be besought of God. It is men's faith that gives most ground for rejoicing and felicitation. Others are to be looked up to for making faith fruitful and rewarding. It is for the preacher of God's word to teach all men. At no time, in no place, and in no way must one be ashamed of the Gospel. A powerful justification of men by God is shown in the Gospel. The just man is the man who believes and trusts in God, while the man who trusts in created things of any sort is impious and unjust; whence it follows that justness is confidence in God, while trust in others is unjustness, connected with a lack of trust in God. What applies to faith applies also to the worship of God. To trust in anyone other than God is idolatry. From trust in God alone true worship of God arises. To know God in any manner but not to worship him is the gravest and most odious impiety. God speaks in his creation, and through it he shows himself to men. To learn of God through his creation, as those that philosophize seek to do, and yet not to worship him, is not only of no avail but does very great harm; from which it follows that it is better not to know God at all than to know him in some degree but not love and worship him. That is an offense against piety. There can be no excuse for any man not to worship God; all nations and peoples from the beginning of the world that have not worshiped God will be found guilty of impiety. If one has known God in any degree and has not at once worshiped him, his mind is darkened and his knowledge is as nothing. The ultimate folly is for a man to have a high opinion of his own wisdom and set a high value on himself. There is no greater proof of folly than to think oneself wise.

Ignorance arises from impiety and the neglect of God, and from impiety and ignorance together, as from a fountain, all other evils flow. The impious forsake God, and once they forsake God, God forsakes them; forsaken by God they fall headlong and rush into every kind of wickedness. Evils arise from a perverted will, a perverted will from ignorance, and ignorance from impiety. The ultimate impiety is the neglect of God; those that neglect God are neglected by him, and neglected by God they perish in numberless ways. From a perverse will arises unnatural perversion. Along with sin the punishment of sin, its wages, grows too. The last end of sin is eternal death, which sinners deserve. Alike deserving of eternal death are those who turn away from God and those who, though they know better, permit other men to turn away from him. It is up to the man who knows the right way to point it out to others and unceasingly summon them back to it, on pain of otherwise sharing in their ruin. (EK, 266–267)

Turning now to the addressee of the letter, Richard Kidderminster, Colet continues:

We garnered these thoughts from the first chapter of the Epistle to the Romans and set them down right away. Nor are these the only ones that could have been noted. From the salutation, for example, others may be gathered: that Christ was promised in the revelations of the prophets; that Christ sanctifies men, and through Christ is the resurrection of both their souls and their bodies; and innumerable others still that are contained in that first chapter, which a keen-sighted man will readily discern and can, if he so desires, dig out. Paul, even taken by himself, seems to me to be as it were a limitless sea of wisdom and piety . . . I have written this, good father, with my own hand, so that your mind, in its golden goodness, can see from this sample how much gold there is hidden in Paul. (EK, 267–268)

Here—*and here only*—can we be sure we are listening to the Colet of the Oxford lectures. In the "Disputatiuncula" Colet is pinned down by a superior opponent and cannot expatiate freely so as to display his own style of thought. By contrast, the priest who called upon Colet that winter evening had heard him lecture in his own preferred style; he naturally expected more in the same vein, with the additional advantage for him that he could copy down exactly the golden sentences that the lecturer "drew forth" from Paul's text. What he expected he got, for Colet reports that while "these few little propositions only skimmed the surface" of Paul's inexhaustible richness, his visitor left well "satisfied."

The visitor's satisfaction with his specimen of Colet's exegetical style during the time of the Oxford lectures was by no means shared by Seebohm and Lupton. They simply could not believe Colet's own words, that this was a specimen of the exegesis of Paul that he gave in his lectures at Oxford. Not that they express their dismay in so many words, of course.

They expatiate lovingly on the enthusiastic witness to the success of the lecturer, but then avert their eyes in embarrassment from what he proudly tells his visitor. When he reaches the heart of the letter, the part we have just read, Seebohm suppresses it entirely, with an uncandid aposiopesis and the bracketed remark "[Here follows a long list.]"[28] Lupton cuts his hero off after seven lines; in contrast to his usual adulation of everything Colet does, he refers to the "golden sentences" by which his hero wished to be remembered in after times as "a long string of similar 'propositions,' " which were apparently not even worth transcribing. This is surely very curious. We can only suppose that at work here is the same cause that made Colet's Victorian biographers glide rapidly over the "Disputatiuncula," the other authentic piece from Colet's Oxford period. In neither place was Colet speaking the part they had assigned to him. They were happy to thrust an anachronistic microphone toward him when he was denouncing wickedness and avarice in the clergy or what he considered the arrogance of St. Thomas Aquinas, and even happier if he chanced to say anything that might suggest historical interests. But when their paragon turned eagerly to allegory and "digging out" hidden moral meanings, the microphone suddenly went dead.

What Colet is doing in the letter to Kidderminster is nevertheless well worth attending to. In hardly more than a page the suppressed heart of the letter gathers up the themes that we have seen in this chapter to be characteristic of Colet's exegesis. Always disdainful of secular scholarship for its own sake, Colet does not see it as his business to give Paul's message a specific historical setting. Instead he gives it a timeless setting in which it addresses the concerns not specifically of first-century Romans but of everyman. The message can be discerned, he says, by "keen-sighted" interpreters, where the keen sight is of course spiritual. He could hardly call himself a spiritual man in his own letter, but it is in this literally enthusiastic spirit that he sets about his task. For the task, he uses the vocabulary with which we have become familiar, almost the whole panoply of terms by which he describes the exegetic enterprise: "effodere" ("dig out"), "eruere" ("extract"), "depromere" ("draw forth"), and "excudere" ("hammer out" or "forge"). The meaning the Apostle intended to convey, he assumed, lay beneath the verbal surface, concealed from unspiritual eyes. The exegete is needed not only to descry it in the first place and then dig it out but finally to give it shape. Near the end of the same letter Colet makes the process explicit. Its first two stages are recognized in the sentence we have already read, in which he speaks of significances "which a keen-sighted man will readily discern and can, if he so desires, dig out." The final stage, described in the conclusion to the letter (EK, 268), is to give it shape by making from "the golden material of Paul" separate "rings." These are the "golden maxims" ("aureae sententiae") that permit the interpreter's insight to assume a form his hearer can carry easily with him and meditate on as occasion allows. In this way that insight is transformed into the "living wisdom" that is Colet's ultimate aim.

Thus the letter to Kidderminster is, so far, thoroughly typical of Colet's exegesis. What remains to be considered is the other use to which "rings" can be put—to form a chain. Rereading the spiritual heart of the letter one soon notices that after a rather rough start the individual *sententiae* are so organized as to constitute a continuous and coherent argument. This, in the metaphor Colet liked to use, is the "semita," the sometimes hidden path taken by Paul that only the keen-sighted spiritual interpreter can follow. On the surface of it, Romans 1 falls into perhaps four sections of unequal length and importance: the salutation (verses 1–7), a prayer that his mission among the Romans will be fruitful (8–15), a statement that man is justified by faith (16–17), and a sharp denunciation of those who have a natural knowledge of God but do not worship him and are therefore punished by being allowed to lapse into unnatural passions (18–32). Colet sees as the key concept one not at all obtruded by Paul but nevertheless implicit, that of piety. Sympathetic to the "caeli enarrant" tradition, Colet followed Paul in supposing that God had revealed himself in some degree to all men. All consequently have the duty to worship him, he continued; the failure so to worship is impiety. From impiety follows ignorance. And if man is ignorant of his nature and duty several consequences make themselves felt. He commits the ultimate folly of thinking highly of himself, making all his knowledge vain. His ignorance of his true nature also perverts his will, which then seeks unnatural satisfactions. Such being the consequences of the ignorance resulting from impiety, those who have clearer knowledge have a duty to recall to the right path those who are ignorant and impious.

So interpreted, the pieces fall into place. It is his revelation that the key to the whole chapter is the concept of "piety" which so pleased Colet and made him think of the letter as a monument to his own creative intimacy with Paul. Once the key is in hand, it can be used to develop further unsuspected meanings latent in the text of the chapter. The potentially unlimited developments starting from the key concept of piety and its opposite justify Colet in saying that the letter only "skimmed the surface" ("delibasse"); for, once the true but latent central concept was known, repeated rereadings would bring more and more discoveries.

It would be an injustice to Colet to speak of his exegesis as simply moralistic. In the letter to Kidderminster he mentions that his visitor hoped also to pick up something of Colet's own "method" ("rationem"), which he could then "imitate." The essence of the method is to isolate the underlying key concepts in the light of which even seemingly disparate elements in the unit of discourse (often longer than one chapter) fall into meaningful relation to one another. But to employ this method the interpreter must be a spiritual man; he has to rely for his initial insight on the fruitful action of grace. Once the key concept is found, however, Colet is not content to rest on an exegetic achievement. Instead he uses it to promote "living wisdom" that will vivify and inspire man to achieve his supernatural destiny. Thus Colet's method, as he saw it, was in principle scientific: the spiritual man interpreted God's infallible text by means of God's infallible guidance. Its results were then put to the service of moral ends.

True to this method, Colet seems regularly to have sought for the underlying theme, what Paul was saying to those who had spiritual ears to hear and eyes to see. Not infrequently Colet says explicitly that a chapter, or what he sees as a unitary group of chapters, is to be read in the light of a given theme. At times he will use a quotation selectively, to buttress his leading idea; he explains, for example, that he has paraphrased a passage from Ficino in such a way as to fit it into the overall theme of the chapter he is elucidating (R, 157). More commonly he will announce either at the beginning or, retrospectively, at the close of a large unit the themes that give it unity. In setting to work on RO, for instance, he identifies three separate fronts on which Paul had problems (RO, 199); then within this larger framework he gives at times a more detailed analysis of the interconnected themes he finds in one of the constituent units. A case in point is chapter 4 of RO, where an unusually long disquisition on its main themes (247–251) precedes a detailed commentary beginning with the first verse.

Colet's quest for themes accounts also for another characteristic of his exegesis. Chapter 4 of RO just referred to is atypical in proceeding through the chapter more or less verse by verse. It is much oftener the case that the discovery of a chapter's theme causes Colet to read it very selectively, emphasizing the verses, sometimes only two or three, that bear clearly on the theme. Chapter 5 in RO is more typical in this respect. It too begins with a sort of introduction centering on the relation between the first Adam and Christ as second Adam, with Moses in an intermediate position. But the chapter itself is read quite selectively within this framework. This method of working is seen also in Colet's handling of the first chapter of First Corinthians. His exegesis is built around the concept of the Mystical Body of Christ. He must have decided that this was for Paul the underlying topic, and the commentary reads as if Colet began by asking himself, What reflections of the great truth of the Mystical Body are to be found in this chapter? Matters less relevant to the theme are hardly glanced at. Again in First Corinthians, notwithstanding the apparent disparity of topics in chapters 12 through 14, Colet finds that the three chapters are a single unit in which Paul is really speaking of spiritual things (C, 264 [272]). And C, like RO, is prefaced by an analytic summary of the work in terms of its underlying themes. In the third of the three Pauline commentaries we possess, the same function is served not by a preface but by a sort of afterword. It will be remembered that Colet originally ended R after chapter 11; his stint concluded, and using the language with which we are now familiar, he finds in looking back that he had "drawn forth" three main themes. Typically, these are phrased in a manner suggesting their importance for an individual's moral life (R, 174).

As a final variation of the quest for themes we may take a rather different piece of work from any considered so far, Colet's commentary on chapter 12 of First Corinthians. This comes from the late part of that commentary, whose chapters, as we saw, were added at different times in different hands and probably from different sources. The chapter in question here differs from all the others in C by having a heading—"Capud duodecimum"—and by sticking far closer to a verse-by-verse development than any of the other chapters do. It may have originated as something like the letter to Kidderminster, a report to a like-minded friend of a discovery made in that limitless sea of wisdom, the writings of Paul. At the outset he intimates his ambitious purpose, which is no less than to "reweave" the text of Paul so as to bring out hidden patterns—as he puts it a little self-consciously, to "consider the weave of the text, or rather the text rewoven" ("textum ipsum, vel retextum, contemplemur"; C, 245 [232]).[29]

In the course of so doing he finds correspondence between the nine "gifts" of the Holy Spirit enumerated in the Vulgate text of Paul and the nine hierarchies of angels (C, 246 [234]); he finds also that there are nine orders of rocks, metals, plants, animals, fish, and birds (252 [248]).[30] Coming now to man, Colet finds him a "microcosm" ("minor mundus") whose superior aspects reflect heaven and whose inferior aspects look toward earth: "The whole church is nothing other than an organ of the Spirit of God, the body, so to speak, of His Spirit." The gifts that come from God serve to raise man up, but at the same time they introduce what Colet ordinarily deplores, namely, a certain multiplicity. From it, however, he now finds that there arises in the church "a union of beauty with usefulness" ("pulchra utilitas et utilis pulchritudo"). Thus while the "gifts" of the spirit involve multiplicity and therefore in a sense degeneration from the one, yet the result is in the end creative: those members farther from the source increasingly lack beauty but compensate for this by ever greater usefulness.

By uncovering this fantasia of correspondences, for the richness of which Colet's text itself must be consulted, Colet is now able to make good on his promise to "reweave" the chapter so as to bring out its pattern. He closes with a remarkable catena of verses from the chapter itself which he puts together in a different arrangement that brings out, almost entirely in Paul's own words, the meaning that had underlain the text all the time but had required the experienced and spiritual eye to bring it out. It is evident that Colet regards this feat with considerable complacency.

Such, then, is the method that interested Colet's contemporaries and secured for his lectures the degree of esteem that they enjoyed—real enough, without being sensational. Because of Colet's commitment to "living wisdom," however, this method finds its complement only when its results can change men's lives. Distillation into golden axioms, or *sententiae*, was one means of doing this. Another was the sermon.

Colet's Sermons

From Erasmus's biographical letter we know that Colet was consciously training himself to preach while still in Italy (A, ll. 277–280). Already at that early period he understood that preaching was the necessary complement to his exegetical studies. With a glance at his sermons, then, we may appropriately close this study of his mature exegesis.

Not much more than a glance, unfortunately, is now possible. Apart from a single sermon delivered under special circumstances, we have only the large amount of incidental sermonizing in the extant writings. These, however, are moral applications of the teachings Colet found in Paul, not sermons proper. I think it is safe to say that these passages must give a very one-sided view of what Colet's preaching style was like. They err—or so I think—not so much in being intemperate and repetitive as in being so relentlessly spiritual that they hardly connect with the lives of most people. The former fault, if such it is, is probably the less serious. In calling the clergy to a high standard and criticizing them when they failed, Colet was by no means alone. Erasmus specifically tells us in the biographical letter that Colet was cautious about public comment on sensitive issues and confided his true feelings to a small inner circle only. The few to whom he did open his heart fully may have found that a little of his vehemence went a long way. Even Colet's devoted editor Lupton, when he had come to the fifth of his five volumes, confesses a little wearily that Colet "in the character of a zealous preacher, or a reformer of abuses . . . might already be sufficiently familiar to us."[31]

Paul recognizes more fully than Colet does that while in principle all men should be, or seek to be, like Christ, in reality many are so "weak" as to require substantial "concessions." According to Colet, however, concessions are available only when an individual has made every effort to rise literally to the example of Christ but despite every effort still finds himself stuck at some lower point in the ascent. Colet does not demand merely that a person never stop before reaching a high spiritual level; he demands that he not stop even then, that he never stop at all. The minimum demanded of everyone is constant effort and constant prayer, in the ardent and continuous desire to ascend further. Anything less, and one "cannot be numbered among the saved" (C, 212 [168]). Nor may people elect to be, in his caustic phrase, "voluntarily sick" (C, 197 [142]); DEH, 200). By this he means they may not drop out of the spiritual race when it has barely begun, confessing themselves to be spiritual invalids who need concessions and will gladly settle for a modest place in paradise. While Colet concedes that there are varying degrees of holiness (CM, 194), he still regards it as the absolute minimum requirement that man try unceasingly to come nearer to God and never lapse into mere formalism. He indignantly refuses to limit the average person's obligations to a sort of Christian core curriculum, with advanced spiritual activities left to specialists. But we have now seen that the writings containing these views were not for the masses but for select spiritual readers. When he addressed the hundreds or thousands of Londoners who admired his sermons he must have taken a different tone.

Though he denies that setting every Christian to imitate Christ's life on earth was giving an "exemplum impossibilitatis" (C, 208 [162]), he knew perfectly well that he, like everyone else, was surrounded daily by people who could sometimes be inspired to greater effort but by and large conceived the everyday life of the everyday Christian in vastly different terms, and he must have made "concessions" to their "weakness" as a regular thing.

Colet was a well-known and highly regarded preacher.[32] We may suppose that he had a fine voice and—considering how often he would preach outdoors at Paul's Cross to large crowds—a strong voice as well. I should imagine that the preaching style he adopted was influenced by his deep conviction of the *disciplina arcani*, the great gulf set between the initiate and those many who still needed to be nursed along on spiritual babyfood. His own idealism and reputation for personal integrity would have lent his sermons force almost irrespective of what he said: listeners who have no intention of pursuing perfection themselves often feel a transitory inspiration in the presence of someone who does pursue it.

In one place, however, I think we catch a glimpse of a powerfully dramatic treatment that would have made an already famous passage unforgettable. Romans 7:15–24 is a *cri de coeur* that strikes a responsive chord even in readers to whom much else in Paul is foreign:

I cannot understand my own behavior. I fail to carry out the things I want to do, and I find myself doing the very things I hate. When I act against my will, that means I have a self that acknowledges that the Law is good, and so the thing behaving in that way is not my self but sin living in me. . . . Though the will to do what is good is in me, the performance is not, with the result that instead of doing the good things I want to do, I carry out the sinful things I do not want. . . . What a wretched man I am! Who will rescue me from the body of this death?

In his earlier work on Romans Colet touched on the passage, though without apparent sympathy or interest (R, 150). But when he returns to it later (RO, 259) he summarizes the whole Pauline passage just quoted in broken, disjointed phrases, as if Paul was sobbing out his despair. Indeed Colet adds, "It appears to me that the devout Paul said this in tears." Paul's anguish culminates in the famous cry "Who will rescue me from the body of this death?" As if to emphasize the dialogue quality implicit in the strife between Paul's two selves, Colet now turns the sequence into dialogue: "In grace and earnestness he replies. . . ." And then, in a passage without parallel in his writings, Colet cries out, like a fascinated spectator at this duel, "Truly and wisely have you answered, Paul!" Like his rapt hearers Colet knew well the experience Paul described, and in this fine passage I think we get a glimpse of the dramatic power that Colet as a preacher could bring to congenial themes. It is a great shame that this dramatic passage is unique in his writings, but a dramatic imagination must often have lent force and dignity to Colet's public sermons.

The one sermon that remains, and the work by which he is best known, is of course a very different matter. It was preached to Convocation, the assembly of the higher clergy of the Province of Canterbury, on the occasion of that body's meeting, for the first time in six years, in January 1510 (it has now been shown that the date regularly given for the sermon, 6 February 1512, is almost certainly wrong).[33] Colet begins the sermon by expressing the sense of unworthiness he feels in addressing his "fathers" and "masters" in the ecclesiastical hierarchy, saying it would seem "almost arrogant" in him to preach to them were it not that he was preaching at the express command of the archbishop. And in concluding he apologizes for anything he has said that seems "excessive" or "intemperate" and asks that any such impression "be pardoned as coming from a man speaking out of zeal, a man grieving at the ruinous state of the church" (OCC, 250). The sermon is often described as epochal, almost unheard of in its candor and the fierceness of its denunciations. Colet's sermon is indeed a strong statement and an eloquent testimony to his convictions. It may be worth while, however, to remind ourselves that criticism of the clergy from within their ranks was no novelty in the generations that preceded the Reformation.

Portraits of what a good bishop or priest should be, and by implication often was not, were virtually a cottage industry.[34] The culprits, for their part, were hardened to criticism, which had to be scathing indeed to make an impression. In probably the same year as the Convocation Sermon Colet's English contemporary William de Melton, chancellor of York, made many of the same criticisms in his *Sermo exhortatorius* (STC 17806, ?1510), which nevertheless attracted no unusual attention.[35] Examples from across the Channel show what really severe criticism of those in high ecclesiastical position could be like. The redoubtable Johannes Geiler of Kaysersberg fiercely denounced the assembled clergy and also the secular lords at the funeral of Bishop Robert of Bavaria before "a throng of princes, counts, bishops, abbots, and other ecclesiastical dignitaries," in a sermon that showed "notable hardihood" because it was delivered in the presence of the deceased bishop's cousin and successor Albert.[36] When it came Bishop Albert's turn to die in 1506 the same preacher was still going strong and delivered this funeral oration too. Coming to the part of the oration where the virtues of the deceased were customarily rehearsed, the preacher declared he was not aware that the deceased had any virtues, and would leave that subject to someone better informed than himself.[37] As another example of plain speaking that makes Colet's effort seem quite restrained, we may glance at a criticism leveled at the pope himself by Dionysius the Carthusian, in an open letter calling for a general council of the Church:

> What I seek Your Holiness surely knows, for it is not in my own name alone that I present myself to Your Holiness but in the name of many, not to say all. The service we ask of you is the reform of the Church. You are the vicar of Christ on earth, who will have to give an account for every soul that is lost. More than anyone else you are obliged to procure the glory of God and to preserve from scandal the weak, who go about everywhere saying that the Pope does not want a council because he does not want his Curia to be reformed, and that the Roman pontiffs have taken an oath not to hold any more councils. If no other reason, then concern for your reputation should bring you to convoke this assembly. . . . Where in the Church can one find anything that is not soiled and corrupt? Does there remain a spark of integrity in ecclesiastics, of nobility in the powerful, of loyalty in the common people? Everything is spoiled and overthrown: from head to foot, all is but one wound. The evil is so great that no private initiative can cure it; it requires the effort of all to extinguish the conflagration that is overwhelming the Church. That is why all the world cries for a council.[38]

Judged by such standards, Colet's sermon is not especially daring. His text is from Paul: "Do not be conformed to this world, but be reformed in the newness of your understanding." After a brief preamble, in which the preacher suggests the gravity of the Church's state by quotations from the prophets and asserts his own unworthiness to address such a gathering, all assembled say the Paternoster together. The sermon itself divides neatly into two parts, the first dealing with the ways in which the Church is actually conformed to this world, and the second with how it may be reformed. The first part is divided into the four evils distinguished in St. John's First Epistle; the illustrations from contemporary ecclesiastical life make it the most quotable portion of the sermon. They are vigorously expressed and strongly felt. At the same time, the plentiful use of scriptural quotations throughout the sermon gives it the air of a theological discourse grounded in biblical truth rather than the expression of one preacher's view. By choosing the quotations, of course, Colet controls the movement of the argument; but he is careful at all times to present his points as much as possible in biblical language.

The second half of the sermon is equally orderly. He opens it by observing that what is needed is not so much that Convocation make more laws as that it remind itself of the laws already made and take steps to put them into effect; these are the two branches of the sermon's second half. Existing laws are introduced one after the other with the same ultimately impressive preface, "Recitentur leges . . ." ("Let the laws be rehearsed . . ."). In conclusion he turns, as he had done already at several points, to his hearers. It is they who must give the example to be followed by the preacher himself and other priests and ultimately by the laity. The sermon is short, for it was intended as the prelude to a meeting on Convocation's business; it closes with the apology already noticed and by the prayer that from Convocation's work good will yet come. The sermon is elegant, clearly articulated, and well suited to the occasion. If it looks a little schematic in print, in actual delivery it would benefit from its clarity of outline when suffused with the preacher's warmth and conviction.

It has become a commonplace to say that Colet's Convocation Sermon was a bombshell. The reason must be that it is often read with strong preconceptions, or even that it is not so much read as read about. From time to time a careful reader recognizes how far the sermon falls below advance notices in regard to doctrine: "[N]one of the later shibboleths of reform appear in Colet's fiery sermon. There is not a word against the Pope, nor the Mass, nor Indulgences, nor vain ceremonies. Nothing is put forward as to the relations between Church and State."[39] But such temperate estimates of the sermon's scope have not exercised much influence. It is therefore interesting to see what the factual record tells about the sermon's contemporary reception. The sermon is certainly "fiery," but in specifics it is recognizable as belonging to a familiar tradition. Those who heard the sermon do not seem to have been upset by it.

The Latin original was printed by Richard Pynson and dated 1511. Pynson was the King's Printer, to which office he had succeeded after the death of the previous King's Printer in May 1508.[40] The royal patent gave the King's Printer prestige,[41] and by the same token inclined him to conservatism. Pynson was decidedly a "safe" printer: "Religious and legal [books] account for some two-thirds of his total output. The rest of his time was spent in producing a considerable number of scholastic manuals. . . . Thus he may be looked upon as being less adventurous than [his predecessor] de Worde."[42] Pynson padded on in his unadventurous way till his death in 1530, with no one apparently finding fault with him. He was not a printer on the lookout for controversial works, and he seems to have regarded the Colet sermon as fairly routine. Still more important, Pynson's view was shared by Convocation itself.

The notes on which John Bale based his bibliographical works include the following neglected entry: "Coletus inter cetera scripsit . . . Sermones in cleri convocatione, li. i" ("Among other things Colet wrote . . . one volume of sermons delivered at the congregations of the clergy")."[43] What is important to note here is that Bale, who had original access to Colet's manuscripts, uses the plural in speaking of his sermons to Convocation. We have also seen that the one surviving sermon delivered before Convocation must date to 1510—not, as earlier assumed, to 1512—and that the most recent Convocation before 1510 was in 1504, before Colet was dean or a member of Convocation. Thus the one surviving Convocation Sermon was not only one of several but indeed the first. It follows that Colet's sermon of 1510, far from being considered a bombshell by those who heard it, was no obstacle to his being invited to deliver sermons before the same body in later years.

Once the canard that Colet's Convocation Sermon was revolutionary has been disposed of, the sermon finds its natural place in this chapter on his exegesis. While not the unique document that Victorian scholars wished to think it, the sermon was thoroughly characteristic of Colet's thought. He read in Paul's contrast between conforming and reforming an application to the requirements of the Church in his own day. In the sermon as in his exegetical works he tried to give biblical passages not merely intelligibility but life; and that meant finding responsive hearers. Colet decided to be realistic about reaching his actual audience, experienced men who had heard a lot of sermons but who, if he could capture their interest, might make a difference. Hence, I think, his elaborate submissiveness, his care to cloak his own convictions in the language of Scripture, the highly visible structure that guaranteed that the speaker was not being carried away by the spirit of criticism. It is more helpful to think of the sermon along these lines than to continue to regard it as a revolutionary challenge. Insofar as Colet could make it so the Convocation Sermon was a success, another small victory for "living wisdom."

8

Colet's Sacramental Universe

Colet's only surviving original treatise is the little book entitled *De sacramentis*.[1] For all of its tangled style, it is full of interest because it brings together and makes explicit the themes that run through all the other writings and sets out clearly the presuppositions that govern Colet's thought. Whatever else the treatise *De sacramentis* is, it is not in any usual sense a treatise on the sacraments. Of the seven recognized in the late-medieval church, only four are treated at all fully, and it soon becomes clear that even these four appear in function of an argument on a quite different subject, or rather pair of subjects.

Lupton's helpless summary of the contents, one thing after another without connection, shows that he failed to see the real subject of the book and could not find a way of concealing what he must privately have thought its incoherence. The subject of *De sacramentis* is in fact a closely intertwined pair of problems that were widely discussed by theological writers: Why was the world created? and, How is fallen man restored from multiplicity and dividedness to unity, and thus to union with God?

These problems arise from certain fundamental premises in Colet's thinking. The premises do not seem to arise from a cognitive act, even though they are duly expressed in the theological language of the Fathers. The ideas we are about to consider were only a peripheral part of the intellectual furniture of Colet's age, but to him they were central in a highly personal way. They are the conceptual expression of dark certainties that possessed him early on and never lost their hold on him. These certainties framed his intellectual and moral universe; they prepared him to accept certain somber patristic conceptions and also to reject with indignation any line of thinking that reposed a measure of confidence in man's own efforts.

More perhaps an attitude than a principle, so deep does it lie, is Colet's attitude to the flesh. None of the Pauline verses on the flesh that he cites fervently and sometimes repeatedly are from epistles on which commentaries by Colet survive. Their inclusion in other writings was thus not obligatory; they were verses that floated free in his mind and became lodged anywhere that a suitable context offered. The clue to his entire outlook probably lies in the way he read the well-known verse from Galatians (5:17) "The spirit lusteth against the flesh" (S, 292; DEH, 249). This warfare of the spirit against the flesh—and, as Paul adds, the flesh against the spirit—often makes it impossible for a person to do what he genuinely wishes to do. The only remedy, Paul says a few verses later (24–25), is to "crucify" the flesh. This remedy Colet cites more often than almost any other biblical passage (S, 294; R, 152, 153; DEH, 244). Flesh, for Colet, is never rosy, never warm, never comforting, indeed never even neutral; flesh is always the principle opposed to spirit, and therefore always to be crucified. When he read in Hebrews 2:14 that "the children are partakers of flesh and blood," he responded instinctively along lines different from those of the biblical writer: Colet assumed that precisely because they are partakers of flesh and blood they must have forsaken God (DEH, 226).

Besides its more general sense as the principle opposed to spirit, flesh had for Colet too the usual sexual sense. While as a young man he was reading and annotating his copy of Ficino's *Epistolae*, his enthusiasm seems to have flagged at times. In a long stretch of sixty-five pages we find only a single marginal comment, but that one is somberly significant: "[P]roclivi sumus ad libidinem" ("We are inclined to lust"; FEM, 126). The letter-essay against which this comment is placed has nothing to do with lust, but deals with the triumphs of Hercules, under the heading "The Life of Heroic Men Is Laborious to Be Sure, but It Is Also Glorious." The healthy, handsome, well-off young reader in his late twenties was trying to concentrate on Ficino but found his imagination wandering in directions having nothing to do with Hercules. As Erasmus intimates (A, ll. 391–392), these struggles remained intense throughout Colet's life. Even during his last few years—in 1516 or later—we find him writing in a very similar vein, "Tanta est fragilitas carnis, tanta pronitas in libidinem" ("So weak is the flesh, so prone to lust"; Trinity College, Cambridge, MS. o.4.44, 39ᵛ).[2] Similarly, the *De sacramentis* shows Colet reflecting on "how prone man is to evil from adolescence onward" (S, 324), where the reference to adolescence shows that he is thinking especially of lust. It is a curious fact that the only pagan god whom Colet names is Priapus (RO, 255).

Exactly why Colet's rejection of the flesh was so intense we simply do not know. Certain obvious features of his early life might seem to offer clues; but we have also to remember that a younger brother brought up in the same household went on to study law and on reaching twenty-one was soon deep into real estate deals. Yet if the reasons for Colet's revulsion from the flesh in the sexual sense must remain speculative, there can be no doubt of the fact. On one occasion he drew up a short list of four horrible kinds of sinners. Not surprisingly, three of the four are poisoners, blasphemers, and assassins; but heading the list are fornicators (DEH, 217). This singling out of fornicators is doubly unusual because it departs both from theological tradition, which regarded adultery as more serious (because a sin against justice was also involved) and also from Dionysius, whom Colet is ostensibly commenting on. Dionysius actually ranks fornicators higher than catechumens, because even though they eventually fell they had already been admitted to first-hand experience of divine realities. Erasmus tells us that in principle Colet reprehended sexual sins less than he did other kinds (A, ll. 460–464), but here we see that he could equate fornicators with devils.

Colet's passionately dualistic conception of a universe polarized between spirit and flesh left him unable to find any good in the things of this world. It also opened up, as we shall see later, a dangerous gap between his really quite comfortable and fortunate personal life and the only judgment of it which, in theory, his ideology permitted. Colet's picture of "this world" was like ours of Jupiter, wrapped in eternal cold fogs, inaccessible to light and warmth and love.

This world had been wretched from the beginning: "From the time of Adam on, the disease [of sin] has grown steadily mightier, and the stain and foul contagion of evil is now so deeply ingrained that its cure is quite beyond man's strength" (R, 147). "This world" is death. The only way to be saved is to be "reborn by grace and baptism" (RO, 235); otherwise one is simply "generating evil in the Devil's privy" (RO, 254). In "this lamentable state of man" (RO, 261), "men's lives, laws, customs, and actions are polluted and filthy" (RO, 260). "The Egypt of this world is ruled by the Pharaoh [the Devil]" (RO, 272). "What shall we say of this bottommost region the earth, where all is black and frigid, contrarious and hostile, this region in which our sojourn is dragged out?" (CM, 185). So horrible is the world that God speedily abandoned it. He came down to it only to overthrow the power of Satan. While on earth he continually looked upward (R, 176–181), and when he returned from it he took his followers with him (C, 209 [164]), leaving the world, as he had found it, full of the multitudinous evils that Colet enumerates: "envy, anger, hatred, rivalry, quarreling, avarice, ambition, strife, wrongdoing, deceitfulness, trickery, robbery, pride, contempt of God and man, self-aggrandizement, gluttony, lust, laziness, vanity, war, murder, destruction" (C, 210 [166]). In short, "Here [in this world] you are in enemy territory, full of implacable opponents commanded by the Devil, a 'roaring lion.' Never does he flag, nor does he sleep. He is ever on the alert, 'seeking whom he may devour' and swallow down" (P, 302, a considerable expansion of 1 Pet. 5:8–9).

This horrified vision of the world as the "bottommost region . . . where everything is black and frigid, contrarious and hostile" is simply the logical inference from the neoplatonist principles that ruled Colet's thought.[3] Neoplatonic thought had been so thoroughly assimilated into Christianity during the patristic period that the biblical view of the goodness of God's creation was all but forgotten by thinkers of a temper congenial to Colet's. This world they regarded as fleeting, evanescent, deceptive, deserving only of repudiation by the Christian.[4]

A further reason, more familiar to Colet's day than ours, is what one scholar has nicely called "the astronomical reason for humility."[5] It is often repeated that the pre-Copernican cosmology gave man the place of honor in the universe, of which this earth was the hub. But looked at more carefully,

> the actual tendency of the geocentric system was, for the medieval mind, precisely the opposite. For the centre of the world was not a position of honor; it was rather the place farthest removed from the Empyrean, the bottom of the creation, to which its dregs and baser elements sank. The actual centre, indeed, was Hell; in the spatial sense the medieval world was literally diabolocentric.[6]

With this we arrive at the fundamental reason for the appalling character of the world as Colet saw it: the world is ruled by demons under the command of Satan. For Colet this is not a figure of speech but a theological fact, the presupposition of the "classical" theory of the Atonement. Colet refers to an idea expressed at the close of the First Epistle of John (5:19) which was of major importance to his own outlook: "We know that we belong to God, but the whole world lies in the power of the evil one" (C, 208 [162]; R, 180, 200). In the first of these three citations Colet asserts that this state of affairs endured till the coming of Christ, but it soon appears that what Christ brought was not the end of the evil one's dominion but rather the possibility of eventual escape from it. The world, that is, did not thereupon become a tolerable place, but its horrors were alleviated by the prospect of escape through uniting oneself with Christ. In the other two passages citing 1 John 5:19, the world is described without qualification as we have just heard Colet characterize it, with grace the only means by which man can be rescued from the evils that beset him in the person of the Devil and his demonic minions.

Well-read in the Fathers and deeply persuaded of the power of the evil one, Colet revived a conception of the Atonement that had been the central one in patristic times. It was a theory neglected by most men in his own time, for it had been replaced by the newer and then orthodox theory that Christ reconciled men to God by the vicarious sacrifice of his own sufferings and death—the theory, it will be remembered, which Erasmus regarded as self-evident in the "Disputatiuncula." Colet, however, continued to find the old theory more meaningful. Satan, according to this patristic theory, acquired dominion over man by seducing him from his allegiance to God through the Fall. Thenceforward the world with all its inhabitants belonged literally and in a sense rightly to him. "Redemption" is "buying back," and if the world was to be bought back a price would have to be paid to the owner. The price was Christ, who was handed over by his Father as a "ransom" to set men free. By a supreme paradox, this was the undoing of Satan, for Christ proved the stronger and overcame sin and death in the person of Satan. He destroyed Satan's power over those who acknowledged himself as their leader and fought under his banner. These, but only these, could hope to escape from Satan's realm; within this realm, however, Satan remained unweariedly and resourcefully active in seeking to turn men away from Christ and make them return voluntarily to the slavery to evil which would bring about their eternal damnation.[7]

Satan's actual dominion over man and his consequent right to a ransom are expressly knowledged by Colet. He says that Christ conquered death and put the Devil to flight, thereby freeing man "without the Adversary's being entitled to complain" ("sine adversarii querela")—his rights over man having been implicitly acknowledged (C, 172 [90]). This Christus Victor theory of the Atonement is set out fully in what are for Colet unusually eloquent terms; they have a flavor of pulpit eloquence about them that may have made their author wish to preserve them on vellum. Christ's victory over the Devil

> was a wondrous victory, for the victorious Devil, by the very fact that he had conquered [man, thus ultimately bringing God to man's rescue], was conquered; so that in both cases the victory was otherwise than as it appeared. Accordingly when God conquered the adversary who had conquered man, man was again reinstated in the liberty and light of God, and the Devil could not justly complain. (DEH, 226)

Colet touches more allusively on the Adversary's owning man when he laments that the failure of the leaders of the Church—in context the bishops and clergy—has caused "Christians to surrender to the Devil and be taken back into slavery" (RO, 229). Devils he speaks of as "the rulers of the darkness of this world" (DEH, 208, 213).

Small wonder, then, that man's true home, his "fatherland" ("patria") is elsewhere. At this point comes into play the pervasive neoplatonic imagery by which Colet represents man's departure from this world as a passage from darkness to light, and at the same time a return home. Since Jesus Christ is "our sun" (C, 253 [250]), as one moves outward and downward from him one draws deeper into the darkness and the cold (cf. C, 163 [72]). Conversely, gazing upon a corporeal image, according to a "definition of love" which Colet endorsed, creates "the desire of returning to the contemplation of that beauty which is divine" (FEM, 90). The "light" that man receives is the "image of that original and purer light" (R, 185). At one point the neoplatonic light imagery is used to portray Christ himself as the lantern that conducts man along the strait way that leads to life. This image combines the light imagery with that of the lost homeland, for the lantern's light makes it possible for man to "return to his Father's house, to which, like an exile, he is summoned back" (R, 206).

The homeland is of course centered in Christ. "Imagine a circle whose center is Christ, the essence of goodness, and whose circumference is less good, while the farther outlying regions are the essence of evil [ipsum malum]" (RO, 264), these last being the world, which still belongs to the Devil. The faithful Christian may and must escape from it "homeward" through grace and unceasing effort: "From it [this world] those who are redeemed betake themselves in all haste to that fatherland to which they are summoned" (RO, 246). No one can come "home," however, unless he is "drawn" by grace (DEH, 208, quoting John 6:44). The person to whom grace is vouchsafed is "drawn" back to heaven "to see there again his father and his fatherland" (C, 207 [160]). Since man's true fatherland is heaven (DEH, 265; R, 187), one cannot get out of "this world" too soon.

Man must choose which will be his home—"this world" or the true "fatherland," where he will "again" see his father. The choice is awesome; its consequences are fateful. Colet represents the choice as still more awesome by neglecting for once his usual stress on man's inborn evil leanings. Instead he gives him a straightforward choice between actively serving Christ and serving the Devil. There is no compromise:

> Whichever direction one goes in, there are those who will carefully encourage his initial steps and confirm him in his choice. It is up to man to choose his direction, to attend to counselors either good or evil, to fall in with one kind of incitement or the other. But in whichever direction he goes, there are all about him immaterial natures that will lead him on in his chosen course. (DEH, 128)

The rhetoric, if not the theology, conveys the impression that the choice, once made, is practically irrevocable. Yet the choice of good, for

Colet, requires much more than good intentions and spasmodic effort. The Christian—this is simply the minimum—must renounce this world and its business and follow Christ without ceasing or looking back. If he fails on this high level he has no fallback position—he fails completely.

By this route we arrive at a further patristic problem that for most people had been settled long before but for Colet remained deeply troubling. This is the problem, which surfaces repeatedly in *De sacramentis*, of *poenitentia secunda*.[8] Is it possible for a sinner to repent and be forgiven, then fall again, and again be forgiven? That Colet should be troubled by this problem is significant. The Church had long since concluded that confession and reconciliation with the Christian community were always available to the sinner who had tried but failed to amend his life, and also that the grace conferred in his repeated confessions would actually strengthen him in his future efforts at atonement. In certain moods Colet himself said much the same thing—not surprisingly since this was simply received dogma. He paraphrased St. John Chrysostom with approval: "To sin is the lot of man; what is devil-like is to remain in the fallen state" ("Peccare humanum est, iacere diabolicum"; S, 324).[9] What is interesting is his recurrent apprehension that the reborn sinner is given only one more chance, that if after that he falls again he is lost.

Colet intensifies the consequences of moral choice to a dramatic degree. He has such a horror of not living up to the spiritual obligations he has taken on himself that he commits himself to the extraordinary assertion that God actually would prefer "that people live as servants to the Devil rather than be slain in war as his enemies" (DCH, 195). One feels that Colet ought to have known there was something wrong with the premises that led to this bleak and deadly conclusion; but I know of no evidence that he did. It comes as no surprise that in the second of his treatises on the Dionysian hierarchies he declared death a matter for rejoicing because it prevents "the danger of a fall into which one might have lapsed had one's life been drawn out longer" (DEH, 256).

From the Fathers Colet took also a final conception that had long since become the merest platitude for most people but somehow remained for him a burning reality. To the early church it had seemed obvious that only those who were themselves holy could be united with Christ and share in the life of his Bride the Church, and thus in the Mystical Body of Christ—both of which figures are very prominent in *De sacramentis*. The passage of centuries had watered down this conviction almost to nothing in actual practice; for Colet, however, the patristic conviction remained as urgent as it had been in the heroic early church. Scorning the compromises that had long since become routine, he continued to insist that the Christian's life be patterned on the holiness of the divine exemplar, that anything less spells damnation.

All of these patristic concepts interwoven into Colet's treatise on the sacraments share two characteristics. They remain unattenuated by what in other quarters might have been considered realism, or simply the undeniable lessons of experience. And they are conceived in his usual absolutist terms. It is not that the concepts we are discussing could not be paralleled in writers of a more adaptable cast: they remained accepted doctrine, after all. But in other writers one could set against such absolutist passages others conceived in a more flexible spirit, passages in which the writer was content to take human nature as it appeared to be and work to improve it little by little, accepting, even if reluctantly, the apparent limits of the possible. In Colet there is nothing else to set against the absolutist principles that we have been considering. There was something in him that might break but could not bend, also that made him wonder, despite the church's reassurances, whether repeated forgiveness really could be extended to undeserving man.

The moral absolutism that drew him to some of the most uncompromising positions of the Fathers was of course reflected in his views on marriage, a subject that is in the very center of his *De sacramentis*. There it becomes a great metaphor for the spiritual marriage of Christ and his Church, Bridegroom and Bride. What goes on earth under the name of marriage is another matter. Colet thought it a good thing that Dionysius, the pupil of Paul, did not even mention matrimony as a sacrament though he included the other six. This must mean, Colet concluded, that marriage was subsumed under the sacrament of orders, through which human beings, considered as feminine with respect to the rush of divine power, were fecundated by the divine Bridegroom (S, 66).

As to marriage in the usual sense, its good points could be covered in a chapter no longer than the chapter Dr. Johnson recited concerning the snakes of Iceland: for Colet, "There is nothing good about marriage" ("nuptiae nihil habent bonitatis"; C, 224 [190]). Marriage is to be avoided if at all possible, but if it is required as a "concession" to the "weak," those so indulged must make the least possible use of its pleasures, those who do otherwise being "loathesome" ("detestandi"; C, 224 [190]). In the past marriage may have had some spiritual justification, but no longer. It was originally needed to fill up "the number of the elect" (144,000, according to Revelation), but the generations of women and men since Eve and Adam had presumably produced this number of the saved by now; hence this excuse for marriage no longer existed.[10] Similarly, in the past marriage had created the Bride, mankind, to whom the Bridegroom was to unite himself, but this too had already happened with Christ's incarnation. As another facet of the same consideration, marriage had earlier served as a figure of the true marriage, which was that of Christ with his Church; but here too, with the fulfillment of the figure the anticipation of it ceased to have significance (C, 225 [192]).

The same kind of absolutist analysis is also brought to bear on the structure to which it is probably least of all suited: human society in its horizontal dimension. Unless men are united with one another through absorption into the Mystical Body of Christ— that is, vertically—they are fatally isolated and antagonistic to one another. Colet's system has no place for, say, a pleasant evening spent with friends or a feast in Mercers' Hall:

> Human beings . . . because of their inherently mortal and carnal nature, are utterly scattered and dispersed. They stand apart from one another by reason of their individual natures and wills; and each person, intent on himself, seeks what he himself wants. . . . There are as many opinions as there are people, as many wills as there are opinions. But there is no help for it— because of that original calamity men are born such that each by nature tends to hold aloof from others and pursue his private advantage. By the innate tendencies of men's fallen nature they turn their backs on the fellowship of society and are borne off in any number of different directions. (CM, 186)

Making laws is of no help, for "in the antagonism of their nature men break these laws and for a long stretch of time observe no laws." Human beings act only on what they see as good for themselves.

What does Colet see as the alternative? The passages we have just reviewed are the premises for an argument that only in the Mystical Body of Christ will man find an organic connection with his fellow man. The reason for the breakdown of order and fellowship, or rather for its never having been attained in secular society since the Fall, is, according to Colet, "motion" ("motus"; CM, 187). Hence the world, if it is to enjoy that static perfection which is the only perfection Colet conceived of, must cease to "move." Colet is forced to propound this radical cure to society's ills because he can find no way of justifying activity in quest of any but supernatural goals; the ideal is static incorporatedness into what is perfect. The dilemma was built into the kind of Christian thinking that Colet understood:

> There was no way in which the flight from the Many to the One, the question of a perfection defined wholly in terms of contrast with the created world, could be harmonized with the imitation of a Goodness that delights in diversity and manifests itself in the emanation of the Many out of the One.[11]

But precisely because the dilemma could not be resolved without challenging either Revelation or reason, it could not be squarely faced. Colet was left with the unsatisfying conviction that God's creation must be good, but that man had to get out of it. And the way to do so was by forsaking the lively bustle of society for motionless incorporatedness.

Thus human society, like that other society, marriage, is subjected to a reductive analysis of an all-or-nothing type. Because Colet could find no absolute value in a kind smile, a beautiful morning, or for that matter a good dinner on the table or a blazing fire on a wet, cold night, he found in them no value at all. His system would require him to consider such small delights as traps or bait to lull our spiritual strivings and put us fatally at ease in "this world" while the "immaterial natures" that surround our dinner table unseen, grin with unholy satisfaction.

Not that Colet himself did not enjoy such things. He was abstemious in certain respects, but we have Erasmus's word for it that Colet liked things around him to be attractive and well done (A, ll. 330–333). We catch what seems to be a glimpse of him at home in an illuminated manuscript of the gospels which he commissioned, dated 1509.[12] He is shown kneeling and venerating an evangelist, in one of a handsome suite of rooms which probably represents the interior of the deanery, warmed by a fire blazing in an enormous fireplace. The problem was that there was no place for these terrestrial good things in a two-valued system whose poles were damnation and salvation, a world in thrall to Satan on the one hand, opposed on the other hand to the ordered perfection of heaven, with nothing in between. One notices that Colet had trouble seeing even Jesus against the background of his life on earth;[13] in fact Colet never shows Jesus doing anything nontheological. Thus though he predictably commends Christ's life to the Christian's imitation (RO, 227) such imitation as he envisions would amount to forsaking the everyday world altogether.

In obvious ways Colet's neoplatonism was the philosophical equivalent of his theological insistence on the nothingness of man. God alone was real, while the earth was distant, dark, and convulsed by contrariety. Colet was aware, however, that other implications of neoplatonist thought were of a tendency far less congenial to him. In *De sacramentis* Colet repeatedly employs the common image of rays to suggest the uniform self-diffusion of the Godhead. However, the same image confers on whatever is illuminated by the divine rays a certain participation in God, a notion that runs counter to Colet's conviction of the valuelessness of man. Colet shows he was aware of this implication by at least once treating Dionysian emanation in a manner that converts continuity into discontinuity. Instead of uniform diffusion Colet distinguishes three stages, which on analysis soon prove to be two. The three stages are God, image, and man, but "image" is simply a makeweight to mask the ontological gap he has thus abruptly opened up between God and Man (DCH, 169).

Colet's version of neoplatonism tends to play up the doctrine of emanation when it dramatizes the absolute centrality of God's all-being, but to play down its unifying implications. Just as with the other structures that we have seen Colet analyzing, here too we have a conception of the universe in which everything distinctively human has been swept away. Late in life Colet summed this ontologically lonely universe into a maxim: "Unless a man can say to himself, I only and God am in the world, he shall have no peace" ("Nisi poterit homo dicere secum ego solus et deus in mundo sum non habebit requiem"; Trinity College, Cambridge, MS. o.4.44, 1^r).

The system of Colet's mental and moral universe was not a system that he had carefully and gradually reasoned his way to. Instead it crystallizes in quasi-objective form what in some sense he had always known or at least felt, the axioms in his patterning of human experience. Certain traditions among those available to him would be for him deeply right, known to be so from the outset. Others would be unthinkable because their premises were unthinkable or because they led to unthinkable conclusions. He read widely, but what little evidence we have suggests strongly that what he recorded was not the systematic structure of other men's systems but rather elements he thought he could use in giving expression to his own outlook.

For example, anyone who takes the trouble to follow up Colet's identifiable extrabiblical borrowings in the originals where Colet read them, soon finds that they rarely lead to fuller contexts that would clarify his intentions. The connection of the passage with its original context has generally been broken. Struck by a phrase, a formulation, an idea, occasionally even a page or two, Colet broke it away from its context and stored the find in his notebooks for future use.

In taking notes from his readings, Colet appears to have followed the method developed by Italian humanist educators in the fifteenth century, that of using *topoi*. In effect subject headings, the *topoi* were a quietly subversive method. The reader did not follow in his notes the structure of the authority he was studying but instead extracted what was of interest to himself: in this sense the method was creative and liberating, for it required the reader to make his own connections among the disparate materials that accumulated in his notebooks. The spoils of one's reading begin to put out new filaments of association and with luck one would find oneself presiding over the emergence of a living new structure that was in a significant sense one's own.[14]

A further pointer to Colet's method of work is offered in a passage of *De sacramentis* itself, the work that mainly concerns us in the present chapter. As so often, we find Colet insisting on the hostility of the spirit to the flesh. What is interesting, however, is that we catch Colet virtually transcribing the whole contents of his notebooks on this theme into his treatise. About five percent of the whole little book (S, 292–294) is made up of the passages of Paul concerning the hostility of the spirit to the flesh;

the passages are in the order in which the books from which they are taken stand in the New Testament, from Romans right through to Colossians. At some point Colet systematically read Paul through with this topos in mind, and when he needed the material for his argument it lay ready to hand in his notebooks.

We find ourselves dealing, then, with an eclectic thinker who on principle does not quote sources and moreover uses his sources in a personal and independent spirit—as Goethe somewhere says, for corroboration. Thus a writer like Colet, and especially in his one treatise that is not a commentary on someone else's text, cannot be approached by the well-trodden way of source study. No matter how full such a study was it would be incapable of giving us the pattern and meaning of the treatise—which, as Lupton's edition unintentionally demonstrates, is by no means obvious.

We will get further by starting at the opposite end from the details of sources, and seeking instead to identify the broad tradition within which he was working. Fortunately this is easy. Though Colet acknowledges no philosophical allegiances in his writings, we have the great advantage of Erasmus's testimony. Everything in Colet's writings confirms Erasmus's account of Colet's strong distaste for one of the two leading traditions that were available to him, the tradition associated with St. Thomas Aquinas. He have already seen some of the reasons for his deep hostility to Thomas. The more fundamental reasons appear if one considers the salient differences between the Thomistic and the Franciscan schools.

Basic to Thomas's philosophy was the effort to establish close links between Christian thought and Aristotle; but we already know what Colet thought of such deference to pagan books. Aquinas interprets Aristotle as virtually a propaedeutic to faith, a natural and necessary complement to it; whereas the great Franciscan doctor Bonaventure thought it hopeless to try to reconcile Aristotle's concept of the universe with the Christian doctrine of creation.[15] Bonaventure's disciple Walter of Bruges took this as his motto:

Dico quod plus credendum est Augustino et Anselmo quam Philosopho; plus adhaerendum est judicio Sancti [Augustini] quam Philosophi, sicut plus credendum est homini existenti in monte, de lumine corporali, quam homini existenti in valle. [I say that more faith should be placed in Augustine and Anselm than in the Philosopher [as Aquinas regularly calls Aristotle]; that one should follow the opinion of the Saint in preference to that of the Philosopher; just as one would trust more to what a man on a mountain peak said about corporeal light than to what a man down in a valley said.][16]

Quite indifferent to concordances between Christian revelation and Aristotle, the Franciscan masters, of whichever school within the order, started from very different premises from those of Aquinas. For them, "the God of the Christian is something very different indeed from the Prime Mover of Book VIII of Aristotle's *Physics*: to attain to him the believer has no need of complicated syllogisms; he feels him within himself as the light of his own life, the soul of his own soul."[17] For the Franciscan thinkers, as of course for Colet, philosophy and theology were intimately united; the Franciscans did not admit a philosophy based on reason only, for to do so would be to exclude the principal source of certain knowledge. They also asserted the primacy of will, and therefore of love, over intellect—a reminder of the topic on which Ficino wrote to Colet during the latter's graduate-school days. The Franciscan doctors insisted on the experiential element in knowledge, and they valued intuition and concreteness rather than abstract essences. Even when the Franciscan and the Thomistic traditions share certain Aristotelian formulas they entertain them in a different manner, the latter regarding them as abstract and impersonal concepts, the former experiencing an inner need for the real and a desire for communion with it.[18] In short, for Aristotle and to a large extent for his follower Thomas,

> everything is necessary; contingency is limited to the terrestrial world and is due simply to the incapacity of matter, which hinders natural causes from carrying out fully the actions that would otherwise be inevitable. For the Franciscan, on the other hand, contingency is at the very root of created being, and the entire cosmic order is suspended in the act of free creation.[19]

For our purposes there is no subject on which the Aristotelian thinkers diverged more fundamentally from the Franciscan school than on the existence of God. On the one hand, Thomas endeavored to demonstrate the existence of God and certain of his attributes as a solid foundation to his metaphysics. Bonaventure, on the other hand, was thoroughly christocentric: his was a religious philosophy "in which God is not a conclusion from other premises, but prior to all conclusions, making them possible."[20] From this difference follows another: that whereas the Aristotelian tradition seeks to separate and distinguish, and thereby to "close all approaches that lead to pantheism," the "Augustinian tradition seeks to connect."[21]

The desire for connection and ultimate unity is best expressed in the principle that for Bonaventure is the essence of metaphysics but to which Thomas nowhere accords any importance,[22] the principle of exemplarism. For Bonaventure the idea of a thing which the intelligence forms within itself is necessarily perceived in relation to the exemplary idea, that which is in God. Franciscan thought is thus inherently vitalistic in the sense that the intelligence is "in quest of the eternal ideas of the things seen by the senses,"[23] their exemplars. Colet would have found the central concept neatly expressed in a work that we know impressed him deeply, Ficino's translation of Plotinus. "More than any others do," Ficino said, "the Platonists posit two worlds: the first is the intelligible world, whose source and exemplar is the divine mind; the second is the sensible world, apparent to the senses, and the reflection of the divine exemplar."[24]

Here is the metaphysical warrant for Colet's profound persuasion that God, who is all truth and all goodness, is above, while everything here below is valueless except as it may point to the divine exemplar. Exemplarism is a central concept of Colet's, and the noun "exemplar" and its adverb "exemplariter" occur frequently (S, 272 [twice], 282 [three times], 284; C, 195 [138], 206 [158], 207 [160]; DEH, 242; DCH, 167 [twice]); yet at one point (RO, 255) Lupton, who apparently never heard of exemplarism, translated "exemplariter" as "for example."

In the Franciscan school, represented for Colet, as we shall see, by Bonaventure, the quest of the divine exemplar is driven by love and therefore ultimately by will, whereas Aquinas's system gives the central role to intellect. Colet's position is stated crisply and briefly: "It is not knowledge but love [*charitas*] that leads to life" (DEH, 219). The question was already an urgent one for him in the days of his Italian studies. The most heavily annotated of all the essay-letters in Ficino's *Epistolae* is "De raptu Pauli," a speculation concerning what Paul learned on being drawn up into the third heaven. Until then Paul had been perplexed, according to Ficino, by whether intellect or love was the more important in bringing man to God. In heaven he literally saw that the celestial beings who burned brightest with love were placed closest to God.[25] The priority of will over intellect, and of love over knowledge, runs close to the surface in many of the annotations in the Ficino volume.[26] It is also the subject on which Colet wrote to Ficino, though the letter he received in reply, a confessedly "mysterious" argument that set intellect over love, probably did not settle the question for him, to judge by the lofty place given to love of the divine in Colet's own writings.[27]

Colet's most important celebration of the priority of will is an unusually long passage in his commentary on the *Ecclesiastical Hierarchy*. There he declares that the whole duty of the higher clergy (because it is for them to guide the lower clergy and ultimately the laity) is simply to ascertain God's will and proclaim it. Man's duty, correspondingly, is to conform his will to the ascertained will of God. The exceptional length of the passage (DEH, 262–265) is a measure of Colet's preoccupation with the key role of will in the organization of the ecclesiastical hierarchy. It is no accident that this theme is echoed in his one surviving sermon, whose Pauline text stresses the need to conform man's will not to this world but to God.

The differences in principle between the great medieval schools entailed also differences in emphasis, worth touching upon because they are the emphases that recur throughout Colet's writings and are notably present in *De sacramentis*.[28] In exalting the greatness of God, Bonaventure tends to stress the "misery" and the "nothingness" of man. His theocentric approach, strongly influenced by Augustine, contrasts with Aquinas's willingness to see man as within certain limits capable of worthy achievement. Also, Aquinas tends to limit God's normal action in the created world to creating it and sustaining it in existence, leaving its regular operation to be governed by law and reason.

In the moral sphere Bonaventure stresses man's habitual wickedness. Good arises from grace, not from the operation of man's own faculties. Bonaventure, like Colet, sees the operation of man's free will as having its fullest scope in sin. The world here below is for him stubbornly recalcitrant to the operation of grace. Hence Bonaventure stresses, as does *De sacramentis*, the long time of preparation that had to intervene between the creation and the re-creation.

This sketch of the many fundamental differences between the Thomistic-Aristotelian school and the Franciscan school shows Colet unambiguously in the Franciscan school. Further, by locating Colet in the tradition exemplified by Bonaventure we acquire also an insight into the line of thinkers to which he belongs. These are the thinkers with whom moral rather than intellectualist emphases are paramount, to whose writings love and will and a lively sense of dependence on God give their distinctive character. Theoretically, within Colet's more immediate time frame, the late fourteenth to the early sixteenth century, he could have found such emphases within the mystic tradition that leads from Meister Eckhart to the Devotio Moderna, passing through Tauler, Suso, Ruysbroeck, and other Rhenish mystics. Yet there is no evidence that Colet was interested in this group. In fact what little evidence there is suggests that Colet, too much the Londoner perhaps, did not find himself much drawn toward the mystic tradition. His beloved Dionysius was a main source of that tradition, but his mystical works are not the ones on which Colet chose to write. Moreover, one passage in the *Celestial Hierarchy*, a treatise on which he did write, concerned the degree of illumination proportioned to each of the hierarchies, a passage which became a *locus classicus* with the mystics.[29] Colet, however, barely glances at the passage in a single sentence (DCH, 186). And though Dionysius expounded the "negative way" to God, and Bonaventure regarded the negative way as superior to the intellectual way,[30] it seems that this kind of experience was not for Colet. He knew the negative way existed (DCH, 172), but he treated Dionysius's mysticism as he treated unassimilable elements in other authors: he simply ignored it.

Instead, Colet belongs to the line of thinkers within his more immediate time frame which "links Petrarch to Lefèvre d'Etaples and Erasmus, and takes in Gerson, Ficino, Pico della Mirandola, Gaguin, Trithemius, and John Colet."[31] If this line of thought is extrapolated backward into time its ultimate Christian sources are the Victorines, Dionysius, and Augustine.

Colet saw Dionysius as a Father of the Church and as the pupil of Paul—neither of which assumptions has stood the test of history. Hence we must consider Dionysius as the early sixteenth-century saw him if we are to understand what Colet found in him. Since the first half of the seventeenth century, scholars have known that the Dionysius whose writings were once so prized was actually a fifth-century figure.[32] He claimed to give an eyewitness account of the execution of Peter and Paul at Rome, to have written letters (which he published) to Paul's disciple Timothy and to Pope Clement, and to have attended with Peter and James the funeral of Mary.[33] Despite, or perhaps because of, these credentials, the Eastern church, which read Dionysius in Greek, doubted almost from the first that the Dionysian writings were genuine. Already at the Colloquy of Constantinople in 532 the Orthodox party rejected them,[34] and striking resemblances to the fifth-century writer Proclus were soon noticed by scholars.[35] The Western church, however, read Dionysius in a series of Latin translations running from John Scotus Eriugena's in the ninth century to those by Ambrogio Traversari (the translator Colet used) and Ficino in the fifteenth.[36] Readers of Dionysius in translation missed the philological clues and failed to assess the historical evidence that alerted the intellectually more advanced East. The few dissenting voices that were raised found no echo, the all but unanimous view being that Dionysius's writings were those of Paul's disciple.

With the gradual increase in the numbers of those who read Greek, however, some misgivings were bound to be felt from time to time; the reactions to them in Colet's circle are interesting. William Grocyn, Colet's friend and a good Greek scholar, gave public lectures on Dionysius, apparently in 1501.[37] Though he began his lectures assuming that the Dionysius of the writings was Paul's disciple, he became convinced as he went along that the opposite was the truth. Because we know Grocyn was right it is easy to assume that his contemporaries accepted his analysis (the lectures themselves are lost). On the contrary, we find that a quarter-century after Grocyn's lectures Dionysius still enjoyed essentially all of his old prestige. In 1525 John Fisher, who knew Grocyn and his views on

Dionysius and had learned Greek, still spoke of Dionysius together with Ignatius, Polycarp, and Clement of Rome as "men of the apostolic age."[38] Moreover Fisher is here writing as a controversialist; in putting Dionysius in the apostolic age he would be exposing himself to rebuttal had not his opponent Luther and the learned world generally still shared this view of Dionysius.

Erasmus seems to have begun to harbor doubts about Dionysius when he began to work seriously on Greek. Already in the *Enchiridion*, dated to 1503, we find him putting some distance between himself and Dionysius, whom he pointedly refers to as "a certain Dionysius."[39] From Erasmus's careful weighing of the evidence in his note 50 to Acts 17:34 (which narrates the conversation of Dionysius by Paul), it is clear what he thought in 1516. Nevertheless, when Luther accused him in 1521 of saying he found Origen and Chrysostom more valuable than Dionysius, Erasmus had, whatever his private reservations, to take the charge seriously and defend himself.[40] In this he was only partially successful. The Theological Faculty of Paris, which already in 1520 had condemned any doubts about Dionysius, renewed the condemnation in 1527, with specific reference to Erasmus.[41]

Though there were ripples of doubt now and then in his circle as elsewhere, Colet continued to share the received opinion of Dionysius. Colet's great regard for him probably explains why William Lily gave one of his children what Lupton calls the "somewhat singular name" of Dionysia;[42] coincidentally or not, Lily was selected as the well-paid high master of Colet's school. His allegiance to Dionysius unshaken, Colet was still quoting him near the end of his life.[43] In an age that estimated the probability of a view by the authority of those who maintained it, it was all but inevitable that the many and great authorities who had vouched for Dionysius over the centuries would suffice to maintain him on his eminence until the "emergence of probability" in the next century.[44]

To return, then, to the religious traditions in which Dionysius continued to hold so high a place. Despite Dionysius's presumed apostolic date the true Christian source of what came to be the Franciscan tradition was rightly held in Colet's time to be Augustine. Dionysius was not cited by Western doctors before Gregory the Great (d. 604), by which time Augustine's commanding position was already established. Colet quotes Augustine relatively often, though Erasmus, aware of Augustine's fundamental importance for Luther, from whom he was trying to detach his correspondent Justus Jonas, told Jonas that toward no one was Colet *iniquior* than toward Augustine (A, 1. 273). Since Erasmus uses the same word in regard to Colet's attitude toward Aquinas, which is unambiguously negative, many writers have concluded that it must be applied in the same negative sense to Augustine. But *iniquus* corresponds quite closely to our use of the word "prejudiced." The context usually settles the sense as negative, "prejudiced against"; but it is also perfectly possible to speak of someone as "prejudiced in favor of" a person. The prepositions that make a final ambiguity impossible in English are not needed in Latin: whichever meaning is intended the dative case is used. Strictly speaking, then, Erasmus was correct in describing Colet's attitude to Augustine by the same word that described his attitude to Aquinas, though for reasons determined by his aim. Colet was no doubt influenced by the contemporary Augustine revival,[45] but he would have been drawn to him in any case.

Besides having wide first-hand knowledge of Augustine, Colet of course drew from him at one or more removes in reading later writers within the Augustinian-Franciscan tradition; for Augustinianism, it has been pithily observed, is the common denominator of every truly Franciscan school.[46] This, I would suggest, may be why Colet—still according to Erasmus—preferred even Duns Scotus to Thomas Aquinas. The Franciscan doctor, for all his famous subtlety, which must have put Colet off, nevertheless shared with Bonaventure the preference for the concrete and the experiential as against the Thomistic abstract essences and intellectualism.

By Colet's time the Franciscan schools in England had displaced Bonaventure in favor of William of Ockham,[47] but Ockham's nominalist stance would have had limited appeal for Colet. Instead Colet responded to the Bonaventure renaissance that was in full swing from the late fifteenth century, especially in northern Europe. The Franciscan pope Sixtus IV, by canonizing Bonaventure in 1482, had at last placed the Franciscan theologian on a footing of equality with the Dominican master St. Thomas Aquinas. Pope Sixtus followed through by proclaiming Bonaventure also a Doctor of the Church in 1488, a distinction which enhanced further the prestige and authority of his teaching.[48]

The extensive influence of Bonaventure in the latter half of the fifteenth century is unmistakable from the number of editions of his works. The great catalogue of incunabula is still far from the letter *T*, so that direct comparisons with the editions of Thomas Aquinas on a full scale are not yet possible. In that catalogue, however, Bonaventure and the pseudonymous writings attributed to him fill 105 columns, while, for purposes of comparison, Boethius and pseudo-Boethius occupy 67 columns, Duns Scotus and pseudo-Duns 29, and Aristotle 115.[49] In the catalogue of incunabula in the libraries of the single country of Belgium, to take an example where direct comparisons of Bonaventure and Thomas are possible, the fifteenth-century editions of Thomas fill 41 columns, those of Bonaventure 39.[50] Bonaventure's influence ran strong also in the manuscript tradition, for over a hundred commentaries under his inspiration were written before 1500.[51]

Colet signals his working in the tradition of Bonaventure by echoing at the beginning of *De sacramentis* the quotation that opens one of Bonaventure's most widely read treatises, the *Breviloquium*, a compendium of his teachings on the whole field of theology. Bonaventure begins by quoting Ephesians 3:15: "for from [Christ] all fatherhood in heaven and on earth take its name"; Colet changes the single word "fatherhood" to "priesthood," for the priesthood of Jesus is to be his subject. A reader of Colet's treatise would understand from this allusion that in his more modest way he too is offering a compendium of his theological views, and this proves to be the case.

In *De sacramentis* Colet deals, as we noted at the beginning of this chapter, with a pair of problems that were much mooted especially in the Franciscan tradition. The Franciscan emphasis on man's nothingness, and the imperative need for him to be incorporated into the Mystical Body of Christ, raised in a particularly acute form the question of why the world had been created at all. Bound up historically with the first question is the question how man is to be restored to God after the original sin set him at variance with God, and separated him both from the natural environment that till then had supported him freely and from his own kind. Though the two questions are intimately related, Colet's standpoint will be clearer if they are discussed successively.

The First Problem:
Why Was the World Created?

So long as God was conceived in anthropomorphic terms the problem of the creation could be resolved in kindred terms. But in proportion as the idea of God was cleared of material and anthropomorphic admixture and he was acknowledged as perfect, all-powerful, and the all-sufficient object of his own contemplation (if the subject-object distinction were conceivable in being utterly at one with itself), it became clear that God could desire nothing other than, nothing "outside," himself. A reality "outside" himself could not exist of its own right but only contingently, dependent, that is, upon God's pleasure but by contributing nothing to it. In short, the development of metaphysics made inconceivable what Revelation proved had actually happened.

The problem had to be tackled at the other end, starting, that is, with the fact that creation had happened and trying to decide why. From the principle of sufficient reason it followed that God had a ground for the creation; it remained only to discover it. The ground could not be an end or purpose, for there was nothing for God to aim at outside his own substance. It was increasingly felt, therefore, that God's perfect goodness must of its nature express itself spontaneously and thus freely in diffusing goodness. This conception goes back at least to Plotinus[52] and is prominent in Dionysius, especially in the treatise *On the Divine Names*. The conception in fact entailed a number of serious difficulties,[53] but as they do not seem to have occurred to Colet we may concentrate instead on the contribution that the axiom regarding the spontaneous self-diffusion of goodness makes to the solution of the problem of the creation.

Diffusion may be regarded as a special case of the principle of plenitude, according to which God's "fullness" is reflected in the fullness of the creation, which must necessarily be filled with all the possible modalities of being. The principle was widely accepted; Colet found it endorsed by Ficino also in one of the essays that he annotated.[54] The Godhead or the One diffuses an image or imitation or vestige of itself. In this manner the One is reflected in images of itself without being essentially multiplied and without being complemented by its own images. The spontaneous diffusion of goodness by Goodness becomes a kind of moral necessity which does not imply unfreedom but rather represents a new domain of moral freedom.[55]

So seen, the entire universe becomes a "temple of God." The concept of *templum Dei*—an expression that occurs repeatedly in *De sacramentis* —was familiar in the West from the "Dream of Scipio" with which Cicero concluded his *Republic*, inspired by the myth of Er with which Plato concluded his *Republic* but more religious and reverential in atmosphere.[56] Thanks to its handling by Macrobius, the "Dream of Scipio" became deeply imbedded in medieval cosmic speculation, becoming part of the tradition associated with Plato's *Timaeus* and *Epinomis*.[57]

Goodness is symbolized, in Colet as in Bonaventure, by a metaphysics of light whose origin is the creating word of Genesis, "Let there be light." Light is the harmonious and harmonizing power that makes possible interaction among initially disparate elements. The more brightly the created thing is illumined (to use Dionysius's term), the more fully capable it is of taking its due place in the divine harmony. Thus as it ascends ever closer to the Light and Oneness, which is its source, the created thing becomes undivided not merely accidentally, as a rock is undivided, but essentially, as a human being is undivided—undivided in such manner that division is unthinkable.[58] The axiom that good is by nature diffusive of itself will prove also to make a powerful contribution to the second of the two problems with which Colet is mainly concerned in *De sacramentis*, the means by which sinful and divided man is restored to union with God.

A Further Complication:
The Problem of Sin

But before we are in a position to trace out Colet's framing of the questions and his proposed solution through the sacraments, we must turn to a central aspect of the problem of creation that forces itself on the Christian thinker. Greek thinkers, including Plato and Plotinus, could discuss the origin of the world without reference to sin, and certain Christian thinkers in the neoplatonic tradition could deal with it through the images of light and darkness, harmony and disharmony.[59] Colet, however, could not leave to one side the role of Satan. He saw him as active and terrible, the endlessly resourceful lord of this world. Central to his discussion in *De sacramentis* is the victory that Christ won over Satan. But would Christ have become man if Adam had not sinned? And from this question it is only a short step to the next: Was man's Fall a preordained part of God's plan?

The question of whether God would have become man had Adam not sinned was thoroughly discussed during the scholastic period. The majority of the doctors—but with two very important exceptions—had concluded that even if Adam had remained sinless Christ would have come, not of course in the passible flesh but in the glorified body he revealed at the Transfiguration. They thus avoided the difficulty that the coming of Christ might appear to depend on the fact of sin, or even that man's fall, which was to call forth God's mercy, was predestined—the position taken nevertheless by Bonaventure's pupil Matthew of Acquasparta.[60] The two great exceptions to this consensus were, however, St. Bonaventure and St. Thomas, who argued that Adam's continued sinlessness would have left Christ's incarnation without a sufficient reason.[61] The point is important for our understanding of the tradition of *De sacramentis*. It is evident that Colet was not dependent on Aquinas, whose account of the creation is worked out on quite different lines from his;[62] instead he follows Bonaventure, with whom even the later Franciscan doctors parted company on this issue.

In following Bonaventure here, Colet is in fact following the twelfth-century Augustinian Hugh of St. Victor, whom Bonaventure held up to the highest admiration in an epigram expressed with his usual fondness for ternaries. It is worth repeating as a reminder that the filiations among medieval doctors which we have been considering are not simply the constructs of modern scholars: Bonaventure was quite conscious of the tradition in which he saw himself working.

The greatest teaching is that of Augustine, the second greatest that of Gregory, while the third teacher is Dionysius. Anselm follows Augustine, Bernard follows Gregory, Richard [of St. Victor] follows Dionysius; because

> Anselm excels in reasoning, Bernard in preaching, Richard in contemplation—but Hugh [of St. Victor] in all three.[63]

Clearly Bonaventure's paradigmatic appreciation of Hugh expresses equally well his own ideals.

Hugh is a transitional figure between the positive theology of the earlier period which worked on isolated problems, and the system-building doctors of the scholastic period. Hugh's *De sacramentis* is the first medieval *summa*,[64] and it soon becomes evident to the reader of Colet's *De sacramentis* that its central concepts derive from Hugh's far larger *summa*.

Hugh and Bonaventure, it will be recalled, believe that God became man only because man had made use of his free will to sin and thus quite literally dissociated himself from the divine Father. They nevertheless insist that the outcome of this cosmic tragedy was creative, following a line of argument that Colet was to make his own. In the fullness of time— Bonaventure had a strong sense that new dispositions needed time to develop—God crowned what Hugh calls his *opera conditionis*, or works of creation, by his *opera restaurationis*, or works of restoration and salvation. Hugh's understanding of the work of restoration is historical and existential, neither drawing a clear line between theology and philosophy nor dealing in abstract essences as the Aristotelian-Thomistic analysis did.[65] In his second preface to *De sacramentis* Hugh makes explicit the connection of the second of Colet's two problems, the restoration of fallen man to union with God, with the sacraments: "The work of restoration is the incarnation of the Word along with all of his sacraments, as well those that preceded, from the beginning of the world, as those that continue them until its end."[66]

Hugh here contrasts the sacraments of the Old Law, which were regarded as basic to human society and therefore in existence from the beginning, with the sacraments that Christ either instituted himself or raised to a new level by associating grace with their conferral. For example, there must always have been a sacrament or sign by which a man and a woman gave themselves to each other in marriage, they argued; likewise there must always have been a felt need for a form of thanksgiving to God.[67] Thus matrimony and the Eucharist are sacraments of the Old Law, by means of which God slowly tightens again the bonds between himself and forsaken man. Out of this concept Colet drew the ultimate motivation for the creation, expressing it in the same threefold form as Bonaventure did: the redemption manifested God's power, his wisdom, and his goodness.[68] What is more, Bonaventure asserted—followed here too by Colet—that the fact of sin made the manifestations of power even more splendid. For it is more difficult—or rather, to avoid anthropomorphic language, it argues greater might—to restore to goodness what has lapsed into evil than to create out of nothing. The underlying conception seems to be that the positive power of God is even further removed from evil, seen as having a kind of negative magnitude of its own, than it is simply from zero or nothing. This theory thus goes beyond the explanation of the incarnation as merely a *reparatio lapsi* and shows it as in addition a positive manifestation of God in his triune aspect.

The Second Problem: How Is Fallen Man Restored to God?

Ready now to confront the second of his two problems in *De sacramentis*, Colet argues that God restores man to unity with himself through the sacraments, in the broad sense in which he uses the term. Colet knew that *sacramentum* originally meant the military oath of the Romans (C, 226 [194]), but far more important for him was its use in a famous pericope (Eph. 5:32) as equivalent, in the Vulgate translation, to *mysterium*. That the sacraments were seven, only seven, and these seven, was defined only a few decades before Colet's birth, in the decree of Pope Eugenius IV "Pro Armenis" (1439); this strict definition followed almost word for word and thus translated into dogma the formulation arrived at by St. Thomas Aquinas. Theologians of a more mystical cast loved to discern in the created world a vast host of signs and affinities and secret correspondences, mysteries that took on their true significance only to the eyes of the discerning. Partly to meet this feeling, no doubt, the seven defined sacraments were surrounded by a host of lesser sacraments called sacramentals, still recognized as such by the Roman Catholic church, while these in turn were surrounded by a limitless penumbra of signs that invited and rewarded speculative insight. Colet himself, though he duly distinguishes the seven sacraments from the others (DEH, 250), strongly leans toward a more comprehensive and capacious sense of what sacraments are: "Whatever is remotely symbolized by a sign perceptible to the senses or by visible tokens is a sacrament" (DEH, 247). Even the early Christian custom of casting lots was for him "a great sacrament" (DEH, 245) — dignified no doubt by its use as the vehicle of God's will in the choice of the Apostle Mathias to replace Judas.

Colet's treatise on the sacraments deals at length with orders and matrimony; in a special sense with reconciliation, as he prefers to call the sacrament of penance; and with baptism. The rest, even the Eucharist, which Colet elsewhere treats as supreme among the sacraments (DEH, 216; cf. C, 242–244 [224–228]), are scarcely mentioned, huddled together into a paragraph at the very end. It is possible that the work was broken off before it could be finished. But I think it more likely that Colet did not find it easy to incorporate all the sacraments into the pattern that he formulated for those he did discuss.

In a sense the Eucharist and baptism are competing symbols of the redemptive action. Stress on baptism, a sacrament received only once, yields a theory of the atonement which stresses the cosmic and decisive character of Christ's liberation of mankind from death and the demonic; whereas stress on the Eucharist, which is a sacrament received repeatedly, tends by contrast to emphasize a progressive redemptive integration. Baptism, moreover, centers on Christ's victory over the Devil, a unique event.[69] The patristic theories of baptism were developed while baptism was still mainly for adults, who went on at once to receive the Eucharist. In this setting the Fathers uniformly saw baptism and not the Eucharist as the primary means of becoming one with Christ.[70] But in later times, especially after the Second Lateran Council in 1139 anathematized the opponents of infant baptism, baptism became almost exclusively a sacrament for infants, and the understanding of what it had once meant largely disappeared. Interestingly, however, Bonaventure retained a strong sense of the older view of baptism; he combined it, as Colet was to do, with nuptial imagery in asserting that baptism effects a spiritual union between God and the soul.[71]

Colet, well read in the Fathers and personally inclined to absolutist positions, also retained a strong sense of the decisive and unique character of baptism. In his treatise he discusses almost exclusively the one-time sacraments of baptism, orders, and, in the special sense that he gave to that sacrament, matrimony. The fourth of the four sacraments that he discusses is reconciliation, which he also saw as ideally a one-time sacrament. As we have seen in other contexts he harbored a lingering inability to accept fully the mercy and forgiveness that the Church taught were extended repeatedly to sinners. For him man was so unworthy as hardly to be conceivable as the recipient of saving grace. Colet's focus on sacraments received only once probably explains the almost complete absence of the Eucharist from his treatise: in this context he did not see his way to giving the Eucharist, which is received repeatedly, the importance that belonged to it in other contexts.

Still, Colet was living in an age deeply influenced by eucharistic theology and piety. The incorporation into Christ which the repeated reception of the Eucharist offered is represented in Colet's *De sacramentis*— characteristically—by what he regards as a one-time experience, incorporation into the Mystical Body of Christ. Deep interest in this conception runs through all his writings; his commentary on the opening chapter of First Corinthians is devoted entirely to this theme, and it appears often elsewhere (R, 190, 208–213, 221; DEH, 223, 244, 249–250, 270; and of course in the short treatise entitled "On the Mystical Body," esp. 187, 194). The Mystical Body was for him more than a metaphor. He conceived it in literal and thoroughgoing fashion. Because the connections of the members of a body with the head and the other members are organic, they must live with the life of that body or else die. Nor, one feels, does Colet draw back from the clear implication that the member, once cut off from the body, cannot be regrafted onto it. For the worthy members of the Mystical Body, moreover, his formulation of their relations to the divine is in terms of the greatest possible intimacies, kinship and marriage. We read in *De sacramentis*:

> Human beings, as brothers or sisters of the daughter of God the Father [the Church], are collectively the spouse of the Son of God; we are sisters to the man in Christ and spouses to the divinity in him. Human beings are also like sisters to this divinity, whom the eternal Son of God espoused so that in the common house of his Father, the church might be to him both sister and spouse.[72]

In an equally extravagant vein Colet expresses the relation of members to Christ in almost pantheistic terms; for example, "that the sons may appear in the sight of God as true, just, and in a sense Christs [*et quidam christi*]" and "one day reign together with Christ in heaven in the company of [*apud*] their common father" (C, 217 [178]). Lupton understandably backs away from the literal translation of "christi" and prints the ambiguous "anointed" instead, taking refuge in the fact that "anointed" is the English for Christ or Messiah (C, p. 82). But the same evasion will not do when we read that men are rendered "gods" ("dii")—we may choose between the capital letter and the small—in the Mystical Body, an assertion that Colet repeats several times (R, 177; CM, 190; DEH, 201). The Mystical Body refers to mankind in its unitary and corporate aspect, an aspect under which one either belongs or one doesn't.[73] It does not really meet the case of the ordinary individual Christian whose recreations are wavering lines with some long-term forward movement but many backslidings. The Mystical Body as Colet understands it offers only the extreme alternatives of either being virtually "gods" and fellow "anointed" or else being cut off and not sharing at all in the life of the body—a dramatic antithesis in which he may have been influenced by Origen.[74] Again one senses Colet's inability to accept fully that repeated forgiveness would be granted for repeated sins, and his lack of understanding for the ordinary workaday Christian. His own sense of the Christian life was cosmic, dramatic, and terrible.

The matrimony metaphor for expressing the reincorporation of fallen and distracted man into Christ is also conceived in all-or-nothing terms. Matrimony as Colet represents it is a one-time commitment for the Bride of Christ, the Church. As in the Mystical Body, so also here the emphasis is on man in his unitary and corporate aspect; "individual," a word which in our day has strongly personal overtones, has for Colet its etymological sense of "undivided." Throughout *De sacramentis* the word "individuum" occurs often—but never in the meaning "individual." The modern sense of the word implies such dividedness as may be necessary for self-realization, but in Colet the meaning is either "concentrated," "not distracted" (as one gives one's "undivided" attention), or "not made up of parts," "single" (like the Latin *simplex*, which also recurs often in the treatise). Man is thus seen as either united or not united to Christ, with no intermediate stages; and if he is united to Christ this is so in virtue of his belonging to the organic collectivity of the Church, the Spouse of the divine Bridegroom.

This strand of thought goes back at least to the Canticle of Canticles and its innumerable spiritual interpretations.[75] It develops also the implications of the enigmatic passage in which Christ speaks of himself (Mark 2:19–20; Matt. 9:15; Luke 5:35) as a Bridegroom (S, 302). Especially influential in this connection was 2 Corinthians 11:2 (quoted by Colet, S, 300; C, 225 [192]), in which Paul speaks of himself as the father who gives his daughter the Church of Corinth in marriage to the Bridegroom Christ. This nuptial mysticism is unknown to Dionysius, in whose works the words "bride" and "bridegroom" do not occur at all, but is rather a development traceable to Origen[76] and St. John Chrysostom, among others.[77]

A Skeleton Key to *De sacramentis*

Such, I think, are the main themes that the reader will meet in turning to the rather opaque text of *De sacramentis*. The title, as we have seen, is not particularly helpful because of the special sense in which Colet used the term "sacraments" and because his strong emphasis on the nonrepeating sacraments gradually convinces the reader that Colet was not trying to produce a conventional treatise on the sacraments. Unhappily, nothing makes it correspondingly clear exactly what he was trying to do. Even the two main problems that underlie the argument are never distinctly stated; they will usually emerge only on repeated readings, and indeed to Lupton they never emerged at all.

Colet's text is virtually continuous in the manuscript, and in any case writers of his day rarely wrote with what we think of as paragraphs in mind. The translation that I offer of the complete treatise in appendix 1 is deliberately as literal as possible, to given an idea of Colet's style when it is not buffered by Lupton's solicitous prose. However, I have sought to accommodate the reader's needs by breaking it into seven sections of very different lengths, each of which carries the main line of the argument a step forward.

The reader who is coming to Colet's only substantial original work for the first time may wish to consult the digest of the argument which follows. Its seven sections correspond to the seven sections into which the translation has been divided. In view of the purpose of this digest, the page references are to the *translation* in appendix 1. For each translated page the Latin original is printed *en face*.

The Argument of *De sacramentis*

1. (pp. 271–277) God is Priesthood and Order.

Priesthood by its very nature offers sacrifice, and the sacrifice it offers is "justice" (Ps. 4:6). Diffusion of this "justice" is the priest's central purpose.

2. (pp. 277–279) The purpose of matrimony is, similarly, to make "justice" fruitful.

Therefore in their true sense Priesthood and Matrimony are the same (compared to which true matrimony, earthly matrimony is merely a shadow).

3. (pp. 279–285) The obstacle to the diffusion of "justice" is sin, and the associated "downward tendency of all things to deformity and evil."

To overcome this obstacle the angelic spirits minister to reconcile man to God by cleansing, illumining, and perfecting him (the threefold process described by Dionysius).

Through the sacraments, the angels convey to man the grace that at any given moment he is capable of receiving. The sacraments are well adapted to man's twofold nature, flesh and spirit, because they make use of a visible sign to signalize an invisible reality.

This ministration produces a gradual progress from "shadow" in the Mosaic Law to "image" in the Christian epoch to "truth" in heaven.

Colet ends this section by emphasizing again that the "exemplar" of all things is in heaven, toward which man is destined slowly to move. The process takes time, and "only God knows" just when each step will lead on to the next.

4. (pp. 285–309) In this long section there is a good deal of repetition and backtracking. But its central subject is God's reasons for creating the world.

The first reason is that it gives scope to God's mercy and power. This explains also the Fall of man, since man thereby rendered himself unworthy of love and union, thus giving occasion for God's mercy. Since, moreover, re-creation out of evil argues greater power than creation out of nothing, the Fall occasioned the exercise of God's power.

The second reason for the creation is that God foreknew that it would ultimately entail the Incarnation, a supreme act of love. Thus the creation and subsequent Fall give scope not only to God's mercy and power but also to his love.

Because there must be some "proportion," something in common, between lover and beloved, the incarnate Christ had to have an unspotted bride.

He would have taken Eve had she been sinless, but she was sullied by sin in the Garden.

In order that his original purpose should not be frustrated, God had to generate out of the sinful flesh that mankind had now become, a bride worthy of himself. This took time. The first step was the Mosaic Law, which rescued man from utter moral confusion. (It had, however, the paradoxical effect of actually increasing evil, since what men had till then been doing unwittingly—the light of nature being for Colet darkness—and therefore blamelessly, was now blameworthy because they knew better.)

In his mysterious good time Christ came to give reality and life to the Law that Moses had outlined but his chosen people had failed to follow.

By the sacraments Christ gave men strength to follow God's will, and by his sacrifice he made them love him and wish to please him.

The sacraments were instituted at his death, and "flowed from his side" (the theory of Augustine), creating the physical basis for union with him.

Thus by his death Christ became both Priest and Bridegroom. He became Priest by the sacrifice of himself, foretold by David in Psalm 4:6, "Sacrifice the sacrifice of justice" (since the Psalms' reference is to Christ). By his espousal of the Church he became Bridegroom also. His sacrifice had therefore produced, at last, a bride worthy of him, a Church "without spot or wrinkle." He made his Bride fertile, and thus stood as male to the Church as female. Within the Church, its superior members correspondingly make fertile those below them. Thus bridegroom and priest prove (like orders and matrimony) to be the same; for the result of each activity is "justice."

Human beings thus become, collectively, the Bride of Christ (the Church).

All the other sacraments "tend toward" matrimony as thus conceived. Through cleansing, illumining, and perfecting man, they make him ready for "this holy wedding."

In concluding "this rather wandering discussion," Colet restates the equivalence of (1) priesthood and matrimony, (2) sacrificing and begetting, and (3) "justice" and progeny.

5. (pp. 305–315) In the light of the foregoing discussion, what is to be said about carnal matrimony?

It is a "remedy" for those unable to follow Jesus in being celibate.

"In the early days of the human race" it was also a type of the true, spiritual matrimony, which in time "scattered and banished" the carnal matrimony that had adumbrated it.

The forming of Eve out of Adam's side foreshadowed the institution of the Church from the blood that flowed from Christ's side.

Now that the true purpose of matrimony is known, carnal matrimony has lost its *raison d'être* and ideally should disappear.

6. (pp. 315–331) Colet now turns to penance and baptism.

To some extent he integrates them into his proposition that all the other sacraments "tend toward" matrimony by discussing penance and baptism as parallel respectively to the Dionysian cleansing and illumining by which men are made fit to be joined in union with Christ.

7. (pp. 331–333) The remaining three sacraments of the Church, the Eucharist, confirmation, and extreme unction, are mentioned very summarily in the last twenty lines. For the two last-named sacraments nothing is given but the traditional proof-texts from Scripture.

This ingenious argument is in effect Colet's personal ecclesiology. Like other inconvenient evidence for his real views it received practically no attention from his Victorian admirers. Lupton left the work untranslated, and even the occasional curious scholar in later times has apparently been deterred by the difficult style and the less-than-lucid exposition. Nevertheless *De sacramentis* deserves the serious attention of those interested in Colet. It displays the hallmarks of his thinking which we have found to characterize his better-known writings. And it has the great importance that it is, for once, not a commentary on another man's work. Instead it is laboriously but candidly original. All the evidence points to its being among the last works that Colet completed, so that it gives a summing-up, in his own personal terms, of the themes that had guided all of his other work. *De sacramentis* gives us in an original treatise the same eclectic, christocentric, and hermetic Colet we have found in his commentaries and his exegesis.

Part III

Vita Activa

9

St. Paul's School: The True "Fellow-Work" with Erasmus

On the last line of his little spiritual treatise "A Ryght Fruitfull Monicion"[1] Colet set side by side two mottoes that summarize its teaching: "Use well temporall thynges," and "Desyre eternall thynges." We have seen that while he aimed at eternal truths he sought to translate them into working terms of "living wisdom." So it was with temporal things. He did not envision possession only, but also putting what he possessed to use.

Ever since his brother Richard's death (between 1503 and 1505), John Colet knew he would inherit from his father, then in his seventies, a very substantial estate. He decided to use a large part of his fortune to found a school in the heart of his native London. Behind the decision lay a tangle of motives that probably not even he could have sorted out completely, and there is no telling which of them weighed heaviest. Emulation may have played some role, for as we will see a number of heads of the great guild companies had founded schools in their native cities. Probably more important, Colet had quite a bit of experience with young people and apparently enjoyed his contact with them. It looks as if he had a good many pupils first and last, for in his will he left all his books printed on paper to be disposed of "to poore studentes and especially to suche as hath bene schollars withe me."[2] Though the *puer senex* model of much Renaissance educational thinking now comes in for criticism for its mingled condescension and repressiveness, its good side apparently predominated in Colet's teaching. The work that he did on Romans, initially for a boy named Edmund apparently in his late teens, shows both a solicitude for the boy's morals (RO, 212) and a vast willingness to take him seriously.

We would naturally like to know more about how Colet related to his pupils. Not surprisingly, the few further wisps of information I have been able to gather point to some successes and some failures. Among the failures was John Dudley, whose later career of intrigue made him a duke under Edward VI but brought him to the block under Mary. Colet became John's guardian after his father, the notorious Edmund Dudley, was executed, when John was about twelve; the boy may have remained in Colet's household several years, but the idealistic dean's teachings obviously made no lasting impression on him.[3]

But while with some pupils Colet's precepts went in one ear and out the other, there were also pupils who were grateful all their lives for what he had taught them. One of these was the "Gaspar" of Erasmus's colloquy "Pia confabulatio." After he was grown up, Gaspar, as narrated in chapter 7 (above), gratefully testified to the religious influence of his old teacher. A treatise written by Thomas Lupset may indeed give us a firsthand glimpse of how Colet behaved toward his pupils, since Lupset has been tentatively identified with Gaspar. The treatise is dedicated to a former pupil of Lupset's, now a grown man, Edmond Withipoole. In a crabbed but touching preface Lupset reveals to his old pupil that he himself had been trained not to show the affection he felt for his pupils, so that only now can he confess to Withipoole the feelings he had toward him in those former days: "Longe I haue ben taught, that the mayster neuer hurtethe his scholer more, than whan he uttereth & shewethe by cheryshyng and cokerynge, the loue that he bearethe to his scholars."

Lupset does not say who "taught" him this, but the lesson may well derive from reflections on his own school days passed in Dean Colet's household. It would be in keeping with Colet's reserved manner but passionate temperament that he should remain similarly aloof while Thomas was his pupil, only to confess to him later that he refrained from showing affection at the time in order not to spoil the lad. Now that Lupset was a teacher himself he told his favorite former pupil that his "lothnesse" at the time to express his affection openly "came . . . of that I loued you." "But nowe in as moche you be of age, . . . I wyl not deferre any longer the expressynge of myne harte, that no lesse louethe and fauourethe you, than yf nature had made you eyther my sonne or my brother." There were certainly times, he recalled, when they had had disagreements; but

if you wyll call to your minde all the frayes, that haue benne betwene you and me, or betwene me and Smythe [another pupil], you shall fynde, the causes euer depended of a care I had for your and his maners [i.e., character development], whan I sawe certayne phantasies in you or him, that iarred from true opinions, the which true opinions, aboue al lernyng, I wolde haue masters euer teche theyr scholers.[4]

The primacy of moral education over strictly academic training sounds like Colet. Both men would conceive it their duty to mask the affection they felt for the more receptive boys in order not to spoil them—another practical exercise in repression.

I am inclined to think that the fondness Lupset felt for his more promising pupils, his emphasis on moral education above all, and the self-restraint he imposed on himself to keep from showing how fond he was of the pupils reflect, partly unconsciously, the practice of Colet himself during the years Lupset spent in his house. In any case one can safely discount the allegation, first made in the eighteenth century, that Colet took pleasure in being harsh to children.[5] The truth seems to be exactly the opposite. In principle and practice no work was dearer to Colet than the education of the still-unspoiled young.

Once Colet decided to found a school in London he had to turn to the question of who would administer the projected school. Though Lupton, who liked to imagine Colet an innovator, thought that the lay trustees of St. Paul's School were an innovation,[6] evidence for the institution of lay trustees goes back at least as far as 1402–1403, when we find the school of Stratford-on-Avon administered by a guild—in practice, the town council.[7] A number of London guild companies also administered schools. The Goldsmiths administered both the Stockport grammar school founded by Sir Edmund Shaa (or Shaw) in 1487–1488 and the Cromer grammar school founded by Sir Bartholomew Read in 1503;[8] the Merchant Taylors acted in the same capacity for the school established at Wolverhampton by Sir Stephen Jennings around 1512.[9] Local lay trustees were also entrusted with schools at Macclesfield (1502–1503)[10] and at Bridgnorth in Shropshire (1503).[11] Finally, the Mercers themselves had been administering the college of their former master Robert Whittington since 1421,[12] and the school at Faryngho (later Farthingoe) since 1443.[13]

Colet's comment (qtd. in A, ll. 366–370) that, all things considered, he found less corruption in "married men of established reputation" than in any other comparable group, is rightly often quoted. There are, however, other than moral reasons for his preferring laymen as governors of the school and as masters. The experience of such schools as those just mentioned showed that the arrangement worked well. Especially in the case of institutions governed by the Mercers, where he was an insider, Colet was in a good position to evaluate trustees' fidelity to testators' intentions under changing circumstances. As a result, his statutes for the school contain a section expressly granting the company liberty to interpret the meaning of the statutes when unforeseeable eventualities should render that necessary.[14]

A further consideration was the changing economic and political climate. As a churchman he was aware that Crown policy was increasingly directed toward suppressing chantries and monasteries under the pretext of merging them with others, whereupon the endowments of the suppressed institutions were sequestered. He perhaps foresaw, correctly, that if authority over schools was entrusted to ecclesiastical bodies, the schools could become a takeover target. And in fact the Chantries Act of 1547 did include ecclesiastically controlled schools in its purview; only St. Paul's and other schools whose statutes specified lay headmasters escaped the meshes of the act. A school placed under the protection of a secular foundation "offered no pretext for the appropriation of its funds," as a modern scholar bluntly puts it.[15] At the time St. Paul's was founded these clouds were still no bigger than a man's hand, but they were there; by 1524, long before the Reformation, Wolsey was specifically empowered by the pope to suppress any monastery in England.[16] Colet was a founder who took the long view.

Colet came into his father's fortune after the latter's death on 1 October 1505. Already by 1508 he had begun to build a large schoolhouse of stone in Paul's Churchyard, where no fewer than 153 boys were to be taught free. Also in 1508 Colet was made free of the Mercers,[17] no doubt in contemplation of their being ultimately asked to become trustees for the school. From a document dated 1 July 1509 it appears that by that date an endowment in real estate was being assembled to support the school.[18] The master's house, a frame building, was erected after 17 August 1510 but before 28 March 1511.[19] The original plan envisioned two teachers, the high master and the "surmaster," as the second master is known at St. Paul's; but by April 1513, after the school had been in operation less than a year, the plan was enlarged to include a chaplain, who, if he was learned, could also serve as a third master. With the chaplain came a decision to endow a chantry in the chapel of St. Mary and St. John, also in Paul's Churchyard, where daily mass was being offered by 10 June 1514.[20]

As preparations went forward Colet entered into formal negotiations with the Mercers to act as trustees. On 9 April 1510 the company was formally apprised of the dean's intention and appointed a committee to work out further details. On 12 April the committee, having submitted a favorable interim report, waited on Colet, who then on 16 April submitted a list of lands in three counties whose revenues were to be allocated to the support of the school. As was usual in such cases Colet also made a substantial donation of lands in London whose revenues would compensate the company for its pains. On the following day the livery considered Colet's proposal and voted to accept the trust.[21] The speed with which this important commitment was made, eight days from start to finish, strongly suggests that the company had been sounded out earlier and an acceptable agreement arrived at, with subsequent approval a formality.

A number of details show that the school became operative in 1512 or not long before. Title to the lands in Buckinghamshire whose revenues were to be used for the support of the school was formally conveyed to the company on 21 July 1511.[22] On 6 September, still in 1511, the dean and chapter of St. Paul's conveyed to the company a small piece of unused land between two buttresses on the east side of the cathedral, to be used as a spot where the 153 boys could relieve themselves. (One wonders what the neighbors thought of the rent, which was one red rose every ninety-nine years.)[23] The schoolhouse was described as "new" on 30 March 1512,[24] and on 15 June 1512 Colet formally attended a meeting of the court of the company and read aloud the proposed articles of governance, which the company promptly accepted.[25]

The large and handsome new structure cast completely into the shade the cathedral school which had been attached to St. Paul's for centuries. The relation of Colet's school to the earlier school is discussed at length in Lupton's biography, which attributes novelty to Colet's foundation at every point. However, Lupton's loyal effort was discredited by the historian of the school[26] and quite demolished a year later by Arthur F. Leach, the leading authority on Tudor schooling.[27] The latter study showed that Colet's foundation was not a completely fresh beginning, as Lupton thought, but simply superseded on a far grander scale the existing cathedral grammar school. Leach's monograph nettled the school's historian, Michael F. J. McDonnell, because Leach concluded that the existing grammar school had been basically a good one which Colet belittled in order to glorify his own foundation.[28] McDonnell returned to the fray with a further volume on the school published posthumously exactly a half-century after his first history.[29] The result of the protracted controversy has essentially vindicated Colet's assertion, made in a petition to Pope Julius II dated simply "1512," that the previously existing cathedral grammar school was "manifestly of no importance" ("nullius plane momenti").[30] The reason for petitioning Rome was that while the cathedral grammar school now was refounded and expanded, and administered by a secular corporation, legal authority over it was still vested in the chancellor of the cathedral. The then chancellor Dr. William Lichfield had already in 1511 voluntarily surrendered his authority over the school to the Mercers, but Colet, well versed in ecclesiastical law, wanted to make certain that no subsequent chancellor could reassert authority over the school. The petition was apparently acted upon favorably; thenceforward the government of the school and the selection of the high masters belonged solely to the company.[31] The singing school of the cathedral, which Lupton, to compound the confusion, failed to distinguish from the cathedral's grammar school,[32] continued to exist for its stated purpose even after the grammar school had been absorbed into Colet's foundation.

Colet seems to have participated actively in running the school's affairs as long as he lived, as is often the case with founders. Notwithstanding the school's statutes, it was he personally who selected the first high master, William Lily, godson of his friend William Grocyn and father of a large family. The high master was exceptionally well paid, receiving, at £20 annually, twice as much, for example, as the high master of the well-regarded Magdalen College School at Oxford, who himself was considered well paid.[33] That the post was considered advantageous is shown by Lily's appointing his son-in-law John Ritwise as a surmaster and thus qualifying him to succeed him under the statutes, as in fact happened on Lily's death. That Ritwise came to Lily's notice in the first place was, however, Colet's doing, for Ritwise had been recommended to him by Erasmus;[34] Colet seems also to have selected and paid the chaplain.[35]

Colet fully trusted the Mercers, but as his father's son he automatically took extra precautions to protect the integrity of his trust. He saw to it that the trust was kept in an entirely separate account from all the Mercers' other dealings—the only such separate account for any trust administered by the company until the nineteenth century.[36] Moreover he introduced his own "servant," or agent, William Newbold, into the company on 15 June 1512, the very day that Colet formally presented the school's statutes for approval by the company.[37] Newbold's job was to keep an eye on the administration of the dean's trust. The successful businessmen who made up the small committee that administered the trust (the master and four wardens only—another precaution) did not take Colet's measures amiss, and Newbold's role was not felt to be an adversarial one. He became an accepted fixture in the company and privy to its inner workings, as shown by his being "admytted" as secretary on 1 February 1522, several years after the dean's death, in which office he continued to serve until his own death some twenty-one years later.[38] In the last analysis, however, Colet knew that after both he and his personal agent were gone the future of the school would depend on the integrity of the Company. This is why, with his insider's knowledge of their workings, he had chosen the Mercers in the first place. As a testator later in the century put it, "Let men give never so large legacies, yet if there be failing in the execution then all comes to nothing."[39]

The Londoners who watched the school buildings go up and in due course saw masters and boys take up their work inside, looked on the structure with pride and doubtless with gratitude. The founder fully shared their pride and liked to refer to the institution as "my school," not infrequently adding that it was built at great expense. Its true purpose, however, was not mainly to give the boys secular schooling. On the facade Colet had this inscription cut: "Schola Catechizationis Puerorum in Christi Opt. Max. Fide et Bonis Literis" ("School for the Instruction of

Boys in the Faith of Christ Best and Greatest, and in Good Literature").[40]
The order in which the school's concerns were stated was conventional,
but that it was deeply felt can be seen from the unusual number of boys
to be educated on the foundation, exactly 153.

Lupton—unwilling to see his subject allegorizing—argued at length[41]
but vainly against the obvious fact that Colet took the number 153 from
the miraculous draft of fishes in John 21:11. Colet himself set great store
by the number. On a manuscript copy of the school statutes he juggled
the numbers until he produced a grand total of holidays and half-holidays
in his school that came to 153.[42] This number had already excited the interest of medieval exegetes.[43] Writers in the monastic tradition, such as
Cassiodorus, saw the fish as Colet did, as symbolizing men "drawn up by
the nets of the Gospel from the stormy depths of this world."[44] Augustine's active fancy noted that 153 is the sum of all the successive numbers
from one to seventeen, and decided that the base number seventeen was
chosen because it summed the commandments in the Decalogue and the
sevenfold spirit of God.[45] A more compelling interpretation of the
number—possibly known to Colet, who seems to have been interested
in number symbolism (cf. C, 252 [248], on the number ten and G, 197,
on the number six)[46]—is that it is a "triangulated" number. If one imagines the largest element in its sum, seventeen, as the base of a triangle
built up of the successively smaller numbers sixteen, fifteen, and so on
and having as its apex the number one, the number thus built up, having
the aspect of a triangle, is by an easy inference seen as sacred because
it represents the Trinity.[47] The unusually specific number[48] of the pupils
points to the evangelical concern that was the reason for the school's
existence.[49]

Colet's School showed certain novel features, but its novelties were
practical and administrative rather than curricular. The master, we have
noted, was exceptionally well paid and was lodged in a newly built house.
Here is at least a hint that Colet was interested in a wide reform then still
in its very early stages, the development of teaching in the schools as itself
a profession. If teaching was to be more than a makeshift or second-best
for a cleric or layman who would have preferred to be doing something
different, it would have to be reasonably well paid, develop a collective
self-esteem, and enjoy public respect as other professions did. As first
steps to such an end Colet at least paid good salaries, the sine qua non
for attracting good people, which also made teaching in the schools possible as a career for married men.[50] His putting the school under a secular
corporation also tended in the long run to the same end. His foundation
was exceptionally large and aimed for practical purposes at the sons of
the rising middle class. The 153 boys on the foundation outnumbered the
seventy scholars plus sixteen choristers on the foundation at Winchester

or the seventy scholars at Eton,[51] though the latter two schools also enrolled considerable numbers of town boys.[52] The fact that Colet's foundation was set in the heart of the capital city also ensured it a strong influence; with an eye to the city's cosmopolitan commercial population, St. Paul's was specifically opened to boys of all nations.[53] Middle-class boys were for a century and a half almost the sole constituency of St. Paul's, unlike more aristocratically oriented schools. As magistrates and servants of the Crown, as members of the learned professions, as merchants, the pupils of St. Paul's could make a difference; Colet hoped to set a distinctively Christian stamp on them early, knowing that in their future careers the boys would have ample scope for their virtues. Of course Colet had no monopoly of this insight; but the size and site of his school increased its influence.

According to Erasmus, Colet shared a widespread conviction that meaningful change would have to come from the generation that was not yet corrupted; the adults could hardly be reached. Referring to a poem of his which sets forth what it means to be a Christian, Erasmus explains to a correspondent that he wrote it in a simple style because it was commissioned for use in Colet's school. Colet, he explained, "finding his own age deplorable in the last degree, fixed on tender youth as the new bottles to which he would entrust the new wine of Christ."[54]

In his hopes for the school the realist and the idealist in Colet came together to the benefit of each component. On one side he was a doer. He exulted in the hopefulness and vitality of his plan. He expected his school to go down the centuries, as it has done, into an inconceivable future. He could not control it beyond its first generation, no matter what precautions he took, and he knew he had to bet on someone or something. Characteristically, he bet on an institution, the Mercers' Company, for Colet was always a man comfortable with structures. Within this framework he bet on the young people and the future. He must have known on some level that the world was not, for him personally, "deplorable in the last degree," though the preacher in him continued to insist that it was. It was a familiar world in which he was highly comfortable and influential, busy, respected, and in his last decade increasingly drawn into political life. But while he did not renounce any of his own advantages he sensed that the system that had treated him so well had lost momentum. Something would have to change, though like most well-situated reformers he probably assumed the existing state of things would last out his time—as it did, barely.

Founding a good school with good teachers and good pupils, like any creative act, carries with it a measure of risk. Even though not necessarily in opposition to religious tradition, a notably humanistic education develops its own momentum and by its nature highlights the possibilities of this-worldly tradition. The pupils are bound to develop a strong sense of all that man can do and demonstrably has done for himself. The great human structures of man's past—literature, law, unfettered speculation about man's nature and destiny, as well as great buildings and paintings and gardens—all this speaks of things potentially subversive to a religious man of Colet's stamp.[55]

Having taken the momentous step of founding a school, Colet, being only human, did what he could to moderate and channel the consequences of his act. His school was not intended to be notably humanistic. His personal and especially his religious conservatism show in the curriculum he adopted for St. Paul's, as compared with the curricula of other schools of earlier foundation. If one adopts the distinction between "humane," or humanistic, schools and "Christian schools" proposed by one historian of Tudor education,[56] then Eton, Winchester, and Wolsey's Ipswich schools, all similar to one another in curriculum, fall into the humanistic category, while St. Paul's falls into the Christian class—a characterization that Colet would have considered a compliment, of course.

The issue on which St. Paul's School, as its founder conceived it, parted company with the more humanistically oriented schools was the role of the Latin and Greek classic writers. That issue was not a novel one in the early sixteenth century. It had been pretty thoroughly thrashed out a hundred years earlier in the *Lucula noctis* of Giovanni Dominici. Dominici, in true scholastic form, set up the discussion as a dispute. To be fair, he took the arguments in favor of the study of the classics from an eloquent humanist partisan, Coluccio Salutati, the chancellor of the Florentine Republic. Salutati's points were then contested by the author, a Dominican friar. His book, written in 1405,[57] is divided into a prologue and forty-seven sections, to correspond with the forty-eight letters of the verse John 1:5, "Lux in tenebris lucet et tenebre eam non comprehenderunt," in Dominici's spelling. The disputants interpreted the verse in characteristically opposite ways; for Salutati the light shining in the darkness was that of classical antiquity dispelling the darkness of ignorance, while for Dominici it was of course the light of Christianity illuminating the pagan darkness. After the prologue Dominici objectively sets out Salutati's arguments in twelve sections; in the remaining thirty-five sections he proceeds to refute them.[58] The book's importance for our subject is twofold. First, Dominici's using the verse John 1:5 to give structure to his argument reminds us that no matter how opposed the interpretations of this verse were, both parties accepted as common ground that the ultimate end of study, at least in principle, was to interpret Scripture. Further, the substance of Dominici's book establishes that the issue was well understood but controversial a century before Colet's "Statutes"; his curriculum was not simply a statement of personal preference, though it was that too, but intentionally programmatic.

Colet's "Statutes" set forth in no uncertain terms "what shalbe taught."[59] After a bow in the direction of "good literature both laten and greke" Colet declares that the authors he wants read are "suych as haue the veray Romayne eliquence joyned withe wisdome specially Cristyn auctours that wrote theyre wisdome with clene and chast laten other [i.e., either] in verse or in prose." The reason for preferring "Cristyn auctours" is very specific: "for my entent is by thys scole specially to incresse knowlege and worshipping of god and oure lorde Crist Jesu and good Cristen lyff and maners in the Children." The same purpose, it will be remembered, was chiseled into the facade of the school building in large letters: this school is a "School for the Instruction of Boys in the Faith," with "Good Literature" mentioned in second place.

From the same section on curriculum it is clear that Colet had well-defined ideas of what "Good Literature" meant. The books he specified come from two sources: texts specially commissioned for the school, "and thenne other auctours Christian as lactancius prudentius and proba and sedulius and Juuencus and Baptista Mantuanus and suche other as shalbe tought convenyent [i.e., thought suitable]." Then follows a rather confused passage that seems intended to distinguish pure Latin idiom, "the olde laten spech and the varay Romayne tong which in the tyme of Tully and Salust and Virgill and Terence was vsid," from barbarism and corruption in formal elements on the one hand, and from immorality on the other. Colet chooses to ignore the fact that there was plenty of immorality in the literature of Cicero's and Vergil's time, and also that the language of "seint Jerome and seint Ambrose and seint Austen" is no longer classical. For him the important criterion is Christian content, which makes the writings of the fourth century classical enough for him, while it causes him to decry much literature of the Golden Age as, in his neologism, "blotterature" which he did "vtterly abbanysh and Exclude oute of this scole."

Colet's was an extreme position. A present-day historian of education finds him "the least adventurous of all his contemporaries" because of his antagonism to classical literature, and adds that "his attitude to pagan authors was still medieval in its proscription."[60] Colet the educator is the same Colet who in exegesis denied to secular scholarship any value in interpreting Scripture, finding that deference to anything outside the Christian tradition was in Paul's phrase "sacrificing to demons" (Acts 16:16). Colet did not regard himself as faced with a conflict between countervailing goods. A conflict would arise only if the opposed ideals in question were of equal consequence. In Colet's school, however, the ethico-religious dimension was paramount. It was to be furthered, if possible, in the best Latin—hence the mention of Cicero and Vergil. But if a choice had to be made in order to avoid "ffylthynesse" and "blotterature," then Latinity was no consideration at all. Juvencus, Sedulius, Proba, and their like were quite good enough for the purpose at hand—in fact better, because their themes were explicitly Christian.

Baptista Mantuanus (1448–1516) is the only modern writer whom Colet groups with his "auctours Christian," but the apparent anomaly disappears when one recalls that he was spoken of as the Christian Vergil, on the strength of his having in common with the other Vergil a birthplace in Mantua. In an early and possibly not quite candid letter to a bishop and patron, Erasmus even professed to see a time coming when Baptista "would not fall far short of his fellow citizen in glory and fame."[61] At least in educational circles the Carmelite poet and theologian did very well during the sixteenth century. Baptista's poems found a place in the schools of the Brethren of the Common Life and also in those of the early Jesuit colleges, while from an allusion in *Love's Labor's Lost* he appears to have made his way as far west as Stratford-on-Avon.[62] Besides the pastorals in which he was thought by some to rival his "fellow citizen," the adaptable Baptista took a leaf from Ovid's book and composed *Fasti*, an alternative to the pagan original which was organized according to the church calendar of saints.

With the exception of Baptista Mantuanus and Lactantius, a prose writer who was another Christian alternative (the Christian Cicero), all Colet's recommended writers appear in similar lists drawn up centuries earlier, one by Alcuin of York at the end of the eighth century and the other by Vincent of Beauvais in the thirteenth century.[63] In fact three of Colet's unadventurous four Christian poets are found in a still earlier list, the "Versus in bibliotheca" of Isidore of Seville,[64] who died in the year 636.

The proof that Colet's attempt to restrict the boys of St. Paul's to explicitly Christian writers was excessively conservative is that it did not work. I presume that while he lived his views on "what shalbe taught" were observed at least in the main, but this brings us down only to the seventh year of the school's existence. After his death, if not even before, some quiet modernization of the curriculum in this respect took place, no doubt with an eye on such foundations as Eton and Winchester.[65] With the death of the hand-picked first high master in 1522, the era of Colet's direct control was over. The fragmentary evidence for the school's first half-century seems to show that the prescription of Christian poets had become a dead letter.[66] In fact the curriculum for 1559, which survives by a fortunate chance, included not one of Colet's four Christian poets, nor yet Lactantius, the Christian Cicero; less than fifty years after Colet's list was drawn up the only survivor was the durable Baptista Mantuanus.[67]

The facts concerning the teaching of Greek at St. Paul's are not quite so clear. The statutes mention in general terms "good literature both laten and greke," but the evidence for when and how long Greek was actually taught is partly conflicting.[68] It is possible that Lily, though a good Greek scholar, found that he and his surmaster had their hands full teaching 153 boys the other necessary subjects, even after being joined by a chaplain who served as second usher a year or two later. Some confirmation that Greek may have had to be sacrificed in the earliest years is afforded by the fact that when Greek is first actually known to have been taught it was being taught by a master brought in especially for the purpose. This was a friend of Erasmus's, Herman Hamelman, who taught Greek during and after 1516, though for how many years is not known.[69] We know that Greek was not being taught in 1559. The reason, however, was the admitted incompetence of the high master to teach it. If it is true, as he claimed, that his inability to teach Greek was perfectly well known when he was hired ten years earlier, this would suggest that back in 1549 Greek was not considered a necessary part of a high master's equipment. If there was a Greekless interlude, perhaps a considerable one, before 1549, one could understand more readily why the high master had been in his place for ten years before the deficiency was made a ground of complaint against him. But to complicate matters, a further, unavowed factor seems to have played a part in the dismissal of the Greekless high master of 1559. Another of the Tudor religious revolutions had just taken place. With Queen Mary's death in 1558 the old religion had been banished once again. The examiners of the school in 1559 were all strong Protestants who may have used the high master's known Greeklessness simply as a pretext for replacing him by a man both more learned and more congenial theologically.[70]

From all this we may perhaps conclude that the teaching of Greek, while a part of Colet's plan from the outset, was carried out only fitfully during the early years. This reading of the evidence is compatible with Colet's emphasis on religious and ethical considerations as a first priority. When Colet himself at length understood the importance of Greek for the study of Scripture, after Erasmus's Greek New Testament appeared in 1516, his school suddenly acquired a qualified teacher of Greek.

If Colet's attitude toward Latin literature of the Golden Age and perhaps also the Greek language was soon superseded in his own school, he was much more successful in the textbooks he specified. Thanks to his friendship with Erasmus, who was living in England while the school was being set up, Colet was able to commission from him a number of schoolbooks. Among the slighter pieces were several "Carmina scholaria"[71] and a "Sermon on the Child Jesus" to be delivered by a boy in the school.[72] Some writers have seen in the latter a reflection of the boy bishop tradition of the later middle ages,[73] but since the anarchic dimension is of course entirely lacking and there is no reference to social problems as such, it seems safer to take the sermon at face value, as an encouragement to children to follow the "perfect child."[74] An image of the Child Jesus was erected over the master's chair, with the inscription "Ipsum audite" (Matt. 17:5) added at Erasmus's suggestion (A, ll. 517–518); it would serve as a stimulus, and perhaps also as a reproach, to the throng of youngsters.[75]

More substantial and far more important was the rhetorical text that Erasmus drew up for the school, *De duplici copia verborum ac rerum*. Though its earlier stages apparently go back as far as 1501 and it was in tentatively complete form already in 1508,[76] the work was not published until Colet commissioned it for his school, in 1512. The book was an immense success, running into hundreds of later editions down through the eighteenth century. It was a happy chance for Colet that the appearance of his name in the book did more to make his name recognized than any other one factor, especially on the Continent. As a textbook, the *De copia* falls into the two parts promised by its title. In the first, the pupil learns to acquire an "abundance of words" ("copia verborum") in chapters that use the many rhetorical figures as patterns whereby he can vary almost at will the expression of a given idea while the idea itself remains unchanged. A masterpiece of sorts is chapter 33, in which the author uses the principles he has taught to demonstrate 194 different ways of saying "I was pleased to get your letter" and 200 variations of "Always, as long as I live, I shall remember you."

The first part of *De copia* is devoted to enlarging the pupil's means of expressing his ideas; the second is devoted to the complementary enterprise of enlarging the number of ideas he has to express ("copia rerum," or "abundance of material"). Here Erasmus gives a fresh treatment to the key element in ancient rhetorical theory, that of "invention," or finding things to say. Though Erasmus does not quote from him, he is clearly thinking of the perfect orator as defined by Cicero's teacher Lucius Crassus—"a man who can speak with fulness and variety on any topic."[77] To be an orator in this wide sense a man had to have, as Cicero had, wide culture, ready wit, and thorough training; Erasmus's *De copia* in both its parts is intended as a long first step in that direction.

The *De copia* owed its great success not only to its pedagogical merit but to its broad-minded conception of Christianity and classical culture as natural allies.[78] It was written by an acknowledged master of its subject, and Erasmus placed his book's technical merits in the service of a far-reaching ideal. He fully shared Colet's sense that it was vital to reach the young; he did not disdain, as scholars such as Budé or later Scaliger did, to take time from weightier studies in order to write texts that would be in the hands of thousands of young men during their most impressionable years. He was far from sharing Colet's rigidity on everything having to do with sex and deliberately recognized its importance for his young audience without giving it disproportionate attention; he unobtrusively encouraged them to take a balanced Christian view of this as of other aspects of real life. Erasmus's educational work, like Colet's, was meant as a contribution to the reforming of men.

Alongside Erasmus's rhetorical texts Colet intended to have a new Latin grammar written for his school. His first idea was to use a grammar written by the scholarly Thomas Linacre. This work, however, which has not survived, must have been deemed unteachable by the headmaster who had to actually get the Latin grammar into his young charges' heads. Linacre replaced it with an essentially new grammar in a simpler form[79] — a work which, after being given the final touches by Erasmus, established itself as a classic in the genre.[80]

Probably Colet, with his wary conservatism, had thought he was playing safe by having these texts specially commissioned for use in his school. If so, he would have felt some disappointments. At bottom, *De copia* takes for granted the ultimate harmony of what is best in pagan culture with Christianity — a conviction to which Colet refused to pay even lip service. Moreover, Erasmus's major contribution to the revision of the Latin grammar was to provide illustrations of the grammatical principles, and he took them from classical writers only — a subtle persistent reminder that would not be lost on the boys. Can Colet's ostentatious slowness in paying Erasmus the agreed-on fifteen angels for *De copia* — Erasmus had to write him an emphatic dunning letter[81] — reflect his feeling that Erasmus had let him down by showing too strong humanist sympathies in his textbook?

A contribution by Colet himself to the texts used in his school was a modest "Cathecyzon" running to some five average-size pages.[82] This little catechism lists first the twelve articles of the Apostles' Creed, then the seven sacraments of the Church and the spiritual effect of each. Then follow three short paragraphs, devoted to love of God, love of self, and love of neighbor; under the last of these headings are mentioned "specyalli my fader and my moder that brought me into this worlde," "the mayster that techeth me," and "my felowes that lerne with me." Next are four one-sentence injunctions, the last two quite touching in the mouths of children: "Whan I shal dye I shal call for the sacraments"; "And in peryl of deth I shal gladly call to be enealed."

The catechism concludes with a list of forty-nine (only coincidentally seven times seven?) miscellaneous precepts, phrased as brief *sententiae* of the sort Colet favored. The boy is urged to fear and love God, "to worship hym and his moder Mary," to avoid such schoolboy vices as swearing and foul language, anger, "ryot," unchasteness, idleness. A good many of the *sententiae* inculcate the virtues that were especially dear to the class from which the pupils were drawn. "Be sobre of meet & drynke." "Dispend measurably [i.e., spend moderately]." "Flee dyshoneste." "Be true in word & dede." "Reuerence thyne elders." "Be alwaye wel occupyed." "Lose no tyme." "Wasshe clene." "Be no slogard." "Awake quyckly." "Enrich thee with vertue." "Lerne dylygently." At the end of the list: "By this waye thou shalte come to grace and to glory. Amen."

When the boys had mastered the "Cathecyzon" in English prose, they were given it again in Latin verse, this time in hexameters by Erasmus. This became the "Institutum Christiani homines [*sic*] which that lernyd Erasmus made at my request."[83] In its elegant Latin verse form the originally rather rustic "Cathecyzon" was soon picked up by other schools and widely diffused all across Europe. With the advantage of Erasmus's name and with its own quietly noncontroversial content it continued to find favor with all confessions even well after the Reformation, until Luther's catechism became classical among Protestants.

In England itself the "Institutum Christiani hominis" probably gave its title to the *Institution of a Christian Man* (1537),[84] which enjoyed official status during the Henrician reformation (though not afterward).[85] Some scholars see the "Institutum" as belonging to the Protestant catechism tradition that culminates in Luther. The Tyrolian humanist and Protestant educator Petrus Tritonius Athesinus made it the second part of a catechism whose first part, also in hexameters, he composed himself.[86] Erasmus's version of Colet's "Cathecyzon" was equally acceptable even after the Reformation to Nicholas Barbonius (*Pedagogium seu morum puerilium praecepta christiana*, 1542) in Catholic Cracow and to Johannes Sulpitius (*De moribus puerorum carmen*, 1553) in Protestant Utrecht, as well as to the England of the *via media* under Elizabeth and her successors.[87]

Colet's other contribution to the textbooks used in his school was equally minor and equally fortunate. He drew up an explanation of the eight parts of speech which he thought would be well suited to beginners, included in a work often called *Coleti Aeditio* (first surviving edition, 1527), which became a standard textbook that was used for many generations.[88] In writing this elementary introduction to grammar, Colet had in mind as usual both educational and pastoral concerns. He wanted texts the youngsters could handle; he wanted them to succeed and see that they could do good work. All the while they would be imbibing the Christian outlook that was the school's real reason for existence. Addressing himself to the children directly, Colet writes that he hopes he has made the eight parts of speech "a lytel more easy to yonge wyttes than (methynketh) they were before. Judgyng that no thynghe may be to softe nor to famylyer to lytel children, specyally lernynge a tongue vnto them al straunge," he did not write

> to shewe ony grete connynge [i.e., knowledge], wyllyng to speke the thynges often before spoken in suche maner as gladli yonge begynners and tender wyttes myght take & conceyue. Wherfore I praye you, al lytel babys, al lytel chyldren, lerne gladly this lytel treatyse. . . . And lyfte vp your lytel whyte handes for me, whiche prayeth for you to god.[89]

There is no need to find "sources" for this warm and unforced passage, but it is worth remembering that Colet was conscious of working in a manner that still had novelty. In the previous age the great exemplar of an important churchman who took time from other duties to concern himself directly with the catechizing and pastoral care of children and young people was the chancellor of the University of Paris, Jean Gerson. Like Colet later, Gerson felt deeply the need to reach young people as much as possible in their own terms. Also like Colet, he apparently enjoyed this side of his work, teaching young people in a manner that would benefit them intellectually and spiritually: "The guidance of souls," he declared, "is the queen of the arts"[90] ("ars artium est regimen animarum")—alluding perhaps to the familiar characterization of theology as queen of the sciences. He also shared Colet's sense of urgency. Nothing else had worked in bringing reform to the Church; it would have to begin with the children.[91] Gerson approached young people with genuine interest and great tact—a tact apparently necessary.

There was a virtual cult of Gerson during Colet's earlier years,[92] and he may well have read with interest Gerson's famous little book on *How to Draw Children to Christ* (*De parvulis trahendis ad Christum*), a subject that lay close to his heart, as the language just quoted shows. By the time Colet's school opened its doors he had occupied one of the most conspicuous pulpits in the realm for seven years and had often preached also at court. He probably understood better than most readers Gerson's answer to critics who told him he would do more good by reaching large numbers through sermons than by spending his time on youngsters. Experience, Gerson replied, had led him to doubt it.[93]

In founding his school, Colet was frankly trying to reach the rising generation, and the curriculum he prescribed quite plainly reflected the school's religious aims. Hence the curriculum was intended to be conservative. It centered on inculcating Christian values and kept the pagan Latin classics at arm's length. Instead of the obvious Roman writers, Colet prescribed safe Christian writers even though their literary merit was inferior. The fact that his recommendations were soon ignored and his handpicked Christian writers were displaced by the classical writers he had sought to exclude, shows that this aspect of his curriculum was unacceptably behind the times in a school that aimed at excellence.

If Colet's curriculum proves him in modern eyes "the least adventurous of all his contemporaries," the fact would not have embarrassed him. He declared proudly, "My entent is by thys scole specially to incresse knowlege and worshipping of god and oure lorde Christ Jesu and good Cristen lyff and maners in the Children." The "entent" of the school is thus the same that guided him in his lectures on St. Paul and his preaching. Colet never gave up preaching, but experience must have convinced him of the resiliency of the Old Adam in grown men and women. Like Gerson before him he eventually placed his hope in the young.

During the years in which St. Paul's was being planned and founded, by a lucky chance Erasmus was living in England. At first sight the extent of Erasmus's participation in the project seems surprising. He not only wrote texts but composed little poems and the lengthy thoughtful sermon on the Child Jesus for delivery by one of the boys. His wish to help make the school a success extended even to such details as suggesting an inscription for the image of the Child Jesus placed over the master's chair. But besides being a major scholar, Erasmus was also one of the most successful textbook writers of the western world. His *Colloquies* taught conversational Latin and much else, and like the *De copia* remained a staple textbook for several hundred years. Erasmus fully shared Colet's conviction that the education of the young was a central task of the age.

I believe that this is the interest that finally brought Colet and Erasmus together as colleagues and equals. Erasmus's contributions to education are such as perhaps only he could have made. But Colet too was in a position to make a unique contribution to the work. He had a large fortune at his disposition, and he knew intimately, as few did, the three worlds that would contribute to the school's success, the mercantile world, the court, and the church. Not only could he establish a school in the most nearly ideal spot in the kingdom, Paul's Churchyard; he was there to guide it and solve the inevitable problems large and small that attend a major foundation. He had personal access to Erasmus himself and, moreover, the gift of finding others to do what they could do better than he. In the latter category belongs his choice of a great guild company to administer the school in the unknown future.

Colet had nothing to teach Erasmus about scriptural exegesis at any stage. Nor can it be seriously maintained any more that their encounters at Oxford were a turning point in the life of a man who marked his thirty-third birthday during his brief visit to that university. But with education, matters stand quite differently. During Erasmus's long stay in England at the time the school was in the planning and building stages, the two men had more chance to get to know each other, and to value each other's good qualities while making allowances for the others. In education they could not be rivals, despite muted differences in their appreciation of the pagan past. Minor problems of personality or educational emphasis would remain minor in respect of the great aim of reform that both men embraced wholeheartedly. Each had his own contribution to make and was in a good position to value the other's contribution, and it is St. Paul's School which for Englishmen made their names indissociable. If theirs was a "fellow-work"—the term proposed by Seebohm so many years ago—that joint work was not the interpretation of the Bible but the education of the young.

10

Politics, Heresy, Final Victory

For a good many generations after his death Colet was remembered primarily for the school he had founded. But for his contemporaries, his importance was due at least as much to his being dean of St. Paul's and a well-known figure at court. Erasmus decided to conclude his account of Colet by dramatizing a scene that focused on the interconnections between Colet's two worlds, the church and the court. This scene will occupy much of our attention throughout the present chapter, and it will be well to have its key passages before us.

"And now, lest Colet's perfect piety should appear in any way incomplete," Erasmus writes to Justus Jonas,

> I will tell you of the storm by which he was assailed. He had never got along well with his bishop. . . . Nor was Colet particularly well liked by most members of his chapter, for he was a stickler for regular discipline; they would constantly complain that he was treating them as if they were monks. . . .
>
> But since the old bishops's hatred—he was then at least eighty—was too intense to be suppressed, he allied himself with two other bishops equally shrewd and no less virulent, and proceeded to bring charges against Colet, using the weapons such people always use when plotting a man's ruin. He delated him to the archbishop of Canterbury after noting down some passages that he had extracted from Colet's sermons. One charge was that he had taught that images were not to be adored. Another was that he had refused to acknowledge the duty of hospitality which Paul praised: Colet agreed with other exegetes in interpreting the first two commands in the Gospel passage [John 21:15–17] "feed, feed, feed my sheep," as meaning feeding by the example of their lives and feeding by preaching God's word; but he disagreed about the third injunction, finding it inconsistent that the Apostles, who were then poor men, should command their sheep to feed

235

them with temporal sustenance. The third charge against Colet was that in a sermon he had spoken of certain persons reading their sermons (an uninspiring practice that is common in England), obliquely criticizing his bishop, who was in the habit of so doing because of his age. The archbishop, who knew very well Colet's gifts, took it upon himself to defend the innocent, the judge thus becoming an advocate; for Colet himself disdained to reply to these charges, and to others that were still more absurd.

The very insubstantiality of the charges is interesting. The first "charge" is nothing but a simple restatement of accepted doctrine, according to which God alone can be adored. What Erasmus meant must be that Colet was accused of denying any cult at all to images, whereas the traditional distinction was that images could be "venerated" but not "adored" (in technical language, they could receive the cult of *dulia* but not that of *latria*).[1] Colet's enemies apparently preferred to interpret his theologically correct objections to image worship as a rejection of images altogether. In reality, we know from his will that the retreat from the world where he intended to pass his last years had its walls decorated with images as an aid to devotion: "*Item* as touchyng my logyng at the Charterhous, I wyll that . . . all paynted images upon the walls remayne to that lodgyng *in perpetuum*."[2] It is almost unnecessary to add that in the austere precincts of the Charterhouse the images that adorned Colet's walls depicted sacred subjects. As for the remaining two charges reported by Erasmus, in Colet's time there was no officially defined interpretation of the passage from John;[3] and of course it was hardly heresy to criticize, even unfairly, preachers who read their sermons. In fact Colet must have known that in earlier days his bishop had been himself a celebrated preacher.[4]

Besides these charges of heresy reportedly lodged by Bishop Fitzjames, William Tyndale (probably influenced by Erasmus's mention of Colet's supposed heretical views) asserted in 1531 that Colet's bishop had accused him of heresy for having translated the Paternoster into English.[5] This charge too fails to stand up under examination. Colet's version is merely a very slightly expanded rendering of the seven petitions of the Lord's Prayer. Its modest pretensions may be judged from the first petition in Colet's paraphrase: "O father in heuen, holowed be thy name amonge men in earth, as yt is among angels in heuen."[6] Simple as it is, Colet's English paraphrase is not known to go back earlier than the 1534 edition of his *Aeditio*; the earliest surviving edition, dated 1527, merely prints the unexpanded Paternoster in Latin.[7] The primacy in translating the prayer into English belongs, as far as is known, to two primers with which Colet had nothing to do, one dated definitely and one probably to 1523 (*STC* 15934, 15935).[8] But in any case the whole basis of Tyndale's charge is false: far from suppressing the Lord's Prayer in the vernacular, the late medieval English church tried hard to make it widely known, as a typical fourteenth-century text makes clear: ". . . And þe Pater noster and þe Crede, / þer offe ye sscholden taken hede, / On Englissch to sege, what it were."[9] Though vernacular translations of the Bible were no novelty on the Continent, persistent Lollard influences made the English church nervous about giving Englishmen access to the Bible in their own language. But this uneasiness did not extend to the Lord's Prayer: in fact Erasmus mentions in passing that Colet preached in St. Paul's a whole series of sermons on the Paternoster (A, ll. 301–305), and the church as a whole was carrying on an intense official campaign to ensure the people's knowledge of the Lord's Prayer.[10]

We are thus confronted with the curious fact that none of the charges reportedly brought against Colet were serious—Erasmus called three of them "absurd"—and in fact Tyndale claimed Colet was considered heretical for doing what at that time the English church was officially engaged in doing. It is easy to see why Tyndale, by 1531 openly committed to Reform, could think he had found in Erasmus's letter evidence that Colet too was persecuted for preaching the Word. But Bishop Fitzjames, who unlike most of his episcopal brethren was a trained theologian rather than a canonist,[11] would have known how weak the charges were which Erasmus says he brought. An experienced administrator, if he were to prefer charges against a prominent fellow churchman, would have had to make a stronger case than that before the archbishop—especially since what Erasmus calls his "hatred" for Colet would be known to Warham. So we are driven to ask, Did Fitzjames really make charges against Colet? If so, are these the charges?

In responding to the first question it is important to recall its context. Erasmus is walking a narrow line. On one hand, in depicting Colet as accused of heresy he is seeking to enlist Jonas's sympathy and interest. On the other hand, it was his object to keep Jonas within the Catholic fold. Hence the only heresies he actually mentions are so unheretical that Colet is clearly well within the doctrinal framework of the traditional church. He emphasizes Colet's rectitude by contrasting him with a malevolent and obscurantist bishop, the role given to Fitzjames. Erasmus probably had some animus against the bishop, for though Richard Fitzjames was not perfect, other evidence shows him in a better light; he was the confessor of the Lady Margaret and sympathized with her enlightened humanistic efforts. That Erasmus was forcing the opposition between the bishop and the dean is shown by the fact that he is wrong in saying that Colet and Fitzjames had never got along. And since Erasmus was living in England at the time he would know the actual facts.

Scattered evidence demonstrates that Fitzjames and Colet were still working well together in 1510, when Colet had already been dean for five years. On September 13 of that year Bishop Fitzjames asked for and received Colet's support in a matter that Fitzjames had been unable to handle for himself. He wanted Dr. John Young to accept the position of master of the house of St. Thomas of Acons, but Young was reluctant.[12] Casting about for an intermediary, Fitzjames called on Colet. The record shows that Colet was put to some trouble in carrying out Fitzjames's commission, but in part thanks to him Fitzjames got his way.[13] Evidence from the same period, circa 1510, shows that Fitzjames trusted Colet on theological as well as personal matters. He empowered Colet to censor books, and Colet exercised that authority officially.[14] We have already seen that modern scholarship puts Colet's first Convocation sermon in 1510, further evidence that at that point Colet and the bishop of London were not at odds. Archbishop Warham, Colet says in the sermon, selected him to give the address that opened Convocation; this would have been an intolerable slight on Colet's own bishop if the two men were known to be enemies, especially since Fitzjames was also dean of Convocation. A further practical proof that in fact the two men were getting on well together is that on 18 August 1510 a well-informed court figure committed the guardianship of his son jointly to four highly placed men, two of them being Fitzjames and Colet. The father in question was Edmund Dudley, the hated tax-gatherer of the preceding reign whom the young Henry VIII executed in a sacrifice to public opinion.[15] Dudley knew his way around the London establishment, and his uniting Fitzjames and Colet as guardians of his son shows he assumed that they would pull together to protect the boy's interests. After Dudley's attainder his goods and chattels fell to the Crown, but it was common practice in such cases to regrant property piecemeal to the natural heirs if they worked their way back into royal favor[16]— hence the necessity of choosing the right guardians.[17]

Fitzjames and Colet were still working together amicably circa 1512, when the bishop's cooperation enabled Colet to solve a perplexing problem. A recent decedent had left the very substantial sum of £100 to St. Paul's School. Colet soon became aware, however, that acceptance of the bequest would entail sharing with others the governance of the school. So he refused the bequest for the school, but enlisted Fitzjames's help in diverting it to the cathedral of which he was dean, so that this handsome sum would not get away (A, ll. 361–366). Perhaps this collaboration between the dean and the bishop in thwarting the testator's intent excited unfriendly comment, for we find Colet maintaining elsewhere that a bishop has a moral right to alter wills that are proved in his court (RO, 243). This doctrine, it may be added, is all the odder when we recall that it flatly if silently contradicts Holy Scripture, which declares, "If a will has been drawn up in due form, no one is allowed to disregard it or add to it" (Gal. 3:15). It appears that even Colet occasionally could hearken to what the Goliardic poet called "The Gospel of the Silver Mark."

A further point, not certain but several times suggested by historians of education, is that Colet may deliberately have imitated Fitzjames's school at Bruton when he established St. Paul's. It is certain that Fitzjames was the principal figure among the joint founders of the Bruton school[18] and had been helping to support it since 1506, well before Colet embarked on his project. When the Bruton school was formally reendowed in 1519 the deed stated that "the said Scolemaster shall teache his scolers Gramer after the gode newe Fourme used in Magdalene College in Oxford or in the scoole at Pawles in London."[19]

This survey of the evidence bearing on the relations between Fitzjames and Colet is instructive. We see that the hostility between the two men was not a matter of personalities, for they worked well together during at least the first seven years of Colet's decanate and perhaps longer, for we shall see that the earliest evidence for hostility between them is not until October 1514.

Entirely overlooked by previous scholars has been documentary evidence proving that in mid-1511 Colet, so far from being accused of heresy, was actually busy himself in trying heretics and condemning them. This evidence is from the unpublished and unfortunately very fragmentary registers of Archbishop Warham, now in Lambeth Palace library. From these registers we learn that on 8 May 1511 Colet was party to the proceedings against John Brown of Ashford and Edward Walker of Maidstone.[20] The trial of these two men was part of an ongoing proceeding against Kentish heretics which extended into the year 1512. The judges on the commission were all well-credentialed men of the ecclesiastical establishment; its president was the archbishop of Canterbury, and its members included several bishops along with Colet, as the register testifies. After their condemnation Brown and Walker were formally turned over to the secular arm; Foxe reports that they were then burned to death.

Thus the records, even in their fragmentary state, prove that in mid-1511 Colet—so far from being suspected of heresy—was actually sitting in judgment on heretics. There is no reason to suppose that this documented occasion was the only one. In fact the antiquarian John Foxe included Colet among the "Persecutors and Judges" of heretics, and as we now see he was right. Lupton buried Foxe's highly interesting assertion in a footnote and regarded it as self-evidently "strange";[21] but the evidence of Warham's unpublished register now proves that Foxe was right and Lupton was wrong. We do not know whether Colet was present when the same commission sat six days earlier, but on that occasion it convicted one Agnes Grebil, a housewife, of having heretical opinions. She was condemned by the testimony of her husband, John, and her two grown sons, aged nineteen and twenty-two, witnesses who she had supposed would never betray her. And on the same day as Agnes Grebil the commission also convicted two others. One of them, William Carder, now expressed sorrow at having departed from Catholic orthodoxy and recanted, but though he was not a recidivist, Warham, contrary to custom according to Foxe, refused his submission. The man tried with Carder, Robert Harrison, submitted only after he was convicted on the testimony of witnesses, and though he then promised to conform, his plea too was refused. Both were turned over to the secular arm and burned to death.[22]

It is worth adding that where Foxe can be tested he has come off well under the scrutiny of modern historians.[23] The unambiguous evidence that Colet was indeed "Persecutor and Judge" throws the traditional account into reverse. Instead of Colet's being the lonely pre-Reformer sympathetic to the Lollards, we find him sitting in commission to judge them. Moreover, the very fact that Colet was named to the commission by the archbishop of Canterbury shows that in the inner ecclesiastical circle to which he belonged, his doctrinal convictions were above suspicion. As to Colet's role in imposing the death sentence that sometimes followed conviction of heresy, each reader will wish to form his or her own opinion. In any case, this new evidence would seem—at least for the period down to 1512 and perhaps later—to dispose of the allegation that Colet was regarded by high churchmen as a heretic. The testimony of colleagues who knew him and worked regularly with him is the most valuable evidence we have for the way in which knowledgeable high-level ecclesiastics regarded their zealous colleague. Such evidence cannot be set aside.

If Fitzjames ever did accuse Colet of heresy, the real reason would not have been a personality conflict, for the two men worked together amicably for years. Yet Erasmus sets his account in a framework of strong personal hostility on the bishop's part, a hostility that we have seen could not have arisen before mid-1512, when we find the two prelates still actively cooperating, and whose first known sign is not until October 1514. What happened between mid-1512 and late 1514 to cause a rupture between the bishop and the dean?

A letter from Erasmus to Colet dated 11 July 1513 has often been read as testifying to a breakdown in relations between Colet and his bishop, but without justification. The main purpose of the letter was to claim the long overdue payment promised to Erasmus for *De copia*. That done, Erasmus adds this paragraph:

> I was sorry to hear from the end of your letter that you are more than usually burdened by the vexations of administration [*molestia negociorum solito grauius vexari*]. Personally, I would wish you as far removed as possible from the affairs of this world. Not that I fear that this world with all its trou-

blesomeness could have any appeal for you or make you its captive. It is simply that I would rather your intelligence, eloquence, and learning were entirely at the service of Christ. If you cannot get free of these problems, be careful not to be drawn deeper and deeper into them. It might be better to accept defeat than to purchase victory at such a high price; the great thing is to enjoy peace of mind. And these are the thorns that go along with wealth. For the present set your clear and unblemished conscience against the idle talk of those who are ill-disposed toward you; concentrate on Christ, one and undivided, and the complexities of the world will disturb you less.[24]

Writers on Colet have too often read back into this text their preconceptions about Colet's troubles with Fitzjames, ignoring the details that do not square with the assumption. Read without preconceptions the text makes clear that those "ill-disposed" were numerous, and the hostile comments they make about Colet were merely "idle talk" ("blatteramentis"), not a term one could apply to charges of heresy. The letter also speaks of the conflict, whatever it was, as one that Colet could still win, though at what Erasmus considered too high a price in loss of peace of mind. It is up to Colet to decide whether to carry on the struggle or let the whole matter go—again, not a choice he would have if Erasmus were talking about accusations of heresy. And, finally, the problem is one of "the thorns that go along with wealth."

The last-quoted phrase makes no sense if referred to charges of heresy. It makes excellent sense, however, if referred to a conflict in which we know from other sources that Colet was deeply and stubbornly engaged— the battle with his own cathedral chapter. The canons, as Erasmus reports in the biographical passage already quoted, resented Colet's trying to "treat them as if they were monks." Colet was "a stickler for regular discipline," while the canons took a more relaxed view of their duties. Colet was dean, but this fact did not give him the authority to govern the chapter. He was a member of the chapter not in his capacity as dean but in his capacity as canon of Mora, one of his numerous benefices.[25] Colet nevertheless took it upon himself to tighten discipline in the chapter, and for that purpose he drafted statutes for the governance of the cathedral clergy. These statutes are often assumed to be remarkable in their reforming efforts, but in reality they were quite traditional.[26] In any case no one was interested in seconding his proposals. Fitzjames never "commended" the statutes[27]—not necessarily, I think, because he did not approve of them but because he had no wish to get himself embroiled in this kind of controversy: administrative experience had given him a healthy respect for the obstructive capabilities of a cathedral chapter. Wolsey, equally judicious, "witnessed" the statutes but did not sign them.[28] Thus the statutes "were, at the time, and remained ever after, a dead letter."[29]

Refusing to concede defeat, Colet nevertheless threw himself, with his usual energy and his usual conviction that his quarrel was just, into a fray that cooler heads declined. In his frustration he adopted such measures as lay within his power. One of the most resented of these was curtailing almost to the vanishing point what was then called hospitality. If Colet chose not to take dinner, the main meal of the day, that was his own affair so far as the canons were concerned. They rebelled when he sought to impose his own abstemiousness on them. The canons' reaction to this measure is explained by an ecclesiastical historian who was himself a dean and understood such situations from the inside:

> The word "hospitality" in the middle ages had a more extensive significa-
> tion than it has at the present time [1867]. . . . In Colet's time, hospitality
> was in a transition state. The various officers at St. Paul's Cathedral re-
> ceived their salaries, and they expected the dean to keep a table for them,
> if not, as in times past, every day, yet probably on every festival of the
> Church, at a time when festivals were numerous. We can easily understand
> how these entertainments in London, among the lower class of the clergy
> and their dependents, degenerated into riotous living, and brought dis-
> credit on religion. The austere dean determined to effect a reform. . . .
> However it is not precisely what you do that gives offence, but an unhappy
> manner of doing it. Colet so conducted his reform as to excite against him-
> self the animosity of all the underlings of his church.[30]

Even this interpretation of Colet's reform lets Colet off too easily, for a later ecclesiastical historian of the nineteenth century has pointed out that there is no evidence that only the "underlings" objected to Colet's proposals and his manner of proposing them. The higher cathedral clergy were also incensed at the dean's ostentatious setting of the good example.[31] The dean, for his part, probably made no secret of his opinion that "in chapters of canons it is almost always the worse group that prevails."[32] As this self-congratulatory opinion got around, it would not help matters.

No doubt Colet's motives were good. Nevertheless an incidental effect of the reform of hospitality was that he would also save a fair amount of money. He had in any case the reputation of being stingy, as Erasmus told him bluntly when he grew tired of reminding the dean of a long over-due debt. "I have to say that there are people, people who are your friends—I have nothing to do with your enemies and attach no importance to anything they say—who speak of you as quite hard and overly frugal in disbursing money."[33] Not, he adds, because of avarice but rather be-cause of the many claims on your funds. This courteous fiction was aban-doned, however, in precisely the place one would have expected to see it maintained, the obituary tribute. There, though what Erasmus considered Colet's hardness with money was decorously muffled by the trans-literated Greek word "philargyria" (A, l. 393), he set off against his dead friend's virtues the fact that he was "not entirely free from the disease of avarice." The canons may have resisted more important reforms be-cause they were associated in their mind with the tactless retrenchment of hospitality by a man who everyone knew could well afford to set a good table.

Colet for his part, like many reformers, claimed merely to be restoring the virtuous customs of old—phrases like "ex antiquo Ecclesiae more" and "veteri Ecclesiae more" recur constantly in his stillborn statutes.[34] The canons, however, had their own ideas of what the olden customs were, and Colet succeeded simply in alienating nearly everyone without achieving anything except to keep alive a low-level feud. It is hard to know where to lay the blame. Even centuries later such unedifying fracases con-tinued in cathedral chapters under similarly pertinacious deans, if one can judge by the impatient recollections of a twentieth-century bishop who had been himself a canon of Westminster:

> The controversy respecting the character and extent of the Dean's authority disturbed my mind, and wasted my time, during the years 1905 and 1906. . . . The Dean must, I think, be judged mainly responsible for its be-ginning, for the friction it occasioned, and for its ineffectiveness. Had he been disposed to act with his colleagues, instead of pursuing a lonely course, there would have been no insuperable obstacle to agreement. If any be dis-posed to discount this verdict as biased, let him reflect on the significant fact, that the entire body of the Canons, though markedly differing in type, temper, and point of view, were united in opposition to the Dean's version of his own authority.[35]

If we roll the dates back four hundred years, from 1905 to 1505, the words just quoted might have been written about Colet.

Nor did Colet's schoolmasterly tone help. Under the heading "Vain Conversations during Choir-Prayer," his regulations specified that the resident canons "are to refrain from vain conversation, guffawing and laughing, and they are to stand up straight in their stalls, concentrated and devout; and they are either to be praying or reading or chanting, mindful that they are in the sight of God and the angels."[36] Colet was fond of regulations—a prohibition was posted in the doorways of his cathedral warning the public, "Hic locus sacer est, hic nulli mingere fas est" ("This is a sacred place—no pissing here")[37]—but much to his annoyance his reg-ulations were not always observed. It is hardly surprising to read in a manuscript of Colet's proposed statutes dated "Paulles, 1611," that one reason they never took effect was that he was "out with the Chapter" at the time they were drawn up.[38]

It is likely, then, that Erasmus's letter usually dated 11 July 1513, which has been read as referring to troubles with Fitzjames, actually refers to Colet's running battles with his chapter. The letter makes no mention of the bishop. Instead, Erasmus associates Colet's troubles with "the vexations of administration." Those "ill-disposed" to him are numerous. And the problem is said to be one of the "thorns that go along with wealth." Erasmus advised him to avoid getting deeper and deeper into the conflict; while it was a battle he perhaps could win, the price would be too high. Since we know independently of Erasmus that Colet was "out with the Chapter," Erasmus's letter reads naturally as if this is the struggle he refers to. Pocketbook issues such as that of the stiff fines imposed for nonperformance of clerical duties and a rich man's tactless refusal of hospitality are far more likely than heresy to be the source of Colet's frustrations in 1513.

The first real evidence that Colet and Fitzjames have become enemies is from a letter written more than a year later, in October 1514. Even here their hostility is referred to only in passing, as part of a single sentence in which Colet reports to Erasmus how things are going along in his world. What is most interesting about the sentence is that it matter-of-factly couples Fitzjames's hostility with the meteoric rise of Thomas Wolsey.

The whole text of Colet's letter runs to only thirteen lines in Allen's edition. Its brevity is probably due to the fact that in the (lost) letter to which Colet was replying Erasmus had dropped a broad hint concerning money. (Colet's carefully laconic response was, "Those who can help do not care to, and those who would like to cannot.") By way of changing the subject and giving the news, Colet reports as follows, referring successively to Warham, archbishop of Canterbury; Wolsey, bishop of Lincoln and newly named archbishop of York; and Fitzjames, bishop of London: "Canterbury is his usual pleasant self, Lincoln now reigns in York, and London continues to harass me."[39] The complain about Fitzjames is more resigned than emphatic, and Wolsey's newest triumph is only what insiders had already foreseen.

The successive mentions of Wolsey and Fitzjames suggest a connection between them which Erasmus was expected to understand. The two prelates were already squaring off against each other. Wolsey was a butcher's son, as his enemies never forgot; but Fitzjames came from a prominent family, to the proper pronunciation of whose name even Proust was to give his attention.[40] But more fundamental than social disparity was the dismay with which the clerical party that Fitzjames headed viewed the power over the church which Wolsey was rapidly acquiring through his influence with the king.

As this fundamental division hardened, it soon became clear to all that Colet was Wolsey's man. At Wolsey's unprecedentedly magnificent installation as cardinal it was Colet who delivered the sermon, though the ceremony took place not in St. Paul's but in Westminster Abbey. Colet did not fail to show his colors in his sermon, of which some notes made by a listener fortunately survive.

It appears from these notes that the sermon fell into three divisions.[41] In the first the preacher expatiated on the means by which the cardinal "obtained to this high honor, chiefly as by his own merits," a topic that led Colet to set forth the "divers and sundrie vertues that he hath used which have been the Cause of his high and joyous promotion to all the Realme." After touching on his second division, the secular authority of a cardinal as prince and judge, Colet turned in his closing division to an appreciative treatment of the cardinal's office in its spiritual aspect. "A cardinal," he declared,

> betokenth the free beames of wisdome and Charitie, which the Apostles received of the holie ghoste on *Whitsundaie*, and a Cardinal representeth the order of *Seraphin* [sic], which continually brenneth [i.e., burns] in the love of the glorious Trinity, And for thies considerations a Cardinal is melie [i.e., meetly, or fittingly] apparreled with redd, which Collour onelie betokenth nobleness.

After the conventional adjuration to the newly installed cardinal to live up to the obligations of his high office (a passage to which Lupton gives quite unjustified prominence), the preacher concluded by painting the picture of what, "accomplishing the same, [the cardinal's] reward will be in the kingdom of heaven. And so ended."[42] Lupton, determined to find in all this an Oxford Reformer, reads the sermon very selectively. He says nothing of Colet's adulation for the red hat, which every insider knew was the reward of relentless politicking. Nor does he comment on Colet's picture of Thomas Wolsey as a seraph burning with love for the glorious Trinity. Instead he finds the sermon "fearless" in its "singleness of purpose."[43] But what had such an enthusiastic eulogist to fear?

The installation of the cardinal was graced with the presence of three archbishops besides Wolsey himself; eight abbots in addition to the *ex officio* abbot of Westminster, the archbishop of Canterbury; and eight named bishops (Fitzjames not among them). The ceremony took place on 18 November 1515 and gave Convocation watchers public evidence that Colet was firmly aligned with the all-powerful cardinal.

A few weeks later, this time behind closed doors, Colet had a private but at least equally momentous occasion to show his loyalty to Wolsey. On this occasion, in December 1515, he was one member of a five-man committee appointed to deal with a set of serious interrelated problems of ecclesiastical and court politics.[44] For some years diocesan bishops had been complaining that the Prerogative Court of Canterbury was invading their rights. Canterbury insisted that when a testator died possessed of lands in more than one diocese, no matter how little the property held outside the diocese where he resided, probate was withdrawn from the diocesan bishop's court and transferred to Canterbury. This mechanism ensured that Canterbury would pocket the fees connected with proving the wills of many wealthy testators. Though Warham had protested against this system while he was a diocesan bishop he changed his tune on becoming primate and rejected all complaints. The diocesan bishops appealed, Fitzjames among them, and the case went for decision to Rome. At this point the Crown became involved. Henry ordered the bishops to withdraw their appeal and submit the matter to himself for decision. The bishops deferred to the royal pleasure, but the archbishop continued to seek a binding decision from the Holy See. Henry responded to this defiance by requesting Convocation to appoint a committee to look into the matter. It was obvious to Convocation that Henry desired a new chancellor who would be more amenable to the royal will, in the person of the newly created cardinal. First, however, Warham would have to step down.

After meeting behind closed doors with the handpicked committee representing the Convocation and including the dean of St. Paul's, Warham did step down. In good humanistic fashion, Thomas More congratulated him on being quit of an onerous and thankless responsibility,[45] and Erasmus is generally assumed to mean Warham when he writes discreetly of "N." (from *nomen*, "name"—we should now write "X"), who is well out of "the royal prison."[46] But Warham was Erasmus's most reliable patron, and of course More subsequently assumed the very position that he congratulated Warham on being rid of. Neither humanist referred to the intense pressure that had been brought to bear on Warham to resign. The fact was nevertheless sufficiently well known: the Tudor chronicler Edward Hall makes it clear that Wolsey pestered Warham with deliberate interference in his primatial jurisdiction in the name of the king,[47] and modern scholars see Warham as forced out of the chancellorship. With Wolsey's accession to the cardinalate, Warham's eclipse was betokened by signs that men like Colet knew how to interpret. Even before his installation Wolsey had a cross carried in front of him in Warham's own archdiocese; after it, he was preceded by two crosses, one in token of his being cardinal and the other of his being archbishop. Warham, by contrast, had no cross borne before him at all when Wolsey was present.[48] Moreover, Wolsey systematically encroached on Warham's prerogatives and paid little attention to the protests of his archiepiscopal brother.[49]

For those who observed such things, Colet's place on the five-man committee that persuaded Warham to resign the chancellorship was as clear a signal as his preaching the installation sermon that Colet had chosen Wolsey's side. This allegiance put Colet in a better position to help his own clients too, though as it happens the one extant request for preferment for a candidate of Colet's was not successful.[50] This of course means little. At any desirable vacancy the cardinal was besieged by a host of well-connected petitioners on behalf of their protégés, only one of whom could be successful.

Wolsey demonstrated his favor toward Colet in a far more significant way shortly after he became chancellor. Though Colet's academic field was theology he was also reasonably well versed in the law. As already mentioned he followed some courses in law at Orléans in the 1490s, apparently on a rather advanced level. Colet was thus suited from several points of view for the eminent place to which Wolsey now raised him, nothing less than a seat on the King's Royal Council. Though the exact date is uncertain it was not long after Wolsey became chancellor on 24 December 1515, and in any case earlier than 18 June 1517. On the latter date Wolsey issued an order that set up a committee of the council to hear and expedite "poor men's causes," and named to that committee seven men, including Colet, all of whom were already councillors. If the seven were named on the basis of aptitude for the newly created committee demonstrated by previous service on the council itself, then the time of Colet's appointment to the latter is pushed back still closer to the date of the cardinal's becoming chancellor. Colet was reappointed to the committee a year later, on 17 June 1518; this appointment apparently remained in effect for the remainder of his lifetime, since the next reappointments were made only after his death in 1519.[51] The fragmentary records of the sittings of the whole council show him present at three meetings, the latest of them on 6 November 1518. Presence lists survive for only two of the meetings of the whole council between the latter date and Colet's death; while he was not present at these meetings, the fragmentariness of the data does not permit any inference as to the extent of his participation in the Royal Council after 6 November 1518.[52] In general, however, it is clear that Colet's role as councillor is associated with Wolsey. The council records surviving from Henry VII's reign are considerably fuller, but they make no mention of Colet.[53] Moreover, Colet appears on Henry VIII's council only after Wolsey becomes its president. Henry VIII, unlike his father, rarely attended council meetings, and Wolsey had essentially a free hand in elaborating its functions and determining its composition. During the entire period during which Colet served on the council, Bishop Fitzjames, who had attended sessions in the days before Wolsey, completed absented himself. Colet's alliance with the cardinal marked him as the bishop's opponent.

Both Fitzjames and Wolsey saw that the institutional Church was threatened by a crisis, but they differed sharply on how to meet it. The Hunne case (1513–1515), with its wide publicity and sensational aftermaths, along with the provisional withdrawal of the immunities traditionally enjoyed by the clerics in minor orders accused of serious crimes, left the church badly shaken. All London, as Fitzjames himself acknowledged, was ranged against the clergy. The obstinate avarice that started the whole Hunne affair, the refusal to have Fitzjames's chancellor acknowledge the jurisdiction of the king's courts when he was accused of murder, and traditionalist clergymen's insistence that no matter what crime a cleric in minor orders might have committed, as one of "the Lord's anointed" he was not to be tried or punished by mere worldly men—all this was too much for the laity and also for some of the clergy. Still more ominously from the ecclesiastical point of view, the king had now intervened in the tangle of issues deriving from the Hunne case and the problem of clerical immunities. What was to be done?

Fitzjames, as we saw in chapter 4, took a hard line. In very short order he condemned Hunne posthumously for heresy and took the offensive by having Abbot Kidderminster preach an intransigent sermon in defense of clerical immunities. By these bold steps Fitzjames may have won the battle, but at the risk of losing the war. Those who took a longer view understood that the status quo could not survive many more such crises, yet it was only a matter of time until the unreformed ecclesiastical structure generated them.

Wolsey understood that major structural reforms were necessary if the church was to retrieve its position and be allowed to continue to manage its own affairs. As the leading authority on his policy has put it, Wolsey "wanted as much practical reform of the church as would at least render possible the continuance of ecclesiastical autonomy. He wanted the church to be reformed by itself or rather by himself, but in no event by parliament." The problem was too urgent to wait for whatever remedies the Fifth Lateran Council, already in its third year of sessions, might produce. England would have to push on with the indispensable reforms on its own, guided of course by Wolsey. "But," adds the same authority, "he had little confidence in reform by the convocation of a province, of which Warham was president and Fitzjames was dean."[54]

Once he had his red hat Wolsey soon forced the hapless archbishop of Canterbury out of the chancellorship, with the assistance of the five-man committee of Convocation which included Colet. The full political implications became clear when the king declared in writing that the ultimate responsibility for Warham's ouster was his,[55] thus endorsing the work of Colet and his fellow committee members. With the king's support, and Warham gone, Wolsey could outflank the conservative clerical party headed by Fitzjames. However, Fitzjames's position as bishop of London and dean of the convocation of the southern province left him with a good many cards to play. If he could not get at Wolsey directly he could harass his allies. In Colet's case the harassment soon turned ugly.

Colet's tendency to extremes would render him an easy victim of an attentive enemy bent on discrediting him. Erasmus acknowledges that Colet was charged with heresy but selects specimen charges that, as we have seen, will not stand examination. He glides rapidly over the fact that there were other charges too—"others still more absurd," as he says (A, l. 555)—and gives no indication of their content. These charges may have been absurd as evidence to prove Colet a heretic, but they were not necessarily trivial in themselves. We have Erasmus's word for it that Colet did not parade his more extreme views before the public at large, but that within ecclesiastical circles he was not so reticent. His views, occasionally incautious in their substance and often intemperate in their expression, would make their way speedily over the short distance that separated his residence from Fitzjames's. "Within cathedral precincts," as a clerical writer on Colet remarks from experience, "the sayings of a dean are likely to be quoted."[56]

Before we turn to charges documented from Colet's own writings, it may be worthwhile to consider a charge that Victorian scholars imputed to Colet, his supposed failure to provide for prayers for his soul after death, which would imply disbelief in purgatory. Examination of this charge will involve us in something of a detour, but it is so often repeated that it cannot be ignored. It would be important if true, but it is not true.

Colet's Victorian biographers were much struck by the fact that his will contains no provisions for masses to be said for himself or the members of his family. The absence of such provision was all the more interesting in the will of a man who was easily rich enough to endow a chantry. Recent scholars have shown, however, that in Colet's time very few new chantries were endowed. This was not necessarily because testators did not wish to do so but because royal policy opposed the further accumulation of wealth in clerical corporations which such bequests produced. Also, the chantry priests themselves were increasingly looked on with disfavor. They were a clerical underclass who were poorly paid and had little beyond the saying of a daily mass to keep them busy; hence some of them spent their ample leisure in unedifying ways. Even chantries were hard to come by, however, because the hordes of priests far outnumbered the foundations.[57] And almost by definition the chantry priests were men without influence, who had to angle for years to land a chantry worth perhaps £8 a year;[58] the priest who had influence would go after something better. Hence a testator who still wanted to found a chantry would find the required mortmain license very difficult to obtain, a difficulty that very nearly brought the foundation of chantries to a halt. Only nine were founded in London and Middlesex together during the long period 1500–1534.[59]

Provisions for obits were far more frequent, but they were often made in a manner that casts some doubt on the spiritual impulses behind them. The carrying out of the testator's provision was often entrusted to livery companies. In return for the company's supervision, the bequest was so structured that after the specified religious duties were carried out a sub-

stantial surplus would remain each year. Part of the surplus went for "potations" for those present at the mass, and the rest went into the company's "box," or general fund.[60]

Another deterrent to foundations for obits or chantries was the recurrent possibility of secularization. Rumors of secularization were abroad
as early as 1450,[61] and gained increasing credibility after the turn of the
century. As a modern student of the subject has concluded, "Despite the
overt expressions of piety of Henry VII and his son, some Englishmen
began to fear that new legislation might be introduced to confiscate the
chantries which had been founded by feoffments or for terms of years."[62]
These facts suggest that even if it were factually correct to say that Colet
did not leave funds for masses to be said for his soul, the commonsense
conclusion would be not that he disbelieved in purgatory but that chantries were not a safe investment.

In reality, however, Colet did endow not one but two chantries, his
influence being great enough to procure the mortmain license denied to
many others. In 1514 he gave a manor to endow a chantry dedicated to
Our Lady Patroness of Boys.[63] This was the second of his chantries, for
he had in effect already endowed a chantry where prayers would be offered for his soul. It will be remembered that a chaplaincy was added very
soon to the original plan for St. Paul's School. Even Lupton, in an off-
guard moment, rightly calls the school chaplain a "chantry-priest."[64] Colet specified that the chaplain "pray for the Children to prosper in good
lyff and in good litterature"; it is inconceivable that after the founder's
death, and probably also in his lifetime, the chaplain would not pray also
for him. This was the standard procedure with other founders of schools,
and Colet's disdaining this spiritual benefit in his own school would have
been instantly notorious. That would indeed have been a weapon for his
enemies, but there was no breath of such a charge by those who were in
a position to know and who were hostile to him.

Our inquiry thus far has led to the conclusion that while Colet was indeed beset by enemies who charged him with heretical views, the charges
that Erasmus saw fit to record are not serious enough to have caused real
trouble. Victorian scholars saw the difficulty and attributed to Colet a contempt for purgatory and masses said on behalf of a wealthy testator's soul,
which would have been serious indeed if it were real. But as has been
shown, these latter-day charges are contradicted by the facts.

The real charges were different both from those that Erasmus detailed
and from those that nineteenth-century scholars imagined. Erasmus was
writing to a correspondent, Justus Jonas, who was on the point of going
over to Luther.[65] Erasmus's strategy for preventing this was to propose
Vitrier and Colet as models of churchmen who criticized the Church's institutions as vigorously as Jonas himself could wish but remained loyal

to the church in matters of defined doctrine. Thus if Colet was charged with errors of doctrine, the letter to Jonas was definitely not the place to set them forth. Erasmus does state, however, that there were other accusations than the trivial ones he specifies, calling the unspecified charges "still more absurd" (A, l. 555). It would not be easy to find charges of heresy more absurd than those Erasmus lists if the adjective is taken to refer to their content. But if "absurd" applies to the likelihood that the charges could be believed, then Erasmus is saying that if the three silly charges cannot be taken seriously, still less could one take seriously graver charges of which he says nothing. This reading would explain why Erasmus felt it necessary to insist, in the same portion of the biographical letter, that "in no way" did Colet favor any "error" (A, ll. 481–482).

Despite Erasmus's protests that Colet never favored any "error" the most recent editor of the letter astutely asks, "Are we really sure?" ("Est-ce bien certain?").[66] The bishops whom Colet execrated, Erasmus says, as "more like wolves than shepherds" (A, 472–473), could easily have drawn up a far more damning dossier of what they considered heresies than any that Erasmus reports. Colet was not by temperament a cautious man. Though he made it a point not to break ranks with the clergy in public, in private circles he could be candor itself. Moreover, "heresy" was a blanket term that covered not only formal doctrinal error but offenses against church discipline or criticism of ecclesiastical authority, pious customs, or traditional beliefs.[67] This broad conception of heresy, combined with Colet's impatient idealism, made him vulnerable, and it would be surprising if his enemies had not taken advantage of their opportunities to entrap him.

Some of Colet's views that would have angered the bishops have already been mentioned—his outrage at money-grubbing clerics who exacted fees for every special spiritual service and at the legalistic bishops who supported them; the worldliness and open ambition of the higher clergy; the scandals epitomized in the Hunne case. These views were, however, widely held and not peculiar to Colet. The reader of Colet's writings will find, in addition, opinions that went well beyond the perennial subject of abuses and were sometimes scarcely reconcilable with the doctrines of the church.

For example, it appears that Colet's view of the pope's position, while fundamentally orthodox, was hedged about with significant, if muted, reservations. He acknowledges the pope as "the vicar of God, the head of the Church" ("vicarius dei, ecclesie capud"; DEH, 222). He likewise accepts in principle the legal primacy of the pope (RO, 263) and sees Pope St. Leo the Great, for example, as holding in his hands "the apostolic reins" (DEH, 197). At the apex of the ecclesiastical hierarchy he places the "pontifex" (singular). Lupton tendentiously translates "pontifex" as "bishop," but in Ambrogio Traversari's translation of Dionysius, on which Colet is commenting, the word is used for *pontifex maximus*, "pope," the term adopted in classicizing ecclesiastical Latin in preference to *papa* (DEH, 198).[68] But while Colet acknowledges the pope's juridical position, a few pages later he comes very close to drawing a dangerous and, to the Church, quite unacceptable distinction. Since he imitates Christ, Colet says, the "pontifex" (again, singular) must manifest holiness in his own person. Should he fail to do so, "he is not the man to occupy the pontifical throne" (DEH, 201). Much later in the same treatise Colet goes so far as to hint, though in the subjunctive mode, that there could be a pope who was not "legitimus." Like the other "pontifices" a pope must be guided in all things by the Spirit, seeking no "lucrum" ("reward") but the harvest of souls; he must not endeavor to effect his own will. "If he be legitimate [*legittimus*] it is not he who acts but God in him. But if he attempt anything of himself he brews poison. Should he then carry out his own intentions and effect what he himself wills, he is recklessly infusing a poison that will kill the church" (DEH, 264–265). In medieval Latin *legitimus* describes a person "enjoying a privileged status determined by a particular body of law"[69] and thus in some degree conditioned by that law. The law in question is often specifically ecclesiastical law: another modern dictionary of medieval Latin defines *legitimus* as "reglé par la loi, conforme à la loi ecclésiastique."[70] By applying the word *legitimus* to the pope, Colet, who had studied the law, implied that the pope's unique status depended on his conformity to ecclesiastical and, *a fortiori*, divine law. Had Colet lived to be confronted with the Act of Supremacy, would he have endured martyrdom in absolute affirmation of the pope's authority over the universal Church?

At all events, the reservation Colet hints at was not without example. In his lifetime, indeed during his stay in Rome, the papacy had reached its modern nadir with the reign of Alexander VI. The question that Colet was concerned with was bound to arise in other men's minds as well; it had in fact a long history and a substantial bibliography,[71] though Victorian writers on Colet liked to think that here too Colet was unique. Two popes had already been found to have uttered heretical pronouncements — Anastasius II in the fifth century and Honorius I in the seventh — and at least the former case was familiar to Colet through its inclusion in Gratian, whom he cites.[72] Colet distinguished between "him who is in appearance a priest with a fleshly tonsure, and him who is secretly tonsured in the spirit" (RO, 228) — a distinction that leads to dangerous inferences concerning the spiritual power of the priest whose tonsure is merely carnal.

"Evil cannot be remedied by evil," as he put it elsewhere, "nor can evil men make good laws" (CM, 186) — again questioning the efficaciousness of ecclesiastical actions *ex opere operato*. In the context of the flare-up of Lollardy during 1511–1512,[73] this theme of Colet's would be highly objectionable to conservative churchmen. Much the same can be said of Colet's bitter comments on the folly of vicarious prayers. Well-off men, Colet says, do not bother to pray themselves but pay others to pray for them. Such people are "supremely stupid" and do not deserve to have others pray for them, if they suppose "they can be saved by other people when they do not do anything to save themselves" (DEH, 261). To express convictions like these, even in private circles, would be to sound like a Lollard sympathizer.

The views quoted have been taken out of context, as they would be if gathered by enemies of Colet. It would be a mistake to conclude that he intended all their implications. His bitterness and near-despair at the state of the church made him sharpen his formulations to an imprudent degree. But though the larger context of his career isolates these utterances as occasional and marginal, they are suggestive of one strand in his thinking.

At least equally pronounced, however, was his affirmation of order. Order was dear to him in celestial and ecclesiastical hierarchies, and also in his deanery and his school and his chapter, in the livery company that his father had governed and of which he himself remained a member, in the capital city of the kingdom, and in the court. At the same time his was not a particularly systematic mind. Colet was a preacher at heart. He had his full share of the impetuosity and extravagances peculiar to that calling, so that those ill-disposed toward him needed only to bide their time. He would make them a present of charges that could be laid against him. Erasmus, in the biographical letter, professed to find these charges absurd, and if they are read in the larger context of Colet's career I feel sure Erasmus was right. But even if largely unjustified the charges were serious; this Erasmus himself acknowledges, as we shall see, by making Colet's final vindication the climax of his biography.

In other ways too Colet's ardent temperament got the better of his prudence. At an indeterminate date between 1512 and 1514 Colet and Erasmus journeyed together to the famous shrine of St. Thomas à Becket at Canterbury. Erasmus published his account of his and Colet's pilgrimage in 1526, at least a dozen years after the actual occasion and seven years after his companion's death. It appeared as an addition to his *Colloquia* entitled "Peregrinatio religionis ergo" ("A Pilgrimage for Religion's Sake").[74] In it a narrator recounts to a friend the reactions of his traveling companion on the pilgrimage, Gratianus Pullus, a pseudonym for John Colet.[75] John, or Johannes, derives from the Hebrew *johanan*, meaning "Jahweh has shown grace."[76] The Latin *pullus* means "colt," close enough in sound to "Colet" to pass muster for the purpose of a pun. I suspect that Erasmus remembered also the pun on the name Polus in Plato's *Gorgias* and in Aristotle's *Rhetoric*—in Greek too Πῶλος means "colt." This literary tradition of punning on the name Pullus would encourage readers to look behind the ostensible name Gratianus Pullus,[77] but even if they failed to see behind the disguised name, the intimates of Erasmus would already know who Gratianus Pullus was because Erasmus had said openly in 1524 that his companion was Colet.[78]

As Erasmus recounts the visit years later, Gratianus Pullus was far from edified by what he found at the shrine. The two men had arrived armed with a letter from William Warham, archbishop of Canterbury, which would ensure them special treatment. Accordingly they were first given a close-up look at the shrine's striking collections of plate and jewels. Colet encouraged their priest-guide to tell stories of St. Thomas's generosity to the poor during his life, and then asked rhetorically whether he didn't agree that the saint would be pleased to see some of this superfluous wealth used to help the poor now. The priest was silent, but his frown and what Erasmus called his "Gorgonian eyes" showed what he would have said had the guests not carried a letter of recommendation from the archbishop.[79]

Worse was yet to come. The important visitors were taken into a sacristy where were preserved "some torn fragments of linen" that obviously the saint had used "to wipe the sweat from his face or his neck, the runnings from his nose, or such other superfluities from which the human frame is not free." When these relics were taken out of their leather-covered box, all who were present "knelt down and worshipped." To Colet, as an important pilgrim, the prior offered as a present one of the used pieces of linen.

> But Gratian, not sufficiently grateful, drew it together with his fingers, not without some intimation of disgust, and disdainfully put it back in the box: pouting out his lips as if imitating a whistle, for he had that trick when something offended him which at the same time he regarded as beneath his notice.

Erasmus probably was secretly amused, though he records only that he felt "shame and fear"; but the prior, "like a sensible man, pretended not to notice it."[80]

Even then Erasmus's embarrassments were not over. On the return journey to London the two companions passed the Herbaldown Hospital, which sheltered a few old men. Hearing pilgrims approaching, one of the inmates rushed out into the road to sprinkle the travelers with holy water. He then held up to them the top part of an old shoe, bound with a brass rim and adorned with an imitation jewel of glass, inviting them to kiss the shoe. Colet was riding on the side nearer the building; though he had been on the receiving end of most of the sprinkling, he had kept his self-control. But the shoe was too much:

He asked the man what he wanted. He replied that it was the shoe of St. Thomas. On that my friend was irritated, and turning to me said, "What, do these brutes suppose we have to kiss every good man's shoe? Why, by the same token they might offer his spittle to be kissed, or who knows what else!" For my part I pitied the old man and gave him a small coin by way of consolation.[81]

The contrast between the friends' reactions is instructive. Colet flared out in anger at the crude exploitation of pious tradition. Erasmus simply commented, "I must admit that it would be better if these things did not happen, but from situations that cannot readily be set right I try to draw whatever positive value I can." With his cooler temperament and deeper understanding he felt sympathy for ordinary men mired in a pseudo-Christian materialism and superstition they had no means of criticizing, much less transcending.[82]

Colet's sense of outrage may seem a little extravagant, but Erasmus had no motive for misrepresenting his reaction. Moreover, the same quick temper in a good cause that Erasmus reports in this colloquy, along with a complete lack of ironic detachment, are evident in all Colet's writings. Besides, Erasmus had had a specimen of the same impatient absolutism in his friend on another occasion that he reports with evident amusement. When Colet read the first book of Erasmus's *Antibarbari*, which contains an attack on rhetoric, he was delighted with it. But when Erasmus told him that the second book was to contain a defense of rhetoric, Colet not only showed no sympathy for the second book but reproached Erasmus for writing on both sides of such important questions. Reporting Colet's impassioned literal-mindedness to another correspondent, Erasmus could only shrug with amusement.[83] Further confirmation of the accuracy of Erasmus's report about the pilgrimage is provided by the fact that among Erasmus's readers in 1526 were such men as Richard Pace, who succeeded Colet as dean, John Fisher, Thomas More, Thomas Lupset, and Polydore Vergil, men who knew Colet well and accepted his quirks but honored his memory. Readers who had known Colet personally would enjoy the scenes that evoked their old friend's manner, but Erasmus's awareness that they were among his readers would restrain any tendency to improve the story too much.

For Colet's enemies the unadorned truth would be quite bad enough. His contempt for the shrine's jewels, or for Thomas's used handkerchief, would soon become known. Colet's rejection of the shrine's wonders could be seen as a criticism of the whole system of commercialized official shrines.[84]

Taken together with his denunciation of litigious bishops, his intimation that even a pope might not be *legitimus*, his bitter outcries during the Hunne case, and his constant criticism of the church's institutional side, Colet's scorn for widely venerated relics would add yet another weapon to his enemies' armory. This array of charges would be more than enough to cause Colet's hard-pressed bishop to try to get Warham to do something about Colet. References to these troubles in the correspondence between Colet and Erasmus begin in late 1514, during which period Warham seems to have been unwilling to give Colet the swift vindication his friends expected.[85] It was increasingly clear to Warham both that Colet was Wolsey's man and that Wolsey aimed to oust Warham from the chancellorship. Within a year, it will be remembered, Colet was to become a member of the five-man committee appointed to bring pressure on Warham to resign in favor of Wolsey. In late 1514, however, Wolsey was not yet lord chancellor and not in a good position to help Colet. After Wolsey was installed as lord chancellor on Christmas Eve of 1515 it would have been far more difficult to attack Colet directly.

The criticisms leveled against the dean which we have examined so far were of greater concern to the church than to the court. There, Colet still enjoyed the favor that the Tudor house had shown his family since old Sir Henry's time; in addition, his denunciations of bishops who cared more for privilege and power than for pastoral care struck a sympathetic chord with laymen, as the Hunne case showed. Colet was harassed, to be sure, but he was still safe.

The hierarchy thought it saw its chance to bring him down when he appeared to enlarge the already ample scope of his criticisms by indicting royal policy as well. However, as the sequel would show, even if the king was not vitally interested in the clerical infighting he was quite aware of it and now turned it dexterously to his advantage.

Erasmus's is our only account of how the clash between Colet and his ecclesiastical enemies came to a head. Fortunately for us he was living almost continuously in England during the critical period he describes and had access to good sources—including Colet himself—about what was a widely discussed crisis. Erasmus shared his contemporaries' sense of the importance of this crisis for Colet's career, and he makes it the climax of his biography of Colet. Colet's death is moved to an earlier point in the narrative so that the final scene can depict his definitive triumph over his attackers.

Though Erasmus's implied dating is probably off by a year or two, the discrepancy is unimportant. Erasmus, writing years after the event, and often casual about chronology, locates the event he is about to describe as coinciding with Henry VIII's preparations for war against France, a fact that points to mid-1513; but he closes his account by saying that thenceforward no one dared attack Colet, whereas Colet was under attack in October 1514.

The true date of the climactic scene in Erasmus's biography is probably 1515. By the end of that year Wolsey was lord chancellor, and the combination of the king's favor and the chancellor's protection made Colet invulnerable from then on. If Erasmus's implied dating to 1513 was intentional, it would be to dramatize Colet's opposition to war. What the biographer wanted was to situate Colet's call for peace in a most unpropitious environment. Then, when Colet's enemies were delightedly anticipating his disgrace, he was triumphantly vindicated by the king himself.

As Erasmus tells the story, Colet's enemies hoped to destroy him by causing him to lose the king's favor. Their chance seemed to come when Colet quoted in a sermon Cicero's dictum that even an unjust peace was preferable to the justest war. They were quick to see here an allusion to Henry's policy of war against France. This was the king's inference as well, for he requested a private interview with the outspoken dean. During the interview, as Erasmus reports what he must have learned from Colet himself, the king first encouraged Colet to "continue to minister by his learning to the morals of an age far gone in corruption, and not withdraw his light from an epoch that was plunged into darkness" (A, ll. 565–568). The king then got down to business. He told the dean that

> he was not unaware what set those bishops against him, nor was he ignorant of how much good Colet had done for the people of England by his life and his sacred learning. He would thwart his enemies' designs, he added, in such a manner that everyone would understand that no one who attacked Colet would go unpunished. At this point Colet thanked the king indeed for his favor, but declined his offer. He did not wish anyone to be the worse on his account; rather than that he would resign the office that he held. (A, ll. 568–575)

Colet's magnanimity and the king's sympathy for him must have remained unknown to his enemies, who saw that he was pardoned on this occasion but did not quite understand why. They bided their time until they could catch him in a still more flagrant indiscretion. Just when the occasion arose is uncertain. All Erasmus says is that it was "some time later," and that "from Eastertide, preparations were under way for a campaign against the French." Though Erasmus speaks of this projected campaign as distinct from the earlier, there was in reality only one campaign at anything like this period[86] — another indication that war against France was used mainly as a literary backdrop to dramatize Colet's idealism in the cause of peace.

In any case Colet, who rarely erred on the side of caution, must have been encouraged to find the king solidly behind him. He took the occasion of a Good Friday sermon to make the still-stronger assertion that warfare was inherently incompatible with Christianity. Though the sermon does not survive, Erasmus summarizes it in part. In keeping with the day, Colet spoke of Christ's paradoxical victory through his death on the cross and then

> exhorted all Christians to serve and conquer under the banner of their king. For the fact is that wicked men who out of hatred or greed fight with other wicked men in mutual slaughter serve not under Christ's standard but under the Devil's. He further showed how hard it would be to die a Christian death when most of those who wage war carry the stain of hatred or greed; and how it is hardly possible for one and the same person to show brotherly love, without which no one will see God, and plunge his sword into his brother's entrails. He added that they should follow Christ as their prince rather than the Juliuses and Alexanders. Much more he declaimed along the same lines, until the king became somewhat uneasy lest this sermon dampen the ardor of the soldiers he was to lead. All the wicked then flocked together, as if at the cry of a bird of ill omen, in the hope that now at last the king's anger could be kindled against Colet. He was sent for by order of the king. He came, and dined in the little Franciscan convent adjoining the palace of Greenwich. When the king learned of this he came down to the convent garden and on Colet's approach dismissed his entire suite. When there remained just the two of them, he told Colet to put his cap on again and converse without restraint. The noble and considerate young man began in this way: "You must not feel any distrust, Dean. I have not summoned you here to interfere with your sacred labors, of which I thoroughly approve, but to disburden my conscience of some scruples, and by your advice do fuller justice to my responsibilities" (A, ll. 579–601).

After this skillful opening, Henry confided that Colet's sermon had caused him misgivings about whether a Christian prince could be justified in going to war. Colet must have tried to lighten the royal conscience by explaining that he had not meant to be understood as speaking absolutely. There were recognized occasions on which a Christian prince would be entitled, even obliged, to go to war; and we may suppose that Colet would mention them to the king. Henry's diplomatic approach showed him as the conscientious prince at the same time that it gave Colet opportunity to "clarify" his teaching on war. Both men emerged with honor intact. Colet readily acceded, Erasmus tells us, to the king's request that on some suitable occasion he would "express his meaning more plainly, for the sake of the rough soldiers, who might otherwise place a wrong construction on his correct statement that there was no such thing as a just war."

Most modern scholars seem to prefer to ignore the political realities of the situation, and doubt that Colet gave the requested public "clarification." The antiquarian Matthew Parker (1504–1575), however, states as a fact that Colet did preach the sermon the king asked for. According to Parker, who had no apparent axe to grind, Colet came to share the king's view that war against France was a defensive war and therefore licit. On mature deliberation, according to Parker, Colet came about "with such eloquence and weight on the right of Christians to wage war, as to inflame not the king and his nobles only, who were already inclined for war against the French, but even the spiritless and timid."[87] In calling attention to Parker's account Lupton also raises certain questions about it, and some later scholars have preferred to regard Colet's public palinode as a myth.[88] Nevertheless, I think it inconceivable as a realistic matter that the king did not get what he delicately requested; Allen too, unconvinced by Lupton, assumes that what the king asked for the king got.[89]

Henry's masterly handling of this small crisis did justice all round. The bishops who had been harrying the dean were unambiguously warned off in the king's final word on the subject, which we will consider shortly. They, along with Colet, were also reminded that the king reserved the right to intervene, as he did in the Hunne case, when ecclesiastical problems took on a political dimension. For his part, Colet would understand that he had had something of a close call from which only the king's personal favor had saved him, and that it was expected that in future his zeal would not lead him into seeming to criticize the king's policy. Colet understood the unspoken message well enough, and there is no indication that he again risked losing the royal protection so dramatically granted him.

The scene in which the king reappears after a private half-hour interview with the dean forms the dramatic close of Erasmus's life of Colet. The king played the scene to the hilt. He and Colet stood together as the returning courtiers formed a circle about them, in delighted expectation of Colet's public humiliation. Instead, the king called for a goblet of wine and drank to the dean.

> He took him in his arms in the kindest possible manner, and before letting him depart he promised him everything one could look for in even the most favorably disposed monarch. Then, turning to the courtiers, he cried in a tone audible to everyone, "Let every man have his own doctor, and show his favor to him. This is the doctor for me!" (A, ll. 613–614)

Discomfited would be too weak a word to describe the enemies who thought they had finally engineered Colet's disgrace. Erasmus describes them—still relying of course, as he must have done throughout, on Colet's own account—as "like wolves open-mouthed, as the saying goes,"[90] baffled of their prey. Colet noticed especially the chagrin of Bishop Edmund Birkhead (or Brygate),[91] probably one of the two bishops with whom Fitzjames had joined forces (A, ll. 539–541) in a concerted attack on Colet. Nevertheless, after the king spoke there remained nothing for Colet's foes to do but reconcile themselves to his triumph. If they hoped he would rashly risk the royal favor by some fresh imprudence in the future, they were to be disappointed. Colet had learned his lesson.

Though Erasmus appreciated the political dimensions of the cabal against his friend, the prominence he gave to Colet's victory was due to its religious dimensions. The gravamen of the attack on Colet, as Erasmus saw it, was Colet's plea for the primacy of love over legalism; far from attacking authority as his opponents claimed he was doing, Colet intended to reassert its New Testament roots in the great commandment of love.

Erasmus's wholehearted concurrence with this framing of the issue appears in the line with which he elected to close his little life of Colet. It seems not to have been observed that in this conclusion Erasmus associates Colet with his divine Master at a parallel point in Jesus' life. Jesus too was beset near the end of his life by enemies, both Pharisees and Sadducees, who tried to trap him into contravening either the word of Scripture or the law of the Roman provincial government. He triumphed over them so signally that the evangelist closes his account with the line, in the Vulgate, "Neque ausus fuit quisquam ex illa die eum amplius interrogare" ("Nor from that day forward did anyone dare question him further"; Matt. 22:46). Erasmus closes the scene of Colet's triumph with an unmistakable allusion to the same line: "Nec ab eo die quisquam est ausus impetere Coletum" ("Nor from that day forward did anyone dare attack Colet"; A, 1. 616).[92]

With this hint one may glance back over the biography and detect a seeming parallel from Jesus' earlier years. In his account of Colet's lectures on Paul at Oxford Erasmus stressed the lecturer's youth ("a iuvene"; A, 1. 290). Colet was then actually in his thirties—no boy by fifteenth-century standards—but Erasmus was glancing at the topos of the youthful Christ teaching in the temple—a topos he had already used in describing the youthful Thomas More lecturing publicly on *The City of God*.[93] The unobtrusive parallels with the life of Christ served to set Erasmus's subject off against the background of a corrupt society that sought to destroy him as Jesus' society had him. By closing his life of Colet as he does, Erasmus encourages the reader—in the first place Jodocus Jonas—to imitate Christ in the assurance that he, like Colet, would win ultimate victory.

Erasmus found nothing in the remainder of Colet's life that called for commemoration. Colet continued to lead a busy, useful, and honored life. He was dean of St. Paul's, a famous preacher, a member of the Royal Council. As we learn from a letter dated 1516, Colet was granted private interviews with Henry VIII whenever he requested them,[94] proof that he continued to stand high in the royal favor. That favor continued to the end.[95] With these advantages, and Wolsey's support, Colet's further advancement seemed inevitable. The deanery of St. Paul's, so desirable in itself, was assumed by Erasmus to lead to greater things still.[96] It must have seemed that Colet had only to be patient. The bishop of London was already an old man; so, for that matter, was the archbishop of Canterbury.

Then his expectations began to take a sharply different turn. He was stricken three times by the mysterious plague, called the sweating sickness, that was sweeping England.[97] His inherited strength of constitution stood him in good stead, but each attack took its toll and left him further weakened, though he continued to work. Finally he succumbed, in Erasmus's account, to a liver infection consequent upon the third and final attack; after lingering for some days on the point of death, he died on 16 September 1519.[98]

"An autopsy [anatomia] revealed nothing unusual, save that the lateral lobes of the liver were overspread with an upright tuftlike growth" (A, ll. 382–383). Cirrhosis of the liver seems precluded by Colet's abstemious habits. It has been suggested to me that certain carcinomas might to the naked eye fit Erasmus's sketchy description;[99] what seems sure is that the condition of the liver which Erasmus reports is not associated with the sweating sickness.[100] The medical interest of the case may help explain why an autopsy was performed; but it is also true that autopsies were coming into fashion. Already in 1410 the body of Pope Alexander V was subject to postmortem examination, and by the sixteenth century there were "innumerable" instances of autopsies on "respected citizens." Such autopsies were of course private, with only two or three physicians present, and they were carried out in the hope of "anatomical discoveries from which medicine could profit."[101] Colet himself, as one of the two licensers of London physicians, may have attended postmortems and authorized his own.[102]

In any case, the body was placed in a tomb that bore, by Colet's express wish, the simplest possible inscription: "IOAN. COL." (A, ll. 384–386). Not long afterward, however, it was embellished with the usual flourish of tributes in verse and prose.[103] Still later it was renewed at the expense of the Mercers' Company but was destroyed in the Great Fire.

The lasting memorial to Colet was the biographical tribute by Erasmus with which our study began. Between Erasmus's departure from England in 1516—except for a brief business trip in the spring of 1517 he never returned—and the dean's death on 16 September 1519, Erasmus conception of Colet began to take on an added dimension. There was no estrangement, but both men increasingly moved in different worlds, especially after Erasmus gained prominence with the Greek Testament of 1516. Colet noticed that while Erasmus stayed in touch with certain English friends he himself was not of this chosen group, and he complained to Erasmus that he neglected him.[104] This was probably true, but at the same time the separation worked to Colet's advantage, at least with respect to posterity. The increased distance between the two men began to work in the mind of the more imaginative of them a kind of alchemy. As his English friend grew more distant, he came to stand out more clearly in outline. His rigidity lent him a certain exemplary quality; it encouraged Erasmus to think of him not only as an individual but also as a type. Hence when Erasmus found occasion to write of Colet he paired him with another man who seemed to him to provide a parallel in the Plutarchan manner. This was the French Franciscan Jean Vitrier, an older contemporary (1456–ca. 1516) whom Colet seems never to have met.[105] From this juxtaposition with Vitrier we gain further hints of the light in which Erasmus saw Colet almost twenty-two years after they first met.

Vitrier was an Observant Franciscan and Guardian of the Franciscan house at Saint-Omer at the time when Erasmus met him, in the late summer of 1501.[106] Lupton, followed by Allen,[107] identified him with the Jean Vitrier who was censured by the Sorbonne in 1498 because of certain passages in his sermons. This has been doubted, however—partly because the Vitrier censured in 1498 was from Tournai rather than Saint-Omer, and partly because it seems "not very credible" that a man who had incurred the censure of the Sorbonne should immediately afterward be named head of a religious community.[108] But for whatever reasons, Erasmus seems to have drawn apart from Vitrier. Though he admired him there is no known correspondence between them—a fact readily explained if Erasmus preferred not to continue his friendship with a controversial figure while he was still making his own reputation.

Only later, when he was famous and Vitrier dead, did Erasmus make reference to him. In 1523 he declared that some two decades earlier he had been much encouraged by the reception given his *Enchiridion* by "the Franciscan Jean Vitrier, who was highly esteemed in that part of the world";[109] and even this guarded phrase reports others' judgments rather than Erasmus's own. Vitrier may be referred to under a pseudonym in the colloquy "The Apotheosis of Johannes Reuchlin,"[110] and Erasmus openly named Vitrier[111] as the model for the ideal preacher described in his "Ecclesiastes" (1535).[112] Though the "Ecclesiastes" was not published till 1535 Erasmus had been working on it intermittently for some dozen years, so that the evocation of Vitrier may go back to the period of the passage concerning the *Enchiridion* already cited. In any case, Erasmus made his regard for Vitrier unmistakable by pairing him with Colet in the biographical sketch addressed to Justus Jonas in 1521.

Especially interesting is the fact that when Erasmus later wrote a short biography of Origen (1536) he described Origen by borrowing from his earlier biography of Vitrier, so closely was Vitrier linked in Erasmus's mind with the great allegorical exegete of the early church.[113] Erasmus thought one page of Origen worth ten of Augustine,[114] and it was through Vitrier that he came to know Origen. Vitrier was thus responsible for the strongly felt presence of Origen in the *Enchiridion militis christiani*, mostly written in the late summer of 1501.[115] This is the only period during which we know that Vitrier and Erasmus were in close intellectual contact; when Erasmus thought back to Vitrier he inevitably associated him with Origen. Origen in turn, as the greatest allegorical interpreter of the Bible, is thus brought indirectly into connection with Colet by Erasmus's association of the two men. In the tripartite association of Colet with Vitrier and Vitrier with Origen we find a valuable pointer to the exegetical tradition with which Erasmus associated Colet. It is as a seeker of hidden significances that Erasmus saw Colet, a worker in the long tradition that extended down the centuries from Origen.

The known facts about Erasmus's relation to Vitrier are perhaps most readily explained if we assume that after the early "decisive"[116] influence due to Vitrier's introducing him to Origen, Erasmus soon outgrew Vitrier the man. He continued the pursuit of what he called "arcane letters"[117] to the end of his life, but for this he no longer needed Vitrier. The Franciscan had a falling-out with his religious superiors not long afterward and passed the remainder of his days, from 1502 to about 1516, in an "exile"[118] during which Erasmus found it imprudent and perhaps uninteresting to disturb him. He did not forget him, however. When he decided to commemorate his old friend Colet, whom also he eventually outgrew, he saw that Vitrier's life could be used to reinforce the same point as Colet's. Both were rigidly good men, strident critics of abuses, who had carried on the work of Christ from within existing church structures. Accordingly he turned both of them into models for the contemplation of Justus Jonas.

Vitrier, as an Observant Franciscan, would be associated with the small minority of Franciscans in England who followed the strict rule. In 1484 the two branches of the order in England had split, and the resulting figures speak for themselves, for the laxer Conventuals took fifty of the fifty-three English houses. Henry VII, however, showed where his sympathies lay by adding to the three Observant houses three more founded at his own expense. One of these was the Franciscan house at Greenwich where Colet dined before the memorable interview with Henry VIII which resulted in his definitive vindication.[119] Like his father and many another layman, Henry VIII approved though he did not imitate those who took the steep path to perfection. Erasmus remembered Vitrier and Colet as men who set high moral standards for themselves and, in season and out of season, demanded of others the same level of commitment.

Both subjects of Erasmus's parallel lives offended the institutionally pious by their criticisms. Vitrier was censured by the Sorbonne— assuming that the Jean Vitrier who was the object of the doctors' ire was Erasmus's Vitrier—and, as we have seen, Colet ran into serious trouble with his diocesan and other bishops. Colet's connections enabled him to ride out the storm, but Vitrier, not so fortunately situated, was soon shunted into permanent obscurity: even the year of his death is uncertain. While prudence may have counseled Erasmus to put some distance between himself and Vitrier, whom he did not acknowledge publicly until the double portrait of 1521, Colet, by contrast, was very much on the ecclesiastical fast track; when Erasmus found he would be returning to England after all, he naturally resumed correspondence with the dean-designate of St. Paul's. He saw Colet during each of his stays in England, and, as I read the evidence, grew closest to him at the period of the founding of St. Paul's School.

The conclusion of Erasmus's double portrait shows, however, that it would be a mistake to suppose that the ampler record of Erasmus's friendship with Colet means that he prized Colet above Vitrier. In comparing his two subjects, the biographer gave the preference to Vitrier:

> It is up to you [he tells his correspondent], to select in each man whatever you think most likely to conduce to true piety. If now you ask which I prefer, I reply that they seem to me equally praiseworthy. It was a fine thing for Colet, with his ample fortune, to follow unwaveringly the call of Christ rather than the call of nature, but it was all the more admirable of Vitrier that in such a mode of life [the monastery] he attained and bore witness to the spirit of the Gospels, like a fish that lived in a bog without taking on a swampy taste. But Colet did have certain qualities that reminded one he was after all a human being, while I never saw Vitrier exhibit the least trace of attachment to human values. If you follow my advice you will unhesitatingly enroll both these men among the saints even if no pope ever canonizes them. (A, ll. 619–630)

Acting then on his own advice, Erasmus addressed a brief and moving prayer to the two "happy souls, to whom I owe so much," and whom he hoped to rejoin in heaven (A, ll. 631–633). With this prayer the six-thousand-word letter closes.

Thus Erasmus's final estimate of Colet is both generous and judicious. He had had more than one experience with traits that showed that Colet, however holy, was "after all a human being." As we saw earlier, he chafed under Colet's tightfistedness and said so openly, to Colet himself and also in the biographical letter. Even before he was ordained, and though he did not need money, Colet accumulated half a dozen highly desirable benefices, three of them entailing cure of souls. Nor did he have qualms about pluralism in later life. He acquired further valuable benefices for himself, and in 1508 he used his influence to have a rich benefice (£20 per annum) granted for life to a favorite pupil who was only thirteen years old.[120] A reading of Colet's last will, which goes on for page after page enumerating the properties of which he stood possessed even after granting many other properties to the Mercers' Company for the endowment of his school, does not suggest indifference to worldly goods.[121] He once confessed that he was deterred only at the last moment from taking an uncle to court in a dispute over property,[122] despite his proclamation to others that "there is no way to go to law without sin, when controversy clouds over the brightness of charity" (C, 198 [126]). By the standards of his time such instances are only minor flecks on a noble portrait; still, they show what Erasmus meant in alluding to the all-too-human traits in his subject.

Erasmus was not put off for long by Colet's flaws, irritating at times but not fundamental. More basic in defining the limits of their friendship were differences of temperament that restricted the imaginative sympathy they could feel for each other. Colet's incomprehension of irony and complete lack of interest in poetry ("cum is a poeticis numeris esset alienissimus"; A, 563–564), for example, were not in the end such a barrier between Colet and the author of *The Praise of Folly* as was Colet's deep-rooted and pervasive concern for order—or rather, structure. For his greater friends Erasmus and More order was open to heuristic experiment, experiment that could call into question the very foundations of society. Not for Colet was the praise of folly or the construction of imaginary kingdoms where a people that had never heard of Christ lived in natural happiness. For Colet structure was primary, and *ordo* was tied to *hierarchia*. The fact is everywhere evident, from his devotion to Dionysius's *Hierarchies* to his penchant for diagrams, with which his manuscripts abound. Everything, for Colet, had to have its fixed place. It seems that his limited imaginative reach, reinforced by his professional experience within the church, made him wish to block off the beckoning possibilities of *ordo* in the sense of organic growth. Instead he understood order only as hierarchy, which assigns a place to each thing depending on its participation in a single agreed-on value.

Something made him uncomfortable with unsanctioned freedoms. Man's limits had been fixed in a sacred book, and only within its permitted bounds might the spirit range in quest of fuller meaning. A wider-ranging quest made no sense when revealed truth was ready to hand. Perhaps his constant struggle against his own strong sensuality (A, ll. 391–392) reinforced his rigid sense of rules. He grossly undervalued everything this-worldly and set a correspondingly extravagant valuation on everything renunciatory and otherworldly: he had to believe that the high price he personally paid was worth paying.

Colet's virtual equation of order with hierarchy may be supposed to raise the question of whether, if he had lived, he would have subscribed the Act of Supremacy in 1534. While I am inclined to consider this a nonquestion—Colet died, after all, fifteen momentous years earlier—it has often been mooted. Modern writers on the period, now that confessional rivalries have subsided, largely agree in seeing Colet not as a Reformer in the old sense but as a "repristinator."[123] If this was Colet's aim he would have been in a much better position as dean of St. Paul's and member of the Royal Council to help bring the church back to its pristine purity than if he had refused to sign the Act, and been deprived and cast into prison. The papal supremacy for which Fisher and More[124] lost their lives may not have been as dear to Colet as it was to them. His personal experience of Rome was during the pontificate of Alexander VI, and his own later experience of routine ecclesiastical administration would perhaps not have prepared him to lay down his life for the Roman supremacy. Only one prominent layman and only one bishop did so, and they were joined by only a small handful of religious, mainly Carthusians. It is true that it was with the Carthusians that Colet had proposed to end his days after retirement (A, ll. 372–376), but it is also true that the Carthusian monastery at Shene, where he built himself a magnificent "nest," enjoyed the special patronage of the Tudor kings.[125] Even apart from the terrible penalties of treason it is at least possible to wonder whether Colet, alone among all other prominent Englishmen, would have felt obligated to make a third with Fisher and More. His exceptionally strong commitment to hierarchical structures, and his close and loyal relation to the king, seem to me to make it doubtful that Colet would have felt obliged to offer such a sacrifice in such a cause.

Colet was less concerned with doctrine than with purity of life. In his most distinctive achievement, the school that he founded, he sought to give institutional embodiment to this deal. The curriculum he drew up showed his characteristic mistrust of humane letters pursued for their own sake. Instead, he wanted such studies subordinated to ethical and ultimately religious aims. He began with the world he knew well, the prosperous middle class of London, which would produce from its rising generation the future servants of the state and church. The church was especially open to the possibility of rapid change because in principle its major offices were held by celibates and not handed down, like landed property, from generation to generation in the same family. The church could be a career open to talents. Vacancies occurred continually, and if there was a suitable supply of educated and virtuous young men one could envision dramatic change for the better within a short period. Colet's school was intended to help meet this need by educating many of the boys who would occupy places of responsibility in the next generation.

Like his work in education, Colet's other activities were dedicated to promoting Christian values, with primary emphasis on virtuous living. Living according to Christ's teachings was his constant theme. It was in English, not in Latin, that he trained himself to preach. Greek studies meant nothing to him when he was young, he had a puritanical aversion to poetry, and his Latin style was at best rough and ready. Still less did he understand the play element in humanistic culture that fascinated some of his contemporaries. Nothing mattered to him, at least in principle, unless it pointed, in Paul's words, to "Christ and him crucified."

While his character was formed and his goals were set early in life, he owed the wider scene on which he moved later to the accident that the mortality among his siblings left him at the age of thirty-eight heir to his father's great fortune. His father's influence with the Tudors also brought Colet the deanery of St. Paul's, and with it one of the most influential pulpits in the kingdom, especially as it entailed preaching at court. But though his scope was enlarged by these opportunities his ideal remained remarkably constant from his twenties on. He preferred to pursue his aims within well-established institutional structures, where he felt at home. In all his areas of activity he made an impression not so much from any novelty of doctrine or teaching but by his unblemished life and fervent eloquence.

To the goods of nature and fortune he added a final stroke of great good luck, his gradually ripening friendship with the most influential scholar and writer of the age. It was Erasmus's biography which made Colet one of the handful of early Tudors who are still memorable as persons. By using Colet's career to point a moral to a reform-minded young proto-Protestant, Erasmus set Colet's life within the reformist framework that was to exercise decisive influence in the Victorian age and beyond. Without Erasmus St. Paul's School would still have given Colet a certain importance, but it was the biography that was to make of him a kind of household name among those interested in the England of Thomas More and Henry VIII. For it was from the biography that Frederic Seebohm selected many of the materials for his imaginary league of Oxford Reformers. And it was Seebohm's book that launched the Victorian Colet on his career as perhaps the longest-running myth in English renaissance studies.

APPENDIXES

1. Colet's *De Sacramentis*: Text and Translation

2. List of Writers Referred to by Colet

Appendix 1
De Sacramentis*
John Colet

I

[A] deo patre per filium cum spiritu sancto sunt, formantur, et perfici-
untur omnia. A sanctissima trinitate omnis consecratio est: videlicet a deo
per filium cum spiritu sancto. Deus verus sacerdos est: a quo omne sacerdotium in celo et in terra nominatur. In deo vere sunt omnia. Extra
deum imitatio est dei. In deo qui eternus est eterna sunt omnia. Illic pa-
ternitas et filiatio et amor et sacerdotium eternum est. Sacerdotium illic
est quidem (vt ita dicam) sacerdotificans, omne enim sacerdotium a deo
est, sacerdotum sacerdote. Sacerdotale munus est[t que]dam dei assidua
imitatio in puritate, luce, et bonitate. Deus ipse est puritas, lux, et bonitas. Post deum hec relucent in angelis quos deus summus sacerdos puri-
ficando, illuminando, et perficiendo sibi consecrauit. Consecrauit autem
et dedicauit sibi, vt angeli in se triunum deum in hac trinitate referant.
Quatenus hec tria eminentissime in deo sunt: deus est ipse qui colitur et
cui sacrificatur. Quatenus sanctificator ille hec propagans creat, illuminat,
perficit: sacerdos est mirifice et sacrificans sibi et aliis sacerdotes consecrans. Effectus illius benignissimi diuini sacerdotii primus in angelis est,
qui in tanto consecratore et summo pontifice euaserunt feliciter sacerdotes consecrati deo ab ipso deo, vt deum deinceps consecratione imitentur.

*The Latin text below is based on British Library Loan Manuscript 55/2 (Duke of Leeds).

On the Sacraments
John Colet

I

From God the Father through the Son together with the Holy Spirit all things have their existence, their form, and their perfection. All consecration is from the most holy Trinity, that is, from God through the Son together with the Holy Spirit. God is the true priest, from whom all priesthood in heaven and on earth takes its name.[1] All things that exist have their true existence in God; all that exists outside him is an imitation of God. In God, who is eternal, all things are eternal; hence fatherhood and sonship and love and priesthood are eternal. Hence it is that priesthood is actually, if I may so express it, priest-making; for all priesthood is from God, the priest of priests. A priest's function is a kind of unflagging imitation of God in purity, light, and goodness. God himself is purity, light, and goodness. After God, these qualities are most manifest in the angels, whom God, the supreme priest, has consecrated to himself by cleansing, illumining, and perfecting them. He has consecrated them to himself, however, in such a way that in themselves the angels reflect the triune God by the trinity of their activity; for those three actions exist preeminently in God. It is God himself who is worshipped and to whom sacrifice is offered. Hence the sanctifier in propagating these three actions himself cleanses, illumines, and perfects; in a wondrous way he is a priest who both sacrifices to himself and consecrates priests for others.[2] The effect of this gracious divine priesthood is first of all in the angels: consecrated by so great a high priest they have gone forth joyously as priests consecrated to God by God himself, in order to imitate God in their turn by

Imitentur (inquam) consecrando sacrificandoque triplici illa racione purgandi, illuminandi, et perficiendi qua ipsi deo sunt consecrati. Propagatio enim oportet sit dei: et illius benignitatis diriuatio. In hoc officio qui sunt, in sancto dei sacerdotio sunt. Quod sacerdotali munere sanctificatur deo, sacerdotis sacrificium est deo acceptatissimum. Velit deus vt sacerdotes sacrificent sibi in sanctificatione, sicut ille sanctificans sacerdotes ipsos sibi [sacrificat]. Propagatio deitatis maximum et precipuum est deo sacrificium. Opus enim est ardentissime charitatis, et ob id quidem opus iustissimum. Iusticia deus placatur mirifice. Hinc illud Daviticum: Sacrificate sacrificium iusticie. Inter se mutuo et sine intermissione angeli sacerdotale munus exercent sacrificantque iusticiam. Item simul extra se fit vt quam latissime in deo iusti appareant. Moliuntur omni conatu in ordine ipso ordinante constantem et iustum ordinem in rebus. Hic effectus sacerdotalis muneris est. Vnde sacerdotium ordo a recentiori ecclesia cognominatum est. Ordinata in ordinatores, ordinatores in ordinem ipsum referuntur. Ordo ipse racio est dei illa omniformis ab intima dei mente deprompta tota et adequata diuinitatis summa ipsa pulchritudo quod ipsum est verbum dei ex alto ore prolatum deum totum intimo exitu plenissime expressissime significans, quo pulcherrimo ordine dictata sunt omnia. In quo ab ordinatis in propagationem ordinis laboratur. Primum et maxime in stabilem et iustum ordinem rerum sacerdotali officio expurgans, illustrans, et perficiens ordo ipse agit et operatur, et in eo deinceps, qui sunt ordines ordine quisque suo. Primus ergo sacerdos est ordo ipse et primus ordo sacerdos ipse. Hic est sacratissimus dei eternus filius cui pater in ore Dauid hec verba habuit: Tu es sacerdos in eternum secundum ordinem Melchisedech, cuius ordinis neque principium neque finis agnoscitur. Itaque eternus sacerdos est dei, ipse deus sacerdotificans. Idem eternus dei ordo, ipse deus ordinans omnia a quo omnis sacerdotalis ordo est et omne ordinatum sacerdotium. Ille ordo et sacerdos primum ordinauit sacerdotium in celis sanctissimorum spirituum, in quibus est illuminatio, purgatio, et perfectio, et inter se maxime ipsorum et omnium.

Sacerdos eciam ille primus et exemplaris in quo sunt omnia, qui ipse est omnia verissime. Is ipsum est etiam sacramentum sacrificans omnia,

further consecration—imitate him, that is, by consecrating and sacrificing in the threefold mode of cleansing, illumining, and perfecting in which they themselves have been consecrated to God. It is fitting that propagation should characterize God and that his goodness should flow outward.[3] Those who are employed in this propagation are in God's holy priesthood. The priest's sacrifice is most acceptable to God because by the power of the priest things are sanctified to God. God wills that priests sacrifice to him in sanctification just as he makes them holy by sanctifying them to himself. The greatest and fundamental sacrifice to God is the propagation of the Godhead, since it is a work of the most ardent love and for that very reason a work most just. By justice God is wondrously appeased. Hence it is that David said, "Sacrifice the sacrifice of justice" [Ps. 4:6]. By sacrificing justice the angels exercise their priestly power upon one another mutually and without ceasing. Likewise they exercise this power outside their own ranks, that in God the just may appear to the widest possible extent. Their every effort is in virtue of that Order who himself ordains a just and stable order in all things. This is what the priestly power produces. Therefore in more recent times the church has called priesthood orders.

Things that are ordered manifest those who have ordered them, and these in turn reflect Order himself. Order himself is the all-shaping plan of God, arising from his inmost mind, complete and expressive of his divinity, itself of supreme beauty; for it is the word of God uttered from his royal lips, signifying God wholly in his inmost expression, fully and manifestly. In this fair order all things find their place. And in it the ordained work to propagate order. First and foremost, Order himself acts and operates through his priestly office to cleanse, illumine, and perfect all things and produce a just and stable order, in which the subordinate orders will act in their turn, each in its own order. Thus the first priest is Order himself, and the first Order is the Priest himself. He is the most sacred, the eternal son of God, of whom the Father spoke through the mouth of David these words: "Thou art a priest forever according to the order of Melchisedech" [Ps. 109:4; qtd. in Heb. 5:6, 6:17], which order knows neither beginning nor end. Accordingly he is the eternal priest of God, himself the priest-making God. The same is the eternal Order of God, God himself who ordains all things, from whom all priestly order takes its being, and all ordered priesthood as well. He who is order and priesthood first ordained the priesthood in heaven of the most holy spirits, in whom there is illumining, cleansing, and perfecting[4] of all, but especially of and among themselves.

That first and exemplary priest,[5] in whom all things exist, who is himself most truly all things—he is also that very sacrament that sanctifies all

omniaque sacramenta faciens que omnia ipsum referant sacramentorum
sacrament[um]. Primum autem conditum sacramentum per quod deinde
omnia alia sacramenta condantur, erat quod ordinem vocant et sacerdotium. In principio a sacerdote ipso et ordine. Consecrauit enim sibi et
apte* astrinxit sacramento felicissimos illos spiritus vt in ipso ordinum
auctore sancte et ordinate commilitent. Militia enim in deo omne sacerdotium est vt in viribus dei, dei creaturam a racionibus deo contrariis vin-
dicent vtque agant vt deus vbique et in omnibus luculente appareat. Quoniam authores malicie nequitieque indesinenter agunt vt sibi ex bono
malum exaugeant: vt quemadmodum deprauerint se ita alia que-
quumque, quoad possunt in incrementum mali deprauent. Celeste sacerdotium consecratur deo, et sacramentali nexu obligatur vt in vno, pulchro
et bono deo vnitatem, pulchritudinem et perfectionem rerum conquirant
et conseruent a racionibus videlicet contrariis multiplicitate, deformitate,
et defectu, que assidue moliuntur in mundo qui sua ipsorum improbitate
apostatarunt ex lucifero illo* factus tenebrifer, diabolus et satellites eius.
Sacratissimi illi [angeli] quos dedicauit sibi deus ipse statim [post] defec-
tionem illorum qui in suum malum corruerunt, in hac rerum vniuersitate
quod dei est templum extant magnifici sacerdotes summi dei et industriosi
exercitus magni dei sabaoth, tales facti a deo vt pro datis uiribus sine intermissione in mundo suapte natura labente conquirant deo iusticiam ius-
ticiamque consacrificent. Quorum assiduitatem in hac parte moysaicum
sacerdotium quod scatet hostiis et immolationibus solertissime adumbrat.
Illi ergo imitantes exemplar et causam omnis sacerdotii ordinem eciam
et iusticiam ipsam in propagatione iusticie dei elab[orant] hoc maxime,
sacrificantes deo et vero suo fungentes officio sacerdotali quod est quidem
in sole deo triplici dei radio purgatorio, illuminatorio, et perfectorio, et
quam late fieri potest et quam longe copiosum iusticie fructum parere et
procreare. Quoniam sacerdotium est certe imitacio dei in amplificatione
iusticie. In eo munere ordines illi angelorum numero nouem (sicuti de-
scribit Dionysius) longe excellunt et antiquitate et veritate. Qui consecrati et consummati ordines in creatura mundi dei templo perfecti sacerdotes sunt sanctissime se in sacrifitiis laudis exercentes. In quo mundo
constituit deus angelos sacerdotes, vt sibi incrementum dei sacrificent in
omnibus, id est simplicem et veram bonitatem. Dei filius summus et eter-

.

---

*MS: apte, with a horizontal crossbar on the descender of the *p*; whence the erroneous
expansion *aperte* in St. Paul's School MS.
*MS: ille.

things, making all things sacraments that reflect him, the sacrament of sacraments. The first sacrament to be instituted, through which all the other sacraments were subsequently instituted, is that which is called orders or priesthood.[6] Its beginning is from the Priest and Order himself. By this sacrament he consecrated to himself and duly organized those happy spirits, to serve as soldiers in holy and ordered fashion under the very author of order. For all priesthood is a warfare in God by which his power rescues his creation from the forces that are hostile to God and brings it about that God appears in his glory everywhere and in all things.[7] Those that procure evil and iniquity, on the one hand, strive unceasingly to win for themselves evil out of good and, having debased themselves, do all they can to debase others as well, so that the domain of evil may be enlarged. The heavenly priesthood, on the other hand, is consecrated to God and bound together by the sacrament [of orders] to attain and preserve through the one, beautiful, and good God the unity, beauty, and perfection of all things, defending them from the opposite condition of multiplicity, deformity, and defect which those of their own number who through their own wickedness apostasized and from being light-bearers have become the bringers of darkness—the devil and his satellites—strive continuously to bring about. Most blessed are those [angels][8] who, immediately after the defection of those who embraced their own ruin, stand forth in this universe, which is the temple of God,[9] as splendid priests of the most high God and the indefatigable army of the great God of Hosts; such they were made by God, to use unceasingly the strength he had given them, even though their own nature might waver, in order to procure justice for God and to make that justice holy. The Mosaic priesthood, which abounds in victims and immolations, ingeniously typifies their efforts in this enterprise. The angels, then, in imitation of the exemplar and cause of all priesthood, Order and Justice himself, labor to propagate the justice of God, especially by sacrificing to God and performing their true priestly office. This is simply to beget and bring forth the abundant fruits of justice, as comprehensively and widely as possible, in that sun that is God, whose triple ray cleanses, illumines, and perfects. For priesthood is assuredly the imitation of God in the diffusion of justice.

In this power the orders of angels, nine in number (as Dionysius describes them), far excel, both for venerableness and for truth. These orders, consecrated and brought to fulfillment in the creation of the world, the temple of God, are perfect priests, devoting themselves in most holy wise to sacrifices of praise. God has constituted the angels priests in the universe, in order that in all things they may sacrifice unadulterated and true goodness to him, thus increasing the godlike element. The Son of God is the supreme and eternal priest, who brought into being both the temple of the universe and the angelic, spiritual, priests. He likewise in-

nus pontifex condens et templum mundi et angelicos et spiritales sacerdotes. Item sacramenta et sacrificia constituens omnia, ipse in omnibus
sacrificantibus sacrificans deo patri suo vt vniuersus mundus nihil sit nisi
templum, sacerdotium, et sacrifitia deo in eo qui ipse est templum templi
et sacerdotii et sacrificii veritas, deo patri suo a quo eterniter accepit omnia; et vt sit templum, sacerdos, et sacrificium. Primus itaque et summus
pontifex est deus ipse cuius sacra est edes templum creature in quo sacerdotes sunt angeli; in quo sacrificium est simplex veraque iusticia quam
vt sacrificent quin immo vt inter sacrificandum ministri sint (pontifex est
enim ipse qui omnia in omnibus consacrificat) in perpetuum sacerdotium
deo consecrantur. Quo fit vt in sacramentis prior et antiquior sit ordo,
et sacerdotium in templo mundi a deo conditum. Pontificia maiestas sacerdotium consecrans eterna est.

II

[S]unt preterea in spiritalibus naturis reliqua sacramenta omnia sed modo
spiritali et angelico: Matrimonium, Penitentia, Baptismus, Confirmatio,
Eucharistia, Extrema vnctio. Nam tanquam vxor dei adherent deo diuini
illi spiritus et fecundantur ab ipso, et fecundati diuino semine diuinam similitudinem propagant. Item vxores in deo viri sunt, aliosque* tanquam
feminas sibi asciscunt et quodam sancto coitu impregnant. Sic a primo viro
et marito maritatio procedit, que est inferioris partis attractio sursum a
superiore et amplexu astrictio vt fecundetur in eo, et pro capacitate ple-
num sit diuina bonitate et iusticia que tota est diriuata, que viros facit vt
hi feminas faciant viragines atque vt sic vicissitudinario matrimonio ius-
tificetur mundus in iusto deo. Finis enim veri matrimonii est fecunditas
iusticie aut ex adhesione que ipsa est iusticia, aut illis que ab ipso iustificantur. Verus vir et maritus est primus ille pontifex in quo est omnis maritatio in fecunditatem omnium vt sterilia queque in se subjecta vel deo
vel subiectis deo alicuius iusticie fructus fiant feratia atque tenera, si spiritali mente examinentur.

Idem est sacerdotium quod matrimonium, et sa[crificatio idem] est
quod prolificatio. Quum enim in mundo prolem iusticie fecisti, sacrificasti
deo. Huius matr[imonii] leuis et inanis umbra est id quod est maris et femine in propagationem carnis de cuius institutione et quid velit dicemus

*MS: aliis: que

stituted all the sacraments and sacrifices, and in all who offer sacrifice he himself offers sacrifice to God his Father, so that the whole world may be in its entirety temple, priesthood, and sacrifice to God in him who is himself the temple of the temple and the truth of priesthood and sacrifice—to God his Father, from whom he received all things eternally, that also there might be temple, priest, and sacrifice. Thus the first and supreme priest is God himself, whose holy house is the temple of creation, where angels are the priests and where the sacrifice is justice simple and true. The angels were consecrated in perpetual priesthood to God in order to sacrifice justice, or rather to participate as ministers in the sacrifice, for it is the Priest himself who sacrifices all things in all. This is why orders, the priesthood founded by God in the temple of the universe, is first and most ancient among the sacraments. The priestly majesty that consecrates priesthood is eternal.

II

All the other sacraments exist among spiritual natures too, but in a spiritual and angelic manner: matrimony, penance, baptism, confirmation, the Eucharist, and extreme unction. For like a wife of God the divine spirits cling to him and are fecundated by him; fecundated by the divine seed, they propagate a divine likeness. Men likewise are wives in God, but take other men to themselves in the capacity, so to speak, of women, and impregnate them in a kind of holy coitus. Thus from the first Man and Husband proceeds marriage, by which the superior part attracts the inferior and enfolds her in his embrace so that she may be fecundated in him and become, to the extent of her capacity, full of the divine goodness and justice, which is wholly derived from God and makes men such that they may in turn produce women,[10] a matrimonial interaction[11] by which the world may be made just in the just God. For the purpose of true marriage is to make justice fruitful, by clinging either to him who is Justice itself or to those who are justified by him. The true Man and Husband is that first high priest in whom is all the marrying by which all are fecundated; so that whatever is in itself barren, once subjected to God or the subjects of God, may become tender and abound in the fruit of justice, when scrutinized with a spiritual mind.

Priesthood is the same thing as matrimony, and sanctification is the same thing as begetting offspring. For when one has begotten offspring of justice in the world, he has sacrificed to God. Of this true matrimony the marriage of male and female for the propagation of the flesh is a vain and empty shadow, whose institution and meaning we shall discuss later

postea prolixius. Nunc autem cursim et leuiter in hoc magno mundi templo sub pontifice deo quomodo celebrantur reliqua sacramenta volumus annotare vt a primis fontibus diriuata oracio influat in id melius quod intendimus. Habemus enim in proposito loqui expressius de sacramentis ecclesie nostre quibus quasi iurati deo nostro in Iesu christo militamus.

III

Penitentia vero que longe rectius reconciliationis sacramentum vocaretur et reditus a deteriori ad id quod melius est, que semp[er] est cum penitencia delicti et confessione peccati et voluntate recompensandi vt confessio etiam et satisfactio possit vocari eque ac penitentia. Illud (inquam) reconciliationis sacramentum (quod posteriori ecclesie placuit penitentiam appellare) in alienatis et lapsis assidue a sacerdotali mundi parte agitur qui spiritus sunt, qui ordines illi releuant et quodque ad suum statum restituunt vt in ordinatis a deo qui ipse est ordo omnia suum ordinem teneant. Ex infirmitate rerum transgressiones et casus sunt frequentes in mundi parte inferiore et corporali. Quod si a superiori et spiritali parte reuocata non sustinerentur, defluxus rerum suapte impotencia in malum et deforme euaderet in nihilum. In hoc ergo magni mundi templo pars illa purgata, illuminata, confirmata, perfecta, pars videlicet illa a deo sibi consecrata et sacerdotalis, pars spiritalis et angelica, sacerdotale munus exercet quasi sacramentali racione, et corpoream partem infirmam et impuram purgat et stabilit quoad fieri possit in esse spiritali, vt pro captu illuminetur et perficiatur in deo: vt a diuisione ad vnum, a deformitate ad pulchritudinem, a defectu ad perfectionem contracta, omnia deum in se referant vt deus qui debet extet omnia in omnibus: in hoc munus et officium sacerdotis est, in hoc sacrificatio grata deo est. Quoniam in hoc est coactio et cooperacio in deo, qui vnum in se pulchrum et bonum mundum velit esse et res omnes a malitia, tenebris, et morte vindicare vt tandem absorpta morte viuant in deo omnia luculenta ordine et perfecta. In quo labore, per angelos qui student consecrare mundum deo, est expurgatio et reconciliacio rerum et baptismalis illuminatio et confirmatio in lumine et denique sua cuiusque quatenus potest capere bonitate impletio et perfectio.

at some length. Now, however, we wish to say something in a cursory and glancing way, about how the other sacraments are celebrated in this great temple of the world under God as high priest, so that the conclusions we reach in these prior matters may lay a firmer groundwork for our subsequent discussion. For we intend to speak more fully concerning the sacraments of our church,[12] by means of which we carry on the battle like men sworn to our God in Jesus Christ.[13]

III

Now penance, which might far more aptly be termed the sacrament of reconciliation or of the return to what is better, always comprises repentance for the fault, confession of sin, and the desire to make amends; and might just as well be called confession or amendment as penance. This sacrament of reconciliation,[14] then, which the church in more recent times has preferred to call penance, is zealously conferred on those who are estranged and lapsed by the priestly part of the world, the spirits who lift up everything to God and restore everything to its place so that under God, who is Order, all things may be ordained in their due order. Owing to natural frailty, sins and transgressions occur frequently in the lower and corporeal part of the world. If the lower world were not lifted up and supported by the higher and spiritual part the downward tendency of all things toward evil and ugliness would, because of men's utter powerlessness, bring him to nothingness.[15] In the universe, therefore, the part that is cleansed, illumined, strengthened, and perfected, that priestly part that God has consecrated to himself, the angelic and spiritual part, exercises its priestly power, so to speak, by means of the sacraments. It cleanses the weak and impure corporeal part and insofar as possible establishes it in spiritual being, which then may be cleansed, illumined, and perfected according to its capacity; thus all things may be brought from dividedness to oneness, from ugliness to beauty, from defect to perfection, and reflect God in themselves, so that he may duly be revealed as all in all. In this lies the power and office of the priest; in this is the sacrifice that is pleasing to God. For through the priest's power men work and act together in God, who wills that the world should be one, beautiful, and good in himself, and that all things should be reclaimed from evildoing, darkness, and death; so that when death is finally superseded all things may live in God, radiant and perfect in their order. Through the angels, who strive to consecrate the world to God, come the cleansing and reconciliation of things, the illumining of baptism and the confirmation in the light, and finally the filling of each person with goodness according to the measure of his capacity and the degree of his perfection. All priestly power has as its sole

Nihil enim aliud vult omne sacerdotale munus nisi diuersorum purgationem in vnitatem et tenebricosorum illuminationem in claritatem et postremo deficientium impletionem in perfectionem, que in spiritalibus naturis fiunt simpliciter et aperte sine consignatione sacramenti sensibilis. In naturis partim spiritalibus partim corporeis cuiusmodi sunt homines eadem fiunt sed adhibitis etiam symbolis et consignaculis sensibilibus, vt corpus in eis habeat etiam quod agat puritatem, lumen, et bonitatem ipsius. In naturis vero que non sunt predite spiritibus eternis, in ipsis pura, pulchra, et bona conditio eorum sine ulteriore significatione est earum temporalis felicitas. Etenim tria sunt genera rerum sub ipsa rerum omnium causa deo: spiritalia penitus sine corporibus temporalibus, et corporea prorsus sine eternis spiritibus, et inter hec media ex temporalibus corporibus et eternis spiritibus constantia. In illis primis sacramentum est quodque res ipsa sacramenti; in secundis res ipsa sacramentum. In mediis his qui sunt homines et res est ipsa aliquatenus et sacramentum quiddam medium scilicet ex spiritali et corporeo compositum medie nature admodum congruum. Hec sunt sacramenta humane societatis in christo ad que aliquando nostra perueniat oracio.

Ex superiore itaque sermone constat sub pontifice templi id est tocius mundi dei filio esse naturas spiritales purgatas in esse simplex et stabile in deo et illustratas omnifaria sapientia et impletas omni bonitate, que purgant, illuminant, et perficiunt purganda, illuminanda, et perficienda in deo.

In qua purgatione (que reconciliacio est) multiplex est ministerium. Vnde in eo versati a Dionysio ministri vocantur. In quibus potes cogitare in magno mundo sed longe meliori nota quam in nobis nostraque ecclesia Hostiarios, Lectores, Exorcistas, Acolitos, Hypodiaconos. Diaconos mihi videtur Dionysius vocare sacerdotes. Et quos nos vocamus sacerdotes et presbiteros, ille pontifices et presules appellat quorum est dominicum corpus conficere et illuminatos complere mysteriis: sacerdotum dyaconorumque illuminare purgatos. Ministrorum primum expurgare, in quibus (vt dixi) hostiarii sunt, qui stant pro foribus templi dei excludentes multiplices, simplices sinentes intrare. Item lectores psalmorum et scripture sacre hi in spiritalibus sunt, qui tacite indicant sine verbo veritatem dei; Exorciste qui energuminos obsessosque a malignis spiritibus soluunt et liberant, quod faciunt angelici spiritus adiurationibus nobis incognitis; Acoliti qui ignem et aquam templo amministrant, quod est factum in mundi templo a celestibus acolitis longe alio et veriori modo; Hypodia-

purpose cleansing diversity into unity, illumining darkness, and finally bringing those who are deficient to the fullness of perfection.

In the case of spiritual natures all this is done simply and openly, without the mark of a sign perceptible to the senses. In natures partly spiritual and partly corporeal, such as those of human beings, the same results are accomplished, but by the use of symbols and sensible signs, so that such natures' corporeal element too may attain its own purity, light, and goodness. As to natures not endowed with eternal spiritual being, their temporal felicity consists in a state of purity, beauty, and goodness not conferred by any external sign. Indeed there are three kinds of beings under God, the true cause of all beings: those wholly spiritual, without temporal bodies; those wholly corporeal, without eternal spirits; and those intermediate, with both temporal bodies and eternal spirits. In the first-mentioned natures the reality of the sacrament consists simply in its essence, while in the second-mentioned the outward sign is the only reality of the sacrament. In the third, that intermediate class that comprises human beings, the sacrament is to some extent the reality itself and to some extent the outward sign,[16] so that it is both spiritual and corporeal, as befits man's dual nature. These are the sacraments of man's fellowship in Christ, to which our discussion will turn in due course.

From what has been said above it is clear that under the Son of God, the high priest of the temple (that is, of the whole world), there are spiritual natures, cleansed to a simple and stable existence in God, illumined with multifarious wisdom, and filled with all goodness; these natures cleanse, illumine, and perfect the beings that are fit to be cleansed, illumined, and perfected in God.

In cleansing, or reconciliation, there is a manifold ministry. Hence those who exercise it are called by Dionysius ministers. Among the ministers in the universe one can think of doorkeepers, lectors, exorcists, acolytes, and subdeacons—but of much greater excellence than those among us, in our church. It seems to me that Dionysius calls deacons priests, and those whom we call priests and presbyters he calls pontiffs and presidents, whose function it is to confer the Eucharist and to fill the illumined with the mysteries, whereas the priests and deacons illumine those who have been cleansed. The primary function of the ministers is to cleanse; among them, as I have said, are the doorkeepers, who stand at the entrance of God's temple to keep out those who are not undistracted, while permitting the undistracted to enter; the readers of psalms and sacred Scripture (readers in the spiritual sense are those who wordlessly point out God's truth); the exorcists, who release and liberate those who are haunted and possessed by evil spirits, as the angelic spirits do by adjurations not known to us; the acolytes, who provide fire and water for the temple, an office that in the temple of the world is performed in

coni in sacrario et dei sanctuario sollicite inseruiunt, quod in sanctuario
et cho[ro] templi mundi fit ineffabiliter.
    Aqua autem et igne lauantur purganturque omnia. Celestis ignis et
aqua est amor et gracia spiritus sancti. Supra hos purgatorios ordines in
mundi sacerdotio potes cogitare qui se habent illic vt apud nos nostri
sacerdotes—vt vocat Dionysius; vt nos vocamus Diaconi—quorum est
purgatos illustrare vt saltem imagines diuine veritatis uideant eisdemque
iniiciantur. Hi in celesti hierarchia sunt potentes et dominantes virtutes
que in media illic hierarchia locantur, a quibus est in mundo illuminatio
sicut ab infima purgatio. Supra hos cogita summum pontificalem ordinem
sub pontificum pontifice deo, a quibus sub deo cuique est perfectionis
ministratio. Illi sunt in mundo perfectione complentes omnia sicut nostri
apud nos debent esse pontifices. Nihil est his excellentius preter ipsum
deum. In his consummatus est numerus ecclesiasticorum ordinum qui
sunt exemplariter in mundi sacerdotio in illis choris angelicis, imaginarie
in humana hierarchia. Apud Moysen eadem erant omnia umbrositer preter hec que sunt et nominantur: episcopi, archiepiscopi, primates, officia,
et administrationes. Atque hi quos modo diximus, facultates sunt potius
quam ordines. Sed de his apud nos iam statim plura diffusius dicemus.
    Hoc ante omnia teneamus in memoria: ad exemplar dei omnia esse,
quem referunt angeli verius: ecclesia nostra imaginarie, ecclesia legalis
umbrose; omnia pr[ius] esse in celo quam in terra. In terra que fiunt ab
imperfecto ad perfectum proficisci. Non potuit enim imago dei depingi
in terra in hominibus nisi prius adumbraretur. In media mundi tabula et
hominum quasi carbone infuscauit atrum quiddam Moyses; depinxit clar-
ius in toto mundo noster Iesus. Primaria idea et exemplar omnium in celis
est, in quam veritatem ibitur* aliquando vt opus a deo ceptum in terris
perficiatur. Quod vt est promotum a moysaica umbra ad christianam
imaginem in terris, ita ab hac imagine ad christianam veritatem in celis
suo tempore promouebitur. Est enim suum cuiusque tempus. Temporis
momenta solus deus nouit. Qui nouit tempora adumbrandi et depingendi,
idem nouit eciam verificandi. Ordo autem, matrimonium, reconciliacio,
baptismus, confirmacio, synaxis, extrema vnctio, et eciam vt hec fiant pur-

*MS: ietur.

a far different and truer manner by the heavenly acolytes. The subdeacons serve zealously in God's shrine and sanctuary, as also, in an ineffable manner, in the sanctuary and choir of the world.

Now, all things are washed and cleansed by water and fire. Love and the grace of the Holy Spirit are the heavenly water and fire. Above those orders whose function in the priesthood of the world is to cleanse may be considered the priests of the other world and of this (so Dionysius calls them—we say "deacons") whose function is to illumine the cleansed so that they are able to see at least images of the divine truth and be inspired by them. In the celestial hierarchy these are the Powers and Denominations and Virtues, whose place is in the middle of the supernal hierarchy; illumining in the world comes from them, as cleansing comes from the lowest hierarchy. Above the middle hierarchy consider the highest, the high-priestly order, under God the highest of high priests. Their work, under God, is the ministration of perfection to each. It is they who fill all things in the universe with perfection, as our bishops are supposed to do among us. None are more excellent than they, save God himself. With these the number of the ecclesiastical orders is complete; among the choirs of angels they exist in the priesthood of the universe in exemplary fashion, while the human hierarchy is their image. In the books of Moses all of them are adumbrated except for those which now exist under the names of bishops, archbishops, primates, officers, and administrators. But these, which we have just spoken of as orders, are really powers rather than orders. Concerning them, as they exist among us, we shall shortly speak more at large.[17]

This above all we must remember, that all things have God for their exemplar; the angels manifest him more truly, our church manifests him in an image, and the church of the Old Law as a shadow.[18] We must remember too that all things exist in heaven before they exist on earth, and that whatever is done on earth moves from the imperfect to the perfect. For the image of God could not have been portrayed on earth, among men, unless it had previously been sketched. It is as though Moses drew a hazy outline on the panel that is the world, using men, so to speak, as his charcoal; and our Jesus then filled in the colors more clearly.[19] The ultimate idea and exemplar of all things is in heaven.[20] This truth is approached when a work begun by God upon earth is brought to perfection. Thus a work that has advanced here on earth from the Mosaic shadow to the Christian image will in like manner advance in due course from this image to the truth of Christ in heaven. But each thing has its own time, and only God knows the moment that belongs to each. He who knows the time for the shadow and the time for the image knows also the time for the truth. In order that orders, matrimony, reconciliation, baptism, confirmation, the Eucharist, and extreme unction and the other things

gatione, illuminatione, et perfectione in illis quoque ordinibus primis sunt hostiarii, lectores, exorciste, acoliti, hypodiaconi, diaconi, presbiteri: tanquam in magno huius mundi templo in celis. Sed illic modo celesti et vere omnia; hic in nobis qui ad illud exemplar componimur, imaginarie. Quorum imaginum nomina sunt que modo diximus et nostre ecclesie sacramenta significantia. De quibus nunc vti in principio statuimus liberius vestigantes magis aliquid quam diffinientes diss[eremus].

IV

[D]iuino erant in mundo angeli scientes et sponte desciscebant a deo. Hic malum cepit in creatura peccatum: scilicet inobedientia, superbia, transgressio. Superbi[entis] a deo est humiliari decidique in malum. Sua sponte longe abiit a deo, cui* erat coniunctissimus, lucifer ille factiosus† secum contrahens in suas partes magnam angelorum cateruam quorum culpa inuenialis et discessus irreuocabilis est quod scienter et sponte commissus erat. Sciens enim spontaneumque peccatum non habet veniam. Est id contra spiritum sanctum quod non remittetur neque in hoc seculo neque in futuro. Hic voluntaria n[ocentia] in mundo et nequitia est malum et stultitiam et diuisionem mortemque machinans assidue, hic maxime inuidie homini cuius gloriam vidit fore. Hinc hic author et propagator mali quem Moyses serpentem callidiorem vocat cunctis animantibus terre que fecerit dominus deus, suasit mulieri falso promisso vt de illecebroso fructu ligni (quod est in medio paradisi) ederet: hoc scitura dea bonum et malum; cui muliercule assensus est vir, iam scius mali, auscultans malum, audiens sociam mulierem que audiuit serpentem maledictum inter omnia animantia terre, pronum, terram comedentem, perpetuum inimicum mulieris, et insidiosum. Hinc humano generi vita erumnosa, dura, difficilis, plena miserie extra paradisum, longe a ligno vite. Homo quia seductus peccauit quodammodo inscius et inuitus peccauit. Vnde non erat ei nihil loci misericordie quum homini erat aliquid excusationis. In serpentem seductorem reiectum peccatum est. Nouit deus optimum tempus miserendi.

Erat faciendum vt qui creauit homines idem recrearet. Creatus erat homo vt esset coniux diuini filii, sed sapiencia dei (de qua exclamat Pau-

*MS: qui.
†MS: factuosus.

that are effected by cleansing, illumining, and perfecting may be accomplished, the first orders contain doorkeepers, lectors, exorcists, acolytes, subdeacons, deacons, presbyters; just as in the great temple of the world in heaven. There, however, everything is true and after a heavenly fashion; while here in this world, which is ordered on the model of the other, everything is an image. The names of the images of these realities are those we have just given, which are those of the sacraments of our church. As we declared at the outset we shall now discuss them, rather in a freely inquiring than in a doctrinaire spirit.

IV

In the divine world the angels had knowledge and yet they departed from God of their own free will. At that moment the evil of sin began in the creation—namely, disobedience, pride, and transgression. It is only fitting that he who in his pride rebelled against God should be cast down and cut off as evil. Factious Lucifer, who had been so closely joined to God, turned from him of his own will, carrying with him a great troop of angels to the other side. Their sin was unforgivable and their fall irrevocable, for they did what they did knowingly and voluntarily; and a conscious voluntary sin cannot find forgiveness. It is the sin "against the Holy Spirit, which will not be forgiven either in this world or in the next" [Matt. 12:32]. With the malice of his wicked will Lucifer is now unweariedly plotting in the world to bring about evil and folly and dividedness and death. He especially hates man, for he sees his future glory. Hence this author and propagator of evil, whom Moses calls "the serpent more subtle than all the beasts of the earth that the Lord God made" [Gen. 3:1], persuaded the woman to eat of the seductive fruit of the tree that stood in the middle of paradise by the false promise that she would be like God and know good and evil. The husband acceded to the promptings of his wretched wife, though already aware that they were evil and that he was listening to evil in listening to his helpmeet, who had listened to the serpent "accursed among all the beasts of the earth, crawling on his belly and eating the earth, always the treacherous enemy of woman" [Gen. 3:14]. Hence the life of humankind, outside paradise and far from the tree of life, is burdensome, hard, difficult, and full of misery. Man sinned because he was seduced; in a sense, he sinned unwittingly and unwillingly. Therefore there was some ground for showing mercy to man, since he had some degree of excuse: the sin was laid upon the serpent who seduced him. God knows the best time to show mercy. It fell out in this way in order that he who created man should also re-create him. Man was created to be the spouse of the divine Son, but the wisdom of God (of which Paul ex-

lus, O altitudo diuitiarum sapientie et scientie dei: quam incomprehensibilia sunt iudicia eius et inuestigabiles vie eius. Quis cognouit sensum domini?) illa sapientia vt tanta misericordia adhuc maior agnosceretur sinit hominem delabi vt non solum creatum* ex nihilo sed etiam recreatum ex malo ducat uxorem vt vniuersa creatura tantam creatoris benignitatem obstupescat et reuereatur.† Creauit et recreauit sibi suam coniugem humanam deus; que bonitatis diuitie sunt tante vt verba defecerint Paulum quibus digne rem tantam exprimeret, sed diuicias et opes misericordie appellat. Si ante casum assumpsisset sibi in vxorem hominem, et propagatio mali et potencia dei in malo discutiendo et in mundo maxima dei sapiencia et misericordia non apparuisset. Transgressiones et mala declarant equitatem et bonitatem dei; iniquitas iusticiam dei commendat & vt idem sentit paulus, Veritas dei in mendatio abundat, in gloriam ipsius. Materia gracie dei malum est vt morbus materia artis medicine in gloriam medici. Antequam illud tantum miraculum assumpte humane nature in creatura mundi ostentaretur sciuit et permisit hominem cadere in nihilum, vt ex tanta humilitate in sublimatione hominis ingentius benefitium et deo dignius manifestissime cognosceretur. Predestinatum erat vt homo creatus decideret seductus ab illo qui decidit non seductus, vt in recreatione rerum in creaturis dei potencia eciam non minor quam in creatione appareret, misericordia autem multo maior quam in creatione; quum multo maius est ex misericordia reuocare a malo quam ex misericordia creare a nihilo. Nam quod non est vt non creetur non est causa, quod autem malum est vt non recreetur* causa est. Magis obstat deo malum in recreatione quam non esse in creatione, vt multo maioris potentie esset recreare mundum a malo quam creare ex nihilo. In creatione pura potentia, in recreatione pura misericordia, in utraque summa sapientia erat: per quam deus et potenter creauit et misericorditer recreauit, vt in mundo tandem simul cum potentia timenda inestimabilis misericordia eiusdem amanda sapientissime effulgeret (vt iterum atque iterum inculcat Paulus) in laudem gracie glorie sue.

Ex tanta ergo humilitate, in creaturis voluit sibi coniugem accipere altissimus deus et infimam naturam racionalem eam quoque in irracionalitatem delapsam, vt suprema illa natura racionalis que inuidia decidit magis in suam miseriam inuidia ardeat. Est enim pena perditis gloria saluatorum, et in his quanto maior est misericordia tanto illis iusticia maior est altiorque vindicta, vt liceat cernere quam ineffabili modo est deus

---

*MS: reatum.
†MS: reueretur.
‡MS: recreatur.

claims, "O the depth of the riches of the wisdom and knowledge of God! how incomprehensible are his judgments and how unsearchable his ways! For who has known the mind of the Lord?" [Rom. 11:33–34])—that wisdom permitted man to fall in order that God's great mercy should be seen to be greater still, in that he took as his bride not merely what he had created from nothing but what he had re-created from evil. The whole of creation was astonished and awestruck at the Creator's great goodness. God created and re-created for himself a human spouse. The riches of his goodness are so great that Paul could find no words to express worthily so great a theme but simply spoke of "the riches and abundance of mercy" [Rom. 2:4]. If before the Fall he had taken mankind as his wife, neither the propagation of evil nor the power of God in dispelling evil nor the great wisdom and mercy of God would have appeared in the world. Sin and evil proclaim the justness and goodness of God, and as again Paul says, "The truth of God abounds in falsehood" [Rom. 3:7]: iniquity commends the justice of God and makes for his glory.[21] Evil gives scope for God's grace, as disease gives scope for the physician's art and makes for his glory. Before he performed that great miracle of taking on human nature in the world, which was his own creation, he knew and permitted the fall of man to nothingness, that by raising man up from that utter dejection he might clearly manifest a mercifulness that was all the grander and worthier of God. It was foreordained that created man should fall,[22] seduced by him who fell without being seduced; so that God's power over his creatures should appear no less in the re-creation than it had in the creation, since it is far greater mercifully to recall man from evil than mercifully to create him from nothing. There is no reason why what does not exist should not be created, but there is reason not to re-create what is evil. Evil is a greater obstacle to God's re-creating than nonexistence is to his creating; so that it would be a matter of much greater power to re-create the world from evil than to create it from nothing. In creation there is pure power, and in re-creation pure mercy, while in both is the highest wisdom; through his wisdom God both created in power and re-created in mercy. Thus along with his fearsome power his boundless and lovable mercy might at length stand revealed in full wisdom in the world (as Paul again and again emphasizes), to the praise of his glorious grace.

The most high God therefore willed to take a bride from the lowness of his creatures and also to take on rational nature, which was not only base in itself but had actually fallen into irrationality; he did this in order that that supreme rational nature that had fallen through envy might burn still more miserably through envy. For the glory of the saved is a torment to the damned;[23] the greater the mercy that is shown to the saved, the greater appears the justice to the damned, and the loftier God's vengeance. Thus one may see in what ineffable manner God is at once just

simul iustus et misericors, et simul quanto magis misericors eo magis iustus, vt in misericordia eius videatur nasci iusticia et esse eadem in deo
misericordia et iusticia in una infinita sapientia.

Longa era declaratio imbecillitatis humane impotentieque resurgendi
per se, antequam eam reuelauit deus vt deserta multo experimento et
suam imbecillitatem confiteretur et diuinam misericordiam agnosceret,
vtque que volens superbire decidit a deo discat humilitate resurgere et
referre omnia deo. Sine lege delira erat, sub lege deliratior; oportuno
tempore in extremo periculo succurrit diuina misericordia et paupercu-
lam naturam hominis obsitam et squalidam quasi manu vel capite appre-
hensam ad se traxit, exuit fedam et tabificam vestem, discussit puluerem,
extersit sordes, purgatam induit nitidam et salutarem vestem nuptialem.
Idem pontifex et maritus consecrauit nuptias, vt qui angelorum pontifex
est idem sit pontifex hominum idemque restauret ecclesias qui construxit.
In creato homine tantarum nuptiarum sacramentum voluit antecedere
eciam ante peccatum vt sanctius sacramentum esset: vt mirabiliter creatus
homo ex nihilo recreati hominis ex malo sit sacramentum. Ade primo
homini in creatione adiecit mulierem ad carnem propagandam: vt ex hoc
primo homini in recreatione intelligatur adiecta femina, ex latere eius recreata redemptione effusi sanguinis in spiritum propagandum cui dicatur,
Crescite et multiplicamini spiritali prole et replete terram et subiicite eam
et dominamini piscibus maris et volatilibus celi et vniuersis que mouentur
super terram. In paradiso creata femina virago erat recreate in terra ecclesie umbra de qua vaticinatus est Adam primus propheta dicens quod
relinquet homo patrem suum et matrem et adherebit vxori sue et erunt
duo in spiritu vno. Nam caro Adam significat spiritum christi. Hoc est sacramentum quod dicit Paulus in Epistola ad Ephesios et pre magnitudine
(vt Ieronimus scribit) non explicat sed vno fere verbo dicit quod est sacramentum in christo et ecclesia malens tantum mysterium tacere quam
de eo loqui diminutius. Iccirco admonet Ephesios vt vxores diligant sicut
christus ecclesiam in sanctificationem earum et fecundationem in spiritu
non in carne. Nam quatenus in coniugio res carnis sit, tanto veritas spiritus
minuitur. Et in paradiso erat maris et femine connubium sine carnali copula, spiritalis coitus sacramentum. Adam autem primus homo creatus et
parens carnalis progeniei umbra erat secundi hominis recreati et parentis

and merciful, and at the same time the greater his mercy is, the greater is his justice; so that it is evident that his justice is born of his mercy, and that in God mercy and justice are the same thing in one infinite wisdom.

Man's weakness and inability to rise again through his own strength became obvious long before God finally relieved it, in order that human nature, abandoned to its own efforts, would recognize both its own powerlessness and the divine mercy, and that that nature which through pride had fallen away from God might learn to rise again in humility and refer all things to God. When humanity did not have the Law it wandered from the true path, and when it had the Law it deviated more. At the fitting moment, when the peril was extreme, God came to the rescue of mankind. He drew to himself poor human nature, covered with filth, as forcefully as if he grasped it by the head or the hand. He removed its foul and putrid garment, scattered the dust, wiped away the dirt, and reinvested humanity in the cleansed garment, a shining and saving wedding garment. As both high priest and husband he consecrated the nuptials, so that he might be the high priest of men as well as of angels, and so that he who built the churches might be the one to restore them. He willed that this great nuptial sacrament should be in created man before the Fall so that the sacrament would be holier, that man wondrously created out of nothing might be the sign of the re-creation of man out of evil. In the creation he gave to Adam, the first man, a wife for the propagation of the flesh; this was to signify that the first man in the re-creation was also to have a woman taken from his side, re-created and redeemed by the shedding of his blood, for the propagation of spirit; to whom it was said, "Increase and multiply" with a spiritual offspring, "fill the earth and subdue it, and be lord over the fishes of the sea and the birds of the heavens and all things that move on the earth" [Gen. 1:28]. The woman created in paradise foreshadowed the church re-created on earth, which Adam, the first prophet, foretold when he said, "A man will leave father and mother and cling to his wife, and they will be two in one"—spirit [Gen. 2:24]; for Adam's "flesh" signifies the spirit of Christ. This is the sacrament of which Paul speaks in the Epistle to the Ephesians and which, because of its grandeur (as Jerome writes),[24] he does not explain, merely saying in a word or two that it is "the sacrament in Christ and the church" [Eph. 5:32], preferring to pass over the great mystery in silence rather than diminish it by speaking about it. On that account he admonishes the Ephesians to "love their wives as Christ does the church" [Eph. 5:25], to sanctify them and make them fruitful in the spirit, not in the flesh.[25] For to the extent that the fleshly element enters into marriage its truth of spirit is lessened. In paradise too there was marriage of male and female without carnal union, a sacrament of spiritual coition. Adam, however, the first created man and the father of fleshly progeny, was the shadow of the second, re-

prolis spiritalis ad numerum stellarum. Erat primus Adam minister dei in propagatione carnis ad mortem, secundus Adam minister dei in propagatione spiritus ad vitam. Primum Adam vocat Paulus in epistola ad Romanos formam futuri, cuius gracia in plures abundauit ex multis delictis in iustificationem vt iusti conregnent in vita per vnum Iesum christum per cuius obedientiam homines iustificantur. Is erat parens et propagator spiritus ad vitam in terris, sicut primus Adam progenitor carnis ad mortem. Quocirca scribit Paulus ad Chorinthios, Sicut in Adam omnes moriuntur ita et in christo omnes viuificantur. Factus est prim[us] homo Adam in animam viuentem, nouissimus Adam in spiritum viuificantem. Primus homo de terra terrenus, secundus homo de celo celestis. In christo ergo non est prolificatio nisi celestis et spiritus. Iam (ait Paulus alibi) neminem cognouimus secundum carnem. Nec carnalis in christo debet esse ulla propagatio sed tota celestis, vt portemus imaginem celestis, et celestis parentis nostri similes simus, qui fecundat suam ecclesiam iniecto in eam diuino semine vt copiosam pariat prolem iusticie ad regnum dei. Qui creauit Adam vt esset imago sui voluit ipse quoddammodo recreari vt (sicut ad Colocenses scriptum est) qui est primogenitus omnis creature idem sit principium, primogenitus ex mortuis, ecclesie caput: vt sit in omnibus ipse primatum tenens, et creatis et recreatis, et plenis et deficientibus, qui defecit ipse maxime vt esset eciam in recreatione et reconciliatione primas sicuti in creatione et plenitudine et perfectione rerum erat primas et primogenitus omnis creature. Quoniam in ipso condita sunt vniuersa perfecta in celis et in terra visibilia et invisibilia, siue throni, siue dominationes, siue principatus, siue potestates; omnia per ipsum et in ipso creata sunt mirifice et omnipotenter, deficiente ipso creatore quodammodo vt creatura reficiatur: vt primogenitus creature sit idem primo regenitus recreature in recreata scilicet humana natura que defecit, ad quam eciam defecit dei filius ipse et factus est filius hominis, vt refecta natura humana fiat filia dei et sponsa filii eterna. Vt decidit homo in carnem ita fuit necesse vt exemeretur ex carne comprehensione spiritus: fiat ex carne spiritalis, carne que regnauit a spiritu victa: vt spiritus existens homo, idoneus esset vt spiritali connubio cum deo ipso coniungeretur cum quo nequaquam coniungi potest nisi sit summe spiritalis. Propor-

created, man, the parent of a spiritual progeny as numerous as the stars. The first Adam was God's minister in the propagation of the flesh that results in death; the second Adam was God's minister in the propagation of spirit that results in life. In his Epistle to the Romans Paul calls the first Adam "the type of him who was to come" [Rom. 5:14], whose grace would abound to many others and justify them after their many crimes so that the just might reign together in life through Jesus Christ alone, through whose obedience men were justified.[26] He it is who is the parent and propagator of the spirit for life on earth,[27] while the first Adam is the begetter of the flesh for death. This is what Paul means in writing to the Corinthians: "As in Adam all men die, so in Christ are all men given life. The first Adam became a living soul, the last Adam a life-giving spirit. The first man came from the earth and was earthly, the second came from heaven and is heavenly" [1 Cor. 15:47]. In Christ therefore there is no engendering save a heavenly engendering of the spirit. For, as Paul says elsewhere, "We know no one according to the flesh" [2. Cor. 5:16]. As is only fitting, in Christ propagation is in no way carnal but altogether heavenly, "that we may bear the image of the heavenly" [1. Cor. 15:49] and be like our heavenly parent who makes the Church fruitful by casting into her his divine seed so that she may bear a copious offspring of justice for the kingdom of God. He who created Adam to be his image willed him to be in a certain sense re-created, so that, as was written to the Colossians, "he who is the first-born of all creation" should be also "the beginning, the first-born from the dead" [Col. 1:15, 18], the head of the church; that he might hold the first place among all, both the created and the re-created, both those that were lacking and those that were full. He emptied himself utterly so as to be preeminent in re-creation and reconciliation just as he was preeminent and the first-born of all the universe in creation and fullness and perfection. "For on him is based everything that is perfect in heaven and on earth, all things visible and invisible, whether Thrones or Dominations, whether Principalities or Powers; all things were created through him and in him" [Col. 1:16] wondrously and omnipotently—the creator unmaking himself in a sense in order that those he created might be remade, that the first-born of the creation might be also the first-born of the re-creation; in that human nature, I mean, which had fallen, to which also the Son of God himself condescended by becoming son of man, in order that refashioned human nature might become the daughter of God and the eternal spouse of the Son. As man fell to the level of the flesh it was necessary that he be redeemed from the flesh by the embrace of the spirit, and that the flesh, which had been dominant, should be overcome by the spirit, so that the emergence of spirit might make man suitable for a spiritual marriage with God himself, with whom no one can be united unless he is in the highest degree spiritual;

tione enim aliqua oportet sint que copulentur. Caro enim longe distat a deo, vt carnalem hominem cum deo coniungi sit impossibile. Hinc Paulus et reliqui apostoli suadent et imperant quoad maxime possunt mortificationem carnis et reuiuificationem in spiritu, semper hoc docentes plane: nisi homines fiant spiritus eos deo vt unus fiat spiritus adherere non posse. Commortuos et consepultos dicit Paulus nos esse cum christo in epistola ad Romanos. Vetus homo noster simul crucifixus est vt destruatur corpus peccati, vt ultra non seruiamus peccato. Est paulo post: Quis me liberabit a corpore mortis huius? Item Sapientia carnis inimica est deo, et prudentia carnis mors. Qui in carne sunt deo placere non possunt. Si christus in vobis est corpus quidem mortuum est propter peccatum, spiritus viuit propter iustificationem. Si spiritu facta carnis mortificaueritis viuetis. Et adhuc postea: Obsecro vos, fratres, vt exhibeatis corpora vestra hostiam viuentem, sanctam, deo placentem, racionabile obsequium, et nolite conformari huic seculo sed reformamini in nouitate spiritus et sensus vestri vt probetis que sit voluntas dei bona et beneplacens et perfecta. Ad Corinth[ios], Animalis homo non sapit ea que dei sunt: stulticia enim est illi et non potest intelligere quia spiritaliter examinatur. Spiritalis autem iudicat omnia. Quem dicit animalem hominem eundem mox postea carnalem dicit et secundum hominem ambulare. Et in .ii. ad Corinth[ios], Semper nos qui viuimus in mortem tradimur propter Iesum vt vita Iesu manifestetur in carne nostra mortali, et in eodem loco, sempter mortificationem Iesu christi in corpore circumferentes, vt et vita Iesu manifestetur in corporibus nostris. Item, Vnus pro omnibus mortuus est christus et in christo omnes mortui sunt vt qui viuunt iam non sibi uiuant sed ei qui pro eis mortuus est et resurrexit. Itaque nos ex hoc neminem nouimus secundum carnem. Si qua ergo in christo noua creatura, vetera transierunt: ecce noua facta sunt omnia. Et illud: Libenter gloriabor in infirmitatibus meis vt inhabitet in me virtus christi. Quum infirmor tunc fortior sum. Ad Galathas, Si hominibus placerem christi servus non essem. Item, Ego per legem legi* mortuus sum vt deo viuam, christo crucifixus sum cruci: viuo iam non ego, viuit vero in me christus. Et illud: spiritu ambulate et desideria carnis non perficietis. Caro enim concupiscit adversus spiritum, spiritus aduersus carnem. Hec enim sibi inuicem aduersantur.

---

*MS: per legem dei (cf. Gal. 2:19).

for there must be some kind of proportion between those who are joined in marriage. The flesh is so far removed from God that it is impossible for carnal man to be united with him. Hence it is that Paul and the other Apostles exert all their powers in pleading and demanding that the flesh be mortified and then revivified in the spirit, always teaching plainly that unless men become spirit they can never so cling to God as to be one spirit with him.[28] We are "dead and buried with" Christ [Rom. 6:4], says Paul in the Epistle to the Romans. "Our old nature has also been crucified, that the body of sin might be destroyed and that we might serve sin no longer" [Rom. 6:6]. A little later he asks, "Who will free me from the body of this death?" [Rom. 7:24–25].[29] Again: "The wisdom of the flesh is enemy to God," and, "The prudence of the flesh is death" [Rom. 8:7, 6]. "Those who are in the flesh cannot please God." "If Christ is in you the body indeed will die to sin but the spirit will live and be justified" [Rom. 8:8, 10]. And still further on: "I beseech you, brethren, through the mercy of God, that you present your bodies as a living sacrifice, holy and pleasing to God, a reasonable service." "And do not be conformed to this world but be reformed[30] in newness" of spirit and "of your mind, that you may determine what is the good and well-pleasing and perfect will of God" [Rom. 12:1, 2]. To the Corinthians he wrote: "The natural man savors not the things that are of God; they are foolishness to him and he cannot understand them, for it takes a spiritual man to discern them; whereas the spiritual man discerns all things" [1 Cor. 2:14, 15]. The one he had spoken of as the "natural" man he soon after refers to as the "carnal" man, "who is guided by human standards" [1 Cor. 3:3]. And in the Second Epistle to the Corinthians he writes, "We who live are always being delivered over to death for the sake of Jesus so that the life of Jesus may be manifested in our mortal flesh"; and in the same place, "We carry always the dying state of Jesus Christ in our bodies so that the living state of Jesus may be manifested in our bodies too" [2 Cor. 4:11, 10]. Again: "Christ died for all men," and in Christ "all men died, so that those who now live do not have their life from themselves but from him who died and rose up again for them. We, accordingly, do not know any man in the flesh. If there has been a new creation in Christ the old has passed away, and behold! all things are made new" [2 Cor. 5:14, 17]. There is also this passage: "I would rather glory in my weakness that the power of Christ might dwell in me. When I am weak, then I grow strong" [2 Cor. 12:9, 10]. To the Galatians he wrote, "If I were to please men I would not be the servant of Christ" [Gal. 1:10]. Again: "Through the law I have died to the law that I might live to God; for Christ I am crucified to the cross; it is not I that live, but Christ lives in me" [Gal. 2:19, 20]. And again: "Walk in the spirit, and do not carry out the desires of the flesh, for these are enemies the one to the other" [Gal. 5:16, 17]. And

Et paulo post, Qui autem sunt christi carnem suam crucifixerunt cum viciis et concupiscentiis. Si viuimus spiritu, spiritu ambulemus. Et post hec: Mihi absit gloriari nisi in cruce domini nostri Iesu christi, per quem mihi mundus crucifixus est et ego mundo, in quo nihil valet nisi noua creatura. Et ad Ephe[sios] scribens deum patrem appellat qui benedixit nos in omni benedictione spiritali in celestibus. Et illud: Deponite vos secundum pristinam conuersationem veterem hominem (qui corrumpitur secundum desideria erroris) et renouamini spiritu mentis vestre: et induite nouum hominem qui secundum deum creatus est in iusticia et sanctitate ueritatis. Et, Nolite contristare spiritum. Et, Implemini spiritu sancto. Est nobis colluctacio aduersus spiritalia nequicie in celestibus, que vincenda sunt armatura dei. Et ad Philippenses: Mihi viuere christus est et mori lucrum. Et illud, Configuratus morti eius, si quomodo ad resurrectionem occurram que est ex mortuis. Si quomodo comprehendam in quo et comprehensus sum a christo Iesu. Que quidem retro sunt obliuiscens ad ea que priora sunt extendens meipsum ad destinatum prosequor brauium superne vocationis in christo Iesu. Ad Collocen[ses]: Nunc gaudeo in passionibus pro vobis vt adimpleantur ea que desunt passionum christi in carne mea. Item, Mortificate membra vestra que sunt supra terram: deponite et expoliate veterem hominem cum actibus suis et induite nouum. Sed quorsum hec testimonia? Nempe vt intelligamus si deo qui spiritus est coniungi et copulari voluerimus, nos necessario mortificata carne spiritales omnino esse oportere et penitus nouos in christo ad formam illius hominis in christo uiuentes qui exemplum dedit vt sequamur vestigia eius qui ob id cause solum assumpsit hominem vt spiritalem et diuinam in homine vitam ostendat hominibus doceatque quam vestem nuptialem induat homo si velit a deo in vxorem duci.

Noc locatur matrimonio deo nisi virgo reiuuenescens spiritu, sine ruga, sine macula aut aliquid eiusmodi, tota sancta et immaculata, casta cum casto, sancta cum sancto, spiritalis et diuina cum spiritu et deo. Cuiusmodi puellam dominus quando de celo prospexit vt videret si esset intelligens aut requirens deum sibi in terris non inuenit quoniam omnes declinauerunt simul inutiles facti sunt: non erat qui fecit bonum, non era usque ad vnum. Fuit igitur necesse sane vt deus creator omnium, quum voluit in terris (misericordia quanta excogitari potest a nemine) vxorem ducere et hominem arctissima copula sibi astring[ere], eam crearet. Creauit pri-

a little further on he says, "Those who are of Christ have crucified their flesh to vices and concupiscence. If we live by the spirit let us walk by the spirit" [Gal. 5:24, 25]. Later he says, "Let me make no boast except in the cross of our Lord Jesus Christ, through whom the world is crucified to me and I to the world," in which "there is nothing of value but the new creation" [Gal. 6:14–15]. And writing to the Ephesians [1:3] he calls God the father who has blessed us with all the spiritual blessings of heaven. And again he says, "Put away your former mode of life and your old self, which was corrupted according to the appetites of error, and be renewed in the spirit of your mind; and put on the new self, which is created according to God's image in the justice and holiness of truth. Do not grieve the Holy Spirit" [Eph. 4:22–24, 30]. Again: "Be filled with the Holy Spirit" [Eph. 5:18]. "Ours is a struggle against the spiritual powers of wickedness on high," which must be overcome by "the weapons of God" [Eph. 6:12, 11]. And to the Philippians Paul writes, "For me, to live is Christ and to die is lucre" [Phil. 1:21]. And again: "I am molded in the pattern of his death if I am in any way to come to the resurrection from the dead and to possess him who possesses me from Christ Jesus. Forgetting what lies behind me I hasten on to what is ahead, to the destined prize of the lofty calling in Christ Jesus" [Phil. 3:10–14]. To the Colossians he writes, "Now I rejoice in my sufferings for you, that I can make up in my own flesh anything that was lacking in the sufferings of Christ" [Col. 1:24]. Likewise he says, "Mortify your members that are on earth" [Col. 3:5]. Cast off and "strip away the natural self with its deeds, and put on the new" [Col. 3:9, 10].

But what is the purpose of these quotations? Simply to make us understand that if we wish to be linked and joined to God, who is spirit, we must needs mortify the flesh and become wholly spirit, utterly renewed in Christ and living in Christ after the pattern of him who gave the example that we might follow in his footsteps; for this purpose only did he become man, to show men the spiritual and divine life in man and to teach them what wedding garment man must put on if he would be taken to wife by God.

None can be wife to God but a maiden reborn in spirit, "without wrinkle, without spot or anything of that kind, altogether holy and immaculate" [Eph. 5:27], chaste bride with chaste husband, holy bride with holy husband, spiritual and divine in the spirit and God. When the Lord "looked down from heaven, to see whether there were any who knew God and sought after him," he found no such maiden on earth; for "all had turned away and were of no use; there was none who did well, not even one" [Ps. 13:2, 3]. It was therefore absolutely necessary for God, creator of all things, when in his inconceivable mercy he willed to take humanity to wife and bind it to him by the closest of ties, to create this wife. He

mum hominem vtero matris virginis Marie, quem secundum Adam coni-
unxit sibi sanctum penitus et sine labe peccati cuiusmodi erat primus
Adam antequam cecidit. In illo dei filius apparuit hominibus vt omnes vo-
lentes credere crearet eiusmodi adscisceretque multos ex peccatoribus
factos iustos in societatem filii sui, in sanctam sibi coniugem que vocatur
ecclesia quam Paulus sepe vocat in christo nouam creaturam: vt sancro-
sanctis nuptiis et diuino coitu homo cum deo (femina homo) in amplexu
tanti uiri et dei summe perficiatur: et que erat sterilis plene fecundetur
in illo misericordi concubitu dei filii: vt quasi semine concepto pariat copiosum fructum in se sanctitatis et iusticie que sunt bona opera, que sepe
Paulus vocat fructus in vitam eternam. Ad Galath[as] scribit, Fructus autem spiritus est charitas, gaudium, pax, paciencia, longanimitas, bonitas,
benignitas, mansuetudo, fides, modestia, continentia, castitas. He virtutes sunt quasi soboles filii dei et ecclesie, opera iusticie quasi filii sunt
dei et sue coniugis ecclesie. Homines vocantur in ecclesiam in partem vxoris dei vt diuino semine impregnentur, et quum antea friguerint iam cale-
ant et ex charitate pariant spisse bona opera et iusticiam que proles est
eterna dei et ecclesie. Homines confratres vel consorores filie dei patris
vna coniunx est filii dei; homini in christo consorores sumus, deitati in
christo coniuges. Illi eciam deitati quasi sorores* quibus nupsit eternus
dei filius, vt ecclesia sit ei in communi patris domo et soror et coniunx.
Soror creata a deo patre† vt eam vxorem ducat filius, eam fecundans iusticia in eternitatem. Itaque ecclesia homini in christo consoror est: deo
filio in christo et soror et coniunx, deo patri filia virago. Sed filia dei virilior
est viris filiis hominum. Deus pater genuit sibi eterna generatione coet-
ernum filium, genuit quidem in se et ex se ipso et quasi coit cum se ipso
vt filium progignat in se ipso vt illo ineffabili modo filio esset simul [pater]
et mater. Genitus autem filius ille eternus dei patris virtus et dei sapientia
quum ceperit amare non potuit esse cui non tradatur vxor. Nam ex amore
implere, perficere, et in alio et cum alio propagare imaginem et simu-
litudinem suam tanta virtus abesse diuinis et diuino filio non potest. Hoc
est matrimonium, coniunctio maris et femine, que si bona est debet esse
prima in primo, vt a primo deinceps que sunt nominentur. Dei filius ergo
primus maritus est, a quo omnis maritatio in celo et in terra nominatur.
Est vir ipse et ipsa masculinitas, femine creature perfectio.

*MS: sores.
†MS: patri.

created the first man in the womb of the virgin mother Mary; he joined to himself this second Adam, who was utterly holy and free from the stain of sin, as the first Adam had been before he fell. In him the Son of God appeared to men, so as to make them willing to believe and thus receive many of the now justified sinners into the fellowship of his Son, that holy spouse of his called the church. Paul often calls the church the "new creation in Christ" [2 Cor. 5:17]. Thus mankind—now the female, so to speak—is supremely fulfilled through the sacred nuptials and divine union with God in the embrace of this great husband and God;[31] and she who was barren was made abundantly fruitful in that merciful cohabitation with the Son of God, so that having conceived as it were by his seed she brought forth in herself abundant fruit of holiness and justice—good works, which Paul often calls fruits unto life eternal.[32] To the Galatians he writes, "The fruits of the Spirit are love, joy, peace, patience, long-suffering, goodness, kindness, gentleness, faith, modesty, temperance, chastity" [Gal. 5:22–23].[33] These virtues are as it were the offspring of the Son of God and his spouse the church. Human beings are summoned into the church to be God's wife, that they may be impregnated by the divine seed and, though previously they were cold, should now be warm and bring forth out of their love good works in profusion, along with the righteousness that is the eternal progeny of God and the church. Human beings, as brothers or sisters of the daughter of God the Father, are collectively the spouse of the Son of God: we are sisters to the man in Christ and spouses to the divinity in him. Human beings are also like sisters to this divinity, whom the eternal God espoused so that in the common house of his Father, the church might be to him both sister and spouse:[34] a sister created by God the Father that his Son might make her his wife, fecundating her with justice eternally. Accordingly the church is to man a sister in Christ, sister and spouse to God the son in Christ, and daughter to God the Father. But this daughter of God is more virile than are the male sons of men. By an eternal generation God the Father begot a Son coeternal with himself—begot him, that is, in himself, and of himself, and as it were by a union with himself, that he might bring forth the Son in himself; in that ineffable manner he is at once father and mother. Now, that eternal Son whom he begot, the power and wisdom of God the Father, could not, when he began to love, be without a wife. For it could not be that the great power of filling with love, perfecting, propagating his own image in and with another—that this should be lacking in things divine and in the divine Son. This is matrimony, the union of male and female; if it is good it ought first to be in him who is first, in order that what succeeds should take its name thence. Therefore the Son of God is the first husband [*maritus*] from whom all marriage [*maritatio*] in heaven and on earth takes its name. He is the very essence of a husband, the very essence of masculinity, who perfects the feminine creation.

Quanquam illi destinata erat coniunx, tamen non statim ei data fuit. Primogenitus ille omnis creature (vt vocat Paulus in epistola ad Collocenses) in quo condita sunt vniuersa in celis et in terra, visibilia et inuisibilia, siue throni siue dominationes, siue principatus siue potestates, omnia per ipsum et in ipso creata sunt. Ille primogenitus creature et imago inuisibilis dei creaturam ad imaginem dei conditam, id est hominem creatum, illico duxisset vxorem, si puella hec lasciua in paradiso non violata fuisset. Qua ob id cause repudiata, mansit viduus vir ille filius dei donec pater genuerat sibi filiam incorruptam quam filio suo nubendam tradat; quam quum voluit ex corrupta carne et adulterata illa in paradiso progignere, vt opus dei ordine procedat magno opus erat preparamento, magno eciam et vario rerum successu. Ante omnia vero opus erat vt tanta res futura digno et congruo sacramento significaretur. Est semper intelligendum sensibilia et carnalia in hominibus, intelligibilium et spiritalium esse sacramenta. Quum prouisum erat Adam casurum cui erat adiecta femina vt ex eo carnalis fluat progenies, simul predestinat[um] erat ex celo virtus processura que comprehendens hominem serperet spiritificans in interitum carnis, que esset alia propago et secunda cui prima illa propago vt vmbra precessit et potentibus intelligere vt sacramentum. Voluit ergo deus in corrupto homine depingere eam veritatem que incorrupto homine euenit suo tempore. Vsus est corruptela mundi pro materia significationis. Veritas significata ex celo tandem contrario cursu se influit in mundum, lapis obiectus fluctibus, lapis offensionis et petra scandali, ad quem delabens mundus se frangit, qui est mundo omnino contrarius et celestis fluuius mundano omnino obiectus, fluuius ille impetuosus qui letificat ciuitatem dei. Hec est restauratio mundi per uim releuantem. Mundo bene creato et condito (vidit deus (inquit) cuncta que fecerat et erant valde bona) ruine ceperunt esse, quas reparaturus erat deus per filium suum et reedificaturus mundum ac quasi nouum mundum facturus, vt nuptie, gloria, regnum sit filio suo qui erat apud patrem antiquus adam. Sed non est bonum hominem esse solum. Dixit ergo dominus deus, faciamus ei adiutorium simile sibi. Hinc Paulus vocat ecclesiam coadiutorem dei in propagacione iusticie: proles enim filii dei et ecclesie coniugis iusticia est. Adam ille antiquus nominauit omnia proprio nomine, quo verbo erant creata omnia. At huic filio dei non erat reperta vxor quam impleret semine diuino in propagacionem iusticie. Ade non inueniebatur adiutor similis eius. Voluit deus Adam in sopore esse in humana carne, ex eius latere edificare mulierem, os ex ossibus et caro ex carne viraginem,

Although the spouse was destined for him, she was not given to him at once. He who is "the first-born of all creation," as Paul cries in the Epistle to the Colossians, "who is the foundation of all things in heaven and on earth, visible and invisible, whether Thrones or Dominations, whether Principalities or Powers, through whom and in whom all things were created" [Col. 1:15, 16]—that first-born of creation would immediately have taken to wife the creation founded in his likeness, that is, created man, were it not that the wanton girl was violated in paradise. For that reason the husband who is the Son of God repudiated her and remained without a wife until the Father begot an incorrupt daughter to give to his Son as wife. Since it was his will to beget her from the flesh that had been corrupted and defiled in paradise, so that God's work would proceed in due order, there had to be a great preparing of the way and a great and complex train of events. Above all it was necessary that the great event to come be signified by a worthy and fitting sacrament. It is always to be understood that the sensory and carnal element in man is a sacrament, or sign, of the intellectual and spiritual. Since God had foreseen the fall of Adam, who had been given a wife in order to have an offspring in the flesh, it was also predestined that a power would come from heaven who would overshadow human nature and proceed to spiritualize[35] men until they died to the flesh. The first race of men would foreshadow this other, second, race, as a sign to those who were able to understand. God wished to depict in corrupt man what in due course transpired in incorrupt man. He used the corrupt world as the material element of the sacrament. The truth that it signifies, however, flows in a countermovement, from heaven down to earth, a stone set against the waves, "a stone to trip over and a rock to stumble against" [1 Pet. 2:8], upon which the fallen world dashes itself; for this celestial stream is entirely opposed to the world and set against everything earthly, "the rushing stream that gladdens the city of God" [Ps. 45:5]. This is the restoration of the world through the power that raises man up. Though the world had been created and established well ("God saw all that he had done, and it was very good" [Gen. 1:31]), it had begun to fall into ruin. Through his Son, God was to repair this destruction and rebuild the world, virtually to make it anew, so that the wedding, the glory, and the dominion might belong to his Son, who in his Father was the first Adam. But, "It is not good for man to be alone. Therefore the Lord God said, Let us make him a helpmeet like to himself" [Gen. 2:18]. This is why Paul calls the church God's helper in the diffusion of justice, for justice is the progeny of the Son of God and the church his spouse. The first Adam gave all things their names, and in that world all things were created. But for this Son of God no wife was to be found whom he could fill with the divine seed for the propagation of justice. "For Adam no helpmeet like to himself could be found." God willed that Adam sleep in his human flesh, that from his side he might build a woman,

propter quam relinquet filius dei patrem suum et matrem et adherebit vxori sue et erunt duo in spiritu vno. Sed vt serpens euam, ita serpens est
qui seducit ecclesiam. Quapropter Paulus ad Corinth[ios], Timeo (inquit)
ne sicut serpens euam seduxit astutia sua ita corrumpantur sensus vestri
et excidant a simplicitate que est in christo qui assumpsit sibi ecclesiam
in vxorem vt non edat de ligno scientie boni et mali, sed adhereat illi simplici fidei a qua si cadat in raciocinationem boni et mali tum cadit a fide
et christo. Despondi vos vni viro (filio dei) virginem castam (simplicitate
fidei) exhibere christo qui relinquit patrem et matrem, id est deum, qui
illum genuit ex seipso vt esset et pater et mater, vt adhereret vxori sue
ecclesie quam sanguine ex latere effuso et morte christi redemptam pater
sibi adoptauit in filiam vt ei nubat filius suus. Ad Romanos, Vos morti-
ficati estis legi [per] corpus christi vt sitis alterius, id est filij dei vna cum
homine assumpto illo, qui resurrexit a mortuis vt vos noui cum illo homine, et coniunx christi fructificetis deo. Hic fructus iusticie est masculina
virtus et filius dei et ecclesie. Vos enim estis membra de membro, id est
homines adherentes homini illi primo vt vna cum illo sitis in vxore dei uniti
et adherentes illi quam vxorem humanam vocat Paulus facturam et creaturam ex nequitia huius mundi. Cuius rei et matrimonij coniunctionisque
feminei hominis cum masculino deo sacramentum (dicit in epistola ad
Ephesios) magnum: illud sanxitum matrimonium Ade et Eue fuisse qui
primi erant homines et in illis primum sacramentum et prima prophetia,
quod illud et carnalia omnia in alio progressu spiritali incepto a christo
perfici debent spiritaliter in finitionem eorum que sunt carnis. Iota dixit
ille secundus Adam et apex vnus non preteriet de lege donec omnia fiant.
Adam diuinum filium, Eua ecclesiam significat. Matrimonium inter
Adam et Euam matrinomium sanctum inter dei filium et ecclesiam in fecunditatem iusticie que proles est dei et ecclesie. Propagatio illa carnalis
ad mortem, hec per christum propagatio iusticie ad vitam. Hec* omnia
sunt signa et sacramenta noui mundi in christo vt nec iota nec apex pre-
tereat donec omnia fiant. Postquam ceciderit homo quam longissime a
deo in nihilum in paranda hac coniuge multum erat laboris et negotii: vt
dei opus ordine procederet summa et serenior pars humani erat reseruata

*MS: hanc.

bone of his bone and flesh of his flesh, a woman for whose sake the Son of God would leave father and mother and cleave to his wife, and they would be two in one spirit. But as a serpent seduced Eve, so there is a serpent that seduces the church. For this reason Paul says to the Corinthians, "I fear that, as the serpent seduced Eve by his wiles, so too your minds will be corrupted and fall away from the singleness that is in Christ" [2 Cor. 11:3]. He took the church as his wife so that she would not eat of the tree of the knowledge of good and evil but adhere to a simple faith; to fall from that to a reasoning about good and evil would mean falling from faith and from Christ. "I have espoused you to one husband," the Son of God, "to present to Christ a virgin who is chaste" [2 Cor. 11:2] (in the simplicity of her faith). To cleave to his wife, the church, he left father and mother (that is, God, who brought him forth from himself and was thus to him both father and mother). The church, redeemed by the shedding of Christ's blood from his side[36] and by his death, was then adopted by the Father as his daughter and married to his Son. To the Romans Paul wrote, "Through the body of Christ you are now made dead to the law so that you may be subject to another" (that is, the Son of God with the human nature he took on), "who rose from the dead" so that you who are now renewed with that man and are the spouse of Christ "might bring forth fruit for God" [Rom 7:4]. This fruit of justice is the masculine power, and the son of God and of the church. For you are members of the member, that is, men who cling to the first man, that you may be with him in God's wife, united and clinging to her whom Paul speaks of as the wife of man, who will bring a creation out of the wickedness of this world. As a consequence of this, and of the union of mankind as wife with God as husband, Paul says in the Epistle to the Ephesians that the solemn marriage of Adam and Eve, who were the first human beings, is "the great sacrament" of the new creation and marriage. In Adam and Eve were both the first symbol and the first prophecy, for this marriage and all things carnal were to be perfected in a further spiritual development beginning with Christ, until those things that are of the flesh should find their fulfillment. The second Adam said, "Not a jot or a tittle will pass away from the law until all these things are accomplished" [Matt. 5:18]. Adam signifies the divine Son and Eve the church; the marriage of Adam and Eve signifies the holy marriage of the Son of God and the church, which causes justice, the progeny of God and the church, to abound. Propagation in the flesh leads to death, but the propagation of justice through Jesus Christ leads to life. All this is a sign and sacrament of the new world in Christ, so that not a jot or tittle will pass away until all things are accomplished. After man fell as far as possible, from God to nothingness, it cost much labor and difficulty to prepare this spouse. In order that God's work might proceed in due order, she who was the

et ea quoque in humano genere ordine fluens donec tandem [p]urissima virgo flos ex radice Iesse fructificauerit Iesum masculum et feminam, in quo erat masculus deus et femineus homo. Id est quod Moyses ait, Faciamus hominem ad imaginem et similtudinem nostram et presit piscibus maris et volatilibus celi et bestiis vniuerseque terre omnique reptili quod mouetur in terra. Et creauit deus hominem ad imaginem et similtudinem suam, ad imaginem dei creauit illum; masculum et feminam creauit eos. Hic est Iesus masculinus deo et femininus humanitate per quam attraxit sibi reliquos homines in completionem coniugis sue, vt incrementum et multiplicacio sit et repletio et subiectio terre per iusticiam. Hic est quem Paulus vocat principium, primogenitus (id est, primoregenitus*), vt sit ipse in omnibus primatum tenens. In quo est factura rerum et refactura inchoata ab homine, que coniunx assumpta est per caput qui homo est a Maria virgine sumptus, cui sunt reliqui vocati homines, membra ex membro, ex quibus omnibus constat vna ecclesia cuius caput est christus, cuius maritus est dei filius.

Que ecclesia vt effingeretur apta ad nuptias antecessit moysaica lex; immo illic vt in breui tabula que est futura ecclesia in mundo significatur a patre facto capite ecclesie et data filio suo in manum agit idem pater in completionem vxoris filii sui. Nemo venit nisi pater traxerit in coniugium; simul filius fecundat in frugem iusticie vere et simplicis tum in deum tum in homines. Itaque eterno genito filio pater in terris genuit filiam ecclesiam et eam locauit matrimonio filio suo. Hinc filius dei apud Marcum se sponsum vocauit dicens, Numquid filii nuptiarum quamdiu sponsus cum illis est possunt ieiunare? Quanto tempore habent secum sponsum non possunt ieiunare. Veniet autem tempus quum auferetur ab eis sponsus et tunc ieiunabunt illis diebus. De his nuptiis est illa parabola apud Matheum: Hominem regem (id est, deum patrem) fecisse nuptias filio suo, vocasse quamplurimos, sed illos indignos non venisse; vocatos multos paucos venisse. Primum ergo quod est in ecclesia nostra est pontifici nostro veritas nuptiarum in qua quia non est significatio sed ipsa veritas. Ideo puto dionysium in ecclesiastica hierarchia de matrimonio tacuisse cuius sacramentum antecessit. Hinc inter deum et ecclesiam vere sunt nuptie, et feminei hominis cum masculino deo fecundissima coniunctio

---

*MS: primoregeniti.

greatest and fairest of human kind, even though still a sharer in the order of humanity, was set apart until, though an unspotted virgin and the flower of the root of Jesse, she brought forth her fruit, Jesus. He was both masculine and feminine, for in him God was the masculine nature and man the feminine. This is what Moses had spoken of: "Let us make man to our image and likeness, and he will be lord over the fishes of the sea, and the birds of the air, and the animals, and the whole earth, and over every reptile that moves upon it. And God created man in his image and likeness, created him in the image of God. Man and woman both, he created them" [Gen. 1:26–27]. This is Jesus, masculine in his divine nature and feminine in his humanity, through which humanity he drew the rest of mankind to himself in order to make his spouse complete, that there might be accession and diffusion and repletion of justice, and the earth might be subject to it. This is he whom Paul calls "the beginning, the first-born" (that is, the first who is reborn), "that he might hold the first place among all" [Col. 1:18]. He fashioned all things and also refashioned them, beginning with man, who was taken as spouse by the head, the man who was born of the virgin Mary. To him the rest of mankind is summoned, the members by the member; of all of these does the church consist, whose head is Christ, whose husband is the Son of God.

To make this church fit for marriage, first came the Mosaic law; indeed, it showed in limited compass what the future church would be in the world, which had been made by the Father, the head of the church. The father presented the church as a bride to his Son and wrought to perfect her. No one comes to this union but those whom the Father has summoned; at once the Son fecundates them to make them bring forth the fruit of true and single justice toward God and man. Accordingly, for his Son begotten in eternity the Father begot on earth a daughter, the church, and gave her in marriage to his Son. This is why in Mark's Gospel the Son of God called himself a bridegroom, saying, "Do you think the men of the bridegroom's party will fast while the bridegroom is still with them? As long as they have the bridegroom with them they may not fast. But the time will come when the bridegroom will be taken from them, and when that time comes they will fast" [Mark 2:19–20]. The parable in Matthew concerns this wedding: "A king" (that is, God the Father) "prepared a wedding for his son" [Matt. 22:2]; he summoned a great many, but being unworthy they did not come; of the many who were summoned, few came. The principal thing about our church is therefore the truth of its marriage to our high priest; this truth is not a symbol merely, but the very truth. I take it that the reason Dionysius says nothing about matrimony in the *Ecclesiastical Hierarchy* is that its sacrament had already come and gone. Hence the true wedding is that between God and the church, the fruitful union of mankind as wife with God as husband. All the other sac-

ad quam omnia sacramenta in ecclesia tendunt vt homines parentur et in illis sanctis nuptiis contineantur sacramentis purgatoriis, illuminatoriis, et perfectoriis. Homo in dei filium assumptus purissimus, illuminatissimus, et perfectissimus erat et vera dei vxor. Is sacerdotium instituit apostolos, qui pentitentia, baptismo, confirmatione, eucharistia, extrema unctione, expurgent, illuminent, perficiant, et talibus sacramentis consignent homines in vxorem christi et dei. Consecrauit primum sibi sacerdotes ad exemplum angelorum pontifex ille et sponsus, qui sunt primi in sponsa dei et quasi mulieris anima vt reliquum sponse corpus conficiant purgatum, illuminatum, et perfectum, ac eiusmodi dignis sacramentis consignent vt sensibili sigillo et impressione spiritalem impressionem agnoscant. Dei filius pontifex noster, vir et sponsus, purgator idem et illuminator et perfector sanxiuit nuptias inter se et sororem suam adoptatam in domum patris sui; instituit sub se filios et pontifices qui reliquam coniugem consecrent deo: que quia corporea et caduca est corporeis sacramentis tanquam retinaculis quibusdam colligauit: penitencia, baptismo, confirmacione, eucharistia, et extrema unctione. Omnia ad hec tendunt vt compleatur coniunx et nuptie christi. Sacerdotes sunt mariti in marito et sacerdote Iesu, et in illo purgantes penitentia, illuminantes baptismo et confirmatione, et perficientes eucharistia et extrema vnctione. Quid est tota ecclesia nisi matrimonium illud spiritale, vir et vxor, ordinati eciam et qui ordinantur* purgatione, illuminatione, et perfectione, vt sordes, tenebre et defectus carnis tollantur a secundo Adam? Pontifex et sponsus se propagat, et in illo omnes pontifices sunt sponsi et agunt in illo pontificale munus et parationem vxoris et fecundationem diuino semine et verbo dei vt eo fecunda ecclesia parens et mater sit iusticie.

Ordo ergo primum est in ecclesia: pontifex enim ipse christus et in illo deinde simul matrimonium; et in illo pontifices et sponsi agentes pontificatum et sponsionem christi vt tales nuptias propagent omniaque contrahant ordine in coniugem christi et in eodem contineantur. Ipsa veritas pontificis est dei filius, qui et angelorum est idem quoque veritas sponsi; superior ecclesie pars in racione pontificis et sponsi illum imitatur, vt in pontifice et sponso deo pontificem et sponsum agat et sacrificet prolemque progignat.† In qua actione, quia idem est sponsus et pontifex, iccirco idem est proles et sacrificium que [iusticia] est que sacrificatur a pontifice et progignitur† a sponso. In qua re idem est sacrificatio et pro-

*MS: ordinentur.
†MS: progingnat; progingnitur.

raments in the church move toward this one: men are born in order that they may be absorbed into this holy wedding by means of the sacraments, which cleanse, illumine, and perfect. The human being who is taken to the Son of God must be entirely cleansed, illumined, and perfected, a true wife of God. God enjoined the institution of priesthood upon the Apostles so that by means of penance, baptism, confirmation, the Eucharist, and extreme unction, they might cleanse, illumine, and perfect, and by these sacraments mark a man as wife to Christ and God. That Priest and Bridegroom first consecrated priests to himself, as he had the angels, to be the first in God's bride, so to speak the soul of the wife. It is their office to cleanse, illumine, and perfect the rest of the body of the wife, by such sacraments as produce also a spiritual impression, through setting a visible seal and impression upon the body. The Son of God, our priest, husband, and bridegroom, he who cleanses and illumines and perfects, has sanctified the nuptials between himself and the sister who has been adopted into the household of his Father. Beneath himself he has placed his sons and priests, to consecrate the rest of the spouse's body to God. Since men are corporeal and mortal, priests use corporeal sacraments as cables to bind them: penance, baptism, confirmation, the Eucharist, and extreme unction. All of them work to make Christ's spouse and his wedding feast complete. Priests are husbands in Jesus, who is Husband and Priest; in him they cleanse through penance, illumine through baptism and confirmation, and perfect through the Eucharist and extreme unction. What is the entire church but a spiritual marriage between the husband, those already ordered, and the wife, those who are being ordered by cleansing, illumining, and perfecting; so that the stains, darkness, and inadequacies of the flesh are removed by the second Adam? The Priest and Bridegroom propagates himself. In him all priests are bridegrooms: they both carry out in him their priestly office, and also procure a wife and make her fruitful by the divine seed and the word of God; so that, thus made fruitful, the church may be parent and mother of justice.

Orders therefore stand first in the church, for the priest is Christ himself and in him accordingly is matrimony also. In him priests and bridegrooms exercise their offices[37] so as to bring about a spiritual wedding with Christ which will draw all things to join together in due order as the spouse of Christ, and to be absorbed in him. The true and essential priest is the Son of God, who is likewise the true and essential bridegroom of the angels. The higher part of the church imitates him in its function as priest and bridegroom, so that in God who is priest and bridegroom it too may be priest and bridegroom and sanctify and bring forth offspring. Because in this activity priest and bridegroom are one and the same, the offspring and the sacrifice are also one and the same. This sacrifice is justice, which is sanctified by the priest and brought forth by the bridegroom.

generacio. Vt enim idem est sacrificans et generans (id est, pontifex et sponsus in summo pontifice et sponso deo christo) ita eadem est actio sacrificatio et prolificatio et eadem oblatio et proles, que est iusticia quam ecclesia sanctificata et fecundata a deo filio et offert et parit prolem et sacrificium. In persona ecclesie Dauid in Psalmo quarto iubet, Sacrificate sacrificium iusticie et sperate in domino. Multi dicunt, quis ostendit nobis bona? Signatum est super nos lumen vultus tui domine.

In quo annotandum est breuiter ibi a propheta tactas esse illas tres virtutes celeberrimas: spem, fidem, et charitatem. Iubet enim speremus qui sumus constituti in spe, singulariter id est simpliciter, et sumus signati lumine fidei quod est signum vultus et veritatis dei, et sacrificate sacrificium iusticie, quod idem sacrificium est et proles dei et ecclesie. Quid enim aliud est sacrificare quam parere, et procreare ex semine et fecunditate dei viuas et pingues hostias vitali sanguine plenas; et id quoque quidnam aliud est quam iuste agere offerreque iusticiam domino illi iusticie iustificanti et fecunditatis domino fecundanti* vt idem sit pontifex iustus iustificans et sponsus fecundus fecundans ecclesiam sponsam, que est gens sancta, et sacerdotalis sacrificans et eadem mater fecunda verbo et semine dei pariens iusticiam, sacrificium, et prolem deo filio parenti genitorique iusticie in sua vxore ecclesia?† Paulus autem agens in Iesu vero pontifice et sponso personam pontificis et sponsi sepe in suis epistolis in quibus se vocat dispensatorem mysteriorum‡ dei et coadiutorem quatenus ad pontificatus officium attinet, scribit in epistola ad Romanos hisce verbis, Audatius autem scripsi vobis fratres ex parte, tanquam in memoriam vobis reducens propter graciam que data est mihi a deo (in quo ago ministerium) vt sim minister Iesu christi in gentibus sanctificans euangelium dei vt fiat oblatio gentium accepta [(] id est iusticia in eis) et santificata in spiritu sancto, in obedientia scilicet deo. Et ad eosdem Ro[manos] (quos velit gentem esse sanctam (nam est sacerdotis sacerdotium propagare): nihil enim est munus et officium cuiusque nisi propagatio eiusdem et qui se sacrificauit deo efficere vt secum alii consacrificent, vt tota ecclesia sit sacerdotium consacrificans iusticiam, id est quisque in ea se iustum viuam hostiam offerat deo) scribit, Obsecro itaque vos fratres per misericordiam dei vt exhibeatis corpora vestra hostiam viuentem, sanctam, deo placen-

---

*MS: iustificant . . . fecundante.
†MS: ecclesie.
‡MS: ministeriorum.

In this activity sanctification and generation are also one and the same. As he who sanctifies and he who generates are one and the same (that is, priest and spouse in the supreme priest and spouse who is Christ God), so the activities of sanctifying and begetting offspring are one and the same, namely, justice. Thus the church, sanctified and fecundated by God the Son, both offers and brings forth offspring and sacrifice. Speaking for the church, David in the fourth Psalm bids us, "Sacrifice the sacrifice of justice, and hope in the Lord. Many will say, who can show us anything that is good? but in fact the sign of your favor, O Lord, is upon us" [Ps. 4:6–7].

In this connection it is to be noted that the prophet here touches briefly upon those three most glorious virtues, hope, faith, and charity.[38] He bids us hope, for "we are grounded singularly" (that is, undistractedly) "in hope," and "we are marked out by the light" [Ps. 4:10] of faith, which is the sign of God's favor and truth. "Sacrifice the sacrifice of justice," for that sacrifice is the offspring of God and the church. For what is sacrifice but begetting and bringing forth, through the seed and fecundity of God, fat living victims, full of the blood of life? And again, what is generation but acting justly and offering this justice to the Lord, who is justice justifying and fecundity fecundating? Thus the just priest justifying will be one and the same with the fecund bridegroom fecundating the church his spouse, which is his holy people. As the priestly bridegroom sanctifies her the church becomes a mother fertile by the word and seed of God, and brings forth justice, sacrifice and progeny to God the Son, parent and begetter of justice in his wife the church. Now Paul, acting the part of priest and bridegroom in the true priest and bridegroom Jesus, more than once speaks of himself in his Epistles as "dispenser of God's mysteries" [1 Cor. 4:1; 2 Cor. 6:4] and a coadjutor in what pertains to the priestly office. In the Epistle to the Romans he says, "I have written to you somewhat boldly here and there, to remind you of the grace that has been granted me by God" (in whom I carry out my ministry) "to be the minister of Jesus Christ among the Gentiles, and show them the holiness of the gospel of God and thus make it an offering that they would accept" (that is, the justice that is in them), "and one that is sanctified in the Holy Spirit" [Rom. 15:15–16], in obedience to God. He wished the Romans to be a holy people—it is after all the priest's role to propagate priesthood—and wrote to them that everyone must take as his duty and responsibility the propagation of priesthood, that those who sacrificed to God might bring others to sacrifice along with them in order that the entire church might be a priesthood sacrificing justice all together, each man offering his own just self as a living victim to God. Therefore, he writes, "through God's mercy I beseech you, brethren, to present your bodies as a living victim, holy and pleasing to God, your reasonable service. And

tem, racionabile obsequium vestrum. Et nolite conformari* huic seculo sed reformamini in nouitate spiritus vestri vt probetis que sit voluntas dei bona, beneplacens, et perfecta. Hic ecclesia inferior superiorem ecclesiam imitatur, et sacrificans se illam sacrificantem se deo contendit referre. Quia nihil est aliud officium in ecclesia quam sacrificatio sui cuiusque deo, et id quoque nihil est aliud quam se filium dei facere. Sacrificare est ergo facere filium summo pontifici et sponso. Et ecclesia est sacerdos et mater. Iusticia est sacrificium et proles. Masculinior pars cum femininiori agit assidue vt a tota simul sacrificium et proles offeratur. Offert masculinior vt gignens, femininior† vt mater et parens. Tota res vna est et simplex, et quasi arbor fructificans. Filioli mei (inquit ad Galathas Paulus) quos iterum parturio donec formetur in vobis christus. Ibi christum sponsum imitatur cuius est in coniuge formare filios iusticie facereque vt coniunx sacerdo[s] offerat filios deo iusta sacrificia iusticie. Est enim ecclesia soror christi et mater et sacerdos iusticie, sponsa et sacerdos paciens non agens. Sunt enim sacrificantes agentes et sacrificantes pacientes. Vna sacrificat agens et pars paciens in ecclesia. Et tota ecclesia (vt Petrus scribit) genus electum, regale sacerdotium, gens sancta, populus acquisitionis est simul vt modo geniti infantes vt crescamus in salutem in similitudinem domini, ad quem accedentes lapidem viuum electum ipsi lapides viui superedificamur,‡ domus spiritalis§ sacerdotium sanctum offerentes spiritales hostias acceptabiles deo per Iesum christum. Hec hostia est suum cuiusque in se sacrificium iusticie deo in christo, que eciam iusticia est filia dei in nobis genita, verbo dei audito et credito et nobis edita.

Huc ergo ventum est tandem vago sermone: vt habeamus matrimonium et sacerdotium in christo omnino esse idem et eandem actionem effectumque habere, sacrificareque esse idem quod gignere, et prolem idem quod sacrificium que iusticia est. Hanc rem matrimonialeque sacerdotium et sacerdotale matrimonium venisse et diriuatum esse in homines ab ipso sacerdote et sponso Iesu christo.

V

In quo ad imitationem ipsius deinceps in reliqua ecclesia procedet simul et idem sacerdotium et matrimonium sanctum sanctificans sanctam ecclesiam deo vt totum officium superioris et masculinioris partis in ecclesia sit studere in sanctificationem inferioris, inferioris autem obedire in om-

*MS: conformare.
†MS: feminior.
‡MS: -edificemur.
§MS: spiritales.

do not be conformed to this world, but be reformed in the newness of your spirit in order to determine what is God's good, well-pleasing and perfect will" [Rom. 12:1–2]. In this the lower church imitates the higher and sanctifies herself in emulation of the way the higher church sanctifies herself to God. For there is no other duty in the church than for each person to sanctify himself to God, which in turn means simply to make oneself a son of God. To sacrifice therefore means to give a son to the supreme priest and bridegroom. And, the church being priest and mother, justice is her sacrifice and offspring. The more masculine part works earnestly with the more feminine part in order that they may jointly offer sacrifice and offspring. The masculine offering is that of the begetter, the feminine is that of the mother and parent. Together they are one single thing, like a fruit-bearing tree. "You are my sons," Paul says to the Galatians, "to whom I give a new birth until Christ is formed in you" [Gal. 4:19]. In this he imitates the bridegroom Christ, who acts to form sons of justice in his spouse and to make his wife a priest who offers sons to God, just sacrifice to justice; for the church is Christ's sister, and the mother and priest of justice. Now, there are some who sacrifice actively and some who sacrifice passively, and she is a passive spouse and priest rather than an active one. The active and passive part sacrifice as one in the church. And the entire church, as Peter writes, is "a chosen race, a royal priesthood, a people that God wants for himself," and we are "like newborn infants who will grow unto salvation" in the likeness of the Lord; "as we draw near to him we are erected like living stones on that chosen living stone, a spiritual household, a holy priesthood, offering spiritual victims that are acceptable to God through Jesus Christ" [1 Pet. 2:9, 2, 4, 5]. This victim is each man's sacrifice in himself to the God of justice in Christ; while this justice is the daughter of God born in us, made manifest to us because we have heard and believed the word of God.

In this rather wandering discourse we have got to the point where we see that matrimony and priesthood are completely the same in Christ and have the same action and effect; that sacrificing is the same as begetting; and that that progeny which is justice is the same as sacrifice. All this amounts to a matrimonial priesthood or a priestly matrimony, which flows to men from Jesus Christ, himself Priest and Bridegroom.

V

In Christ and in imitation of him the rest of the church will in turn come to this holy priesthood and matrimony, sanctifying the whole church to God. Thus the whole duty of the higher and more masculine part of the church is to work for the sanctification of the lower, while the duty of the

nibus vt sanctificetur. Id est quod Paulus latenter suadet in epistola ad Ephesios quum viri et mulieris officium docet, mulieris scilicet officium obedire in omnibus viro in sanctificationem s[uam] ab illo in domino. Viri* autem (qui caput est mulieris sicut ecclesie christus) diligere vxorem et ad exemplum christi seipsum tradere pro ea sanctificans eam et mundans lauachro aque gracie in verbo vite, vt exhiberet ipse sibi gloriosam vxorem non habentem maculam neque rugam aut aliquid eiusmodi sed sanctam et immaculatam. Nam in christo sponsum esse est illum imitari et santificationem corporis sui agere, id est mulieris, in eternitatem: sicut in prima generatione mulier egit corruptionem capitis sui viri in mortalitatem. Item fecundare adherentem sibi coniugem et implere iusticia, vt sicut exhibuimus membra nostra seruire immuniditie et iniquitati ad iniquitatem: item nunc exhibeamus membra nostra seruire iusticie in sanctificationem. Iesus enim castus sponsus, propagator spiritus, extat nobis exemplum. Omnis actio in ecclesia debet esse imitacio illius vt non sit in ea quicquam nisi quod ipsum est in illo verius, nec debet esse in ecclesia nisi quod ab illius veritate diriuetur. Ille maritus est ecclesie in santificationem eius qui caput illius seipsum tradidit pro e[a] vt illam sanctificet et impleat fetu iusticie. In hunc finem debet esse quisque maritus in ecclesia in domino in sanctificationem vxoris sue et castum coniugium, vt sicut ab Adam peccatore profluxit carnalis generatio in mortem ita ab Adam iusto profluat spiritalis generatio in vitam eternam.

Carnalis autem generatio tametsi mollitudini hominum in prima epistola ad Corinth[ios] ab apostolo indulgetur necessitate magis quam voluntate: tamen ipsa non est res christi, nec ea nec eius prolificatio in christianitate requiritur necessario, tametsi necessario mollibus et infirmis permittitur. Est enim illa res hominis creati in damnationem, non recreati hominis in christo in salutem. Racio enim sacramenti in eo, modo adsit veritas ipsa matrimonii, euanescat et abeat necesse est. Materiam regeneracionis satis suppeditasset paganitas si in ea parte ecclesia omnino sterilis fuisset. Nec erat timendum ne tota paganitas christianizet: quum nunc quoque sub ipso nomine christianitatis maxima pars hominum paganizet. Veritas sincera semper rara est et in paucis. Et perrexisset generatio carnalis in filiis hominum, et simul ex eisdem generatio spiritalis a filiis dei. De qua re consulentibus Corinthiis in epistola respondit Paulus, Incontinentibus vitande fornicationis causa, ex indulgenciis licere eis vxores suas

*MS: viro.

lower is to obey in all things so that it will be sanctified. This is what Paul is covertly urging[39] in the Epistle to the Ephesians when he is explaining the obligations of husband and wife: it is the woman's obligation to obey her husband in all things so that she will be made holy by him in the Lord. For his part the husband, who is the head of his wife as Christ is of the church, must love his wife and, following Christ's example, give himself over for her sake, sanctifying and "cleansing her in the font of the water" of grace "in the word of life" [Eph. 5:26], that he may present his wife in her glory, without spot or wrinkle or anything similar, but rather holy and unspotted. For to have been espoused in Christ is to imitate him and to effect the eternal sanctification of his body, which is his wife, whereas in the original creation the woman had wrought the mortal corruption of her husband and head. Likewise he is to fecundate the wife who cleaves to him and fill her with justice, in order that, just as we have given our members to the service of uncleanness and iniquity and thereby become ourselves iniquitous, now we should devote our members to the service of justice and thereby become holy. Jesus indeed, the chaste spouse and propagator of spirit, sets us the example. Everything that is done in the church should be in imitation of him, so that there will be nothing in her which is not more truly existent in him and nothing which does not flow from his truth. He is the church's husband who sanctifies her; as her head he has given himself for her, to make her holy and to fill her with the off-spring of justice. This is the end toward which every husband in the church should work, the sanctification of his wife and a chaste marriage. Thus, as carnal generation resulting in death flowed from the sinful Adam, so spiritual generation resulting in eternal life flows from the just Adam.

Though in the First Epistle to the Corinthians the Apostle conceded carnal generation to man's weakness, reluctantly but as a matter of necessity, still it is not part of Christ's order. There is no need for it to be required among Christians, though it is necessarily permitted to the weak and feeble; nor is the resulting offspring needed. Carnal generation belongs rather to man as he was created unto damnation than to man as he was re-created in Christ unto salvation. Once the true nature of matrimony appears, the *raison d'être* for the sacrament in re-created man will necessarily vanish and disappear. The pagans would supply ample material for regeneration even if the church were altogether barren in that respect. Nor need there be any fear that all pagans will become Christians, for now the majority of men, though they call themselves Christians, act like pagans. True sincerity is always rare and is met with in few. While carnal generation would continue among the sons of men, a spiritual regeneration by the sons of God would also arise from among them. Paul answered the Corinthians in a letter when they asked him about this question. In order to obviate fornication those who cannot contain may be per-

tenere si habent, si non habeant ducere et in matrimonio rem mutuo reddere quando libidinis ardor et necessitas vrget. Verum hec inuitus permittit qui voluit omnes esse sicut ipse erat virgo et suadet, quatenus per infirmitatem impotentiamque continendi licet, disiugatis tum viduis tum virginibus soluti et liberi maneant deo. Beatiores eos dicit si sic permanserint quia virgines et vidue quietius et simplicius vacabunt deo vero marito suo. Verum in omnibus non est sanitas quidem, et egrotis indulgendum est ex ecclesie misericordia. Vnusquisque proprium donum habet, alius quidem sic, alius vero sic. In tanta infirmitate non audet Paulus laqueum iniicere optimis, necnon indulgere aliquatenus deteriori. Quod facit ea lege vt homines ea licentia vtantur. Siquidem qui velint potius sani esse et tales vt indulgentia nihilo egeant, alioquin sponte videntur egrotare et insanire; quod est in ecclesia christiana detestabile vt aliquis scilicet sponte langueat mulieretque quum sumus vocati in virilem dignitatem non vt turpe aliquid et carnale muliebriter agamus. At imbecillioribus et non valentibus agere quod melius est, ipsum tametsi malum est tamen egroto non est malum modo medicina indulta vtatur non amplius quam suus morbus exposcat. Quum videt omnes in ecclesia ad exemplum christi celebes esse oportere, tamen simul videt omnes non posse. Quapropter, vt velit potentes celibes viuere, ita impotentes permisit refrigerio sui ardoris vti. Optandum est tamen vt tota christianitas esset in celibatu: quod optauit ipse Paulus quando dixit, Vellem vos omnes esse sicut ego sum. Quoniam sancta ecclesia christi tota spiritalis non requirit nisi matrimonium spiritale et spiritalem prolificationem in marito nostro Iesu christo in quo carnales homines sunt facti spiritales vt propagationem non agant nunc nisi, angelorum more ad exemplum christi, spiritalem iusticie.

In superiori parte ecclesie in christo est ordo et matrimonium (vt ita dicam) masculinum quod vocatur sacerdotium, quod ipsum est eciam sponsus in sponso, quod partitur* in varios ordines. Sunt presbiteri quos Dionysius vocat pontifices, diaconi quos idem sacerdotes appellat. Sunt eciam quos ille vocat ministros, in quibus sunt subdiaconi, accoliti, exorciste, lectores, hostiarii, qui omnes exercitantur in purgatione sicut sacerdotes diaconique in illuminacione, et postremo sicut illi pontifices in perfectione et consummatione. Nam totum officium viri est in purgatorum illuminatione fide, et perfectione eorundem charitate. Purgatio tendit in simplicitatem et constantiam spei. In psalmo quarto est, Constituisti

---

*MS: patitur.

mitted, as a concession, to keep the wives they have; those who have no wives may marry, and in the married state they may render what is due each to the other when necessity and the heat of passion so require. He permitted this reluctantly, for he would have preferred that everyone be as he was, a virgin.[40] He urges those who are unmarried, whether widows or maidens, to remain single and free for God so far as their weakness and inability to contain will permit. He says that those who so remain are happier, because widows and maidens have more peace and leisure for God, who is their real husband. Yet not everyone enjoys good health, and the church in her mercy makes concessions to those who are ill. "Every person has his own gift, one person this and another that" [1 Cor. 7:7]. In view of this great weakness Paul does not risk laying what might be a snare for the best people, though at the same time he does not in the least countenance their weak side; this he achieves through the principle that he lays down for making use of this permission. Those who have the will to be healthy and are not such as to require any concession could appear to fall ill and lose their health by choice; and it would be a detestable thing in the Christian church for anyone to choose to languish like a woman, for we are called to manly greatness, not to act basely and carnally in a womanish way. But as to those who are weaker and have insufficient strength to do what is best, a thing that may be an evil in itself may yet not be an evil for someone who is ill, provided that he uses the remedy granted to him in no greater measure than is required by the disease. Though Paul sees that everyone in the church should remain celibate, after the example of Christ, yet at the same time he sees that not everyone can. Hence, while he wishes everyone to live celibate who is able, he has allowed to those who are unable a means of cooling their passion. And yet it is to be wished that the whole Christian world were celibate, a wish Paul himself expressed when he said, "I would that you were all as I am" [1 Cor. 7:7]. For Christ's holy church, being entirely spiritual, needs only spiritual marriage and spiritual engendering of offspring in our husband Jesus Christ. In him carnal men are made spiritual, so that their only propagation now would be, like that of the angels, after the example of Christ, a spiritual propagation of justice.

In the higher part of the church in Christ is orders, and a kind of masculine matrimony that is called priesthood. It is the specifically sponsal element in the spouse, and is divided into various orders. There are the presbyters, whom Dionysius calls pontiffs; the deacons, whom he calls priests; and then those he calls ministers, including subdeacons, acolytes, exorcists, lectors, and doorkeepers, all of these last being occupied in cleansing, as the priests and deacons are occupied in illumining and the pontiffs in perfecting and consummating. The husband's whole duty lies in illumining by faith those who have been cleansed, and perfecting them in charity. Cleansing works to produce the concentration and stability of

me singulariter in spe. Illuminatio effectum suum habet fidem vt in lumine dei videamus lumen et in enigmate veritatem et in imagine vultum. Quod lumen fidei (vt in illo eodem psalmo testatur Dauid) signatum est super nos et est imago vultus dei et veritatis. Perfectionis autem finis est sacrifitium iusticie ex charitate. Hec molitur superior pars ecclesie et vna cum eadem obedit et patitur inferior pars matrimonii et sacerdos feminea vt pariat et sacrificet filios iusticie deo.

De ordine loquitur Dionysius, de matrimonio tacet: vel intelligens sacerdotium matrimonium esse, vel sua taciturnitate nos docens non aliud in ecclesia christi matrimonium esse oportere quam sacerdotium. Carnale matrimonium, quod erat spiritalis sacramentum, modo choruscante veritate discussum est et abiisse. Antecessit illud olim in primordio humani generis et in paradiso cepit diuine coniunctionis et humane symbolum, christi eterni sponsi et ecclesie coniugii signum et sacramentum. Que quidem ecclesia virago in somno illo in viuifica carne ex illius costa et latere formata erat mulier dei, vnde sanguis redemptionis sponse et aqua ablutionis eius in omni sanctificatione effluxit vt illam sanctificaret mundans eam lauachro aque in verbo vite in seipso vt exhiberet ipse sibi gloriosam ecclesiam non habentem maculam neque rugam nec aliquid eiusmodi sed sanctam et immaculatam, vt tota sancta adhereat sancto illi deo quem mirificauit dominus vt in illo cum illo mirabiliter euadat vnus spiritus. Testatur in epistola ad Ephesios Paulus viraginem illam sumptam de latere viri: carnem ex carne, et os ex ossibus illius propter quam relinquet homo patrem et matrem et adherebit vxori sue, magnum esse sacramentum in christo et ecclesia, in qua nemo coniugatur coniunctione significante sed significata, non carnali sed spiritali, non sacramento sed veritate, omnes ad imitacionem christo in omnibus vt quisque diligat vxorem sicut christus ecclesiam in vxoris sanctificationem in veritate. Matrimonium et sacerdotium idem est, et in superiore parte ecclesi[e] ac masculina eius officium est purgare, illuminare, et perficere, vt tota ecclesia pariat et sacrificet prolem iusticie deo. At hec de ordine et matrimonio sufficiant.

VI

[V]ti modo diffuso sermone ostendimus superior ecclesie pars in christo masculinior et actiuior sacerdos est et sponsus, pater et genitor iusticie

hope. The fourth Psalm says, "You have founded me singularly in hope" [Ps. 4:10]. The result of illumining is faith, which enables us to "see the light in the light of God" [Ps. 35:10], the truth in the mystery, the countenance in the image. This light of faith, as David asserts in the same Psalm, is "signed upon us" [Ps. 4:7], the sign of God's favor and truth. Finally, perfection brings about the loving sacrifice of justice. These are the endeavors of the higher part of the church; the lower partner in the marriage, the feminine priest, obeys along with her and suffers in order to bring forth and sanctify sons to the God of justice.

Dionysius discusses orders but is silent about matrimony, either because he considers them the same or because his silence is intended to teach us that no other kind of marriage but priesthood would belong in the church of Christ.[41] Once true matrimony burst upon us, carnal matrimony, which was the symbol of spiritual matrimony, would be dispelled and disappear. It had come at the beginning, in the early days of the human race, and this symbol of the union between God and man, the sign and sacrament of the marriage between Christ the eternal bridegroom and the church, was first seen in paradise.[42] As Adam slept, the church, the woman, was formed as the wife of God in the life-giving flesh from his rib and his side, whence flowed the blood that would redeem his spouse and the water that would wash her in all holiness; "thus he sanctified her, cleansing her in the font of the water of the word of life, in himself, in order to have a glorious church without spot or wrinkle or anything of that sort, but holy and unspotted" [Eph. 5:26–27]. Being entirely holy she would cling to the holy God in whom and with whom the Lord had amazingly brought it about that her spirit would wondrously become one. Paul declares in the Epistle to the Ephesians that the wife was taken from the side of her husband, flesh of his flesh and bone of his bone, for whose sake "he would leave father and mother and cleave to his wife," and this is "the great sacrament in Christ and the church" [Eph. 5:32], in which one is bound not by the bond that is merely a sign but by the bond that is thereby signified, not by a carnal but by a spiritual bond, not merely symbolically but in truth — all of them imitating Christ in all things, so that everyone will love his wife as Christ does the church, so that his wife is made holy in truth. Matrimony is the same as priesthood, and its function in the higher, masculine part of the church is to cleanse, illumine, and perfect, so that the whole church will bring forth and sanctify offspring for the God of justice. But let this suffice for orders and matrimony.

VI

As we have now shown at some length, the higher part of the church, that which is more active and masculine in Christ, is both priest and bride

in inferiore parte ecclesie que est femininior* et magis passiua et quasi sponsa ac mater in qua iusticia formari debeat. Iusticia autem est fides deo per christum et charitas dei et proximi. Hec ex deo ipso est hominibus electis, illis quos deus irradiat vt fide respiciant illum et reament et ex fide hominibus bene agant. Radius dei et lucet et calet suauissime. Hic in deo vera bonitas est et bona veritas. In hominis anima idem radius est fidelis amor deo et amans fides. Sed vt nihil possit lucere et calere nisi prius sit (Est autem quodque simplicitate et veritate, nam diuisio et multiplicitas mors est) vt aliquid ergo illuminetur fide et concaleat amore dei et proximi, oportet illud recreetur prius quasi ex nihilo et a multiplicitate puluereque ad simplicitatem, a diuisione morteque ad vnitatem et vitam contrahatur vt sit in tali esse et puncto vt diuino radio attingi possit illuminarique et perfici in summo sole deo qui est in Iesu christo. Est enim in homine quod suum est proprium indiuiduum et simplex, quod mala et multiplici racione obductum et inuolutum vacillat secum et titubat, qua extraria conditione oportet spolietur homo omnino, et expurgetur illud intimum indiuiduum vt in se redeat et extet nudum, purum, et simplex, ac nunc subtractis omnibus impedimentis et abrepto omni onere quod deorsum detrusit, solutum et liberum in se libere et summe constet abductum iam ab omni diuisa et multiplici conditione, et expositum deo alte in racione simplici et indiuidua et in se penitus nuditer et aperte: vt tale apparens in deo, in deo summo sole statim attactus diuino radio illuminetur et calefiat. Hoc indiuiduum in homine Paulus vocat hominem interiorem, Saluator in euangelio hominis oculum: qui si simplex fuerit totum corpus lucidum erit. Simplicitas huius indiuidui hominis et anime vnitas et esse in deo per christum est spes, que est illa nuda et simplex expositio et apparitio humane anime deo omni graui appendice abstracto vt leuis et libera nunc anima secum constet in se intime et in deo stabiliter coniuncta vni et vnifico deo, et ab illo solo dependens et ab eodem cert[e] expectans omnia. Que sperans expectatio est anime suum esse spiritale: potencia, firmitas, et constancia purgationis finis, christiani hominis initium qua imprimis quisque christianus et tota ecclesia quasi fixa et stabilita est in puncto essentia spiritali vt deinde altius in lumen et perfectionem sui promoueatur. De ecclesia inquit Dauid in psalmo quarto, Tu domine singulariter in spe constituisti me. Quum quis implicatur rationibus deo con-

---

*MS: feminior.

groom, father and progenitor of justice in the lower part of the church, the more feminine and passive part, which is like the bride and mother in whom justice must be formed. Now, justice is faith in God through Christ, and love of God and one's neighbor. It comes from God himself to those whom he has chosen, those whom God so shines upon that they reflect him in faith and love, and from this faith do good to their fellow men. The ray of God imparts a delicious warmth and light. In God this ray is good truth and true goodness. In the soul of man it is faithful love of God and loving faith.[43] But as nothing can impart light and warmth unless it already exists—exists, that is, in singleness and truth, for dividedness and multiplicity means death—anything that is to be illumined by faith and glow with the love of God and neighbor, must first be re-created, so to speak out of nothing, and to pass from multiplicity and materiality to singleness, from dividedness and death to oneness and life; then it will exist in the manner and in the position in which it can be reached by the divine ray, and illumined and perfected in the supreme sun God, who is in Jesus Christ. There is in man an undivided and single element, which belongs to his nature. If it is obscured and weakened by evil multiplicity it wavers and falters. A man must rid himself entirely of this hampering[44] condition and restore inmost undividedness so as to be once more himself and appear naked, pure, and simple. With all these hindrances removed and the weight shaken off that had weighed him down, let him be fully and utterly himself, liberated now and free from any condition of dividedness or distraction, exposed to God on high in singleness and undividedness, naked and open in himself. The man who appears thus in the sight of God the supreme sun is receptive to the divine ray and derives from it light and warmth. This element of undividedness in man Paul calls "the inner man" [Eph. 3:16], while the Savior calls it in the Gospel "the eye of man," which "if it be single the whole body will be light" [Matt. 6:22]. Hope is the singleness of this undivided man, the unity of his soul, and his being in God through Christ. Hope is the simple and absolute exposure of the human soul to God, disburdened of everything that had weighed it down, so that now it appears, weightless and free, as it is in its inmost being and in God: unshakably linked to God, who is one and renders one, dependent solely on him, and from him expecting confidently all things. The hope and expectation of these things is the soul's spiritual essence, the strength and firmness and constancy that result from cleansing, the starting point of Christian man. It is primarily in hope that every individual Christian and the church as a whole are as it were fixed and settled in a state of spiritual reality from which they are in a position to advance higher toward light and perfection. Of the church David says in the fourth Psalm, "O Lord, you have founded me singularly in hope" [Ps. 4:10]. When a man pursues purposes that run counter to God's, in the folly and

trariis stulticia et nequitia huius mundi non est sui compos, et ita diuiditur et distrahitur vt in solo deo vno et indiuiduo sperare non possit. Primus ergo labor et negotium est sacerdotti in ecclesia vt expurget et purificet homines in simplicitatem et spem deo vt desperare desinant et sperare incipiant, vt remotis dispositionibus contrariis quum iam in summa spe sint a deo, hoc ipso sint regeniti vt inde simul promoti perficiantur. Quod docet diuus Petrus in epistola ad dispersos Iudeos sic exorsus, Benedictus deus et pater domini nostri Iesu christi qui secundum misericordiam suam regenerauit nos in spem viuam per resurrectionem [Iesu christi ex mor-] tuis in quo homines simul resurgunt per potentiam patris a vita moribunda, interminata* desperatione, in spem viuam vt in patre genitore quisque iam sperans sit viuens et habeat esse vnitatis et simplicitatis in patre cui vnitas et potentia attribuitur per quem potenter est in spe et stabiliter purgatoria vi ministrorum dei. Ad Collocenses inquit Paulus, immobiles a spe euangelii quod accepistis. Est in hac spe immobilitas et paterna constantia que est proprie in esse et vnitate, que vnitas patris est et potentis genitoris, in quo potenter viuunt homines qui ministri sunt dei, quorum opus est (vt scribit Paulus ad Hebreos) introductio melioris spei per quam proximamus ad deum. Nam soluti in mundo longe absunt a deo. Et qui in multis mundi rebus sunt distracti diuersa spe et expectatione earum, ii reuera non sunt, et desperantes deum nihil sunt. Vt recolligantur et reuniantur spe vni deo per quam ad deum proximent, despectis et abiectis omnibus in quibus sperauerunt terrenis, multiplicibus et diuisis distrahentibusque homines, vt sit (inquam) recollectio et introductio in spem meliorem per quam proximent deo, est labor et officium paterne administrationis et spiritalis regenerationis in deo. Et in hoc paterni sacerdotii in ecclesia est prima actio, vt desperationis puluerem discutiat et depellat adversantia et impedientia omnia diuinam reformationem nudetque quasi statuam humanam nouo colore depingendam, procreet hominem in suam ipsius simplicem vnitatem, educat ab aquis huius mundi in spiritum dei, ab imo terre in altum celi: vt in monte spei extet vicinus deo vt ab illo illustretur et exornetur, exuat vetustatem male olentem ex fece huius mundi, et induat [vestem nitidam], abradat a vase amarum saporem veteris imbutionis vt sit nouum vas suauissimi vini dei; spoliet et detrahat

---

*MS: interminite.

wickedness of this world, he is not in command of his faculties and is so divided and distracted that he cannot hope solely in God, who is one and undivided. It is therefore the first task of priests in the church to cleanse and purify man so that he becomes single and hopes in God; he must cease to despair and begin to hope so that, once his contrarious dispositions are removed and he places all his hope in God, he may be reborn by this very fact and be able to advance at once from this state to perfection. This is the teaching of St. Peter in his Epistle to the Jews of the Diaspora, beginning with these words: "Blessed is God and the Father of our Lord Jesus Christ, who in his mercy has brought us forth again to a living hope, through the resurrection of Jesus Christ from the dead" [1 Pet. 1:3]. In him men rise again through the power of the Father from a life in death of boundless despair, so that everyone who now hopes in God the Father may have life and partake of the essence of oneness and singleness in the Father, whose attributes are oneness and singleness and through whom comes strong and unshaken hope, by way of the cleansing power of his ministers. Paul says to the Colossians, "Do not budge from the gospel hope that you have received" [Col. 1:23]. In this hope is the stability and fatherly constancy that belongs properly to being and oneness. This unity is that of the Father, the potent sire in whom men live potently as ministers of God whose task it is, as Paul writes to the Hebrews, "to bring in a better hope, through which we can come closer to God" [Heb. 7:19]. For those who are absorbed in the world are at a great distance from God. And those who are distracted among the many affairs of this world, with varying hope and expectation regarding these affairs, do not truly exist, for since they do not hope in God they are nothing. It is the task and the duty of paternal ministry and spiritual regeneration in God to gather men together again into a oneness of hope in the one God. Through this hope they come closer to God, once they have scorned and put away all the varied and divisive things of this world in which they had set their hope and by which they had been distracted—so that, as I say, they may be gathered together again and brought to a better hope that will make them closer to God. This is the first activity of the paternal priesthood in the church, to shake off the dust of despair and to rout everything that opposes and stands in the way of a divine reformation, and to strip off the old coating, just as one does with a manmade statue that is to be painted afresh. Man must be brought forth to singleness and unity, drawn out of the waters of this world into God's air, from the depths of earth to the heights of heaven. Thus he may stand forth on the mount of hope, close to God, by whom he will be enlightened and adorned. He must then put off his old nature, stinking with the filth of this world, and put on [a clean garment];[45] he must scour the bitter taste of his former potations from the drinking vessel so that it can be a new vessel containing now the de-

fedam et squalidam vestem quam ipse sibi homo rudi arte ex terra huius mundi contexuit et induat eam nouam et celestem ex materia gracie lucis spiritus sancti digitis contextam. Sit anima penitus simplex, vna, indiuidua, in vnam partem duntaxat et vnice intenta in vnum deum mera et indiuisibili spe, puncto hoc spei constans in deo et hac radice alte infixus in terra viuentium vt radicatus spe pulchre crescat fide et charitate fructificet vtiliter et spisse bona opera in vitam eternam. Primus ergo effectus sacerdotii in humiliori ecclesie parte est spes deo qui finis est purgationis, que eadem spes eciam humilitas, subiectio, et obedientia est deo, vt ab illo in diuinam formam exaltetur. Hec sunt que vel spes ipsa est vel spem indiuisibiliter comitantur, et simul in ea emergente anima ex hoc mundano mari se ostentant, videlicet puritas, nuditas, simplicitas, vnitas, potentia, constantia, stabilitas, firmitas, radicatio, humilitas, subiectio, obedientia, essentia, generatio, filiatio, vita, initium, fundamentum, et eiusmodi omnia que principii racionem habent et inchohationis solliditatem. Est enim certe homo sperans deo purus, nudus, simplex, in se vnus, radicatus humiliter, subiectus obedienter, generatus in esse firmo, potenti, constanti, stabili, filius dei viuus iam inchoatus et fundatus alta et sollida spe, vt in reliquum edificium perficiatur. Vt homo reducatur in hanc et obedientem spem elaborant ministri assidue docentes ex sacris literis quam sperandum est in deo, quam simul que mundi sunt desperranda et abiicienda. Hi hostiarii, lectores, exorciste et id genus hominum qui in inferiori ecclesia in purgandis hominibus spiritaliter se exercent. Cathecumeni vero vocantur qui sic instruuntur, et illa operatio cathe[c]izatio vocatur. In epistola ad Galathas precipit Paulus, Communicet is qui cathecizatur verbo ei qui se cathecizat in omnibus bonis. Oportet doceatur vt abrenunciet que sunt huius [mundi] omnia vt in spem soli deo deinceps se recipiat. Hoc significat depositio vestium et hominis nudatio in nouum indumentum, vt peniteat male acte vite, vt confiteatur se peccasse, vt habeat voluntatem redimendi tempus et recompensandi illa mala cum bonis in deo et satisfaciendi modo deinceps contrario, vt bonitatis lanx que erat ante depressa iusta satisfactione peccatorum lancem adequet, immo potius superet iusticie causa vt erat ante superata. Quum enim confessorum peccatorum te peniteat tui, salus esse non potest quidem nisi

lightful wine of God. Let him take off and throw away the foul and filthy garment that with the untutored skill of a mere man he wove for himself from the earth of this world, and put on the new and heavenly garment made of grace and light, woven by the fingers of the Holy Spirit. Let his soul be entirely single, one and undivided, with all her energies bent solely on one concern only, on the one God, with absolute indivisible hope; firm on her base of hope in God, and with root sunk so deep in the earth of the living that thus rooted in hope it can grow flourishingly in faith and make fruitful in charity a useful and bountiful harvest of good works so as to attain eternal life. Thus the first effect of priesthood upon the lower part of the church is hope in God, which results from cleansing. This same hope is also humility, obedience, and subjection to God, so that by him man may be exalted to a divine form. The following qualities are either parts of hope itself or its inseparable concomitants, and make their appearance as the soul emerges from the sea of this world: purity, unadornedness, simplicity, unity, power, constancy, stability, firmness, rootedness, humility, subjection, obedience, essence, generation, filiation, life, being, foundation, and all the qualities that contribute to a beginning and make it solid. Assuredly a person who hopes in God is pure, unadorned, single, one with himself, deeply rooted, obediently subject, and generated in a being that is firm, powerful, constant, and stable; he is a living son of God now well started and founded on deep and solid hope, ready for the completion of the rest of the structure. Ministers work assiduously to bring a person to this obedient hope, teaching him from sacred Scripture how he must hope in God and at the same time reject and withdraw his confidence from the things of this world. These ministers are the doorkeepers, lectors, exorcists, and others of this kind who are engaged in cleansing men spiritually in the inferior church. Those who receive instruction from them are called catechumens, and the work that they do is called catechizing. In the Epistle to the Galatians Paul prescribes, "He who is being catechized should share everything good that he has with his catechist" [Gal. 6:6]. He must be taught to renounce all the things of this world and have recourse to hope in God alone. This he signifies by putting off his garments and stripping himself to receive new clothing, with sorrow for the evil life he has led; admitting that he has sinned and desiring to make good use of his time, making amends to God by good deeds for the evil deeds he has done, and offering satisfaction by taking a future course opposite to that which he took in the past. In this way a just satisfaction will cause goodness no longer to be outweighed by sin; indeed its justice may turn the scales in favor of goodness, which was outweighed before.[46] When one is sorry for the sins he has confessed, there is still no forgiveness unless one makes good use of his time by mak-

redimas tempus, recompenses, et satisfacias, exurgas vt superes sicut eras superatus. Pugnes, proternas, vinces malum, cum bono superes, vt iusta compensatione sit pro malis tuis satisfactio in bonitate, vel re vel voluntate: vt emergente in te ea iusticia a iusto deo apprehendare. Quid ergo est cuique peccato contrarium et sua cuique vitio que propria virtus diligenter docendi sunt cathecumeni vt discant in meliori vita pro malis bona recompensare et pro peccatis in iusticie operibus satisfacere vt simul cum iusticia sit misericordia dei; vt erat in peccatis libido et voluptas ita pro eisdem dolor et tristicia sit et quidem animo angor et corporis cruciatus qui vt ignis expurget labes peccatorum et eradicet funditus vt iterum non pullulent. Dum in manibus ministrorum est aliquis vt purgetur vtque colluuiem peccatorum lachrimis lauet et abstergat, vel cathecumenus, vel penitens, vel energuminus, vel apostata, tametsi is rursus sit in ecclesia tamen non numeratur, nec est ex hierarchia et corpore christi, in quo nemo* esse potest nisi purgatus et perfectus. Vnde constat omnes malos christianos non esse in ecclesia sed extra vt purgentur. Et interea dum peccatorum contagione infecti sunt eis non licere nec mysteria audire nec sacramenta aspicere, quoniam prophanos et fedos habent oculos. Que sunt ad vite eruditionem audire possunt, vti sunt ex sacris literis cantus et lectiones. At quum sacramenta aguntur longe propellantur; fedi enim et turpes illuminari non possunt vt videant sacra que nemo recte discernit nisi illuminatus fide vt in lumine dei lumen videat; fidei autem acies in peccatorum flumine extinguitur. Fide spectantur sacramenta et eorum mysteria intelliguntur. Vt autem credamus, sine peccato [simus] oportet. Infuscatur enim et obtenebratur fides in peccatorum caligine et fumo. Ait ille, Adhuc in peccatis vestris estis. Donec ergo deponatur tetra illa et detestabilis vestis scelerum et dolorum ac tristicie facibus comburatur et pro ea vicissim nudus ille modo induat nitidam et amabilem vestem nuptialem, in mensa celestium dapum et sacramentorum dei non discumbat. De hac re distincte tanquam de sacramento non loquutus est Dionysius quoniam est potius via et paratio ad sacrament[um quam] sacramentum: vt exuere antecedit induere et reconciliatio amicitiam et procuratio adeptionem et curatio sanitatem et lotio ac tersio nitorem. Iusta illa misericordia et misericors iusticia non miseretur quidem nisi in iusticia. Confessionem quum videt peccatorum, penitentiam, et satisfactionem, tum

---

*MS: in quo est nemo.

ing amends and offering satisfaction, rising up again to win the victory even after being vanquished. He must contend against evil, lay it low, and overcome it by good, in order that his amends of justice, whether in intention or in fact, may make satisfaction in goodness for his evil deeds. Thus as justice emerges[47] in him the God of justice will take him to himself. Catechumens must therefore be taught carefully what is the opposite quality to a given sin, and which virtue is the appropriate counterweight to a given vice.[48] In this way they may learn to lead a better life by returning good for evil and making amends for their sins by works of justice, that God's mercy may be invoked as well as his justice. As sins bring keen pleasure they must also cause grievous sorrow, trouble in the mind and affliction in the body, which like fire will cleanse away the stigma of sin and root it out so completely that it will not fester anew. During the period when a person is committed to the ministers for cleansing, to wash away the residue of his sins with tears—whether that person be catechumen, penitent, apostate, or a man possessed by the devil—notwithstanding that he is again in the church he is not so reckoned; nor is he of the hierarchy or the body of Christ, for no one can be in it who is not cleansed and perfect. From this it is obvious that no wicked Christians can be in the church, but that they must be cleansed while still without. Meanwhile, while they are still infected by the contagion of sin, they may not hear mass or lay eyes upon the sacraments, for their eyes are profane and unclean. They may hear instruction that would prepare them to change their life, such as chants and readings from Holy Scripture. But when the sacraments are being administered they must be driven off, for the base and unclean cannot receive the illumination needed to perceive the mysteries, which no one can know how rightly to look upon who is not illumined by faith and who cannot "see the light in the light of God" [Ps. 35:10]. It is by faith that the sacraments are seen and their mysteries understood; however, the eye of faith is closed by the flux of sin. But if we are to have faith we must be without sin, for faith is sullied and darkened by the mists and fumes of sin. As Paul says, "You are still in your sins" [1 Cor. 15:17]. Until one doffs the disgusting and detestable garment of sin and shame and burns it in the flames of repentance, and instead strips himself in order to receive the clean and lovely wedding garment, he must not partake of the heavenly banquet of the sacraments. Dionysius does not distinctly speak of this as a sacrament because it is rather preparing the way for the sacrament than the sacrament itself; just as one has to take off the old clothes before he can put on the new; has to be reconciled before friendship can be restored; has to care about having something before he can acquire it; has to have his disease cured before he can be healthy again; has to be washed and polished before he can again be shining. Just mercy and merciful justice will not show mercy save in justice. But when he sees

miseretur iuste et misericorditer iustificat. Et hoc quoque quotienscunque hanc iusticie voluntatem in nobis deprehendit confessionis, penitencie, et satisfactionis, [quanquam] fidefragi sumus et amicitia professa deficimus et a gradu stationis nostre miseri delabimur. Sed illa supra quam excogitare potest indulgens pietas dei (que non vult mortem peccatoris sed vt conuertatur et viuat) quotienscunque ex casu resurgimus pudore et dolore affecti quod turpe decidimus et correptis armis iterum bona spe in spiritalem hostem animositer irruimus dux nostre militie diuina illa pietas nostram industriam et voluntatem debellandi non recusat: quinimmo amplectitur, fouet, laudat, coronat. In hac milicia christiana necesse est pro natura belli vicissitudinaria* sit victoria: vt cadere non sit damnabile sed prostratum velle iacere. Statim si resurgas quanquam non es comparandus cum illis qui numquam ceciderint tamen quum nolis victus iacere miles non es inutilis. Non tam succenset tibi quod cecidisti quam gratam habet resurrectionem tuam. Peccare humanum est (ait Chrisostomus) iacere diabolicum. Rogante Petro, O Saluator, septiesne duntaxat peccanti ignosceret: respondit misericordia ipsa, immo septuagesiessepties. Et proposuit parabolam in qua docuit non ignotum ei fore qui non ignoscit. Quotiens ergo fidefragi sumus, quotiens vt canis reuersus ad vomitum, vt sus lota in volutabro luti, tametsi posteriora sunt peiora prioribus, tamen deus qui cognoscit figmentum nostrum, qui cognoscit quam homo pronus est ad malum ab adolescentia, quotiens diluere sordes et mundare nos volumus et ad fidem redire, non repudiat sed de centesima oue inuenta gaudet plus quam de nonagintanouem que non errauerunt et ecclesia mulier vxor dei cum vicinis gaudet magis de dragma inuenta quam de omnibus quam possidet, et pater ille de reuerso filio qui perdite dissipauit substantiam suam tamen dicenti, peccaui in celum coram te, iam non sum dignus vocari filius tuus: tantopere exultauit omnibus leticie signis exhibitis (stola, annulo, calciamentis, vitulo, vt magis non potuit) dicens, Hic filius meus mortuus erat et reuixit, perierat et inuentus est. Est saluatoris audienda et colenda sentencia quod gaudium erit coram angelis dei super vno peccatore penitentiam agente et se purgante vt videat

*MS: vicicitudinaria.

confession of sins, repentance, and satisfaction, then he will show mercy justly and mercifully justify. He does this every time that he perceives in us the desire for justice, for confession, repentance, and satisfaction; even though we break our faith and fail to live up to the friendship we have promised him and backslide miserably from the position we had promised to maintain. But in God's inconceivably indulgent goodness, which aims not at the death of the sinner but at his conversion and life, no matter how many times we rise after such a fall, overcome by shame and grief at having fallen so basely, and again with good hope seize arms with which boldly to charge our spiritual enemy, he who directs our endeavors and is divine goodness itself will not refuse his help to our effort and desire to give battle; on the contrary, he embraces, encourages, and praises us, and gives us the victory. It is inevitable because of the nature of the conflict, that in this Christian warfare victory will go now to one side and now to the other. What is damnable is not to fall but to remain down voluntarily. If one rises up again at once, even though he is not to be compared with those who never fell, still the fact that he will not lie down and accept defeat shows that he is a soldier not without value. For God will not so much be angry at your having fallen as rejoice at your getting up again. "To sin is the lot of man," says Chrysostom; "what is devil-like is to remain in the fallen state."[49] When Peter asked, "Savior, ought one to pardon the sinner as many as seven times?" Mercy himself answered, "No, but rather seventy times seven" [Matt. 18:21, 22]. And he propounded the parable in which he taught that he would not forgive anyone who was unforgiving. Therefore no matter how often we break our faith, no matter how often we "return like the dog to his vomit, or the washed sow to wallowing in the mud" [2 Pet. 2:22], and even if still worse things follow, nevertheless God, who "knows the way we have been fashioned" [Ps. 102:14], who knows how prone man is to evil from adolescence onward,[50] on every occasion when we wish to wash away our filth, to cleanse ourselves and return to the faith, does not disown us but rejoices more at the hundredth sheep who has been found than at the ninety-nine who were never lost [Luke 15:3ff.]; and the church, his wife, rejoices with her neighbors more in the drachma she has found than in all the rest of her possessions. So it was also with the father whose son returned after recklessly squandering his father's wealth but then said to him, "I have sinned against you before heaven; I am no longer worthy to be called your son" [Luke 16:2]. Yet the father greatly rejoiced and showed his happiness in every possible way (ceremonial robe,[51] ring, footwear, fatted calf— everything he could possibly do), saying, "This is my son who was dead and has come back to life, who was lost and has been found." We must hear and cherish the Savior's words, that "there will be rejoicing among the angels of God over one sinner who repents" [Luke 15:10] and

sacramenta dei vt alienatus reconcilietur deo. Cuius reconciliationis que fit confessione delicti, penitencia, et recompensatione, ecclesia sacramentum instituit vt quemadmodum ad veterem abolendam maculam statutum est sacramentum ita noua immaculatio* suum sacramentum habeat. Radio dei fiunt omnia, qui in sacramentis euadit sensibilis in corporum eciam purgationem.

Purgatio, illuminatio, et perfectio omnis est sacramenti effectus, et radius ille dei benignus nihil aliud agit nisi auocationem hinc et illuc in celum reuocationem, illuminationem nostri cum tenebrarum depulsione. In quo est hoc valde notandum nullius sacramenti esse ex proposito et intento depellere tenebras et sordes diluere, sed lumen infundere per se, quod necessario fuga tenebrarum comitatur. Hinc baptismus, quod sacramentum est aduenientis spiritus in hominem purgatum et regignentis deo, a Dionysio vocatur sacramentum illuminationis quia adest iam spiritus lucidus qui dicit, hic est filius meus dilectus in quo mihi bene complacui. In qua illustratione obscuritas omnis et macula discutitur. Aqua illa intinctionem gracie significat et obruitionem que nos absorbet in spiritum et facit vt secundum carnem in fide mortis christi moriamur, viuamus autem et sentiamus spiritu iam toti spiritales, regeniti spiritu sancto dei ideo baptisma illuminationis et regenerationis vocatur. Infantes baptizati nubeculam originalis iniusticie aduentu luminis habent propulsam, modo que sequutura est vita sacramento responderit.

Adulti autem vt illuminentur, que ipsi scientes commiserint peccata et agnoscunt et confitentur et dolent et satisfaciunt. Item qui recasu in tenebras lumen extinxerunt, his non solum fides sed voluntaria confessio, meror, et recompensatio est necessaria. Hic oportet sit spontanea relictio peccatorum. Volunt autem quos deus vult in cuius bona voluntate volunt. Ille operatur in nobis et velle et perficere. Quos deus vult agnoscere et abrenunciare peccata ii abrenunciant in deo. Et quos deus soluit, relaxat, et dimittit, ii se soluunt et relaxant, in deo et confitentes ac odientes peccatorum vincula, erumpunt et exeunt in deo. Huius diuine solutionis, liberationis, et remissionis sacerdotum ministerio oportet sit sacramentum et signum aliquod venerabile misericordis voluntatis dei qui immittit in hominem uoluntatem soluendi et agnoscendi et abiiciendi peccata. Veruntamen quanquam in deo vult esse liber, tamen res non conficitur nisi medio sacramento ministrato a ministris dei, quod testis efficax simul

*MS: immaculatione.

cleanses himself so that he can look upon the sacraments of God and, no longer an outcast, be reconciled with God. This reconciliation, which is effected by confession of sins, repentance, and making amends, has been instituted by the church as a sacrament;[52] thus, just as a sacrament was instituted to wipe away the stain of original sin, so the restoration of sinlessness was to have its sacrament too.[53] All things are brought about by the ray of God, which becomes visible in the sacraments, in order that bodies too may be cleansed.

Cleansing, illumining, and perfecting are the consequence of every sacrament, and God's loving ray works precisely to call us away from this world and call us back to heaven, to illumine us by driving away the darkness. In this connection we should specially note that there is no sacrament whose express purpose and intent is to dispel the darkness and wash away stains; the fundamental purpose of the sacraments is to infuse light, which necessarily results in banishing the darkness. Hence baptism, which is the sacrament of the coming of the Spirit into cleansed man and his rebirth to God, is called by Dionysius the sacrament of illumining, for the spirit of light is now present, who says, "This is my beloved son, in whom I am well pleased" [Matt. 3:17; 17:5]. In this brightness all obscurity and uncleanness disappear. The water signifies being plunged into grace, an immersion that absorbs us into the spirit and causes us to die to the flesh in the faith of Christ's death but to live and breathe in the spirit, being now entirely spiritual and reborn in the holy spirit of God; which is why baptism is called the sacrament of illumination and regeneration. Baptized infants have the cloud of original sin dispelled by the coming of the light, provided that their subsequent life is in keeping with the sacrament.[54]

But for adults to be illumined they must confess and acknowledge the sins they have knowingly committed, repent of them, and make amends. Similarly those who by relapsing into darkness have extinguished the light must not only have faith but must freely confess, feel grief, and make amends. They must leave their sins voluntarily and instead will what God wills, in whose good pleasure is their will. He it is who brings us both to will and to accomplish. Those who God wills should acknowledge and renounce their sins, do renounce them in God. Those whom God frees, forgives, and dismisses free themselves and are forgiven in God; confessing and detesting the shackles of sin, they break loose and go forth in God. It is fitting that there should be a sacrament for this divine release, liberation, and remission through the ministry of priests, as a kind of adorable sign of God's merciful will that makes men desire to be free and to confess and cast off their sins. And yet, even though men wish to be free in God, this cannot be accomplished except by means of the sacrament administered by God's ministers, as efficacious witness of both God's and

et diuine et humane voluntatis remittendi. Hinc sacramentorum sacramenta, racio ipsa sacramentificans deushomo ille noster Iesus christus qui iecuit sacramenta inter deum et homines testes et federa coeuntium voluntatum, qui remisit ipse et relaxauit peccatorum vincula, eciam remissionis peccatorum et reconciliationis hominum sibi quos vult deus reconciliari, instituit sacramentum voluitque diuinam voluntatem in homine et humanam voluntatem in deo oportuna racione consignari. Itaque post resurrectionem suam (vt testatur Ioannes) mittens discipulos suos legatos insufflauit et dixit eis, Accipite spiritum sanctum cuius sacramentum erat flatus ille. Et addidit, Quorum remiseritis peccata peccata remittuntur eis et quorum retinueritis retenta sunt. Retinentur vero que non remittuntur, non remittuntur que non remittit homo ille qui est in vinculis peccatorum agnoscens et confitens peccata sua. Que vero ille agnoscit et confitetur audiens sacerdos, medius inter deum et hominem qui intelligit ex voluntate dei hominis illius voluntatem se soluere, quot soluta et confessa peccata audit illam solutionem contestatur et hominis voluntatem in deo et dei voluntatem in homine et remissionem peccatorum sacerdotali officio tum signis tum verbis comprobat. Que autem non remittit ille peccator nec confitetur, illa sacerdos non remittit. Hoc certissimum est, omnis remissio primum est a deo cuius solius est peccata remittere qui monet hominem vt se soluat a peccatis, qui vult vt intercedente sacerdote humiliatione, confessione, impositione manuum, inuocatione sancte trinitatis, sacris christi verbis recitatis—videlicet, remittuntur tibi peccata tua— mysterium diuine voluntatis testificetur vt inter deum et hominem qui respondet diuine voluntati, sacramenti testimonium extet. Hoc sacramentum reconciliationis et remissionis non inepte vocari potest qua homo benigna dei gratia reconciliatur deo, quod recentior ecclesia vocat penitencie sacramentum. In quo vides ex istis verbis quidnam racionis habet quod inter deum et hominem se soluentem in deo a peccatis, intermedius est sacerdos et audiens et remissionem auditorum a deo contestans: et quid sit illud, quorum remiseritis peccata remittuntur, quorum retinueritis retinentur. Que non soluit ipse homo retenta sunt et sacerdos contestatur retenta esse quia ea remissa esse non contestatur. Vult in terris deus testificationem eorum que in celis fiunt ab ipso erga homines quod sacerdotali munere exhibetur.

man's desire for the remission.[55] Hence he who is the sacrament of sacraments, the sacramental principle himself, our God-Man[56] Jesus Christ, who set the sacraments between God and man as witness and covenant of the harmony of their wills, he who himself forgave and remitted the bonds of sin and instituted the sacrament of the forgiveness of sins and the reconciliation to himself of those whom he willed to be reconciled—he, then, willed that the divine will in man and the human will in God should be symbolized in a suitable way. Accordingly, after his resurrection, as John testifies, he sent his disciples as his ambassadors. "He breathed on them and said to them, 'Receive the Holy Spirit,' " of whom his breathing was the sign. And he continued, "Whose sins you shall forgive they are forgiven them, and whose sins you shall retain they are retained" [John 20:22–23]. The sins that are not forgiven are retained, and they are not forgiven because the sinner himself, who is in the toils of sin, does not forgive them by acknowledging and confessing them. The sins that are forgiven are the sins that the sinner acknowledges and confesses to a listening priest, who is God's intermediary and knows that the man's own will frees itself through God's will. The priest bears witness to the forgiveness of whatever sins he hears confessed and confers absolution; and in his priestly role he confirms, by both words and signs, man's will in God and God's will in man, and the forgiveness of the sins. But whatever sins the sinner does not forgive by confessing them, the priest does not forgive either. Thus it is most certain that all forgiveness comes from God, who alone can forgive sins; for it is he who exhorts man to free himself from sin. God wills that the mystery of the divine will be testified to by the intercession of the priest, and by means of the submission, confession, laying on of hands, invocation of the holy Trinity, and recitation of Christ's words "Your sins are forgiven you"; and that the witness of the sacrament should be plain as between God and the person who obeys his will. That sacrament by which through God's gracious favor man is reconciled to God is not unfittingly called the sacrament of reconciliation and forgiveness; in more recent times the church calls it the sacrament of penance. From what has been said one can see that it is logical for the priest to be the intermediary between God and the man who frees himself from sin in God, and that the priest should listen and bear witness to God's forgiveness of the sins he has heard; and it has now also been shown what those words mean, "Whose sins you shall forgive they are forgiven them, and whose sins you shall retain they are retained." The sins that the person himself does not forgive are retained, and the priest bears witness to their retention by not bearing witness that they have been forgiven. God wills that what he does in heaven regarding human beings should be testified to on earth; and this witness is borne by the priestly office.

$$\left\{\begin{array}{l}\text{Deus: remittens vincula peccatorum.}\\\text{Sacerdos: medius, sacramento confirmans.}\\\text{Homines: se soluentes in deo.}\end{array}\right.$$

Quecunque alligauerint et soluerint saltem ministri fideles in deo qui intelligunt quid deus agit in hominibus, ea ligantur et soluuntur in celis. Qui (vt docet Corinthios paulus) apostoli, sacerdotes, et spiritalior ecclesie pars ministri duntaxat sunt christi et dispensatores ministeriorum dei in quibus requiritur fidelitas maxima; alioquin quod agunt non confit in celis. Audire confessionem debet sacerdos et sentire penitudinem que est tam necessaria vt ab ea reconciliationis sacramentum cognomen habeat.* In Euangelio Luce iubet Saluator: remittatur peccatori quotiescunque modo penitet. Verba illius hec sunt, Si peccauerit in te frater tuus increpa illum, et si penitentiam egerit dimitte illi. Et si septies in die peccauerit in te et septies in die conuersus fuerit ad te dicens, Penitet me: dimitte illi. De confessione spiritus Isaie ait, Dic tu iniquitates tuas vt iustificeris. Recompensatio in contrario semper debet esse vt pro malo satisfactio fiat in bono et vt contrarium contrarium vincat. Auaritia redimenda est liberalitate et elemosina, Luxuria et crapula continentia et Ieiunio. Negligentia dei, oratione assidua vt iniusticia tua deus misereatur tui. Item pro voluntate, in omnibus in corpore dolor ferendus est, vt dolor et cruciatus carnis delectationem eradicet, quem dolorem vocat Paulus compassionem. Si tamen compatimur (inquit) vt glorificemur, Non sunt condigne passiones ad futuram gloriam. Omnia hec ad sacramentum reconciliationis pertinent vt redeamus in graciam et in ecclesiam introeamus simusque in ea aliquod membrum sanctum christi in sanctificato corpore suo et iam illuminato baptismo,† quod lumen sacramento remissionis recuperamus, quod est lumen fidei vt conspectis sacris dei eis credamus et viuamus pro racione sacrorum.

VII

Baptismus autem (vt tradit Dionysius[)] datus a sacerdotibus et illuminat purgatos et fidem dat, hoc est fidem a deo infusam consignat. Confirmatio vero testatur spiritus sancti firmam dationem. Hoc sacramentum potest vocari donorum spiritus sancti. Nam est sacramentum donationis spiritus

---

*MS: habet.
†MS: baptismato.

$\left\{\begin{array}{l} \text{God: undoes the shackles of sin.} \\ \text{Priest: as intermediary confirms the sacrament.} \\ \text{Human beings: forgive themselves in God.}^{57} \end{array}\right.$

Whatever is bound or loosed by those who are, at the minimum, faithful ministers in God[58] and understand what God is effecting in man, is bound or loosed also in heaven. As Paul taught the Corinthians, these apostles, priests, and more spiritual members of the church are no less than "ministers of Christ and dispensers of the ministry of God" [1 Cor. 4:1]. In them the highest faithfulness is required; otherwise what they do is not ratified in heaven. A priest ought to hear one's confession and ascertain that one is penitent, a condition that is so necessary that the sacrament of reconciliation takes therefrom its very name. In the Gospel of Luke the Savior commands that the sinner be forgiven as often as he repents. His words are these: "If your brother sins against you, rebuke him; and if he repents, forgive him. And if he sins against you seven times a day and seven times a day turns to you and says, I am sorry, forgive him" [Luke 18:3–4]. Concerning the confession of the spirit Isaiah says, "Tell me the wrongs you have done, that you may be justified" [Isa. 43:26].[59] Nevertheless, amends must always be made, so that satisfaction for the evil that has been done is made through good, and the good eliminates its opposite. Avarice can be redeemed by liberality and almsgiving, lust and drunkenness by continence and abstemiousness, and neglect of God by assiduous prayer that God will forgive unrighteousness. Similarly, instead of pleasure one should endure bodily pain in all things, so that delight may be rooted out by the torment of the flesh and by the great sorrow that Paul calls fellow suffering. "If we suffer with him," he says, "we shall be glorified with him." "These fellow sufferings are not worthy to be compared with the glory that is to come" [Rom. 8:17–18]. All this has to do with the sacrament of reconciliation, by which we return to grace and enter the church and are made members of Christ in the church, his sanctified body now illumined by baptism. We recover this light, which is the light of faith, through the sacrament of forgiveness, that having looked upon the sacred mysteries of God we may believe in them and live according to them.

VII

Now, we read in Dionysius that baptism is administered by priests and gives faith and light to those who have been cleansed; that is, it testifies to the infusion of faith by God. Confirmation testifies to the abiding conferral of the Holy Spirit and may be called the sacrament of the gifts of

inde tractum et institutum, quod Samarie baptizatis erat postea ab apostolis missus qui eis impositis manibus daret spiritum sanctum: alioquin in ecclesia non censerentur. Sacramentum communionis in communi pabulo carnis et sanguinis quod sacramentum coniuncti et vnitatis est: confirmatorum et spiritificatorum est in christo in summa vnitate coaltio et connutritio. Vocamur enim vt purgemur, illuminemur, perficiamur spiritu, connutriamur, conuiuamus, compugnemus, conuincamus, conglorificemur. Hec vis charitatis spiritalium hominum. Postremo extrema vnctio (que quondam fiebat eciam cadaueribus, nunc autem in extrema vita quatenus coniectura suspicari possumus) sacramentum est perfuncti laboris ac militie et purgationis affliciti corporis, et affert in egritudine presentiam et consolationem spiritus sancti, de qua Iacobus loquutus est hisce verbis: Tristatur aliquis vestrum, oret; equo animo est, psallat. Infirmatur quis in vobis, inducat presbiteros ecclesie et orent super eum vngentes eum oleo in nomine domini. Crebra est vnctio in ecclesia, que est crebra admonitio frequentis spiritus sanc[ti] cuius aduentum, operationem, effectum sacramenta denotant credentibus, in eorum salutem sempiternam.

the Holy Spirit. For the sacrament of the conferring of the Holy Spirit is taken from and based upon the fact that at Samaria the Apostles sent, subsequently to the people's baptism, a representative empowered to lay hands upon them and thereby confer on them the Holy Spirit; otherwise they would not have been considered to belong to the church. The sacrament of communion, the sacrament of unity and oneness in the shared food of flesh and blood, is the common sustenance and nourishment of those who are confirmed and spiritualized in the most intimate unity in Christ. For we are called to be cleansed, illumined, and perfected in the spirit, to be nourished together, live together, contend together, conquer together, be glorified together. Such is the power of love in spiritual man. Finally, extreme unction (which formerly used to be conferred even on corpses[60] but is now conferred at the close of life, insofar as that can be conjecturally determined) is the sacrament of work accomplished, and of the service and the cleansing of the afflicted body; in the midst of sickness it brings the presence and consolation of the Holy Spirit. James speaks of it in these words: "Does one of you grieve? Let him pray. Is he cheerful? Let him sing. Is anyone sick among you? Let him summon the elders of the church to pray over him, anointing him with oil in the name of the Lord" [James 5:13–14]. Anointing is a frequent practice in the church, for it is a constant reminder of the presence of the Holy Spirit, whose advent, operation, and effect the sacraments signify to whose who believe, unto their eternal salvation.[61]

Appendix 2
List of Writers
Referred to by Colet

The following list gathers Colet's certain or probable references to authors other than the biblical writers, pseudo-Dionysius Areopagita and Marsilio Ficino.

1. *Acts of John* (in *The Apocryphal New Testament*, trans. M.R. James [Oxford: Clarendon, 1950] secs. 96, 97). DCH, 170; DEH, 199.

   Marjorie O'Boyle, *Erasmus on Language and Method in Theology* (Toronto: Univ. of Toronto Press, 1978), 110, finds that Colet is apparently the only other writer of Erasmus's time who makes use of the conception of Christ as choreographer found in the apocryphal *Acts of John*.

2. Anselm of Canterbury, St. *Proslogion* 1. FEM, 107.

   At the foot of a page in his copy of Ficino's *Epistolae* Colet wrote, "credas ut intelligas," an evident echo of Anselm's famous maxim "Credo ut intelligam."

3. [pseudo-]Aristeas, "Letter of Aristeas to Philocrates." R, 177.

   Lupton is entirely silent about the nature of his work. It purports to have been written by a Greek at the court of Ptolemy Philadelphus (287–246 B.C.); the actual date of composition is put by the most recent editor around 100 B.C. (André Pelletier, S.J., ed., *Lettre d'Aristée à Philocrate* [Paris: Ed. du Cerf, 1962], 58). Although it is best known for its account of the origins of the Septuagint, the "Letter" has another main topic, the one that interested Colet: a thoroughgoing allegorical interpretation of the prescriptions in the Old Testament regarding unclean animals. These allegories are sampled with much gusto by Frederic W. Farrar, *History of Interpretation* (London, 1886), 128 n. 4.

4. Augustine, St.
   a. *Contra Gaudentium* II.2.3–4.4 (in *CSEL* 53:256–259). C, 179 [104] (not previously identified as a quotation).
   b. *Tractatus in Johannem* IV.3 (in *CC*, Ser. Lat. 36:32). C, 204 [154] (not previously identified as a quotation).
   c. *Enarrationes in Psalmos* CIV.12 (in *CC*, Ser. Lat., 40:1543). R, 160.

      The passage cited by Lupton from Augustine's *Opus imperfectum contra Julianum* (R, p. 36 n. 1) expresses a different thought and is not the passage Colet refers to, as the wording shows. Colet: "deus . . . malis nostris, ut ab Aurelio Augustino praeclare est dictum, bene utitur, sicuti nos suis bonis male." Augustine, *in Ps*. CIV.12: "quomodo deus utatur bene malis operibus hominum, sicut illi contra male utuntur bonis operibus dei." Augustine, *contra Julianum*: "Deus vero tam bonus est ut malis quoque utatur bene; quae Omnipotens non sineret si eis bene uti summa sua bonitate non posset." For a parallel to R, 160, see DCH, 196.
   d. *Sermo XXIX ex ineditis* (cf. David Lenfant, *Concordantiae Augustinianae*, 2 vols. [1656–1665; reprint, Brussels: Culture et civilisation, 1982], vol. 2, Sig. Ddd 1). R, 180.

      Lupton's suggestion that Colet "seems to be referring" to Augustine, *Confessions* 13, chapters 7–9, is in error; Colet quotes the cited passage from *Sermo XXIX* almost word for word. Because Lupton did not follow Colet's thought at this point, his translation is also in error.
   e. *Tractatus in Johannem* XL, or perhaps LXXIX. RO, 230.

      Colet credits the thought to "St. Augustine," but it is very general: "Faith is the virtue by which things that are not seen, are believed." The sample texts above are suggested by Lupton, but others would do equally well.
   f. *Sermo CCCLV, de vita et moribus clericorum* 5 (in PL, vol. 39, col. 1572). RO, 245.

      Atypically, Colet himself gives the reference. He also notes that the passage is cited in Gratian (see below in this list).
   g. *De gratia et de libero arbitrio* 7 (in PL, vol. 44, col. 886), RO, 253.

      Lupton's suggested sources, *Ps. 70, Serm. 2* and *Ps. 102*, are less probable because the passages belong to a different context from Colet's, which is similar to that of *De gratia*.
   h. *De civitate Dei*. Probable general references in "civitatem dei in Christo Jesu" (CM, 189) and "nova dei civitas et celestis" (R, 176).

5. Baptista Mantuanus. Cited by Colet (as "Joannes carmelitanus") in R, 158, for Latin equivalents of the Greek *anathematizo*. Like Lupton before me, I have been unable to verify the reference.

6. Chrysostom, John, St.
   a. *De laudibus Pauli*, Homilia VII. R, 224.
      See p. 130 above.
   b. *Homilia XXVI in Matthaeum* 325b. S, 324.
      See above, p. 191.

7. Cicero.
   a. *De oratore* 2.36.2. Letter from Colet to Christopher Urswick, ca. 1492 (Wallace K. Ferguson, "An Unpublished Letter of John Colet, Dean of St. Paul's," *American Historical Review* 39 [1934]: 699).
   b. *De officiis* I.7. RO, 230, 261.
   c. *De natura deorum* II.15. G, 176; C, 251 [246].
      Source identified by Lupton (C, p. 18 n. 1).
   d. *Epp. ad Familiares* VI.vi.5. A, ll. 559–560.

8. [pseudo-]Clement I, Pope. *Recognitiones* I.7 (trans. Thomas Smith, in *The Ante-Nicene Library*, vol. 8 [New York: Scribner's, 1906], 73–212). R, 223.
   See p. 127 above.

9. Council of Chalcedon (451 A.D.). OCC, 247.
   Sacrorum conciliorum nova et amplissima collectio, ed. Giovanni Domenico Mansi, 31 vols. (Florence and Venice, 1759–1798), 6:1226.

—. Democritus. See note at end of this list.

10. Durand, Guillaume. *Rationale divinorum officiorum*. Alluded to in DEH, 203.

11. Erasmus, Desiderius.
    a. *Adagia* 370, "Actum agere." C, 183 [114], in the form "agere actum."
       Regarded by Lupton as a quotation from Erasmus, but perhaps merely a commonplace.
    b. *Novum instrumentum*. The borrowings by Colet in Trinity College, Cambridge, MS. o.4.44, first noticed by Seebohm though denied by him to Colet, are collected by Lupton in R, p. 230.

12. Gratian. *Decretum*, Pars II, cap. 17, q. ult. RO, 245.
    Passage cited by Colet, containing reference to item 4.f above.

—. Heraclitus. See note at end of this list.

13. Ignatius Martyr, St.
    a. *Letter to the Magnesians*. DEH, 207.

Though Colet cites the letter by author and title, Lupton rightly observes that what he gives is a paraphrase rather than a quotation.

b. *Letter to the Romans.* DEH, 257.

Lupton observes (DEH, p. 139 n. 1) that Colet gives the passage the same twist, seemingly not intended by Ignatius, as pseudo-Dionysius gives it in *De divinis nominibus* IV.12 (in *Oeuvres complètes du pseudo-Denys l'Aréopagite*, ed. and trans. Maurice de Gandillac [Paris: Aubier, 1943], 106), and he thinks Colet may have taken it at second hand from Dionysius.

14. [pseudo-]Ivo, Bishop of Chartres. R, 224.

Cited, as Lupton notes (R, p. 127 n. 2), as the author of a manuscript chronicle history of France which in reality was written by Hugo Floriacensis.

15. Jerome, St.

a. *Epistolae*, to Algasia. R, 158.

b. *Adversus Jovinianum* I.49. C, 224 [190].

Cited in a marginal note, of uncertain authorship, in Cambridge University Library MS. Gg.iv.26; the thought of Colet is similar to that in Jerome, but there are no verbal parallels.

c. *Comm. in Epistolam ad Ephesios libri tres* (in PL, vol. 26, col. 569). S, 288.

16. Lactantius. *Divinae institutiones* II.9. RO, 256.

17. Leo the Great, Pope, St. *Homiliae* LXXIX.1. DEH, 197.

18. Macrobius. *In Somnium Scipionis* I.2. G, 182.

19. Origen.

a. *Comm. in Epistolam ad Romanos* III (in PG, vol. 14, col. 928). RO, 232; R, 138; DEH, 236–238.   This passage is part of a long unacknowledged quotation, first noted by Lupton, from Pico della Mirandola, *Oration* (in *The Renaissance Philosophy of Man*, ed. Ernst Cassirer [Chicago: Univ. of Chicago Press, 1948], 250–252).

b. *Comm. in Epistolam ad Romanos* I (in PG, vol. 14, cols. 861–863). RO, 203.

c. *Comm. in Epistolam ad Romanos* IV (in PG, vol. 14, col. 979). RO, 268.

d. *Comm. in Epistolam ad Romanos* VII (in PG, vol. 14, cols. 1155–1156). R, 172.

e. *Comm. in Epistolam ad Romanos* VIII 14, col. 1197). R, 172.

f. *Comm. in Joannem* II (in PG, vol. 14, col. 146). G, 171.

g. *Comm. in Joannem* VI (in PG, vol. 14, cols. 290–291). RO, 250.

20. Ovid.
    a. *Metamorphoses* VII.20–21. C, 196 [140].
    The allusion to Ovid's familiar tag "video meliora proboque, / Deteriora sequor" is implied by Colet in the opposition "ut quam maxime possint sequantur meliora, deteriora quam maxime fugiant." Cf. S, 278: "reditus a deteriori ad id quod melius est."
    b. *Metamorphoses* XIV.445 (noted by Lupton). R, 146.

21. Perotti, Niccolò. *Cornucopiae* (enlarged ed. [Venice, 1499]).
    From this widely used reference work Colet took definitions and etymologies of several words, including *prevaricator* (RO, 222; Colet's spelling: *privaricator*), *abolere* (RO, 266), and *testamentum* (RO, 243). To the above, all noted by Lupton, may be added the derivation of *mentula*, "penis" from *mens*, "mind" (RO, 224), which Lupton probably also noticed but decided not to record. Constance Blackwell, "Niccolò Perotti in England—Part I: John Anwykyll, Bernard André, John Colet and Luis Vives," *Res publica litterarum* 5 (1982): 20–21, draws attention to Colet's use of Perotti's entry *fides* (RO, 261). Jayne points out that Colet owes his etymology of *palinodia* to Perotti (FEM, 114).

22. Philo Judaeus. *Quod mundus sit incorruptibilis.* G, 168.
    Referred to by title only.

23. Piccolomini, Aeneas Sylvius (later Pope Pius II). *Historia Bohemica.*
    See the discussion of this work on pp. 53–57 above.

24. Pico della Mirandola.
    a. *Heptaplus* 1. C, 257 [258].
    b. *Heptaplus* 4. R, 185–186.
    c. *Apologia.* R, 138 (sidenote).
    d. *Hexaemeron*, "Praefatio ad lectorem." G, 170–171.
    e. *Oratio* (see item 19.a above). DEH, 236–238.

25. Plato. *Timaeus* 30D. R, 186.

26. Plotinus. *Enneas* 1.1. R, 146.

27. Polycarp of Smyrna, St. *Epistola ad Philippienses.* DEH, 204–205.
    Something is wrong with the reference, which is given by Colet; like Lupton, I have been unable to verify it.

28. Suetonius.
    a. *Vita Claudii* 15. R, 201.
    b. *Vita Claudii* 40. R, 201.

29. Terence. *Heautontimorumenos* 77. P, 295.
    Colet's sentence "Nihil quod fratris est, alienum a se esse putet" alludes unmistakably to the well-known line in Terence "Humani

nil a me alienum puto"; but the Terentian line is so familiar out of context that quoting it need not be taken as proving familiarity with the play.

30. Thomas Aquinas, St. *Summa theologiae* 1ª1ᵃᵉ, q. 75, a. 5 et passim. Not recognizing the principle "Quicquid recipitur, recipitur per modum recipientis" as a maxim of Scholastic philosophy, Lupton looked for it in vain in Augustine (C, p. 13 n. 1); but O'Kelly and Jarrott correctly identify it (C, 295 n. 28). Colet quotes the maxim, with slight variations in the wording, four times: R, 150, 164; C, 167 [80], 178 [100].

31. Varro. Letter to Urswick (see item 7.a above).
Colet attributes to Varro the sentiment that history is "ministra leticie" ("a bringer of joy"). I have not succeeded in verifying this statement. If it was made by Varro, a learned and prolific scholar but no stylist, it was uncharacteristic of him and of his time. Even when Pliny the Younger, born almost 175 years after Varro, writes that "historia quoquo modo delectat" ("history is in every way delightful"; Ep. v.8), his editor remarks that this is "an unusual attitude towards written history in antiquity" (A. N. Sherwin-White, *The Letters of Pliny: A Historical and Social Commentary* [Oxford: Clarendon, 1966], 333) and cites no parallels.

32. Vergil.
   a. *Eclogae* 2.68. R, 204.
   b. *Aeneis* 1.26 (but misquoted in a form that does not scan). RO, 204.
   This verse is also quoted (correctly) by Ficino in the passage in his *Epistolae* (Ficino, "De raptu Pauli," in *Prosatori latini del quattrocento*, ed. Eugenio Garin [Milan and Naples: Ricciardi, 1952], 936) where Colet's annotations are heaviest.

Note: At C, 248 [238], Colet says, "I know not whether to laugh with Democritus or to weep with Heraclitus when I see . . ." (similar wording but without mention of the names, DEH, 246–247). However, the pairing of the laughing and the weeping philosopher, already established in Juvenal x.28–52 (Cora E. Lutz, "Democritus and Heraclitus," *Classical Journal* 49 [1954]: 309–314), was a commonplace and need not imply a reference to their writings; see R. H. Bowers, "Democritus and Heraclitus in Elizabethan Literature," *Southern Folklore Quarterly* 22 (1958): 139–143. Jayne (31 n. 4) remarks in another context that the paired names appear several times in Ficino's *Epistolae*.

Notes

Chapter 1.
A Case of Mistaken Identity

1. Thomas Harding, *A Reioindre to M. Jewels Replie* (Antwerp, 1566), 44ᵛ.

2. Erasmus to John Fisher, 17 October 1519, in Allen, 4:94, Ep. 1030. (For Allen, see Abbreviations at the front of this volume. Citation of the letter numbers permits cross-reference to the recently published French and English translations of the correspondence.) Unless otherwise indicated, all translations from Allen in the text are mine.

3. Circumstantial evidence inclines the leading authority on Vitrier to think he died "toward 1516" (Godin, *Vies*, 103–104; see Abbreviations at the front of this volume).

4. Some of Erasmus's efforts to keep Jonas from embracing Luther's position are described in Martin Lehmann, *Justus Jonas, Loyal Reformer* (Minneapolis: Augsburg, 1963), 17–35, but the letter on Vitrier and Colet is not mentioned. In any case it made no decisive impression on the addressee, for Colet's name does not appear in the index to Jonas's published correspondence: *Der Briefwechsel des Justus Jonas*, ed. D. Gustav Kawerau, 2 vols. (Halle, 1884–1885).

5. H. A. Enno van Gelder, in *The Two Reformations in the 16th Century* (The Hague: Nijhoff, 1961), 185, notes that during the crucial first generation of the Reformation in England, no one is known to have called himself a follower of Colet. Carl S. Meyer, in "John Colet's Significance for the English Reformation," *Concordia Theological Monthly* 34 (1963): 410–418, similarly denies Colet any influence on the Reformation; but he goes much too far in the opposite direction in finding Colet "a precursor of the Counter-Reformation" (417).

6. William Tyndale, *Answere vnto Sir Thomas Mores Dialoge*, ed. H. Walter (Cambridge, 1850), 168.

7. Hugh Latimer, "Seventh Sermon on the Lord's Prayer," in his *Sermons*, ed. G. E. Corrie, 2 vols. (Cambridge, 1844–1845), 1:440.

8. John Bale, *Illustrium majoris Britanniae scriptorum . . . summarium* (Ipswich, 1548), qtd. in Knight, 225, note k (for Knight, see Abbreviations at the front of this volume). Knight reports that the detail about the king's intervention was added in Bale's enlarged edition (Basel, 1557–1559).

9. Henry de Vocht, *Earliest English Translations of Erasmus' Colloquies 1536–1566* (Louvain: Librairie universitaire, 1928), xlix–lii. Even at this early date—not long after 2 July 1533—the translator, upon being reminded of Colet through the dialogue (Erasmus, *Peregrinatio religionis ergo*), felt it necessary to assure his potential patron that Colet "hathe ben longe a way, yet his gostly searveces be nat so clene worne a way or exiled, thorow oblivion, owte off menes brestes, but that yff thei now see hime, thei will knoliage theire kinsman, theire frende, theire ffather in god and for old acquantaunce receve hyme lovingli" (British Library Harleian MS. 6989, fol. 45^{r-v}, qtd. in Donald W. Rude, "On the Date of Sir Thomas Elyot's *The Education or bringinge vp of children,*" *Papers of the Bibliographical Society of America* 71 [1977]: 63–64).

10. John Foxe, *Acts and Monuments*, ed. Josiah Pratt, 8 vols. (London [1877]), 4:230–235.

11. Henry Wharton, *Historia de episcopis et decanis Londinensibus* (London, 1695), 233–237.

12. *The Phenix*, 2 vols. (London, 1707–1708), 2:1–12.

13. White Kennett, notes for a biography of John Colet, British Library Lansdowne MS. 1030, fol. 2.

14. G. V. Bennett, *White Kennett 1660–1728, Bishop of Peterborough* (London: S.P.C.K., 1957), 174.

15. Bruce Mansfield, *Phoenix of His Age: Interpretations of Erasmus c1550–1750* (Toronto: Univ. of Toronto Press, 1979), 269.

16. Mansfield, 271.

17. Mansfield, 272.

18. As noted also by Lupton, *Life*, 204 n. 1 (see Abbreviations at the front of this volume).

19. Knight [iii].

20. In the long versified list of English humanists by John Leland, first published in 1589 but written before 1549 (possibly as much as twenty or twenty-five years before), Colet is simply one of eight "lights of learning" ("lumina doctrinae") who followed Grocyn to Italy and returned with "treasures." Leland was apparently a pupil in St. Paul's School in 1520 or a little earlier and would be aware of the traditions concerning Colet. See Hoyt H. Hudson, "John Leland's List of Early English Humanists," *Huntington Library Quarterly* 2 (1939): 301–304.

21. See Christopher Wolle's preface to the anonymous German translation of Knight's *Life* (Leipzig, 1735) [13], in which Colet's claims to distinction are set forth. In effect, they are his friendship with Erasmus and his contribution to "laying the first foundation stone for the Reformation in England."

22. *Lords Journal* 1:86, qtd. in Joel Hurstfield, *Freedom, Corruption and Government in Elizabethan England* (Cambridge: Harvard Univ. Press, 1973), 45.

23. Brooks Adams, *The Law of Civilization and Decay*, 2d ed. (New York, 1896), 268.

24. F. M. Powicke, "The Reformation in England," in *European Civilization: Its Origin and Development*, vol. 4, ed. Edward Eyre (Oxford: Oxford Univ. Press, 1936), 353. The furore caused by this sentence caused Powicke to tone it down somewhat upon separate publication of his study (*The Reformation in England* [London: Oxford Univ. Press, 1941]); here the "one definite thing" is "that it was an act of state" (p. 1).

25. J. Lewis May, *The Oxford Movement* (London: Bodley Head, 1933), 286.

26. Herbert Hensley Henson, in *The Church of England* (Cambridge: Cambridge Univ. Press, 1939), while calling the church "reformed," adds that it "refuses fellowship with all other reformed churches" (p. 1).

27. This is the title of the definitive third edition (1887; reprint, London, 1896). In the first edition the title ran: *The Oxford Reformers of 1498: A History of the Fellow-Work of John Colet, Erasmus, and Thomas More* (London, 1867).

28. J. A. F. Thomson, *The Later Lollards 1414–1520* (Oxford: Oxford Univ. Press, 1965), 162.

29. "John Colet, Dean of St. Paul's," *American Church Quarterly Review* 21 (1869): 202.

30. Qtd. in J. H. Lupton, editor's foreword to *Opuscula*, x (see CM in Abbreviations at the front of this volume).

31. Robert L. Schuyler, "John Richard Green and His *Short History*," *Political Science Quarterly* 64 (1949): 350.

32. Frederic Seebohm, *The Spirit of Christianity: An Essay on the Christian Hypothesis* (1876; reprint, London: Longmans, Green, 1916); the book (which was privately printed in 1876) expresses "the current of his thought between the years 1866 and 1876" (viii).

33. Seebohm, *Spirit of Christianity*, 142.

34. Seebohm, *Spirit of Christianity*, 132.

35. Seebohm, *Spirit of Christianity*, 167.

36. Hugh E. Seebohm, preface to *Oxford Reformers*, Everyman's Library ed. (London: Dent, 1914), vii, viii; this edition omits most of the annotation.

37. See H. D. A. Major, *English Modernism: Its Origin, Methods, Aims* (Cambridge: Harvard Univ. Press, 1927), chap. 3 "English Modernism and Its Immediate Predecessors," esp. 37.

38. Alan M. G. Stephenson, *The Rise and Decline of English Modernism* (London, S.P.C.K., 1984), 24–25.

39. *Church Gazette* (14 Oct. 1899), 715; qtd. in Stephenson, 61.

40. J. C. Hardwick, "John Colet," *The Modern Churchman* 15 (1925): 184.

41. Michael Glazebrook, "The Second Reformation," *The Modern Churchman*, July 1914; qtd. in Stephenson, 103.

42. Auguste Humbert, *Les origines de la théologie moderne: I. La renaissance chrétienne (1450–1521)* (Paris: Gabalda, 1911), 212.

43. *Acta Apostolicae Sedis* 3 (1911): 278.

44. *Acta Apostolicae Sedis* 4 (1912): 57.

45. Sir Paul Vinogradoff, "Obituary.—Frederick Seebohm (1833–1912)," in Vinogradoff, *Collected Papers*, 2 vols. (Oxford: Clarendon, 1928), 1: 273–274.

46. Stephenson, 296.

47. Stephenson, 17.

48. Sears Jayne has added to the documentary basis for an interpretation of Colet by publishing extensive marginalia, with commentary (1963); and Bernard O'Kelly has published an improved text and translation of one of Colet's works, with annotations largely by Catherine A. L. Jarrott (1985). J. B. Trapp has made significant studies in the Colet manuscripts (1975, 1976). P. S. Allen's edition of Erasmus's *Opus epistolarum* (1906–1958) has done much to correct the chronological framework, especially for the early relations between Colet and Erasmus; on the latter topic Allen in turn has been critically challenged by Fokke (1978). Of essays on Colet perhaps the most valuable are those by Rice (1952) and Porter (1966), neither of which has attracted the attention it deserves. For these and other titles see Abbreviations (above) and Works Cited (below).

49. Publishers' statement on the flyleaf of Lupton's *Life* (1887).

50. Karl Bauer, "John Colet und Erasmus von Rotterdam," in *Festschrift für Hans von Schubert zu seinem 70. Geburtstag*, ed. Otto Scheel (Leipzig: M. Heinsius, 1929), 157–158.

51. Karl August Meissinger, *Erasmus von Rotterdam*, 2d ed. (Berlin: Nauck, 1948), 97–98.

52. Allen, 4:507; cf. 3:413.

53. E.g., Marcel A. Nauwelaerts, trans., *La correspondance d' Erasme*, vol. 4 (Brussels: Presses académiques européennes, 1970), 590; and Walter Delius, *Justus Jonas 1495–1555 (Berlin: Evangelische Verlagsanstalt, 1952)*, 29. See especially André Godin, *L'homéliaire de Jean Vitrier* (Geneva: Droz, 1971), 12 n. 59; "De Vitrier à Origène," in *Colloquium Erasmianum: Actes du Colloque international réuni à Mons du 26 au 29 octobre 1967* (Mons, France: Centre universitaire de l'État, 1968), 47– 57; and his edition of Erasmus, *Vies*, 9–13, the fullest and best discussion.

Chapter 2.
"As the Tree Is Planted . . ."

1. Erasmus to John Fisher, 17 October 1519, in Allen, 4:94, Ep. 1030.

2. E.g., on learning of the execution of Sir Thomas More, Erasmus declared, "In More I seem to perish myself, to such an extent were we, as Pythagoras has it, one soul in two bodies" (Erasmus to Peter Tomiczki, 31 August 1535 in Allen, 11:221, Ep. 3049); but a persuasive case has been made that the early biographer Thomas Stapleton was correct in saying that the friendship between the two men "decreased and grew cool" as More plunged into the fight against heresy (see Richard Marius, *Thomas More: A Biography* [New York: Knopf, 1985], 331).

3. Cf. Donald A. Stauffer, *English Biography before 1700* (Cambridge: Harvard Univ. Press, 1930), 42, 271.

4. John Stow, *A Survey of London, Reprinted from the Text of 1603*, ed. C. L. Kingsford, 2 vols. (Oxford: Clarendon, 1971), 1:252.

5. Erasmus to Bonifatius Amerbach, 6 July 1532, in Allen, 10:59, Ep. 2684.

6. Two of these friends were Polydore Vergil (see *The Anglica Historia of Polydore Vergil* A.D. *1485–1537*, trans. and ed. Denys Hay [London: Royal His-

torical Society, 1950], 146) and George Lily, whose father, William, was the first headmaster of Colet's school and knew Colet well (Knight, 220n).

7. Clara E. Collet, "The Family of Dean Colet: Summary of Facts Obtained from the Records of the Mercers' Company," *Genealogists' Magazine* 7 (1935–1937): 243.

8. *Calendar of the Patent Rolls, Henry VII*, vol. 2 (London: H.M.S.O., 1963), 199.

9. John B. Gleason, "The Birth Dates of John Colet and Erasmus of Rotterdam: Fresh Documentary Evidence," *Renaissance Quarterly* 32 (1979): 73–76.

10. For a factual outline of Colet's life see the article by J. B. Trapp, "Colet, John," in *Contemporaries of Erasmus: A Biographical Dictionary of the Renaissance and Reformation*, ed. Peter Bietenholz, 3 vols. (Toronto: Univ. of Toronto Press, 1985–1987), 1:324–328.

11. *Cal. Pat. Rolls, Henry VII*, 2:275; cf. *Calendar of the Close Rolls, Henry VII*, vol. 2 (London: H.M.S.O., 1916), 339.

12. Text of the will is in Knight, 398–400.

13. William Ralph Inge, "John Colet," in his *Lay Thoughts of a Dean* (New York: Scribner's, 1926), 3.

14. Philippe Ariès, *Centuries of Childhood: A Social History of Family Life* (New York: Knopf, 1962), esp. chap. 2.

15. "Pedigree of the Colet Family," in Lupton, *Life*, facing 1; on the date, 313.

16. For discussion see David Stannard, *Shrinking History* (New York: Oxford Univ. Press, 1980).

17. F. Grossmann, "Holbein, Torrigiano and Some Portraits of Dean Colet," *Journal of the Warburg and Courtauld Institutes* 13 (1950): 215, and figure facing 206.

18. Perhaps the only reference to "father" outside a theological context is DEH, 270: the son "reveres" ("colat"; Lupton translates this more coldly as "respects") both his natural father and godfather, the former for having made him "a son of man" and the latter for having made the baptismal promises on his behalf. But then he adds that his natural father "did a work of the flesh for his own pleasure rather than for the good of his offspring"—ambivalent, and perhaps also envious.

19. Jerome Kagan, *The Development of the Child* (New York: Basic Books, 1984), 4–10.

20. Supplementary to the details on the Knyvet family in Lupton's *Life* and Mary L. Mackenzie's *Dame Christian Colet: Her Life and Family* (Cambridge: Privately printed, 1923) is Colin Richmond, *John Hopton: A Fifteenth Century Suffolk Gentleman* (Cambridge: Cambridge Univ. Press, 1981), 124 n. 76.

21. Mackenzie, 24–25.

22. J. B. Trapp, "Knyvet, Christian," in *Contemporaries of Erasmus* 2:267.

23. Mackenzie, 63, 65.

24. Peter Laslett, *Family Life and Illicit Love in Earlier Generations* (Cambridge: Cambridge Univ. Press, 1977), 218–221.

25. See J. B. Trapp, "Dame Christian Colet and Thomas More," *Moreana*, nos. 16–17 (1967): 103–114.

26. Lupton, *Life*, 13.

27. Lupton, *Life*, 311, hesitates between these alternatives; Sir John Watney (clerk of the Mercers' Company), *An Account of the Mistery of Mercers of the City of London Otherwise the Mercers' Company* (London: Privately printed, 1914), 86, makes Henry the third son.

28. Lupton, *Life*, 3, 311.

29. *VCH Buckinghamshire*, vol. 2 (1908); 370; repeated in vol. 3 (1925) 27 (for VCH, see Abbreviations at the front of this volume).

30. Collet, 242.

31. Mackenzie, 4.

32. *Acts of Court*, ix (see Abbreviations at the front of this volume).

33. T. F. Reddaway and Lorna E. M. Walker, *The Early History of the Goldsmiths' Company 1327–1509* (London: Edward Arnold, 1975), 147.

34. *Acts of Court*, 382 (17 December 1510).

35. Mercers' Hall, Wardens' Account Book, 1347, 1391–1464; letter of Miss Jean Imray, archivist of the Mercers' Company, to Prof. J. B. Trapp, 7 February 1980; kindly communicated to me by Professor Trapp.

36. Lupton, *Life*, 4.

37. Cf. *Acts of Court*, xvi.

38. E.g., Werner Sombart, *The Quintessence of Capitalism*, trans. M. Epstein (1915; reprint, New York: Howard Fertig, 1967), 153–167.

39. Reddaway and Walker, 192 (a case dating from 1494). It was not the loan at interest as such but the failure to observe its terms that brought the transaction within the cognizance of the Warden's Court. For this reason records of loans at interest are rare.

40. Reddaway and Walker, 99.

41. Reddaway and Walker, 151. Practices documented among the Goldsmiths cannot have been unknown to the Mercers and other major companies, all of which were subject to similar economic pressures.

42. Reddaway and Walker, 47.

43. Reddaway and Walker, 36.

44. Jean M. Imray, " 'Les bones gentes de la Mercerye de Londres': A Study of the Membership of the Mediaeval Mercers' Company," in *Studies in London History Presented to Philip Edmund Jones*, ed. A. E. J. Hollaender and W. Kellaway (London: Hodder and Stoughton, 1969), 173.

45. William F. Kahl, *The Development of London Livery Companies: An Historical Essay and a Select Bibliography* (Boston: Baker Library, Harvard Graduate School of Business Administration, 1960), 25.

46. Jean M. Imray, "The Merchant Adventurers and Their Records," *Journal of the Society of Archivists* 2 (1960–1964): 459.

47. *Acts of Court*, xi–xii.

48. *Acts of Court*, 66, 67.

49. *Acts of Court*, 47 (4 February 1461).

50. *Acts of Court*, 88 (11 September 1475).

51. *Acts of Court*, 47.

52. *Acts of Court*, 58–59 (23 July 1463).

53. *Acts of Court*, 147 (24 April 1483).

54. *Acts of Court*, 290 (31 August 1485).

55. *Acts of Court*, 51–52.

56. *Acts of Court*, xviii, for the circumstances of the loan.

57. *Acts of Court*, 54–56 (12 June 1461).

58. *Acts of Court*, 96 (9 June 1477).

59. *Acts of Court*, 95 (18 December 1476).

60. Alfred B. Beaven, *The Aldermen of the City of London Temp. Henry III.–1908*, 2 vols. (London: Eden Fisher, 1908–1913), 2:15.

61. *Acts of Court*, 188–189.

62. *Acts of Court*, 217–218.

63. *Acts of Court*, 121.

64. *Acts of Court*, 148 (12 May 1483).

65. *Acts of Court*, 187 (19 January 1489).

66. *Acts of Court*, 650 (12 March 1498).

67. *Acts of Court*, 130–134.

68. Beaven, 2:167.

69. *Acts of Court*, 139.

70. Beaven, 2:167.

71. Beaven, 2:xxi.

72. Beaven, 1:154.

73. Lupton, *Life*, 9.

74. Beaven, 1:17.

75. Lupton, *Life*, 10.

76. Beaven, 1:90.

77. Benjamin Varley, *The History of Stockport Grammar School* (Manchester: Manchester Univ. Press, 1946), 10.

78. Beaven, 1:324.

79. Beaven, 1:278.

80. Lupton, *Life*, 10.

81. Mary Albertson, *London Merchants and Their Landed Properties during the Reigns of the Yorkists* (Philadelphia: Privately printed, 1932), 58.

82. E. J. Burford, *Bawds and Lodgings: A History of the London Bankside Brothels c.100–1675* (London: Peter Owen, 1976), 108.

83. Jean-Louis Flandrin, "Mariage tardif et vie sexuelle: Discussions et hypothèses de recherche," *Annales: Economies, sociétés, civilisations* 27 (1972): 1351–1378.

84. Reddaway and Walker, 15–16. See also Sylvia Thrupp, *The Merchant Class of Medieval London* (Chicago: Univ. of Chicago Press, 1948), 130–132.

85. Erasmus to Bonifatius Amerbach, 6 July 1532, in Allen, 10:59, Ep. 2684.

86. Colet to Erasmus, 20 June 1516, in Allen, 2:259, Ep. 423.

87. See Rachel Giese, "Erasmus' Knowledge and Estimate of the Vernacular Languages," *Romanic Review* 28 (1937): 10–12; and esp. Jacques Chomart, *Grammaire et rhétorique chez Erasme*, 2 vols. (Paris: Les Belles Lettres, 1981), 1:144–146. According to Erasmus, English is practically all monosyllables, and English orators do not so much speak as "bark" (Chomart, 1:145 n. 114).

88. Trapp, "Dame Christian Colet," 106.

89. *Cal. Close Rolls, Henry VII* 2:339 (6 July 1508).

90. Knight, 399.

91. Knight, 403.

92. Mackenzie, 58.

93. Mackenzie, 49–51.

94. *Acts of Court*, 486 (14 December 1519).

95. F. R. H. Du Boulay, *An Age of Ambition: English Society in the Late Middle Ages* (London: Nelson, 1970), 90ff.

96. C. V. Malfatti, *Two Italian Accounts of Tudor England* (Barcelona: n.p., 1953), 40 (from the year 1497); *A Relation, or Rather a True Account of the Island of England . . . About the Year 1500*, Camden Society Publ. 37, trans. C. A. Sneyd (London, 1847), 24.

97. *A Relation*, 44. The translator also cites (113) the reference in William Harrison's preface to Holinshed's *Chronicles* (1577) to "the great silence that is used at the tables of the honorable and wyser sort, generally all over the realme."

98. Except for the material on Perotti, the material in the two following paragraphs is from Seymour Byman, "Child Raising and Melancholia in Tudor England," *Journal of Psychohistory* 6 (1978): 67–92. Byman (88 n. 24) gives a list of Tudor works on child rearing; they are surprisingly numerous and homogeneous.

99. Guillaume Boaistuau, *Theatrum Mundi* (London, 1566), Ciii^{r-v}.

100. See appendix 2 (below).

101. Niccolò Perotti, *Cornucopiae*, enlarged ed. (Venice, 1499), 542.

102. DCH, 172 (Colet's expansion on *Oeuvres complètes du pseudo-Denys l'Aréopagite*, ed. and trans. Maurice de Gandillac [Paris: Aubier, 1943], 188).

103. Jean-Claude Margolin, ed., Erasmus, *De pueris statim ac liberaliter instituendis* (Geneva: Droz, 1966), 543 n. 508, observes, however, that Erasmus in his portraits of Warham, More, and Fisher attributes to them also the same frugality at table and moderation in drinking.

104. *Acts of Court*, 125 (5 January 1480).

105. *Acts of Court*, 127 (13 and 17 January 1480).

106. *Acts of Court*, 237 (10 December 1494).

107. *Acts of Court*, 240–241 (16 February 1495).

108. *Acts of Court*, 101, 103–104 (22 and 24 December 1477).

109. Knight, 277.

110. John Le Neve, *Fasti Ecclesiae Anglicanae 1300–1541*, vol. 5 [St. Paul's, London], compiled by Joyce M. Horn (London: Athlone, 1963), 49.

111. "Memorandum quod magister Johannes Colet sacre theologie professor decanus ecclesie sancti Pauli London' electus fuit secundo die mensis Junii anno Christi millesimo quingentesimo quinto" (Proceedings of the Cathedral Chapter of St. Paul's, London, Guildhall Library MS. 25, 187 [formerly St. Paul's Cathedral MS. A 53/29]). Allen, 4:xxii, quotes a manuscript written for Colet dated 20 June 1506 "et decanatus sui anno primo"; hence several weeks passed between Colet's election and his actual assumption of his duties on 21 June 1505 (at the earliest). Lupton (*Life*, 120 n. 4) is mistaken in thinking Colet was acting as dean as early as 1504.

112. Cf. *Acts of Court*, 101, 150, 306.

Chapter 3. "... So It Grows"

1. Nicholas Orme, *English Schools in the Middle Ages* (London: Methuen, 1973), 308–309, lists the schools.

2. Cf. Ernst-Wilhelm Kohls, *Die Schule bei Martin Bucer* (Heidelberg: Quelle & Meyer, 1963), 29.

3. Skelton, qtd. in J. H. Hexter, "The Education of the Aristocracy in the Renaissance," *Journal of Modern History* 22 (1950): 2.

4. Alonso Hernández, *Historia partenopea* (Rome, 1516), qtd. in Erasmus, *Tratado del niño Jesús y en loor del estado de la niñez (Sevilla, 1516)*, ed. Eugenio Asensio (Madrid: Castalia, 1969), 27.

5. Fritz Caspari, *Humanism and the Social Order in Tudor England* (Chicago: Univ. of Chicago Press, 1954), chap. 6.

6. Ludwig Dringenberg, rector of the school in Strassburg (Alsace) from 1441 to 1477, cited by Kohls, 24.

7. Robert Browning, in *The Cambridge History of Classical Literature*, vol. 2, *Latin Literature*, ed. E. J. Kenney (Cambridge: Cambridge Univ. Press, 1982), 695–696.

8. R. S. Stanier, *Magdalen School: A History of Magdalen College School Oxford*, Oxford Historical Society Publ. n.s. 3 (Oxford: Oxford Univ. Press, 1940), 28–29.

9. Lupton, *Life*, 15–20, gives details about both schools.

10. "Statutes of St. Paul's School," Lupton, *Life*, 277.

11. T. W. Baldwin, *William Shakspere's Small Latine & Lesse Greeke*, 2 vols. (Urbana: Univ. of Illinois Press, 1944), 2:702–705, argues persuasively that the school Colet founded in 1512 had eight forms; there is no reason to suppose this number departs from previous practice. Knight, 113, note c, also states that Colet's foundation had eight forms.

12. Malcolm Seaborne, *The English School: Its Architecture and Organization* (Toronto: Univ. of Toronto Press, 1971), 14.

13. Strickland Gibson, ed., *Statuta antiqua Universitatis Oxoniensis* (Oxford: Oxford Univ. Press, 1931), lxxxv, lxxxvii.

14. J. Howard Brown, *Elizabethan Schooldays: An Account of the English Grammar Schools in the Second Half of the Sixteenth Century* (Oxford: Blackwell, 1933), 24.

15. From a Berkshire document dated 20 July 1526, translated by T. W. Baldwin, in his *William Shakspere's Petty School* (Urbana: Univ. of Illinois Press, 1943), 34. I have made a few minor stylistic changes in the translation.

16. See Warren Wooden, "The Topos of Childhood in Marian England," *Journal of Medieval and Renaissance Studies* 12 (1982): 179–194.

17. The single exception is the O'Kelly and Jarrott edition of C (see Abbreviations at the front of this volume).

18. Sombart, pt. 5, chap. 7.

19. Josephine W. Bennett, "Andrew Holes: A Neglected Harbinger of the English Renaissance," *Speculum* 19 (1944): 322; *A Relation*, 44.

20. G. D. Squibb, *Doctors' Commons: A History of the College of Advocates*

and Doctors of Law (Oxford: Clarendon, 1977), 124. The influence of this close-knit group of men is studied by J.K. McConica in *English Humanists and Reformation Politics* (Oxford: Clarendon, 1965), 51–53.

21. Polydore Vergil, 146.

22. E.g., T. E. Bridgett, *Life of Blessed John Fisher, Bishop of Rochester* (London, 1888): "Mr. Seebohm . . . has drawn a Pseudo-Colet" (99n). H. Maynard Smith, *Pre-Reformation England* (London: Macmillan, 1938), entitles one section of a chapter "The So-called Oxford Reformers" (451). After detailing some of Seebohm's mistakes, Albert Hyma, "Erasmus and the Oxford Reformers (1503–1519)," *Nederlands archief voor kerkgeschiedenis*, n.s. 38 (1951), adds, "A surprisingly large number of British writers continue to heap praises on Seebohm's antiquated work" (65–66). Germain Marc'hadour, in *Moreana* 17 (1980), observes that Seebohm's work now possesses "no more than an historical interest" (151).

23. "The questionist was the scholar who was engaging in those exercises that accompanied his admission to the bachelor's degree," according to John M. Fletcher, "The Teaching of Arts at Oxford, 1400–1520," *Paedagogica Historica* 7 (1967): 440.

24. W. Robert Godfrey, "John Colet of Cambridge," *Archiv für Reformationsgeschichte* 65 (1974): 7–9.

25. Josephine W. Bennett, "John Morer's Will: Thomas Linacre and Prior Sellyng's Greek Teaching," *Studies in the Renaissance* 15 (1968): 73, finds that fifteen or sixteen was the normal age for going up in the time of Linacre, an older contemporary of Colet; other writers mention ages from fourteen to seventeen.

26. In the year 1503–1504 the proctors authorized payment of 8*d.* to the vicar of Trumpington for writing the letter sent to Sir Henry; the vicar received 20*d.* for the letter he wrote to the king (Mary Bateson, ed., *Grace Book B, Part I, Containing the Proctors' Accounts and Other Records of the University of Cambridge for the Years 1488–1511* [Cambridge: Cambridge Univ. Press, 1903], 194).

27. Godfrey, 10 n. 23, with references. See further H. C. Porter, in *Erasmus and Cambridge: The Cambridge Letters of Erasmus*, trans. D. F. S. Thomson, with introduction, notes, and commentary by H.C. Porter (Toronto: Univ. of Toronto Press, 1963), 24.

28. *Erasmus and Cambridge*, 195 (Erasmus to Henry Bullock, 22 August 1516; in Allen, 2: 328, Ep. 456.)

29. James D. Tracy, " 'Against the Barbarians': The Young Erasmus and His Humanist Contemporaries," *Sixteenth Century Journal* 11 (1980): 6 n. 15, cites four humanist attacks on Alexander.

30. Erasmus to a Friend, ?1489, in Allen, 1:123, Ep. 31.

31. Walter J. Ong, S. J., *Ramus, Method, and the Decay of Dialogue* (Cambridge: Harvard Univ. Press, 1957), 56–57.

32. Qtd. in Ong, 332 n. 10. Joseph P. Mullally, *The Summae Logicales of Peter of Spain* (Notre Dame, Ind.: Univ. of Notre Dame Press, 1945), includes a text and translation of the *Parva Logicalia*.

33. Ong, 62.

34. John R. H. Moorman, *The Grey Friars at Cambridge* (Cambridge: Cambridge Univ. Press, 1952), 121–123.

35. W. A. Pantin, "The Conception of the Humanities in England in the Period of the Renaissance," in *Les universités européennes du XIVᵉ au XVIIᵉ siècle, aspects et problèmes: Actes du Colloque international à l'occasion du VIᵉ centenaire de l'Université Jagellone de Cracovie 6–8 mai 1964* (Geneva: Droz, 1967), 105–108.

36. Montagu Burrows, "Memoir of William Grocyn," in *Oxford Historical Society Collectanea*, 3 vols. (Oxford, 1885–1896), 2:347.

37. Lisa Jardine, "Humanism and the Sixteenth Century Cambridge Arts Course," *History of Education* 4 (1975): 16–31, shows that for the Cambridge of 1535–1590 the list of the titles of books owned by those who died in residence during that period "amplifies considerably the basic outline of the course as laid down by university and college statutes" (16), and suggests that newer subjects not in the curriculum nevertheless became the object of systematic study. Cf. also Margery H. Smith, CSJ, "Some Humanist Libraries in Early Tudor Cambridge," *Sixteenth Century Journal* 5 (1974): 15–34.

38. Pantin, 103.

39. Godfrey, 12.

40. Pantin, 105, relying on case histories in the archives rather than the regulations in the statutes; for the statutory regulations see Gibson, 48–50, who however also observes (453) that some students evaded the full statutory requirement.

41. D. S. Chambers, "The Economic Predicament of Renaissance Cardinals," *Studies in Medieval and Renaissance History* 3 (1966): 287–313, documents the arguments by which contemporaries justified pluralism and emphasizes (309–311) that pluralism was not necessarily associated with corruption.

42. *The Letters of Richard Fox 1468–1527*, ed. P. S. Allen and H. M. Allen (Oxford: Clarendon, 1929), 93.

43. Maynard Smith, 35.

44. Thomas Starkey, *A Dialogue between Reginald Pole and Thomas Lupset*, ed. Kathleen M. Burton (London: Chatto and Windus, 1948), 127; qtd. in M. Smith, 35. In fact, Colet's cure of Dennington was being served in 1499, while he was studying at Oxford, by a parochial chaplain of whom complaint was made in his own parish for neglecting chancel and vicarage (Christopher Harper-Bill, "Dean Colet's Convocation Sermon and the Pre-Reformation Church in England," *History* 73 [1988]: 194).

45. Francis Maddison et al., *Essays on the Life and Work of Thomas Linacre c. 1460–1524* (Oxford: Clarendon, 1977), xxii, xliii–xliv.

46. George B. Parks, *The English Traveler to Italy*, vol. 1 (Rome: Ed. di Storia e Letteratura, 1954), 465.

47. As suggested by Jayne, 7.

48. A letter from Colet to Christopher Urswick, in Wallace K. Ferguson, "An Unpublished Letter of John Colet, Dean of St. Paul's," *American Historical Review* 39 (1934): 699, shows that Colet and Urswick had been together in Rome; Urswick had been there at least since the election of Alexander VI in August 1492. Another source shows Urswick at Etaples, eleven miles south of Boulogne and a regular port of embarkation for England, on 3 November 1492. The overland journey would hardly have taken much less than forty days (cf. Parks, 1:497–498), so that Urswick must have left Rome, and Colet have arrived there, by late Sep-

tember (see Thomas A. Urwick, *Records of the Family of Urswyk, Urswick, or Urwick* [St. Albans: Privately printed, 1893], 96).

49. Brian Newns, "The Hospice of St. Thomas and the English Crown 1474–1538," *The English Hospice in Rome*, spec. issue of *The Venerabile* 21 (May 1962): 160.

50. Max Heimbucher, *Die Orden und Kongregationen der katholischen Kirche*, 3d ed., 2 vols. (Paderborn: Ferdinand Schöningh, 1933–34), 1: 417–419.

51. Newns, 190.

52. Vincent J. Flynn, "Englishmen in Rome during the Renaissance," *Modern Philology* 36 (1938): 131.

53. First cited from the manuscript source by Adrian Gasquet, *A History of the Venerable English College, Rome* (London: Longmans, 1920), 24; but overlooked by later writers. Roberto Weiss, "Englishmen in Rome," *The Times Literary Supplement* (London) 34 (1935): 596, rediscovered the entry printed in Pietro Egidi, ed., *Necrologi e libri affini della provincia romana*, 2 vols. (Rome: Istituto Storico Italiano, 1908–1914), 2:176.

54. Lionel Rothkrug, *Religious Practices and Collective Perceptions: Hidden Homologies in the Renaissance and Reformation*, spec. issue of *Historical Reflections/Réflexions Historiques* 7.1 (Spring 1980): 72 and n. 255.

55. Newns, 156–157.

56. Like Lupton before me, I have tried without success to verify the statement made by J. S. Harford, *Life of Michael Angelo*, 2 vols. (London, 1857), 1:57, that "Tiraboschi [*Storia letteraria d'Italia*], vi, pt. 2, p. 382, edit. Roma, 4º, 1784," or indeed any other passage in the work, records that Colet stayed in Florence.

57. Armand Grunzweig, ed., *Correspondance de la filiale de Bruges des Medicis*, pt. 1 (Brussels: Lamertin, 1931), xxii, xxxvii.

58. *Calendar of Pleas and Memoranda Rolls of the City of London*, vol. 6 (London: H.M.S.O., 1961), 116–117.

59. For the writers Colet cites see appendix 2.

60. See the map of "English Routes to Italy" in Parks, facing p. 48.

61. Parks, 513, 526.

62. Parks, 526–527.

63. Hidetoshi Hoshino, *L'arte della lana in Firenze nel basso medioevo* (Florence: Olschki, 1980), 253.

64. *Gesamtkatalog der Wiegendrucke*, 8 vols. to date (Leipzig: Hiersemann, 1925–1979), 8:402.

65. What follows is my reconstruction of the correspondence. As described below, Jayne (see FEM in Abbreviations at the front of this volume) takes a different view (18–21).

66. In an effort to make sense of this passage Jayne renders it, "sustain me in this half-life." Nothing is impossible in Colet's Latin, but this translation seriously strains the meaning of "partiali" and ignores "tui" altogether. Clearly something is wrong with Colet's text. The context requires something like "sustain me in this life bereft of you"; hence Colet may have meant to write not *partiali* but *privata*, "deprived," which can govern the genitive *tui*, "of you."

67. Ficino's letters are printed in Jayne, 81–83; quotation at 81.

68. Jayne, 37 n. 1.

69. Jayne, 130 (quoted text), 20–21 (discussion).

70. Jayne, 20.

71. Cf. Roberto Cessi, "Paolinismo preluterano," *Rendiconti dell'Accademia Nazionale dei Lincei*, Cl. di scienze morali, storiche e filologiche, 8th ser. 12 (1957): 3–30.

72. Emile V. Telle, *Erasme de Rotterdam et le septième sacrement* (Geneva: Droz, 1954), 206.

73. Arnaldo della Torre, *Storia dell'Accademia Platonica* (Florence: Carnesecchi e Figli, 1902), 830–832.

74. Kenneth R. Bartlett, " 'Worshipful Gentlemen of England': The *Studio* of Padua and the Education of the English Gentry in the Sixteenth Century," *Renaissance and Reformation*, n.s. 6 (1982): 236.

75. See Leland Miles, *John Colet and the Platonic Tradition* (La Salle, Ill.: Open Court, 1961), esp. 35–43, 46–51, 54–60, 70–79.

76. See Armando F. Verde, *Lo studio fiorentino 1473–1503*, vol. 3 in 2 pts. (Pistoia: Memorie Domenicane, 1977).

77. See Aloysius Andrich, *De natione anglica et scota iuristarum Universitatis Patavinae ab a. MCCXXII p. Ch. n. ad a. MDCCXXXVIII* (Padua, 1892).

78. Ferguson, 696–699. On Urswick's intellectual style see J. B. Trapp, "Christopher Urswick and His Books: The Reading of Henry VII's Almoner," *Renaissance Studies* 1 (1987): 48–70, esp. 57 for *Historia Bohemica*.

79. On this comment from Erasmus's biography see *Vies*, 73 n. 497.

80. The manuscript copy that Urswick later had made from the printed volume Colet sent him is now in the Princeton University Library (*Historia Bohemica*, Medieval & Renaissance MS. 89).

81. Joseph Macek, *Jean Hus et les traditions hussites (XVᵉ–XIXᵉ siècles)* (Paris: Plon, 1973), 294–295, shows how the Hussite movement became detached from its revolutionary origins as it moved westward, conveyed no longer in Czech but in Latin, and expressing lofty conceptions appealing to ecclesiastical intellectuals.

82. Erasmus to Martin Lypsius, 7 May 1518, in Allen, 3:320, Ep. 843.

83. Rudolf Říčan, "Die tschechische Reformation und Erasmus," *Communio viatorum* 16 (1973): 188.

84. Paul de Vooght, "Un épisode peu connu de la vie d'Erasme: Sa rencontre avec les hussites bohèmes en 1519–1521," *Irénikon* 47 (1974): 27–47.

85. Foxe, 230.

86. Aeneas Silvius Piccolomini, *Historia Bohemica* (Cologne, 1532), 69.

87. Piccolomini, 73.

88. Piccolomini, 74–76.

89. Piccolomini, 76.

90. Richard G. Salomon, "Poggio Bracciolini and Johannes Hus: A Hoax Hard to Kill," *Journal of the Warburg and Courtauld Institutes* 19 (1956): 174–177.

91. Eugenio Garin, ed., *Prosatori latini del quattrocento* (Milan and Naples: Ricciardi, 1952), 228–241.

92. Qtd. in Ernst Walser, *Poggius Florentinus: Leben und Werke* (Leipzig: Teubner, 1914), 68 n. 1.

93. Roberto Ridolfi, *Cronologia e bibliografia delle prediche*, vol. 1 of *Bibliografia delle opere del Savonarola*, ed. Piero Ginori Conti (Florence: Fondazione Ginori Conti, 1939), 64.

94. Thrupp, 188–189.

95. See Carl S. Meyer, "Henry VIII Burns Luther's Books, 12 May 1521," *Journal of Ecclesiastical History* 9 (1958): 173–174.

96. Patrick Collinson, "The Role of Women in the English Reformation Illustrated by the Life and Friendships of Anne Locke," in *Studies in Church History*, vol. 2 (London: Nelson, 1965), 263.

97. J. B. Trapp, "John Colet, His Manuscripts and the ps.-Dionysius," in *Classical Influences on European Culture 1500–1700*, ed. R. R. Bolgar (Cambridge: Cambridge Univ. Press, 1976), 214 n. 8.

98. Typical is Friedrich Dannenberg, *Das Erbe Platons in England bis zur Bildung Lylys* (Berlin: Junker und Dünnhaupt, 1932): "[Colet's] complete mastery of Greek is not open to the slightest doubt. In fact one may take it as certain that Colet knew all of the [Greek] works he cited in the original" (66). And as recently as 1983 a study of the period declared that Colet was actually "a leading scholar of Greek" (Jasper Ridley, *Statesman and Saint: Cardinal Wolsey, Sir Thomas More, and the Politics of Henry VIII* [New York: Viking, 1983], 43).

99. J. Bennett, "John Morer's Will," 75–76.

100. Colet to Erasmus, 20 June 1516, in Allen, 2:257, Ep. 423.

101. More to Erasmus, 22 September 1516, in Allen, 2:347, Ep. 468.

102. Erasmus to Reuchlin, 29 September 1516, in Allen, 2:351, Ep. 471.

103. Richard Pace, *De fructu qui ex doctrina percipitur: The Benefit of a Liberal Education*, trans. and ed. Frank Manley and Richard S. Silvester (New York: Ungar, 1967), 126.

104. Allen, 2:350. Jarrott (C, pp. 36, 61 n. 27), who wrongly assumes that Colet knew Greek, overlooked this document. André Chastel remarks that at this period it was the mode for writers ignorant of Greek to obtrude a few Greek words into their text (*Revue des études grecques* 69 [1956]: xiii–xiv).

105. For a recent discussion see Jaroslav Pelikan, *The Christian Tradition: A History of the Development of Doctrine*, 4 vols. to date (Chicago: Univ. of Chicago Press, 1971–1984) 1:333–339.

106. Martin Dorp to Erasmus, 27 August 1515, in Allen, 2:132, Ep. 347.

107. C. Spicq, *Equisse d'une histoire de l'exégèse latine au moyen âge* (Paris: Vrin, 1944), 92.

108. Spicq, 196–197.

109. Hubert Jedin, *Geschichte des Konzils von Trient*, 4 vols. in 5 (Freiburg i. B.: Herder, 1949–1975), 2:79–82.

110. L. D. Reynolds and N.G. Wilson, *Scribes and Scholars: A Guide to the Transmission of Greek and Latin Literature*, 2d ed. (Oxford: Clarendon, 1974), 138.

111. Qtd. in Lupton, *Life*, 45.

112. Jacques Boussard, "L'Université d'Orléans et l'humanisme au début du XVIe siècle," *Humanisme et renaissance* 5 (1938): 210.

113. Erasmus to Faustus Andrelinus, 20 November 1500, in Allen 1:312, Ep. 134.

114. Deloynes to Erasmus, 26 November 1516, *Correspondance d'Erasme*, 2:529.

115. *Correspondance d'Erasme* 2:528.

116. M. Cuissard, "L'étude du grec à Orléans, depuis le IXe siècle jusqu'au milieu du XVIIIe siècle," *Mémoires de la Société archéologique et historique de l'Orléanais* 19 (1883): 645–840.

117. Cf. Ricardo García Villoslada, S.J., *La Universidad de París durante los estudios de Francisco de Vitoria O.P. (1507–1522)* (Rome: Universitas Gregoriana, 1938).

118. Raymond Marcel, "Introduction et succès du platonisme en France à l'aube de la Renaissance," in *The Late Middle Ages and the Dawn of Humanism Outside Italy: Proceedings of the International Congress, Louvain, May 11–13, 1970*, ed. G. Verbeke and J. IJsewijn (Louvain: University Press, 1972), 93.

119. On Gaguin's circle see Jean-Pierre Massaut, *Josse Clichtove, l'humanisme et la réforme du clergé*, 2 vols. (Paris: Les Belles Lettres, 1968), 1:144–166.

120. Alphonse Le Roy, "Gaguin (Robert)," in *Biographie nationale . . . de Belgique*, vol. 7, (Brussels, 1880–1883), 418–423.

121. Erasmus to Henry of Bergen, 7 November 1496, in Allen, 1:163, Ep. 49. See also Eugene Rice, Jr., "Erasmus and the Religious Tradition," *Journal of the History of Ideas* 11 (1950): 405.

122. *L'Immaculée Conception de la Vierge Marie: Poème de Robert Gaguin*, ed. and trans. Alcide Bonneau (Paris, 1885), xii–xvii, xxiv.

123. *L'Immaculée Conception*, xxiv.

124. Franco Simone, "Robert Gaguin e il suo cenacolo umanistico," *Aevum* 13 (1939): 410–476, esp. 461, 467.

125. A revealing instance is in a letter written by Thomas More to Erasmus when Colet was making a belated effort to learn Greek. More first suggests that Erasmus send Colet a word of encouragement but then thinks better of the idea: "It might be quite enough to leave him to decide for himself. As you know, out of contrariness he will often refuse to listen to a suggestion even if it is something he would have been strongly inclined toward if left to his own devices" ("Credo fore vt pergat et peruadat nauiter, maxime si tu ab Louanio vsque stimules; quanquam fortasse satius erit eum impetui suo permittere. Solet vt scis, disputandi gratia repugnare suadentibus, etiam si id suadeant in quod ille sua sponte maxime propendeat"; 22 September 1516 in Allen, 2:347, Ep. 468).

126. If one can judge by the tone and content of DEH, 256.

127. RO, 204; R, 204 (the latter instance misquoted in a form that does not scan).

128. Lupton, *Life*, 282.

Chapter 4. The Colet Manuscripts

1. Seebohm, *Oxford Reformers*, 33 n. 2, records only his own view, saying nothing about the weighty evidence militating against it. He also ignores Lupton's conscientious discussion (appendix to R, pp. 229–232). The remainder of the present paragraph depends on Lupton's discussion.

2. R, p. 230.

3. For Gale see Sir Michael McDonnell, *The Annals of St. Paul's School* (London: Privately printed, 1959), 245–258.

4. Gale's note reads in full:

Videtur esse opus Joannis Coleti Decani S^{ti} Pauli Lond:
Multa hic plane eadem sunt cum iis quae scripsit manu sua Coletus, in libro qui servatur in Capitulari domo Ecclesiae S^{ti} Pauli: atque adeo haec sunt quasi secundae curae.
Multa hic parum emendata scribuntur, quo vitio Coletus laborabat. Ea subinde notantur, et corriguntur.
Ordo Epistolarum S^{ti} Pauli non est idem hic, qui est in illo altero libro manu Coleti scripto.

T. G.

5. The passages in S are these: "idem est sacerdotium quod matrimonium" (276); "sacrificatio idem est quod prolificatio" (276); "idem est sponsus et pontifex" (304); "idem est proles et sacrificium que iustitia" (306); "idem est sacrificatio et progeneracio" (306); "matrimonium et sacerdotium in christo omnino esse idem" (308).

6. R. E. Latham, *Revised Medieval Latin Word-List from British and Irish Sources* (London: Oxford Univ. Press, 1965).

7. *Ortus Vocabulorum* (London, 1500 [STC 13829]); reprint, ed. R. C. Alston ([Menston, Yorkshire: Scolar, 1968]) sig. PP, p. viii. (For STC see Abbreviations at the front of this volume.)

8. Albert Blaise, *Dictionnaire latin-français des auteurs chrétiens* (Strasbourg: Le latin chrétien, 1954); id., *Dictionnaire latin-français des auteurs du moyen âge* (Turnholt: Brepols, 1975), a "continuation" (p. v) of the former work.

9. For this fact I am indebted to a computer search of the database for the Corpus Christianorum edition of the works of Augustine kindly authorized by the editors of the Augustinus-Lexikon, Stuttgart.

10. Polydore Vergil, 146.

11. *A Catalogue of the Manuscripts Preserved in the Library of the University of Cambridge*, 6 vols. (Cambridge, 1856–1867), 3:171, describes MS. Gg.iv.26 as "written in several different hands." J. B. Trapp, "Notes on Manuscripts Written by Peter Meghen," *The Book Collector* 24 (1975): 85, thinks the manuscript is "partly in the autograph of John Colet . . . partly perhaps in the hand of Meghen . . . with additions and corrections by Colet."

12. Knight, 401.

13. The term is suggested by Trapp, "John Colet, His Manuscripts," 205–221.

14. For the facts of Meghen's career see J. B. Trapp, "Meghen, Peter," in *Contemporaries of Erasmus* 2:420–422.

15. The existing confusion about this date has recently been settled by the palaeographical study of Andrew J. Brown, "The Date of Erasmus' Latin Translation of the New Testament," *Transactions of the Cambridge Bibliographical Society* 8 (1984): 351–380.

16. In Colet's time St. Paul's had a famous scriptorium (W. Sparrow Simpson, "A Newly Discovered Manuscript Containing Statutes Compiled by Dean Colet for the Government of the Chantry Priests and Other Clergy of St. Paul's," *Archaeologia* 52 [1890]: 152). See also P. S. Allen, *The Age of Erasmus* (Oxford: Clarendon, 1914), 141.

17. Erasmus to Peter Gilles, 18 November 1516, in Allen, 2:385, Ep. 391.

18. Erasmus to Colet, ca. 5 March 1518, in Allen, 3:241, Ep. 786.

19. Robert Peters, "The Contribution of the Eastern Fathers to the Intellectual Equipment of the English Clergy during the Sixteenth Century," in *Miscellanea Historiae Ecclesiasticae, IV* (Louvain: Bibliothèque de la Revue d'histoire ecclésiastique, 1972), 93–112.

20. Max Schär, *Das Nachleben des Origenes im Zeitalter des Humanismus* (Basel and Stuttgart: Helbing & Lichtenhahn, 1979), 159–160.

21. D. P. Walker, "Origène en France au début du XVIe siècle," in *Courants religieux et humanisme* (Paris: P.U.F., 1959), 101.

22. Schär, 247.

23. Schär, 190.

24. For Colet's citations of Origen see appendix 2.

25. It may be worth adding that only in the Trinity manuscript, so far as I have noticed, does Colet ever use a Greek accusative ending for a Latin word. Hence the form "hypocrisin" (53^v), if it is not a minim error, may be a tiny trophy from his effort to learn Greek.

26. Illustrated in plate 26, facing p. 81, of Trapp, "Manuscripts Written By Meghen."

27. A. Brown, 354–356.

28. A. Brown, 354, 361.

29. Jayne, Appendix A, "The Identification of Colet's Hand," assembles relevant evidence but does not take account of the manifest differences in handwriting within the manuscript. Trapp, "Manuscripts Written by Meghen," 85, mentions the possibility that Meghen's hand may also be found there.

30. For description of the manuscript see O'Kelly and Jarrott, C, 19–21.

31. ". . . adductus fui tandem ut promitterem quod est ceptum modo me perrecturum." The translation in the text conveys my sense of the passage; however, the ambiguous position of "modo" in the sentence and the relativity of its meaning (it designates a short period either before or after the time of its associated verb) makes Lupton's translation also possible: ". . . promise that I would go on with what I had before begun" (R, p. 58).

32. See the critical apparatus *ad loc.* in *Biblia Sacra iuxta Vulgatam versionem*, 2 vols., ed. Robert Weber, O.S.B. (Stuttgart: Württembergische Bibelanstalt, 1969), 2:1772.

33. It is especially odd that Colet should be uncertain about this text, because it was well-known as one of the proof-texts for the existence of purgatory. See Ludwig Ott, *Grundriss der Dogmatik*, 4th ed. (Freiburg i. B.: Herder, 1959), 576.

34. Lupton's characterization of the handwriting of C as "a neat, careful hand, changing gradually to a hasty, more running hand," is quite inadequate to the facts. By his own account he seems to have worked most of the time at two removes from the holograph, for he used a copy, borrowed from Seebohm, of the cleaned-up Emmanuel College copy of the holograph (C, p. vii). Lupton makes only minimal reference to the difficult and sometimes even chaotic holograph, which caused trouble even to Meghen.

35. When Paul wrote, "The belly is for food and food for the belly," commentators agree that he meant that the appetite for food is a natural one and therefore benefits the body, whereas fornication, substituting union with a prostitute for

the true desire of union with God, does not benefit the body. But Colet, disciplined to the taking of only one meal a day, responded to the mention of food for the belly with a conditioned reflex, "Conquer gluttony!"—which was not Paul's point.

36. Polydore Vergil, 146.

37. Eugene F. Rice, Jr., ed., *The Prefatory Epistles of Jacques Lefèvre d'Etaples and Related Texts* (New York and London: Columbia Univ. Press, 1972), 558–559.

38. Lupton, foreword to *Opuscula*, vii.

39. Jayne, 27.

40. Jayne, 37.

41. The extreme tightness of this proposed chronology, together with the nearly complete silence proposed for the following nineteen years, has also struck Miles, *Colet and the Platonic Tradition*, 201 n. 123.

42. Eugene F. Rice, Jr., review of *John Colet and Marsilio Ficino*, by Sears Jayne, *Renaissance News* 17 (1964): 107–110.

43. Listed by John Pits, *Relationum historicarum de rebus anglicis tomus I*, ed. William Bishop (Paris, 1619), 691.

44. Qtd. in H. C. Porter, "The Gloomy Dean and the Law: John Colet, 1466–1519," in *Essays in Modern English Church History in Memory of Norman Sykes*, ed. G. V. Bennett and J. D. Walsh (London: A. and C. Black, 1966), 32–33.

45. Porter, 18–34.

46. For the facts of the Hunne case I follow the careful recent account by Stefan J. Smart, "John Foxe and 'The Story of Richard Hun, Martyr,' " *Journal of Ecclesiastical History* 37 (1986): 1–14, supplemented by details from Porter, 18–34, and Maynard Smith, 83–90. Details from other sources are noted as they appear.

47. G. G. Coulton, *Ten Medieval Studies* (Cambridge: Cambridge Univ. Press, 1930), 126–129, 131.

48. For the legal issues generally, and the strength of the technical case against Hunne particularly, see the instructive Appendix B, "The Affairs of Richard Hunne and Friar Standish," by J. Duncan M. Derrett, in More, *CW*; vol. 9 (1979) (see Abbreviations at the front of this volume).

49. Smart, 2–4.

50. The original reading, replaced in Hall's *Chronicle* by "any clerk," as M. Smith observes (86 n. 1).

51. On Kidderminster see David Knowles, *The Religious Orders in England*, 3 vols. (Cambridge: Cambridge Univ. Press, 1948–1959), 3:92–95.

52. Porter, 22.

53. Above, 73–74.

54. See the similar distinction between good prelates and illegitimate ones below, 251–252.

Chapter 5. Erasmus and Colet

1. C, p. xvi.

2. Cf. Pelikan, 1:245–246.

3. For a detailed speculative analysis of the structure of Ep. 109 see G. J. Fokke, S. J., "An Aspect of the Christology of Erasmus of Rotterdam," *Ephemerides Theologicae Lovanienses* 54 (1978): 166–168.

4. Ernest W. Hunt, *Dean Colet and His Theology* (London: Publ. for The Church Historical Society by S.P.C.K., 1956), unaccountably takes no notice of Erasmus's "Disputatiuncula" (cf. 91).

5. Erasmus to Colet, December 1504, in Allen, 1:405, Ep. 181.

6. Fokke, 182–183.

7. Erasmus's predilection for diminutives is illustrated by the extensive list drawn from a single treatise by Jean-Claude Margolin, ed., *Declamatio de pueris statim ac liberaliter instituendis* (Geneva: Droz, 1966), 618–619.

8. Erasmus's use of patristic sources in the "Disputatiuncula" is studied by James D. Tracy, "Humanists among the Scholastics: Erasmus, More, and Lefèvre d'Etaples on the Humanity of Christ," in *Erasmus of Rotterdam Society Yearbook*, vol. 5 (Oxon Hill, Md.: Erasmus of Rotterdam Society, 1985), 30–51. I am indebted to Professor Tracy for prepublication access to an earlier version of his paper.

9. Here as elsewhere in this treatise Erasmus basically follows, though with an individual accent, the traditional view; cf. Martin Elze, "Das Verständnis der Passion Jesu im ausgehenden Mittelalter und bei Luther," in *Geist und Geschichte der Reformation: Festgabe Hanns Rückert zum 65. Geburtstag*, ed. Heinz Liebing and Klaus Scholder (Berlin: de Gruyter, 1966), 132. Elze (129) quotes Augustine, *De vera religione* 16,32, an interpretation of Jesus' entire life as *disciplina morum*, teaching men how they should live.

10. On "propassion" as used by the Stoics and in early Christian literature see the note by Clarence H. Miller, ed., More, *De Tristitia Christi*, in More, *CW*, vol. 14 (1976), pt. 2, p. 1024.

11. Cf. Fokke, 175–185, and Giovanni Santinello, *Studi sull'umanesimo europeo* (Padua: Antenor, 1969), 77–116.

12. On Erasmus's christology see John B. Payne, *Erasmus: His Theology of the Sacraments* (Richmond, Va.: John Knox, 1970), 54–70.

13. Fokke, 183.

14. Eugene F. Rice, Jr., "John Colet and the Annihilation of the Natural," *Harvard Theological Review* 45 (1952): 141–163.

15. Santinello observes that it is Erasmus, not Colet, who uses a philological method: "Erasmus, that is, uses his authorities critically. He does not follow them unquestioningly but records their consensus or disagreement and, in the case of Jerome, seeks to determine what weight to give an affirmation, based on the context in which it appears and the method that the authority himself employs" (104).

16. Erasmus, *Adagiorum collectanea* (Paris, 1500), a.iii^v: "Neminem adeo uiribus antecellere: ut unus pluribus par esse possit. Nec fortissimo quidem uiro pudendum esse: multitudini cedere." This adage, which became no. 439 in the standard numbering, was greatly enlarged in later editions.

17. Cf. Emile V. Telle, "Trois contes érasmiques et une note sur More," *Moreana*, nos. 15–16 (1967), "Erasme et Caïn," 63–68.

18. Erasmus to John Sixtin, November 1499, in Allen, 1:268–271, Ep. 116.

19. *P. Vergilius Maro Aeneis Buch VI*, 6th ed., ed. Eduard Norden (Darmstadt: Wissenschaftliche Buchgesellschaft, 1976), 144.

20. Vergil, *The Aeneid*, trans. Robert Fitzgerald (New York: Random House, 1983), VI, ll. 45–55 (p. 161), ll. 76–80 (p. 162).

21. Seebohm, *Oxford Reformers*, 98–99.

22. Lupton, *Life*, 102; see also C, p. xvi n. 3.

23. Allen, 1:246.

24. Lupton, *Life*, 103.

25. Erasmus to Robert Fisher, 5 December 1499, in Allen, 1:273, Ep. 118.

26. Cicero, *De oratore* XIX.62; noted by Godin, *Vies*, 113.

27. *Erasmi opuscula*, ed. Wallace K. Ferguson (The Hague: Mouton, 1933), 29; for the date, 27.

28. Yvonne Charlier, *Erasme et l'amitié d'après sa correspondance* (Paris: Les Belles Lettres, 1977), 113. In February 1504 Erasmus wrote to his friend Jean Desmarais (Paludanus) a long set-piece in defense of flattery under certain circumstances, citing among others the Stoics, Plato, and St. Paul (Erasmus to Jean Desmarais, February 1504, in Allen, 1:398–403, Ep. 180). A sensitive recent account of Erasmus during the period of his early encounters with Colet is by Robert Stupperich, *Erasmus von Rotterdam und seine Welt* (Berlin and New York: de Gruyter, 1977), 33–68.

29. Erasmus to Antony of Bergen, 16 March 1501, in Allen, 1:352, Ep. 149.

30. Cf. Margaret Mann Phillips, *The 'Adages' of Erasmus: A Study with Translations* (Cambridge: Cambridge Univ. Press, 1964), 51.

31. The adages "With unwashed hands" and "With unwashed feet," similar in meaning, are nos. 854 and 855 in the standard numeration; the phrases reappear also in no. 2386 (*Adagia*, in ASD, II, 5:284; for ASD, see Abbreviations at the front of this volume).

32. Erasmus to Colet, in Allen, 1:248–249, Ep. 108. Allen, followed in the French and English translations of the *Epistolae*, supposes this letter to be the opening gun in the disputation on Christ's Passion. However, Fokke, 164 n. 15, points out that the only connection of Ep. 108 with the disputation is the mention of the name of Charnock. The letter reads more naturally as Erasmus's response to a complaint that he had let Colet down by refusing to lecture on the Scriptures at Oxford; in which case the letter belongs to the end of Erasmus's stay at Oxford (ll. 104–105 show that he was writing from there), that is, probably early November 1499, after Ep. 116. Erasmus says in Ep. 108 that he is detained partly by winter weather and that he expects to return to Paris "soon" (ll. 102–103).

33. The suggestion of Delio Cantimori, preface to Erasmus, *Elogio della pazzia*, ed. Tommaso Fiore (Turin: Giulio Einaudi, 1964), x–xiv; endorsed by Silvano Cavazza, "La cronologia degli 'Antibarbari' e le origini del pensiero religioso di Erasmo," *Rinascimento*, 2d ser. 15 (1975): 178 n. 3.

34. Peter Iver Kaufman, "John Colet's *Opus de sacramentis* and Clerical Anticlericalism: The Limitations of 'Ordinary Wayes,' " *Journal of British Studies* 22 (1982): 4 n. 12; cites Roland Bainton, *Erasmus of Christendom* (New York: Scribner, 1969), 62, who reverses the traditional view by suggesting that Erasmus threw himself into Greek studies partly in reaction to Colet's neglect of them.

35. For a balanced evaluation of the evidence on this issue see Craig R. Thompson, "Erasmus and Tudor England," in *Actes du Congrès Erasme . . . Rotterdam 27–29 octobre 1969* (Amsterdam and London: North-Holland, 1971), 29–68; reference to Colet, 32.

36. Writing to an intimate friend in 1500, Erasmus mentions matter-of-factly that he has for a long time been impatient to devote himself to the study of sacred literature ("ad quas tractandas jamdudum mihi gestit animus"; Erasmus to James Batt, 11 December 1500, in Allen, 1:321, Ep. 138).

37. Hermann Dibbelt, "Erasmus' griechische Studien," *Gymnasium* 57 (1950): 63.

38. Jerry H. Bentley, *Humanists and Holy Writ: New Testament Scholarship in the Renaissance* (Princeton: Princeton Univ. Press, 1983), 117–118.

39. See also Peter I. Kaufman, "John Colet and Erasmus' *Enchiridion*," *Church History* 46 (1977): 296–312.

40. Seebohm, *Oxford Reformers*, 174 n. 1 (emphasis in the original).

41. Erasmus to John Botzheim, 30 January 1523, in Allen, 1:5, Ep. 1. Colet may have extended an open invitation to return to England, for in mid-1501 a visit to Colet is mentioned in a list of alternatives from which Erasmus could choose, all of them represented as being for one reason or another unattractive. In mid-1501 Erasmus writes to a fellow-countryman, "Sometimes I think of returning to England, to spend a month or two on the holy mysteries of theology [*in theologiae sacris*] together with my friend Colet, for I am aware how useful that might be to me; but I am still put off by the 'infamous cliffs' [Horace, *Odes* 1.3.20] on which I've already shipwrecked once [an allusion to the confiscation of almost all his money upon his previous departure from England, a disaster Erasmus's friends heard about again and again]" (Erasmus to James Tutor [or Voecht], 18 July 1501; in Allen, 1:368, Ep. 159). Three considerations help in deciding how serious was the project of going to see Colet again. The first is a comparison of the quoted text with that of Ep. 157. To make sure that at least one letter gets through to Tutor, Erasmus tells his correspondent in Ep. 159, he is repeating "essentially the same content, if not in the same words," as Ep. 157, which he had written to Tutor one day earlier and sent by a different messenger. Ep. 157, however, which Erasmus regarded as containing everything of consequence that was being repeated in Ep. 159, makes no mention of Colet. The second piece of evidence is the contrast between Erasmus's languid appreciation of England and his eagerness to travel to Italy. After his enumeration of places he could go to but does not particularly wish to visit, including England and Colet, he turns by way of contrast to the country he intensely desires to visit but has no means of reaching: "I am as eager as ever to see Italy—but, as Plautus says, it's not easy to fly without feathers." Had anyone given Erasmus an open invitation to visit Italy, he would not have been lingering indecisively in Tournehem writing these words to Tutor. A third consideration is all but decisive: he and Colet did not even correspond for the following three years.

42. Cf. Jean Hoyoux, "Les moyens d'existence d'Erasme," *Bibliothèque d'humanisme et renaissance*, n.s. 5 (1944): 17.

43. Erasmus to Colet, December 1504, in Allen, 1:405–406, Ep. 181.

44. Erasmus to Colet, December 1504, in Allen, 1:405–406, Ep. 181.

45. Irmgard Bezzel, "Sechs neu entdeckte Widmungsexemplare des Erasmus von Rotterdam und ihre Empfänger," *Gutenberg-Jahrbuch* 55 (1980): 89. Hoyoux, 34–41 gives a long list of Erasmus's dedications, the same volume sometimes being dedicated by Erasmus to more than one person; but the list is not free from errors of detail.

46. Thompson, 34–35, n. 27.

47. Allen, 1:229.

48. The *Lucubratiunculae* is put in February 1503 by, among others, *Bibliotheca Catholica Neerlandica Impressa 1500–1727* (The Hague: Nijhoff, 1954), 3; Charles Béné, "Erasme et Cicéron," in *Colloquia Erasmiana Turonensia*, 2 vols. (Toronto: Univ. of Toronto Pr., 1972), 2:573, 579; Raymond Marcel, "L'Enchiridion militis christiani: Sa genèse et sa doctrine, son succès et ses vicissitudes," in *Colloquia Erasmiana* 2:630; *Erasmus en zijn tijd: Tentoonstelling ingericht ter herdenking van de geboorte . . . van Erasmus te Rotterdam*, 2 vols. (Rotterdam: Museum Boymans-Van Beuningen, 1969), 1:67; *Tentoonstelling Dirk Martens 1473–1973* (Aalst: Stedelijk Museum—Oud Hospitaal, 1973), 270 (the bibliography is "as far as possible in chronological order" [261]); and Cavazza, 173 n. 1. Except for Vittorio de Caprariis, cited in the following note, the only writer known to me who dates the *Lucubratiunculae* to 1504 (without discussion) is Jean Rouschausse, ed., *Erasmus and Fisher: Their Correspondence 1511–1524* (Paris: Vrin, 1968), 20 n. 7.

49. Vittorio de Caprariis, "Il 'Panegyricus' di Erasmo a Filippo di Borgogna," *Rivista storica italiana* 65 (1953): 204n, declares for the date 1504 because that is the date of Erasmus's "Panegyricus," which he supposes to have formed part of the *Lucubratiunculae* but which is in fact a separate work. No copy of the *Lucubratiunculae* is recorded in North America, but its contents are accurately listed in Wouter Nijhoff and M. E. Kronenberg, *Nederlandsche bibliographie van 1500 tot 1540,* 3 vols. ('s-Gravenhage: Nijhoff, 1923) 1:303–304. I have used the copy in the British Library.

50. Alain Derville, "Vitrier," in *Biographie nationale . . . de Belgique*, vol. 38, suppl. 10 (Brussels: Bruylant, 1974), 809–816, with references to the fundamental researches of André Godin. See also Godin's annotations to Erasmus's life of Vitrier in *Vies*, 26–45.

51. See the revealing anecdote in Erasmus to Colet, 29 October 1511, in Allen, 1:479, Ep. 237, and the comment by Porter in *Erasmus and Cambridge*, 77.

52. Colet to Erasmus, ca. June 1517, in Allen, 2:599, Ep. 593.

53. The letters forming the correspondence are conveniently enumerated by Jayne, 158.

54. LB 9:86 (see Abbreviations at the front of this volume).

55. Seebohm, *Oxford Reformers*, 123.

56. *Dissertatio theologica, in qua sententiam vulgo receptam, esse Sacrae Scripturae multiplicem interdum sensum litteralem, nullo fundamento satis firmo niti demonstrare conatur Joannes Theodorus Beelen* (Louvain, 1845).

57. Seraphinus M. Zarb, O.P., "Utrum S. Thomas unitatem an vero pluralitatem sensus litteralis in Sacris Scripturis docuerit?" *Divus Thomas* (Piacenza) 33 (1930): 337.

58. St. Augustine, *De doctrina christiana* III 27 (cited by Beelen, 40 n. 10).

59. F. Ceuppens, O.P., "Quid S. Thomas de multiplici sensu litterali in Sacris Scripturis senserit?" *Divus Thomas* (Piacenza) 33 (1930): 169–171.

60. Cf. Beelen, 101–112.

61. Karlfried Froehlich, " 'Always to Keep the Literal Sense in Holy Scripture Means to Kill One's Soul': The State of Biblical Hermeneutics at the Beginning

of the Fifteenth Century," in *Literary Uses of Typology from the Late Middle Ages to the Present*, ed. Earl Miner (Princeton: Princeton Univ. Press, 1977), 29–32. This article studies seventy-five written opinions on the Eighth Assertion extracted by Jean Gerson from Jean Petit's arguments in defense of the recent assassination of the Duke of Orléans, brother of the King of France, at the instigation of Duke Jean of Burgundy. Petit's arguments, submitted to the Council of Constance (1414–1418), included a nonliteral interpretation of "Thou shalt not kill." It is significant that fifty-one respondents favored the Assertion quoted in the title of Froehlich's article, while only twenty-four condemned it.

62. Froehlich, 45–47.

63. Beelen, 78–85.

64. ". . . omnia ita sunt tecta ut infinitarum sentenciarum et verborum data est materia, in quoque fere cuique licet dicere quid velit, modo inter se concinna dicat."

65. On Stafford see Porter in *Erasmus and Cambridge*, 76; Thomas Becon, *Works*, ed. J. Ayre, 3 vols. (Cambridge, 1843–1844), 2:425–426; Hugh Latimer, *Sermons*, ed. G. E. Corrie, 2 vols. (Cambridge, 1844), 2:xxvii.

66. Patrick Collinson, *Archbishop Grindal 1519–1583* (Berkeley, Los Angeles, London: Univ. of California Press, 1979), 40–41.

67. Hector Boece to Erasmus, 26 May 1528, in Allen, 7:400, Ep. 1996.

68. Rouschausse, 19.

69. Erasmus to Colet, probably November 1499, in Allen, 1:248, Ep. 108 (see chap 5, n. 32, above).

70. Daniel Bellamy, *On Benevolence: A Summary of the Life and Character of Dean Colet. A Sermon* (London, 1756), 15.

71. Marie Delcourt, "Recherches sur Thomas More: La tradition continentale et la tradition anglaise," *Humanisme et renaissance* 3 (1936): 12–42.

72. E.g., Joachim Camerarius (1500–1574) wrote in 1553 that "if it happened that a person elicited a letter from Erasmus to himself this was regarded as an enormous title to honor and celebrated as a remarkable triumph. And if on top of that one could converse or associate with Erasmus, and have access to him, the person so favored regarded himself as blessed on earth" (qtd. in Allen, 3:405).

73. Published by Erasmus as an appendix to his own *Apologia* (Basel, 1520), 139–141, under the heading "Epistolae aliquot eruditorum virorum ex quibus perspicuum quanti sit Eduardi Lei virulentia." Abridged translation in Seebohm, *Oxford Reformers*, 468–469.

74. On this topic see Robert P. Adams, *The Better Part of Valor: More, Erasmus, Colet, and Vives, on Humanism, War, and Peace, 1496–1535* (Seattle: Univ. of Washington Press, 1962), 69–72; and James D. Tracy, *The Politics of Erasmus: A Pacifist Intellectual* (Toronto: Univ. of Toronto Press, 1978), 32–33, 148.

75. Erasmus, *Adagia*, 974.

76. Especially the "Pia confabulatio." Bucer would presumably not have recognized the name John Colet under the pseudonym Gratianus Pullus in "Peregrinatio religionis ergo," where Colet is the main figure (see below, chap. 10).

77. Martin Greschat, "Martin Bucers Bücherverzeichnis von 1518," *Archiv für Kulturgeschichte* 57 (1975): 178–182.

78. Bucer, *Deutsche Schriften*, ed. Robert Stupperich, vol. 1 (Gütersloh: Mohn, 1960), 284.

79. "Haec divinus ille & doctissimus vir Johan. Coletus Anglus, per Erasmum Rott. identidem et merito sane celebratus, probe sensit, ut testatur eius ad Erasmum Epistola" (p. [11]).

80. Martin Bucer, *Enarrationes perpetuae, in sacra quatuor evangelia, recognitae nuper & locis compluribus auctae* (n.p.) [B2ᵛ]; same text except that the concluding words are "ad Erasmum hac de re Epistola."

81. Constantin Hopf, *Martin Bucer and the English Reformation* (Oxford: Blackwell, 1946), 51–52.

82. Cf. Hastings Eells, *Martin Bucer* (New Haven: Yale Univ. Press, 1931), and Johannes Müller, *Martin Bucers Hermeneutik* (Gütersloh: Mohn, 1965). Müller, 142–148, outlines the characteristics of Bucer's exegesis.

83. Allan H. Gilbert, "Martin Bucer on Education," *Journal of English and Germanic Philology* 18 (1919): 321–345; esp. 326–327, 330, 340.

84. Eells, 65.

85. Müller, 67 ("Enthistorisierung des Evangeliums").

86. Adolphus Ward, in *Cambridge History of English Literature*, 15 vols. (Cambridge: Cambridge Univ. Press, 1907–1927), 14:79.

Chapter 6.
The Enterprise of Exegesis

1. Lupton, *Life*, 64.

2. Sixtus Senensis, *Bibliotheca sancta* (Lyons, 1591), o5ᵛ.

3. M. Pontet, *L'exégèse de S. Augustin prédicateur* (Paris: Aubier, 1946), 82.

4. Garry Haupt, ed., More, *A Treatise on the Passion*, vol. 13 of More, *CW*, lii. Charles Béné, in ASD, V, 2:12–14, describes the history of the term and the breadth of its meaning.

5. Tomas Hägg, *The Novel in Antiquity* (Berkeley, Los Angeles, London: Univ. of California Press, 1983), 162–163.

6. Early opinions are collected in PG, vol. 1, cols. 1179–1184 (see Abbreviations at the front of this volume).

7. Erasmus to John Longland, 3 March 1527, in Allen, 6:469, Ep. 1790.

8. On revision Colet realized that Chrysostom made the statement merely to illustrate how Paul's unwavering faith increased his daring in carrying out his work; he came to see that Chrysostom was writing an encomium, not a history. See St. John Chrysostom, "Liber . . . de laudibus Beati Pauli Apostoli, Homilia VII," in *Opera Venerabilis Bedae* (Basel, 1537), 5:1175.

9. Once, Colet says here, Christians were few but sincere; later "a mass of people poured into a nominal rather than genuine Christianity." Colet's point is not the perplexing problem that these new members, many of them backsliders under earlier persecutions, presented to the fourth-century church but merely the distinction, a favorite with him, between the minority of "sincere" Christians and the much greater number of nominal Christians ruled by the devil and destined for hell.

10. Edward A. Cerny, *Firstborn of Every Creature (Col. 1:15)* (Baltimore: St. Mary's Univ., 1938), xvii.

11. Cf. Alfred Hockel, *Christus, der Erstgeborene: Zur Geschichte der Exegese von Kol 1, 15* (Düsseldorf: Patmos-Verlag, 1965), 95–97.

12. Spicq, 199.

13. St. Ignatius, Epistle to the Philadelphians (longer version), chap. 54 in *The Ante-Nicene Fathers*, 10 vols. (Buffalo, 1885–1887), 1:81.

14. Clement of Alexandria, *Stromata*, 36 (PG, vol. 8, cols. 1152–1153).

15. Jean-Pierre Massaut, *Tradition et critique à la veille de la Réforme en France* (Paris: Vrin, 1974), 140–148.

16. Spicq, 123–124.

17. Spicq, 200.

18. *Oeuvres du pseudo-Denys*, 209B (p. 210).

19. Bentley, 156–158. On the discussion see also Jarrott's note to Colet's text, C, p. 335, n. 7.

20. PL, vol. 196, cols. 665–684; see cols. 665–674, 679 (see Abbreviations at the front of this volume).

21. L. Vischer and D. Lerch, "Die Auslegungsgeschichte als notwendige theologische Aufgabe," in *Studia patristica*, vol. 1 (Berlin: Akademie-Verlag, 1957), 414.

22. PL, vol. 158, col. 528. Anselm's principle is also asserted by St. Bonaventure, *Opera omnia*, 10 vols. (Quaracchi: Collegium S. Bonaventurae, 1883–1902), 4:138.

23. Bonaventure, 5:388, qtd. in Henri de Lubac, S.J., *Exégèse médiévale: Les quatre sens de l'Ecriture*, 4 vols. (Paris: Aubier, 1959–1964), 4:270.

24. The distinction is drawn by Beryl Smalley, *The Study of the Bible in the Middle Ages*, 2d ed. (Notre Dame, Ind.: Univ. of Notre Dame Press, 1964), 293.

25. Jean Leclercq, *The Love of Learning and the Desire for God*, 2d ed. (New York: Fordham Univ. Press, 1974), 87–109.

26. ASD, V, 2:193.

27. More to a Monk, ca. 1519–1520, in More, *C*, 192 (see Abbreviations at the front of this volume).

28. K. W. Humphreys, *The Library of the Franciscans of Siena in the Late Fifteenth Century* (Amsterdam: Erasmus, 1978), 20.

29. Barry Collett, *Italian Benedictine Scholars and the Reformation: The Congregation of Santa Giustina of Padua* (Oxford: Clarendon, 1985), 8.

30. Smalley, 293.

31. Hugh of St. Victor, *De arca Noe morali* IV.6 (PL, vol. 176, col. 672).

32. The four senses of Scripture were transmitted in the well-known distich "Littera gesta docet, quid credas allegoria, / Moralis quid agas, quo tendas anagogia." (For this tradition see Lubac, 1:23–39.) For metrical reasons the tropological sense is here called *allegoria*, producing confusion with *allegoria* in the wider sense in which I use the term.

33. Nicholas of Lyra and St. Albert the Great, qtd. in Spicq, 249–250.

34. Jean Steinmann, *Richard Simon et les origines de l'exégèse biblique* (Paris: Desclée de Brouwer, 1960), 38.

35. Anthony Nemetz, "Literalness and the *sensus litteralis*," *Speculum* 34 (1959): 78–80.

36. T. S. K. Scott-Craig, "The Literal Sense," *History of Ideas News Letter* 1 (1955): 11–12.

37. W. Schwarz, *Principles and Problems of Biblical Translation: Some Reformation Controversies and Their Background* (Cambridge: Cambridge Univ. Press, 1955), 173–174.

38. Hans Urs von Balthasar, "Le mysterion d'Origène," *Recherches de science religieuse* 26 (1936): 561.

39. Schwarz, 173–174.

40. The parallel is pointed out by George V. Jourdan, *The Movement towards Catholic Reform in the Early XVI Century* (London: John Murray, 1914), 113–114.

41. Samuel Berger, *La Bible au seizième siècle* (Paris, 1879), 29; cited by Jourdan, 114 n. 1.

42. See appendix 2.

43. George A. Kennedy, *Greek Rhetoric under Christian Emperors* (Princeton: Princeton Univ. Press, 1983), 241–254.

44. Don Cameron Allen, *Mysteriously Meant: The Rediscovery of Pagan Symbolism and Allegorical Interpretation in the Renaissance* (Baltimore and London: Johns Hopkins Univ. Press, 1970), 9–10, with references.

45. Patristic arguments for the study of ancient writers are summarized by E. Harris Harbison, *The Christian Scholar in the Age of the Reformation* (New York: Scribner's, 1956), chap. 1.

46. Editor's introduction to *Saint Basil on the Value of Greek Literature*, ed. N. G. Wilson (London: Duckworth, 1975), 14.

47. Luzi Schucan, *Das Nachleben von Basilius Magnus "ad adolescentes": Ein Beitrag zur Geschichte des christlichen Humanismus* (Geneva: Droz, 1973), 64.

48. Wilson, introduction to *Saint Basil*, 14.

49. Schucan, 116.

50. St. Augustine, *De doctrina christiana* II.19ff. (*CC*, Ser. Lat., 33:54ff.; see Abbreviations at the front of this volume).

51. Origen, *Comm. in Epist. ad Rom.* I (PG, vol. 1, vols. 861–863), similarly asserts that the gentiles' failure to worship the true God, whom they had come to know, made them deserve punishment. The parallel is not, perhaps, close enough to warrant its being considered a source.

52. For Colet, faith generated warmth ("calor"); see *De sacramentis*, passim (appendix 1).

53. References collected in John Maxwell Edmonds, ed., *The Fragments of Attic Comedy*, 3 vols. in 4 (Leiden: Brill, 1957–1961), 3B:626.

54. Edmonds, 3B:627 note g.

55. Jean-Pierre Massaut, "Erasme et saint Thomas," in *Colloquia Erasmiana Turonensia*, 2 vols. (Toronto: Univ. of Toronto Press, 1972), 2:593–603, surveys the evidence, finding that on the whole Erasmus accords Aquinas a place well below the Fathers. Sometimes, however, he mentions Aquinas in the same breath with them. In his New Testament, Erasmus says, he has had sometimes to disagree with great authorities: "I show that in some passages Hilary erred, Augustine erred, Thomas erred. . . . They were very great men, but they were after all men" (Erasmus to Henry Bullock, 22 August 1516, in Allen, 2:325, Ep. 456).

56. Godin (*Vies*, 65) surveys the use of *enthousiasmon* in Erasmus's other writings.

57. Years later both men changed their positions regarding the reasons for the acceptability of Abel's sacrifice. In the *Paraphrasis* of Hebrews (1520), LB 7:1187, Erasmus adopts Colet's theory (as pointed out by Bauer, 176–178); he must have reconsidered Colet's position when he published Colet's letter in October 1518. Meanwhile Colet for his part had developed an altogether different explanation for the acceptability of Abel's sacrifice (RO, 249).

58. Ronald A. Knox concludes his *Enthusiasm* (London: Oxford Univ. Press, 1950), with a paradoxical evocation of Erasmus.

59. Cf. Erasmus, "Ratio verae theologiae," in *Ausgewählte Werke*, ed. Hajo Holborn and Annemarie Holborn (Munich: Beck, 1933), 191: "Quid enim tam dispar et discrepans a stilo prophetarum, Christi et apostolorum quam hoc, quo qui Thomam et Scotum sequuntur, nunc de rebus divinis disputant?"

60. Edward L. Surtz, S.J., " 'Oxford Reformers' and Scholasticism," *Studies in Philology* 47 (1950): 549. Notwithstanding its title, this article deals only with Aquinas (547).

61. Paul O. Kristeller, "Florentine Platonism and Its Relations with Humanism and Scholasticism," *Church History* 8 (1939): 201, 205.

62. Erasmus to Louis Platz (31 July 1520), in Allen, 4:319, Ep. 1127.

63. Erasmus to John Slechta (23 April 1519), in Allen, 3:552, Ep. 950.

64. Erasmus, "Ratio verae theologiae," 183.

65. Christian Dolfen, *Die Stellung des Erasmus von Rotterdam zur scholastischen Methode* (Osnabrück: Meinders und Elstermann, 1936), 86–87.

66. Dolfen, 88. Erika Rummell, *Erasmus' Annotations on the New Testament: From Philologist to Theologian* (Toronto: Univ. of Toronto Press, 1986), 76–80, finds that Erasmus usually treated Aquinas disdainfully, but she does not give any weight to his numerous citations of Aquinas in the *Annotationes*.

67. Cf. Wayne Shumaker, *The Occult Sciences in the Renaissance* (Berkeley, Los Angeles, London: Univ. of California Press, 1972), esp. 186–190. For the strength of occult traditions in sixteenth-century English intellectual circles see Mordechai Feingold, "The Occult Tradition in the English Universities of the Renaissance: A Reassessment," in *Occult and Scientific Mentalities in the Renaissance*, ed. Brian Vickers (Cambridge: Cambridge Univ. Press, 1984), 73–94.

68. Helda Bullotta Barracco, "Saggio bio-bibliografico su Enrico Cornelio Agrippa di Nettesheim," *Rassegna di filosofia* 6 (1957): 237–238.

69. Lupton, *Life*, 201.

70. Henricus Cornelius Agrippa, *Opera*, 2 vols. (Lyons, 1531), 2:510.

71. Agrippa, 2:512.

72. Agrippa, 2:595.

73. On the significance of "pentagram" see Shumaker, 144, and the diagram reproduced from Agrippa, 1:193, by Shumaker, 141.

74. Cf. Charles M. Nauert, Jr., *Agrippa and the Crisis of Renaissance Thought* (Urbana: Univ. of Illinois Press, 1965).

75. Lupton later wondered (*The Influence of Dean Colet upon the Reformation of the English Church* [London and Cambridge, 1893], 22 n. 2) whether Agrippa's real purpose in visiting England may have been to visit Colet; to which the answer must be no (see following note).

76. For Agrippa's career at this juncture see Josef Strelka, *Der burgundische Renaissancehof Margarethes von Österreich und seine literarhistorische Bedeutung* (Vienna: A. Sexl, 1957), 65–67.

77. Allen, 9:350.

78. Paola Zambelli, "Cornelio Agrippa, Erasmo e la teologia umanista," *Rinascimento*, 2d ser. 10 (1970): 30 n. 1.

79. François Secret, *Les kabbalistes chrétiens de la renaissance* (Paris: Dunod, 1964), 228–229.

80. Colet to Erasmus, June 1517, in Allen, 2:599, Ep. 593.

81. Shumaker, 136–137.

82. Allen, 2:350.

83. On this period of Reuchlin's career see Hans Rupprich, "Johannes Reuchlin und seine Bedeutung im europäischen Humanismus," in *Johannes Reuchlin 1455–1522: Festgabe seiner Vaterstadt Pforzheim zur 500. Wiederkehr seines Geburtstages*, ed. Manfred Krebs (Pforzheim: Selbstverlag der Stadt Pforzheim, 1955), 24–34.

84. A. S. Pease, "Caeli Enarrant," *Harvard Theological Review* 34 (1941): 163–200.

85. Marsilio Ficino, *Epistolae* (Venice, 1495), fol. cxxxvi^r.

86. The angels are introduced into the stories by Dionysius. Colet shows no interest in the fact that neither Gen. 41:1–7 nor Dan. 2 makes mention of them.

87. Karl Henrich Graf, "Jacobus Faber Stapulensis," *Zeitschrift für die historische Theologie* 22 (1852): 25–28.

88. DCH, p. 25 n. 1. The passage was canceled when Colet added the continuation called by Lupton "Chapter 16."

89. Cf. Frederic Henry Chase, *Chrysostom: A Study in the History of Biblical Interpretation* (Cambridge, 1887), 41–45.

90. Pico della Mirandola, *Oration on the Dignity of Man*, in *The Renaissance Philosophy of Man*, ed. Ernst Cassirer et al. (Chicago: Univ. of Chicago Press, 1948), 250–252.

91. A sound recent summary is Douglas Powell, "Arkandisziplin," in *Theologische Realenzyklopädie*, vol. 4 (Berlin and New York: De Gruyter, 1978), 1–8. The term *disciplina arcani* was first used by Melchior Cano in 1563.

92. Browning, 771 provisionally identifies Firmicus Maternus the writer on astrology with Firmicus Maternus the Christian polemicist.

Chapter 7. "Living Wisdom"

1. *Oeuvres du pseudo-Denys*, 228.

2. Thomas M. Greene, "Petrarch and the Humanist Hermeneutic," in *Italian Literature, Roots and Branches: Essays in Honor of Thomas Goddard Bergin*, ed. Giose Rimanelli and Kenneth John Atchity (New Haven: Yale Univ. Press, 1976), 210.

3. Pits, 691.

4. Lupton's correct identification of Colet's allusion here (C, p. 67 n. 1) is ignored by Jarrott. The triple cord gave rise to a number of allegorical interpreta-

tions. That endorsed by Colet was seldom found in earlier authorities. It appears first in Bede (*CC*, Ser. Lat., 119A:208) and was picked up from him, word for word, by Hrabanus Maurus (PL, vol. 109, cols. 171, 440). (Heinz Meyer and Rudolf Suntrup, *Lexikon der mittelalterlichen Zahlenbedeutungen* [Munich: Fink, 1987], col. 261.) Colet's phrasing is, however, quite different from Bede's.

5. Lupton, C, p. 109, n. 3, observes that the same interpretation is found in St. Bernard and other spiritual writers.

6. Allegorical and historical interpretations are anthologized by St. Thomas Aquinas, *Catena aurea in quatuor evangelia*, ed. Angelico Guarienti, O.P., new ed., 2 vols. (Turin and Rome: Marietti, 1953), 2:571–572.

7. See James Samuel Preus, *From Shadow to Promise: Old Testament Interpretation from Augustine to the Young Luther* (Cambridge: Belknap-Harvard Univ. Press, 1969), pt. 1, "Medieval Hermeneutics to 1513," 9–149.

8. Cf. Matt. 13:18–23 (who however softens the effect by omitting "so that") and Luke 8:11–15.

9. Isa. 6:9–10.

10. John 12:40.

11. Acts 28:26–27.

12. Umberto Eco, "Simbolo," in *Enciclopedia Einaudi*, vol. 12 (Turin: Einaudi, 1981), 877–915; quotation at 904.

13. See above, 53–57.

14. The concept of tradition during this period is studied from opposed points of view by George H. Tavard, *Holy Writ or Holy Church* (New York: Harper, 1959), esp. chap. 4, "The Fifteenth-Century Dilemma"; and Helmut Feld, *Die Anfänge der modernen biblischen Hermeneutik in der spätmittelalterlichen Theologie* (Wiesbaden: Steiner, 1977), esp. chap. 2, "Der franziskanische Armutsstreit im 14. Jahrhundert," and chap. 8, "Johannes Gerson."

15. Cf. Heb. 5:12–14. As already noted, Colet unhesitatingly accepted Paul's authorship of Hebrews.

16. In Colet's time this passage was generally considered "a carefully constructed definition of faith" (Bentley, 29).

17. Heinrich Denifle, O.P., *Die abendländischen Schriftausleger bis Luther über Justitia Dei (Rom. 1:17) und Justificatio* (Mainz: F. Kirchheim, 1905).

18. Leclercq, 230–231.

19. *Oeuvres du pseudo-Denys*, 565D–569D (Gandillac's translation, 324–326).

20. *The Colloquies of Erasmus*, trans. Craig R. Thompson (Chicago: Univ. of Chicago Press, 1965), 37.

21. John Archer Gee, *The Life and Works of Thomas Lupset* (New Haven: Yale Univ. Press, 1928), 35–41; less plausibly Preserved Smith, *A Key to the Colloquies of Erasmus* (Cambridge: Harvard Univ. Press, 1927), 6, suggests a Continental pupil of Erasmus's named Gaspar Ursinus Velius. The ASD editor seems not to know Gee's suggestion.

22. Marsilio Ficino, in Plato, *Opera omnia quae exstant*, trans. Ficino (Frankfurt, 1602), 407.

23. Marsilio Ficino, in Plotinus, *Operum philosophicorum omnium libri liv in sex enneados distincti*, trans. Ficino (Basel, 1580), 41.

24. Marsilio Ficino, "De raptu Pauli," in *Prosatori latini del quattrocento*, ed. Eugenio Garin (Milan and Naples: Ricciardi, 1952), 932–969 (Latin text facing Ficino's own Italian trans.); quotation at 964.

25. Spicq, 213–215.

26. Lupton, *Life*, 92.

27. For the full Latin text of the letter see Knight, 265–269; the suppressed portion is on 266–268.

28. Seebohm, *Oxford Reformers*, 46.

29. Bonaventure also uses *retexere* in describing his exegetic aims (Etienne Gilson, *La philosophie au moyen âge*, 2d ed. [Paris: Payot, 1947], 440). The O'Kelly and Jarrott edition fails to see what Colet is doing in this chapter and translates the cited Latin words as "to the text itself, or rather, to an analysis of it."

30. Lupton has a valuable long note on the unnatural natural history that Colet draws on here: C, pp. 127–128n.

31. Lupton, foreword to *Opuscula* [v].

32. See John Brown, "John Colet and the Preachers of the Reformation," in his *Puritan Preaching in England* (New York: Scribner's, 1900), 35–63.

33. Michael J. Kelly, "Canterbury Jurisdiction and Influence during the Episcopate of William Warham, 1503–1532" (Ph.D. diss., Cambridge University, 1963), 112 n. 2., makes the following points regarding the dating of the sermon. (1) War was the chief business on the agenda in 1512, but Colet, despite his strong feelings on war, does not mention the subject at all. (2) Colet asserts that he does not know what will be done in the assembly, whereas the agenda in 1512, concerning issues associated with war, was well known in advance. (3) He calls for laws against simony; such laws were in fact enacted during the Convocation of 1510, and it would make no sense to call for them again only two years later. (4) He deplores the fact that general and provincial councils are not called, but this complaint would have lost its force by 1512: the bull for the Fifth Lateran Council was issued 15 July 1511, and proctors for England were appointed in 1512. Colet must be referring to the long hiatus between the Convocations of 1504 and 1510, as well as to the much longer period during which no general council of the Church had been called.

34. For bibliography and discussion see Gigliola Fragnito, "Cultura umanistica e riforma religiosa: il 'De officio viri boni ac probi episcopi' di Gasparo Contarini," *Studi veneziani* 11 (1969): 1–115, and Hubert Jedin, *Il tipo ideale di vescovo secondo la riforma cattolica*, ed. Giuseppe Alberigo (Brescia: Morcelliana, 1985).

35. Melton's criticisms are summarized in John B. Gleason, "The Earliest Evidence for Ecclesiastical Censorship of Printed Books in England," *The Library* 6th ser. 4 (1982): 139.

36. L. Dacheux, *Un réformateur catholique à la fin du XVᵉ siècle: Jean Geiler de Kaysersberg, prédicateur à la cathédrale de Strasbourg (1468–1510)* (Paris, 1876), 33.

37. Dacheux, 482–485.

38. Dionysius the Carthusian, *Opera minora*, 2 vols. (Cologne, 1532), 1:43–44; qtd. by K. Krogh-Tonning, *Der letzte Scholastiker: Eine Apologie* (Freiburg i. B.: Herder, 1904), 6.

39. Arthur W. Jenks, "John Colet," *Anglican Theological Review* 1 (1919): 363.

40. E. Gordon Duff, *The Printers, Stationers and Bookbinders of Westminster and London from 1476 to 1535* (Cambridge: Cambridge Univ. Press, 1906), 162.

41. On the office of King's Printer see Robert Steele, ed., *Tudor and Stuart Proclamations*, 2 vols. (Oxford: Clarendon, 1910), 1:xxxiv–xxxvii.

42. H. S. Bennett, *English Books and Readers 1475 to 1557* (Cambridge: Cambridge Univ. Press, 1952), 191.

43. *Index Britanniae Scriptorum: John Bale's Index of British and Other Writers*, ed. R. L. Poole and Mary Bateson (Oxford: Clarendon, 1902), 195.

Chapter 8. Colet's Sacramental Universe

1. The title Lupton gives the treatise, *De Sacramentis Ecclesiae*, has no authority. It is simply the title of the manuscript now in the library of St. Paul's School, London, which Lupton used as his copytext; he did not know of the existence of the original. The title of the original (in British Library Loan MS. 55/2 [Duke of Leeds]) from which his manuscript was copied reads "De Sacramentis Part." What is meant by the last four letters, not a Latin word as they stand, is unclear. In more important respects than the title, Lupton's edition, his first venture in editing Colet, leaves much to be desired. It offers no translation, though Colet's style is especially difficult here as he is wrestling with the expression of an intricate argument and the reader has no Paul or Dionysius to fall back on in determining his meaning. Lupton's copy departs from its original in some fourteen readings, and he makes fifty-two additional errors on his own, ranging from minor slips to misread words and the accidental omission of whole lines.

2. I must confess some wonder at the selectivity by which Catherine A. L. Jarrott, "Erasmus's Annotations and Colet's Commentaries on Paul: A Comparison of Some Theological Themes," in *Essays on the Works of Erasmus*, ed. Richard L. DeMolen (New Haven: Yale Univ. Press, 1978), concludes that "to Colet the world of the Christian is not a vale of tears but a grace-filled love-filled existence of endless opportunity for spiritual growth" (131).

3. See Miles, *Colet and the Platonic Tradition*, passim, and J. B. Trapp, "An English Late Medieval Cleric and Italian Thought: The Case of John Colet, Dean of St. Paul's (1467–1519)," in *Medieval English Religious and Ethical Literature: Essays in Honour of G. H. Russell,* ed. Gregory Kratzman and James Simpson (Dover, N.H.: Brewer, 1986), 233–250.

4. Heinz Robert Schlette, *Die Nichtigkeit der Welt: Der philosophische Horizont des Hugo von St. Viktor* (Munich: Kösel, 1961), 11–15.

5. Arthur O. Lovejoy, *The Great Chain of Being* (Cambridge: Harvard Univ. Press, 1936), 122.

6. Lovejoy, 101–102.

7. Gustaf Aulén, *Christus Victor*, trans. A. G. Herbert (1931; reprint, New York: Scribner's, 1969), is the standard study. For a brief account see Pelikan, 1:148–151.

8. Bernhard Poschmann, *Paenitentia secunda: Die kirchliche Busse im ältesten Christentum bis Cyprian und Origenes: Eine dogmengeschichtliche Untersuchung* (Bonn: Peter Hanstein, 1940).

9. Lupton's proposed identification of the source of this quotation is merely a loose parallel; the actual source is St. John Chrysostom, *Homilia XXVI in Matthaeum* 325B. Though Colet did not know it, Chrysostom in his turn took the passage from Aristophanes (*Clouds,* 126), a favorite author of the saint's whose works, a contemporary of Colet's assures us (Benjamin F. Rogers, ed., *Acharnians* [London: Bell, 1930], lii), he used as a pillow. Colet could follow Chrysostom in many things, but not in that.

10. David Burr, "Olivi on Marriage: The Conservative as Prophet," *Journal of Medieval and Renaissance Studies* 2 (1972): 186–187.

11. Lovejoy, 83–84.

12. Reproduced in Allen, vol. 4, facing p. 516.

13. As observed by William O. Clebsch, "John Colet and Reformation," *Anglican Theological Review* 37 (1955): 169.

14. R. R. Bolgar, *The Classical Heritage and Its Beneficiaries* (Cambridge: Cambridge Univ. Press, 1954), 269–270.

15. Bruno Nardi, "L'aristotelismo della scolastica e i francescani," *Scholastica ratione historico-critica instauranda: Acta Congressus Internationalis Romae Anno Sancto MCML celebrati* (Rome: Pontificum Athenaeum Antonianum, 1951), 615–616.

16. Qtd. in Leo Veuthey, O.F.M. Conv., "Les divers courants de la philosophie augustino-franciscaine au moyen âge," in *Scholastica,* 630.

17. Nardi, 620.

18. Veuthey, 631–632.

19. Nardi, 623.

20. Paul Tillich, *A History of Christian Thought* (New York: Harper and Row, 1968), 85. See Werner Dettloff, O.F.M., " 'Christus tenens medium in omnibus': Sinn und Funktion der Theologie bei Bonaventura," *Wissenschaft and Weisheit* 20 (1957): 28–42, 120–140.

21. Etienne Gilson, *La philosophie de saint Bonaventure,* 2d ed. (Paris: Vrin, 1943), 235–236.

22. Gilson, *Philosophie de Bonaventure,* 157.

23. Veuthey, 639.

24. Ficino, in Plotinus, 17: "Duos Platonici praecipue mundos ponunt: Primum intelligibilem scilicet, divinam mentem mundi huius principium et exemplar: secundum sensibilem, hanc scilicet sensibus manifestum, divini exemplaris imaginem."

25. Ficino, "De raptu pauli," 932–936.

26. See the valuable discussion in Jayne, chap. 4.

27. The voluntarist element in Colet's writings is stressed by Peter Iver Kaufman, *Augustinian Piety and Catholic Reform: Augustine, Colet, and Erasmus* (Macon, Ga.: Mercer Univ. Press, 1982), 60–81.

28. The following list of Franciscan features is from Evangéliste de Saint-Béat, O.F.M. Cap., "Etudes sur saint Bonaventure," *Etudes franciscaines* 2 (1899): 382–400.

29. Gandillac, *Oeuvres du pseudo-Denys*, 223 n. 1.

30. *De triplici via* III.13, in *The Works of St. Bonaventure*, trans. José de Vinck, 5 vols. (Paterson, N.J.: St. Anthony Guild Press, 1960–1970), 1:93.

31. Jean-Pierre Massaut, "Mystique rhénane et humanisme chrétien d'Eckhart à Erasme: Continuité, convergence, ou rupture?" in *The Late Middle Ages and the Dawn of Humanism Outside Italy: Proceedings of the International Congress, Louvain, May 11–13 1970*, ed. G. Verbeke and J. IJsewijn (Louvain: University Press, 1972), 114–115.

32. C. A. Patrides, "Renaissance Thought on the Celestial Hierarchy: The Decline of a Tradition," *Journal of the History of Ideas* 20 (1959): 155–166; supplemented by his "Renaissance Views on the 'Unconfused Orders Angellick,' " *Journal of the History of Ideas* 23 (1962): 265–267.

33. O. Speyr, *Die literarische Fälschung im heidnischen und christlichen Altertum* (Munich: Beck, 1971), 56, 81, 231, 289.

34. René Rocques et al., eds., Introduction to ps.-Dionysius Areopagita, *La hiérarchie céleste* (Paris: Cerf, 1958), vii.

35. Ir. Hausherr, S.J., "Doutes au sujet du 'Divin Denis,' " *Orientalia Christiana periodica* 2 (1936): 489–490.

36. Martin Grabmann, "Die mittelalterlichen lateinischen Übersetzungen des Pseudo-Dionysius Areopagita," in *Mittelalterliches Geistesleben: Abhandlungen zur Geschichte der Scholastik und Mystik*, 2 vols. (Munich: Max Hueber, 1926–1936), 1:450–466.

37. They are referred to as "recent" in a letter assigned on internal evidence to about November 1501 (More, *C*, 4).

38. John Fisher, *Sacri sacerdotii defensio contra Lutherum (1525)*, ed. Hermann K. Schmeink (Münster i. W.: Aschendorff, 1925), 63.

39. *The Enchiridion of Erasmus*, trans. and ed. Raymond Himelick (Bloomington: Indiana Univ. Press, 1963), 107. See also Massaut, *Tradition et critique*, 182–183.

40. Erasmus to Peter Barbirius, 13 August 1521, in Allen, 4:561, Ep. 1225.

41. František Novotný, *The Posthumous Life of Plato* (Prague:Academia, 1977), 384.

42. Lupton, *Life*, 147 n. 1.

43. Colet to Erasmus, ca. June 1517, in Allen, 2:599, Ep. 593.

44. Ian Hacking, *The Emergence of Probability* (Cambridge: Cambridge Univ. Press, 1976), 33–34, discusses the analogous case of critical attacks on the Donation of Constantine, which also failed to make much impact because the Donation was supported by authority.

45. See Heiko A. Oberman, *Masters of the Reformation: The Emergence of a New Intellectual Climate in Europe*, trans. Dennis Martin (Cambridge: Cambridge Univ. Press, 1981), chap. 6, "The Augustine Renaissance in the Later Middle Ages."

46. Veuthey, 629.

47. Martin Grabmann, "Der Einfluß des hl. Bonaventura auf die Theologie und Frömmigkeit des deutschen Mittelalters," *Zeitschrift für Aszese und Mystik* 19 (1944): 22.

48. Georg Steer, "Die Rezeption des theologischen Bonaventura-Schrifttums

im deutschen Spätmittelalter," in *Bonaventura: Studien zu seiner Wirkungsgeschichte* (Werl i. W.: Dietrich Coelde, 1976), 146–156, esp. 147.

49. *Gesamtkatalog der Wiegendrucke.*

50. *Catalogue des livres imprimés au quinzième siècle des bibliothèques de Belgique*, 4 vols. (Brussels: Pour la Société des bibliophiles et iconophiles de Belgique, 1932).

51. Evangéliste de Saint-Béat, O.F.M. Cap., "L'école franciscaine et ses chefs, s. Bonaventure et le B. Scot," *Etudes franciscaines* 1 (1899): 463.

52. For the history of the axiom see J. Pehaire, "L'axiom 'bonum est diffusivum sui' dans le néoplatonisme et le thomisme," *Revue de l' Université d'Ottawa* 1 (1932): 5*–30*.

53. Lovejoy, 84.

54. Ficino, Epistolae, xlvi^v–xlvii^r. See also FEM, 104.

55. Klaus Kremer, "Das 'Warum' der Schöpfung: 'quia bonus' vel/et 'quia voluit'?: Ein Beitrag zum Verhältnis vom Neuplatonismus und Christentum an Hand des Prinzips 'bonum est diffusivum sui,' " in *Parusia: Studien zur Philosophie Platons und zur Problemgeschichte des Platonismus: Festgabe für Johannes Hirschberger*, ed. Kurt Flasch (Frankfurt a. M.: Minerva, 1965), 247–249.

56. C. S. Lewis, *The Discarded Image: An Introduction to Medieval and Renaissance Literature* (Cambridge: Cambridge Univ. Press, 1964), 24.

57. Pierre Boyancé, *Etudes sur le Songe de Scipion* (Bordeaux: Feret, 1936), 115–116.

58. José de Vinck, trans., *Breviloquium*, in *Works of St. Bonaventure* 2:79n.

59. John H. Gay, "Four Medieval Views of Creation," *Harvard Theological Review* 56 (1963): 243–273.

60. Iohannes-M. Bissen, O.F.M., "De motivo Incarnationis: Disquisitio historico-dogmatica," *Antonianum* 7 (1932): 331–332.

61. Bernardinus a S. Ioanne Rotundo, O.F.M. Cap., "Thesis franciscanae de motivo primario Incarnationis expositio," *Collectanea franciscana* 4 (1934): 546.

62. Gay, 261–267.

63. Bonaventure, *De reductione artium ad theologiam*, in *Opera omnia* 5:321.

64. On Hugh see especially Jean Chantillon, "Une ecclésiologie médiévale: L'Idée de l'Eglise dans la théologie de l'école de Saint-Victor au XIIe siècle," *Irénikon* 22 (1949), esp. 123–126, 400–401, 407–410, which show significant parallels between Victorine thought and Colet's.

65. Schlette, 25–27.

66. Hugh of St. Victor, Prologus ii to *On the Sacraments of the Christian Faith (De Sacramentis)*, trans. and ed. Roy J. Deferrari (Cambridge: Mediaeval Academy of America, 1951), 3–4.

67. R. R. Marett, *Sacraments of Simple Folk* (Oxford: Clarendon, 1933), chap. 1, esp. 6–8.

68. Romano Guardini, *Die Lehre des heil. Bonaventura von der Erlösung* (Düsseldorf: Schwann, 1921), 33–34.

69. George H. Williams, *Anselm: Communion and Atonement* (St. Louis: Concordia, 1960), 9–12.

70. Williams, 17.

71. St. Bonaventure, *In IV Sent.* 6.1.un.5, cond. in *Opera omnia* 4:145; qtd. in Daniel Culhane, *De corpore mystico doctrina Seraphici*, (Mundelein, Ill.: Privately printed, 1934), 75.

72. On the sister-spouse (*soror-coniunx*) theme see Carl Kérenyi, *Zeus and Hera* (Princeton: Princeton Univ. Press, 1975), chap. 5.

73. Guardini, 136.

74. Origen, *Comm. in Ep. ad Rom.* (a work Colet mined extensively—see appendix 2) III (PG, vol. 14, col. 921). After citing John 10:35 Origen continues (in Rufinus's Latin translation of the fifth century): "Those, therefore, to whom the word of God is spoken are declared by the Lord in the Gospel to be not men but gods." And a few sentences below: "non erant homines, sed dii." Origen's commentary diverges here from the literal meaning, in context, of Jesus' rabbinical argument. Colet adopts the view expressed by Origen.

75. Helmut Riedlinger, *Die Makellosigkeit der Kirche in den lateinischen Hoheliedkommentaren des Mittelalters* (Münster i. W.: Aschendorff, 1958), 2–3, points out that the Canticle was, after the Psalms and Paul's Epistles, the book most frequently commented on in the middle ages. Of the 77 commentaries of known authorship, 45 come from the period 1200–1500; in addition there survive 126 anonymous commentaries dating from 700 to 1500.

76. Josef Schmid, "Brautschaft, heilige," *Reallexikon für Antike und Christentum* 2 (1954): 529–534.

77. Schmid, 548.

Chapter 9. St. Paul's School

1. Reprinted in Lupton, *Life*, 305–310.

2. Colet, qtd. in Knight, 402.

3. Edmund Dudley, *The Tree of Commonwealth*, ed. D. M. Brodie (Cambridge: Cambridge Univ. Press, 1948), 16 n. 3.

4. Thomas Lupset, *An Exhortation to Yonge Men, Perswadinge Them to Walke in the Pathe Way That Leadeth to Honeste and Goodnes* (*STC* 16936; London, 1535), reprinted in Gee, 235–236.

5. Margolin, ed., Erasmus, *De pueris instituendis*, 551 n. 567, traces back to Knight's biography of 1724 the application to Colet of a passage in the *De pueris instituendis* about a teacher's deliberate harshness to pupils. I would add that it is unlikely that Erasmus would think of someone in Colet's high position as a "teacher." In any case the application to Colet is gratuitous: Knight tended to connect Erasmus as closely as possible with the English scene.

6. Lupton, *Influence of Colet*, 52.

7. Arthur F. Leach, *VCH, Lancaster*, vol. 2 (1908), 590.

8. Reddaway and Walker, 177, 180.

9. Kenneth Charlton, *Education in Renaissance England* (London: Methuen, 1965), 92.

10. Arthur F. Leach, "St. Paul's School before Colet," *Archaeologia* 62, pt. 1 (1910): 207.

11. Charlton, 92.

12. William Herbert, *The History of the Twelve Great Livery Companies of London*, 2 vols. (1834–1837; reprint, New York: Augustus M. Kelley, 1968), 1:235. Cf. *Acts of Court*, 59, 116, 141, 230–232, 244; the last two references are from Colet's lifetime.

13. Leach, "St. Paul's School before Colet," 208.

14. Colet, "Statutes," in Lupton, *Life*, 281–282.

15. F. W. M. Draper, *Four Centuries of Merchant Taylors' School 1561–1961* (Oxford: Oxford Univ. Press, 1962), 242.

16. Ridley, 169.

17. Watney, *Mercers' Company*, 87.

18. McDonnell, *Annals*, 32–33.

19. McDonnell, *Annals*, 41.

20. McDonnell, *Annals*, 49–52.

21. *Acts of Court*, 360–364.

22. *Acts of Court*, 393.

23. McDonnell, *Annals*, 44–45.

24. *Acts of Court*, 401.

25. *Acts of Court*, 404.

26. Sir Michael McDonnell, *A History of St. Paul's School* (London: Chapman and Hall, 1909), 1–7, 23–32.

27. Leach, "St. Paul's School before Colet."

28. Leach's basic theses, in the light of which he tended to discuss particular problems in the history of early English schooling, are discussed by Jo Ann Hoeppner Moran, *The Growth of English Schooling 1340–1548: Learning, Literacy, and Laicization in Pre-Reformation York Diocese* (Princeton: Princeton Univ. Press, 1985), chap. 1.

29. See above, note 18 for this chapter.

30. McDonnell, *Annals*, 48.

31. McDonnell, *Annals*, 42–43, 47–49.

32. See McDonnell, *History*, 23.

33. Stanier, 8–10.

34. McDonnell, *History*, 88.

35. Cf. McDonnell, *Annals*, 60.

36. Jean M. Imray, *The Charity of Richard Whittington: A History of the Trust Administered by the Mercers' Company 1424–1966* (London: Athlone, 1968), 75 n. 1.

37. *Acts of Court*, 403.

38. *Acts of Court*, 3, 572. McDonnell, *Annals*, 56, errs in putting Newbold's death in 1540.

39. Peter Clark and Paul Slack, eds., *Crisis and Order in English Towns 1500–1700: Essays in Urban History* (Toronto: Univ. of Toronto Press, 1972), 20.

40. Knight, 373.

41. Lupton, *Life*, 164–166.

42. Lupton, *Life*, 166; but see Baldwin, *Shakspere's Small Latine*, index references under "Whittinton," for a fuller explanation of half-holidays.

43. For interpretations by well-known writers see Aquinas, 2:588–589.

44. Cassiodorus, *Institutes,* ed. R. A. B. Mynors (Oxford: Oxford Univ. Press, 1963), I.i.7; p. 13.

45. St. Augustine, *Tractatus in Johannem*, 122; cited by Robert M. Grant, "One Hundred Fifty-Three Large Fish (John 21:11)," *Harvard Theological Review* 42 (1949): 273–275.

46. On the exceptional significance of these numbers see John MacQueen, *Numerology: Theory and Outline History of a Literary Mode* (Edinburgh: Edinburgh Univ. Press, 1985), 1.

47. Grant.

48. The only reference to the number 153 that I have run across outside the Christian tradition, and which I give for what it is worth, is that the Roman Hermippus, feeling himself getting old, cut himself off from companions of his own age and, by mingling only with the young, lived to 153 years (Harvey Cushing, *The Life of Sir William Osler*, 2 vols. [Oxford, Clarendon, 1925], 1:667).

49. Baldwin, *Shakspere's Small Latine* 2:705, notes that if the school had eight forms plus a group of catechumens taught by the chaplain, the total number of children would have been nine (i.e., eight plus one) times seventeen, for a total of 153. But this calculation works only on the assumption that all nine groups were of exactly the same size.

50. Karl Hartfelder, "Das Ideal einer Humanistenschule (Die Schule Colets zu St. Paul in London)," *Verhandlungen der . . . Versammlung[en] deutscher Philologen und Schulmänner* 41 (1892): 180–181.

51. Sir Cyril Picciotto, *St. Paul's School* (London and Glasgow: Blackie, 1939), 7.

52. McDonnell, *History*, 39.

53. Colet, "Statutes," 277.

54. Erasmus to John Botzheim, 30 January 1523, in Allen, 1:6, Ep. 1.

55. Cf. Eugenio Garin, *L'educazione in Europa, 1400–1600* (Bari: Laterza, 1957), 78.

56. Stanier, 43–46.

57. Iohannes Dominici, *Lucula noctis*, ed. Edmund Hunt (Notre Dame, Ind.: Notre Dame Univ. Press, 1940), xiv.

58. For the argument see Franco Simone, "La coscienza della rinascita negli umanisti," *La rinascita* 3 (1940): 184–186.

59. Colet, "Statutes," Lupton, *Life,* 279–280.

60. Charlton, 55.

61. Erasmus to Henry of Bergen, 7 November 1496, in Allen, 1:163, Ep. 49.

62. William Shakespeare, *Love's Labor's Lost* IV.ii.95–102. Cf. Baldwin, *Shakspere's Small Latine* 1:643.

63. Leach, "St. Paul's School before Colet," 208.

64. A. F. L. Raby, *Christian Latin Poetry* (Oxford: Clarendon, 1927), 126.

65. McDonnell, *History*, 45, 53, notes that the "Carmen de moribus" written by Lily and included in Colet's *Aeditio*, describes familiarity with Vergil, Terence and Cicero as indispensable to an educated person; from which he infers that they were already being read in the school in the lifetime of Lily (d. 1522).

66. M. L. Clarke, *Classical Education in Britain 1500–1900* (Cambridge: Cambridge Univ. Press, 1959), 5–6.

67. McDonnell, *Annals*, 75–76.

68. The chief evidence is reviewed by McDonnell, *History*, 48–50.

69. McDonnell, *Annals*, 60–61, citing *The Pauline*, no. 225 (June 1916): 81.

70. McDonnell, *Annals*, 81–82.

71. *The Poems of Erasmus*, ed. C. Reedijk (Leiden: Brill, 1956), 297–300.

72. Knight, 285–302, gives the Latin text; an anonymous English translation ca. 1540 is excerpted by Elizabeth M. Nugent, ed., *The Thought and Culture of the English Renaissance: An Anthology of Tudor Prose 1481–1555* (Cambridge: Cambridge Univ. Press, 1956), 345–348.

73. Cf. Helmut Exner, *Der Einfluss des Erasmus auf die englische Bildungsidee* (Berlin: Junker & Dünnhaupt, 1939), 108n.

74. Erasmus, *Tratado del niño Jesús y en loor estado de la niñez (Sevilla, 1516)*, ed. Eugenio Asensio (Madrid: Castalia, 1969), 36–37.

75. James H. Rieger, "Erasmus, Colet and the Schoolboy Jesus," *Studies in the Renaissance* 9 (1962): 182–194.

76. H. W. Garrod, "Erasmus and His English Patrons," *The Library*, 5th ser. 4 (1949): 3.

77. L. P. Wilkinson, in *Cambridge History of Classical Literature* 2:236.

78. J. K. Sowards, "Erasmus and the Apologetic Textbook: A Study of *De duplici copia verborum ac rerum*," *Studies in Philology* 55 (1958): 122–135; esp. 134.

79. Kristian Jensen, "*De emendata structura Latini sermonis*: The Latin Grammar of Thomas Linacre," *Journal of the Warburg and Courtauld Institutes* 49 (1986): 109–125, gives a detailed account of Linacre's innovations and his indebtednesses to traditional grammars.

80. D. F. S. Thomson, "Linacre's Latin Grammars," in *Essays on the Life and Work of Thomas Linacre c.1460–1524*, ed. Francis Maddison et al. (Oxford: Clarendon, 1977), 24–31, clarifies the features of Linacre's grammatical writings which made them impractical for the schoolroom. On "Lily's Grammar" and its influence see G. A. Padley, *Grammatical Theory in Western Europe 1500–1700* (Cambridge: Cambridge Univ. Press, 1976) 24–27.

81. Erasmus to Colet, 11 July 1513, in Allen, 1:526, Ep. 270.

82. Reprinted in Lupton, *Life*, 285–289.

83. Colet, qtd. in Lupton, *Life*, 279.

84. Conjectured independently by Lupton, *Influence of Colet*, 4–9, and Baldwin, *Shakspere's Petty School*, 35.

85. Charles Lloyd, ed., *Formularies of Faith Put Forth by Authority during the Reign of Henry VIII* (Oxford, 1825), iv–v, points out that nothing antecedent to the reign of Edward VI carried authority in the later church. Lupton's contention, in *Influence of Colet*, 4–10, that the "Cathecyzon," via the *Institution*, influenced the English Reformation would be vitiated by the *Institution*'s loss of legal status in any event, but it also disregards the fact that while the "Cathecyzon" is five pages long the *Institution* runs to forty (Lloyd, 89–129) and is an entirely different kind of work, highly confessional in character. The *Institution* moreover fails to follow the "Cathecyzon" in perhaps the only unusual feature of the latter,

its putting Orders and Matrimony before Baptism and the rest, an order Colet defends elsewhere (S, 302–305) which goes back ultimately to Dionysius.

86. Ferdinand Cohrs, "Der humanistische Schulmeister Petrus Tritonius Athesinus," *Mitteilungen der Gesellschaft für deutsche Erziehungs- und Schulgeschichte* 8 (1898): 264–265.

87. Ferdinand Cohrs, ed., *Die evangelischen Katechismusversuche vor Luthers Enchiridion*, vol. 4 (Berlin: A Hofmann, 1902), 418–419.

88. The complex bibliographical history of the *Aeditio* has now been worked out in *STC²*, vol. 1 (1986).

89. Colet, qtd. in Lupton, *Life*, 290–291.

90. Jean Gerson, *Oeuvres complètes*, ed. Palémon Glorieux, 10 vols. (Paris: Desclée, 1960–1973), 9:678.

91. Michael Kaufmann et al., eds., *Aegidius Romanus' de Colonna, Johannes Gersons, Dionys des Kartäusers und Jakob Sadolets pädagogische Schriften* (Freiburg i. B.: Herder, 1904), 92 n. 4, with refs.

92. J. B. Schwab, *Johannes Gerson* (Würzburg, 1858): "It would be hard to find a theologian whose writings enjoyed such wide diffusion after the discovery of printing"; qtd. by Garry Haupt, ed., in More, *CW* 13 (1976): xlv n. 4.

93. Gerson, 9:681.

Chapter 10.
Politics, Heresy, Final Victory

1. Karl Rahner and Herbert Vorgrimler, *Theological Dictionary*, trans. Cornelius Ernst, O.P. (New York: Herder and Herder, 1965), 480.

2. Colet's will, qtd. in Knight, 402.

3. *A Catholic Commentary on Holy Scripture* (London: Nelson, 1953), 1017.

4. Philip Hughes, *The Reformation in England*, 3 vols. (London: Hollis and Carter, 1952–1954), 1:78.

5. William Tyndale, *Answere vnto Sir Thomas Mores Dialoge*, ed. Henry Walter (Cambridge, 1850), 168; first published in Antwerp, 1531 (*STC²* 24437).

6. Lupton, *Influence of Colet*, 66, reprints the entire paraphrase in twelve lines.

7. *Coleti Aeditio*, ed. R. C. Alston (1527; reprint, Menston: Scolar, 1971), A4ᵛ.

8. Charles C. Butterworth, *The English Primers (1529–1545)* (Philadelphia: Univ. of Pennsylvania Press, 1953), 305, 308.

9. Qtd. in G. H. Russell, "Vernacular Instruction of the Laity in the Later Middle Ages in England: Some Texts and Notes," *Journal of Religious History* 2 (1962): 103. On the Paternoster see esp. 102–109.

10. On this campaign see Florent G. M. A. Aarts, ed., *e Pater Noster of Richard Ermyte: A Late Middle English Exposition of the Lord's Prayer* (The Hague: Nijhoff, 1967), cii–cxiii.

11. Hughes, 1:81.

12. On Young see John Watney, *Some Account of the Hospital of St. Thomas of Acon, in the Cheap, London, and of the Plate of the Mercers' Company* (London: Privately printed, 1892), 63–66, 84–87.

13. *Acts of Court*, 375–376.

14. Gleason, "Ecclesiastical Censorship," 138–140.

15. J. S. Brewer, *Letters and Papers, Henry VIII*, vol. 1 (London, 1862), 179.

16. J. R. Lander, "Attainder and Forfeiture, 1453 to 1509," *Historical Journal* 4 (1961): 124.

17. The goods and chattels of Dudley were granted to the same four guardians, presumably for this reason, on 18 Sept. 1514 (Brewer, 885).

18. Fox, 117.

19. Qtd. in T. Scott Holmes, *VCH, Somerset*, vol. 2 (1911), 449.

20. Lambeth Palace Library MS [unnumbered], The Registers of the Archbishops of Canterbury: William Warham (1503–1532), 173, 174.

21. Lupton, *Life*, 144 n. 1; his reference is to Foxe, 5:217.

22. Warham's sentence of Carder is printed in Foxe, 5:651 n. 3. The sentence followed a customary form.

23. J. A. F. Thomson, "John Foxe and Some Sources for Lollard History: Notes for a Critical Appraisal," in *Studies in Church History*, vol. 2 (London: Nelson, 1965), 251–257. For the modern conclusion that Foxe "was an industrious historian who did not invent evidence for partisan ends" and deserves to be regarded "as a historical source rather than as a propagandist" see also A. G. Dickens and John Tonkin, with Kenneth Powell, *The Reformation in Historical Thought* (Cambridge: Harvard Univ. Press, 1985), 49, with further refs.; and, more generally, Warren W. Wooden, *John Foxe* (Boston: Twayne, 1983), chap. 3, "The *Acts and Monuments*: Literature and Propaganda."

24. Erasmus to Colet, 11 July 1513, in Allen, 1:527, Ep. 270.

25. Maynard Smith, 457.

26. E. F. Carpenter, in W. R. Matthews and W. M. Atkins, eds., *A History of St. Paul's Cathedral and the Men Associated with It* (London: Phoenix House, 1957), 112, finds that Colet's statutes "do not in fact differ greatly from their predecessors' " of earlier centuries.

27. Carpenter, in Matthews and Atkins, 114.

28. W. Sparrow Simpson, ed., *Registrum statutorum et consuetudinum Ecclesiae Cathedralis S. Pauli Londinensis* (London, 1873), 418–419.

29. Sparrow Simpson, xlix.

30. Walter Farquhar Hook, *Lives of the Archbishops of Canterbury*, 12 vols. (London, 1860–1876), 6:288–289.

31. Cf. Sparrow Simpson, xlix.

32. Given as Colet's opinion by Erasmus, *De recta latini graecique sermonis pronuntiatione*, ed. M. Cytowska, in ASD, I, 4 (1973): 24.

33. Erasmus to Colet, 11 July 1513, in Allen, 1:526–527, Ep. 270.

34. Sparrow Simpson, chaps. 4, 14, 20, 28, 49.

35. Herbert Hensley Henson, *Retrospect of an Unimportant Life*, 3 vols. (London: Oxford Univ. Press, 1942–1950), 1:83.

36. Sparrow Simpson, 240.

37. Carpenter, in Matthews and Atkins, 110.

38. Sparrow Simpson, 418–419.

39. Colet to Erasmus, 20 October 1514, in Allen 2:37, Ep. 314.

40. Marcel Proust, *A la recherche du temps perdu*, Pléiade ed., 3 vols. (Paris: Gallimard, 1954–1966), 3:35.

41. Cf. Lupton, *Life*, 195.

42. Qtd. in Richard Fiddes, *The Life of Cardinal Wolsey*, 2d ed. (London, 1726), separately paginated "Collections," 201–202. Lupton, *Life*, 195–198, quotes most of the text, in normalized spelling.

43. Lupton, *Life*, 198.

44. On this see Alfred A. Mumford, *Hugh Oldham 1452[?]–1519* (London: Faber & Faber, 1936), 99–100.

45. More to Warham, January 1517, in More, *C*, 86, Ep. 31. Cf. also More to Erasmus, 17 February 1516, in Allen, 2:195, Ep. 388.

46. Erasmus to Ammonius, 5 June 1516, in Allen, 2:246, Ep. 414.

47. J. D. Mackie, *The Earlier Tudors 1485–1558* (Oxford: Clarendon, 1952), 295.

48. A. F. Pollard, *Wolsey* (1929; reprint, London: Collins, 1965), 57.

49. Edward Carpenter, *Cantuar: The Archbishops in Their Office* (London: Cassell, 1971), 125–126.

50. Lupton, *Life*, 226–227.

51. John A. Guy, *The Cardinal's Court* (Hassocks: Harvester, 1977), 41–42.

52. William Huse Dunham, Jr., "The Members of Henry VIII's Whole Council, 1509–1527," *English Historical Review* 59 (1944): 208.

53. C. G. Bayne, ed., *Select Cases in the Council of Henry VII.*, completed by W. H. Dunham, Jr., Publ. Selden Society 75 (London: Quaritch, 1958), xxii, gives the total number of councillors named in extant documents as 227; Colet's name is not among them.

54. Pollard, 54–55.

55. Pollard, "Additions and Corrections" (posthumously published in the 1965 reprint ed. of *Wolsey* from the marginalia in the author's copy of the 1929 edition), 373.

56. M. Smith, 456.

57. K. L. Wood-Legh, *Perpetual Chantries in Britain* (Cambridge: Cambridge Univ. Press, 1965), 269, records that "the number of cantarists at the time [of the suppression of the chantries] is traditionally given as 2374."

58. Alan Kreider, *English Chantries: The Road to Dissolution* (Cambridge: Harvard Univ. Press, 1979), 26–27.

59. Kreider, 75.

60. George Unwin, *The Guilds and Companies of London* (London: Allen and Unwin, 1938), 206–208.

61. Guy Fitch Lytle, "Patronage Patterns and Oxford Colleges c.1300–c.1530," in *The University in Society*, ed. Lawrence Stone, 2 vols. (Princeton: Princeton Univ. Press, 1974), 1:147.

62. Kreider, 84.

63. *VCH, Hertford*, vol. 4 (1914), 32.

64. Lupton, *Life*, 277 n. 3, 131–132.

65. Walter Delius, "Justus Jonas und Erasmus," *Theologia viatorum* 1 (1948–1949): 71–79.

66. Godin, *Vies*, 69 n. 462.

67. Pelikan, 4:61.

68. Colet's terminology is not wholly consistent. He refers to Durandus bishop of Mende as "episcopus" rather than "pontifex" (DEH, 203), but a few pages later he employs "pontifex" in the sense of "bishop": "Agit igitur pontifex quisque in sua ecclesia . . ." (DEH, 207).

69. J. F. Niermeyer, *Mediae Latinitatis lexicon minus* (Leiden: Brill, 1954–1976).

70. *Novum glossarium mediae latinitatis ab anno DCCC ad annum MCC*, Fasc. "L" (Copenhagen: Munskgaard, 1957). Leland Miles, "Protestant Colet and Catholic More," *Anglican Theological Review* 33 (1951): 31, observes that Colet's emphasis on interior religious experience, reinforced by his platonism, tended to place him in positions at least potentially inconsistent with orthodox formulations.

71. Pelikan, 4:107–109, with refs.

72. RO, 245 (omitted from Lupton's quite incomplete list of the authors cited by Colet [*Life*, 67 n. 1]).

73. J. A. F. Thomson, *Later Lollards*, 162.

74. Erasmus, "Peregrinatio religionis ergo," L. -E. Halkin et al., eds., in ASD, I, 3 (1972): 470–494; on Colet see 488–492.

75. P. Smith, 40. In a more solemn vein Erasmus etymologized Colet's surname also with the Hebrew "coheleth" ("preacher"); but this was after Colet's death (Erasmus to Thomas Lupset, 23 August 1521, in Allen, 4:569, Ep. 1228).

76. E. G. Withycombe, *Oxford Dictionary of English Christian Names*, 3d ed. (Oxford: Clarendon, 1977).

77. Plato, *Gorgias*, ed. E. R. Dodds (Oxford: Clarendon, 1959), 226, note on *Gorgias* 463e2; to which I owe the further reference to Aristotle's *Rhetoric* 1400b20.

78. Erasmus, *Modus Orandi Deum* (1524), in LB 5:1119–1120.

79. For a fully annotated translation see Erasmus, *Pilgrimages to Saint Mary of Walsingham and Saint Thomas of Canterbury*, 2d ed., trans. and ed. John Gough Nichols (London, 1875), 45–46. With minor alterations this translation is quoted for the extracts that follow.

80. Erasmus, *Pilgrimages*, 50–51.

81. Erasmus, *Pilgrimages*, 53–54.

82. For alternative statements of the problem see G. G. Coulton, "The Plain Man's Religion in the Middle Ages," in his *Ten Medieval Studies* (Cambridge: Cambridge Univ. Press, 1930), 189–200, and François Rapp, "Essor ou déclin de la piété?" pt. 3, chap. 4 of *L'Eglise et la vie religieuse en occident à la fin du moyen âge* (Paris: P.U.F., 1971).

83. Erasmus to John Sapidus, ca. June 1520, in Allen, 4:279, Ep. 1110.

84. However, Walter M. Gordon, "The Religious Edifice and Its Symbolism in the Writings of Erasmus, Colet, and More," *Moreana* 22 (1985): 16, 18–19, thinks Colet's reaction did not imply condemnation of wealthy shrines as such.

85. P. S. Allen, "Dean Colet and Archbishop Warham," *English Historical Review* 17 (1902): 303–306.

86. A. F. Pollard, *Henry VIII* (London: Longmans Green, 1951), 52–53.

87. Matthew Parker, *Antiquitates Britannicae* (1572–1574; reprint, London, 1605), 307, qtd. in Lupton, *Life*, 191–192 (Lupton's translation).

88. R. Adams, *Better Part of Valor*, 71–72, 318–319 n. 31. Tracy, *Politics of Erasmus*, 32–33, 148, seems to reserve judgment.

89. Allen, 3:580.

90. Erasmus, *Adagia* 1258. However, as Liddell and Scott's *Greek-English Lexicon* observes s.v. χάσκω, the phrase λύκος ἔχανεν was a proverbial way of describing "disappointed hopes." Elsewhere Erasmus uses "χανῶν expecto" in an everyday context (Erasmus to Richard Pace, 22 October 1518, in Allen, 3:425, Ep. 887).

91. Because the fact bears on the date of the incident Erasmus is describing, it should be noted that Godin, *Vies*, 81 n. 578, incorrectly gives the date of Birkhead's consecration as bishop—Birkhead is described by Erasmus as a bishop in the scene under discussion—as 15 April 1513; the true date is 29 May 1513 (John Le Neve, *Fasti Ecclesiae Anglicanae 1300–1541*, vol. 11 [The Welsh Dioceses], compiled by B. Jones [London: Athlone, 1965], 39). Hence the date of the scene Erasmus describes must be later than 29 May 1513.

92. Erasmus's own translation of Matt. 22:46 brings the verbal parallel still closer. In both the 1516 and the 1519 editions of his Greek New Testament he replaced the Vulgate's "illa die" by "eo die."

93. Godin, *Vies*, 51 n. 277. Godin notes (75 n. 508) that the motif of envy, frequent in Plutarch's parallel lives, appears also in the lives of Vitrier and Colet.

94. Erasmus to Reuchlin, 27 August 1516, in Allen, 2:331, Ep. 457.

95. In a letter to Sir Henry Guildford dated 15 May 1519, Erasmus politely attributes the high opinion Guildford has formed of him to "the conversation of D. John Colet and other friends" (Allen, 3:585, Ep. 966). Guildford was a lifelong personal friend of the king and at that period his equerry; his continued friendship with Colet testifies to Colet's continued favor with the king.

96. Erasmus to John Botzheim, 16 May 1520 (with reference to Richard Pace's recent appointment as dean of St. Paul's), in Allen, 4:262, Ep. 1103.

97. The references to the sweating sickness from Erasmus's correspondence (London, 1540 ed.) are assembled by Christian Gottfried Gruner, *Scriptores de sudore anglico superstites* (Jena, 1847), 434–439.

98. His will was proved in the Prerogative Court of Canterbury because he died possessed of properties in three counties besides London (*Index of Wills Proved in the Prerogative Court of Canterbury 1383–1558*, comp. J. C. C. Smith, 2 vols. [London, 1893], 1:133).

99. I owe the suggestion to Dr. Ilza Veith, professor emeritus of the history of medicine, University of California School of Medicine, San Francisco.

100. G. Schwers, in *Individu et société à la renaissance: Colloque international, tenu en avril 1965* (Brussels: Travaux de l'Institut pour l'étude de la renaissance et de l'homme, 1967), 291. Schwers's comment is apropos of Hyacinthe Brabant's "L'homme malade dans la société de la renaissance," in the same volume, 259–273.

101. William S. Heckscher, *Rembrandt's* Anatomy of Dr. Nicolaas Tulp (New York: New York Univ. Press, 1958), 45. For Colet as licenser of physicians in virtue of being dean of St. Paul's see Lupton, *Life*, 227 n. 2.

102. During the building of the new St. Paul's Cathedral the body was again the object of examination. "In 1680, or thereabouts, when the wall was taken down, the said coffin [of lead] was discovered, for it laid in the said wall about two feet and a half above the surface of the floor. . . . Some of the Royal Society, who out of curiosity went to see it, did thrust a probe or little stick into a chink of the coffin, which bringing out some moisture with it, found it of an ironish taste, and fancied that the body felt soft and pappy like brawn." Anthony à Wood, *Athenae Oxonienses*, ed. Philip Bliss, 4 vols. (London, 1813–1820), 1:27.

103. Lupton, *Life*, 236.

104. Colet to Erasmus, ca. June 1517, in Allen, 2:599, Ep. 593.

105. The best account of Vitrier is *Vies*, 88–110.

106. Alain Derville, "Jean Vitrier et les religieuses de Sainte-Marguerite," *Revue du nord* 42 (1960): 229.

107. Allen, 3:372 n.3; see also Derville, "Vitrier et les religieuses," 229.

108. Johannes Beumer, S. J., "Erasmus von Rotterdam und seine Freunde aus dem Franziskanerorden," *Franziskanische Studien* 51 (1969): 122.

109. Erasmus to John Botzheim, 30 January 1523, in Allen, 1:20, Ep. 1.

110. Erasmus, *L'apoteosi di Giovanni Reuchlin*, ed. Giulio Vallese (Naples: R. Pironti, 1949), 92–95. The silence *ad loc.* of the ASD edition of the *Colloquia* suggests disagreement.

111. Allen, 4:509 n.62.

112. LB 5:987.

113. Godin, "De Vitrier à Origène," 47–57.

114. Erasmus to John Eck, 15 May 1518, in Allen, 3:337, Ep. 844.

115. Cf. Raymond Marcel, "L'Enchiridion militis christiani," 613–646.

116. Charlier, 115. The ample proof is given by André Godin, *Erasme lecteur d'Origène* (Geneva: Droz, 1982).

117. Erasmus to Edmund, beginning of 1502, in Allen, 1:378, Ep. 168: "Confido enim me posthac toto pectore in arcanis literis libenter versaturum."

118. *Vies*, 20.

119. Roberto Lecchini, *I Francescani e la rinascita inglese* (Modena: TEIC, 1975), 25.

120. Gee, 35–41.

121. *Index of Wills* 1:133; full text in Knight, 400–409.

122. Erasmus to Jodocus Gaverius, 1 March 1523, in Allen, 5:239, Ep. 1347.

123. Clebsch, 167–176.

124. Marius, 432–433 and 456–457, has however recently argued that More did not set the high value on the papal supremacy which most writers have attributed to him.

125. Roy Midmer, *English Mediaeval Monasteries (1066–1540)* (Athens: Univ. of Georgia Press, 1979), s.v. "Sheen."

Appendix 1. Colet's *De sacramentis*

1. Colet begins his treatise with a double allusion: (1) to Eph. 3:15 ("the Father of our Lord Jesus Christ, from whom all fatherhood in heaven and on earth takes its name") and (2) to St. Bonaventure's *Breviloquium*, which opens with a quotation of Eph. 3:15. Eph. 3:32, on "the great sacrament," is a central text in the present treatise; and *De sacramentis* summarizes Colet's theological outlook, just as the *Breviloquium* is a succinct statement of Bonaventure's theological position.

2. Colet exploits the semantic overlap between *sacrificium* and *sanctificatio*, both of which can mean "making holy."

3. On the axiom "Good is diffusive of itself," see above, 204.

4. Only in this passage does Colet alter the otherwise invariable order of the three actions—presumably an error.

5. An exemplar is "that according to which something else is made in such wise that it imitates the exemplar" (Richard P. McKeon, ed., "Glossary," in *Selections from Medieval Philosophers*, 2 vols. [New York: Scribner's, 1929–1930], 2:454). Exemplarism is a key concept in Colet's treatise, linking it with the Franciscan tradition and especially with Bonaventure. See Iohannes-M. Bissen, O.F.M., *L'exemplarisme divin selon s. Bonaventure* (Paris: Vrin, 1929).

6. As the following discussion shows, Colet, following pseudo-Dionysius, considers order both in the very broad sense of God's ordering of the universe and in the narrower, specifically Christian sense of holy orders. In the broad sense orders are logically prior, as a sort of final cause, to the other manifestations of God's will.

7. For Bonaventure, God "made the sensible world in order to manifest himself [*ad declarandum seipsum*]" (qtd. in Gilson, *La philosophie au moyen âge*, 442).

8. Lupton prints merely "illi quos," but in the MS these two words are separated by a blank, due to erasure, which is large enough to accommodate about six letters; I conjecture *angeli*.

9. On the tradition underlying the use of "temple of God" in the sense of "the universe," see 204 above.

10. The Latin, "feminas . . . viragines," suggests that the males in this "holy coitus" recapitulate the original Creation, for in the Vulgate translation Eve is called "virago."

11. On Colet's repeated use of the unusual word *vicissitudinarius* see 69–70 above.

12. I.e., the seven sacraments first officially defined as such by Pope Eugenius IV in the decree "Pro Armenis" (1439). On the term *sacramenta ecclesiae* see Roy J. Deferrari et al., *A Lexicon of St. Thomas Aquinas*, 5 vols. in 3 (Washington: Catholic Univ. of America Press, 1948–1953), s.v. "sacramentum (2)."

13. A reference to the original meaning of *sacramentum*, "soldier's oath."

14. On "reconciliation" as the early name for the sacrament see Bartolomé María Xiberta, O. Carm., *Clavis Ecclesiae: De ordine absolutionis sacramentalis ad reconciliationem cum Ecclesia* (Rome: Collegium Sancti Alberti, 1922), 66.

15. This sentence is a strong but thoroughly characteristic statement of man's nature and powers as seen by Colet.

16. Colet unselfconsciously employs the regular scholastic terminology, according to which *sacramentum* is the outward sign and *res* is the inward grace signified and conferred under that sign. This terminology was developed only in the twelfth century and became standard among the medieval doctors (A. Landgraf, "Beiträge der Frühscholastik zur Terminologie der allgemeinen Sakramentenlehre," *Divus Thomas* [Vienna] 29 [1951]: 3–34).

17. In fact, Colet does not return to this topic.

18. The development from shadow to image to truth is fundamental to Colet's thought in this treatise and recurs frequently. It is clearly implicit in Heb. 8:4–5; for later times it was perhaps reinforced by Pliny's encyclopedic *Naturalis historia*, preserved intact all through the middle ages, which gives a history of painting in terms of those who used outline only, those who added colors, and finally those who added also shading (35.3).

19. Colet struggles to express the same idea in DEH, 204; Lupton's translation (p. 58) shows that he did not understand.

20. On this strand in Colet's thought see Miles, *Colet and the Platonic Tradition*, 37–40.

21. The thought expressed in the preceding two sentences is closely paralleled in St. Bonaventure, *Breviloquium* 7.7 (*Opera omnia* 5:289; English translation by de Vinck, *Works of Bonaventure* 2:304), who demonstrates how the creation and the re-creation manifest God's wisdom, mercy, and justice. It will be recalled that Colet begins De sacramentis with the same scriptural quotation with which Bonaventure begins the *Breviloquium*.

22. Christ's incarnation, for some theologians, was independent of Adam's sin and determined on other grounds; for others, it depended on the fact of the original sin. Colet here ranges himself among the latter; see 205 above.

23. A commonly held conception at that period; cf. Peter Lombard, *Sent. IV* (PL, vol. 192, col. 692); Thomas Aquinas, *Summa theologica*, Suppl. q. 94, a. 3, using Ps. 58:11 Vulg. (= 59:10) as a proof-text. For a survey of this doctrine in the middle ages see Charles H. Grandgent, "Quid Ploras?" *Annual Reports of the Dante Society* (Cambridge, Mass.) 42–44 (1926): 8–18. D. P. Walker, *The Decline of Hell* (London: Routledge and Kegan Paul, 1964), 29–30, notes that the happiness afforded the saved by contemplating the torments of the damned was a traditional answer to the question of the utility of hell after the Last Judgment. He adds that the conception became virtually obsolete in the seventeenth century, in consequence of changing attitudes toward other people's sufferings.

24. *Commentariorum in Epistolam ad Ephesios libri tres* (PL, vol. 26, col. 569), where Jerome attributes the thought to his friend St. Gregory of Nazianzus.

25. Colet characteristically spiritualizes a passage that most pre-scholastic commentators took as a proof-text of the sacramentality of earthly marriage, seen as prefiguring the union of Christ and the church (Pietro Colli, *La pericope paolina ad Ephesios V.32 nella interpretazione dei SS. Padri e del Concilio di Trento* [Parma: Fresching, 1951], 117–119).

26. Colet here adopts the New Testament writers' sense that Jesus' uniqueness lies in his perfect obedience to the Father rather than in the moral perfection of

his human life; indeed it is noteworthy that Colet nowhere expressly commends to his audience the imitation of Jesus' recorded life on earth. Cf. Oliver Chase Quick, *Doctrines of the Creed* (New York: Scribner's, n.d.), 172: "The Bible does not speak the language of moral philosophy, and even in its portrait of Jesus Christ it sets before us no ideal of human goodness *as such*. In the Bible . . . perfection for man consists in obedience to God's revealed will" (emphasis in the original; the author was Regius Professor of Divinity in Oxford University).

27. A slip for "in heaven"?

28. Here begins a long catena of quotations from the Pauline Epistles regarding the conflict between spirit and flesh. Colet gives them in sequence as the Epistles stand in the New Testament, beginning with Romans and ending with Colossians; evidently he read through the Pauline Epistles expressly to collect the texts pertinent to his subject and now empties his notebook. On this practice see Bolgar, 267–275, and August Buck, "Die 'studia humanitatis' und ihre Methode," *Bibliothèque d'humanisme et renaissance* 19 (1959): 273–290.

29. From the twelfth century on, this reference to liberation from death was often interpreted as the forgiveness of sins brought about by the sinner's repentance (Z. Alszeghy, S.J., "La penitenza nella scolastica antica," *Gregorianum* 31 [1950]: 278–280).

30. The foregoing words of Paul are the text for Colet's surviving Convocation Sermon.

31. This nuptial metaphor appears also in C 172 [90]: "adorandum miraculum quod deus ipse coierit cum humana natura." For the tradition see Richard A. Baer, Jr., *Philo's Use of the Categories Male and Female* (Leiden: Brill, 1970), 14–64, 94–95.

32. For an extended parallel to the thought of this passage see DEH, 239–242, 248–249.

33. In enumerating twelve fruits of the Holy Spirit Colet follows the Latin text. The Greek text gives nine, the extra three in Colet's list being synonyms that had crept into the Latin text.

34. On this *soror et coniunx* theme see above, 209.

35. The strained Latin of the original, "serperet spiritificans," seems intended to highlight the opposition between the serpent (*serpens*) who wrought the destruction and him who "would proceed" (*serperet*) to undo it.

36. Colet here draws on the traditional interpretation according to which the Church was founded when the water and the blood flowed from the side of the crucified Christ (John 19:34), symbolizing baptism and the Eucharist (cf. Karl Hermann Schelke, "Taufe und Tod: Zur Auslegung von Römer 6, 1–11," in *Vom christlichen Mysterium: Gesammelte Arbeiten zum Gedächtnis von Odo Casel OSB*, ed. Anton Mayer et al. [Düsseldorf: Patmos-Verlag, 1951], 10). This tradition was confirmed at the final session of the Council of Vienne, 6 May 1312. There Pope John XXII declared that the chronology of the account given by John 19:33–35 concerning the piercing of Christ's side was correct (as against the manuscripts that placed the piercing after Matt. 27:49, when Jesus was still alive). The soldier did not open Christ's side until he was dead, the pope said further, in order that the immaculate bride, the Church, could be formed from his side as Eve had been from Adam's (Ewald Müller, *Das Konzil von Vienne 1311–*

1312: Seine Quellen und seine Geschichte [Münster i. W.: Aschendorff, 1934], 353–355).

37. In the sense required here, "the office of a bridegroom," "sponsio" seems to be unknown to the dictionaries.

38. The traditional order of these virtues is faith, hope, charity (as given in 1 Cor. 13:13). Colet reverses the positions of the first two in order to institute a triple parallel—psychological, theological, and historical—which is worked out in detail in DCH, 188–190. Of primary interest in *De Sacramentis* is the parallel with the sequence *umbra/imago/veritas*, "image/shadow/truth."

39. Regarding "latenter suadet": at R, 202 Colet uses the very similar phrase "latenter docet" ("covertly teaches"), likewise to reveal a meaning that Paul conceals from the superficial reader who does not have the spiritual eyes to see the meaning concealed beneath the text. Always maintaining the superiority of the spiritual meaning to the literal (cf. also DEH, 238–239), Colet preened himself most, as we have seen in chap. 7, on the feats of exegesis by which he elicited from Paul meanings hidden from the common exegete.

40. With his strong preference for virginity, Colet ignores patristic evidence and later argument that Paul was a married man; see above, 132.

41. In hesitating to treat matrimony as on a footing with the other sacraments Colet was not alone. For the vigorous discussion in the fourteenth century see Burr, 183–204.

42. The use of "symbolum," "signum," and "sacramentum" as virtual synonyms within a single sentence illustrates Colet's indifference to terminological precision.

43. Such language, which Colet is fond of here and elsewhere in his writings, though awkward enough, suggests, almost mimics, the impulse of the universe toward oneness and fusion, toward a vital center where all significances collapse into the ineffable real.

44. The word here translated, "extraria" (misread by Lupton as *externa*), in the usage of Christian writers often implies a reference to Satan, the "stranger" and enemy par excellence.

45. At this point the MS has a gap, due to erasure, long enough to accommodate two words. Lupton proposed *sinceram nouitatem*, apparently because it is a Pauline phrase. I suggest *vestem nitidam* because the same two words follow "induat" also on p. 288 above; Colet is given to repeating himself verbally.

46. The translation gives what Colet meant to say but not, as the Latin text shows, what he did say. For a parallel instance of his saying the opposite of what he meant see Jayne, 121 n. 2.

47. Lupton prints: "ut energens [a misprint for *emergens*] in te ea justitiâ a justo Deo apprehendare," but he does not try to translate it. An easy emendation is the ablative absolute *emergente*, which yields the translation in the text. Cf. "emergente anima ex hoc mundano mari" (S, 320).

48. The same advice is given in R, 195: "let us overcome a wicked disposition by its opposite, and evil by good" ("contrarium contrario vincamus, et malum bono"). For Chrysostom too, one of Colet's preferred writers, repentance ("metanoia") includes cultivation of the virtue opposed to the sin repented of

(*Homilies on the Gospel According to Saint Matthew*, in vol. 10 of *Select Library of the Nicene and Post-Nicene Fathers*, ed. Philip Schaff [New York: Scribner's, 1903], 66).

49. On this passage, derived ultimately from Aristophanes, see above, chap. 8 n. 9 (Lupton's note is wrong).

50. Man's "proneness to evil" is a leitmotif in Colet; see above, 186–191.

51. In medieval Latin this word (*stola*) connotes "robe of immortality" (*Works of Bonaventure* 2:164n).

52. The phrasing is probably unconsidered; it was *sententia certa* that all the sacraments were instituted by Christ, a doctrine formally defined by Trent (Ott, 403–404).

53. A commonly received idea; cf. Thomas Aquinas, *Summa theologica* III, q. 84, a. 3, for penance as sacramental parallel to baptism.

54. Colet presumably means here not that the "character," or indelible mark, of baptism is conditional upon the quality of the recipient's subsequent life but that the light given in baptism may later be lost through evildoing.

55. In the early church the repentant sinner was reconciled to the church only after performing a public penance. From the eighth century onward this practice became increasingly obolescent under changed social circumstances, and by the tenth or eleventh centuries it had become the rule to grant absolution immediately after confession, at a point when the satisfaction imposed on the sinner had not yet been made; the penance required of him was normally performed privately. Hence the cause of forgiveness, which had previously been regarded as the performance of satisfaction, had to be rethought. Forgiveness was now increasingly attributed to the sinner's inward repentance at the time he confessed, a change which in turn required a change in the conception of the priest's role. (On these developments see Karl Müller, "Der Umschwung in der Lehre von der Buße während des 12. Jahrhunderts," in *Theologische Abhandlungen, Carl von Weizsäcker zu seinem siebzigsten Geburtstag gewidmet* [Freiburg i. B., 1892], 287–320, esp. 299–313.) From Peter Lombard on, mainstream theologians espoused the doctrine, which Colet also accepts, that in effect the source of the sinner's forgiveness is in himself but that ecclesiastical law requires the priest's witness (Constantin von Schäzler, *Die Lehre von der Wirksamkeit der Sakramente ex opere operato* [Munich, 1860], 270–271, 352). The form of absolution by the priest—"*Ego te absolvo* . . ."—acquired binding force only with the decree "Pro Armenis" of Eugenius IV in 1439 (art. "Beichte," in *Theologische Realenzyklopädie*, vol. 5 [Berlin and New York: de Gruyter, 1980], 417). Colet betrays some uneasiness in trying to reconcile the frequently mentioned self-forgiveness of the repentant sinner with the requirement that "a listening priest" "bear witness" to the fact of forgiveness, sometimes but not always implying that in the absence of such official witness there is no forgiveness.

56. The term *deushomo* appears also in DEH, 262; Colet uses its Greek equivalent *theanthropos* too, in the roman alphabet and variously misspelled (R, 179; C, 172 [90]). Origen coined the latter term (Berthold Altaner, *Patrology*, trans. Hilda C. Graef [New York: Herder and Herder, 1960], 232)—a point I owe to O'Kelly, C, p. 292. Colet will have had the word from an intermediary writing

in Latin, perhaps Augustine. (Cf. PL, vol. 35, col. 2011; and *CSEL* 44:575 and 57:144; see Abbreviations at the front of this volume.)

57. Besides this recapitulatory table, placed directly in the text, *De sacramentis* contains a number of others, most of them longer, which are not included in the present text. As his other manuscripts show, Colet was fond of such tabular summaries, but in this he was by no means unique; cf. More, *CW* 13:285.

58. Here as elsewhere Colet places more emphasis on the moral quality of the minister than the orthodox doctrine of the efficacy of the sacraments *ex opere operato* would seem to justify. A partial explanation is that he is reflecting the thought of Dionysius, one of whose very few divergences from later orthodoxy is his seeming denial of the efficacy of the sacraments *ex opere operato* (Gandillac, *Oeuvres du pseudo-Denys*, 32 n. 63).

59. The passage from Isaiah is here translated so as to support the meaning Colet derives from it. In context, however, it means, "What can you say in your own behalf concerning your wrongdoings?" The development of the thought in this and the following five sentences is easy to follow. Apparently Colet meant to say that while confession to a priest is desirable, in order that he may in his judicial capacity assess the penitent's contrition, Luke's Gospel shows us Christ commanding lay persons to "forgive" those who confess to them, and Isaiah shows God commanding that sins be confessed directly to him. Though confession to a priest therefore cannot always be necessary, it is always necessary to make amends, irrespective of the mode of confession. If this interpretation is correct, Colet is simultaneously acknowledging the practice of confession to laymen and of course confession directly to God, and yet defending the church's central role in the administration of penance.

60. Colet mentions this fact hurriedly also in DEH, 255–256; in both passages he merely repeats the testimony of Dionysius (556C [*Oeuvres du pseudo-Denys*, 316]), who is similarly brief.

61. A notably close parallel to this sentence, "Crebra est vnctio in ecclesia, que est crebra admonitio frequentis spiritus sancti," is in DEH, 266: "Unguenti usus est frequens in christiana ecclesia . . . quod unguentum spiritum sanctum significat." The parallel is a final reminder of the closeness in spirit, and probably in date, of Colet's treatise on the sacraments and his work on the ecclesiastical hierarchy.

Works Cited

Manuscripts

Cathedral Chapter of St. Paul's, London. Proceedings. Guildhall Library MS. 25, 187. (Formerly St. Paul's Cathedral MS. A 53/29.)

Colet, John. Corpus Christi College, Cambridge, Parker MS. CCCLV. (Contains RO and G.)

————. Cambridge University Library MS. Gg.iv.26. (Contains R, EK, CM, C, and DCH.)

————. Trinity College, Cambridge, MS. o.4.44. (Contains unpublished apophthegms, unpublished "abbreviations" of the Pauline Epistles, and P.)

————. Emmanuel College, Cambridge, Library MS. 3.3.12. (Contains C.)

————. British Library Loan MS. 55/2 (Duke of Leeds). (Contains DCH, DEH, and S.)

————. St. Paul's School Library, London, MS [unnumbered]. (Contains DCH, DEH, and S.)

Kennett, White. Notes for a biography of John Colet. British Library Lansdowne MS. 1030.

Piccolomini, Aeneas Silvius. *Historia Bohemica.* Mediaeval & Renaissance MSS, MS. 89. Princeton University Library.

"The Registers of the Archbishops of Canterbury: William Warham (1503–1532)." Lambeth Palace Library, London.

Printed works

For works cited in the notes in abbreviated form see Abbreviations at the beginning of this volume. For some items not cited in this study see the bibliographies in Jayne (below) and in *The New Cambridge Bibliography of English Literature*, vol. 1 (Cambridge: Cambridge University Press, 1974), cols. 1790–1792.

Aarts, Florent G. M. A., ed. Þe Pater Noster of Richard Ermyte: A Late Middle English Exposition of the Lord's Prayer. The Hague: Nijhoff, 1967.

Adams, Robert P. The Better Part of Valor: More, Erasmus, Colet, and Vives, on Humanism, War, and Peace 1496–1535. Seattle: University of Washington Press, 1962.

Agrippa, Henricus Cornelius. Opera. 2 vols. Lyons, 1531.

Albertson, Mary. London Merchants and Their Landed Properties during the Reigns of the Yorkists. Philadelphia: Privately printed, 1932.

Allen, Don Cameron. Mysteriously Meant: The Rediscovery of Pagan Symbolism and Allegorical Interpretation in the Renaissance. Baltimore and London: Johns Hopkins University Press, 1970.

Allen, P. S. The Age of Erasmus. Oxford: Clarendon, 1914.

———. "Dean Colet and Archbishop Warham." English Historical Review 17 (1902): 303–306.

Alszeghy, Z., S.J. "La penitenza nella scolastica antica." Gregorianum 31 (1950): 275–283.

Andrich, Aloysius. De natione anglica et scota iuristarum Universitatis Patavinae ab a. MCCXXII p. Ch. n. ad a. MDCCXXXVIII. Padua, 1892.

Ariès, Philippe. Centuries of Childhood: A Social History of Family Life. New York: Knopf, 1962.

Aulén, Gustaf. Christus Victor. Translated by A. G. Herbert. 1931. Reprint. New York: Scribner's, 1969.

Baer, Richard A., Jr. Philo's Use of the Categories Male and Female. Leiden: Brill, 1970.

Bainton, Roland H. Erasmus of Christendom. New York: Scribner, 1969.

Baldwin, T. W. William Shakspere's Petty School. Urbana: University of Illinois Press, 1943.

———. William Shakspere's Small Latine & Lesse Greeke. 2 vols. Urbana: University of Illinois Press, 1944.

Bale, John. Index Britanniae Scriptorum: John Bale's Index of British and Other Writers. Edited by R. L. Poole and Mary Bateson. Oxford: Clarendon, 1902.

Balthasar, Hans Urs von. "Le mysterion d'Origène." Recherches de science religieuse 26 (1936): 513–562.

Bartlett, Kenneth R. " 'Worshipful Gentlemen of England': The Studio of Padua and the Education of the English Gentry in the Sixteenth Century." Renaissance and Reformation, n.s. 6 (1982): 235–248.

Basil, St. Saint Basil on the Value of Greek Literature. Edited by N. G. Wilson. London: Duckworth, 1975.

Bateson, Mary, ed. Grace Book B, Part I, Containing the Proctors' Accounts and Other Records of the University of Cambridge for the Years 1488–1511. Cambridge: Cambridge University Press, 1903.

Bauer, Karl. "John Colet und Erasmus von Rotterdam." In Festschrift für Hans von Schubert zu seinem 70. Geburtstag, edited by Otto Scheel, 155–187. Leipzig: M. Heinsius, 1929.

Bayne, C. G., ed. Select Cases in the Council of Henry VII. Completed by W. H. Dunham, Jr. Publication of the Selden Society, 75. London: Quaritch, 1958.

Beaven, Alfred B. *The Aldermen of the City of London Temp. Henry III.–1908.* 2 vols. London: Eden Fisher, 1908–1913.

Becon, Thomas. *Works.* Edited by J. Ayre. 3 vols. Cambridge, 1843–1844.

Beelen, Joannes Theodorus. *Dissertatio theologica, qua sententiam vulgo receptam, esse Sacrae Scripturae multiplicem interdum sensum litteralem, nullo fundamento satis firmo niti demonstrare conatur Joannes Theodorus Beelen.* Louvain, 1845.

"Beichte." In *Theologische Realenzyklopädie* 5:411–439. Berlin and New York: de Gruyter, 1980.

Bellamy, Daniel. *On Benevolence: A Summary of the Life and Character of Dean Colet. A Sermon.* London, 1756.

Béné, Charles. "Erasme et Cicéron." In *Colloquia Erasmiana Turonensia,* 2 vols., 2:571–579. Toronto: University of Toronto Press, 1972.

Bennett, G. V. *White Kennett 1660–1728, Bishop of Peterborough.* London: S.P.C.K., 1957.

Bennett, H. S. *English Books and Readers 1475 to 1557.* Cambridge: Cambridge University Press, 1952.

Bennett, Josephine W. "Andrew Holes: A Neglected Harbinger of the English Renaissance." *Speculum* 19 (1944): 314–335.

———. "John Morer's Will: Thomas Linacre and Prior Sellyng's Greek Teaching." *Studies in the Renaissance* 15 (1968): 70–91.

Bentley, Jerry H. *Humanists and Holy Writ: New Testament Scholarship in the Renaissance.* Princeton: Princeton University Press, 1983.

Bernardinus a S. Ioanne Rotundo, O.F.M. Cap. "Thesis franciscanae de motivo primario Incarnationis expositio." *Collectanea franciscana* 4 (1934): 546–563.

Beumer, Johannes, S.J. "Erasmus von Rotterdam und seine Freunde aus dem Franziskanerorden." *Franziskanische Studien* 51 (1969): 117–129.

Bezzel, Irmgard. "Sechs neu entdeckte Widmungsexemplare des Erasmus von Rotterdam und ihre Empfänger." *Gutenberg-Jahrbuch* 55 (1980): 89–96.

Biblia Sacra iuxta Vulgatam versionem. Edited by Robert Weber, O.S.B. 2 vols. Stuttgart: Württembergische Bibelanstalt, 1969.

Bibliotheca Catholica Neerlandica Impressa 1500–1727. The Hague: Nijhoff, 1954.

Bissen, Iohannes-M., O.F.M. "De motivo Incarnationis: Disquisitio historico-dogmatica." *Antonianum* 7 (1932): 313–336.

———. *L'exemplarisme divin selon s. Bonaventure.* Paris: Vrin, 1929.

Blackwell, Constance. "Niccolò Perotti in England—Part I: John Anwykyll, Bernard André, John Colet and Luis Vives." *Res publica litterarum* 5 (1982): 13–28.

Blaise, Albert. *Dictionnaire latin-français des auteurs chrétiens.* Strasbourg: Le latin chrétien, 1954.

———. *Dictionnaire latin-français des auteurs du moyen âge.* Turnholt: Brepols, 1975.

Boaistuau, Guillaume. *Theatrum Mundi.* London, 1566.

Bolgar, R. R. *The Classical Heritage and Its Beneficiaries.* Cambridge: Cambridge University Press, 1954.

Bonaventure, St. *Opera omnia*. 10 vols. Quaracchi: Collegium S. Bonaventurae, 1883–1902.

———. *The Works of St. Bonaventure*. Translated by José de Vinck. 5 vols. Paterson, N.J.: St. Anthony Guild Press, 1960–1970.

Boussard, Jacques. "L'Université d'Orléans et l'humanisme au début du XVIᵉ siècle." *Humanisme et renaissance* 5 (1938): 209–230.

Boyancé, Pierre. *Etudes sur le Songe de Scipion*. Bordeaux: Feret, 1936.

Brabant, Hyacinthe. "L'homme malade dans la société de la renaissance." In *Individu et société à la renaissance: Colloque international, tenu en avril 1965*, 259–273. Brussels: Travaux de l'Institut pour l'étude de la renaissance et de l'homme, 1967.

Brewer, J. S., ed. *Letters and Papers, Henry VIII*. Vol. 1. London, 1862.

Bridgett, T. E. *Life of Blessed John Fisher, Bishop of Rochester*. London, 1888.

Brown, Andrew J. "The Date of Erasmus' Latin Translation of the New Testament." *Transactions of the Cambridge Bibliographical Society* 8 (1984): 351–380.

Brown, J. Howard. *Elizabethan Schooldays: An Account of the English Grammar Schools in the Second Half of the Sixteenth Century*. Oxford: Blackwell, 1933.

Brown, John. "John Colet and the Preachers of the Reformation." In his *Puritan Preaching in England*, 35–63. New York: Scribner's, 1900.

Bucer, Martin. *Deutsche Schriften*. Edited by Robert Stupperich. Vol. 1. Gütersloh: Mohn, 1960.

———. *Enarrationes perpetuae, in sacra quatuor evangelia, recognitae nuper & locis compluribus auctae*. N.p., 1530.

———. *Enarrationum in evangelia Matthaei, Marci & Lucae, libri duo*. Strasbourg, 1527.

Buck, August. "Die 'studia humanitatis' und ihre Methode." *Bibliothèque d'humanisme et renaissance* 19 (1959): 273–290.

Bullotta Barracco, Helda. "Saggio bio-bibliografico su Enrico Cornelio Agrippa di Nettesheim." *Rassegna di filosofia* 6 (1957): 222–248.

Burford, E. J. *Bawds and Lodgings: A History of the London Bankside Brothels c.100–1675*. London: Peter Owen, 1976.

Burr, David. "Olivi on Marriage: The Conservative as Prophet." *Journal of Medieval and Renaissance Studies* 2 (1972): 183–204.

Burrows, Montagu. "Memoir of William Grocyn." In *Oxford Historical Society Collectanea*, 3 vols., 2:332–380. Oxford, 1885–1896.

Butterworth, Charles C. *The English Primers (1529–1545)*. Philadelphia: University of Pennsylvania Press, 1953.

Byman, Seymour. "Child Raising and Melancholia in Tudor England." *Journal of Psychohistory* 6 (1978): 67–92.

Calendar of Pleas and Memoranda Rolls of the City of London. Vol. 6. London: H.M.S.O., 1961.

The Cambridge History of Classical Literature. Vol. 2, *Latin Literature*. Edited by E. J. Kenney. Cambridge: Cambridge University Press, 1982.

Cantimori, Delio. Introduzione. In *Elogio della pazzia*, by Desiderius Erasmus, edited by Tommaso Fiore, x– xv. Turin: Giulio Einaudi, 1964.

Carpenter, Edward. *Cantuar: The Archbishops in Their Office*. London: Cassell, 1971.

Caspari, Fritz. *Humanism and the Social Order in Tudor England*. Chicago: University of Chicago Press, 1954.

Catalogue des livres imprimés au quinzième siècle des bibliothèques de Belgique. 4 vols. Brussels: Pour la Société des bibliophiles et iconophiles de Belgique, 1932.

A Catalogue of the Manuscripts Preserved in the Library of the University of Cambridge. 6 vols. Cambridge, 1856–1867.

A Catholic Commentary on Holy Scripture. London: Nelson, 1953.

Cavazza, Silvano. "La cronologia degli 'Antibarbari' e le origini del pensiero religioso di Erasmo." *Rinascimento* 2d ser. 15 (1975): 141–179.

Cerny, Edward A. *Firstborn of Every Creature (Col. 1:15)*. Baltimore: St. Mary's University, 1938.

Cessi, Roberto. "Paolinismo preluterano." *Rendiconti dell'Accademia Nazionale dei Lincei*, Cl. di scienze morali, storiche e filologiche, 8th ser. 12 (1957): 3–30.

Ceuppens, F., O.P. "Quid S. Thomas de multiplici sensu litterali in Sacra Scriptura senserit?" *Divus Thomas* (Piacenza) 33 (1930): 164–175.

Chambers, D. S. "The Economic Predicament of Renaissance Cardinals." *Studies in Medieval and Renaissance History* 3 (1966): 287–313.

Chantillon, Jean. "Une ecclésiologie médiévale: L'idée de l'Eglise dans la théologie de l'école de Saint-Victor au XIIᵉ siècle." *Irénikon* 22 (1949): 115–138; 395–411.

Charlier, Yvonne. *Erasme et l'amitié d'après sa correspondance*. Paris: Les Belles Lettres, 1977.

Charlton, Kenneth. *Education in Renaissance England*. London: Methuen, 1965.

Chase, Frederic Henry. *Chrysostom: A study in the History of Biblical Interpretation*. Cambridge, 1887.

Chomart, Jacques. *Grammaire et rhétorique chez Erasme*. 2 vols. Paris: Les Belles Lettres, 1981.

Clark, Peter, and Paul Slack, eds. *Crisis and Order in English Towns 1500–1700*. Toronto: University of Toronto Press, 1972.

Clarke, M. L. *Classical Education in Britain 1500–1900*. Cambridge: Cambridge University Press, 1959.

Clebsch, William O. "John Colet and Reformation." *Anglican Theological Review* 37 (1955): 167–177.

Cohrs, Ferdinand. "Der humanistische Schulmeister Petrus Tritonius Athesinus." *Mitteilungen der Gesellschaft für deutsche Erziehungs- und Schulgeschichte* 8 (1898): 261–271.

———, ed. *Die evangelischen Katechismusversuche vor Luthers Enchiridion*. Vol. 4. Berlin: A Hofmann, 1902.

Collet, Clara E. "The Family of Dean Colet: Summary of Facts Obtained from the Records of the Mercers' Company." *Genealogists' Magazine* 7 (1935–1937): 242–243.

Collett, Barry. *Italian Benedictine Scholars and the Reformation: The Congregation of Santa Giustina of Padua*. Oxford: Clarendon, 1985.

Colli, Pietro. *La pericope paolina ad Ephesios V.32 nella interpretazione dei SS. Padri e del Concilio di Trento.* Parma: Fresching, 1951.

Collinson, Patrick. *Archbishop Grindal 1519–1583.* Berkeley, Los Angeles, London: University of California Press, 1979.

———. "The Role of Women in the English Reformation Illustrated by the Life and Friendships of Anne Locke." In *Studies in Church History* 2:258–272. London: Nelson, 1965.

Contemporaries of Erasmus: A Biographical Dictionary of the Renaissance and Reformation. Edited by Peter Bietenholz. 3 vols. Toronto: University of Toronto Press, 1985–1987.

Coulton, G. G. *Ten Medieval Studies.* Cambridge: Cambridge University Press, 1930.

Cuissard, M. "L'étude du grec à Orléans, depuis le IXe siècle jusqu'au milieu du XVIIIe siècle." *Mémoires de la Société archéologique et historique de l'Orléanais* 19 (1883): 645–840.

Culhane, Daniel. *De corpore mystico doctrina Seraphici.* Mundelein, Ill.: Privately printed, 1934.

Cushing, Harvey. *The Life of Sir William Osler.* 2 vols. Oxford: Clarendon, 1925.

Dacheux, L. *Un réformateur catholique à la fin du XVe siecle: Jean Geiler de Kaysersberg, prédicateur à la cathédrale de Strasbourg (1468–1510).* Paris, 1876.

Dannenberg, Friedrich. *Das Erbe Platons in England bis zur Bildung Lylys.* Berlin: Junker & Dünnhaupt, 1932.

de Caprariis, Vittorio. "Il 'Panegyricus' di Erasmo a Filippo di Borgogna." *Rivista storica italiana* 65 (1953): 199–221.

Deferrari, Roy J., et al. *A Lexicon of St. Thomas Aquinas.* 5 vols. in 3. Washington, D.C.: Catholic University of America Press, 1948–1953.

Delcourt, Marie. "Recherches sur Thomas More: La tradition continentale et la tradition anglaise." *Humanisme et renaissance* 3 (1936): 12–42.

Delius, Walter. *Justus Jonas 1495–1555.* Berlin: Evangelische Verlagsanstalt, 1952.

———. "Justus Jonas und Erasmus." *Theologia viatorum* 1 (1948–1949): 71–79.

della Torre, Arnaldo. *Storia dell'Accademia Platonica.* Florence: Carnesecchi e Figli, 1902.

Denifle, Heinrich, O.P. *Die abendländischen Schriftausleger bis Luther über Justitia Dei (Rom. 1,17) und Justificatio.* Mainz: F. Kirchheim, 1905.

Derville, Alain. "Jean Vitrier et les religieuses de Sainte-Marguerite." *Revue du nord* 42 (1960): 207–239.

———. "Vitrier." In *Bibliographie nationale . . . Belgique*, vol. 38, suppl. 10, Brussels: Bruylant, 1974. 809–816.

Dettloff, Werner, O.F.M. " 'Christus tenens medium in omnibus': Sinn und Funktion der Theologie bei Bonaventura." *Wissenschaft und Weisheit* 20 (1957): 28–42, 120–140.

de Vocht, Henry. *Earliest English Translations of Erasmus' Colloquies 1536–1566.* Louvain: Librairie universitaire, 1928.

de Vooght, Paul. "Un épisode peu connu de la vie d'Erasme: Sa rencontre avec les hussites bohèmes en 1519–1521." *Irénikon* 47 (1974): 27–47.

Dibbelt, Hermann. "Erasmus' griechische Studien." *Gymnasium* 57 (1950): 55–76.

Dickens, A. G., and John Tonkin, with Kenneth Powell. *The Reformation in Historical Thought*. Cambridge: Harvard University Press, 1985.

Dionysius Areopagita. *Oeuvres complètes du Pseudo-Denys l'Aréopagite*. Edited and translated by Maurice de Gandillac. Paris: Aubier, 1943.

Dolfen, Christian. *Die Stellung des Erasmus von Rotterdam zur scholastischen Methode*. Osnabrück: Meinders & Elstermann, 1936.

Dominici, Iohannes. *Lucula noctis*. Edited by Edmund Hunt. Notre Dame, Ind.: Notre Dame University Press, 1940.

Draper, F. W. M. *Four Centuries of Merchant Taylors' School 1561–1961*. Oxford: Oxford University Press, 1962.

Du Boulay, F. R. H. *An Age of Ambition: English Society in the Late Middle Ages*. London: Nelson, 1970.

Dudley, Edmund. *The Tree of Commonwealth*. Edited by D. M. Brodie. Cambridge: Cambridge University Press, 1948.

Duff, E. Gordon. *The Printers, Stationers and Bookbinders of London and Westminster from 1476 to 1535*. Cambridge: Cambridge University Press, 1906.

Dunham, William Huse, Jr. "The Members of Henry VIII's Whole Council, 1509–1527." *English Historical Review* 59 (1944): 187–210.

Eco, Umberto. "Simbolo." In *Enciclopedia Einaudi* 12:877–915. Turin: Einaudi, 1981.

Edmonds, John Maxwell, ed. *The Fragments of Attic Comedy*. 3 vols. in 4. Leiden: Brill, 1957–1961.

Eells, Hastings. *Martin Bucer*. New Haven: Yale University Press, 1931.

Egidi, Pietro, ed. *Necrologi e libri affini della provincia romana*. 2 vols. Rome: Istituto Storico Italiano, 1908–1914.

Elze, Martin. "Das Verständnis der Passion Jesu im ausgehenden Mittelalter und bei Luther." In *Geist und Geschichte der Reformation: Festgabe Hanns Rückert zum 65. Geburtstag*, edited by Heinz Liebing and Klaus Scholder, 127–151. Berlin: de Gruyter, 1966.

Erasmus, Desiderius. *Adagiorum collectanea*. Paris, 1500.

———. *Apologia*. Basel, 1520.

———. *L'apoteosi di Giovanni Reuchlin*. Edited by Giulio Vallese. Naples: R. Pironti, 1949.

———. *Ausgewählte Werke*. Edited by Hajo Holborn and Annemarie Holborn. Munich: Beck, 1933.

———. *The Colloquies of Erasmus*. Translated by Craig R. Thompson. Chicago: University of Chicago Press, 1965.

———. *De pueris statim ac liberaliter instituendis*. Edited by Jean-Claude Margolin. Geneva: Droz, 1966.

———. *The Enchiridion of Erasmus*. Translated and edited by Raymond Himelick. Bloomington: Indiana University Press, 1963.

———. *Erasmi opuscula*. Edited by Wallace K. Ferguson. The Hague: Mouton, 1933.

——. *Pilgrimages to Saint Mary of Walsingham and Saint Thomas of Canterbury*. 2d ed. Translated and edited by John Gough Nichols. London, 1875.
——. *The Poems of Erasmus*. Edited by C. Reedijk. Leiden: Brill, 1956.
——. *Tratado del niño Jesús y en loor del estado de la niñez (Sevilla, 1516)*. Edited by Eugenio Asensio. Madrid: Castalia, 1969.
Erasmus and Cambridge: The Cambridge Letters of Erasmus. Translated by D. F. S. Thomson, with introduction, notes, and commentary by H. C. Porter. Toronto: University of Toronto Press, 1963.
Erasmus en zijn tijd: Tentoonstelling ingericht ter herdenking van de geboorte . . . van Erasmus te Rotterdam. 2 vols. Rotterdam: Museum Boymans-Van Beuningen, 1969.
Evangéliste de Saint-Béat, O.F.M. Cap. "L'école franciscaine et ses chefs, s. Bonaventure et le B. Scot." *Etudes franciscaines* 1 (1899): 290–304, 457–469.
——. "Etudes sur saint Bonaventure." *Etudes franciscaines* 2 (1899): 382–400.
Exner, Helmut, *Der Einfluss des Erasmus auf die englische Bildungsidee*. Berlin: Junker & Dünnhaupt, 1939.
Farrar, Frederic W. *History of Interpretation*. London, 1886.
Feingold, Mordechai. "The Occult Tradition in the English Universities of the Renaissance: A Reassessment." In *Occult and Scientific Mentalities in the Renaissance*, edited by Brian Vickers, 73–94. Cambridge: Cambridge University Press, 1984.
Feld, Helmut. *Die Anfänge der modernen biblischen Hermeneutik in der spätmittelalterlichen Theologie*. Wiesbaden: Steiner, 1977.
Ferguson, Wallace K. "An Unpublished Letter of John Colet, Dean of St. Paul's." *American Historical Review* 39 (1934): 696–699.
Fiddes, Richard. *The Life of Cardinal Wolsey*. 2d ed. London, 1726.
Fisher, John. *Sacri sacerdotii defensio contra Lutherum (1525)*. Edited by Hermann K. Schmeink. Münster i. W.: Aschendorff, 1925.
Flandrin, Jean-Louis. "Mariage tardif et vie sexuelle: Discussions et hypothèses de recherche." *Annales: Economies, sociétés, civilisations* 27 (1972): 1351–1378.
Fletcher, John M. "The Teaching of Arts at Oxford, 1400–1520." *Paedagogica Historica* 7 (1967): 417–454.
Flynn, Vincent J. "Englishmen in Rome during the Renaissance." *Modern Philology* 36 (1938): 121–138.
Fokke, G. J., S.J. "An Aspect of the Christology of Erasmus of Rotterdam." *Ephemerides theologicae Lovanienses* 54 (1978): 161–187.
Fox, Richard. *The Letters of Richard Fox*. Edited by P. S. Allen and H. M. Allen. Oxford: Clarendon, 1929.
Foxe, John. *Acts and Monuments*. Edited by Josiah Pratt. 8 vols. London [1877].
Fragnito, Gigliola. "Cultura umanistica e riforma religiosa: il 'De officio viri boni ac probi episcopi' di Gasparo Contarini." *Studi veneziani* 11 (1969): 1–115.
Froehlich, Karlfried. " 'Always to Keep the Literal Sense in Holy Scripture Means to Kill One's Soul': The State of Biblical Hermeneutics at the Beginning of the Fifteenth Century." In *Literary Uses of Typology from the Late Middle Ages to the Present*, edited by Earl Miner, 20–48. Princeton: Princeton University Press, 1977.

Gaguin, Robert. *L'Immaculée Conception de la Vierge Marie: Poème de Robert Gaguin.* Edited and translated by Alcide Bonneau. Paris, 1885.

Garin, Eugenio. *L'educazione in Europa, 1400–1600.* Bari, Laterza, 1957.

———, ed. *Prosatori latini del quattrocento.* Milan and Naples: Ricciardi, 1952.

Garrod, H. W. "Erasmus and His English Patrons." *The Library,* 5th ser. 4 (1949): 1–13.

Gasquet, Adrian. *A History of the Venerable English College, Rome.* London: Longmans, 1920.

Gay, John H. "Four Medieval Views of Creation." *Harvard Theological Review* 56 (1963): 243–273.

Gee, John Archer. *The Life and Works of Thomas Lupset.* New Haven: Yale University Press, 1928.

Gerson, Jean. *Oeuvres complètes.* Edited by Palémon Glorieux. 10 vols. Paris: Desclée, 1960–1973.

Gesamtkatalog der Wiegendrucke. 8 vols. to date. Leipzig: Hiersemann, 1925–1979.

Gibson, Strickland, ed. *Statuta antiqua Universitatis Oxoniensis.* Oxford: Oxford University Press, 1931.

Gilbert, Allan H. "Martin Bucer on Education." *Journal of English and Germanic Philology* 18 (1919): 321–345.

Gilson, Etienne. *La philosophie au moyen âge.* 2d ed. Paris: Payot, 1947.

———. *La philosophie de saint Bonaventure.* 2d ed. Paris: Vrin, 1943.

Gleason, John B. "The Birth Dates of John Colet and Erasmus of Rotterdam: Fresh Documentary Evidence." *Renaissance Quarterly* 32 (1979): 73–76.

———. "The Earliest Evidence for Ecclesiastical Censorship of Printed Books in England." *The Library,* 6th ser. 4 (1982): 135–141.

Godfrey, W. Robert. "John Colet of Cambridge." *Archiv für Reformationsgeschichte* 65 (1974): 6–17.

Godin, André. "De Vitrier à Origène: Recherches sur la patristique érasmienne." In *Colloquium Erasmianum: Actes du Colloque international réuni à Mons du 26 au 29 octobre 1967,* 47–57. Mons: Centre universitaire de l'État, 1968.

———. *L'homéliaire de Jean Vitrier.* Geneva: Droz, 1971.

Gordon, Walter M. "The Religious Edifice and Its Symbolism in the Writings of Erasmus, Colet, and More." *Moreana* 22 (1985): 15–23.

Grabmann, Martin. "Der Einfluß des hl. Bonaventura auf die Theologie und Frömmigkeit des deutschen Mittelalters." *Zeitschrift für Aszese und Mystik* 19 (1944): 19–27.

———. "Die mittelalterlichen lateinischen Übersetzungen des Pseudo-Dionysius Areopagita." In *Mittelalterliches Geistesleben: Abhandlungen zur Geschichte der Scholastik und Mystik,* 2 vols., 1:449–468. Munich: Max Hueber, 1926–1936.

Graf, Karl Heinrich. "Jacobus Faber Stapulensis." *Zeitschrift für die historische Theologie* 22 (1852): 3–86, 165–237.

Grandgent, Charles H. "Quid Ploras?" *Annual Reports of the Dante Society* (Cambridge, Mass.) 42–44 (1926): 8–18.

Grant, Robert M. "One Hundred Fifty-Three Large Fish (John 21:11)." *Harvard Theological Review* 42 (1949): 273–275.

Greene, Thomas M. "Petrarch and the Humanist Hermeneutic." In *Italian Literature, Roots and Branches: Essays in Honor of Thomas Goddard Bergin*, edited by Giose Rimanelli and Kenneth John Atchity, 201–224. New Haven: Yale University Press, 1976.

Greschat, Martin. "Martin Bucers Bücherverzeichnis von 1518." *Archiv für Kulturgeschichte* 57 (1975): 162–185.

Grossman, F. "Holbein, Torrigiano and Some Portraits of Dean Colet." *Journal of the Warburg and Courtauld Institutes* 13 (1950): 202–236.

Gruner, Christian Gottfried, ed. *Scriptores de sudore anglico superstites*. Jena, 1847.

Grunzweig, Armand, ed. *Correspondance de la filiale de Bruges des Medicis*. Pt. 1. Brussels: Lamertin, 1931.

Guardini, Romano. *Die Lehre des heil. Bonaventura von der Erlösung*. Düsseldorf: Schwann, 1921.

Guy, John A. *The Cardinal's Court*. Hassocks: Harvester, 1977.

Hacking, Ian. *The Emergence of Probability*. Cambridge: Cambridge University Press, 1976.

Hägg, Tomas. *The Novel in Antiquity*. Berkeley, Los Angeles, London: University of California Press, 1983.

Harbison, E. Harris. *The Christian Scholar in the Age of the Reformation*. New York: Scribner's, 1956.

Harding, Thomas. *A Reioindre to M. Jewels Replie*. Antwerp, 1566.

Hardwick, J. C. "John Colet." *The Modern Churchman* 15 (1925): 178–184.

Harper-Bill, Christopher. "Dean Colet's Convocation Sermon and the Pre-Reformation Church in England." *History* 73 (1988): 191–210.

Hartfelder, Karl. "Das Ideal einer Humanistenschule (Die Schule Colets zu St. Paul in London)." *Verhandlungen der . . . Versammlung[en] deutscher Philologen und Schulmänner* 41 (1892): 166–181.

Hausherr, Ir., S.J. "Doutes au sujet du 'Divin Denis.' " *Orientalia christiana periodica* 2 (1936): 484–490.

Heckscher, William S. *Rembrandt's* Anatomy of Dr. Nicolaas Tulp. New York: New York University Press, 1958.

Heimbucher, Max. *Die Orden und Kongregationen der katholischen Kirche*. 3d ed. 2 vols. Paderborn: Ferdinand Schöningh, 1933–1934.

Henson, Herbert Hensley. *The Church of England*. Cambridge: Cambridge University Press, 1939.

———. *Retrospect of an Unimportant Life*. 3 vols. London: Oxford University Press, 1942–1950.

Herbert, William. *The History of the Twelve Great Livery Companies of London*. 2 vols. 1834–1837. Reprint. New York: Augustus M. Kelley, 1968.

Hexter, J. H. "The Education of the Aristocracy in the Renaissance." *Journal of Modern History* 22 (1950): 1–20.

Hockel, Alfred. *Christus, der Erstgeborene: Zur Geschichte der Exegese von Kol 1,15*. Düsseldorf: Patmos-Verlag, 1965.

Hopf, Constantin. *Martin Bucer and the English Reformation*. Oxford: Blackwell, 1946.

Hoshino, Hidetoshi. *L'arte della lana in Firenze nel basso medioevo*. Florence: Olschki, 1980.

Hoyoux, Jean. "Les moyens d'existence d'Erasme." *Bibliothèque d'humanisme et renaissance*, n.s. 5 (1944): 7–59.

Hudson, Hoyt H. "John Leland's List of Early English Humanists." *Huntington Library Quarterly* 2 (1939): 301–304.

Hugh of St. Victor. *On the Sacraments of the Christian Faith (De Sacramentis)*. Translated and edited by Roy J. Deferrari. Cambridge: Mediaeval Academy of America, 1951.

Hughes, Philip. *The Reformation in England*. 3 vols. London: Hollis and Carter, 1952–1954.

Humbert, Auguste. *Les origines de la théologie moderne: I. La renaissance chrétienne (1450–1521)*. Paris: Gabalda, 1911.

Humphreys, K. W. *The Library of the Franciscans of Siena in the Late Fifteenth Century*. Amsterdam: Erasmus, 1978.

Hunt, Ernest W. *Dean Colet and His Theology*. London: Publ. for The Church Historical Society by S.P.C.K., 1956.

Hurstfield, Joel. *Freedom, Corruption and Government in Elizabethan England*. Cambridge: Harvard University Press, 1973.

Hyma, Albert. "Erasmus and the Oxford Reformers (1493–1503)." *Nederlandsch archief voor kerkgeschiedenis*, n.s. 25 (1932): 69–92, 97–134.

———. "Erasmus and the Oxford Reformers (1503–1519)." *Nederlands archief voor kerkgeschiedenis*, n.s. 38 (1951): 65–85.

Imray, Jean M. " 'Les bones gentes de la Mercerye de Londres': A Study of the Membership of the Mediaeval Mercers' Company." In *Studies in London History Presented to Philip Edmund Jones*, ed. A. E. J. Hollaender and W. Kellaway, 155–178. London: Hodder and Stoughton, 1969.

———. *The Charity of Richard Whittington: A History of the Trust Administered by the Mercers' Company 1424–1966*. London: Athlone, 1968.

———. "The Merchant Adventurers and Their Records." *Journal of the Society of Archivists* 2 (1960–1964): 457–467.

Index of Wills Proved in the Prerogative Court of Canterbury 1383–1558. Compiled by J. C. C. Smith. 2 vols. London, 1893.

Inge, William Ralph. "John Colet." In *Lay Thoughts of a Dean*, 3–20. New York: Scribner's, 1926.

Jardine, Lisa. "Humanism and the Sixteenth Century Cambridge Arts Course." *History of Education* 4 (1975): 16–31.

Jarrott, Catherine A. L. "Erasmus's Annotations and Colet's Commentaries on Paul." In *Essays on the Works of Erasmus*, edited by Richard L. DeMolen, 125–144. New Haven: Yale University Press, 1978.

Jayne, Sears. *John Colet and Marsilio Ficino*. Oxford: Oxford University Press, 1963.

Jedin, Hubert. *Geschichte des Konzils von Trient*. 4 vols. in 5. Freiburg i. B.: Herder, 1949–1975.

———. *Il tipo ideale di vescovo secondo la riforma cattolica*. Edited by Giuseppe Alberigo. Brescia: Morcelliana, 1985.

Jenks, Arthur W. "John Colet." *Anglican Theological Review* 1 (1919): 355–370.

Jensen, Kristian. "*De emendata structura Latini sermonis*: The Latin Grammar of Thomas Linacre." *Journal of the Warburg and Courtauld Institutes* 49 (1986): 106–125.

John Chrysostom, St. "Liber . . . de laudibus Beati Pauli Apostoli, Homilia VII." In *Opera Venerabilis Bedae* 5: 1136–1176. Basel, 1537.

"John Colet, Dean of St. Paul's." *American Church Quarterly Review* 21 (1869): 193–204.

Jonas, Justus. *Der Briefwechsel des Justus Jonas*. Edited by D. Gustav Kawerau. 2 vols. Halle, 1884–1885.

Jourdan, George V. *The Movement towards Catholic Reform in the Early XVI Century*. London: John Murray, 1914.

Kagan, Jerome. *The Development of the Child*. New York: Basic Books, 1984.

Kahl, William F. *The Development of London Livery Companies: An Historical Essay and a Select Bibliography*. Boston: Baker Library, Harvard Graduate School of Business Administration, 1960.

Kaufman, Peter Iver. *Augustinian Piety and Catholic Reform: Augustine, Colet, and Erasmus*. Macon, Ga.: Mercer University Press, 1982.

———. "John Colet and Erasmus' *Enchiridion*." *Church History* 46 (1977): 296–312.

———. "John Colet's *Opus de sacramentis* and Clerical Anticlericalism: The Limitations of 'Ordinary Wayes.' " *Journal of British Studies* 22 (1982): 1–22.

Kaufmann, Michael, et al., eds. *Aegidius Romanus' de Colonna, Johannnes Gersons, Dionys des Kartäusers und Jakob Sadolets pädagogische Schriften*. Freiburg i. B.: Herder, 1904.

Kelly, Michael J. "Canterbury Jurisdiction and Influence during the Episcopate of William Warham, 1503–1532." Ph.D. diss., Cambridge University, 1963.

Kennedy, George A. *Greek Rhetoric under Christian Emperors*. Princeton: Princeton University Press, 1983.

Kérenyi, Carl. *Zeus and Hera*. Princeton: Princeton University Press, 1975.

Knowles, David. *The Religious Orders in England*. 3 vols. Cambridge: Cambridge University Press, 1948–1959.

Knox, Ronald A. *Enthusiasm*. London: Oxford University Press, 1950.

Kohls, Ernst-Wilhelm. *Die Schule bei Martin Bucer*. Heidelberg: Quelle und Meyer, 1963.

Kreider, Alan. *English Chantries: The Road to Dissolution*. Cambridge: Harvard University Press, 1979.

Kremer, Klaus. "Das 'Warum' der Schöpfung: 'quia bonus' vel/et 'quia voluit'?: Ein Beitrag zum Verhältnis vom Neuplatonismus und Christentum an Hand des Prinzips 'bonum est diffusivum sui.' " In *Parusia: Studien zur Philosophie Platons und zur Problemgeschichte des Platonismus: Festgabe für Johannes Hirschberger*, edited by Kurt Flasch, 241–264. Frankfurt a. M.: Minerva, 1965.

Kristeller, Paul O. "Florentine Platonism and Its Relations with Humanism and Scholasticism," *Church History* 8 (1939): 201–211.

Krogh-Tonning, K. *Der letzte Scholastiker: Eine Apologie*. Freiburg i. B.: Herder, 1904.

Lander, J. R. "Attainder and Forfeiture, 1453 to 1509." *Historical Journal* 4 (1961): 119–151.

Landgraf, A. "Beiträge der Frühscholastik zur Terminologie der allgemeinen Sakramentenlehre." *Divus Thomas* (Vienna) 29 (1951): 3–34.

Laslett, Peter. *Family Life and Illicit Love in Earlier Generations.* Cambridge: Cambridge University Press, 1977.

Latham, R. E. *Revised Medieval Latin Word-List from British and Irish Sources.* London: Oxford University Press, 1965.

Latimer, Hugh. *Sermons.* Edited by G. E. Corrie. 2 vols. Cambridge, 1844–1845.

Leach, Arthur F. "St. Paul's School before Colet." *Archaeologia* 62, pt. 1 (1910): 191–238.

Lecchini, Roberto. *I Francescani e la rinascita inglese.* Modena: TEIC, 1975.

Leclercq, Jean. *The Love of Learning and the Desire for God.* 2d ed. New York: Fordham University Press, 1974.

Lehmann, Martin. *Justus Jonas, Loyal Reformer.* Minneapolis: Augsburg, 1963.

Le Neve, John. *Fasti Ecclesiae Anglicanae 1300–1541.* Vol. 5 (St. Paul's, London), compiled by Joyce M. Horne. London: Athlone, 1963. Vol. 11 (The Welsh Dioceses), compiled by B. Jones. London: Athlone, 1965.

Le Roy, Alphonse. "Gaguin (Robert)." *Biographie nationale . . . de Belgique,* 7:418–423. Brussels, 1880–1883.

Lewis, C. S. *The Discarded Image: An Introduction to Medieval and Renaissance Literature.* Cambridge: Cambridge University Press, 1964.

Lloyd, Charles, ed. *Formularies of Faith Put Forth by Authority during the Reign of Henry VIII.* Oxford, 1825.

Lovejoy, Arthur O. *The Great Chain of Being.* Cambridge: Harvard University Press, 1936.

Lubac, Henri de, S.J. *Exégèse médiévale: Les quatre sens de l'Ecriture.* 4 vols. Paris: Aubier, 1959–1964.

Lupton, Joseph H. *The Influence of Dean Colet upon the Reformation of the English Church.* London and Cambridge, 1893.

Lutz, Cora E. "Democritus and Heraclitus." *Classical Journal* 49 (1954): 309–314.

Lytle, Guy Fitch. "Patronage Patterns and Oxford Colleges c.1300–c.1530." In *The University in Society,* edited by Lawrence Stone, 2 vols. 1:111–149. Princeton: Princeton University Press, 1974.

McConica, J. K. *English Humanists and Reformation Politics.* Oxford: Clarendon, 1965.

McDonnell, Sir Michael. *The Annals of St. Paul's School.* London: Privately printed, 1959.

———. *A History of St. Paul's School.* London: Chapman and Hall, 1909.

Macek, Joseph. *Jean Hus et les traditions hussites (XVᵉ–XIXᵉ siècles).* Paris: Plon, 1973.

Mackenzie, Mary L. *Dame Christian Colet: Her Life & Family.* Cambridge: Privately printed, 1923.

McKeon, Richard P., ed. *Selections from Medieval Philosophers.* 2 vols. New York: Scribner's, 1929–1930.

Mackie, J. D. *The Earlier Tudors 1485–1558.* Oxford: Clarendon, 1952.

MacQueen, John. *Numerology: Theory and Outline History of a Literary Mode.* Edinburgh: Edinburgh University Press, 1985.

Maddison, Francis, et al. *Essays on the Life and Work of Thomas Linacre c. 1460–1524.* Oxford: Clarendon, 1977.

Major, H. D. A. *English Modernism: Its Origin, Methods, Aims.* Cambridge: Harvard University Press, 1927.

Malfatti, C. V. *Two Italian Accounts of Tudor England.* Barcelona: n.p., 1953.

Mansfield, Bruce. *Phoenix of His Age: Interpretations of Erasmus c1550–1750.* Toronto: University of Toronto Press, 1979.

Marcel, Raymond. "L'Enchiridion militis christiani: Sa genèse et sa doctrine, son succès et ses vicissitudes." In *Colloquia Erasmiana Turonensia,* 2 vols. 2:613–646. Toronto: University of Toronto Press, 1972.

——. "Introduction et succès du platonisme en France à l'aube de la renaissance." In *The Late Middle Ages and the Dawn of Humanism Outside Italy: Proceedings of the International Congress, Louvain, May 11–13, 1970,* edited by G. Verbeke and J. IJsewijn, 89–99. Louvain: University Press, 1972.

Marett, R. R. *Sacraments of Simple Folk.* Oxford: Clarendon, 1933.

Marius, Richard. *Thomas More: A Biography.* New York: Knopf, 1985.

Massaut, Jean-Pierre. "Erasme et saint Thomas." In *Colloquia Erasmiana Turonensia,* 2 vols, 2:581–611. Toronto: University of Toronto Press, 1972.

——. *Josse Clichtove, l'humanisme et la réforme du clergé.* 2 vols. Paris: Les Belles Lettres, 1968.

——. "Mystique rhénane et humanisme chrétien d'Eckhart à Erasme: Continuité, convergence, ou rupture?" In *The Late Middle Ages and the Dawn of Humanism Outside Italy: Proceedings of the International Congress, Louvain, May 11–13, 1970,* edited by G. Verbeke and J. IJsewijn, 112–130. Louvain: University Press, 1972.

——. *Tradition et critique à la veille de la Réforme en France.* Paris: Vrin, 1974.

Matthews, W. R., and W. M. Atkins, eds. *A History of St. Paul's Cathedral and the Men Associated with It.* London: Phoenix House, 1957.

May, J. Lewis. *The Oxford Movement.* London: Bodley Head, 1933.

Meissinger, Karl August. *Erasmus von Rotterdam.* 2d ed. Berlin: Nauck, 1948.

Meyer, Carl S. "Henry VIII Burns Luther's Books, 12 May 1521." *Journal of Ecclesiastical History* 9 (1958): 173–187.

——. "John Colet's Significance for the English Reformation." *Concordia Theological Monthly* 34 (1963): 410–418.

Meyer, Heinz, and Rudolf Suntrup. *Lexikon der mittelalterlichen Zahlenbedeutungen.* Munich: Fink, 1987.

Midmer, Roy. *English Medieval Monasteries (1066–1540).* Athens: University of Georgia Press, 1979.

Miles, Leland. *John Colet and the Platonic Tradition.* La Salle, Ill.: Open Court, 1961.

——. "Protestant Colet and Catholic More." *Anglican Theological Review* 33 (1951): 30–42.

Moorman, John R. H. *The Grey Friars at Cambridge.* Cambridge: Cambridge University Press, 1952.

Moran, Jo Ann Hoeppner. *The Growth of English Schooling 1340–1548: Learning, Literacy, and Laicization in Pre-Reformation York Diocese.* Princeton: Princeton University Press, 1985.

Müller, Ewald. *Das Konzil von Vienne 1311–1312: Seine Quellen und seine Geschichte.* Münster i. W.: Aschendorff, 1934.

Müller, Johannes. *Martin Bucers Hermeneutik.* Gütersloh: Mohn, 1965.

Müller, Karl. "Der Umschwung in der Lehre von der Buße während des 12. Jahrhunderts." In *Theologische Abhandlungen, Carl von Weizsäcker zu seinem siebzigsten Geburtstag gewidmet,* 287–320. Freiburg i. B. 1892.

Mullally, Joseph P. *The Summae Logicales of Peter of Spain.* Notre Dame, Ind.: Notre Dame University Press, 1945.

Mumford, Alfred A. *Hugh Oldham 1452[?]–1519.* London: Faber and Faber, 1936.

Nardi, Bruno. "L'aristotelismo della scolastica e i francescani." In *Scholastica ratione historico-critica instauranda: Acta Congressus Internationalis Romae Anno Sancto MCML celebrati,* 607–626. Rome: Pontificum Athenaeum Antonianum, 1951.

Nauert, Charles M., Jr. *Agrippa and the Crisis of Renaissance Thought.* Urbana: University of Illinois Press, 1965.

Nemetz, Anthony. "Literalness and the *sensus litteralis.*" *Speculum* 34 (1959): 76–89.

Newns, Brian. "The Hospice of St. Thomas and the English Crown 1474–1538." *The English Hospice in Rome,* spec. issue of *The Venerabile* 21 (May 1962): 145–192.

Niermeyer, J. F. *Mediae Latinitatis lexicon minus.* Leiden: Brill, 1954–1976.

Nijhoff, Wouter, and M. E. Kronenberg. *Nederlandsche bibliographie van 1500 tot 1540.* 3 vols. 's-Gravenhage: Nijhoff, 1923.

Novotný, František. *The Posthumous Life of Plato.* Prague: Academia, 1977.

Novum glossarium mediae Latinitatis ab anno DCCC ad annum MCC. Fasc. "L." Copenhagen: Munskgaard, 1957.

Nugent, Elizabeth M., ed. *The Thought and Culture of the English Renaissance: An Anthology of Tudor Prose 1481–1555.* Cambridge: Cambridge University Press, 1956.

Oberman, Heiko A. *Masters of the Reformation: The Emergence of a New Intellectual Climate in Europe.* Translated by Dennis Martin. Cambridge: Cambridge University Press, 1981.

O'Boyle, Marjorie. *Erasmus on Language and Method in Theology.* Toronto: University of Toronto Press, 1978.

Ong, Walter J., S.J. *Ramus, Method, and the Decay of Dialogue.* Cambridge: Harvard University Press, 1957.

Orme, Nicholas. *English Schools in the Middle Ages.* London: Methuen, 1973.

Ortus Vocabulorum. 1500. Reprint, edited by R. C. Alston. Menston, Yorkshire: Scolar, 1968.

Ott, Ludwig. *Grundriss der Dogmatik.* 4th ed. Freiburg i. B.: Herder, 1959.

Pace, Richard. *De fructu qui ex doctrina percipitur: The Benefit of a Liberal Education.* Translated and edited by Frank Manley and Richard S. Sylvester. New York: Ungar, 1967.

Padley, G. A. *Grammatical Theory in Western Europe 1500–1700*. Cambridge: Cambridge University Press, 1976.

Pantin, W. A. "The Conception of the Humanities in England in the Period of the Renaissance." In *Les universités européennes du XIVe au XVIIe siècle, aspects et problèmes: Actes du Colloque international à l'occasion du VIe centenaire de l'Université Jagellone de Cracovie 6–8 mai 1964*, 101–113. Geneva: Droz, 1967.

Parks, George B. *The English Traveler to Italy*. Vol. 1. Rome: Ed. di Storia e Letteratura, 1954.

Patrides, C. A. "Renaissance Thought on the Celestial Hierarchy: The Decline of a Tradition." *Journal of the History of Ideas* 20 (1959): 155–166.

——."Renaissance Views on the 'Unconfused Orders Angellick.' " *Journal of the History of Ideas* 23 (1962): 265–267.

Payne, John B. *Erasmus: His Theology of the Sacraments*. Richmond, Va.: John Knox, 1970.

Pease, A. S. "Caeli enarrant." *Harvard Theological Review* 34 (1941): 163–200.

Pehaire, J. "L'axiome 'bonum est diffusivum sui' dans le néoplatonisme et le thomisme." *Revue de l'Université d'Ottawa* 1 (1932): 5*–30*.

Pelikan, Jaroslav. *The Christian Tradition: A History of the Development of Doctrine*. 5 vols. Chicago: University of Chicago Press, 1971–1989.

Peters, Robert. "The Contribution of the Eastern Fathers to the Intellectual Equipment of the English Clergy during the Sixteenth Century." In *Miscellanea historiae ecclesiasticae, IV*, 93–112. Louvain: Bibliothèque de la Revue d'histoire ecclésiastique, 1972.

The Phenix. 2 vols. London, 1707–1708.

Phillips, Margaret Mann. *The 'Adages' of Erasmus: A Study with Translations*. Cambridge: Cambridge University Press, 1964.

Picciotto, Sir Cyril. *St. Paul's School*. London and Glasgow: Blackie, 1939.

Piccolomini, Aeneas Silvius. *Historia Bohemica*. Cologne, 1532.

Pico della Mirandola. "Oration on the Dignity of Man." In *The Renaissance Philosophy of Man*, edited by Ernst Cassirer et al., 223–254. Chicago: University of Chicago Press, 1948.

Pits, John. *Relationum historicarum de rebus anglicis tomus I*. Edited by William Bishop. Paris, 1619.

Plato. *Gorgias*. Edited by E. R. Dodds. Oxford: Clarendon, 1959.

——. *Opera omnia quae exstant*. Translated by Marsilio Ficino. Frankfurt, 1602.

Plotinus. *Operum philosophicorum omnium libri liv in sex enneados distincti*. Translated by Marsilio Ficino. Basel, 1580.

Pollard, A. F. *Henry VIII*. London: Longmans Green, 1951.

——. *Wolsey*. 1929. Reprint. London: Collins, 1965.

Pontet, M. *L'exégèse de S. Augustin prédicateur*. Paris: Aubier, 1946.

Porter, H. C. "The Gloomy Dean and the Law: John Colet, 1466–1519." In *Essays in Modern English Church History in Memory of Norman Sykes*, edited by G. V. Bennett and J. D. Walsh, 18–34. London: A. and C. Black, 1966.

Poschmann, Bernhard. *Paenitentia secunda: Die kirchliche Busse im ältesten Christentum bis Cyprian und Origenes: Eine dogmengeschichtliche Untersuchung*. Bonn: Peter Hanstein, 1940.

Powell, Douglas. "Arkandisziplin." In *Theologische Realenzyklopädie* 4:1–8. Berlin and New York: De Gruyter, 1978.

Powicke, F. M. *The Reformation in England*. London: Oxford University Press, 1941.

———. "The Reformation in England." In *European Civilization: Its Origin and Development*, edited by Edward Eyre, vol. 4. Oxford: Oxford University Press, 1936.

Preus, James Samuel. *From Shadow to Promise: Old Testament Interpretation from Augustine to the Young Luther*. Cambridge: Belknap-Harvard University Press, 1969.

Quick, Oliver Chase. *Doctrines of the Creed*. New York: Scribner's, n.d.

Raby, A. F. L. *Christian Latin Poetry*. Oxford: Clarendon, 1927.

Rahner, Karl, and Herbert Vorgrimler. *Theological Dictionary*. Translated by Cornelius Ernst, O.P. New York: Herder and Herder, 1965.

Rapp, François. *L'Eglise et la vie religieuse en occident à la fin du moyen âge*. Paris: P.U.F., 1971.

Reddaway, T. F., and Lorna E. M. Walker. *The Early History of the Goldsmiths' Company 1327–1509*. London: Edward Arnold, 1975.

A Relation, or Rather a True Account of the Island of England . . . About the Year 1500. Camden Society Publication 37. Translated by C. Sneyd. London, 1847.

Reynolds, L. D., and N. G. Wilson. *Scribes and Scholars: A Guide to the Transmission of Greek and Latin Literature*. 2d ed. Oxford: Clarendon, 1974.

Říčan, Rudolf. "Die tschechische Reformation und Erasmus." *Communio viatorum* 16 (1973): 185–206.

Rice, Eugene F., Jr. "Erasmus and the Religious Tradition." *Journal of the History of Ideas* 11 (1950): 387–411.

———. "John Colet and the Annihilation of the Natural." *Harvard Theological Review* 45 (1952): 141–163.

———. Review of *John Colet and Marsilio Ficino*, by Sears Jayne. *Renaissance News* 17 (1964): 107–110.

———, ed. *The Prefatory Epistles of Jacques Lefèvre d'Etaples and Related Texts*. New York: Columbia University Press, 1972.

Ridley, Jasper. *Statesman and Saint: Cardinal Wolsey, Sir Thomas More, and the Politics of Henry VIII*. New York: Viking, 1983.

Ridolfi, Roberto. *Cronologia e bibliografia delle prediche*. Vol. 1 of *Bibliografia delle opere del Savonarola*, edited by Piero Ginori Conti. Florence: Fondazione Ginori Conti, 1939.

Riedlinger, Helmut. *Die Makellosigkeit der Kirche in den lateinischen Hoheliedkommentaren des Mittelalters*. Münster i. W.: Aschendorff, 1958.

Rieger, James H. "Erasmus, Colet and the Schoolboy Jesus." *Studies in the Renaissance* 9 (1962): 182–194.

Rocques, René, et al., eds. Ps.-Dionysius Areopagita, *La hiérarchie céleste*. Paris: Cerf, 1958.

Rothkrug, Lionel. *Religious Practices and Collective Perceptions: Hidden Homologies in the Renaissance and Reformation*. Spec. issue of *Historical Reflections/Réflexions historiques* 7, no. 1 (1980).

Rouschausse, Jean, ed. *Erasmus and Fisher: Their Correspondence 1511–1524.* Paris: Vrin, 1968.

Rude, Donald W. "On the Date of Sir Thomas Elyot's *The Education or bringinge vp of children.*" *Papers of the Bibliographical Society of America* 71 (1977): 61–65.

Rupprich, Hans. "Johannes Reuchlin und seine Bedeutung im europäischen Humanismus," in *Johannes Reuchlin 1455–1522: Festgabe seiner Vaterstadt Pforzheim zur 500. Wiederkehr seines Geburtstages,* edited by Manfred Krebs, 10–34. Pforzheim: Selbstverlag der Stadt Pforzheim, 1955.

Russell, G. H. "Vernacular Instruction of the Laity in the Later Middle Ages in England: Some Texts and Notes." *Journal of Religious History* 2 (1962): 98–119.

Salomon, Richard G. "Poggio Bracciolini and Johannes Hus: A Hoax Hard to Kill." *Journal of the Warburg and Courtauld Institutes* 19 (1956): 174–177.

Santinello, Giovanni. *Studi sull'umanesimo europeo.* Padua: Antenor, 1969.

Schär, Max. *Das Nachleben des Origenes im Zeitalter des Humanismus.* Basel and Stuttgart: Helbing und Lichtenhahn, 1979.

Schäzler, Constantin von. *Die Lehre von der Wirksamkeit der Sakramente ex opere operato.* Munich, 1860.

Schelke, Karl Hermann. "Taufe und Tod: Zur Auslegung von Römer 6, 1–11." In *Vom christlichen Mysterium: Gesammelte Arbeiten zum Gedächtnis von Odo Casel OSB,* edited by Anton Mayer et al., 9–21. Düsseldorf: Patmos-Verlag, 1951.

Schlette, Heinz Robert. *Die Nichtigkeit der Welt: Der philosophische Horizont des Hugo von St. Viktor.* Munich: Kösel, 1961.

Schmid, Josef. "Brautschaft, heilige." *Reallexikon für Antike und Christentum* 2 (1954): 528–564.

Schucan, Luzi. *Das Nachleben von Basilius Magnus "ad adolescentes": Ein Beitrag zur Geschichte des christlichen Humanismus.* Geneva: Droz, 1973.

Schuyler, Robert L. "John Richard Green and his *Short History.*" *Political Science Quarterly* 64 (1949): 321–354.

Schwarz, W. *Principles and Problems of Biblical Translation: Some Reformation Controversies and Their Background.* Cambridge: Cambridge University Press, 1955.

Scott-Craig, T. S. K. "The Literal Sense." *History of Ideas News Letter* 1 (1955): 11–12.

Seaborne, Malcolm. *The English School: Its Architecture and Organization.* Toronto: University of Toronto Press, 1971.

Secret, François. *Les kabbalistes chrétiens de la renaissance.* Paris: Dunod, 1964.

Seebohm, Frederic. *The Oxford Reformers John Colet, Erasmus, and Thomas More: Being a History of Their Fellow-Work.* 3d ed. London, 1896.

———. *The Spirit of Christianity: An Essay on the Christian Hypothesis.* 1876. Reprint. London: Longmans, Green, 1916.

Shumaker, Wayne. *The Occult Sciences in the Renaissance.* Berkeley, Los Angeles, London: University of California Press, 1972.

Simone, Franco. "La coscienza della rinascita negli umanisti." *La rinascita* 3 (1940): 163–186.

——. "Robert Gaguin e il suo cenacolo umanistico." *Aevum* 13 (1939): 410–476.

Simpson, W. Sparrow. "A Newly-Discovered Manuscript Containing Statutes Compiled by Dean Colet for the Government of the Chantry Priests and Other Clergy of St. Paul's." *Archaeologia* 52 (1890): 144–174.

——, ed. *Registrum statutorum et consuetudinum Ecclesiae Cathedralis S. Pauli Londinensis*. London, 1873.

Sixtus Senensis. *Bibliotheca sancta*. Lyons, 1591.

Smalley, Beryl. *The Study of the Bible in the Middle Ages*. 2d ed. Notre Dame, Ind.: Notre Dame University Press, 1964.

Smart, Stefan J. "John Foxe and 'The Story of Richard Hun, Martyr.' " *Journal of Ecclesiastical History* 37 (1986): 1–14.

Smith, H. Maynard. *Pre-Reformation England*. London: Macmillan, 1938.

Smith, Margery H., CSJ. "Some Humanist Libraries in Early Tudor Cambridge." *Sixteenth Century Journal* 5 (1974): 15–34.

Smith, Preserved. *A Key to the Colloquies of Erasmus*. Cambridge: Harvard University Press, 1927.

Sombart, Werner. *The Quintessence of Capitalism*. Translated by M. Epstein. 1915. Reprint. New York: Howard Fertig, 1967.

Sowards, J. K. "Erasmus and the Apologetic Textbook: A Study of *De duplici copia verborum ac rerum*." *Studies in Philology* 55 (1958): 122–135.

Speyr, O. *Die literarische Fälschung im heidnischen und christlichen Altertum*. Munich: Beck, 1971.

Spicq, C. *Equisse d'une histoire de l'exégèse latine au moyen âge*. Paris: Vrin, 1944.

Squibb, G. D. *Doctors' Commons: A History of the College of Advocates and Doctors of Law*. Oxford: Clarendon, 1977.

Stanier, R. S. *Magdalen School: A History of Magdalen College School Oxford*. Oxford Historical Society Publication n.s. 3. Oxford: Oxford University Press, 1940.

Stannard, David. *Shrinking History*. New York: Oxford University Press, 1980.

Starkey, Thomas. *A Dialogue between Reginald Pole and Thomas Lupset*. Edited by Kathleen M. Burton. London: Chatto and Windus, 1948.

Stauffer, Donald A. *English Biography before 1700*. Cambridge: Harvard University Press, 1930.

Steele, Robert, ed. *Tudor and Stuart Proclamations*. 2 vols. Oxford: Clarendon, 1910.

Steer, Georg. "Die Rezeption des theologischen Bonaventura-Schrifttums im deutschen Spätmittelalter." In *Bonaventura: Studien zu seiner Wirkungsgeschichte*, 146–156. Werl i. W.: Dietrich Coelde, 1976.

Steinmann, Jean. *Richard Simon et les origines de l'exégèse biblique*. Paris: Desclée de Brouwer, 1960.

Stephenson, Alan M. G. *The Rise and Decline of English Modernism*. London: S.P.C.K., 1984.

Stow, John. *A Survey of London. Reprinted from the Text of 1603.* Edited by C. L. Kingsford. 2 vols. Oxford: Clarendon, 1971.

Strelka, Josef. *Der burgundische Renaissancehof Margarethes von Österreich und seine literarhistorische Bedeutung.* Vienna: A. Sexl, 1957.

Stupperich, Robert. *Erasmus von Rotterdam und seine Welt.* Berlin and New York: de Gruyter, 1977.

Surtz, Edward L., S.J. " 'Oxford Reformers' and Scholasticism." *Studies in Philology* 47 (1950): 547–556.

Tavard, George H. *Holy Writ or Holy Church.* New York: Harper, 1959.

Telle, Emile V. *Erasme de Rotterdam et le septième sacrement.* Geneva: Droz, 1954.

———. "Trois contes érasmiques et une note sur More. Erasme et Caïn." *Moreana*, nos. 15–16 (1967): 63–68.

Tentoonstelling Dirk Martens (1473–1973). Aalst: Stedelijk Museum—Oud Hospitaal, 1973.

Thomas Aquinas, St. *Catena aurea in quatuor evangelia.* New ed. Edited by Angelico Guarienti, O.P. 2 vols. Turin and Rome: Marietti, 1953.

Thompson, Craig R. "Erasmus and Tudor England." In *Actes du Congrès Erasme . . . Rotterdam 27–29 octobre 1969,* 29–68. Amsterdam and London: North-Holland, 1971.

Thomson, D. S. F. "Linacre's Latin Grammars." In *Essays on the Life and Work of Thomas Linacre c.1460–1524,* edited by Francis Maddison et al., 24–35. Oxford: Clarendon, 1977.

Thomson, J. A. F. "John Foxe and Some Sources for Lollard History: Notes for a Critical Appraisal." In *Studies in Church History* 2:251–257. London: Nelson, 1965.

———. *The Later Lollards 1414–1520.* Oxford: Oxford University Press, 1965.

Thrupp, Sylvia. *The Merchant Class of Medieval London.* Chicago: University of Chicago Press, 1948.

Tillich, Paul. *A History of Christian Thought.* New York: Harper and Row, 1968.

Tracy, James D. " 'Against the Barbarians': The Young Erasmus and His Humanist Contemporaries." *Sixteenth Century Journal* 11 (1980): 3–22.

———. "Humanists among the Scholastics: Erasmus, More, and Lefèvre d'Etaples on the Humanity of Christ." In *Erasmus of Rotterdam Society Yearbook* 5:30–51. Oxon Hill, Md.: Erasmus of Rotterdam Society, 1985.

———. *The Politics of Erasmus: A Pacifist Intellectual.* Toronto: University of Toronto Press, 1978.

Trapp, J. B. "Christopher Urswick and His Books: The Reading of Henry VII's Almoner." *Renaissance Studies* 1 (1987): 48–70.

———. "Dame Christian Colet and Thomas More." *Moreana,* nos. 16–17 (1967): 103–114.

———. "An English Late Medieval Cleric and Italian Thought: The Case of John Colet, Dean of St. Paul's." In *Medieval English Religious and Ethical Literature: Essays in Honour of G. H. Russell,* edited by Gregory Kratzmann and James Simpson, 233–250. Dover, N.H.: Brewer, 1986.

———. "John Colet, His Manuscripts and ps.-Dionysius." In *Classical Influences on European Culture 1500–1700*, edited by R. R. Bolgar, 205–221. Cambridge: Cambridge University Press, 1976.

———. "Notes on Manuscripts Written by Peter Meghen." *The Book Collector* 24 (1975): 80–96.

Tyndale, William. *Answere vnto Sir Thomas Mores Dialoge*. Edited by H. Walter. Cambridge, 1850.

Unwin, George. *The Guilds and Companies of London*. London: Allen and Unwin, 1938.

Urwick, Thomas A. *Records of the Family of Urswyck, Urswick, or Urwick*. St. Albans: Privately printed, 1893.

van Gelder, H. A. Enno. *The Two Reformations in the 16th Century*. The Hague: Nijhoff, 1961.

Varley, Benjamin. *The History of Stockport Grammar School*. Manchester: Manchester University Press, 1946.

Verde, Armando F. *Lo studio fiorentino 1473–1503*. Vol. 3 in 2 parts. Pistoia: Memorie Domenicane, 1977.

Vergil. *The Aeneid*. Translated by Robert Fitzgerald. New York: Random House, 1983.

———. *P. Vergilius Maro Aeneis Buch VI*. 6th ed. Edited by Eduard Norden. Darmstadt: Wissenschaftliche Buchgesellschaft, 1976.

Vergil, Polydore. *The Anglica Historia of Polydore Vergil* A.D. *1485–1537*. Translated and edited by Denys Hay. London: Royal Historical Society, 1950.

Veuthey, Leo, O.F.M. Conv. "Les divers courants de la philosophie augustino-franciscaine au moyen âge." In *Scholastica ratione historico-critica instauranda: Acta Congressus Internationalis Romae Anno Sancto MCML celebrati*, 627–652. Rome: Pontificum Athenaeum Antonianum, 1951.

Villoslada, Ricardo García, S.J. *La Universidad de París durante los estudios de Francisco de Vitoria O.P. (1507–1522)*. Rome: Universitas Gregoriana, 1938.

Vinogradoff, Sir Paul. "Obituary.—Frederic Seebohm (1833–1912)." In Paul Vinogradoff, *Collected Papers*, 2 vols. 1:272–276. Oxford: Clarendon, 1928.

Vischer, L., and D. Lerch. "Die Auslegungsgeschichte als notwendige theologische Aufgabe." In *Studia patristica* 1:414–419. Berlin: Akademie-Verlag, 1957.

Walker, D. P. *The Decline of Hell*. London: Routledge and Kegan Paul, 1964.

———. "Origène en France au début du XVIe siècle." In *Courants religieux et humanisme*, 101–119. Paris: P.U.F., 1959.

Walser, Ernst. *Poggius Florentinus: Leben und Werke*. Leipzig: Teubner, 1914.

Watney, Sir John. *An Account of the Mistery of Mercers of the City of London Otherwise the Mercers' Company*. London: Privately printed, 1914.

———. *Some Account of the Hospital of St. Thomas of Acon, in the Cheap, London, and of the Plate of the Mercers' Company*. London: Privately printed, 1892.

Weiss, Roberto. "Englishmen in Rome." *The Times Literary Supplement* (London) 34 (1935): 596.

Wharton, Henry. *Historia de episcopis et decanis Londinensibus*. London, 1695.

Williams, George H. *Anselm: Communion and Atonement*. St. Louis: Concordia, 1960.

Withycombe, E. G. *Oxford Dictionary of English Christian Names*. 3d ed. Oxford: Clarendon, 1977.

Wood, Anthony à. *Athenae Oxonienses*. Edited by Philip Bliss. 4 vols. London, 1813–1820.

Wood-Legh, K. L. *Perpetual Chantries in Britain*. Cambridge: Cambridge University Press, 1965.

Wooden, Warren. *John Foxe*. Boston: Twayne, 1983.

———. "The Topos of Childhood in Marian England." *Journal of Medieval and Renaissance Studies* 12 (1982): 179–194.

Xiberta, Bartolomé María, O. Carm. *Clavis Ecclesiae: De ordine absolutionis sacramentalis ad reconciliationem cum Ecclesia*. Rome: Collegium Sancti Alberti, 1922.

Zambelli, Paola. "Cornelio Agrippa, Erasmo e la teologia umanistica." *Rinascimento*, 2d ser. 10 (1970): 29–88.

Zarb, Seraphinus M., O.P. "Utrum S. Thomas unitatem an vero pluralitatem sensus litteralis in Sacra Scriptura docuerit?" *Divus Thomas* (Piacenza) 33 (1930): 337–359.

Index